A CRITICAL COMMENTARY
ON
THE BOOK OF DANIEL

A CRITICAL AND EXEGETICAL COMMENTARY ON THE BOOK OF DANIEL

WITH INTRODUCTION, INDEXES AND A NEW ENGLISH TRANSLATION

By R. H. CHARLES

D.D. (DUBLIN), D.LITT. AND
HON. D.D. (OXFORD), HON. LL.D. (BELFAST)
ARCHDEACON OF WESTMINSTER
FELLOW OF THE BRITISH
ACADEMY

Wipf & Stock
PUBLISHERS
Eugene, Oregon

Wipf and Stock Publishers
199 W 8th Ave, Suite 3
Eugene, OR 97401

A Critical and Exegetical Commentary on the Book of Daniel
By Charles, R. H.
ISBN: 1-59752-675-4
Publication date 5/4/2006
Previously published by Oxford University Press, 1929

THIS ALSO
TO MY WIFE
WITHOUT WHOSE HELP
THIS CONTRIBUTION TO
THE BOOK OF DANIEL
COULD NEVER HAVE
SEEN THE LIGHT

PREFACE

As in my Commentary on Revelation so also in this Commentary I have been often obliged to break with the traditions of the elders—alike ancient and modern—and to pursue my path unaccompanied by any of my great predecessors in this field of research. But there is no great scholar in the past who has made contributions to our knowledge of this Old Testament Seer, to whom I am not under the deepest obligations. These obligations have been duly recorded where I am conscious of them and the occasion required. I have not, however, made it a practice to enumerate all the scholars who have supported any particular emendation or interpretation I have adopted. No more have I done so, when the suffrages of all the learned world are against me, and when I have had to reject their guidance, and pursue my own solitary path. But in any real contribution I may have made in this work to the emendation and interpretation of Daniel, I can seldom make any claim to merit, seeing that with the exception of Dr. Montgomery in his Commentary in the International Critical Commentary Series, all my forerunners in the study of Daniel have been handicapped in many respects owing to the lack of an Aramaic grammar [1] which dealt with the historical development of the language, a lack which it is now possible in a great degree to make good through the discovery of the invaluable Elephantine papyri and various isolated inscriptions. But since no attempt was made till last year to supply this lack, I was obliged to make a first hand study of the *CIS*, the Elephan-

---

[1] Kautzsch's splendid grammar (1884) is limited to Biblical Aramaic. It was not till 1927, when Baumgartner published his very admirable and compressed study ' Das Aramäische im Buche Daniel ' in the *ZATW* 1927, 81–133, that a comprehensive view of the development of Aramaic from the eighth century B. C. to the first century B. C. was laid before the world of scholars. In the same year Bauer and Leander published their *Gramm. d. Biblisch-Aramäischen*, which, though not so able and stimulating, is very helpful to the student of Aramaic. Unfortunately my Commentary had been sent into the Oxford Press six months before these works appeared, and I had to pursue my work independently. Happily I have been able to avail myself of their help in my Introduction, though from time to time I have been obliged to adopt different views both in respect of the grammar and the actual extent of the original text.

tine papyri and other, for the most part, fragmentary survivals of Aramaic from the eighth century down to the second century B.C. The results of this study are given in §§ 17–21 of the Introduction. Some months after my Commentary had been sent to the Oxford Press, I had the great satisfaction of receiving from Professor Baumgartner an elaborate sketch of this development which confirmed in the main the conclusions at which I had already arrived, and helped to enrich my own treatise. Fortunately for my readers and myself my Introduction was only in part written though a vast accumulation of materials, digested and undigested, was at my disposal for the completion of this task in the briefest form possible. I need hardly add that Professor Baumgartner's conclusions and mine own do not always agree, but in the main they lead to the same goal. Moreover, though his treatment of individual forms is often fuller than mine, there are several distinctive idioms which he has failed to recognize.

Without such a study of the development of Aramaic we cannot interpret our author. The importance of such an historical study of Aramaic may be illustrated by two out of nearly thirty expressions. In Aramaic down to 300 B.C.—in fact down to the second century B.C., so far as I can discover, the Aramaic order of words in mentioning an Oriental monarch was always 'Nebuchadnezzar the King': but never 'King Nebuchadnezzar'. The impression given is that there was only one King. The rest were Kinglets, petty rulers. Ezra, which in its present form is dated by Driver c. 300 B.C., always reproduces this idiom faithfully. Cf. Introduction, § 20. dd. But Daniel, in keeping with the usage of the second century B.C., uses the later order of this phrase 'King Nebuchadnezzar' once out of every three times. Neither Baumgartner nor Montgomery nor anyone else so far as I know has noticed this fact. Again in Daniel the proper preposition after the verb 'to say' in addressing a Divine Being or a semidivine (as an Eastern monarch) was 'before'—not 'to'. See Introduction, § 20. w. This usage is common in the New Testament and always in the Targums, as Dalman points out. Even in Egypt a subject never spoke 'to' the King, but 'before' him. Now the interpolator of 4^{3-7a} $(6-10a)$ in Daniel has not the slightest knowledge of the author's usage, and actually represents the great Eastern potentate Nebuchadnezzar as reporting his address to the wise men in the following phrase: 'I told the dream BEFORE them ', $4^{4\,(7)}$. A similar blunder occurs in the next verse. It is worth observing that the LXX omits this passage and thus confirms the above conclusion. This passage includes other idioms conflicting with our author's usage. Accordingly a large section of the Introd. is devoted to the grammatical development of Aramaic idioms, so far as these have any bearing on the Aramaic of our text.

With regard to the Versions I have made the best use I could of them in their present condition. But they all require to be critically edited. Notwithstanding, their evidence, even as they are, is invaluable. Owing to the lack of space I have not discussed them, save in the case of the pre-Theodotion version, of which a genuine fragment is, I feel convinced, preserved in Justin Martyr, *Dial.* 31. See Introd., § 13 (c) n. : § 25. I have not even mentioned the three Additions to the Versions. They and their bibliography are dealt with in the *Apocrypha and Pseudepigrapha* which I edited for the Oxford Press in 1913.

Furthermore, though I had intended to give a brief historical sketch of the history of the Eastern Empires, so far as our author was concerned with them, for the same lack of space I have been obliged to relinquish this intention. At the same time these historical questions have been concisely dealt with in the special Introductions to Chapters 5 and 6 and in Introd. § 26.

Notwithstanding recent attempts to establish the sixth century date of our author, I cannot but regard it as an absolutely hopeless task. Even linguistically it is now possible to prove the later date.

Again I may remark that though many of the greatest Semitic scholars have edited Daniel, not one of them seems to have had a first hand knowledge of the characteristics of Apocalyptic outside Daniel. It is not strange, therefore, that they fail often to observe special characteristics of this type of literature. I may add three examples out of many, wherein such a knowledge is indispensable. In $11^{41,\,44}$ there are two interpolations, which are impossible in literature of this type. The apocalyptist never designates the national enemies of Israel by their actual names, especially when the events occur near or in the time of the actual writer. Again no apocalyptist was ever guilty of the incredible irreverence of calling God 'an old man' (Dan. 7^9), an irreverence which is camouflaged by the splendid English phrase 'an ancient of days'. Yet no commentator save myself has ever censored this impossible phrase, as I did in my small Commentary. Since then I have found my early emendation of that phrase into 'like unto an ancient of days' actually in Clem. Alex., *Paed.* ii. 10 (*c.* A. D. 200) and in the LXX in 7^{13} (*c.* 145 B. C.).

In publishing this Commentary my chief claim is, so far as possible, to recover the oldest form of the text, and to interpret that text in conformity with the usages of Jewish Apocalyptic.[1]

When the renderings in the Translation differ from those in the Commentary, as they do in a few cases, the former are to be accepted as my final conclusions and not the latter.

Finally I cannot refrain from expressing my deep gratitude, first of all to the Secretary of the Press and his assistants and next to the Printer, the readers and compositors for their unfailing courtesy, patience, and skilled service in the publication of a Commentary and Translation, which involved a continuous revision of the entire text, and which has proved to be the most difficult of all my studies, in an experience of nearly forty years of research in apocalyptic literature.

R. H. C.

4 LITTLE CLOISTERS, WESTMINSTER ABBEY
    August 1928.

[1] By a special arrangement made in 1912 with Messrs. T. C. and E. C. Jack I reserved the right of reproducing in this larger Commentary paragraphs or sections contained in the small Commentary which was published in the Century Bible in 1913.

CONTENTS

§ 8. There is one idiom in 2^{46}-6 which belongs so far as existing evidence goes to the second century B.C. It does not occur in 7, but there is no occasion for its occurrence there. 7 could, if it were a wholly isolated document, be regarded as older than 2^{4b}-6 from the stand-point of language. *page* xliv

§ 9. Since 2^{4b}-7 come from one and the same hand, there is no conceivable ground for the author's forsaking the vernacular language of his day, i.e. Aramaic, *in his appeal to the majority of his countrymen who understood that vernacular only* and having recourse in 1-2^{4a} and 8-12 to Hebrew which was understood by a very small educated minority. Such a change of language would have defeated the main object of our author, who was issuing a trumpet call to his countrymen as a whole. *page* xlv

§ 10. 1-2^{4a} and 8-12 are translations into Hebrew from the original Aramaic: there were three distinct translators at work, 1-2^{4a} from the first: 8-10, 12 (?) from the second and 11 from the third. *page* xlvi

§ 11. Why was the translation of 11 (+12?) entrusted to a very faulty Hebrew translator rather than to the translators of the earlier chapters. *page* xlviii

§ 12. Approximate date of the translation of 1-2^{4a}, 8-12 into Hebrew—either before 161 B.C. or at latest 153 B.C. *page* xlix

§ 13. The Versions. (*a*) and (*b*) the LXX and Th. I have herein followed Swete's edition of *The Old Testament in Greek*. (*c*) A pre-Theodotion Version. Evidence as to its existence before the Christian Era. Readings from it in the New Testament, Ep. Clem., Justin Martyr, who quotes 7^{9-28} from it. See p. cxvi sqq. Hermas, Clem. of Alex. (*d*) Practical rejection of Chapters 4-6 of the LXX by most modern scholars as a means of recovering the original text. But the present editor cannot accept this view and holds that it is just in these chapters that the LXX, though very corrupt, makes its greatest contribution. (*e*) Versions of Aquila and Symmachus. (*f*) the Peshitto. (*g*) The Syriac version of Paul of Tella. (*h*) Old Latin. (*i*) Vulgate. (*k*) Sahidic and Bohairic. (*l*) Ethiopic. *page* l

§ 14. Massoretic Text—its essentially secondary character. Frequently secondary to a better text implied by the versions. (*a*) MT in twelve passages without the support of the LXX, Th., Pesh., and Vulg., though the three last generally support it. (*b*) and (*c*) Without the support of the LXX, Th., Vulg., and Josephus. (*d*) Defective where the LXX and Th. supply the missing date—a date required by our author's usage elsewhere. See § 4. (*e*) MT is wrong in a few passages when only a single version as Th., Pesh., or Vulg. preserves the original. (*f*) MT is frequently untrustworthy, when the LXX alone preserves the original. (*g*) Text of MT is not unfrequently dislocated. (*h*) MT contains many obvious interpolations, some of which originated in marginal glosses. (*i*) MT has occasionly replaced one Hebrew word by another having a different or wrong meaning or else by an older Hebrew equivalent. (*k*) Misuse of Hebrew words in the MT. (*l*) Wrong or later order of words in the Aramaic. (*m*) Misuse of phrases in MT. *page* lix

INTRODUCTION

§ 1. *Short Account of the Book.*

(*a*) *Historical Antecedents.* In the closing years of the Syrian domination of Palestine, Antiochus Epiphanes sat on the throne of Syria. With his invasions of Egypt and other countries we are not here concerned, but only with his dealings with the Jews. His ambition was to hellenize the various provinces and peoples of his great empire. In this aim he met with little opposition except in Judea, and even there he secured without difficulty the support of the hellenizing High Priests. Thus the High Priest Jason, a creature of Antiochus, who had superseded his brother, the faithful High Priest Onias III, set up a Greek gymnasium in Jerusalem, to join in the games of which the very priests abbreviated the sacred services of the Temple. Through his agency also contributions were sent for the celebration of the festival of Heracles at Tyre. Jason was succeeded by Menelaus, who had secured the High Priesthood by the promise of a huge sum of money to Antiochus, a sum which he was unable to raise save through plunder of the Temple treasury. For rebuking this treacherous act, Onias III, referred to above, paid for his fidelity with his life. In 170 B.C., while Antiochus was warring in Egypt, the rumour that he had fallen encouraged the exile Jason to make an attempt to recover the High Priesthood. This attempt led to much bloodshed in Jerusalem, and Antiochus on his return treated the Jews with the utmost severity.

Multitudes of men, women, and children, were put to the sword, and thousands were sold into slavery. This visit of Antiochus closed with his seizure of the last treasures of the Temple. Thus the Jews suffered from without as well as from within, but the cup of their sorrow was not yet full. Two years later Antiochus marched with a vast force into Egypt with the intention of making the kingdom of the Ptolemies a province of his own Empire.

But when his plans seemed on the eve of fulfilment he was met by envoys from Rome, who required him, on the penalty of joining issue with the Republic itself, to withdraw at once

from Egypt. Enraged and embittered, Antiochus turned home-
ward, resolved now to devote all his power to the hellenization
of Judea. With this object in view he forbade the observance
of the Sabbath and the practice of the rite of circumcision. The
sacrifices of the Temple were done away with, and every form
of Jewish worship and ceremonial. The sacred books were
destroyed, and the Temple dismantled and laid waste. The
walls of the city were overthrown, and a fortress erected commanding the Temple enclosure. But the culminating horror of
this awful time was yet to come. On the 15th of December,
168 B.C., a heathen altar was planted on the site of the great
altar of burnt offering, in honour of Olympian Zeus. On the
25th of the same month the profanation of the sacred precincts
was consummated by the sacrifice of swine on the altar. Furthermore, every city and village was required to build temples and
raise idolatrous altars on which swine were to be sacrificed
daily.

At last the anguish of the faithful Jews became unendurable
and an insurrection burst forth at Modein, under the leadership
of Mattathias and his five stalwart sons. All that were zealous
for the Law and the Covenant speedily joined them, and amongst
these notably the Hasidim, or the league of the pious ones. This
small body of Jews met with many marvellous successes. Notwithstanding, in the face of the vast forces of Syria, the Jews
could repose no hope in their own powers. If they were to
succeed it could not be in reliance on an arm of flesh. Now it
was just at this crisis, this hour of mingled hope and despair,
that the Book of Daniel 'appeared with its sword-edge utterance,
its piercing exhortation to endure in face of the despot, and its
promise, full of Divine joy, of near and full salvation. No dew
of heaven could fall with more refreshing coolness on the parched
ground, no spark from above alight with a more kindling power
on the surface so long heated with a hidden glow. With winged
brevity the book gives a complete survey of the history of the
kingdom of God upon earth, showing the relations which it had
hitherto sustained in Israel to the successive great heathen
empires of the Chaldaeans, Medo-Persians, and Greeks—in
a word, towards the heathenism which ruled the world; and
with the finest perception it describes the nature and individual
character of Antiochus Epiphanes and his immediate predeces-

sors so far as was possible in view of the great events which had just occurred. Rarely does it happen that a book appears as this did, in the very crisis of the times, and in a form more suited to such an age, artificially reserved, close and severe, and yet shedding so clear a light through obscurity, and so marvellously captivating. It was natural that it should soon achieve a success entirely corresponding with its inner truth and glory. And so, for the last time in the literature of the Old Testament, we have in this book an example of a work which, having sprung from the deepest necessities of the noblest impulses of the age, can render to that age the purest service; and which by the development of events immediately after, receives with such power the stamp of Divine witness that it subsequently attains imperishable sanctity[1].

(b) *Pseudonymous character of the Book.* The pseudonymous character of this book has been a source of great trouble to many, but to the student who is acquainted with the facts of the time, it is obvious that, if the book were to realize the end it aimed at, it could not have been otherwise than pseudonymous.[2] Owing to the Law having achieved an absolute supremacy, the calling of the prophet had ceased to exist, and there was no room for a religious teacher, except in so far as he was a mere exponent of the Law. From this it followed that all real advances to a higher theology could appear only in works of a pseudonymous character. Accordingly, when a man of God felt that he had a message to deliver to his people, he was obliged to cast it in this form. And thus it was that the brilliant visionary, to whom we owe the Book of Daniel, issued under the name of an ancient worthy this book of transcendant worth not only to his own, but to all after ages. It has taught to mankind many imperishable lessons, and of these there is none nobler than the incomparable testimony of the three Confessors when, in answer to Nebuchadnezzar's demand: 'What god can deliver you out of my hands', they reply: 'We have no need to answer thee in this matter; for there is a God whom we serve, who is able to deliver us . . . and he will deliver us out of thy hands, O King: but if not . . . we will not serve thy god nor worship the golden image which thou hast set up' (3^{17-18}).

[1] Ewald, v. 305 (translated by Stanley).
[2] See fuller treatment of this question in § 2.

(c) *Originally written in Aramaic, 1–2⁴ᵃ, 8–12 were translated into Hebrew at latest before* 153 B.C. The Book of Daniel was, as I hope to prove, written originally in Aramaic, and 1–2⁴ᵃ and 8–12 were subsequently translated into Hebrew.[1] In these chapters the Aramaic original was superseded by the Hebrew. Now since the book is divided into *narratives* (1–6) and *visions* (7–12), we should expect that this division of the book as to its subject matter would correspond with the linguistic division of the book. But a comparison of the above facts shows that this is not so. Hence Dalman has ascribed 1–6 to an earlier writer and 7–12 to our author. A redactor then took the two works in hand and translated 1–2⁴ᵃ into Hebrew and 7 into Aramaic and issued the two works as one. This hypothesis, though it has been developed in various forms by Torrey, Hölscher, Preiswerk, and Montgomery, is very arbitrary, save in so far as it maintains that 1–2⁴ᵃ is a reversion into Hebrew. With Montgomery's hopeless attempt to distinguish the Aramaic of 7 from that of 2⁴ᵇ–6 I have dealt exhaustively in § 7.

The conclusion that Daniel was written originally in Aramaic is confirmed by the fact that there appear to be three distinct types of Hebrew in 1–2⁴ᵃ and 8–12, the first appearing in 1–2⁴ᵃ, the second in 8–10, 12 (?), and the third in 11. See §§ 10–11. If the conclusions of the present writer are valid in this respect, then the hypothesis of a Daniel written originally in Hebrew may be dismissed from further consideration.

The Book of Daniel was an appeal to the majority of the faithful Jews. If this appeal were to be successful, it could only appear in Aramaic. The knowledge of Hebrew in the second century B.C. was confined to a very small body of scholars.

From Aramaic 1–2⁴ᵃ and 8–12 were rendered into Hebrew by three different translators—probably before 161 B.C. or at latest before 153 B.C. Without such a translation from the vernacular into Hebrew in the opening and closing sections the book could not have won its way into the Canon.

(d) *The book suffered much from interpolations and dislocations.* From the beginning to the end the book has suffered at the hands of interpolators.[2] One of the earliest interpolations 12¹²⁻¹³

---

[1] For various hypotheses advanced in explanation of the bilingual character of Daniel, see § 5 (a)–(f).

[2] See § 14, h.

must have been made as early as 164 B.C., but 12^{11} was earlier still. The book originally ended with the encouraging words in 12^{10}, 'they that be wise shall understand'. These are likewise an answer to Daniel's prayer in 12^8 for the gift of understanding the divine mysteries. Thus the book closes with the theme which pervades it from the beginning (cf. 1^{17}) that divine en-lightenment attends on unflinching obedience to the Divine Will.

But not only did the book suffer at the hands of glossers and interpolators, but also of careless copyists and redactors. Thus we find frequent dislocations of the text.[1] Of these we may mention here the two most important, i.e. 1^{20-21}, which in the original text followed immediately after 2^{49a} and 3^{31-33} (4^{1-3}) after 4^{34}.[2] The first of these dislocations must have taken place in the Aramaic before the translation of $1-2^{4a}$ into Hebrew.

(e) *The Versions.* About twenty years after the publication of the book it was translated into Greek This Greek version, known as the Septuagint or LXX,[3] has been preserved to us in a single very corrupt Greek MS. of the eleventh century A.D., but happily it was translated into Syriac about the year A.D. 617.

In the meantime, probably in the latter half of the first century B.C. a second Greek translation—which on various grounds we call pre-Theodotion[4]—was made from the bilingual text under the guidance of the older translation. But by this time the bilingual text had undergone disastrous dislocations in 4-6. Accordingly, since all versions save the oldest LXX Version are derived from this later bilingual text, they all attest the same dislocations in these chapters. But this pre-Theodotion text has not survived independently but only in quotations of the first and second centuries A.D., and in the Version of Theodotion, of which it formed in a large measure the basis.

The Version of Theodotion, which belongs to the second century A.D. approximates closely to the Massoretic text, but implies in some two score or more passages a purer form of the Semitic text. The Peshitto and Vulgate Versions were made from a still later form of the Semitic text than that used by Theodotion. The two Egyptian Versions—the Sahidic and Bohairic—and the Ethiopic are versions of Theodotion.

Beside the above versions there is the Syriac Version of Paul

---

[1] See § 14, *g*.
[2] See Commentary, pp. 79-86.
[3] See § 13, *a*.
[4] See § 13, *c*: § 25.

of Tella[1] and the fragments of the versions of Aquila and Symmachus, which are to be found in Field's *Origenis hexaplorum quae supersunt*, 1875.

(*f*) *The Massoretic text.* This text is essentially of a secondary character. As we have already briefly stated and given some grounds for the statement, the Massoretic consists partly of a corrupt form of the original Aramaic ($2^{4\,b}$–7) and partly of Hebrew versions of the remaining sections. In §§ 6–11 I have furnished what I hold to be conclusive evidence for this statement. Thus half the Massoretic is, to begin with, itself a version, a Hebrew version of the original Aramaic, and both halves of the book, the original Aramaic half and the remaining half consisting of a Hebrew version from three hands, have been very imperfectly transmitted. That this is so should cause no surprise. The Book of Daniel as all other pseudonymous writings was especially exposed to corruptions, interpolations, dislocations, and other evils incident to literature of this description, as a work composed in secret and by an unknown author at a special crisis in the national history, though claiming to have been written some centuries earlier by some notable worthy of Israel, and copied and circulated, in some cases no doubt, under the seal of secrecy during its first or even second decades. It was during this critical period when the book met the clamant needs of the faithful and when, passing with incredible rapidity from hand to hand, it kindled anew the courage of its readers to face overwhelming odds, and inspired them with a loyalty that feared nothing so much as disloyalty to the God of their fathers—it was just during this period that the book suffered so grievously at the hands of its copyists alike in respect of dislocations, interpolations, and other depravations of the text. It was during this period that the dislocation of the text in 1^{20-21} occurred.[2] How early the most disastrous dislocation of all supervened, i.e. that in chap. 4 cannot be definitely determined.[3]   In the LXX

---

[1] See § 13, *g*.

[2] See Commentary, p. 52 seqq.

[3] See Commentary, p. 79 seqq. I am inclined to believe that this disastrous dislocation was effected soon after the publication of the book in the copy from which the MT and the later versions are derived. But happily the LXX was made from a copy which still preserved the original *order* of the text, though in other respects its corruptions are all but incredible. The closing words of this chapter are preserved by the LXX in three distinct forms!

'.e. *c.* 145 B.C.) the order of the text is still that of the original.
is not until we come down to the second century A.D. that
e dislocated text is attested, and in due course came to be
:epted by the Jewish Church and subsequently by the Christian
authentic. But this dislocation may have originated in a copy
old or still older than that from which the LXX was
ıranslated.

For the scores of corruptions in the MT, where the older and
truer text is preserved in the Versions, the reader can consult
the foot-notes in the Translation or the more critical list of these
in § 14. From a comparative study of the MT and the Versions
we cannot escape the conclusion that the present form of the
MT is in many respects later than the fourth century A.D.

But the MT is not only dislocated and corrupt. The very
words of the text have at times been replaced by others which
either misrepresent the meaning of the original word or else by
others which cannot be used in the sense assigned to them in
their new context. See § 14, *i-k.* The MT contains phrases,
where the Semitic order is wrong or not .that of our author.
It also misuses phrases : see § 14, *l-m.*

For the relation of the MT to the various versions the reader
can consult the genealogical tree in § 15.

(*g*) The date of the work has been implicitly assumed in all
the preceding paragraphs. Since the question is dealt with fully
in § 16 there is no occasion for recapitulating the main arguments
here.

§ 2. *Why did Apocalyptic become Pseudonymous in Judaism?*

The fact of a religious teacher issuing his work under the
name of another has been a source of profound difficulty to most
biblical students in the past and to a large section at present.

(*a*) If the book is really pseudonymous, many scholars would
declare and indeed have categorically declared that the book is
a forgery. It must be confessed that the grounds which scholars
have in the past adduced for the use of pseudonymity by Jewish
teachers have quite failed to justify themselves at the bar of the
ordinary conscience. It is of no avail to state that such writers
were wholly devoid of literary ambition and were only concerned
that their teaching should be accepted. No more will it avail to

argue that they were merely making use of a literary form that
was common throughout antiquity, as in Egypt already in the
third century B.C., i.e. in the *Demotic Chronicle,* first edited by
Spiegelberg. For a discussion on 'Hebrew and Egyptian
Apocalyptic Literature' see McCown in the Harvard *Theol.
Rev.*, 1925, 357–411 (quoted by Montgomery, p. 77). But if
the Jewish writers of Apocalyptic pursued the same lofty and
religious aims as the older prophets, as unquestionably they did,
how is it that they did not come forward with their message
in their own persons? Their failure to do so is certainly not due
to any fear of sharing the fate that had befallen so many of the
prophets and that would assuredly have befallen them if they
had delivered their message in person (cf. Zech. 13^3 seqq.).
The religious leaders of the Maccabean period had no such
fear of death; they were only too ready for martyrdom as we
know from actual history.

(*b*) The real grounds, therefore, for pseudonymity must be
found elsewhere. Into these, which I have discussed at some
length in the second edition of my *Eschatology,* pp. 196–206,
I cannot enter here. I will, however, for the sake of the reader,
summarize my results.

From the time of Ezra onwards, the Law made steady progress
towards a position of supremacy in Judaism. And just in proportion as it achieved such supremacy, every other form of
religious activity fell into the background. This held true even
of the priesthood, which in due course became subordinate to
the teachers of the Law. But in an infinitely higher degree was
it true of prophecy. When once the Law had established an
unquestioned autocracy, the prophets were practically reduced
to the position of being merely its exponents, and prophecy,
assuming a literary character, might bear its author's name or
be anonymous. But when a book of prophecy brought disclosures
beyond or in conflict with the letter of the Law, it could hardly
attain to official recognition or a place in the Canon. This was
the case as we know with Ezekiel, which narrowly escaped being
declared apocryphal by Jewish scholars (Shabb. 13^b, Men. 45^a)
as late as the first century of the Christian era. The next claim
made by the Law was that it was all-sufficient for time and
eternity, alike as an intellectual creed, a liturgical system, and a
practical guide in ethics and religion. Thus theoretically and

practically no room was left for new light and inspiration or any fresh and further disclosure of God's will ; in short, no room for the true prophet—only for the moralist, the casuist, or the preacher. How then from the third century B.C. onward was the man to act who felt himself charged with a true message from God to his day and generation ? The tyranny of the Law, and the petrified orthodoxies of his time, compelled him to resort to pseudonymity.

(c) And if these grounds had in themselves been insufficient for the adoption of pseudonymity, there was the further ground —the formation of the Canon. When once the prophetic Canon was closed no book of a prophetic character could gain canonization as such, nor could it gain a place among the sacred writings at all unless its date was believed to be as early as the time of Ezra. On this ground again the prophetic type of man was forced to resort to pseudonymity to obtain a hearing, and so to issue his work under the name of one of Israel's ancient worthies of a date earlier than Ezra or at all events contemporary with him.

In Ps. 74^9 the words 'there is no prophet more', whether they are authentic or merely a gloss, express the belief that the time was characterized by the absence of true prophets. In 1 Macc. this belief is still that of the people as a whole ; for in 4^{46}, 9^{27}, 14^{41} no decision on great questions could be arrived at 'untill a prophet should come'.

Such pseudonymous works were said to have been concealed in some secret place (*in loco abscondito*, 4 Ezra 12^{37}) and not made known till the crises with which they dealt had arrived. Thus our author represents the following command being given to Daniel in 12^4, 'Thou, O Daniel, shut up the words and seal the book even unto the time of the end'—the end being the advent of the Kingdom, which in the view of the writer was immediately impending. The secret and esoteric character of this literature is enforced in 4 Ezra 14^{44} seqq. 'The 24 books (i.e. the O.T.) that thou hast written publish . . . but the 70 last thou shalt keep to deliver to the wise among the people'.

All Jewish Apocalypses were pseudonymous from 200 B.C. to the thirteenth century A.D., but not all Christian, the greatest among the latter being the N.T. Apocalypse.[1]

---

[1] See also § 16 (*ad initium*) on the question of pseudonymity of Jewish Apocalypses.

§ 3. *Points in common between Prophecy and Apocalyptic*[1] *and points of Divergence.*

(a) The forms of the prophetic experiences as beheld by the inner eye, or heard by the inner ear, as well as their literary expression, must take their character largely from the spiritual and literary standards of the time. This psychical experience of the prophet was generally one of sight or of sound; that is, in the psychical state he either saw certain things or heard certain things. Now the things so seen or heard he could grasp only so far as his psychical powers and the spiritual development behind him enabled him to do so; that is, in the case of a heavenly vision he could at the best only partially apprehend its significance. To the things seen he perforce attached the symbols more or less transformed that these naturally evoked in his mind, symbols that he owed to his own waking experience or the tradition of the past; and the sounds he heard naturally clothed themselves in the literary forms with which his memory was stored.

And yet, however successful the prophet might be in setting forth his visionary experiences, he laboured, as we have pointed out, under a double disadvantage. *His powers of spiritual perception* were generally unequal to the task of apprehending the full meaning of the 'heavenly vision', and *his powers of expression* were frequently unable to set forth the things he had apprehended.

Now these visions and trances belong both to prophecy and apocalyptic. Furthermore, just as the prophet came not unfrequently to use the words, 'Thus saith the Lord', even when there was no actual psychical experience in which he heard a voice, and his sole wish was to set forth the will of God which he had reached by other means, *so the term 'vision' came to have a like conventional use both in prophecy and apocalyptic.* It is of especial importance to remember this in connexion with chapter 11, which of course is not to be taken as a literal vision. The Seer is attempting to represent the course of events *sub specie aeternitatis!* A like attempt on a larger scale will be found by the reader in 1 Enoch 89-90.

---

[1] In the above section I have only mentioned a few of the characteristics common to prophecy and apocalyptic. For a detailed comparison see the second edition of my *Eschatology*, 1913, pp. 178-206.

(b) But prophecy and apocalyptic need to be distinguished in regard to their eschatologies.[1] Eschatology in the first place must not be confounded as it often has been by careless writers with apocalyptic. Eschatology is strictly the doctrine of the last things, and the eschatologies of prophecy and apocalyptic differ. The eschatology of prophecy dealt only with the destiny of Israel *as a nation* and the destinies of the Gentile nations, so far as this world was concerned, it had no message of comfort *for the individual* beyond the grave. Sheol was the final and everlasting abode alike of nations and individuals from the standpoint of prophecy.

Every advance on this heathen conception is due to apocalyptic. The belief in a blessed future life is the contribution of apocalyptic and not of prophecy. No hint of it is to be found in O. T. phophecy. But the apocalyptist on the other hand found that it followed necessarily from his conception of God. Apocalyptic was a Semitic philosophy of religion and concerned itself with the questions of whence ? wherefore ? whither ? It sketched in outline the history of the universe and of the angelic and human worlds, the origin of evil, its course and ultimate over-throw. It was thus apocalyptic and not prophecy that was the first to grasp the great idea that all history, human, cosmological, and spiritual is a unity—a unity that follows inevitably as a corollary to the unity of God as enforced by the O. T. prophets. Thus whereas prophecy deals with the present destinies of individuals and nations, and their future destinies as arising organically out of the present *and on the present earth* without reference to the life of the individual after death, apocalyptic dealt with the past, the present, and the future as linked together and forming one whole, and thereby sought to justify the ways of God to man. Prophecy, it is true, looked forwards to a blessed future of the nation, pure and noble from the ethical standpoint but materialistic. But in apocalyptic this hope was gradually transformed, till the expectations of the faithful were fixed, not on any transitory individual blessedness in an eternal Messianic kingdom on this present earth, but to an eternal personal blessedness in a new heaven and a new earth. This transference of the hopes of the faithful from the material world took place

[1] See my *Eschatology*[2] 177 seqq., where the above questions are more fully dealt with.

about 100 B.C. 'The writer of the Book of Daniel had not yet reached this stage of spiritual development. The eternal kingdom of God according to his view is to be established on the present earth, and only the pre-eminently righteous are to rise to enjoy eternal life upon it. The writer further believed that he could determine the exact date of the advent of this kingdom.[1] When this prediction in 8^{14} failed of fulfilment, two appendixes were added, the first (12^{11}) by the author (?) The second 12^{12-13} by a reviser, who wrote not from the standpoint of the author, i. e. sixth century, B. C. but from that of the second century B. C. (c. 165-164), in which he states that Daniel should survive its coming[2] and share in its everlasting blessedness.

'We have now to ask how did this expectation arise? It cannot be explained from the standpoint of prophecy. Prophecy is a declaration, a forthtelling, of the will of God—not a foretelling. Prediction is not in any sense an essential element of prophecy, though it may intervene as an accident—whether it be a justifiable accident is another question. Prophecy, therefore, takes no account of days or months or years or millenniums. 'It sets forth God's Will and declares in no uncertain note the things which must follow on the fulfilment or the violation of this Will. Since it is only beings morally responsible, who are capable of the conscious fulfilment or violation of this Will, it follows that the development of such beings depends, not on any mechanical divisions of time, but on the steady acceptance or rejection of the Will of God as the law of their being, in the course of which they reach the consummation of life eternal or else of annihilation. Life so considered is essentially a never ending growth in goodness and in knowledge, in the realization of the Will and Being of God. But annihilation is a deliberate suicide in the profoundest sense of the term. If it occurs in the case of any moral being, it is due to his persistent and continuous rebellion against the laws of the Divine life, till at last he extinguishes life in all

---

[1] In Daniel there are three conflicting dates in 8^{14}, $12^{11, 12}$, the second and third being extensions of the first, which were added subsequently to the book, in the hope that by such adjournments the text might be brought into agreement with historical fact. The book ended originally and rightly with 12^{10}.

[2] Ezekiel was a forerunner of apocalyptic and in large measure an apocalyptist himself. He declared that the captivity would last forty years (Ezek. 4^6), and he expressed in the last words that came from his pen the conviction that he would survive its advent (29^{21}).

its senses—spiritual, moral, intellectual, and ontological. Thus annihilation is self-entailed and not the result of any arbitrary prescript of the Divine Being. Prophecy, I may repeat, is not concerned with any definite periods of time but only with the development of character and its issues. Hence our Lord declares in terms that cannot be mistaken : 'Of that day or that hour knoweth no one, not even the angels, neither the Son, but the Father' (Mark 13^{32}).'

'So far we have dealt with prophecy and its rejection of determinism and prediction. How then did determinism, and prediction come to be all but essential elements of apocalyptic? A partial explanation can here be given. When the Canon of the Law and of the prophets was closed, every jot and tittle of these books came to be regarded as infallibly inspired. But there were many unfulfilled prophecies and this according to the orthodox view was impossible. The most tragic instance of such unfulfilled prophecy or rather of prediction was that of Jeremiah, who foretold that after 70 years (Jer. 25^{11}, 29^{10}) Israel was to be restored to their own land ($24^{5, 6}$), and there enjoy the blessings of the Messianic Kingdom under the Messianic King ($23^{5, 6}$). But this prophecy was not fulfilled. I have called this a tragic error on the part of Jeremiah, since it gave birth to an endless succession of idle reinterpretations in order to justify the original forecast, these reinterpretations beginning with our author and extending down all the centuries to our own day. 'It is tragic too that the most spiritually-minded of all the O.T. prophets should have given the sanction of his great name to this radical misconception of his prophetic office. That Ezekiel, Haggai, and Zechariah should have adopted this mechanical view of the Divine rule of the world is not strange ; for the mechanical conception of the prophet's office is manifest in later O.T. prophecy and comes to a head in the Book of Daniel.'

(c and d)'Two further points of divergence should here be mentioned. First the prophet spoke *in his own person*, when he addressed his contemporaries. Secondly he delivered his Divine message mainly in respect to the present and only in respect to the future as arising organically out of the present. He, therefore, sought to lead into the ways of righteousness the individuals, nations, or countries of his own time, addressing them definitely by their respective names, or else, if they deliberately pursued their evil ways, he fulminated God's judgements against them. In apocalyptic the case was otherwise. The seer, *writing in the name of some ancient worthy*, sought to justify the ways of God to man *by rewriting history in the form of prediction*. Such a method required him to avoid the mention of any individual, nation, or country by its specific name. These were denoted by symbols. In most Jewish apocalypses this method is pursued without exception from start to finish. But in a few apocalypses, as in Daniel, it is only in dealing with his own generation and a few generations earlier that the seer rigorously followed the above method and confined himself absolutely to the use of symbolic terms. See note in Comm., pp. 281-3.

§ 4. *The Book divided into ten Sections— each dated by the Author.*[1]

(*a*) The method pursued by our author in the dates he assigns to the narratives and visions—ten sections in all—must be mastered, so far as possible, if the reader is to ascertain the right text in several passages. We shall discover, as we advance, that to every narrative and vision a definite date is assigned. This date is given at the beginning of each section, save in the case of the fifth, where the date is given at the close of the section. For Belshazzar's feast synchronizes with the day of his death in 538 B.C.

The book falls naturally into two parts, chapters 1-6 consisting of narratives, which follow each other chronologically, beginning with the third year of Jehoiakim, King of Judah, while 7-12 consist of visions, which also follow each other chronologically beginning with the first year of Belshazzar.

The first half of the book consists of an Introduction 1$^{1-19}$ and five narratives, which are embodied in chapters 2-6. The second half consists of four visions, embodied respectively in chapters 7, 8, 9, and 10-12^{10}. There is thus an Introduction and nine distinct sections, or ten sections, if we reckon the Introduction as one of them, into which the book naturally falls.

---

[1] The division of the Bible into chapters and verses was first made by Stephen Langton who afterwards became archbishop of Canterbury and died in A.D. 1228. This division was singularly infelicitous in the case of 10-12, which are concerned with one vision only and not three as the division into three chapters would lead the reader to suppose.

(b) Next in the oldest Version—the LXX—each section begins with a definite date, with the exception of the fifth, but even there it is given by implication at its close. The much later Version—that of Theodotion, which in its present form is nearly three centuries later than the LXX, contains all these dates save that in the fourth section. There is no valid ground for questioning the genuineness of these dates on the ground that the MT, which in its present form is not older than the fourth century A.D., omits two of them.

(c) This method of our author is apparently abandoned in 11^1, where in the midst of a section a date is given. But that there is no valid objection to a reference to a past event by the angel see my Comm. *in loc.*

(d) Now that we have on fairly reasonable grounds recognized our author's method of dating his narratives and visions, it becomes our duty to consider the divergence of the MT from this method in 3^1 and 4^1, where the dates are lacking. Since the evidence already furnished as to the observance of this method by our author is reasonably conclusive, we might without further inquiry describe the MT as here untrustworthy. And this criticism we shall find on an examination of the passages justified on other grounds.

(e) The sections with their dates are as follows:

Section I: Introduction, i. e. 1^{1-19}. *In the third year of Jehoiakim* (1^1).

Section II: i. e. 2^{1-49a}, 1^{20-21}, 2^{49b}. Nebuchadnezzar's first dream —*in the second year of his reign* (2^1).

Section III: i.e. 3^{1-30}. Nebuchadnezzar *in the eighteenth year of his reign* (3^1) sets up a golden image to do honour to his god and to celebrate his victories, which image all his subjects are required to worship.

Section IV: i. e. $4^{1-2, \, 7b-34}$, 3^{31-33} (see pp. 79–82). Nebuchadnezzar's second dream, *in the eighteenth year of his reign* (4^1) —in which his humiliation follows within the same year close on the heels of his guilty pride.

Section V: i.e. 5^{1-30}. Belshazzar's feast on the same day as his death (i.e. in 538 B. C.).

Section VI: i.e. 6^{1-29} (5^{31}, 6^{1-28}). Darius thereupon becomes King and reorganizes the entire empire 'being about threescore and two years old' (6^1 (5^{31})). Conspiracy against Daniel and its failure.

Section VII : i.e. 7. Daniel's first vision of the four world
Empires, i.e. *in the first year of Belshazzar* (7¹).

Section VIII : i.e. 8. Daniel's second vision in which fuller
disclosures are given regarding the vision in 7, *in the third
year of the reign of Belshazzar the King* (8¹).

Section IX : i.e. 9. Daniel's third vision, in which Gabriel
explains to him the meaning of the seventy weeks *in the
first year of Darius* (9¹).

Section X : i.e. 10–12¹⁰. Daniel's fourth vision *in the third year
of Cyrus* (10¹), which contains a survey of oriental history
from the time of Cyrus to that of Antiochus Epiphanes with
a forecast of the age of everlasting blessedness on the
present earth on the death of Antiochus Epiphanes.

It will be observed that Daniel's visions take place in the
reigns of Belshazzar, Darius, and Cyrus. The narratives
(chapters 1–6) are recounted in chronological order from the
first year of Nebuchadnezzar to the first year of Darius. The
visions are also recounted in the chronological order of their
occurrence from 'the first year of Belshazzar' to 'the third year
of Cyrus' (chapters 7–12).

§ 5. *Problems connected with the later bilingual character of
the Book of Daniel. Written originally in Aramaic.
Wide divergence between the Versions of the LXX
and Th.*

I shall begin with a short statement of the facts. This statement will be followed by a brief sketch of the various theories
which have been offered for the solution of these problems.
It is possible, indeed, that none of the theories advanced is in
itself adequate, and that it may be necessary to invoke the joint
aid of two or more of them. For as the problem is complex it
is possible that the solution must likewise be complex.

I. The first notable difficulty in the Book of Daniel is connected with its use of two languages. Chapters 1–2⁴ᵃ and 8–12
are written in Hebrew, and 2⁴ᵇ–7²ᵇ in Aramaic. The difficulties occasioned by this diversity of language are somewhat
accentuated by the fact that in the first six chapters Daniel is
spoken of in the third person, whereas in the latter six he is
represented as generally speaking in the first. But even in 7¹

Daniel is spoken of in the third person, but in 7^2 the writer is obliged to use the first person since the subject-matter of 7–12 naturally prescribes it, dealing as it does with Daniel's visions from start to finish. Daniel is the foremost personality throughout the visions: whereas in 1–6 sole and dominant human personalities there are none: there are a number of lesser personalities, such as Nebuchadnezzar, Belshazzar, Darius, Daniel, Hananiah, Misael, and Azariah. There is no difficulty, therefore, in the fact that Daniel is spoken of in the third person in 1–6, and that he speaks in the first in 7–12. In fact the change is exactly what we should expect from the change in the subject-matter.

Having shown that what was supposed to point to a difference of authorship really tends to support the unity of authorship, we must now address ourselves to the real difficulties—the chief of which is the fact that with the change of language there is no corresponding change of subject-matter. This is the main difficulty. A like change of language is found in Ezra 4^8–6^{18}, 7^{12-26}, which is Aramaic, and 6^{19}–7^{11} which is Hebrew: but there this change can be explained from the subject-matter.

How then is the change of language in Daniel to be explained? Are we to explain it as due to diversity of authorship or origin, in the case of the sections in question, and thus assume that these sections were originally written in the language in which they have been transmitted to us? or, rejecting this hypothesis and assuming the literary unity of the book, are we to believe that this present difference of language is not original, but that the book was first written in Hebrew, and that the loss of certain chapters of the Hebrew original was subsequently made good from the Aramaic translation? or conversely, that the book was written in Aramaic and subsequently translated into Hebrew, and that the Hebrew translation was in part destroyed and the missing portions supplied from the Aramaic original? or, finally, that the present Hebrew renderings of chapters 1–2^{4a}, 8–12 were deliberately substituted for their Aramaic originals in order to gain an entrance for the book into the canon of the Holy Scriptures; for Hebrew, of course, was regarded as the sacred language.

II. The second notable difficulty connected with Daniel centres in the wide divergence between the two Greek Versions, i.e.

Note: No - just that EZRA was the redactor.

The LXX which is 3 centuries older.

THE BOOK OF DANIEL

those of the LXX and Theodotion. Where this divergence appears, which is the more trustworthy? Here also full consideration must be given to the theory that, whereas Theodotion's Version is practically based on the MT text, that of the LXX is said by two recent scholars to have been made from a Hebrew original throughout. This problem is dealt with in the individual divergencies as they arise.

In the present connexion we can only enumerate the theories that have been advanced to explain the diversity of language in the text of Daniel.

(*a*) Some scholars (Kliefoth, *Dan.*, p. 44; Keil, *Dan.*, p. 14) were of opinion that Aramaic was the vernacular of Babylonia, and was accordingly used in the sections relating to that country.

But this theory cannot for a moment be sustained. The cuneiform inscriptions prove that the language of Assyria and Babylonia was indeed Semitic, but a Semitic language distinct from Biblical Aramaic.

The latest connected inscription of this nature is that of Antiochus Soter, 280–260 B.C. Gutbrod (see Prince's *Book of Daniel*, p. 11, note) is of opinion that this Semitic language of Assyria was spoken until Hellenic times. As a language of the learned it may have survived till the second century B.C. In connexion with this theory we may notice the popular but now discredited fallacy, that the Jews forgot their Hebrew in Babylonia and spoke 'Chaldee' on their return to Palestine— a discredited fallacy we repeat; for we know from Nehemiah that Hebrew was the nominal language of the Jews in Jerusalem in 430 B.C. (Neh. 13²⁴).

Biblical Aramaic, misnamed Chaldee, was not brought across the Syrian desert by the Jews, but they 'acquired gradually' the use of it 'from their neighbours in and about Palestine' (Driver, *Dan.*, p. lix) after their return from the captivity.[1]

(*b*) Other scholars seek to explain *diversity of language by diversity of origin*. Thus this theory finds its starting-point and justification in the various attempts that have been made to analyse Daniel into different independent elements. Spinoza (*Tractatus theologico-politicus*, ed. 1674, p. 189) was the first to deny

---

[1] See Wright, *Comparative Grammar*, 1890, p. 16; Kautzsch, *Gramm. des Bibl. Aram.*, §§ 1, 2, 6. Bauer-Leander, p. 4 sqq.

the integrity of the book on the ground of the difference of language. Thus he writes: 'Transeo ad Danielis librum ; hic e dubio ex capite ipsius Danielis scripta continet. Unde m priora septem capita descripta fuerint nescio. Possumus icari, quandoquidem praeter primum Chaldaice scripta sunt, Chaldaeorum Chronologiis.' A distinct advance was made, n Sir Isaac Newton recognized the difference in character ween 1–6 and 7–12. In his *Observations upon the Prophecies of Daniel and the Apocalypse of St. John*, 1733, p. 10 (edited afresh by Sir William Whitla in 1922, p. 145) he writes: 'The book of Daniel is a collection of papers written at several times. The six last chapters contain Prophecies written at several times by Daniel himself; the six first are a collection of historical papers written by others. . . . The first chapter was written after Daniel's death . . . the fifth and sixth chapters were also written after his death.'

Note :

Beausobre (*Remarques sur le nouveau Testament*, 1742, p. 70) assigns 7–12 to Daniel but not 1–6. He observes that the author of 1–6 writes in the third person, not as the author of 7–12 in the first.

J. D. Michaelis (*Deutsche Uebersetzung des Alten Testaments*, 1781, vol. x, p. 22) threw doubts on the antiquity of 3–6 and was the first to draw attention to the presence of many Persian words 'which one could hardly expect before the time of Cyrus and the Greek words before the time of Alexander the Great'.

Eichhorn (*Einleitung*[4], § 615) regarded 2^{4b}–6 as a tradition about Daniel written by a Jew at an early date, and 1–2^{4a}, 7–12 as a subsequent addition written by a Jew in the time of Antiochus Epiphanes.

One of the most reasonable theories offered under this head is that of Meinhold (*Die Composition des B. Daniel*, 1884, and *Beiträge zur Erklärung des B. Daniel*, 1888 in Strack-Zöckler's *Kurzgef. Kommentar*, 1889). According to Meinhold, chapters 2^{4b}–7, were a piece of narrative written in Aramaic about 300 B.C. about Daniel and his history. These chapters a writer of the Maccabean age accommodated to the needs of his own time, and having prefixed 1–2^{4a} as an introduction to 2^{4b}–7, he supplemented these with chapters 8–12, containing visions of his own composition with special references to the persecutions of Antiochus, and issued the whole as a bilingual work. Bertholdt

BUT NEWTON STILL Thinks calls Book of DANIEL + its prophecies A Bsolutely critical to its rel. to Rev.

(*Daniel neu übersetzt und erklärt*, 1806) discovers nine distinct sources, of which the last is 10-12 written in the time of Antiochus Epiphanes. His analysis is accepted by Augusti.

Barton (*The Composition of the Book of Daniel* reprinted from the *JBL*, XVII, 62-86, 1898) discovers four sources, A, B, C, A^2, and a redactor. To the last he assigns 1, 2^{49}, 6^1, $12^{5-10, 13}$ and regards a few phrases in $6^{29\,b}$, 9^{21}, $10^{1, 9}$, $12^{11, 12}$ as later glosses.

Another form of this theory is that enunciated by Dalman (*Die Worte Jesu*, p. 11, 1898). Dalman supposes that 1-6 and 7-12 existed independently. The former was written in Aramaic, giving an account of Daniel's experiences and those of his companions at the court of Babylon. In a work in which the visions of the King of Babylon were interpreted, Aramaic, which was the *lingua franca* of the whole East at that time, was naturally considered suitable. The second part of the book, 7-12, was written in Hebrew, as its recounts Daniel's own visions with their interpretation by an angel, who of course would use only the sacred language. The redactor then took the two works in hand, and translated $1-2^{4\,a}$ into Hebrew and 7 into Aramaic, and compressed into one whole the two halves which were distinguished by their contents. Dalman's solution of the difficulty was arrived at independently by Torrey (*Notes*, I. 249), who, together with Hölscher ('Die Entstehung des B. Dan.', *Theol. Stud. u. Krit.*, 1919, p. 113) and Preiswerk (*Die Sprachenwechsel im B. Dan.*, 1902), maintains that $1-2^{4\,a}$ is a reversion into Hebrew.[1]

Montgomery (*The Book of Daniel*, p. 90, 1927) states that Dalman's solution is 'the only one that recommends itself' to him. On p. 95, however, he becomes doubtful and 'is therefore inclined to leave it an open question whether 7 is a distinct composition, a forerunner of the apocalypses in the following chapters even without deletion of verses which would relate it to the Maccabaean age'.

(*c*) The third theory is that which commands the assent of Driver, Behrmann, and Kamphausen, though it is to be observed that Driver with his usual caution and judgement does not absolutely commit himself to it, but only terms it as 'relatively the best' among the explanations offered. According to Kamphausen (*Encyc. Bibl. I.* 1005) 'the author has introduced

---

[1] So also Ryssel, *TLZ*, 1895, 560 (quoted from Montgomery, p. 91 *n*).

the Chaldeans as speaking *the language which he believed to be customary with them*: afterwards he continues to use the same language on account of its greater convenience both for himself and for his original readers, both in the narrative portions and in the following (seventh) chapter, the piece in companionship to chapter 2: for the last three visions 8, 9, 10–12, a return to Hebrew was suggested by the consideration that this had of old been the usual sacred language for prophetic subjects'. According to Behrmann, the Chaldeans, that is, the learned priestly class among the Babylonians, are introduced as speaking Aramaic in 2⁴ᵇ in order to give a local colouring. But to this the rejoinder is obvious. The distinction between Western and Eastern Aramaic had not yet arisen, see § 18. Aramaic was practically the same in our author's time in East and West. To ascribe to such a scholar as our author such ignorance of the situation and of the linguistic problem, as do Driver, Behrmann, and Kamphausen, is simply incredible. How can they do so in face of the fact that in 1⁴ it is said clever and chosen Jewish youths required three years to learn the literature and tongue of the Chaldeans. The tongue of this language could hardly therefore be a form of Aramaic, but rather Babylonian, a Semitic language very different from the Hebrew, or, it might be, even a non-Semitic Sumerian preserved in many of the marginal texts in the cuneiform script. That Babylonian was an unknown language is stated in Jer. 5¹⁵.

If, therefore, we may presume that our author was familiar with his Jeremiah, and if, as Lenormant informs us, he had 'an excellent knowledge of Eastern usages', we may reasonably conclude, first, that he does not confound Babylonian with Aramaic, and, secondly, that he would be very unlikely to represent the Chaldeans as speaking a language which according to this theory was *familiar* to both Jew and Chaldean. The words 'in Aramaic' in 2⁴ are therefore with Oppert, Lenormant, Nestle, Prince, and Marti to be rejected as an interpolation. Driver holds that this excision is probably right.

On the above grounds, therefore, we feel bound to conclude that the change of language in Daniel did not originate with its author. From considerations of a different nature we have previously shown that it was impossible that this change could be explained by diversity of origin.

Two other theories are possible ; and these ascribe the present form of the book not to its author, nor to a diversity of origin of its different sections, but to the fortunes it met with after its publication.

(*d*) The first of these theories, which is advanced by Lenormant, Bevan, Zeydner, Von Gall, Paul Haupt, Prince, and Barton, is that Daniel was originally written in Hebrew. But as the author lived in a time of intense excitement, and the book was evidently meant, not for a small circle, but for all 'the holy people' (see especially 11³³, 12³), 'the author himself or one of his associates' (Bevan, *Dan.*, p. 27) translated the book into the Aramaic vernacular, since the Hebrew language was then unintelligible to the ordinary people. 'But if the book was originally written throughout in Hebrew, why', Bevan asks 'has it reached us in its present form ?' To this he answers : 'The most plausible supposition is that a portion of the Hebrew text having been lost, a scribe filled up the gap by borrowing from the Aramaic version.'

Objections to this theory have been advanced by Driver and Marti. The former maintains that this theory 'does not account for two facts (which can hardly both be accidental) that the Aramaic part begins in chapter 2 just where the Aramaic language is mentioned, and breaks off just at the end of a chapter'¹ (*Dan.*, p. xxii). Marti further asserts that the Aramaic section does not convey the impression of being a translation, that the assumption of such an accident as the theory makes is a mere makeshift, and that it is not at all probable that a book, which was written when the Maccabees were gaining the upper hand, should be translated and yet not secured against destruction. These objections have some weight, but are by no means conclusive. But if it can be shown that the Hebrew sections (see § 10) come from three distinct hands, then this theory ceases to be tenable.

(*e*) The preceding theory has assumed a further development in the hands of Riessler and Jahn. These scholars maintain that chapters 2–7 of the version of the LXX were made directly from the Hebrew, and not from the Aramaic, as was that of

¹ Since the book was not divided into chapters till the middle ages, it would be better to transform this phrase into the form 'at the end of a vision', or 'section'.

Theodotion, and that the Hebrew text presupposed by the LXX is more original than the Aramaic of the Massoretic text, and formed moreover the Hebrew source from which the Aramaic version was translated in a revised form. The facts are altogether against this theory.

(*f*) We have now practically considered every possible ex-planation except that of Marti and Wright following in the steps of Huetius and Bertholdt. Marti (and herein the present writer agrees with him) is of opinion that the book was originally written wholly in Aramaic. Thus he contends that while on the one hand, the Aramaic section of Daniel does not give the impression of a translation, and nowhere points to a Hebrew original, the Hebrew sections, on the other hand, favour the hypothesis of an Aramaic original since they contain frequent Aramaisms. Marti, after advancing various grounds for the truth of his hypothesis proceeds to argue that no book written wholly in Aramaic could have been admitted into the Canon, as Hebrew was regarded as the sacred language, but since its exclusion from the Canon could with difficulty be contemplated on account of the importance of its subject-matter, the beginning and end of the roll were translated into Hebrew. At verse $2^{4\,a}$ the translator found occasion to bring his translation into Hebrew to a close, for the time being, as the Chaldeans were now repre-sented as speaking, and to resume his translation into Hebrew with chap. 8 because in chap. 9, which is closely connected with 8, the prayer of Daniel had already made its way into the text in a Hebrew dress.

In the opinion of the present writer this interpolation was made either when certain chapters of the book were being translated into Hebrew or after they had been so translated and before they were translated into Greek.

When once the beginning of Daniel and its closing chapters were written in Hebrew, it could be adopted into the Canon just as the book of Ezra.

§ 6. *The Book of Daniel was written originally in Aramaic,*
    and, though the author made use of oral or written sources,
    in the narratives, these were so fundamentally recast by
    him linguistically, if not in other respects that $2^{4\,b}$–6 must
    be regarded as coming from his hand no less surely than

This is the correct heresy

the vision in 7. *With the Hebrew sections which are translations by different hands from the original Aramaic we shall deal with in §§ 9, 10.*

(a) If we accept the Maccabean date of Daniel, and recognize that the author's burning appeal to be steadfast even unto death on behalf of God and country is directed *to his countrymen as a whole, and not to a small body of scholars* amongst them, who knew Hebrew as well as Aramaic, then the conclusion is inevitable that the entire work was written in the vernacular of his time, that is, in Aramaic, and this conclusion becomes more self-evident, as we pursue our investigations.

This conclusion does not exclude the use in the narrative sections of traditions which came down to our author either orally or by means of written sources. But, though in all probability their contents go back in part to the Persian period, as may be reasonably inferred from the numerous Persian words —seven of them denoting specific Persian officials—the Aramaic is not of the Persian period nor yet of any period earlier than the last half of the third century B.C. or rather the first half of the second century B.C., as also the historical references in chapter 11 postulates.

(b) The Aramaic of 7 is not to be attributed to a different author from that of 2⁴ᵇ-6. *Both belong to the same date and are the work of one and the same author.* To Dalman's division of Daniel into two distinct books, i.e. 1-6 and 7-12 we have already drawn attention. This hypothesis has been adopted also by Torrey and Montgomery (pp. 90, 95). But Sellin (*Introd. to O.T.* (Engl. Transl.), 1923, p. 233 seq.) more wisely connects 7 with 1-6, assigning 1-7 to a pre-Maccabean period but suggesting that 7 was brought up to date by insertions referring to Antiochus. Hölscher adopts a kindred hypothesis, and ascribes, with the exception of certain additions, 1-7 to the third century B.C.

To the date assigned to these chapters (or in part to a still earlier date) the present writer has no objection to make, if the date refers not to the present Aramaic form of these chapters but to the traditions embodied in them. From generation to generation they were transmitted, growing no doubt with each age, till at last their significance was recognized by our author and through his genius they were recast in a new and immortal setting, which inspired a dying world with fresh hope and an unconquerable faith.

But, so far as I am aware, no exhaustive criticism of Dalman's (i. e. also Torrey's and Montgomery's) hypothesis, which I am convinced is absolutely groundless, has yet appeared. I proceed, therefore, to deal with this hypothesis which would break up the book into two parts and commit, what appears to me to be the unintelligible error of assigning 2^{4b}-6 and 7 to different authors.[1]

---

[1] The chief grounds for this hypothesis are as follows :

(a) The King's name in 7^1 is spelt בלאשצר, whereas in $5^{1, 2, 9, 22, 29}$ it is spelt בלשאצר. But this fact in itself is of no importance in the face of the overwhelming evidence which I furnish for the unity of authorship. Besides in 5^{30}, 8^1 some MSS. of the MT spell the name exactly as in 7^1. Marti corrects this spelling both in 5^{30} and 7^1 but Bär and Strack reproduce the MT. In both these passages the abnormal spelling probably originated in the slips of a scribe.

(b) Again it is urged that the predominant use of Ithpe. and Ithpa. in 7 over against the Hithp. forms in 2^{4b}-6 points to difference of authorship. But what are the facts ? There are seven verbs בהל, זמן, חרך, מלא, רום, רחץ and שכח in 2^{4b}-6 which have the Hithp. forms. But on the other hand there are three verbs שנא 3^{19}, שמם 4^{16}, and יעט 6^8, which have the Ithp. forms. Furthermore to show the freedom with which either form was used we have only to compare 2^{34} and 2^{45} where the same verb (גזר is used—in the former passage with the Hithp. form, in the latter with the Ithp. We might compare with this last fact the use of the Aph'el of קום in 3^1, though the author elsewhere uses the Haph'el. In the face of this evidence no conclusion can be drawn from the appearance of Ithp. forms twice in 7, i.e. אתעקרו 7^8, אתכיות 7^{15}.

(c) Again Dalman emphasizes the fact that עליון is a Hebrew word. This is quite true. But as Montgomery (p. 308) observes : ' In this probably current term of the day the Saints preferred the Hebraic to the Aramaic word.' It is true that, owing to his view that 7 was originally written in Hebrew, he adds : ' Or the Hebrew word may have slipped in from the Hebrew original of the chapter.' His first suggestion appears to be the only tenable one, seeing that the evidence for 7 being in Aramaic originally and from the same hand as 2^{4b}-6 is so overwhelming. Thus we regard the phrase קדישי עליונין in $7^{18, 25, 27}$ as original. The Hebrew phrase in the *Zadokite Fragments* (18-8 B.C.) 9^{33} קדושי עליון is probably suggested by our text, just as in 16^3 'shall loose ... their knots' (קשריהם...יתר) is suggested by 5^{12} משרא קטרין of our text, but in both passages the Aramaic is rendered into Hebrew. There are also other real Hebraisms in our text : cf. 2^{10} יוכל whereas the true Aramaic form is יכל 5^{16}.

(d) It is strange that the champions of the original Hebrew of 7 have failed to notice that the phrase ' answered and said ' which occurs in each of the five preceding chapters does not occur in 7 ; for though the MT attests it in 7^2, I have excised it, since the LXX, Th. and Vulg. omit it. But this fact does not make for a Hebrew original, seeing that, as it is essentially a Hebrew idiom and is quite unknown in later Jewish Aramaic (Dalman, *Worte Jesu*, p. 19), its absence

§ 7. *Chapter 7 from the same author as* 2⁴ᵇ-6.

It seems impossible to question this fact in the face of the evidence that follows. Let us compare the use of words, phrases, syntactical usages, order of words in 7 with those in 2⁴ᵇ-6. There is not a single verse in the entire chapter (i.e. 7) which does not contain from one to four of the words, phrases, or typically idiomatic usages which are found in 2⁴ᵇ-6. Further, the order of the words in 7 is the same as that in 2⁴ᵇ-6. On the other hand, 2⁴ᵇ-6 contains an idiom which appears to belong distinctively to the second century B. C. Since it is absent from 7, this latter chapter could linguistically be older in this respect than 2⁴ᵇ-6. But they do not admit of division. Neither is a fore or after the other.

(*a*) *Individual words.*

אֱדַיִן 'then' 7¹⁹ : 19 times in 2⁴ᵇ-6.

אַחֲרֵי 'after' 7²⁴ : 2²⁹, ⁴⁵.

אָחֳרִי 'other' (fem.) 7⁵, ⁶, ⁸, ²⁰ : 2³⁹ (bis). Earlier form was אחרה : see Cowley 15³².

אחרן 'other' 7²⁴ : 2¹¹, ⁴⁴, 3²⁹.

אֲלוּ 'lo' 7⁸ (bis) : 2³¹, 4⁷, ¹⁰—always in the description of a vision. In 7², ⁵, ⁶, ⁷, ¹³ we find also אֲרוּ but not in 2⁴ᵇ-6. With it we might compare הרי in Mishnaic Hebrew, which bears the same meaning as אלו in 2⁴ᵇ-6 and הלו in fourth century B.C. Aram. See Cooke 73 A¹. The fact that אֲרוּ does not occur in 2⁴ᵇ-6 does not militate against unity of authorship.

דִי (= ὅτι *recitativum*) does not occur in 7, but neither does it occur in 3-4.

from this chapter is just as incomprehensible on the hypothesis of a Hebrew original as of an Aramaic. Dalman goes against the evidence, when he asserts that the formula in question was probably unknown in genuine Aramaic, seeing that our author supports it in 2⁴ᵇ-6 and also the Aramaic version of Aḥiḳar 45, 110, 118, 121 (fifth century B.C.). But idioms that occur in one or more chapters of 2⁴ᵇ-6 do not occur in the others : cf. דִי = ὅτι *recitativum* (see § 20 *u*) : also לְ *c. Inf.* = finite verb only in 2¹⁸, 5¹⁶, and לְ *c. Inf.*, where this phrase is preceded by *vav* and a finite verb, and by דִי = finite verb only in 2¹⁸, 6¹⁶ (see § 20 *t*.). Hence we cannot conclude from the absence of this phrase from 7 that 7 is not from the same hand as 2⁴ᵇ-6. Besides it may originally have occurred even in 7 ; for the LXX and the pre-Theod. version in 7¹⁶ ἀποκριθεὶς δὲ λέγει μοι presuppose עֲנָה וְאָמַר לִי where the MT omits the first verb. These may be right. In that case this idiom occurs in 7. But since it does not recur in the visions in 8-12, the probability is against its genuineness here. But is its absence due to the Hebrew translators?

אלין 'these' 7^{17} : 2^{44}, $6^{3,\,7}$ but not in 3–5. אֵלֶּין 2^{40} (Ginsburg).
In D only אִנּוּן [7^{17}] : 2^{44}, 6^{25}.

אתה 'to come' 7^{22} : 3^{26}.

דִּכֵּן 'this' $7^{20,\,21}$: 2^{31}. Only in Dan. and after noun.

באדין 'then' $7^{1,\,11}$: 24 times in $2^{4\,\mathrm{b}}$–6.

באתר 'after' $7^{6,\,7}$: 2^{39}. The older form is באשר.

בגו or בגוא 'in the midst of' 7^{15} : 3^{25}, 4^{7}, &c.

הדק (Haph.) 'to shatter' $7^{9,\,19,\,23}$: $2^{34,\,40,\,45}$, 6^{25}. In 7^{23}, 2^{40} used of the Fourth Kingdom.

הודע (Haph.) 'to cause to know' 7^{16} : 2^{5}, &c.

חבל (Hithpaʿal) 7^{14} : 2^{44}, 6^{27} (always of the kingdom of God).

ל before impersonal yet definite object 7^{2} : $2^{34,\,35}$, 3^{19}, &c.

מן in comparisons *different from* $7^{3,\,7,\,19,\,23,\,24}$: 4^{13}. Used partitively : חד מנהון 7^{16} : 6^{3}. Cf. $2^{33,\,41,\,42}$.

עד 'until' (prep.) $7^{18\,(\mathrm{bis})\,26}$: 2^{20}, $6^{15,\,27}$, 'during' $7^{12,\,25}$: $6^{8,\,13}$.

עד־די 'until' (conj.) $7^{4,\,9,\,11,\,22}$: 2^{34}, 4^{30}, 5^{21}.

עדה 'to pass away' (of a kingdom) 7^{14} : 4^{28}. Haph. 'to take away' (c. acc. of thing) $7^{12,\,26}$: 5^{20}.

קבל 'to receive' 7^{18} : 6^{1} and exactly in the same connexion : 2^{6}.

קדם 'before' $7^{10\,(\mathrm{bis}),\,13}$: also $7^{8,\,20}$ in the very idiomatic sense in which it is used in $2^{4\,\mathrm{b}}$–6. See § 20 *w*.

רברבן 'great' (fem. pl.) $7^{3,\,7,\,8,\,20}$: 2^{48}.

סלק 'to come up' 7^{3} : 2^{29}.

(*b*) *Phrases.*

אמיא אמיא ולשניא 'peoples, nations, and languages' 7^{14} : 3^{4}.

בעה c. מן of pers. 7^{16} : $2^{16,\,49}$.

דמה followed by ל 'to be like' 7^{5} : 3^{25}.

דת = Jewish religion 7^{25} : $6^{6(5)}$.

זיוי ישתנון עלי 'my countenance was changed' 7^{28} : same phrase in $5^{10\,(6,\,9)}$.

חזוא די ליליא 'vision[1] of the night' $7^{2,\,7,\,13}$. (So LXX and

---

[1] Our author never seems to have used the plural. The LXX has the plural only once in 7^{2}, where it has καθ' ὕπνους νυκτός. But this very phrase is in Is. 29^{7} a rendering of the sing. חזון לילה. The MT preserves the sing. only in 2^{19}, 7^{2} ; but there are occasional attestations of the original text in the later versions : in Th., Pesh., and Vulg. Thus the sing. is preserved in the Pesh. 2^{28}, 4^{10}, in the Pesh. and Vulg. in 4^{7}, in Th. and Vulg. in 4^{10}, in Pesh. and Vulg. in 7^{1}. Further Th. omits the phrase in 4^{7}. Th. and Vulg. attest the plural, in 2^{28}, 4^{2}, $7^{1,15}$, but,

Vulg. in $7^{7, 13}$: in 7^2 LXX has ὕπνους νυκτός but sing. in 4^{10}, 9^{21}: Th. has sing. in $7^{2(a), 13}$, but in 7^7 om.: Pesh. in $7^{2, 7}$ but om. in 7^{13}: Vulg. in $7^{7, 13}$ but in 7^2 agrees with MT.). There can hardly be a doubt that the MT in reading the pl. in $7^{7, 13}$ is corrupt, and that in these two passages we should read as in 2^{19}, seeing that none of the versions read the pl. and that the LXX in 7^2 does not necessarily imply the pl.

חזוי ראשי על משכבי 'the †visions of my head†[1] upon my bed' $7^1 : 2^{28}$.

חזוי־ראשי יבהלנני 'the †visions of my head† troubled me' $7^{15} : 4^2$.

חלם חזה 'saw a dream' $7^1 : 2^{26}$, $4^{2, 6, 15}$.

כל־דנה 'all this' $7^{16} : 5^{22}$.

לבב אנש יהיב לה 'a man's heart was given to it' $7^4 : 4^{13}$ לבב היוא יתיהב לה.

מלכותה מלכות עלם 'his kingdom is an everlasting kingdom 7^{27}: so exactly in 3^{33}, whereas in 4^{31}, where the redactor is at work the phrase is different. Yet in 7^{14} we find 'his dominion is an everlasting dominion which shall not pass away'. See note in the Translation on 7^{14}.

מנה מלכותא 'from the same kingdom' 7^{24}: same idiom in $3^{6, 7, 8, 15}$, $4^{30, 33}$.

מן־קדם 7^8: same phrase in 2^{15}, 6^{27}.

עד־סופא 'unto the end' $7^{26} : 6^{27}$—in both passages in the same connexion.

פלח ל 'to serve' (a deity) $7^{14, 27} : 3^{12, 14, 18, 28}$.

רעיוני יבהלנני 'my thoughts troubled me' 7^{28}: same phrase in 4^{16}, $5^{6, 10}$.

השניה זמנין 'to change the times' 7^{25}: same phrase in 2^{21}.

the Pesh. only in 4^2, 7^{15}. Hence we conclude that the plural in the MT in 2^{28}, $4^{2,7,10}$, $7^{1,15}$ should be emended into the sing. These plurals are the result of a slow process, which finally reached its present form in the MT. See further evidence under חזוא in the Aram. Index.

[1] 'Visions of the head' is a non-Semitic expression and was not introduced into the text of our author earlier probably than the first century B.C. It does not occur once in the LXX. Th. supports the MT in 2^{28}, 4^2, $7^{1,15}$ but omits it in 4^7 and substitutes 'in a vision of the night' instead in 4^{10}. Pesh. supports the MT in 2^{28} (sing.) $4^{2,7}$ (sing.) ^{10} (sing.), 7^{15}, and the Vulg. in all six passages Here we have the intrusion into the text of a non-Semitic phrase. The true Semitic expression is that in Jer. 23^{16} חזון לבם 'a vision of their own heart'.

(c) *Verbal prefixes and tenses.*

אתעקרו 7[8], אתכרית 7[15]: so in other verbs in 2[45], 3[19], 4[16], 6[8]. Yet התֿ occurs 17 times elsewhere in 2[4b]-7. See § 20 *l.* h (*ad fin.*), and once or more in I[α], II[α]. Next the Hoph'al occurs in 7[4, 5, 11] and in 4[33 (bis)], 5[13, 15, 20], 6[24]. Only once in Ezra.

יהיבת 7[27] used as fut. just as השכחנא 6[6] (fut. perf.).

(d) *Order of words : in* 2[4b]-6 *as compared with that in* 7.

	Average per Chap. in 2[4b]-6.	Chap. 7.
Subj. + verb 48 : 26 : 38 : 29 : 33 = 174	35	35
Obj. + verb 34 : 10 : 25 : 30 : 8 = 107	21	14
Verb + subj. or obj. 50 : 38 : 36 : 48 : 43 = 215	43	22

The average length of each of the first six Chapters is 34 verses. Chap. 7 has only 28. Thus the order of the words in 7 agrees on the whole well with that in 2[4b]-6. The greatest difference arises where the verb comes first. But herein Chap. 5, in which the verb comes first 48 times in 31 verses, agrees almost exactly with Chap. 7, in which the verb comes first in 43 in 28 verses. The greatest variation is apparent in the case of the position of the object. Observe that in Chap. 6 it comes first only 8 times.

Next let us compare 2[4b]-6 and 7 in regard to the six different combinations of subj., verb, and object.

	Chapters 2[4b]-6	Chap. 7
(1) Subj. + obj. + verb =		1
(2) Subj. + verb + obj. = 12	average c. 2½ in each Chap.)	3
(3) Obj. + subj. + verb = 2		
(4) Obj. + verb + subj. = 2		1
(5) Verb + subj. + obj. = 2		
(6) Verb + obj. + subj. = 1		1

When there is a combination of subj., verb, and obj., this order is the most common of all, and herein the average of 2[4b]-6 and 7 agree very closely.

If we take account of the fact that 2[4a]-6 consists of narratives, and 7 of visions, the agreement in order is surprising.

But independently of this last argument, the former arguments based on the same idiomatic use of the same particles, phrases, verbal forms, and syntactical usages is conclusive. In the view of the above arguments the unity of 2^{4b}–7 can hardly be regarded as other than an established fact.

The entire Aramaic sections are then from one and the same hand. Yet there is a difference between 2^{4b}–6 and 7. The subject-matter of 2^{4b}–6 has in the main come down to our author through oral (?) tradition : but 7 represents an immediate vision of the author. It is, therefore, all the more remarkable that the language in which the traditions were expressed, has influenced the style and usage of our author only in a few cases, if really at all. The Aramaic throughout 2^{4b}–7 is that of our author. Montgomery (p. 96) admits this fact in regard to 1–6. He writes : 'there is no reason to dispute the assumption of one literary hand for the whole' (i.e. 1–6). I have sought to prove by the evidence furnished above that not only has 2^{4b}–6 but also 7 come from one and the same writer. In fact the evidence, which proves that 7 is from the same hand as 2^{4b}–6, is stronger than the evidence that can be adduced in support of any one ot chapters 2–6 being the work of the same author as the remaining four. Sellin (*Introd. to O.T.*, 1923 (Eng. Transl.), p. 233 seq.) and Hölscher ('Entstehung des B. Daniel', *Theol. Stud. und Krit.*, 1919, 119 seq.) admit this unity of authorship but combine with this expression of their judgement the hypothesis that 1–7 was written in the third century B.C., and that subsequently in times of the Maccabees 7 was adapted to these times by the insertion of references to Antiochus and other personages of that period. This hypothesis as to the date is accepted by Montgomery, but it conflicts with the overwhelming evidence in favour of one and the same writer being the author of 2^{4b}–6 and 7—not only in respect of language and idiom, but also, we may justly assume, in respect of the order in which the events are recorded and the special lessons, moral and religious, which they are designed to convey.

§ 8. *There is an idiom in 2^{4b}–6 which belongs distinctively to the second century B.C., which, however, owing to the subject does not occur in 7.*

If we were forced to distinguish between the authorship and dates of 2^{4b}–6 and 7, as we are not, we should, so far as the language is concerned, be obliged to conclude that, though 7 could from the standpoint of *language* have been written as early as the latter half of the third century B.C., the linguistic evidence of 2^{4b}-6 decidedly favours a date, not earlier than the first half of the second century B.C. For the specific evidence of this nature see § 20 *dd* on the phrase 'Nebuchadnezzar the King'. But the linguistic and other evidence postulates the same author and the same date.

§ 9. *Since 2^{4b}-6 and 7 come to us in Aramaic from one and the same hand, we naturally conclude that the narratives i.e. 1–6 and the visions, i.e. 7–12 were written as a whole in Aramaic, seeing that 7, which contains a vision, is preserved to us in its original Aramaic.*

Since 7, which records the first of the visions is written in Aramaic, *there is no rational or conceivable ground* for the author's forsaking the vernacular language of his day and having recourse to Hebrew for his remaining three visions in 8–12, seeing that his visions, no less than his narratives, were addressed—*not to a small educated minority who understood Hebrew but—to the uneducated many who only understood Aramaic.* No historian of this period can question the fact that one of the chiefest forces in achieving the overthrow of the great Syrian empire by some 10,000 Jewish warriors or more, and so in preserving a personal and spiritual religion for all after times, was this very book with which we are dealing. To get in touch with his countrymen and to bring home to them the ideals for which they stood, *the author of Daniel could not do otherwise than write in Aramaic.* Only through the medium of the vernacular was this possible, and the vernacular of his day was Aramaic.

As the second century (before 160 B.C.) sections of 1 Enoch were written in Aramaic, so likewise we naturally infer that Daniel as a whole was written in Aramaic and that both Daniel and 1 Enoch (earliest sections) were addressed to the people at large.

But, granting that 2^{4b}-7 were originally written in Aramaic, how comes it that 1–2^{4a} and 8–12 have been transmitted to us in Hebrew? This is the next problem which calls for solution.

§ 10. $1-2^{4a}$[1] *and* $8-12$[2] *are translations into Hebrew from the original Aramaic, and the translations were made by three different hands.*

We have already seen that some scholars have held that the entire book was written originally in Hebrew. If this were so, and if the integrity of the book, save in the case of a few interpolations, cannot, as most of the foremost scholars[3] have argued, be questioned, it follows undoubtedly that these Hebrew sections should exhibit one and the same literary style and idiom, as the work of one and the same author. But this is far from being so, and it is the contention of the present editor that $1-2^{4a}-6$ and $8-12$ must be assigned to at least three different writers, or rather, if with most of the foremost scholars we hold fast to the integrity of the book, to at least three *translators.* If we can prove diversity of style in the Hebrew sections, it follows inevitably that the book of Daniel, if we accept its integrity, was not written originally in Hebrew but in Aramaic, and that the translation of the Aramaic was entrusted to several translators, just as the LXX translation of the books of Samuel and Kings can, as Thackeray (*JTS.*, iv. 245, 398, 578; viii. 262) shows, be traced to three different hands and the LXX translation of the books of Jeremiah and Ezekiel can similarly be traced in the case of each to two independent translators. See also Thackeray, *Gram. of the O.T. in Greek*, pp. 10-12.

It is now our task to prove that $1-2^{4a}$ was not translated into Hebrew by the translator or translators of 8-12.

$1-2^{4b}$. I have dealt with the characteristic differences between

---

[1] For Aramaisms in $1-2^{4a}$ see p. 3.

[2] For Aramaisms in 8 see p. 197, § 6: in 10 see p. 253, § 2: in 11, see p. 269 seq. (c): in 12 see p. 324, iii.

[3] Montgomery (p. 21 *ad. fin.*) regards 'the large proportion of Persian words in the Aramaic section of the book' as 'an argument for the distinction of the first and second half of the volume', and as pointing 'to the origin of the first part in Babylonia, not Palestine'. But this argument is irrelevant. The subject-matter of 1-6 requires the presence of Persian words denoting Persian officials, since, though we should expect Babylonian names for these officials, the kernel of the narratives assumed an oral or literary form in the Persian period, whereas the visions (7-12) were psychical experiences of the second cent. B.C. Besides, so far as idioms susceptible of a more or less definite date occur, these are to be found in $2^{4b}-6$ and not in 7, and these idioms tend to prove that the former section is not earlier than the second cent. B.C. See § 20 *w, dd*: also § 14 (*u*) seeing that Montgomery accepts $4^{3-7a(6-10a)}$ as authentic.

the Hebrew of 1–2⁴ᵃ and 8–12 on pp. 1–3, 8–9, 23, 53 (*ad fin.*).
It will suffice, therefore, to mention the chief of these here.

(*a*) In 1², ¹⁸, ²⁰ (i.e. within 24 verses) we find *vav* consecutive
with the Impf. which is also *vav* apodosis, whereas in 8–12
(containing 133 verses) *this rare Classical Hebrew idiom* does not
once occur. But in 8–12 there is an alternative form of this
idiom. Thus when the verb is separated from the *vav* apodosis
at the beginning of the clause by a noun, pronoun, or adverb,
the Imperf. is replaced by the Perf. tense. There are thus two
absolutely distinct forms of this idiom in the Hebrew sections of
Daniel. In 1–2⁴ᵃ (i.e. in 24 verses) the first form occurs three
times : whereas in 8–12) (i.e. in 133 verses) only the second form
of this idiom occurs and that only twice—i.e. in 10⁴, ⁹. On these
two forms of this idiom see Driver, *Tenses*³, § 127 seq. No scholar,
however, has hitherto observed that the first form of the idiom
is confined to 1–2⁴ᵃ and the second to 8–12. The significance of
this fact can hardly be exaggerated. In itself it postulates two
different translators.

(*b*) The Hebrew translator of 1–2⁴ᵃ uses twice the *oratio obliqua*
instead of the *oratio directa* after אמר: in 1³ ויאמר ‥‥ להביא¹ and
again in 2². Cf. also 1¹⁸. But in the 133 verses in 8–12 אמר is
not once followed by ל c. Inf., but by the *oratio directa*. In
Biblical Aramaic (see p. 2 (*b*)) the former construction occurs
9 times, though not once in the *Aram. Pap.* edited by Cowley,
whereas the latter construction occurs almost hundreds of times.
אמר followed by ל c. Inf. is a Hebrew construction—for the most
part late. Yet compare 1 Sam. 24¹¹, 1 Chron. 21¹⁷ where both
constructions are found in the same verses. The original
Aramaic of Daniel may have been influenced by the Hebrew.
The Targ. of 1 Sam. 24¹¹ reproduces the first construction.
Here again the style of 1–2⁴ᵃ is clearly marked off from that
of 8–12.

(*c*) The translator of 1–2⁴ ᵇ uses אדני—a Divine designation not
found in 8–12.

(*d*) In 1⁵, ¹⁹ עמד לפני = 'to serve': in 8–12 it = 'to withstand'.
See p. 324 *ad fin.*

For other evidence to the same effect refer to the pages
mentioned above.

---

¹ In the Targ. on Esth. 1¹⁰⁻¹¹ גזר is used as a rendering of אמר and is followed as in the Hebrew by ל c. Inf., and אמר in the Targ. on Esth. 4¹³,¹⁵ by
the same construction.

8–12. Within this section we must distinguish the Hebrew of 11 from that of 8–10, 12. On p. 268, § 1 (*a*) (see also p. 275) as Driver (*Tenses*³, §§ 171, 175 Obs.) has pointed out, attention is drawn to the fact that the jussive is used 9 times in chap. 11 'without any recollection of its distinctive signification', and not once throughout the remaining five Hebrew chapters. On this ground alone we should in the main be justified in ascribing the Hebrew of 11 to a translator other than the translator of 8–10, 12. 8–10, 12 are distinguished from 1–2⁴ᵃ, as we have shown above, by the fact that they do not use a Classical Hebrew idiom used in 1–2⁴ᵃ but an alternative form of it, independently of other grounds. But 11 is marked off from all the other Hebrew chapters in that it exhibits the frequent *misuse* of a well-known Hebrew idiom. For other grounds see p. 268 seq. (*b*).

§ 11. *Why was the translation of* 11 (+ 12 ?) *entrusted to a very faulty Hebrew scholar rather than to the translators of the earlier chapters?*

An indisputable explanation for this change of translator cannot be furnished, but on the whole it is not improbable that, since this chapter dealt with comparatively recent and contemporary history from 336 to 166 B.C., in which the author assumes on the part of his readers a more minute and detailed history of events than anywhere else in his work, the task of rendering this chapter into Hebrew demanded indeed a Hebrew scholar, but in still greater measure a historian who had an intimate knowledge of this period of history. The combination of both linguistic and historical knowledge was apparently not easy to find at the time in question, but, since in such a detailed narrative, historical knowledge was of more importance than a good Hebrew style, the duty of translating it appears to have been entrusted to a very second-rate Hebraist, who counterbalanced his linguistic shortcomings by a reasonably good knowledge of the history with which the vision dealt.

The translator of 11 may also have been the translator of 12. But no definite conclusion, so far as I can see as yet, can be arrived at on this question. The misuse of the jussive form so frequent in 11 does not recur in 12. But in another respect he shows as great ignorance of Hebrew usage, when he identifies הַיְאֹר with the Euphrates, whereas before 200 B.C. it was used only of the Nile.

§ 12. *The approximate date of the translation
of 1–2⁴ᵃ, 8–12 into Hebrew.*

On pp. 52-4 I have advanced several reasons, which appear to me conclusive, that 1^{20-21} originally followed 2^{49a}. There is no need for recapitulating those reasons here. The lucidity of the Seer's thought and the clear sequence of his ideas, which are manifest throughout in the enforcement of his main thesis, appear to make imperative the restoration of 1^{20-21} to their legitimate place in the Seer's argument, as I have done in my Commentary and Translation.

If then we accept this early dislocation of the text, it must have occurred between 164 and 145 B.C. or thereabouts. The ground for the latter date is to be found in the LXX, a translation which was made of these Hebrew chapters about 145 B.C. When this translation was made, the above dislocation had already taken place. But it had taken place some, if not many years earlier, seeing that the first Hebrew translator found 1^{20-21} already in their present, untrue, and unhistorical context. By these adjectives I mean that 1^{20-21} occupy a place in the traditional text inconsistent alike with the clear intention of the Seer and the historical traditions at his disposal. For the study of many years has convinced me that the Seer was not only a religious genius but a consecutive and logical thinker, and most scholars will agree that in the composition of 2^{4b}-6 he laid under contribution the historical traditions of his day, whether oral or written.

Now as regards the date of the partial translation into Hebrew, it is possible that the six chapters 1–2⁴ᵃ, 8–12 were so translated before the death of Judas Maccabaeus in 161 B.C. The original of the entire book of Daniel was of course in the Aramaic vernacular, but, if the book was to be embodied in the Canon and made of lasting significance, this end could not be achieved otherwise than by commending itself in a Hebrew form, at all events in its opening and closing chapters, to the scholars of the day, who could admit its canonical authority, as they did of the bilingual Ezra, though they refused to include it in the canon of the prophets.

If, owing to the turbulence of the time, this date of the Hebrew translation of the six chapters be regarded as too early, it may be referred to the time of Judas' successor, Jonathan, when

3266 d

as 1 Macc. 9[73] states : ' The sword was now at rest in Israel and Jonathan dwelt at Michmash. And Jonathan began to judge the people ; and he destroyed the ungodly (i.e. the Hellenizers) out of Israel.' This period of peace closes with the year 153 B.C. This year may constitute the *terminus ad quem* of the translation.

The three translators probably worked simultaneously. They had one and the same object, and that was to gain a canonical recognition of the book. To the Hebrew translator of 8–10 we owe the clumsy interpolation of the beautiful prayer in 9[4–19], see p. 226 seq., and possibly the enumeration of the actual national enemies of the Maccabean dynasty in 11[41, 43] a thing impossible in Apocalyptic.

§ 13. *The Versions.*

The present work does not admit of any adequate criticism of the various versions. Individual readings, as they arise are dealt with in this Commentary, and so far as the LXX, Th., and Syro-Hexaplar texts are concerned the present editor has based his work on Swete's *O.T. in Greek*, 498–575.

It is, however, our duty to give a short account of the versions by the help of which we can arrive at a more trustworthy text than that of the MT. For from the selection of readings in § 14 [(a)–(f)], in which the MT. is in the greater number unquestionably inferior to that of the four chief versions taken collectively or of three, or two, or even of one of them, the reader cannot escape drawing the inference that the MT. is to a great extent untrustworthy, and needs to be corrected by these versions.

The chief versions of the book of Daniel are : the Greek versions, i.e. (*a*) the LXX, and (*b*) Theodotion, (*c*) the lost pre-Theodotion, (*d*) the fragmentary remains of Aquila and Symmachus : the two Syriac versions, (*e*) the Peshitto, and (*f*) that of Paul of Tella, (*g*) the Old Latin, (*h*) the Vulgate, (*i*) the Sahidic and Bohairic, (*k*) the Ethiopic.

The Greek Versions—the LXX and Th. These two versions (*a*) and (*b*) are of great value for the reconstruction of the Text, notably the former. As we are aware, the LXX unhappily is preserved only in an almost incredibly corrupt MS., i.e. the Codex Chisianus, attributed by some experts to the ninth and by others to the eleventh century. This Codex once belonged to Pope Alexander VII, a member of the Chigi family, but it was not till more than a century after his death that the *editio princeps* of this MS. was published in Rome in 1772. Its publication was undertaken by Vincent de Regibus and Joseph Bianchini, and finally carried through the press by the labours of Simon de Magistris (de Maîtres). Many editions have subsequently appeared, the most recent of which is that of Dr. Swete, who, to the great convenience of scholars, prints the versions of the LXX[1] and Theodotion on opposite pages, and appends at the foot of the LXX version the variants from the Syriac version of Paul of Tella. This version is of no slight interest. It was made by or for Paul, bishop of Tella, in the year 616–617 from a hexaplar text. Thus it attests the condition of the LXX text as it existed at the beginning of the seventh century. As regards the date of the LXX version of Daniel, it is probable that it was made in the latter half of the second century B.C. *c.* 145.

(*b*) The date and relations of Theodotion's version of Daniel are far from easy to determine. According to Irenaeus, Theodotion was an Ephesian, but according to Epiphanius, a native of Pontus and a disciple of Marcion, where he adopted Judaism, while Jerome reports that he was probably a Jew who had espoused Ebionitic Christianity. Epiphanius assigns the period of his activity to Aurelius Commodus. As this Commodus reigned from A.D. 180 to 192, and as Marcion flourished about 150, the version of Theodotion, if we may trust Epiphanius, was written towards the close of the second century A.D. The *Paschal Chronicle* follows Epiphanius and ascribes the work of Theodotion to the year A.D. 184. The above date is very doubtful, and is in all probability one or more decades too late. But even if we could establish as early a date as 150, it would not materially lessen the difficulties which embarrass the relations of this version with that of the LXX. For we find that a great variety of readings, which we class under (*c*), and which are peculiar to Theodotion as against the LXX, are found already in quotations from Daniel in the first century of the Christian era.

Before entering, however, on this large question, we should observe that prior to Jerome's time[2] the Church discarded the

---

[1] Swete reproduces the Codex Chisianus as published in Cozza's *Sacrorum Bibliorum vetustissima fragmenta graeca et latina*, vol. 3, 1877.

[2] *Praef. in Dan.* Danielem prophetam iuxta LXX interpretes . . . ecclesiae non

use of the LXX version of Daniel in favour of that of Theodotion. How this came about Jerome could not tell. The way for such radical action had already been prepared by the action of Origen, whose citations from Daniel, as Dr. Gwynn writes (*Dict. of Christian Biography*, iv. 974), 'agree almost *verbatim* with the text of Theodotion now current', a fact that accords well with the announcement made by Origen, in the ninth volume of his lost *Stromata*, that he intended to use this version. (Jerome on Dan. 4⁶).

But Theodotion's version was used by several of the Fathers before Origen's time. Clement of Alexandria used Theodotion with occasional readings from the LXX.

In North Africa Tertullian's (*ob.* 240) references to Daniel are based mainly on the LXX version, though in a few cases he cites Daniel according to Theodotion. His contemporary Cyprian (*ob.* 258), Burkitt states, took his citations from the Old Latin translation of Daniel according to the LXX, which was already corrected according to Theodotion's version (cf. *De op. et elem* 5. ed. Hartel, p. 377).[1]

At an earlier date Hippolytus, the pupil of Irenaeus, adopted this version in his Commentary on Daniel about A.D. 202. Hippolytus was here following in the footsteps of his master Irenaeus, who was the first among the Fathers to quote Daniel 9²⁴⁻⁷ as a Messianic prophecy according to Theodotion's version.

(c) *Pre-Theodotion Version.*[2] We have thus far only mentioned writers who lived subsequently to the date usually assigned to Theodotion. But the Theodotion type of text was clearly familiar to writers of an earlier date. Thus in Hermas there is one

---

legunt, utentes Theodotionis editione et hoc cur acciderit nescio. . . . Hoc unum affirmare possum, quod multum a veritate discordet. Cf. *Contra Ruff.*, ii 33.

[1] See Bratke, *Das neu entdeckte 4. Buch des Dan. Comm. von Hippolyt.*, Bonn, 1891.

[2] In this recognition of a pre-Theodotion version of Daniel I follow in the steps of many scholars of the last hundred years. Credner (*Beiträge zur Einl. in die bibl. Schriften*, 1838, ii. 261–272) put forward the conjecture that there was an Early *Christian* version of Daniel, on which the New Testament quotations were based, as well as some of Justin Martyr's. Gwynn (*DCB*, iv. 976) disagrees with Credner's hypothesis. Strongly influenced by Salmon's view (*Introduction*, p. 548 sqq.) that 'there is no clear evidence that St. John had ever seen the so-called version' of Daniel, he shows by a variety of evidence (with all of which I cannot indeed agree) that the Greek text is clearly a *Jewish* and not a Christian translation. 'Side by side with the Christian LXX, there was current among the Jews from pre-Christian times, another version of Daniel,

undoubted reference (*Vis.* iv. 2. 4) to Theodotion's version of Daniel 6²² and possibly to others.

But the existence of Theodotion's readings before the time of Theodotion is still more clearly established by the long extract Justin Martyr (*ob. c.* 163) gives in his *Dial. c. Tryph.* 31 from Dan. 7. This extract while fundamentally in agreement with the LXX, presents us with a score of distinctively Theodotion words and phrases, and at least as many readings peculiar to the LXX. That Justin has quoted twenty verses from this pre-Theodotion Version I have sought to prove in § 25.

That this combination of the two distinct types in not due to pure eclecticism or defective remembrance on the part of Justin has been shown by Burkitt (*Old Latin and Itala,* p. 22 sqq.), since we find the same admixture in the Latin version in Tertullian's reproduction of the same passage. But earlier still, Clement of Rome (1 Cor 34⁶, *c.* A.D. 96) shows acquaintance (Dan. 7¹⁰ ἐλειτούργουν, LXX ἐθεράπευον) with Theodotion in a citation from the passage of Daniel just referred to, and Barnabas (*Ep.* 4⁵) recalls Theodotion's rendering of Dan. 7²⁴ more closely than that of the LXX.

But still more memorable is the attestation given by certain passages of the N.T. to the existence of a pre-Theodotion text.

The citations from the N.T. are here mainly confined to Revelation : but we should not ignore Matt. 21⁴⁴ (=Luke 20¹⁸) λικμήσει from Th. 2⁴⁴ : Matt. 28³ τὸ ἔνδυμα αὐτοῦ λευκὸν ὡσεὶ χιών from

more deserving of the name, claiming to belong to the LXX collection and similar in general character to the LXX versions of other books of the Hagiographa; that this was the version known to the author of the Book of Baruch (or the Greek translator of it); and to St. Matthew, St. Mark,...St Clement, and to Hermas ; and that it was also the version on which Theodotion founded his.' Swete (*Introd. to the Old Testament,* p. 48 sq.) writes with reserve on this question, but in his Commentary on the Apocalypse, p. cliv sq., he practically accepts Salmon's view and writes : 'the Greek text of Daniel known to the Apocalyptist came nearer to the Theodotionic than to the Chigi text.' Thackeray in his *Septuagint and Jewish Worship,* 1921, p. 24 sqq., admits the necessity of assuming a pre-Theodotion translation. The many parallels between 1 Baruch (later half of first century A.D.) and this translation where it diverges from the LXX can thus easily be explained.

Montgomery (p. 50) in closing a discussion of this question concludes that 'there existed some such body of received translation (i.e. Theodotionic) before the Christian age', but he urges that 'we must not too quickly assume a written version'. He advances the hypothesis of 'a Hellinistic oral Targum' But the hypothesis does not explain the facts.

Th. 7⁸: James 1¹² μακάριος ἀνὴρ ὃς ὑπομένει=Th. 12¹²(?): Heb. 11³³ ἔφραξαν στόματα λεόντων : cf. Th. 6²³ ⁽²²⁾ ἐνέφραξεν τ. στόματα τῶν λεόντων.

For the existence of a pre-Theodotion text, which was in part based on the LXX and a redacted edition of the Hebrew-Aramaic text of Daniel the following evidence, which could be given in greater fullness, may be adduced.

Revelation. There are several passages in the Apocalypse which show a dependence on a pre-Th. text.

In 1⁷ ἰδοὺ ἔρχεται μετὰ τ. νεφελῶν τοῦ οὐρανοῦ agrees with Th. 7¹³. Here the LXX has ἰδοὺ ἐπὶ τ. νεφελῶν τοῦ οὐρανοῦ . . . ἤρχετο.

In 1¹³ γίνεσθαι μετὰ ταῦτα. Cf. Th. 2²⁹, ⁴⁵ γενέσθαι μετὰ ταῦτα.

9²⁰ τὰ εἴδωλα τὰ χρυσᾶ καὶ τὰ ἀργυρᾶ καὶ τὰ χαλκᾶ καὶ τὰ λίθινα καὶ τὰ ξύλινα. Cf. Th. 5²³ where exactly the same enumeration is given save that the adjectives are all in the masc., being dependent on τοὺς θεούς. Here the LXX has only τὰ εἴδωλα τὰ χειροποίητα.

10⁴ σφράγισον. Th. 8²⁶ σφράγισον τ. ὅρασιν. LXX different.

10⁶ ὤμοσεν ἐν τῷ ζῶντι = Th. 12⁷. LXX ὤ. τ. ζῶντα.

11⁷ ποιήσει μετ᾽ αὐτῶν πόλεμον καὶ νικήσει αὐτούς. Th. 7²¹ ἐποίει πόλεμον μετὰ τ. ἁγίων καὶ ἴσχυσεν πρὸς αὐτούς. LXX πόλεμον συνιστάμενον πρὸς τ. ἁγίους καὶ τροπούμενον αὐτούς.

11¹³ ἔδωκαν δόξαν τ. θεῷ τ. εὐρανοῦ. Cf. Th. 2¹⁹ εὐλόγησεν τ. θεὸν τ. οὐρανοῦ. LXX differs.

16¹⁸ θλίψις οἵα οὐ γέγονεν ἀφ᾽ ἧς γεγένηται ἐν τῇ γῇ— Th. 12¹ οἷος οὐκ ἐγένετο ἀφ᾽ οὗ οἱ ἄνθρωποι ἐγένοντο ἐπὶ τῆς γῆς. The last three words are peculiar to Rev. and Th.

19⁶ φωνὴν ὄχλου and Th. 10⁶ φωνὴ ὄχλου (LXX θορύβου).

20⁴ κρίμα ἐδόθη αὐτοῖς. Th. 7²² τὸ κρίμα ἔδωκεν ἁγίοις.

20¹¹ τόπος οὐχ εὑρέθη αὐτοῖς = Th. 2³⁵: but LXX ὥστε μηδὲν καταλειφθῆναι ἐξ αὐτῶν.

In Rev. there are some passages which show the influence of the LXX. I have dealt with these in my Comm. on Rev., and in any case this subject does not call for treatment here.

But the circulation and use of the pre-Theodotion text for nearly a century after the N.T. Apocalyse cannot be ignored. They confirm the conclusions already arrived at.

Ep. Clement, xxxiv. 6 (c. A.D. 96) Μύριαι μυριάδες παρειστήκεισαν αὐτῷ καὶ χίλιαι χιλιάδες ἐλειτούργουν αὐτῷ. In Th. 7¹⁰ we find χίλιαι χιλιάδες ἐλειτούργουν αὐτῷ καὶ μύρ. μυριάδες παριάτήκεισαν αὐτῷ. Here Th. agrees with the LXX save in reading ἐλειτούργουν where the

LXX has ἐθεράπευον. Clement as Rev. 5¹¹ inverts the order of the numerals, 'thousand thousands' and 'ten thousand times ten thousand'.

Justin Martyr (A.D. 100–163) shows an admixture of Th. and the LXX, or a revised LXX, or the actual use of the pre-Theodotion version in his *Dial.* 31. That neither of the first hypotheses is correct I am fully convinced so far as *Dial.* 31 is concerned, in which we find twenty consecutive verses of Daniel, i.e., 9⁹⁻²⁸. Since the problem is a difficult one, I have treated it at some length in § 25 (*a*), and furnished what appears to be conclusive evidence that Justin has in this passage drawn his quotations from the pre-Theodotion version, though in a few other passages he has used the LXX.

Again in *Dial.* 110. 7 he follows the LXX 11³⁶ ἔξαλλα λαλήσει where Th. has λαλήσει ὑπέρογκα.

Shepherd of Hermas, *Vis.* iv. 2. 4 (A.D. 140–155), Ὁ Κύριος ἀπέστειλεν τὸν ἄγγελον αὐτοῦ . . . οὗ τὸ ὄνομά ἐστιν Σεγρί, καὶ ἐνέφραξεν τὸ στόμα αὐτοῦ, ἵνα μή σε λυμάνῃ. Here Hermas follows a pre-Th. text. In Th. 6²³⁽²²⁾ we have ὁ θεός μου ἀπέστειλεν τ. ἄγγελον αὐτοῦ καὶ ἐνέφραξεν τὰ στόματα τῶν λεόντων καὶ οὐκ ἐλυμήναντό με. I have underlined the words in Hermas dependent on a pre-Th. text. Even the word Σεγρί, as Rendel Harris has pointed out, recalls the verb סגר 'shut' (the mouth). See *DCB.* iv. 601. The clause containing this word may have originated in a gloss. Here the LXX is different.

Irenaeus (*c.* A.D. 180) *Adv. Haer.* v. 25. 4 quotes Th.'s version of Dan. 8²⁵, as well as v. 25. 3 from Th. 7²³ sqq.

Clem. Alex. (A.D. 150–210), ed. by Stählin, 1906).

Dan. 2²⁷⁻⁸: *Strom.* i. 4 (330 P). Purely Th. save for the addition of δύναμις τοῦ before ἀναγγεῖλαι.

7⁹: *Paed* ii. 10 (235 P). ἐτέθησαν, φησί, θρόνοι καὶ ἐκάθισεν ἐπ᾽ αὐτῶν ὡσεὶ παλαιὸς ἡμερῶν καὶ τὸ ἔνδυμα αὐτοῦ ὡσεὶ χιὼν λευκόν. Here Clem. reproduces Th. over against the LXX. But it does more: it gives the true apocalyptic designation of God ὡσεὶ παλ. ἡμερῶν, though all other authorities save the LXX 7¹³ omit the ὡσεί or its Aramaic original.

8¹³⁻¹⁴: *Strom.* i. 21 (408 P) = Th.

9²⁴⁻⁷: *Strom.* i. 21 (393 P) = Th. with some divergences. He corrects Theodotion's καὶ ἀπαλεῖψαι καὶ τοῦ ἐξιλάσασθαι into καὶ τοῦ ἀπαλεῖψαι καὶ τοῦ ἐξιλάσασθαι. The first verb was originally a gloss.

12^{11-12}: *Strom.* i. 21 (409 P) = Th. with one or more slight divergences.

For the existence of two such versions we have a partial analogy in the two Books of Esdras in the LXX. A further and better analogy to the existence of two different versions of the Book of Daniel, which in fact represent in a minor degree two recensions of that book, may be found in the Testaments of the Twelve Patriarchs, of which there are two distinct Greek versions, one of which is represented by three MSS., and the other by six.

If the scope of this work admitted of it, we should now have to inquire : did these two versions go back to different Semitic originals ; or did the notable variations between these two versions arise within the Greek itself? But though we cannot advance here the detailed evidence of the Semitic text and of the Greek versions, we can state the conclusions arrived at from the above evidence. These are, that if the Semitic text in its present form is as old as the Christian era, or even as ancient as 50 B.C., then there existed side by side with it another and earlier form of the Semitic text, of which the LXX form in the Chigi MS. presents us with a valuable, though corrupt rendering. It is possible to prove that the vast majority of the corruptions in this version can be traced to a Semitic background.

This statement holds in regard to chapters 1–3, 7–12, and its cogency has been recognized to a considerable extent by all the foremost scholars.

(*d*) But with regard to chapters 4–6 the case is different. Here the foremost scholars have in most cases relinquished the study of these chapters in despair. Thus Bevan writes on p. 46 : ' In chapters 3–6 . . . the original thread of the narrative is often lost in a chaos of accretions, alterations, and displacements.'

The same view is practically set forth by Behrmann on p. 30 seq. of the introduction to his edition. Bludau (*Alexandrinische Uebersetzung des Buches Daniel*, p. 154, 1897) states as his opinion, after a critical examination of the LXX, that chapters 4–6 are to be named 'a revision rather than a translation'. This verdict is quoted with approval by Marti in his edition, p. xix.

On p. 31 Bludau includes chapter 3 in this criticism. It is

less corrupt indeed than 4-6. In regard to these the translator is said to have sometimes filled the role of a translator, sometimes of a paraphrast, and sometimes of an epitomizer. To these adverse critics of 4-6 we may now add Montgomery, *Book of Daniel*, p. 38, 1927. He thinks (p. 37) that 3-6 circulated as an independent and pre-Maccabean collection of stories, as Bevan had already suggested.

But with the above conclusions the present writer cannot agree. A long sustained and minute study of the text and versions has led him to conclude that it is just in these chapters that the LXX makes its greatest contribution to the recovery of the original text over against the late redacted text of the MT. particularly in chapter 4 and to a less extent in 5. The bulk of the evidence for this conclusion cannot of course be given here, but some of the grounds are enumerated in the introduction to chapters 4-6. The LXX, however, which has been reproduced in Hexaplaric form, needs to be critically edited.

In fact, in many instances it attests an older and purer form of the LXX text. It retains the critical signs introduced by Origen into the text, i.e. the asterisk, and obelus, and the metobelus, which have as a rule been omitted in the Codex Chisianus.

(*e*) I have occasionally referred to the fragments of the versions of Aquila and Symmachus in the Commentary, but have no space to deal with them here.

(*f*) *The Peshiṭo Version* belongs to the same type of version as Theodotion, and therefore agrees for the most part with the Massoretic text. It is reproduced from practically identical texts in the London and Paris Polyglots and by Lee in 1823. A photographic reproduction of the Ambrosian MS. was published by Ceriani in 1876. Of course it diverges at times from all known authorities, and in one case may single-handed represent the original, i.e. in 11⁴.

(*g*) *The Syriac Version of Paul of Tella.* This slavishly literal rendering of Origen's Hexaplaric text was made at Alexandria in the years 616-617 by Paul of Tella. It is preserved in an eighth century MS., and was published by Bugati in 1788.[1]

---

[1] This version was first made known to the world of scholars by Andreas Masius (*ob.* 1573) from a MS. which has since been lost. But another MS. was preserved at Milan, which Ceriani published in photographic facsimile, *Codex*

This Syriac version is of great value in the correction of the Codex Chisianus.

(*h*) *The Old Latin.* According to Burkitt (*Rules of Tyconius,* p. cxvi) 'The Old Latin brings us the best independent proof we have that the Hexaplar signs introduced by Origen can be relied on for the reconstruction of the LXX. Passages in Hexaplar MSS. to which is prefixed the asterisk (※) profess to be no part of the original LXX but to have been added from other sources. *No such passage is found in any genuine form of the African Latin.*' For a very extensive list of O.L. Patristic quotations see Ranke, *Fragmenta versionis sacrarum scripturarum latina antehieronymiana,* Vienna, 1868; *Par palimpsestorum wirceburgensium,* 1871 (i.e. the Wurzburg Fragments); *Stutgardiana versionis sacrarum scripturarum latinae antehieronymianae fragmenta,* Vienna 1888; Dold, Konstanzer altlateinische Propheten, Leipzig, 1923, in *Texte u. Arbeiten herausgegeben durch die Erzabtei Beuron,* 1 Abt., Heft 7–9; also Montgomery's enumeration (in his Comm.) of O.L. Fragments from all sources, p. 29 seqq., which he says amounts to three-fourths of the entire book. A comprehensive and critical study of these fragments and their bearing on the LXX is much to be desired.

(*i*) *The Vulgate Version.* This version was made in the years 319–405. It is most closely related to the Massoretic text and to Theodotion. Sometimes it agrees with the Massoretic against Theodotion, and sometimes conversely, whilst in others it seems to take an independent line. In $6^{25\,(24)}$ it may be the only authority which preserves the original text. In 9^{24} it apparently does so also in conjunction with the LXX.

(*k*) The Sahidic and Bohairic versions are translations of the Th. as Sir Herbert Thompson informs me. I have not been able to make any use of them.

(*l*) The Ethiopic version of Daniel, published last year in Paris by Oscar Löfgren, appeared too late to be of service to this edition. It is itself a version of Th., and a very free and at times unintelligible version of it. It differs from Th. in reading 'vision' and not 'visions' (4^2, 7^{15}). It reproduces the non-Semitic expression 'vision of the head' in 2^{28} (COW) 4^2 (A$_1$ A$_2$ L$_2$), 7^{15} and certain MSS. of 7^1.

syro-hexaplaris Ambrosianus 1873. See Swete, *Introd. to the Old Testament,* pp. 112–13.

§ 14. *The Massoretic Text—its essentially
secondary character.*

The Massoretic text of our author may on the whole be
regarded as representing the substance of the original, but in
scores or rather hundreds of passages it is wholly untrustworthy
as to the form of the original and occasionally as to its subject-
matter. But to be more definite, we are obliged to maintain
that it is very often inferior to the LXX, Th., Pesh., and Vulg.,
and that, if it is our aim to recover as far as possible the original
Aramaic of 2^{4b}–7, or the primitive form of the Hebrew version
of the remaining chapters, we must have constant recourse to
the above versions.

The great scholars of the past and present, who have devoted
their energies to the recovery and interpretation of Daniel, have
as a rule overlooked the fact that this work belongs not to the
prophetic type of O.T. literature but to the Apocalyptic, and that,
whereas O.T. prophecies, which dealt with contemporary nations
and individuals under their actual designations, were *first spoken
and then committed to writing* under the names of their respective
authors, Jewish apocalypses were *first written and not spoken*,
and written, moreover, under the names not of their actual
authors but of various ancient worthies who lived some 400 to
4000 years (according to Jewish chronology) before the actual
period of the respective authors of these apocalypses.

Jewish apocalypses thus dealt in the main with the individuals
and nations of the past down to their authors' actual period and
*generally with these under symbolic designations. When the writer
approaches his own period this rule held absolutely.* Personal or
national names were then absolutely eschewed and only symbolic
designations used. Hence, as we shall see later, the clauses in
Dan. $11^{41, 44}$ mentioning nations contemporary with the writer of
Daniel are, as even tyros in apocalyptic literature will recognize,
interpolations made 161 or at latest before 145 B.C., when the LXX
was translated, and when the Jews could hold their own with
their national enemies. Since Jewish apocalypses after the third
century B.C. were in all cases pseudonymous,[1] this pseudonymity
must for some years, if not for one or more generations, have
exposed the text to corruptions, interpolations, dislocations, and

---

[1] Not so the great Christian Apocalypse. See my Comm. I, p. xxxviii sqq.

manifold other evils incident to the reproduction and circulation of pseudonymous works. In the case of Daniel, not only was it composed in secret as all Jewish apocalypses, but the earliest scribes who copied it must have worked in secret—not only to escape discovery on the part of the agents of Antiochus and the Hellenizing Jews, but also of the main body of the faithful remnant, to which the writers themselves belonged. During this period, when Daniel was being copied by scores of scribes, some of whom were not improbably illiterate, errors of every kind must have crept into the text. This fact cannot be ignored, when we come down to the LXX version, which, though made within twenty years after the composition of the original, teems with corruptions of every variety. But, notwithstanding these, no student of Daniel can fail to recognize that this version is invaluable to him in his efforts to recover the oldest form of the text. This fact will grow in impressiveness as his study advances, till at last he reaches the conviction, based on unquestionable evidence, that between the earliest form of this text which is preserved in a mutilated form in the LXX and that which is preserved in the MT there yawns a deep and at times an impassable gulf. Furthermore, he wins the assurance that, whereas the MT and the versions, which support it, represent the editing and recasting of the text by a scholar, or rather by a body of scholars through successive generations from possibly as early as 145 B.C. down to A.D. 400, the LXX represents the honest attempt of one, or possibly more scholars, to render into Greek the corrupt bilingual text of Daniel, a text so corrupt that they found the task of giving an intelligible version at times utterly beyond them, and so had to content themselves with simply reproducing in Greek the bilingual text that lay before them with its innumerable corruptions and with its frequent dittographs or occasional tritographs.

We have now to justify by actual evidence this general sketch of the relations existing between the early text of Daniel as in the main represented by the LXX and its later edited form, as it appears in the MT.

(a) *Corruptions in the MT according to the Versions. The MT is in a dozen of passages without the support of a single version, LXX, Th., Pesh., or Vulg., though the latter three as a rule support it.* This evidence of the later versions suggests that in certain passages the MT is not older than the fourth century A.D. In some of these passages, the evidence of the context is all but conclusive in itself apart from the documentary evidence.

3[17]. LXX, Th., Pesh., Vulg., and context require two emendations of the MT : 'We have no need to discuss this question ; ⌐for⌐ there is a God, whom we serve, who is able to deliver us ... out of thy ⌐hands⌐. But if not, be it known unto thee, O king, that we will not serve thy god.' This is the answer of the three Confessors to the king's arrogant question : 'What god is there that shall deliver you out of my hands?' It gives the strongest and fullest reply conceivable. 'We have no need to answer thee in this matter ; ⌐for⌐ the God whom we serve can deliver us and He will deliver us out of thy ⌐hands⌐.' Contrast this text with the MT which gives the hopelessly weak text : 'We have no need to answer thee in this matter : †if† our God whom we serve be able to deliver us, he will, &c.' See pp. 68–70.

7[7, 13]. 'Vision of the night' : so LXX, Pesh., and Vulg. Th. also in 7[13], and in 7[2] in two MSS. MT wrongly reads 'visions of the night' in 7[7, 13]. See Transl. 2[19] n.

8[2]. Here the versions require the excision of the clause in the MT ['and it was so when I saw']. This is a mere tautology drawn from 8[15].

8[14]. 'Unto him' as also the context requires : MT 'unto †me†'.

8[21]. 'The he-goat'. Cf. 8[8]. Here the MT incorporated a Hebrew gloss השעיר. See p. 216.

9[20]. 'Sins' (bis). MT 'sin' (bis).

9[23]. 'Tell ⌐thee⌐'. Versions +2 Heb. MSS. MT 'tell'.

9[26]. 'Together with'. Here one Heb. MS. (עִם) and Aq. support the four versions. MT 'people' (עָם).

10[19]. 'Be strong and of a good courage (versions +6 Heb. MSS). MT 'be strong : yea be strong'.

12[2]. 'The dust of the earth'. MT 'a land of dust'.

(b) LXX (original text of), Th., Vulg., Joseph. read 'Mene, Tekel, Peres' while the interpretation in MT 5[26–28] requires this reading. Yet MT reads 'Mene, Mene, Tekel, Upharsin'. Here the weight of evidence against the MT is no less strong than that under (a).

(c) LXX, Th. (in part), Vulg., Joseph. (in part).

2[34]. ⌐'from a mountain'⌐. Only MT and Pesh. om. Justin, Dial. 70 and Cypr. Test. II. 17 also contain the phrase. But the definite phrase 'the mountain' in 2^{45} postulates the previous mention of the indefinite phrase.

2^{45}. ⌜'the clay, the iron'⌝. MT reads 'the iron, the clay'. See note on p. 43.

$6^{25\,(24)}$. 'were cast ... they, their wives and their children'. The evidence for 'were cast' is found in the four authorities above cited. For 'they, their wives and children' we have the LXX, Pesh., and Vulg. אִנּוּן (i.e. 'they') by this emendation of the text is restored to the only usage it has elsewhere in Biblical Aramaic. For the order 'their wives and their children' which is the more normal order in the O.T. we have the support of the LXX, Pesh., Vulg., and Cypr. Test. III. 20, whereas the MT and Th. give the reverse order, which is the normal Greek one. For the Semitic order in the Papyri, fifth century B.C., see Cowley $30^{25,\,29}$, 31^{14}. MT reads 'they cast them (אָנּוּן) ... their children and their wives'. Pesh. supports MT in reading 'cast them' but disagrees with what follows.

8^8. ⌜'horns'⌝. So first three authorities. MT. om.

8^{17}. ⌜'and stood'⌝. So first three authorities. MT. om.

(d) LXX and Th.

3^1. ⌜'in the 18th year'⌝. MT, Pesh. and Vulg. om. But this dating of the narratives and visions is characteristic of our author. Hence in 4^1 where only the LXX preserves the date, it must be followed against all the later authorities. See § 4.

$6^{14\,(13)}$. ⌜'before his God'⌝. The LXX and Th. differ in form here but presuppose this phrase. MT om.

$6^{16\,(15)}$. om. 'came tumultuously to the king and'.

8^{13}. ⌜'is taken away'⌝. So LXX and Th. MT om.

10^{13}. 'I left him ⌜with the prince⌝'. So LXX and Th. MT 'I was left'.

11^{17}. ⌜'But shall make an agreement with him'⌝. LXX, Th., and Vulg. MT 'and upright ones with him and he shall do'.

11^{26}. ⌜'his anxieties'⌝. LXX and Th. MT corrupt.

(e) Even a single later version has occasionally to be followed when the context supports it.

Thus in 2^{35} read with Th. 'the clay, the iron'. MT against the entire context reads 'the iron, the clay'.

Again in $6^{25\,(24)}$ with Vulg., *adducti sunt*, read הֵיתָיוּ 'were brought' and not הַיְתִיו 'they brought'.

Possibly in 11^{41} we should read with the Pesh. שְׁאֵרִית 'remnant'

instead of ראשית, 'chief': and certainly in 5¹⁹, it alone amongst
the versions reads rightly 'kept alive', where Th. and Vulg.
read ἔτυπτεν. Here unhappily the LXX is defective.

(ƒ) LXX—even when it stands alone—possesses for the
recovery of the text as it existed between 165–145 B.C. a critical
value transcending all the other versions collectively.

This version has been quoted already under the first four
headings (a–d) in conjunction with other versions. I shall now
quote some of the passages where it stands alone in preserving
the text.

2²⁸, 4² ⁽⁵⁾, ⁷ ⁽¹⁰⁾, ¹⁰ ⁽¹³⁾, 7¹, ¹⁵. In these six passages we have in MT
a non-Semitic expression 'visions of the head', where we should
expect 'visions of the heart'. Cf. Jer. 23¹⁶. But in none of
these passages does this non-Semitic expression occur in the
LXX. It appears in the addition of the redactor twice in the
MT, i.e. in the interpolation 4² ᵇ⁻⁷ᵃ (4⁵ ᵇ⁻¹⁰ᵃ), which was unknown to the LXX. In 4¹⁰ ⁽¹³⁾ the LXX reads 'in my vision '
(ἐν τῷ ὕπνῳ μου) where MT, Pesh., and Vulg. have 'in the visions
of my head upon my bed', but Th. 'in the vision of the night
upon my bed'. In 7¹ the LXX reads ὅραμα εἶδε παρὰ κεφαλήν =
'he saw a vision near his head', while in 7¹⁵ it reads 'in the
vision of the night'. The words that follow are as the asterisk
shows borrowed from a later version. It is noteworthy that in
these six passages the plural 'visions' does not occur in the
LXX: nor elsewhere in the original text save in 7² καθ' ὕπνους
νυκτός. But in Isa. 29⁷ this pl. renders a Hebrew sing.: see notes
on 7⁷, ¹³ below.[1]

3¹. ⌐'When he had brought under his rule cities and provinces
and all that dwell upon the earth from India to Ethiopia.'⌐ This
clause gives Nebuchadnezzar's reason for erecting the great
image on the plains of Babylon.

4¹. ⌐'In the eighteenth year of his reign.'⌐ Here the usage of
our author requires a date; see § 4.

4²⁻⁷ ᵇ ⁽⁵⁻¹⁰ ᵇ⁾. Here the LXX (supported by Josephus) alone
preserves the true order of the text, which brings to light the
dislocations, interpolations, and losses of the MT. See Transl.,
p. 356.

---

[1] In our author the phrase 'visions of the head' is always secondary: so
likewise is 'visions of the night'. He never uses 'vision' in the plural. Our
author uses two forms of the phrase conveying this idea. See note on 2¹⁹
(Translation).

5[11]. ⌐'Whose name is Daniel, one of the exiles of Judah '.¬
Here Josephus supports the LXX and the context postulates
some such statement. Cf. also Th. 1[3], 5[13].

6[4 (3)]. ⌐'And he prospered in the king's business which he
carried out.'¬ So LXX—a clause which explains the king's
wish to promote Daniel. It is stupidly transposed to 6[29(28)] by
the redactor. See Comm., p. 150, sqq.

6[7 (6)]. Here with LXX (ἐναντίον τοῦ βασιλέως) we should emend
'said to him' (לֵהּ) into 'said before him' (קדמוהי). Cf. 3[32], 6[22],
where ἐναντίον is a rendering of קדם in a like context. See note,
p. 154, ad fin.: also § 20, w.

6[29 (28)]. Here the LXX alone preserves the original. ⌐'So
Daniel was set over the kingdom of Darius. And king Darius
was gathered to his people. And Cyrus the Persian received
the kingdom.'¬ The MT is a confused medley of two distinct
types of text. See pp. 151–2.

7[7]. 'In a vision of the night.' So LXX, Pesh., Vulg., Th.,
om. MT reads 'in visions of the night.' In this last passage
Th. and Vulg. support LXX, Pesh., om.

7[8]. ⌐'he made war with the saints.'¬

7[13]. 'in the vision of the night.' So LXX, Th., Vulg. Pesh.
om. MT reads as in 7[7].

7[17]. ⌐'Shall be destroyed from off.'¬ MT has the impossible
reading, 'shall arise out of'. See pp. 189–90.

10[11]. [Which is Hiddekel]. LXX om. this false and mistaken
gloss in the MT, Th., and Vulg. The Pesh. rightly interprets
it as the Euphrates.

11[34]. ⌐'In the city and many in their *several* homesteads.'¬ MT
and dependent versions wholly corrupt: 'Many shall join
themselves to them with flatteries'. See note on pp. 310–11.

(g) Dislocations of the text of the MT.

1[5a] should be read after 1[5b]: 1[20–21] after 2[49a]: [2[28a] after 2[30]:]
3[31–3] (4[1–3]) after 4[34] as the LXX shows : 5[7–9], which in the MT
is dislocated, interpolated, and defective, should be read as
follows with the help of the LXX and Josephus, 5[7a, b, 8a, 9, 8b],
[7c]. See notes *in loc.* and in translation: 6[19 (18)] should be read
thus, 6[19a, d, b, c]: 10[20–21] in the order 10[20a, 21a, 20b, 21b]: 11[4, a, b, c]
[d, e, f], in the order 11[4a, b, c, e, f, d].

*(h) Interpolations in MT, some of which originated
in marginal glosses.*

1². 'to the house of his god': 2²⁴, 'he went': 2⁴⁰ 'and as
iron that crusheth': 3²³: 4³⁻⁷ᵃ, these last verses being against
the context: also against the grammar of our author and against
the LXX which omits them: 4⁷ᵇ: 4⁹ᵇ: 4¹⁵ (an addition by the
redactor to make the text harmonize with the previous interpolation 4³⁻⁷ᵃ: 4³¹⁻⁴—a recast of the original text by the
redactor and in this edition relegated to the notes: 5⁷ 'and the
king answered and said to his wise men of Babylon'. LXX
does not admit of this clause. Josephus omits it: 5¹⁰ 'by reason
of the words of the king and of his lords': 5¹² 'whom the king
named Belteshazzar': 6⁵⁽⁴⁾ 'neither was there any error or
fault found in him'; 6¹³⁽¹²⁾ 'concerning the interdict of the
king': 6¹⁶⁽¹⁵⁾ 'came tumultuously to the king and': see note
in the Transl. *in loc.*: 6²⁹⁽²⁸⁾ conflate and inconsistent text in MT:
see notes *in loc.*: 7¹ 'visions of his head' and 'he told': 7² 'Daniel
answered and said': 7¹⁹ 'and went forth': 7¹¹ 'I beheld'—the
second one, : 7¹⁸ 'for ever and': 8² 'and it was so when I saw':
also 'and I saw in the vision': 8²¹ duplicate expression in Class.
Heb. 'the he-goat': 8²⁴ 'but not by his own power': 8²⁷ 'fainted
and': 9⁴⁻²⁰—the interpolated prayer drawn probably from
existing Hebrew liturgies: 10⁴ 'which is Hiddekel': 10⁸ 'and
I retained no strength': 10⁹ 'on my face': 10¹⁰ contains a
conflation of glosses: 11¹⁵ 'not' interpolated before 'withstand'
against LXX, Th., Pesh.: 11³⁵ 'and to make them white: 11⁴¹
'Edom and Moab and the chief of the children of Ammon': 11⁴³
'and the Libyans and the Ethiopians shall be in his train'—these
last two contemporary enemies of Judah—being impossible in
a pseudepigraph: 12² 'shame and': 12¹⁰ 'and make themselves
white': 12¹¹ and 12¹²⁻¹³ are the earliest interpolations in the book.

The reader can find these interpolations dealt with in the
foot-notes to the English translation, and at length in the Commentary.

*(i) Replacement of one word by another in MT having a different
or wrong meaning, or by an earlier Hebrew equivalent.*

In 6⁷⁽⁶⁾ the MT has seemingly replaced קרבו (so LXX, Th.,
Pesh., and even the Vulg., though in a corrupt form, and

Josephus; see pp. 152–4). Thus no version or other authority supports הרגשו in this passage from the 2nd cent. B.C. to the 4th A.D. In 6^16(15) the MT, which has against it, the LXX and Th., and the context as it appears in LXX and Josephus, inserted this verb (see p. 154). But the context not only of the LXX and Josephus throughout, but even of MT in 6^15(14), here presupposes the presence of Daniel's enemies during the whole interview till sunset and not of their departure and tumultuous return according to the inconsistent narrative of the MT.

In 6^28 b (27 b), as the LXX as well as the context prove, the text was recast by some redactor or the Massoretes by a conflation of clauses, which in part belonged originally to 6^4 (3) and 6^29 (28). Hence we must restore הֲקִים in place of הצלח which was borrowed from 6^4 (3), and translate 'Daniel was set over the kingdom of Darius' instead of 'this Daniel prospered in the reign of Darius'. See pp. 150–2.

In 7^17 the MT has יקומון מן instead of יאבדון מן as the LXX and the mythical conception behind the text require. The four kingdoms do not 'arise from the earth' but are 'destroyed from off the earth'. Th. has both readings, but corrects the מן into על and so escapes making a statement in glaring contradiction with 7^3 and the myth in question.

In 9^24 the original Hebrew rendering למחות (so LXX ἀπαλεῖψαι, and Vulg. *delere*) 'to blot out', 'to forgive wholly' was replaced by an early reviser by the legalistic verb לכפר 'to forgive' (but as a rule not freely, but for a consideration, a sacrifice or penalty of some sort). Montgomery (p. 374) quotes Driver and seeks to justify לכפר as connoting at once the legal and religious implications of this verb. But this seems inadmissible here, seeing that, though the LXX uses about ten verbs to render כפר, it never elsewhere uses any form of ἀλείφειν, simple or compound, to do so. Nor does the Vulg. use *delere* to render it. This conclusion is valuable. When Th. made his version (c. A.D. 150) he found למחות already displaced by לכפר and so he rendered the latter by τοῦ ἐξιλάσασθαι τ. ἀδικίας. Subsequently a scribe added the LXX rendering of למחות in the margin, i.e. καὶ ἀπαλεῖψαι τ. ἀδικίας, which a later scribe incorporated in the text of Th. without adapting it to its new context by inserting τοῦ before the verb. When a few years later Clem. Alex., *Strom.* i. 21 (393 P) quotes 9^24 from Th. he assimilates the intrusion to its new context by inserting the τοῦ. Thus in Th. we have a conflate text, which is later reproduced in the Bohairic, Sahidic, and Ethiopic versions.

In 11²⁴ the LXX reads εἰς μάτην = לְשָׁוְא which is an obvious corruption of לשעה 'for a time', a pure Aramaism (cf. 3⁶˒ ¹⁵), which, however, was used in Mishnaic Hebrew. But the Massoretes or some earlier revisers replaced this Aramaic phrase by the Classical Hebrew עַד עֵת.

(k) Misuse of Hebrew words.

In 10⁴, 12⁵˒ ⁶˒ ⁷, יְאֹר which is used to denote the Nile throughout the O. T. is used by the Hebrew translator to denote the Euphrates.

In 11²¹˒ ³⁴ †חלקלקות† appears to be either a misuse of this word which means 'slippery places': cf. Jer. 23¹²; Ps. 35⁶: or a corruption of חלקות 'flatteries'. See pp. 297-98. But as the LXX shows it is a corruption of חלקתו = κληροδοσία. There appears, therefore, to be no justification for attributing the meaning of 'flatteries' to this word in Hebrew.

In 12¹³ עמד is said in the Lexicons to mean 'to rise in the resurrection'. But this meaning in Hebrew cannot be justified elsewhere, and seems to be due to the interpolation of the appendices 12¹¹˒ ¹²⁻¹³. The context requires us to translate 'thou shalt stand' in thy lot, i.e. live to inherit it in the coming kingdom. Thus the interpolator has here forgotten that he should be writing from the standpoint of the 6th cent. B.C., and not as a contemporary of the Maccabees, when the coming of the kingdom was due.[1]

(l) Wrong order of words.

In 4¹⁵ ⁽¹⁸⁾ דנה חלמא should according to our author's usage be translated 'this is the dream', and not 'this dream'. In the latter sense the demonstrative follows (eleven times) and does not precede its noun.

In 4¹⁵ ⁽¹⁸⁾ the MT reads 'King Nebuchadnezzar'. Unfortunately the LXX omits this phrase, but inasmuch as Th., Pesh.,

---

[1] The LXX renders תעמד here by ἀναστήσῃ just as it renders it in 12¹ of Michael and seven times elsewhere, where it can have no reference to the resurrection. The technical Hebrew term of the second century B.C. used in reference to the resurrection is הקיץ as in Daniel 12²; Isaiah 26¹⁹: or קום Isa. 26¹⁴˒ ¹⁹.

and Vulg. read 'Nebuchadnezzar the King', we may justly assume that the MT has introduced this late order, which does not apparently occur in Semitic texts before the 2nd cent. B. C. For the passages where this late order occurs elsewhere in our author, see § 20 *dd.* The ancient order still persists in our author two times out of three.

(m) Misuse of phrases.

In 3^{24} the MT and versions corruptly read 'said unto the king' where according to our author's usage we should expect 'said before the king'.

It also commits the astounding error of making Nebuchadnezzar say in $4^{4\,(7)}$ 'I told the dream before (!) them', and similarly in $4^{5\,(8)}$, though קדם = 'before' in such contexts in our author can only be used in the case of divine or semi-divine beings. See § 20. *w.* But these verses are an intrusion. They are wanting in the LXX.

In 7^9 MT with all the versions uses the wrong apocalyptic form עתיק יומין 'an old man'. See note on p. 182. Clem. (*Paed.* ii. 10) quotes the true expression ὡσεὶ παλαιὸς ἡμερῶν = כעתיק יומין 'like an old man', though where he got it I do not know. The LXX, however, in 7^{13} preserves the right apocalyptic form ὡς παλαιὸς ἡμερῶν. See note on 7^9 (Translation).

§ 15. Textual Authorities of the Book of Daniel and their respective Relations represented on a Genealogical Table.

Aramaic Archetype of the Book of Daniel, 165 B.C.

|

This Archetype reproduced by many scribes with glosses, and dislocations including that of 1^{20-21} from its original context after 2^{49a}, and additions such as those of 12^{11-12} which imply three editions within six months.

|

New edition of Daniel with the translation of $1-2^{4a}$ and 8–12 into Hebrew, in which translation three scholars took part—possibly as early as 161 B.C., but in any case within a decade later.

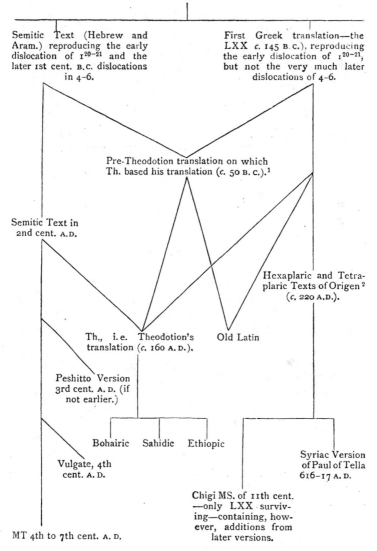

Semitic Text (Hebrew and Aram.) reproducing the early dislocation of 1$^{20-21}$ and the later 1st cent. B.C. dislocations in 4-6.

First Greek translation—the LXX $c.$ 145 B.C.), reproducing the early dislocation of 1$^{20-21}$, but not the very much later dislocations of 4-6.

Pre-Theodotion translation on which Th. based his translation ($c.$ 50 B. C.).[1]

Semitic Text in 2nd cent. A.D.

Hexaplaric and Tetra-plaric Texts of Origen[2] ($c.$ 220 A.D.).

Th., i.e. Theodotion's translation ($c.$ 160 A. D.).

Old Latin

Peshitto Version 3rd cent. A. D. (if not earlier.)

Bohairic   Sahidic   Ethiopic

Vulgate, 4th cent. A. D.

Syriac Version of Paul of Tella 616-17 A. D.

Chigi MS. of 11th cent. —only LXX surviving—containing, however, additions from later versions.

MT 4th to 7th cent. A. D.

---

[1] For 20 verses of this translation (7$^{9-28}$) see § 25 a.

[2] For studies and conclusions as to later Hexaplaric Revisions, see Montgomery, *J.B.L.*, 1925, pp. 289-302, 'The Hexaplaric Strata in the Greek Texts of Daniel'; Benjamin, *J.B.L.*, 1925, pp. 303-26, 'Collation of Holmes-Parsons, 23 (Venetus), 62, 147, in Dan. from Photographic Copies'; Gehman, *J.B.L.*, 1925, pp. 327-52, 'The Polyglot Arabic Text of Dan. and its Affinities'.

§ 16. *Date of the Book.*

As a result of modern research it is now generally agreed amongst scholars that the Book of Daniel was written about or shortly before 165 B.C.

Inasmuch as the Advent of the Kingdom did not take place at the date furnished in 7^{14}, a reviser or possibly the author in a new edition of the book adjourned this date in an appendix 12^{11} which extended the 1150 days to 1290. Subsequently on the failure of this extention, another reviser added a second appendix 12^{12-13}, which extended the original 1150 days to 1335 days. Thus within less than six months three editions of this book appear to have been issued.

The chief reasons for these conclusions as to the date are as follows:

I. *There is no evidence in Jewish literature written before 190 B.C. of the existence of the Book of Daniel.*

1. The position of the book amongst the Hagiographa and not amongst the Prophetical works indicates that the Book of Daniel was introduced into the Jewish Canon after the collection of the Prophets had been closed, and this was done apparently not earlier than the third century B.C.

The Jewish Canon consists of three divisions: first, the Law or Pentateuch, the first formal collection of sacred books; secondly, the Prophets, consisting of the historical books, Joshua, Judges, Samuel, Kings, and the Prophets properly so called, Isaiah, Jeremiah, Ezekiel, and the twelve Minor Prophets.

The exclusion of Daniel from this second division is sufficient to prove that this book did not exist when the Canon of the Prophets was completed. Moreover, Daniel's use of the phrase '*the* books' in 9^2, seems to indicate that the prophetic canon was already closed. It is to be observed also that even in the Hagiographa Daniel is enumerated near the end after Esther.

2. The silence of Jesus the son of Sirach (*c.* 190 B.C.) touching Daniel may prove that Daniel was unknown to him. This writer, in his list of Israel's worthies, chapters 44–50 mentions Isaiah, Jeremiah, Ezekiel, and the twelve Minor Prophets collectively, but says not a word of Daniel. If Daniel had been known to him, with his roll of achievements which were almost

without a parallel in the O.T., the writer could hardly have said, as in 49¹⁵, that no one had ever been born like Joseph.

3. External testimonies to the existence of Daniel begin with the years 145–140 B.C., and they increase in number in subsequent years. Testimonies from 145 B.C.–A.D. 120, including the N.T.

1 Enoch. 6–36 there are several parallel phrases to those in Daniel: i.e. in 1 En. 8³, 14¹⁴, ¹⁸, ¹⁹, 60³, ⁴ 21⁵, corresponding to allied phrases in Dan. 5¹², 8¹⁷, ¹⁸, 7⁹, ¹⁰, ¹⁶; but 1 En. 6–36; is of earlier date than Daniel. In 89⁴⁰, 90²⁰ (before 161 B.C.) the phrase 'pleasant and glorious land' may be partly dependent on Dan. 8⁹, 11¹⁶, ⁴¹ 'the glorious land' of our text, but it can be wholly accounted for by Jer. 3¹⁹; Ezek. 20⁶, ¹⁶; Zech. 7¹³; Mal. 3¹².

On the other hand 1 En. 104² 'shall shine as the lights of heaven' (104–95 B.C. or as late as 70–64 B.C.), appears to be suggested by Dan. 12³ 'shall shine as the brightness of the firmament . . . and . . . as the stars'.

Sibyllines III. In the third book of the Sibyllines 388–400 (145–140 B.C.) there is a manifest reference to Antiochus Epiphanes as 'a man clad with a purple cloak upon his shoulders, fierce, unjust, born of a thunderbolt'. The race he sought to destroy was that of his brother Seleucus IV (186–176 B.C.), by whose son Demetrius I, the son of Antiochus, the 'one root' shall be cut off, Antiochus V, Eupator. The reference to the 'ten horns' in 7⁷ of our text is no less obvious. For the Greek text and a fuller treatment of it, see the Comm., p. 167 seq.

Testaments of the XII Patriarchs (109–107 B.C.). The following passages testify to his use of our author, T. Jos. 3⁴ οἱ νηστεύοντες διὰ τ. θεὸν τοῦ προσώπου τ. χάριν λαμβάνουσιν: cf. Dan. 1¹⁵. T. Sim. 2⁸ ἀπέστειλε τ. ἄγγελον αὐτοῦ καὶ ἐρρύσατο αὐτόν: Dan. 3²⁸; T. Jos. 13⁵ τρίτος γὰρ ἦν ἐν ἀξιώματι παρὰ τῶν Φαραὼ ἀρχόντων: Dan. 5⁷, 'shall rule as one of three'. T. Jos. 19¹² ἡ γὰρ βασιλεία αὐτοῦ βασιλεία ἔσται αἰώνιος, ἥτις οὐ παρελεύσεται, which clearly is based on Dan. 7¹⁴, which, however, reads 'dominion' instead. Is this right? T. Lev. 6² συνετήρουν τοὺς λόγους τούτους ἐν τῇ καρδίᾳ μου: Dan. 7²⁸ 'I kept the matter in my heart', and in the LXX of Dan. in 4²⁵ τοὺς λόγους ἐν τῇ καρδίᾳ συνετήρησε. T. Lev. 16¹ ἑβδομήκοντα ἑβδομάδας: Dan. 11²⁴. T. Reub. 1¹⁰ καὶ οἶνον .. οὐκ ἔπιον καὶ κρέας οὐκ εἰσῆλθεν ἐν τῷ στόματί μου καὶ πᾶν ἄρτον ἐπιθυμίας οὐκ ἔφαγον: Dan. 10³; T. Jos. 19⁷ ἐγένετο .. εἰς βοήθειαν (of Judas Maccabaeus):

Dan. 11³⁴ where the Maccabees are said to be a 'little help'. T.
Lev. 5⁶: Dan. 10¹³, ²¹, 12¹. T. Benj. 10⁸ ἀναστήσονται οἱ μὲν εἰς δόξαν,
οἱ δὲ εἰς ἀτιμίαν : Dan. 12². Here T. Benj. 10⁸ supports the text
arrived at in my Commentary.

Thus the Testaments are valuable for the criticism of the text
in Dan. 7¹⁴ and 12².

The *Book of Jubilees*, which belongs to the same period as
the *Testaments* uses throughout the scheme of year weeks—
each year week consisting of seven years. This chronological
scheme seems to have been supplied by Dan. 9²⁴. The word
'week' (= week of years) has not this sense elsewhere in the
O.T., though Lev. 25⁴, 26³⁴, ³⁵ had prepared the way for it.

1 Maccabees, c. 137–105 B.C. In 1⁹ ἐπλήθυναν κακὰ ἐν τῇ γῇ
agrees in part with the MT of Dan. and in part with the LXX :
see Comm., p. 332 seq. 1¹⁵ ἀπέστησαν ἀπὸ διαθήκης ἁγίας = Dan. 11³⁰,
where LXX and Th. give different but equivalent renderings
of עֵזְבֵי בְּרִית קֹדֶשׁ. 1¹⁸ ἔπεσον τραυματίαι πολλοί = Dan. 11²⁶ : 1⁵⁴
βδέλυγμα ἐρημώσεως = Dan. 11³¹ in LXX but βδέλυγμα ἠφανισμένον in
Th. In Dan. 9²⁷ both the LXX and Th. have βδ. τῶν ἐρημώσεων.
In 12¹¹ LXX and Th. have τὸ (< Th.) βδ. τῆς (< Th.) ἐρημώσεως.
None of these renderings are accurate. See Comm. p. 252 :
2⁵⁹,⁶⁰ imply a knowledge of Dan. 3, 6 ; 4⁴³ ἐκαθάρισαν τὰ ἅγια =
Dan. 8¹⁴. There are other echoes of Dan. in this book.

1 Enoch 37–70 (before 64 B.C.). For the unique interpretation
of the last oppressors of the Jews designated in Daniel as the
fourth kingdom, see p. 168 seq.

Psalms of Solomon (70–30 B.C.). In 3¹⁶ of this book an exact
reproduction of Dan. 12² is found : ἀναστήσονται . . . εἰς ζωὴν αἰώνιον
(so LXX—ἐξεγερθήσονται Th.).

Book of Wisdom (50 B.C.–A.D. 10). In 3⁷ it is said that on
the day of visitation the righteous 'shall shine' (ἀναλάμψουσιν),
which is based apparently on Dan. 12³, where Th. has λάμψουσιν.

In the *Assumption of Moses* (A.D. 17–29) 8¹ the words 'such
as has not befallen them from the beginning until that time' is
drawn from Dan. 12¹. The writer of this work regarded the
Fourth Empire in Dan. as the Roman Empire 10⁸.

In the *Zadokite Fragments* there are echoes of our text and
phrases apparently drawn from it. Thus with הָעֹמְדִים בְּאַחֲרִית
הַיָּמִים 6² : cf. Dan. 12¹³ לְקֵץ הַיָּמִין . . תַעֲמֹד; with קְדוֹשֵׁי עֶלְיוֹן 9³³, cf.
Dan. 7²⁵,²⁷ קַדִּישֵׁי עֶלְיוֹנִין; with (מִצְוֹתָיו) עֹשֶׂה חֶסֶד לְאֹהֲבָיו וּלְשֹׁמְרֵי 9⁴⁹, cf.

Dan. 9[4] מצוחיו ולשמרי לאהביו החסד.. שמר; with היהודה מרשיעי 9[49],
cf. Dan. 11[32] ברית מרשיעי; with מצרפותיו בימי 9[49], cf. Dan. 12[10]
רבים יצרפו : also 11[35], with קשריהם חרצובות כל יתר 'loose all the
bonds of their knots' 16[3], cf. Dan. 5[12] קטרין משרא. The numbers
of chapters and verse refer to my edition of the *Fragments*.
Some scholars assign these *Fragments* to the latter half of the
second century B.C. : the present writer to the latter half of the
first century B.C.

2 Baruch (27–31) before A.D. 70. Here 2 Bar. 28[1] presupposes
Dan. 12[10].[1]

4 Ezra. There are in this composite work many allusions to
Dan. The most interesting is in 12[10-12] (A.D. 80–120), where
the writer plainly implies that the angel in his identification of
the fourth kingdom (Dan. 7[7-8, 17-19, 23 sqq.]) with the Greek
empire was wrong, since it was to be identified with the Roman
(see Comm. p. 169)—a view which agrees with that which
prevails throughout the N.T. The same identification appears
in 11[38].

In the following passages 4 Ezra is in certain phrases dependent on Daniel : 5[15] = Dan. 8[18], 10[10] : 6[35] = Dan. 10[2] : 7[33] =
Dan. 7[9] : 7[97] = Dan. 12[3] : 7[125] = Dan. 12[3] : 9[25] = Dan. 10[3] : 10[29] =
Dan. 8[17,18], 10[9,10,15] : 13[6] = Dan. 2[45]. This list could be increased. It shows that in many respects 4 Ezra is more closely
allied to Daniel than 2 Baruch. The latter is an early representation of the Talmudic attitude towards the doctrine of works
and forgiveness.

---

[1] In 39[5-8] the fourth empire is, as in 4 Ezra, identified with Rome : cf. also
36[6-10]. But 34–40 was written before A.D. 70. Josephus, *Ant.* x. 11. 7, who
follows the older interpreters, identifies the fourth Empire with the Greek (καὶ
δὴ ταῦτα ἡμῶν συνέβη παθεῖν τῷ ἔθνει ὑπὸ Ἀντιόχου τοῦ Ἐπιφανοῦς, καθὼς εἶδεν ὁ
Δανίηλος). But in the sentence that follows immediately thereon (bracketed
by Niese as an interpolation), he gives the later interpretation and identifies
this Empire with Rome, as does also Rev. 13 : and 'Aboda zara 1[6]. In the
Jer. Targ. II on Gen. 15[18] the fourth kingdom is also identified with Rome
under the symbol 'Edom', a symbol used by the Talmudists for Rome. The
four empires according to the original myth came up from the sea (Dan. 7[3]).
But a later form of this myth represents them as arising out of the earth as in
the late MT text of Dan. 7[17], where the LXX, however, preserves the true text,
and Th. combines the two conflicting myths in his conflate version. In the
very composite work, 4 Ezra, not only does the fourth empire, i. e. Rome, arise
out of the sea, 11[1], but in 13[3] even the Messiah is to do so, and 'fly with the
clouds of heaven '—a conflation and confusion of thought and expression.

It is unnecessary to pursue this line of investigation farther. Before 165 B.C. Jewish literature shows no knowledge of the existence of such a book as Daniel, whereas from 145 B.C. onwards the use of this book by later writers grows steadily in volume and in their appreciation of its sovereign importance in its bearing on the future destinies of the world.

Thus from external testimony we conclude that the Book of Daniel was written between 190-140 B.C.

II. *Internal evidence as to the date of the book.*

First the writer's inaccurate acquaintance with the events of the exile and the immediately subsequent history; 2. his accurate knowledge of the third century B.C. and the first thirty-four years of the second century B.C., for which he is accepted by historical critics as an authority of the first rank; and 3. the vague generalities which mark the transition of the narrative as it passes from the region of history into that of prediction about the years 167-165 B.C. These facts can hardly be explained unless on the assumption that the book was written between the years 167-165 B.C.

1. The above facts are manifest to every unbiased student of the work, and the proofs of these statements will be found in the Commentary in connexion with the passages concerned. It follows as a matter of course that the author would have a more accurate acquaintance with the history of his own time than with that of preceding centuries. If the book had been written at the time of the exile, the most accurate part of the book would be that which dealt with the events from the time of Nebuchadnezzar to that of Cyrus, but this is just the part of the book which is least historical. The most important inaccuracies are as follows :

(*a*) The transportation of Jehoiachim in the third year of his reign : see note on 1^2. .

(*b*) The use of the term Chaldeans, not in its ethnic sense, but as denoting a learned class amongst the Babylonians : see note in 1^4.

(*c*) The assumption that the court language at Babylon was Aramaic : see note on 2^4 ; but the text here may not be original.

(*d*) The designation of Nebuchadnezzar as 'the king of kings ' : see note on 2^{37}.

(*e*) The use of the term 'satraps ', see note on 3^2.

(*f*) The representation of Belshazzar as the absolute sovereign of Babylonia, the son and successor of Nebuchadnezzar ; whereas he was only a vassal king under his father Nabuna'id : see pp. 108–113, and § 25. b.

(*g*) The mythical Median Empire of Darius, which our author represents as following immediately on that of Babylon and the mythical king Darius : see pp. 138–146.

From the above facts it follows that our author had a very inaccurate knowledge of the history of the Babylonian period as it appears in the Cuneiform records, and that for his knowledge of this period he was indebted to contemporary tradition in which the events of Babylonian history often appear in a distorted form. Of the Persian period his knowledge appears to be scant if not also untrustworthy : see note on p. 273.

2. But when we come down to the Greek period, the case is wholly different and our author becomes here an actual historical source. This holds good whether we consider the sections that deal with the Egyptian campaigns of Antiochus (11^{25-39}) and his persecution of the Jews : his representation of Antiochus, who became to aftertimes the prototype of the Antichrist, his account of the desecration of the altar of burnt offering (Dec. 15, 168 B.C.) : his reference to the Maccabean revolt, which he designates as 'a little help' (11^{34})—a fact which shows that he is acquainted with the first Maccabean victories. In this period our author is an historian of the first rank.

3. But at its close he ceases to be an historian. He does not record but predicts the death of Antiochus Epiphanes, and the details of the prediction both as to time and place conflict with actual facts (see notes on 11^{45}). The rededication of the Sanctuary, Dec. 25, 165 B.C., was to him still in the future. (See note on p. 212.)

The limits of the date are, therefore, easy to determine. The book must have been written before 165 B.C. ; for we cannot ascribe the victories of Judas Maccabaeus over Apollonius and Seron to a later date. These victories at all events must be in the background according to 11^{34}.[1]

---

[1] Other facts point in the direction of a late date. An exilic date for the book is excluded by its use of many words derived from the Persian. Persian words only slowly came to be used in Aramaic. In the Aramaic translation of the Behistun Inscription of Darius I there are none save proper names. The

§ 17. *Ezra considerably earlier than Daniel, though linguistically they have much in common.*

(a) *Idioms common to E. and D.*

לְ *cum Inf.* = finite verb, expressing purpose, obligation, or the like—not earlier than 400 B.C. See § 20. *t.* But in D. there is a further development of this idiom as is there shown. E. and D. agree in never using כל with suff. after the noun. Both E. and D. use the proleptic suffix : see § 20. *p*—a usage already established in the latter half of the fifth century. E. and D. use suff. with Prep. before a noun—a usage unknown before 400 B.C. Both use אנון (E. once, D. three times) a late formation, where א takes the place of ה and ן of ם: see § 20. *h.* Both agree in using ע for ק and ר for ז exclusively : see § 20. *d.* Both agree in placing the acc. before or after the Inf. that governs it. But this usage goes back to the fifth century. Again, E and D. have two ways in expressing the same idea, and in one of these ways they agree in disagreeing with the like construction in the fifth century B.C. Papyri. Thus (1) in Ezra 5[13] and 6[3] we have בשנת חדה לכורש = 'in the first year of Cyrus'. (2) In 4[24]

fact that nearly half of the Persian words in Daniel consist of names of great Persian officials suggests the hypothesis that the narratives in which seven out of the eight occur, first came into being in the Persian period, and were transmitted partly orally and partly in MSS. down to the Greek period. The Persian words are : גדבריא 3[2], דת 2[9], אדרגזריא 3[2], אזדא 2[6], אחשדרפניא 3[2], אפדן 11[45], המינכא 5[7] (*Qr.*), זן 3[6], נבזבא 2[6] (5[17]), סרכין 6[3], הדבריא 3[2], הדם 6[8], הדבריא 6[8], פתגם 3[16], רו 2[18], תפתיא 3[2], תפתיא 3[2]. We should observe that some scholars find 20 Akkadian and 8 Persian words in Ezra, and that G. R. Driver discovers 30 Akkadian and 20 Persian in the *Aram. Pap.* (Cowley). The original source of many of the words is still a matter of debate.

For a list of loan words from the Akkadian—variously estimated from 12 to 30, many of which have already occurred in the Old Testament books before 200 B.C.—see Montgomery, p. 20. Furthermore there are three words of Greek origin קיתרס (= κίθαρις), פסנתרין (ψαλτήριον), סומפניא (συμφωνία). It is only natural to assume that these words—especially the third—did not obtain currency in the East till after the time of Alexander the Great.

Again, the fact that our author has wrongly combined 2 Kings 24[1,2] with 2 Chron. 36[6,7] (see note on 1[1]) postulates a date not earlier than 300 B.C., while the eschatology demands a much later date.

Finally, whereas the linguistic evidence does not admit of an earlier date than 250 B.C. it suggests a date more than half a century later, as will appear when the linguistic problems come to be dealt with.

שנת שת למלכות דריוש 'the sixth year of the reign of Darius'.
With no. (2) cf. D. 6[29(bis)], and with (1) cf. D. 7[1] בשנת חדה
לבלשאצר. But E. and D. herein differ in every passage but one
from the fifth century Aramaic in respect of this construction.
This exception occurs in a papyrus dated 495 B.C. (Cowley 1[1]),
where the Aramaic for 'in the 27th year of Darius the king'
we find שנת . . . לדריוש just as in E. and D. But nowhere else
in that century nor earlier can I find this construction which
persists in E. and D. The normal and practically universal
construction was that which is found in Cowley 2[1], 5[1], 7[1], 8[1],
14[1], 20[1], 21[3], 30[19,21,30], 31[4], 32[7], 35[1,6]. Thus the normal construction was after mentioning the name of the year to add the
king's name without its being preceded by ל, but this construction
never occurs in E. nor D.

Points wherein E. and D. differ. E. uses אֵלֶּה 'these' 5[15] :
cf. Cowley 2[13], 7[10], 13[13], &c., Jer. 10[11]. But D. uses אלך 'these'
3[12,13,21,22], &c., which E. 4[21], 6[8(bis)] also uses. But D. uses the
very late formation אלין or אלֵּן 2[40, 44], 6[3, 7], 7[17]—unknown to E.
or earlier authorities. E. uses דֵּךְ 'this' 5[16], &c. : but D. uses דא
in the same sense, and also דכן 'this', 'that', 2[31], 7[20,21] (as the
equivalent of either being of common gender).

Archaistic survivals in D. : the jussive forms : see § 20. *s.* מרא :
see p. 51. Much of the content of the narratives comes from
Persian times through tradition (cf. Persian official terms), but
the form is late.

Though D. exhibits a mingling of old and new elements, *it is
the newer elements that determine the date.* Since the Aramaic
of D. does not admit of any period earlier than 300 B.C., which is
that of E. in its present form (though probably brought up to
date in certain words and idioms by later scribes), D. must be
considerably later, seeing that it contains some of the latest
developments in Aramaic. On purely linguistic grounds it
would not be unreasonable to fix its *terminus a quo* at 200 B.C.
But its exact date cannot be determined on linguistic grounds
more nearly than some decades before or after 200 B.C.

(*b*) *Grounds for regarding D. as later than E.*

(1) E. preserves the ancient form המו, but D. always uses the
later form המון.

(2) E. uses frequently the ancient suffixes כם־ (six times out of
seven) and הם־: D. uses *only* the latest כן־ and הן־.

(3) E. uses קְדָם pretty much in the same general sense as fifth century Aramaic writers, whereas D. has developed a meaning peculiar at all events in the second century, but familiar in later times : see § 20. *w.*

(4) E. uses לְ only six times before an acc., whereas D. uses it constantly : see § 20. *l.*

(5) D. uses מִנְּהוֹן . . . מִנְּהוֹן 'some . . . others', 2[33, 41, 42], for the first time (?).

(6) E. has the reflexive prefix *hit-* (i. e. התְ-) four times and *'it-* (i. e. את) only once, and that in a noun 4[15, 19], whereas D. has *hit-* seventeen times and *'it-* six. This is instructive. Baumg., p. 108 seq., Bauer-Leander, § 34 (*g*), (*h*), conclude that this prefix was originally *'it-*, but on the analogy of the Hiph'il and Haph'el forms came to be written *hit-* alike in Hebrew and Aramaic. Thus only once is *hit-* found in I[a] (eighth century : see Cooke 63[14]). In *Eg. Aram. Eph.* II. 237 (see p. 401, l. 13) we find הזדהרו. But towards the close of the fifth century *'it-* is frequent : cf. Cowley 21[6] אזדהרו, &c. In course of time the *hit-* was displaced by *'it.* This process is manifest in E. as compared with D. and the later dialects. Thus, to repeat, whereas E. has *hit-* four times and *'it-* only once, and that in a noun ; D. has *hit-* seventeen times and *'it-* six. Thus *hit-* occurs relatively more often in E. than in D. In the later dialects it vanishes almost altogether. D. thus here attests a later stage of development in Aramaic. See p. xci, n. 1.

(7) It is questionable whether a Hoph'al form occurs before 400 B.C. It occurs only once in E., but nine times in D.

(8) דִי (= ὅτι *recitativum*) occurs several times in D., see § 20 (*u*), but not in periods I–III so far as I am aware.

(9) אמר is frequently followed by the indirect narration, i.e. לְ c. *Inf.* 2[46], 3[13,19], &c., see § 20. *cc*, but not in I–III[a]. In the latter אמר is followed by the direct narration.

(10) In all inscriptions and papyri before 300 B.C. (or possibly 200 B.C.) and in E., the following order, when a king's personal name and his official designation are mentioned together, is without exception 'So and so the king'. Yet five times in D. we find the late order 'King so and so'. In fact the MT attests this late order six times, but in the sixth all the versions are against it. See p. § 20. *dd.*

(11) In E. גברין 4[21], 5[4], &c., preserves its original meaning

'men', but in D. 3[8,12,20] it has been so far weakened as to mean only 'certain ones'. This decadence is a sign of lateness.

(12) When כל is connected with a noun in D., it always precedes it, but the emphatic form follows it in E. 5[7] : see § 20. *r.* In D. the emphatic form is used in D. without a noun : in the Aram. Papyri it precedes or follows its noun.

(13) The equivalent of the English phrase 'named B' would in the Aramaic of Daniel (cf. 2[26], 4[5,16]) be דִּי שְׁמֵהּ בּ״. But this is a late idiom, and is found in the Syriac of the N.T. The older Aramaic equivalent would be בּ״ שְׁמֵהּ : cf. Ezra 5[14]. Ezra (fourth century B. c.) herein agrees with the fifth century B. c. alike of the East and West. See § 20. (z). ˙

(14) Proleptic use of suff. ten times in D., only once in E. See p. cvii, *ad med.*

§ 18. *The Differentiation of Aramaic into Eastern*[1] *and Western cannot from existing documents and inscriptions be established before first century B. C., if so early. Aramaic 800 B. C.–A. D. 100 cannot be distinguished into different dialects on geographical grounds,*[2] *but should be treated as a whole as presenting various stages of development.*

To this conclusion I had come some time ago, and I am glad to see that Baumgartner (p. 124), after quoting Wilson with

---

[1] The distinctive differences between Eastern and Western Aramaic, such as the use of the *n* as prefix instead of *j* in third Sing. and Pl. Impf. and the displacement of the absolute by the emphatic, which thereupon loses its characteristic force, cannot be *proved* to have existed before the Christian Era. No doubt *colloquially* such changes must have taken place earlier but they have not yet been discovered in any kind of literature.

Wilson ('Aramaic of Daniel,' *Princeton Bibl. and Theol. Studies*, p. 268) rightly shows that the preformative in *j* was used very early in Eastern Aramaic. Thus in CIS II. 43[5], seventh century, we find יעל ביום = *in diem producet*. He adduces also proper names which attest this form : II. 39[2] נבירבן, II. 47 יבחראל, &c. The Assyr. Letter 11 יאתה 'he will come', יהתב 'he will return', &c. Baumg. (p. 124) quotes others from Assyria given by Lidzbarski, *Urk.* 16, 3[6], 19, 5[4], &c.

[2] As Baumg. (p. 131 seq.) points out, Biblical Aramaic presents a Western Aramaic character, when affinities with the later Western dialects are recognized, such as the Fast Roll (see Dalman, *Gram. d. Jüd.-Palaest. Aramäisch*, p. 8), Targ. Onk. and Jon., though too much weight must not be attached to this fact, whereas the Eastern Aramaic dialects—Babylonian Aramaic, Syr. and Mandaean—are further removed from it. But so also are the later Western Aramaic dialects— i.e. the Palestinian Talmud, the Midrashim, Dalman's 'Galilean' Dialect (p. 16 seqq., 41), and the Christian Palestinian.

approval, which he rarely does, concludes justly: ' So ist
tatsächlich in alter Zeit keinerlei Unterschied zwischen Ost
und West zu beobachten.' In Bauer-Leander's *Gram. d.
Biblisch-Aram.*, p. 5, the same view is expressed: ' Offenbar
hat es damals die Unterschiede zwischen Ost-und Westaramäisch
noch nicht gegeben, oder diese waren so gering, dass sie in der
Schrift kaum in die Erscheinung traten'.

Local dialectical differences of course arose, but in the main
the Aramaic of the East and the West was the same, and with
some exceptions underwent the same stages of linguistic development. Aramaic as the language of commerce and diplomacy
was the *lingua franca* of the ancient world alike in the East and
the West. I have dealt with the linguistic question from this
standpoint in the sections that follow.

From the above considerations, which I hope to establish in
due course, it follows that Daniel could, so far as the language
itself goes, have been written in the East as well as in the West.
Its place of origin must be determined on other grounds.

§ 19. *Five Periods of Aramaic from 800 B.C. to A.D. 100,
of which Ezra* (= *III*^{a}) *and Daniel* (= *IV*) *represent two.*

In dealing with the different stages of development in Aramaic
from 800 B.C. to A.D. 100, account will be taken only of such
idioms and characteristics in I, II, III, and V as bear on the
Aramaic of Daniel, and in a secondary degree of the Aramaic
of Ezra.

Before I enumerate the main authorities for I, II, and V,
I will state at the outset one main conclusion to which this
investigation leads, and this is that, though there are local
differences and idiosyncrasies throughout the Aramaic speaking
world, *there is no essential difference between the Western and
Eastern dialects.* If this conclusion is valid, then it follows that
*from linguistic grounds in themselves it is not possible to determine
whether Daniel was written in the East or West. On the other
hand the comparison of these different periods will serve to fix
within narrow limits the date of its composition.*

The authorities, from which these conclusions are drawn, are
not exhaustive, but they are so representative that they justify
such conclusions. In this study I have not wittingly ignored
any important inscription or papyrus bearing on the questions
at issue.

I. 800 to 500 B. C.

(a) *Aramaic in the West*—Northern Syria : Zinjirli Inscriptions (Hadad, Panammu, Bar-rekub, and Zakar). Of these the Hadad and Zakar Inscriptions date before 750 B. C. : the Panammu and Bar-rekub between 745 and 727 B. C. See Cooke 61–63 for the first three, and Lidzbarski, *Eph.* iii. 1–11, for the fourth : also Torrey, *JAOS*, 1917, 35 seqq., for a study of the fourth.

Nerab Inscriptions (S.E. of Aleppo) seventh century : Cooke 64–5.

(β) *Aramaic in the East*, i. e. Assyria. Aramaic Letter (seventh century) in time of Assurbanipal. See Lidz., *ZA*, Bd. xxxi, 1917–18, 193 seqq. : revised and republished independently under the title *Altaramäische Urkunden aus Assur*, 1921. Also Aramaic inscriptions on weights, seals, and in contracts : see CIS II. 1–52 : in Babylon II. 53–71 ; in Assyria or Syria II. 73–83—eighth–seventh century, II. 84–107 seventh–fourth century.[1]

II. 500–400 B. C.

(a) *Aramaic in the West :*

Aramaic Papyri (*Aramaic Papyri of the Fifth Century B. C.*, Cowley, 1923). This most important collection of Aramaic documents from Assuan and Elephantine with the exception of 'The Words of Aḥikar' and 'The Behistun Inscription' had their origin in Egypt—mainly in Elephantine. Earlier edited with facsimiles by Sachau, *Aramäische Pap. und Ostraka*, 1911.

Saqqara Inscription : CIS II. 145 (Cooke 76).

(β) *Aramaic in the East.* 'Aramaic Indorsements on the Documents of the Murašû Sons of Nippur on the Euphrates' : see *O.T. and Semitic Studies in Memory of W. R. Harper*, 1908, I. 287–321, by A. T. Clay : also Lidz., *Eph.* II. 203–210 ; III. 12–19.

---

[1] This division overlaps the next in point of time. The inscriptions in CIS II. 1–107 are not in chronological order. Thus while II, 21–31, 30, 40, 42, 46–49 are ascribed to the seventh century, II. 13, 32 are ascribed to the eighth. In the Babylonian inscriptions, while II. 58 definitely belongs to the sixth century, II. 59 is ascribed to the seventh : II. 71 to the fifth century. On the Aramaic in the contracts, see J. H. Stevenson, *Assyrian and Babylonian Contracts with Aramaic Reference Notes*, 1902 : also Lidz., *Eph.* II. 200 sqq.

(γ) *Aramaic in Asia Minor*, i. e. in Kesejek Keojew near Tarsus. Fifth century. See Torrey, *JAOS*, 35, 1915, 370 seqq. Jagdinschrift, fifth–fourth century: Lidz., *N.E.* 446, Cooke 68: Limyra, c. 400 B.C. CIS II. 109. Guzneh, fifth century: see *Eph.* III. 64: Montg., *JAOS*, 1907, 164–167.

(δ) *Aramaic in Arabia*, i. e. the *Tema and Hegra Inscriptions*, fifth century: CIS II. 113–121. For the chief Tema Inscription see Cooke 69.

(ε) Jer. 10^{11}.

III (α). Aramaic sections in Ezra 4^8–6^{18}, 7$^{12-26}$—designated E. Fourth century towards its close: Papyrus Luparensis: CIS II. 146: Cooke 77.

(β). *Lettres d'Uruk* (third century)—Thureau-Dangin, 1922. For the decipherment of this cuneiform script in Aramaic I have followed P. Jensen's *Der aramäische Beschwörungstext in spät-babylonischer Keilschrift*, 1926.

(γ). Inscription in Aram. from Taxila on the Hydaspes: fourth century.

IV. Aramaic section in Daniel 2$^{4\,b}$–7: second century—beginning of—designated D.

V (α). Nabataean. CIS II. 157–489: 1472 seqq. : Lidzbarski, *Eph.* II. 73–6; 251–68. First century B.C.—second century A. D.

(β) Palmyrene : see Lidzbarski, *Eph.* II. 77–80, 269–320.

In the above five periods there is on the whole a steady development, which at last reaches its final stage in the Targums. In the East the evidence is only partially adequate.

Amongst the five periods there is the closest connexion between III^α (i. e. E.) and IV (i. e. D.). But even in the case of these two documents D. shows definitely a later stage of development than E.

§ 20. *A survey of the grammatical development of the forms of words (including endings and prefixes) and of phrases during these five periods.*

(a) *Endings of masc. and fem. nouns in* א *or* ה, whether the absolute or emphatic states during the different periods of Aramaic will be found in Baumg. 90–3. Though the differences are marked they are not decisive enough to be cited on the present question.

(*b*) *Ending of 1 Pl. Pf.*

I. Ends always in ן.

II[a]. Always (?) in ן: cf. Cowley אמרן 40[2]; גלין 37[8]; הוין 30[15], 31[14]; הודעין 30[29]; החוין 26[7]; חזין 30[17], 31[16].

III and IV. Always in נא (as later in the Fast Roll and Onkelos).

V. In Nabataean always נא־.

(*c*) *Pronoun* ־ן = 'us' as verbal suffix.

II[a]. ־ן = 'us': see Cowley החוין 30[16] (Haph'el) 'caused us to see' (so Cowley) or 'caused us to know' (Sachau). But the later form occurs in the corresponding passage in 31[15] חוינא (Pa'el).

(*d*) ־ן (noun suffix) = 'our': Cowley 17[1,5], 30[1,2,18,23], &c. מראן 'our lord'; 20[10, 13], 30[15, 26] בנין 'our sons': 20[10, 13] בנתן 'our daughters': 38[8] בתין 'our houses': 37[8—9] אנפין 'our face': 2[9], 20[8, 9] לבבן 'our heart'. And so always in the fifth century. But just as in the case of the verbal suffix, so in that of the noun suffix we find the beginnings of the change of ־ן into נא־, but not till the fourth (?) or rather the third century B.C. Thus we find תרדמנא 'our dream' in CIS II. 129[1(b)]: ביתנא 'our house' Cowley 81[110]. The text is uncertain.

III[a], IV, and V. In these the above suffix is always written נא, and does not seem to be earlier than the third century (save in III[a]).[1] Even in respect of the ending of the 1 Pl. Pf. the usage in III[a] and IV does not date earlier than the close of the fifth century.

(*e*) Certain letters displaced by others in the course of development ז—ד.

I[a]. ז always in North Syria (so also in Arabia and mostly in Asia Minor, Abydos, Cilicia).

I[β]. Assyr.–Babylonian. ז in the Assyr. Letter and mostly in texts in CIS. But as early as the eighth century ד is found: cf. CIS II. 77 B. 2. Moreover there is no doubt that ד was frequently used to transliterate ז in Aramaic names occurring in Cuneiform Inscriptions (see Baumgartner, p. 95).

II[a]. ד is attested in Egypt as early as 484 B.C.: see Cowley 2[17,19], 3[23], and occasionally in later papyri. Baumgartner finds 55 in all. In Cowley I find 52, of which 14 are nouns, 12 verbs,

---

[1] Here as in the case of other forms the present text may owe these to later redactions.

6 pronouns, 7 adverbs, and 3 adjectives. On the other hand ז
occurs 300 times or more. It is true that only a small minority
of these are verbs, nouns, or adjectives. They are predominantly
pronouns, either relative, demonstrative, or personal.
III[a]–IV. ד always save in E. 7[21]. In D. 6[23] scholars are
divided as to the linguistic origin of זכו—Aram. or Akkadian?.
V[a,β]. ד has displaced ז in Nabataean (save in one inscription : see CIS II. 349[1,2,4], which is assigned to 70 B.C.), Palmyrene and late literary dialects.

ז—ד. To return to II[a] we find within one and the same
document and sometimes in actually the same line of the
document ז and ד used side by side : thus in 14[6] (Cowley) we
have זי and דכא in immediate conjunction. For various explanations of this change see Nöldeke (*Die semitischen Sprachen*[2] (1899)
32 seq.), who holds that the ז in the Zinjirli and Assyrian
inscriptions and documents is due to Akkadian influence, and
'that to the Arabic *ḏ* amongst the Aramaeans a *ḏ* of old corre-
sponded'. This view, Baumg. (*op. cit.* 98), whom I have just
quoted, rejects on the ground that the prevalence of this ז over
the entire empire from Egypt and Arabia to Asia Minor and
India renders it impossible. He is of opinion either that 'im
ältesten Aramäisch ז gesprochen, d. h. die Spirante *ḏ* im
Kanaanäischen zu *z* verschoben wurde, oder . . dieses ז nur ein
Notbehelf war, um den *ḏ*-Laut auszudrücken, für den die phoe-
nikische Schrift eben kein eigenes Zeichen besass'. The
fluctuations between ז and ד in the East back to the eighth
century favour in his opinion the latter view, and these fluctuations furthermore even in the Cuneiform texts—sometimes with
ז but mostly with ד—point to the fact that this specific Aram. *ḏ*
sound, being itself foreign to the Assyrians was transliterated
now one way, now another. Lidzbarski (*Eph.* II. p. 240 : cf.
Nöldeke, *ZA*, 20, 138) writes : ' es ist denkbar, dass im V. Jahr-
hundert der Uebergang von ז (= ṣ) zu ד in der lebenden Sprache
bereits stattgefunden hatte, in der Schrift zwar im Allgemeinen
noch nicht zum Ausdruck gebracht wurde, sich aber doch hie
und da einschlich ' : cf. *Eph.* III. pp. 79, 106.[1]

---

[1] I have given Baumgartner's and Lidzbarski's view at considerable length.
But I cannot understand how it is that the change from ז to ד took place in nouns,
verbs, and adjectives earlier and more frequently rather than in the pronouns and
relatives, which were immeasurably in more constant use. Surely the commonest
particles and words would be the first to exhibit this change.

The same change was taking place in the East. ז is still preserved in the Murašû documents (fifth century), but ד takes its place on the Uruk text.

The conclusion then as to the use of ד in D. is that *its use of* ד *is of no importance whatever in itself: but it is of overwhelming importance that it uses* ד *only* just as do the Nab., Palm., and literary dialects. *This fact disjoins it from the literature of the fourth century and earlier*, and connects it essentially with that of the second and later centuries. *The transformation of* ז *into* ד *is final and complete.*

ע.—ק.

ערק—ק in Iᵃ (North Syria) ארק : Hadad Panammu and Bar-rekub Inscr. See Cooke, 61⁵, 62¹⁴, 63⁴ : Zakar B²⁶.

Iᵝ. In *Assyr. and Baby.* CIS II. 1–4, 7, 11, 28, 35.

IIᵝ. *Aram. in East* (i.e. Murašû Indorsements, No. 5).

IIᵞ. Jer. 10¹¹, where it is followed by ארעא in the same verse.

IIᵃ. *Aramaic in West*: Egypt. זי לערקה 'to meet' (later Aram. לעורע), see Cowley: Beh. 4, 10, 31, 38, 40. On p. 269, No. 3⁶, we find זי לערעה.

קמר 'wool' Cowley 20⁵, 36³, 42⁹, but עמר 15⁷,¹⁰. Again עק in Cowley 20⁵, &c., but אע in IIIᵃ, IV.

ארק Cowley 6⁵⁻⁷,¹²⁻¹⁵, 8¹¹⁻²⁴, 9³,⁵,¹⁴ : but ארעא 5⁵, 6¹⁶, 15¹⁹, 30⁹, &c.

Thus the change of ק into ע, which appears only in D., began in the West in the fifth century, though not found in the East in that century. D appears therefore to be later than 400 B. C. according to existing documents.

ס.—שׁ.

Iᵃ. שׁ, i.e. שׁים in Iᵃ Zakar A¹,⁹ : I⁽ᵝ⁾ CIS II. 10 פרשׁ (= 'half a mina ').

IIᵃ. שׁ is the rule, but three or more times in Cowley 37⁷ סברת Aḥ. 100, 104 (סַפִּין), 147 (תסתכל).

IIIᵃ–IV. ס occurs occasionally (cf. D. 7²⁵ יסבר), but the older שׁ is preserved as a rule, and D. is herein older than Vᵃ,ᵝ .

Vᵃ has שׁ often, and Vᵝ less frequently.

ת.—שׁ.

שׁ in Iᵃ North Syria: Zakar B 15 seq. אשׁר 'inscription', but אתר in the Safa texts *Eph.* III, p. 10). אשׁור = ' Assyria ', Cooke (Panammu and Bar-rekub) 62⁷,¹², 63⁹.

Iᵝ. Assyr. Lett. 16 שׁקל, but in 11 יהתב ' he will give up '.

I⁷ (Babylonian): CIS II. 13, 14, 43 שקלן.

IIᵃ. Cowley 17² אתר 'place': Aḥ. 3–5, 8 אתור 'Assyria'.
But שׁקל is found about twenty-two times and never תקל as in D.,
though the verb תקל 'to weigh' is found five times. The use of
תקל in D. 5²⁵·²⁷ tends to show that it is later than 400 B. C.

(*f*) Assimilation of *n*. IIᵃ נ is preserved frequently in IIᵃ.
See כנכר (talent) in Cowley 26¹⁷, 30²⁸: ענזא 'goat' 33¹⁰: Aḥ.
118 (*bis*), 119, 31²⁷: צנפר 'bird' Aḥ. 91, 98, 199: yet ככרן in
50⁹, 83²⁹.

IIIʸ. E 7²² ככרין : so also עין 6¹⁷.

IV. צפַּר 'bird', 4⁹·¹¹·¹⁸·³⁰.

(*g*) מרא : so in Iᵃ. Cooke 63³ + 6 times: Zakar.

IIᵃ. Cowley: always and very frequently except in 34⁶
(מריהם).

IIIʸ. In the Taxila Inscription מראן 9, 12.

IV. Four times מרא iu Ginsburg's text 1926, even in 2⁴⁷.
But in 4¹⁶·²¹ the *Qr.* reads מרי 'my Lord' as in Vᵃ·ᵝ.

Vᵃ·ᵝ begin to omit the א before suffixes and between the
shewa and full vowels. In Syr. and Targ. the א is always
omitted.

(*h*) *Pronouns personal and demonstrative.*

Iᵃ·ᵝ אנך 'I' (Cooke 61¹), אנכי (62¹⁹), אנה (63¹). Zakar A²:
Lidz., *Eph.* III. p. 3, A².

IIᵃ. אנה always. אנחן and אנחנה 'we'.

IIIᵃ, IV, Vᵃ. אנה. אנחנה (E. 4¹⁶) 'we': once אנחנא 5¹¹. In
IV always אנחנה.

Iᵃ. את 'thou': Cooke 64⁵, 65⁸.

Iᵝ. Assyr. Letter 2 את.

IIᵃ. אנת 'thou': אנתם only with Imper. 21⁴, 38⁵·⁶, 80.

IIIᵃ. אנתה (E. 4¹⁶, 7²⁵), &c. ⎫
IV. אנתא : pl. אנתון D. 2⁸. ⎬ Peculiar to E. and D.
Vᵝ. אנת. ⎭

המו 'they'.

In I, II, IIIᵃ nom. and acc. (in IIIᵃ nom. once; acc. eight
times).

IV always המון (acc. only D. 2³⁴·³⁵, 3²²).

Hence IV, i. e. Daniel—not earlier than 300 B.C. Here a
great gulf divides IIIᵃ and IV.

אנון 'they', 'those', Pl. of הוא.

I–II have no such form.

III–IV. E. 5^4 : D. 2^{44}, 6^{25}, 7^{17} : only in nom.; for D. 6^{25} is corrupt. But in D. אנון seems to be only a demonstrative since in 7^{17} the clause appears to be an interpolation.

אנון is a late formation with א for ה and ן for ם.

דֵּ, דָּ 'that'.

II. Before or after noun.

III. דָּךְ, דֵּךְ after noun only: not in IV.

IV. דכן after noun only and only in D. 2^{31}, $7^{20,21}$.

זנה 'this'.

I. See Zinj. 63^{20} (Cooke). After noun: when it precedes the noun it is not an attribute but the subject itself: cf. Nerab 64^3, 65^2 (Cooke).

II^a. Fifth Cent. Pap. Always זנה save in 16^9, where it occurs as דנה. Always(?) after noun save in 30^{20}, 31^{19} (contrast $35^{7,8}$, 43^4 for the usual order in this phrase), Aḥ. 60.

II$^\delta$. זנה after noun in Tema Inscription: CIS II. $113^{4,\ 22,\ 23}$.

III^a–IV. Always as דנה, and always after noun except in E. 5^4. The other exception occurs in an interpolation in D. 4^{15}. In D. this demonstrative is always after the noun (eleven times). If 4^{15} were authentic we should have to translate 'this is' as in 4^{21}, $5^{25,26}$.

זא 'this' fem. before or after noun in II^a: after noun in II$^\gamma$ CIS II. 113^{13}. But since it does not occur in III^a–IV it does not call for further consideration here.

אִלֵּךְ 'those': before or after noun.

II^a. Before (16^4, 20^8, &c.) or after (Aḥ. 56, 58) noun : CIS II 145 B^6.

III^a, IV after noun : in III^a four times : in IV ten times.

אלה 'these'.

II^a. After noun : Cowley 2^{13}, &c. : II$^\epsilon$ Jer. 10^{11}.

III^a. E. 5^{15} precedes noun.

IV. Does not occur.

דכן IV only and after noun.

אִלֵּין. Pl. of דנה.

IV only : before (2^{44}, [1] 7^{17}) or after noun $6^{3,7}$.

V$^\beta$. אלן.

Thus D. has דכן המון, and אלין peculiar to itself. With E. it

---

[1] But is the position of אלין in 2^{44} due to the fact that it follows כל in the construct כל אלין מלכותא.

has the late form אֲנוּן. These facts make the composition of the former unlikely before 300 B.C. But the form הִמּוֹן disconnects D. with the older Aramaic, and connects it definitely with the later.

(i) *Suffixes.*

כֹם־ or כֹום־.

הֹם־ or הֹום־.

I. Oldest forms as above: cf. Cooke, Zinj. Hadad 61²⁹.

IIᵃ. כֹום־ or כֹם־ always.

הֹום־ nearly 100 times: but between 435–407 B.C. הֹן־ occurs six times: i. e. 16⁴, 30¹¹, 31¹⁰, 34⁶,⁷,¹ 37¹⁴: that is, once in about twenty times. Thus the change of *m* into *n* has just begun to occur *at the close of the fifth century.* Observe that in CIS II. 145²,³ (Cooke 76), end of fifth century, we find הֹם־.

IIᵉ. Jer. 10¹¹ הֹום־,

IIIᵃ (i. e. Ezra). כֹום־ five times: 5³,⁹, 7¹⁷,¹⁸,²⁴. כֹן־ once: 7²¹. הֹום־ eleven times: 5³,⁴,⁵,⁸,⁹,¹⁰(ter), 6⁹, 7¹⁶,²⁴. הֹן־ thirteen times: 4⁹,¹⁷,²⁰,²³, 5¹,²(bis),³(bis), 6⁶,¹³,¹⁸(bis).

Thus the suffixes end in *m* sixteen times: in *n* fourteen.

IV. (i.e. Daniel). In this work the *m* never occurs. The final stage is reached.

Vᵃ (Nab.). כֹם־ and הֹם־.²

Vᵝ (Palm.). כֹן־ and הֹן־.

The conclusion that D. belongs to the third century or later follows obviously from the above facts. Yet Wilson (p. 280) states that ' Ezra, being composed largely of letters between the Eastern Aramaeans and the Western, uses both (forms)'. Further on p. 279 he writes: ' All Aramaic documents of any age written in the East used *n* instead of *m*.' Let us examine this statement. If it is right, then the parts of Ezra written in the West should have *m* and those in the East *n*. But what are the facts? The narrative portions written in the West, as we presume, have the suff. ending in *n* in 4⁹,¹⁷,²⁰,²³, 5¹,²(bis),³(bis),⁶,¹⁷(bis), whereas the letters *written in the East* by the king or a Persian

---

¹ Observe that in 34⁶ (c. 407 B.C.) we have one suffix ending in *m* and another in *n*.

² This survival in Nab. belongs to the beginning of the Christian era: see CIS II. 198¹,²,⁷ : 199³ : 202³. This solitary survival, however we may explain it, has its analogies elsewhere. Thus of all the languages and dialects which owe their origin to Latin, only one, the Sardinian preserves the original hard sound fo *c* = Greek κ.

governor in the West have this ending once in 7^{21}. When Tattenai (Ustani in the Contract Tablets) interrogates the Jews in 5^{3-4} he uses the suff. ending in *m*. After Tattenai's question the narrative is resumed in 5^5, in which the suff. ends once in *m*. Then in 5^{6-10}, Tattenai's letter to Darius, the ending in *m* occurs six times and never once in *n*. This is surely strange in the letter to the king from a Persian governor, who according to Wilson always used an ending in *n*. In the informal answer of Darius (521–485 B.C.) to Tattenai these suffixes occur twice ($6^{6,9}$), but 6^6 is doubtful, and in 6^9 the ending in *m* is used.

The next Aramaic section 7^{12-26} consists of a letter of Artaxerxes (464–424 B.C.), in which there are eight suffixes, five ending in *m* and three in *n*, according to Ginsburg's text as well as Kittel's. Thus in two letters emanating presumably from the Foreign Office in Babylon in the fifth century six suffixes end in *m* and four in *n*.

The above facts prove that suffixes ending in *m* were used in Babylon in the fifth century, and that the ending in *n* was beginning to displace the *m*, just as it did in the West in the same century.

But there is further evidence as to the form of these suffixes as used in the Foreign Office in Babylon. The Behistun Inscription was made by the order of Darius in 510 B. C. to commemorate the achievements by which he consolidated his power. The Aramaic version of this inscription was according to Cowley (p. 249 seq.) 'no doubt done officially by the great king's own scribes, and sent out to the chief men of the provinces . . . soon after the inscription was engraved . . . the official Aramaic copy sent out by Darius, say about 510 . . . these Jews of Elephantine, being a literary people, thought it worth while to recopy and to preserve it as an historical record'. Now what do we find in this fifth century copy of a Babylonian document? Just this—that the suffix ending in *n* never occurs, whereas the ending in *m* occurs in lines 3, 6, 9, 11, 29, 33, 42, 44. A study of Aḥiḳar's story translated into Aram. in Babylon about 450 B. C. testifies to the same fact; for the suffix ending in *n* is not found in it. The evidence of these two independent documents strengthens the surmise that the *n* ending in Darius' letter is due to later influences.

Hence on purely linguistic grounds we conclude that D., in which the suffix *m* does not occur at all, cannot have been written earlier than the latter half of the third century. On other grounds it must be assigned to the first half of the second century.

Thus alike in East and West *m* was the primitive ending. In the fifth century (if the letters in E. are trustworthy, as I believe on the whole they are) the transition from *m* to *n* begins both in the East and the West, and in D. the transition reaches its final stage.

(*k*) *Causative Forms of Verbs*.

Haph'el.

I$^\alpha$. Haph'el exclusively and not Aph'el.

II. Haph'el all but exclusively. Baumg., p. 106, reckons eighty connected with over thirty verbs in II$^\alpha$. Aph'el only in one or more exceptional cases : cf. Cowley 34^6 אתבו (?) : Sachau, Tafel 65. 1^{3,4} : Lidz., *Eph*. III. 257 *n*. For further information consult Baumg., p. 106.

III$^\alpha$ (i. e. E.). Haph'el 6^5 תְּחַת : 6^1 : but Aph'el אחת in 5^{15}. On Bauer-Leander's treatment of this question see pp. 170–5.

IV (i. e. D.). Always Haph'el except in three cases : 3^1 אֲקִימֵה, 4^{11} אחרו, 5^{12} אחוית.

V$^\alpha$. Nab. Always Aph'el, except in CIS II. 349^2 : 70 B. C. : 161. 1^1.

V$^\beta$. Palm. Aph'el with one exception. Baumg., p. 106.

Thus III$^\alpha$ and IV are closely allied to I$^\alpha$, II. But IV less so than III$^\alpha$.

Imperfect and Participial Forms—Haph'el and Aph'el.

I$^{\alpha,\beta}$, II$^\delta$. ה (i. e. Haph'el forms) is generally preserved, but syncopated only in Zinj. Hadad 16, 28.

II$^\alpha$. Baumg. reckons thirty-eight with ה against nine where there is syncopation. See also Sachau I. 270 sq.

III$^\alpha$. The same scholar finds ten with ה against five where it is syncopated.

IV. Baumgartner finds twenty-nine with ה, against sixteen where it is syncopated. Where this syncopation occurs Bauer-Leander (against Brockelmann, *Grundriss* I. 563 sq.) treats the forms as Aph'els. See p. 61 seq. *p-r*, 113 *b*, *c*, *e*.

V$^{\alpha,\beta}$. Aph'el.

Thus III and IV occupy an intermediate stage between I, II, and V. See Baumgartner, p. 107.

Reflexive Stems in התֿ and אתֿ.

I[a]. Only in the Bar-rekub Inscription (Cooke 63[14]) do we find התֿ and in the Nerab (Cooke 65[4]) אתֿ.

II[a]. Baumg., p. 108, gives several examples in אתֿ which belong to the close of the fifth century.

III[a]. התֿ four times; only once 4[15] in a substantival form.

IV. התֿ seventeen times[1]: אתֿ six.[2]

V[a, β]. אתֿ.[3]

The later dialects have only אתֿ with a very few exceptions.

Baumg. infers from the above facts that אתֿ was the primitive prefix alike in Hebrew and Aramaic: that subsequently התֿ was developed after the analogy of the Hiph'il-Haph'el in the Perfect, but that ultimately התֿ was displaced by אתֿ in Aramaic.

(*l*) *Hoph'als.* The Hophals are mainly or only found in III[a], IV.

I[a]. Is מומת in Cooke 61[26] (Hadad) a Hoph'al?

II[a]. In Cowley 20[7] הפקרו is with some doubt taken to be a Hoph'al: Lidzbarski assents. But this does not occur elsewhere in the fifth cent. papyri.

III[a]. Once (i. e) E. 4[15].

IV. Nine times: 4[33(bis)], 5[13,15,20], 6[24], 7[4,5,11].

(*m*) Verbs לֿא and לֿה.

I[a]. These two classes of verbs are as a rule distinguished. See Baumg., p. 113.

II[a]. Verbs in לֿה still preserve their characteristics as a whole, while those in לֿא show a clear tendency to adopt those of the former.

III[a], IV. In these periods the two classes have practically coalesced, and the distinctions in the use of the א and ה no longer concern the two classes, but rather constitute grammatical categories. Herein III[a], IV stand markedly aloof from I[a], II[a], and have reached almost the same stage as V[a, β] (i. e. Nab. and Palm.).

---

[1] Baumg. wrongly reckons only 14. But we find the התֿ in the following verbs : בהל (3 times), נזר (i. e. 2[34]), זמן (1), חרך (1), מלא (1), רום (1), רחץ (1), שבח (8), i. e. 17 times.

[2] In 2[45] אתגזרת, 3[19] Kt. 4[16], 6[8], 7[8,15].

[3] In V[a] the sense and text are doubtful in CIS II. 186[4].

On Wilson's statement (p. 286 sq.) of these relations I cannot refrain from quoting Baumgartner's criticism (p. 115): 'The whole construction is a mass of caprice (voller Willkür): it ignores the general development as a whole, and stands frequently in contradiction with the facts.'

(*n*) *Derived Infinitives.*

II$^\alpha$. There is the first, which is absolute and ends in ה, the the second ends in ת in the construct or before a suffix. For the former see Cowley 9[6] לְזַבְּנָה 'to sell': for the latter 15[30] לתרכותה.

III$^\alpha$. Both the absolute and construct forms occur in E. For a secondary form of the construct, cf. לְהִנְזְקַת E. 4[22]. As a noun התנדבות עמא E. 7[16].

IV. Absolute להצלה D. 3[29], but in 6[16] להצלותה. Another form of the construct is אֲחָוָיַת D. 5[12] as in E. 4[22].

V$^\beta$. Palm. and Syr. use the construct for the absolute.

Thus III$^\alpha$ and IV herein preserve older forms and usages.

(*o*) *Absolute and Emphatic States.*

Though these are carefully distinguished in III$^\alpha$, IV, the usage varies in I$^\alpha$, II$^\alpha$.

I$^\alpha$. Thus in Cooke 62[14] (Panam.) we have רבעת ארק = 'the four quarters of the earth', whereas in 63[4] (Bar-rekub) רבעי ארקא with exactly the same meaning. In 63[14-15] מלכיא, 63[20] ביתא. There are other examples of the emphatic state, and in the Nerab inscriptions of the seventh century (Cooke 64[3,6-7,12]). Other examples of the absolute, used where later Aramaic inscriptions employed the emphatic, will be found in 61[15, 20, 25].

II$^\alpha$. Here the same uncertainty in the use of these states discloses itself. In 13[11] we have the absolute בית where III$^\alpha$, IV, and generally I$^\alpha$ would have used ביתא. Cf. also 8[8] (ארק): באשה (= 'with fire') in 30[12] does not differ from באשתא 31[11], and yet both are employed exactly in the same context and in describing the same event. Again in 30[12] we have 'basons of gold and silver' (זהבא וכסף emphatic and absolute states together!), and in 10[9-10] 'silver and gold, bronze, and iron' all in the absolute state. Yet there are clear signs of a distinction between the two states appearing in I$^{\alpha,\beta}$ which comes to be the rule in III$^\alpha$, IV. On the other hand, in III$^\alpha$, IV as in Hebrew, words designating materials known everywhere, or special ideas (Kautzsch, § 79 *c*) [1] appear in the emphatic (except in D. 2³², 3¹; E. 7¹⁵, ¹⁶) as 'gold and silver' (וכספא דהבה E. 5¹⁴), and 'wine' D. 5¹. 'Gold' is used nineteen times in E. and D. in the emphatic state, and four times (twice in D. 2³², 3¹) in the absolute state, but in D. 2³², 3¹ the absolutes are rightly used as distinguished from the emphatics in 2³⁸ and 3⁵, ⁷, &c. which follow. The same holds good of E. 7¹⁵, ¹⁶ as distinguished from 7¹⁸. Things which are unique are necessarily in the emphatic state: so שמשא 'the sun' in D. 6¹⁵. But in IIᵅ out of twelve instances of its occurrence, it is only once in the emphatic state.

From the above facts it follows that there is a steady development from a loose use of these two forms (in Iᵅ, IIᵅ) to a careful differentiation of them, such as we find in IIIᵅ, IV. In this respect IV is much later than IIᵅ.

WORDS AND PHRASES USED IDIOMATICALLY.

(*p*) *Proleptic use of Suffix* introducing a genitive.

Iᵅ. Unknown in the oldest Aramaic.

IIᵅ. It appears often in the latter half of the fifth century. See Cowley 15¹⁸⁻¹⁹ (אסחור זי בביתה 'in the house of Ashor'), 15³⁰ (440 B.C.): 28³, ¹³ (411 B.C.): 30¹⁰⁻¹¹, ¹⁸⁻¹⁹ (408 B.C.): 31¹⁸ Aḥ. 3: Beh. 5, 20, 28, 43.

IIIᵅ–IV. This use is well established in E. and D.: also in Later Aramaic dialects, in Syriac, also in Ethiopic.

Thus E. and D. can hardly have been written before 450 B.C.

Suffix with Preposition before a Noun.

Iᵅ–IIᵅ. Unknown in these periods.

(*q*) III–IV. First we have בֵּהּ זמנא D. 3⁷,⁸, 4³³, 7²⁴; E. 5³ 'at that same time'. Next we have the repetition of the preposition בֵּהּ בְּדָנִיֵּאל D. 5¹² 'in the same Daniel'. Cf. 5³⁰; E. 4¹¹ (after עַל). This idiom is found frequently in Syriac. Cf. Cur. in Matt. 21¹⁹: Pesh. in Matt. 26⁷⁴ ܟܘ ܚܡܣܐ 'at the same moment': Luke 2⁸, &c. IIᵅ 3⁷, ⁸ could possibly express the same sense by בוכם זמנא; cf. 9², 20⁴, 65³.

---

[1] Kautzsch, § 79 *c* rightly includes בשרא D. 2¹¹, עשׂבא 4²², חמרא 5¹ under this category, but not דהבה וכספא E. 5¹⁴, where the emphatics are due to the relative clause which follows: see *op. cit.*, § 79 *e*.

Thus neither I$^\alpha$ nor II$^\alpha$ appear to have used this idiom so well known in later Aramaic. Hence E. and D.—not earlier than the fourth century.

(*r*) כל with suff.

I$^\alpha$. כל with suff. after its noun.[1] See Cooke 62^{19} ביתה כלה ' his whole house ': also in 62^{17}.

II$^\alpha$. See Cowley Aḥ. 12 כלה אתור יעט ' counsellor of all Assyria ': also 55. This idiom is found in Heb.: cf. 2 Sam. 2^9; Jer. 13^{19}; Isa. 9^8, &c.: in Syr. (where the ' all ' with suff. can follow or precede its noun): in Nab. after. Cf. CIS II. 219^5, 350^5.

III$^\alpha$, IV. But in E. and D. כל is not found with suff. after its noun. In D. 7^{19} it is used with suff. but without a noun כלהון ' them all '. In the emphatic state (כלא) it is used without a noun in D. 2^{40}, 4$^{9, 18}$, or after its noun in apposition as in E. 5^7. In D., when כל is connected with a noun, it always precedes it. It is remarkable that, though as far West as Egypt and East as Babylon in the fifth century כל was used with suff. after its noun, it is never so used in III$^\alpha$, IV.

(*s*) *Jussives used alike in East and West.*

I$^\alpha$. *In the West.* The jussive assumes the following forms: ליתכה (Hadad: Cooke 61^{23} eighth century, ' let him pour it out '). Again in 61^{24} למנע(י)ל ' let him withhold ': also in 61^{30} לתגמרו ' make ye an end of ': 61^{31} לכתשה(י) ' let him crush her ' (?). This idiom is found also in Sabaean: see Cooke, p. 169. In Arabic the lamedh is placed before the subjunctive to express purpose. It follows from the above facts that in Aramaic when ל[2] was placed before the Imperf. it had a jussive force—both in the 2nd and 3rd persons, and apparently with any verb. Since no Imperf. is found in -*un* in the Zinjirli and Nerab inscriptions it is inferred that at this period only the 3rd pl. ending in -*u* was known.

I$^\beta$. Assyr. Letter, l. 8 למחנו ' let them grind '.

II$^{\alpha, \delta}$. The jussive is found in fifth century inscriptions: see

---

[1] In II$^\alpha$ כלא (emphatic) is found before its noun: Cowley 30^{29} or after it 26^{17}, 30$^{11, 12}$. In 39^i we find אלהיא כל—surely a slip for כלא in this fifth century letter.

[2] Lidz., *Eph.* II. 220 finds the form ליקטל ' let him slay ' on a papyrus fragment. He thinks it refers to the garrison in Elephantine. Since it contains the pronominal form המו ' them ', it seems to belong to the fourth century or earlier. Yet Lidz. connects it with other fragments referring to Mithridates.

Cowley 30⁶ (31⁶) יהעדו 'let them remove': Aḥ. 146 אל תהעדי
'remove not'. In the Tema Inscription (II⁶) (see Cooke 69¹⁴)
we find ינסחוהי 'may they pluck him out'.

III*ᵃ*, IV. The jussive form recurs in III*ᵃ* (E.) 4¹², ¹³, 5⁸, 7²⁶,
and in IV (D. 2²⁰, ⁴¹, 3¹⁸, 5¹⁷) and elsewhere, but apparently these
forms have no jussive force save in D. 2²⁴ אל תהובד 'do not
destroy', 5¹⁰ אל יבהלוך 'let them not trouble thee': זיויך אל ישתנו
'let not thy countenance be changed'. Here the אל has probably
been the means of preserving the jussive. Without the אל it
occurs in Jer. 10¹¹ יֵאבַדוּ (fourth century?). See note on
p. 94 seqq.

If we ask why the ל was used in later Aramaic such as E.
and D. only with the verb הוה or הוא, Meinhold, Bevan, and
others hold that Jewish teachers deliberately adopted this
archaism in the case of this verb in order to avoid the likeness
of יהוה to the Divine Name. This view may possibly be accepted
on the ground that, though ל was originally prefixed to either
the 2nd or 3rd persons, from the fourth century onwards it is
prefixed only to the 3rd Sing. masc. or the 3rd Pl. masc. or fem.
of הוה, and of no other verb; for in the case of no other verb was the
3rd pers. Sing. masc. and the 3rd masc. and fem. Pl. similar to
the Divine Name.[1] The 3rd fem. sing. תהוה or תהוא occurs
several times in III*ᵃ*, IV: cf. D. 2⁴⁰, ⁴², &c.: E. 6⁸.

In the Palestinian Talmud and the Midrashim such forms
are found as להוי, ליכול, ליפק, but as Stevenson (*Gram. Pal. Aram.*,
p. 49) observes: 'they seem to occur generally in certain special
types of sentence, e.g. in those expressing a purpose (after ד and
דְּלָא) or a wish (see Dalman, p. 264 seq.).'. It is found also in
Mandaean and possibly also in Assyrian. See Driver, *Tenses*³,
§ 204.

In any case the conclusion is that only a few instances of the
jussive survive in IV and there only after אל, and none at all in
III*ᵃ*, if the MT is trustworthy.

(*t*) ל *with Infinitive used independently or after* רי *to express
purpose.*

I–II. Not found at all so far as I am aware.

III*ᵃ*. E. 6⁸. די לא לבטלא 'that they might not be hindered'.

---

[1] Baumgartner, p. 125 *n*, rejects this view, on the ground that it fails to explain
plural forms such as להון and להוין. Yet see Wright, *Comp. Gr.*, 1890, p. 183 f.

IV. D. 6¹⁶. לא להשניא . . . . די 'that (no interdict) should be changed'.

D. 2¹⁶. ופשרא להחויא . . . . די 'that . . . . and so he would make it his task (i.e. 'undertook.') to show the interpretation '.

5¹⁵. ופשרה להודעתני . . . . די 'that . . . and they made it their task (i. e. 'undertook') to show the interpretation thereof'.[1]

2¹⁸. ורחמים למבעא 'and so they made it their task (i.e. 'undertook') to implore compassion '.

It will be observed that in the first two passages (E. 6⁸, D. 6¹⁶) ל c. Inf. follows די immediately: in the next two it follows a clause introduced by די and therefore seems to be alike dependent on the די. But to the present writer this does not appear to be the true explanation. Here ל c. *Inf.* and introduced by *vav*, though following a clause dependent on די is not to be regarded as dependent on the די but as constituting an independent clause parallel with like clauses before it. This explanation is confirmed by 2¹⁸, where no די precedes this very peculiar construction, but the independent clause דניאל . . ל . . חברוהי מלתא הודע.

Thus this idiom in D. (2¹⁶, ¹⁸, 5¹⁵) is a stage farther advanced than in E. (6⁸, D. 6¹⁶) where it is undoubtedly dependent on די.

This idiom, which, so far as I can discover, is not found in I–II is found in Hebrew. It occurs in 1 Chron. 5¹ ולא להתיחש לבכרה ' and the genealogy must not be reckoned for the birthright'. Cf. also 15² לא לשאת 'none may carry'. Sometimes it denotes futurity without sense of aim or purpose: cf. 2 Chron. 30⁹ ולשוב ' and they shall return '. In Eccles. 3¹⁵ אשר להיות כבר היה 'what is to be hath already been'. It is frequent in late Hebrew: cf. Aboth 4³¹ (ed. Taylor).

Thus E. and still more D. have developed an idiom unknown in Aramaic before the fourth century so far apparently as existing records go.

In 9² we have, as I take it, another example of this idiom : אשר . . . למלאות 'which were to be accomplished': see note *in loc.*: also *Comm.*, p. 131.

(*u*) די = ὅτι *recitativum*: cf. IV (i. e. D. four times only—2²⁵, 5⁷, 6⁶, ¹⁴ (like כי and אשר in Hebrew)), but not in I, II, III, so far as I can discover.

---

[1] I take this clause—not as dependent on די but as parallel with the preceding clause ' the wise men . . have been brought in before me '.

(*v*) נברין כשדאין 'certain Chaldeans': only so used in IV, i. e.
D. 3⁸, ¹², ²⁰. Here נ stands in apposition just as אנשים in Hebrew
in Judges 19²² where אנש is corrupt for אנשים: cf. 20¹⁶:
Deut. 13¹⁴.

(*w*) קדם 'before'. The use of this word is very significant in
connexion with the verb אמר. ל *c.* pers. is used after אמר about
twenty times. In these passages kings use ל after this verb in
addressing their officials, officials use it in the same connexion
to one another: in a few passages the three Jewish Confessors
and the great nobles use it in the MT in addressing the king in
3⁹ MT, Th., Vulg., Pesh., but LXX om., 3¹⁶, ⁺²⁴⁺, 6⁷ ⁽⁶⁾, ¹⁶ ⁽¹⁵⁾. But
3⁹ is an interpolation, being omitted by the LXX: in 6⁷ ⁽⁶⁾ we
should with the LXX read קדם and not ל. Of the remaining three
3¹⁶, ²⁴, 6¹⁶ ⁽¹⁷⁾ we can explain the use of ל in 3¹⁶. It is used by
the three Jewish Confessors, who are facing immediate death
for the sake of their faith, and so address Nebuchadnezzar as
they would any other man. In 6¹⁶ ⁽¹⁵⁾ the great nobles having
secured a law designed to destroy Daniel are indifferent to the
ceremonious language usual in addressing a king, and so in their
insolence they use ל and not קדם, though when earlier they were
seeking to secure this law 6⁷ ⁽⁶⁾ (LXX) they used קדם. Only in
⁺3²⁴⁺ is this rule not observed. It seems therefore to be a primitive
corruption. In 2²⁵ קדם has just been used and so ל is used after
אמר to avoid a repetition of it. But ל is never used after אמר
when God is addressed. Hence not only on this but mainly on
other grounds 4³² ⁽³⁵⁾ must be excised as an interpolation.
Further, as we have just seen, קדם is used after אמר and not ל,
when the king is addressed, unless there are special grounds for
not doing so.

The proper preposition which should be used after אמר when
addressing God is קדם. See our author. The beginnings of
this usage in Aramaic appear in Iᵃ i.e. Nerab 2: see Cooke
65² where קדם is used in addressing the god Sahar. In IIᵃ
it is used mainly when God (Cowley 30²⁷),[1] kings (30², 32⁵), or
governors (32³, 37⁵) are addressed: or friends Aḥ. 141. In IIIᵃ
(i. e. E.) קדם is used before the chancellor, 4²³, before the king, 4¹⁸,

---

[1] In Cowley we find the later usage in connexion with the Egyptian gods:
72⁶ (CIS II. i. 146⁶) 'before 'Aḥor': 72¹⁵ 'before Apuaitu' as well as before
the God of Israel: קדם אלה שמיא 38²⁻³. The first papyrus is not dated but the
second is fifth century B.C.

g

before God, 7^{19} (though after a different verb). On the other hand אמר ל is used of Cyrus in addressing his officials, 5^{15} : and likewise of the Persian governors in addressing the Jews, $5^{3,4,9}$. Thus we see a steady approach to the usage in Daniel.

Having grasped our author's usage of this phrase, we recognize that the interpolator of $4^{3-7a\,(6-10a)}$ had not the slightest conception of it. Thus he represents the great Nebuchadnezzar as saying with regard to the soothsayers and Daniel, whose destruction he had decreed on arbitrary grounds in 2^{13} : ' I told the dream *before* them', $4^{4\,(7)}$: ' I told the dream *before* him', $4^{5\,(8)}$. This passage which is omitted by the LXX contains other idioms conflicting with our author's usage.[1]

(*x*) ל *before the accusative or direct object.*

II^{a}. On this use Cowley, p. 14, remarks : 'the use of ל to mark the object is not common in these texts'. Cf. 5^{9}, $13^{2,\,5}$, [$15^{3,\,27}$], Aḥ. 1. It is really very infrequent.

III^{a}. In E. it occurs six times $5^{9,\,10,\,12}$, 6^{7}, $7^{24,\,25}$.

IV. In D. ל is used before the acc. about forty times and all but as a rule before personal objects : $2^{10,\,12,\,14,\,19,\,24,\,25,\,48,\,49}$, 3^{18}, $4^{22\,(25)}$, &c. (thirty-three times), but not in †$2^{13,\,18}$†, 3^{28} and †6^{25}†.[2] In $2^{34,\,35}$, 3^{19}, $5^{2,\,23}$, 7^{2} it is used before impersonal but defined objects. ל bef. acc. more than twice as often relatively in D than in E.

This usage distinguishes definitely the style of D. from E., and exhibits a much later stage of linguistic development.

(*y*) *Use of* כהל *and* יכל.

For convenience sake we shall consider together these two verbs, which have the same meaning.

I. Not found.

II^{a}. When these verbs are used in the Impf., they are followed by another verb in the Impf. without a conjunction : cf. Cowley

---

[1] On the usage of *before* in relation to the Deity in the Targums and Syriac, see Driver *Samuel*, p. lxx sqq. ; Dalman, *Worte Jesu*, 171-4 (English translation 209-13), who states that in Egypt subjects never spoke 'to' the king but 'in his presence', and that the Targums never represent man as speaking 'to' but 'before' God.

[2] I have bracketed the passages in $2^{13,\,18}$, 6^{25} as corrupt. There is the authority of some of the versions for so doing in the case of 2^{13}, 6^{25}. In 2^{18} by reading יְהוּבְדוּן instead of יְהוֹבְדוּן (as Lambert, *Rev. des Études juives* 54 (1893), p. 269 sq. proposes) the usage of the author could be recovered. In 3^{28} however the context is against any emendation. See Bauer-Leander, p. 339 sqq.

1⁴ (495 B.C.), 5⁶ (471 B.C.), 6¹² (465 B.C.) down to the latest
15³¹ ⁽³⁵⁾ (441 B.C.), whereas the earliest example of כהל followed
by ל *c*. Inf. is to be found in 28⁷⁻⁸ (where eleven words separate
the verb and the Inf.) (411 B.C.), and Aḥ. 17. Yet in Aḥ. it is
twice followed by the Impf. without a conjunctive in 26 (?), 81.

IIIᵃ. These verbs do not occur.

IV. When these verbs are combined with another verb in D.,
the latter is in the Inf. *c*. ל, as in the Targums : cf. 2²⁶, ⁴⁷, 6²¹, &c .
Thus the ancient usage,¹ all but universal in IIᵃ is not once
attested in IV.

Again this verb is used in the sense of ' to get the mastery of '
in D. 7²¹ with ל and a suffix. This usage is not found in Iᵃ, IIᵃ,
IIIᵃ, though it is frequent in Heb. (with ל and a noun) and in
the Targums.

In IIᵃ we have the same early Aramaic usage in connexion
with צבי 'to desire ' in 18²⁻³ צבית אהנצל ' I desire to take away '.⁴
In IV, i. e. D. 7¹⁹ it is followed by ל *c. inf*. So also in Syr. but
not in Iᵃ, IIIᵃ, nor yet in Heb.

Thus D. exhibits only the later construction of כהל and צבי in
Aramaic.

(*z*) די שמה בלטשאצר 'who was named B.', D. 2²⁶.

In IIᵃ (Cowley) in 28⁴ we have פטוסירי שְׁמֵהּ ' one named
Petosiri '. Cf. 28⁵, ⁸⁻⁹, ¹²⁻¹³, 33¹⁻⁵. Aḥ. 1, 18 ; Beh. 2, 7, 12, 22, 25,
27, 35. Cowley on Aḥ. 1 says this is a Persian idiom.: but it is
Hebr. as well. One example of this idiom occurs in IIIᵃ, i. e.
E. 5¹⁴ שמה ששבצר 'one named Sheshbazzar'. The converse
order is found in Aḥ. 4–5 and Beh. 17.

As above remarked this idiom is not found in Iᵃ, IV. In
D. 2²⁶ we have דִּי שְׁמֵהּ בֵּלְטְשַׁאצַּר—an idiom which recurs in 4⁵, ¹⁶.
In the older Aramaic this would have been simply שְׁמֵהּ "ב.
In the Hebrew of D. 10¹ "ב שמו נקרא אשר we have a partial
approach to this. This latter idiom is found in the Pesh. in
Luke 19², though the Greek has simply ὀνόματι καλούμενος. Cf. also
Mark 14³² ; and elsewhere.

In Hebrew there are two constructions in the main. When
the proper name precedes, the first idiom runs as follows
שמו גלית 'one named Goliath ': cf. Sam. 17⁴, ²³ ; 2 Sam. 20²¹, &c.

---

¹ Yet this ancient usage occurs a few times in Hebrew : see Num. 22⁶
אוכל נכה (where we should read נוכל) ' we are able to smite ': Lam. 4¹⁴.

When the proper name does not precede, the idiom is different. The conjunction always precedes the phrase. though the meaning remains unaffected. ושמו לבן LXX ᾧ ὄνομα Λαβάν 'one named Laban'. Cf. Judges 13², 17¹; Ruth 2¹, &c. These two Hebrew idioms are reproduced exactly in the Targums and generally in Syriac.

In D. 5¹² we have another Aramaic construction די מלכא שָׂם שְׁמֵה בל״ but this clause comes from the hand of the reviser or a scribe. The construction in Ezra 5¹⁴ די פחה שָׂמֵהּ 'whom he appointed governor' is different.

Thus the above idioms used in Babylon, Palestine (E.) and in Egypt are not found in D., the idioms of which are late.

The idiom in D. 2²⁶, 4⁵, ¹⁶ is reproduced literally in the Pesh.

(aa) התיב = 'to return' (acc. of answer).

Iᵃ. Not found.

IIᵃ. Used only in the sense of 'to return', 'to restore': Cowley 15²³, 20⁷.

IIIᵃ. 5⁵, ¹¹ 'to return' (with acc. of answer).

IV. 3¹⁶ 'to answer' (without acc.), but in 2¹⁴ with cognate acc. In Hebrew השיב = 'to answer' with or without an acc.

(bb) מנהון . . . מנהון 'some . . . others'.

I, IIᵃ, IIIᵃ. Not found.

IV. i. e. D. 2³³, ⁴¹, ⁴²ᵃ. Cf. מִנָּה . . . מִן־קצת 2⁴²ᵇ.

(cc) אמר followed by direct narration only in I, IIᵃ (about 100 times), IIIᵃ (= 'told them: Do so and so').

IV followed by the indirect narration, i. e. לֹ c. Inf. (= 'told them to do so and so') D. 2⁴⁶, 3¹³, ¹⁹, ²⁰, 5², 6²⁴. There are of course plenty of instances of אמר followed by the direct narration —2⁴, ⁷, &c. But D. stands here alone among the authorities mentioned.

(dd) נבוכדנצר מלכא 'N. the King'. This is the true ancient order of the words—never 'King N.'.

Iᵃ. Unfortunately the phrase does not occur.

IIᵃ. Always observes the above order.

IIIᵃ. So also E.: cf. 4⁹, ¹¹, ²³ (where the order of R.V. is wrong), ²⁴, 5⁶, &c.

IV. The ancient order is forsaken in 2²⁸, ⁴⁶, 3¹⁶, 5⁹, ¹¹, 6¹⁰ for 'King N'. In 3¹⁶ the MT separates 'King' and 'Nebuchadnezzar', but LXX,¹ Th., Vulg. connect them and in this order,

---

¹ LXX adds βασιλεῦ.

but not so the Pesh., and also in [4^{15}] against Th., Pesh., and
Vulg. That this late order had asserted itself in the second
century B.C. is clear from the above evidence as well as from the
fact that the LXX has this late order in 2^{48}, 4$^{1, 34\,b}$ where the
MT omits βασιλεύς.

This late order appears to be not older than the second
century B.C. In reference to oriental potentates it has not been
discovered, so for as I am aware, in works *emanating from the
East earlier than the second century B. C.* In I Macc. we have
the older order in 3^{27}, 6^{16}, 10$^{15, 48, 55, 59, 68, 88}$, 11$^{2, 38, 52}$, 12^{39}, 13$^{31, 34}$,
14^1, 15^{22}, and the later in 6^{55}, 10$^{18, 25}$, 11$^{8, 16, 18, 30, 32}$, 13^{36}, 14^{38}, 15^2.
Now I Macc. belongs to the latter half of the second century B.C.
In 2 Macc., which was written probably at the close of the second
century B.C. or in the first half of the first century the later order
appears in 11^{22}, 14^4 and the earlier in 5^{18}. In I Esdras (first
century B.C.) both orders occur and likewise in Judith (close of
second century B.C.) and in Bel and the Dragon first century
B.C. (Th.). The later order appears on the coins of Alexander
76–67 B.C. : Antigonus 40–37 B.C. and Herod the Great 37–4 B.C.,
See Schürer, *GJV*^{3} I. 287, 355, 397. In Josephus both orders
appear without any special significance in either case : cf. *Ant.*
x. 10, 3 : 11, 1 : xi. 1, 3 for ὁ βασιλεὺς Ναβοκοδρόσορος and x. 11, 4 :
xi. 1, 3 for the converse order ; similarly with regard to Cyrus :
xi. 1, 1 and xi. 1, 3. The significance of this idiom is unknown
to Josephus : as also to his predecessors back to the second
century B.C. In the Greek historians the order is βασιλεὺς Ξέρξης :
see Herodotus (484–425 B.C.) viii. 24 : also Thucydides i. 129 :
viii. 5, 37 (*bis*). This is the true Western order. In Polybius
(204–122 B.C.) the Oriental order is reproduced in his *Hist.*
xxvii. 17, 33 : xxxi. 11, 1, when speaking of Antiochus
Epiphanes, but the Western order when speaking of Ptolemy
Philometor, xxviii. 10, 8. Thus Greek historians follow their
own usage with regard to this idiom : but Oriental writers
observe the older order which was the real order down to the
second century B.C.

The evidence of this order of words seems in itself conclusive
as to the Book of Daniel being not earlier than the second
century B.C.

(*ee*) *Participle used as finite Verb.*

I^a. In the 120 lines or thereabouts of the Zinjirli (Hadad,

Panammu, and Bar-rekub) Inscriptions, eighth century, the participle does not appear to occur once : nor yet is the participle used in the two Nerab Inscriptions (Cooke 64, 65) consisting of fourteen and ten lines respectively.

I$^{\beta}$. Assyr. Letter: seventh century. Here also finite verbs are used apparently always.

II^{a}. *Aram. Pap.* (Cowley). I have not counted up the occurrences of the participle. But if we should say that it occurs once for every thirty times a finite verb occurs, even that might be considerably beyond the limit. Besides the participle, in many of the cases where it does occur, does not take the place of a finite verb.

II$^{\delta}$. Tema Inscription, fifth century, CIS II. 113. In the seventeen lines preserved of this inscription there are no participles.

III^{a} (i.e. E.). End of fourth century. In sixty-seven verses finite verbs (simple (93) and compounded with הוה (14), occur 107 times: participles occur as finite verbs twenty-four times: i.e. less than once in every five times.

IV^{a} (i.e. D.). In 199½ verses there are 99 participles [1] describing a past action as Historic Pres. or Impf. It occasionally alternates with the finite verb in the same sentence 4^{4}, 5^{1}, 6^{7}, and is used in the statement of general truths 2^{21}. This extended use of the participle is found in the Palestinian Talmud and the Midrashim and to a less degree in the Targums. [2]

Thus D. belongs herein to the later Aramaic, and is absolutely sundered in this respect from the older Aramaic.

(*ff*) כָּל-קְבֵל in III^{a} and IV. This is merely a corruption of כְּלָקֳבֵל.

II^{a}. קבל only twice. לקבל and די לקבל twelve times. לקבל as early as the sixth to fifth century: see Abydos Ins., Cooke 67.

III^{a}. כל-קבל only once as a Prep. in E. 7^{17}, but twice as Conj. 4^{14}, 7^{14} when followed by די. לקבל as Prep. 4^{16} : as Conj. when followed by די 6^{13}.

IV. D. כל-קבל 2$^{12, 24}$, 3$^{7, 8, 22}$, 6^{10} as Prep. But thirteen times as Conj. when followed by די. לקבל five times as Prep. As a conjunction כלקבל די occurs twice in E. 4^{14}, 7^{14}, but in D.

---

[1] See Burney, *Aram. Origin of Fourth Gospel*, p. 89.
[2] Stevenson, *Gram. of Pal. Jewish Aram.*, p. 56.

thirteen times. Thus a form בכלקבל (רי) which occurs only three times as Prep. or Conj. in E. has become so popular later that it is found nineteen times in D. The corrupt form has been reproduced in the Targums: cf. Ps. Jon.; Gen. 28[17]; Ruth 4[4]: and בל־קבל זי in Eccles. 5[15].

§ 21. Order of Words.[1]

I. In I[a] the verb as a rule precedes the subject or object.

In the Hadad Inscription

    the verb precedes the subj. (13 times), object (8), subj. + obj. 1 = 22 times.

    the subject precedes verb (2), verb + obj. (1), obj. + verb (1) = 4 times.

    the object precedes verb (2) = 2 times.

Thus the verb precedes subj., or obj., or both combined nearly four times oftener than the subj., or obj., or both combined, precede the verb. Note, that although the verb nearly always comes first, yet the Inscription shows a freedom in the order of the words which forecasts the later developments : i.e.

    (1) Subj. + obj. + verb 61[23].

    (2) Subj. + verb + obj. 61[20].

    (5) Verb + subj. + obj. 61[2–3].

The numbers (1), (2), (5) point to three of the six different combinations found in IV (i.e. D.).

In the Panammu Inscription

    Verb precedes subj. (5 times) or obj. (14) = 19 times.

    Subj.   ,,   verb (2)   = 2 ,,

    Obj.   ,,   ,, (2)   = 2 ,,

The verb precedes subj. or obj. or both combined five times oftener than the subj. or obj., or both combined precede the verb. We find also the combinations

    (4) Obj. + verb + subj. 62[1]

    (6) Verb + obj. + subj. 62[17, 19] but obj. in these cases a suffix.

---

[1] When the subject is contained in the inflected verb, it is generally not included in the reckonings that follow, unless it is actually added in the text, as it is occasionally, for the sake of emphasis. Similarly in relative clauses. Verbal suffixes are included in the reckonings. Participles, when they represent finite verbs, are treated as such. I do not take account of the constantly recurring words ואמר . . ענה. The subject as a rule follows the first verb. The above numbers make no claim to being literally exact, since the inscriptions are so frequently defective and undecipherable, but they are true in the main.

In the Bar-rekub Inscription

verb precedes obj. or subj. or both combined (4) = 4 times.

subj. „ verb (2) = 2 „

Here the verb precedes subj. or obj. or both combined twice as often as the converse order. We find also the combinations : (2) subj. + verb + obj. 63^{20} : (6) verb + obj. (suff.) + subj. 63^{5-6}.

In the Zakar Inscription

verb precedes subj. or obj. or both combined = 20 (?)

subj. „ verb or obj. = 4 (?)

We find also the combinations (2) subj. + verb + obj. and (6) verb + obj. + subj.

In the Nerab Inscription I verb precedes subj. or obj. 5

subj. „ verb 2 (?)

Here also we find the combinations (2) subj. + verb + obj. and (5) verb + subj. + obj.

I^β. *In the Aramaic Letter from Assyria*, the text of which is defective in many parts, the tendency above represented is more pronounced, and the verb almost as often follows the subj. or obj. as it precedes them.

Verb precedes subj. 2 (ll. 8, 11)

„ „ obj. 7 (ll. 5, 6, 8, 11, 12 (*bis*), 16)

Subj. precedes verb 3 (ll. 10, 11, 17)

Obj. „ „ 2 (ll. 8, 19)

Obj. + verb + subj. 1 (l. 7)

Subj. + verb + obj. 1 (l. 17)

This summary does not claim to be exhaustive. At the best it is only approximately accurate. The numbers will vary accordingly as we restore a very defective text. In this inscription the subj. or obj. or both combined precede the verb 7 times, while the verb precedes the subj. or obj. 9 times.

I propose to deal here with four fifth-century documents given by Cowley, i. e. 27, 30, 37 and the words of Aḥiḳar.

II^α. *Cowley 27.* *c.* 410 B.C. This papyrus consisting of twenty-four lines is the draft of a letter to the satrap Bigvai or Arsames, and emanates from the Jewish colony at Elephantine. It complains of the damage done to them and their temple by the Egyptians.

In this papyrus the subj. precedes the verb 12 times.

„ obj. „ verb 3 „

„ verb „ subj. 3 „

Here the verb precedes the subj. or obj. or both once in six times. The combination (1) subj. + obj. + verb occurs twice.

Cowley 30. 408 B. C. Petition to the Governor of Judaea from the Jews in Elephantine.

The subj.	precedes the verb	20 times	}	40
„ obj.	„	„ 20 „		
„ verb	„	obj.		10
„ verb	„	subj.		1

Thus the subj. or obj. or both combined precede the verb four times as often as the converse order. We observe also the following combinations—(1) subj. + obj. + verb 1 : (2) subj. + verb + obj. 3 : (3) obj. + subj. + verb 2. In 30^{18} we have the proleptic use of suffix—not found in I.

Cowley 37. c. 410 B. C. A letter.

The subj.	precedes the verb		7 times.
„ obj.	„	„	2 „
„ verb	„	subj. or obj.	12(?),,

Thus the verb is oftener first than the subj. or obj. or both combined. We note the following combinations— (1) subj. + obj. + verb 1 : (2) subj. + verb + obj. 2 : (3) obj. + subj. + verb 1.

Cowley : Words of Aḥikar. c. 430 B. C.

I have only taken account of the narrative portion of Aḥikar lines 1–78), and not of the proverbs that follow.

Subj.—verb	27	} 33
Obj.—verb	6	
Verb—subj.	7	} 33
Verb—obj. (mainly suffixes)	26	

Thus the verb is just as often first as the subj. or obj. or both combined.

The following combinations occur—

(1) Subj. + obj. + verb 1
(2) Subj. + verb + obj. 4
(3) Obj. + subj. + verb 3
(6) Verb + obj. + subj. 1

Finally the acc. precedes the inf. which governs it in 63, 192, but follows it in 120, 122, 123, 193, and ל precedes the acc. in l. 1 חכם לברה 'taught his son'.

II⁷. *Cilicia (S.E.).* Fifth–fourth century. See Lidz., *N.E.*
446 : Cooke 68. This inscription consists of six lines.

In l. 5. we have the order obj.+verb+subj., and in l. 6
verb+subj.

Cilicia in neighbourhood of Kesejek Keojew fifteen miles NE.
of Tarsus. See Torrey, *JAOS,* vol. 35, 1915, pp. 370–74.

This inscription consists of five lines. In l. 1, obj.+verb+
subj. : in ll. 3–4 subj. (a relative)+obj.+verb : in l. 5 verb+obj.
(*cum* ל)+subj. In l. 5 we have *vav* before the verb יבעה, which
Torrey declares is simply redundant, comparing Kalam l. 12.
Is it the *vav* apodosis ?

Cilicia—i. e. *Limyra.* See CIS II. 109: Lidz., *N.E.* 446.
Limyra in Cilicia. Fifth–fourth century B.C.

Obj.+subj.+verb.

This is a bilingual inscription—in Aramaic and Greek. The
Aramaic order diverges from the Greek. In the latter we have
['A]ρτίμας ... προκατεσκευάσατο τὸν τάφον [τοῦτον], whereas the Aramaic·
reads : עבד ... רתים[א] זנה אסתורנא.

III*ᵃ*, i.e. *Ezra* 4⁸⁻⁶¹⁸, 7¹²⁻²⁸. In present form—close of
fourth century B.C., but probably earlier idioms are displaced
by idioms of a later date.

Subj.+verb 49 ⎫
Obj.+verb 26 ⎬ 75.
Verb+subj. or obj. 64.

Thus verb precedes subj. or obj. or both combined slightly less
frequently than the subj. or obj. or both combined precede the
verb.

The following combinations occur :

(2) Subj.+verb+obj. 6
(3) Obj.+subj.+verb 1
(5) Verb+subj.+obj. (twice with ל) 3
(6) Verb+obj.+subj. 2

In other words four out of the six combinations of subj., verb,
and obj. in D. are found in E., only, nos. (1) and (4) not occurring.

Proleptic use of suff. once, i. e. in 5¹¹. When the Inf.
governs an acc. it precedes it seven times : i.e. 4²¹, ²², 5²,¹⁷, 6⁸,¹²,
7¹⁵ ; and also follows it seven times : i.e. 4¹⁴, 5³(*bis*), ⁹(*bis*), ¹³, 7²⁴.

IV. i.e. *Daniel* 2⁴⁶-7.[1]

Subj. + verb   *c.* 208 ⎫
Obj. + verb   *c.* 120 ⎬ *c.* 328.
Verb + subj. or obj.   *c.* 237.   ⎭

Thus the verb precedes subj. or obj. or both combined about once in three times. The following combinations of subj., verb, and obj. occur two times out of five:

(1) Subj. + obj. + verb   15
(2) Subj. + verb + obj.   29
(3) Obj. + subj. + verb   2
(4) Obj. + verb + subj.   10
(5) Verb + subj. + subj.   5
(6) Verb + obj. + subj.   6

Proleptic use of suff. occurs ten times ($2^{20,44}$, $3^{8,25,26,28,29}$, 4^{23}, $6^{25,27}$), but only once in E.

As in E., the acc. follows the Inf. *c.* לְ sixteen times, i.e. $2^{12,14,24,26,47}$, $3^{2,13,19,20}$, $4^{3,23}$, $5^{2,7}$, $6^{8(bis)}$, 7^{25} ; and precedes it twenty-one times : $2^{9,10,16,18,27,46}$, $3^{16,32}$, $4^{15,34}$, $5^{8(bis),15(bis),16(quater)}$, $6^{5(bis),24}$.

Conclusion. In all the above authorities the order of the old Aramaic is essentially the same as in Hebrew, save in the Aramaic letter which Lidzbarski assigns to the time of Assurbanipal (*circa* 660 B.C.). But the change of order which may be due to the influence of Akkadian is slight as compared to that in D. This letter is valuable,[2] but the writer seems to have been subject to different influences. Thus in l. 15 we have שבי שבה three times, which may be explained as Aramaic (Cooke 62⁸). It is at the same time good Hebrew as to diction, though the order would possibly have been different : i.e. וישב שבי. On the other hand there is the Jussive למחנו 'let them grind', which is essentially Aramaic. The pronoun המו frequently occurs, which is also old Aramaic.

---

[1] Baumgarten ('Das Aramäische im Buche Daniel,' p. 128 in *ZAW*, 19) adopts a different method of calculation, and arrives at the following results in D :—

Subj. occurs before predicate as compared with its occurrences after it *c.* 120 : 80.

Obj. occurs before predicate as compared with its occurrences after it *c.* 80 : 70.

Obj. occurs before Inf. as compared with its occurrences after it *c.* 20 : 16.

[2] In l. 12 we have the words which are so important for the right translation of 3¹⁴ in our text : הצדא הני מליא אלה 'Are these things true ?'

So far then as our present authorities go, we may conclude
that the change in the order of Aramaic which is so marked
in the fifth cent. and later, began in the seventh or at all events
in the sixth cent. If we might argue back we might infer that the
oldest Hebrew and Aramaic agreed on the whole as to the order
of words. Later developments, as we shall see, support this
inference.

II. When we proceed to the next period we find that the
change in the order of the words already observed in the
Aramaic letter from Assyria grows much more pronounced in
the centuries that follow, and that in this respect a gulf lies
between the period I and its successors from 500 B. C. onwards.

§ 22. *Seeing that the Hebrew sections are translated from an
Aramaic original, naturally Aramaisms are discover-
able in the Hebrew, especially as the translators were not
Hebraists of the first order.*

Aramaisms in 1–2⁴ᵃ. רב 1³ : מַדַּע 1⁴ : אשר למה = ' lest ' 1¹⁰ :
גיל 1¹⁰=Heb. דור : חיב not elsewhere in OT. Good fifth-century
B. C. Aramaic : מִנָּה—late Heb. but good Aram.

Aramaisms in 8–12. אבול 8²,³,⁶ (LXX, Pesh., Vulg.) = 'gate',
where MT has Heb. אובל ' river ', save that Vulg. has a different
rendering in 8³.

צפיר 8⁵, ²¹ : היך 10¹⁷ Aram. whereas the Heb. is אֵיךְ : כְּתַב—an
Aramaism in late Hebrew 10²¹ : רְשַׁם ' to inscribe '—pure Aramaic
—not elsewhere in O.T.: cf. 5²⁴, ²⁵, 6¹⁰, ¹¹ sqq.— עמו עם מלך 11¹¹—
cf. 5¹² for this frequent Aramaic duplication of the preposition :
טְקֻף 11¹⁷—an Aram. word in late Hebr. : התחברות 11²³—an
Aramaised Inf. : כמנים 11⁴³.

There are several renderings in the LXX which imply an
Aramaic original. It is enough here to refer to the notes on
11²⁰, ²⁴.

§ 23. *Chronological Tables.*

I. *Neo-Babylonian Kings and Notable Events.*

IV. *Events in Jewish history from the time of Jehoiakim to the death of Antiochus Epiphanes.*

Jehoiakim rebels against Nebuchadnezzar. Judea laid waste by
the inroads of hostile nations including the Chaldaeans
(2 Kings 24$^{1-4}$). [According to 2 Chron. 36$^{6-7}$ Nebuchadnezzar himself invades Judea, and carries off Jehoiakim and
some of the vessels of the Temple to Babylon—a tradition
thus existed as early as 300 B.C. which in part forms the   B.C.
basis of Dan. 1$^{1-2}$] 602
Jehoiakim carried captive to Babylon with all the sacred vessels
of the Temple 597
Captivity of Zedekiah and destruction of Jerusalem . . 586
First return of exiles under Cyrus 538
Second return with Ezra 458
Conquest of Palestine by Alexander the Great . . . 332
Struggle between Ptolemy I and Antigonus over the possession
of Palestine, which results in Palestine becoming a province
of Egypt for nearly 100 years 301
The marriage of Antiochus II with Berenice, the daughter of
Ptolemy II (Dan. 11^6) 248
Fresh wars between Ptolemy III and Seleucus II (Dan. 11$^{7\ sqq.}$) 246
Antiochus III makes himself master of Palestine but is forced
to retire from it through his defeat at Raphia by Ptolemy IV 217
Conquest of Palestine by Antiochus III 202
Despite the attempts of Egypt (200 B.C.) this conquest main-
tained (Dan. 11$^{13\ sqq.}$) by the battle of Paneion . . 198
Cleopatra, daughter of Antiochus III, married to Ptolemy V
(Dan. 11^{17}) 193

§ 24. *Theology.*

(*a*) Although this book is the forerunner and herald of most subsequent apocalyptic developments, it is not by any means the earliest, but it is by far the greatest of the O.T. apocalypses. Its outlook, however, is in the main confined to this world. Its hopes are directed, not to the afterworld, with its retributions for the individual, but to the setting up of a world-empire of Israel which is to displace the heathen, to a Messianic kingdom on earth. Accordingly, it extends neither promise nor threatening to *the individual as such,* but only to those individuals who have *in an extraordinary degree* helped or hindered the advent of the kingdom. But the resurrection is mechanically conceived. It is not represented as the unique prerogative of all the righteous —the martyrs, the saints, and teachers (12²) as it was originally conceived, but it has been degraded into a mere mechanical device for bringing the pre-eminently righteous into the eternal Kingdom of God, and for bringing due retribution on the Jewish apostates in the form of a resurrection to everlasting contempt, i. e. in Gehenna. As for the majority of the nation, who are neither over-much righteous nor over-much wicked, their lot is of no concern to the writer, and Sheol remains their eternal abode. Sheol, which is called the land of dust (12²), retains its O. T. heathen character as a non-moral region. It thus possesses a peculiar character in our author. It is the *intermediate* abode of the very good and of the very bad in Israel, and the *eternal* abode of the rest of Israel and of all the Gentiles. The eschatological outlook of the individual is very imperfectly conceived, or at all events very imperfectly delineated. For we might ask, are the risen righteous to live for ever in the Messianic kingdom? The supernatural character of the kingdom certainly implies this (cf. 7¹⁷,¹⁸), and yet the description in 7¹⁷,¹⁸, where the continued existence of 'the peoples, nations, and languages' as subject to this kingdom is difficult to reconcile with the immortality of the righteous individual upon the earth, is quite reconcilable with the eternity of the Messianic kingdom.

(*b*) *The advent of the kingdom catastrophic.* We have, however, overlooked the manner in which the kingdom is to be introduced. It is to be catastrophic. When evil reaches its culmi-

nation, and the need of the saints is greatest ($7^{21,22}$, 12^1), when
the Antichrist in the person of Antiochus Epiphanes is warring
down the saints, God Himself will intervene, and the throne of
judgement be set up (7^9), and the world powers overthrown
($7^{11,12}$), and the kingdom of the saints shall be set up, which
shall break in pieces all the kingdoms of the world (2^{44}), and
make all the surviving nations their subjects. It is to share in
this kingdom that all the pre-eminently righteous, among whom
of course Daniel and his friends are included, are to rise in the
resurrection (יקיצו 12^2). But according to 12^{13} quite a different
conception is introduced. There (unless we take עמד as
meaning 'to rise in the resurrection', which it never does in
Hebrew or, as Hitzig has already pointed out, in any Semitic
dialect[1]), Daniel hopes *to survive the advent of the kingdom*, and
to have his special inheritance in it (ותעמד לגרלך 12^{13}), just as
Ezekiel does in Ezek. 29^{21}, and St. Paul in 1 Thess. 4^{15}. But,
since it is impossible to entertain the supposition that our author
expected to live for over 400 years, then we must conclude
either that he has forgotten his rôle as presumably writing in
the sixth century B. c., or that 12^{13} is an interpolation from the
same hand that inserted 12^{12}. This interpolator writes from the
standpoint of the second century B. c. and not from that of
the sixth century. The book thus closes in 12^{10} with a special
promise that Daniel's prayer in 12^8, that he might be enabled
to understand, shall be granted—'none of the wicked shall
understand, but they that be wise shall understand' (12^{10}).
12^{13} is in part modelled on 12^9 'Go thy way, Daniel', and 12^4
'to the time of the end'. But the interpolator of 12^{12-13} did not
understand the technical meaning of the author's phrase 'the
time of the end' (עת קץ) in 12^4 and also in 12^9, 8^{17}, $11^{35, 40}$, which
has always in his use a reference to the advent of the kingdom.
Instead of this phrase, which he should have employed in 12^{13},
he adopted from our author another phrase, which he supposes
had the same meaning, i. e. 'the end of the days'. But this
phrase, whether written as קץ הימים as in the interpolation in 12^{13},

---

[1] It will not do to rejoin with Bevan that 'if this belief were new in the days
of the author, a fixed technical term may have been wanting'. The belief was
not new within a limited circle of Judaism, and the right technical term (i.e. הקיץ)
was not wanting; for it appears in our author (12^2) as well as in Is. 26^{19}: cf.
also Jer. $51^{39, 57}$; Job 14^{12} for its use of awaking after death.

or as קץ הימים in 1¹⁵, ⁵, ¹⁸, 4³⁴ ⁽³¹⁾ never has this technical meaning
in our author.   In our author it always marks the conclusion of
a definite period in the lives of the persons, whose history he is
recounting, but it never refers to the advent of the kingdom.
He could rightly have used another phrase of our author here
'the latter days' אחרית יומיא 2²⁸ in Aramaic and אחרית היומים
10¹⁴ in Hebrew.   But he chose just the wrong phrase for his
purpose. Furthermore the Hebrew verb עמד retains its usual and
apparently universal meaning, if we interpret the passage aright.

   (c) *Growing transcendentalism in the conception of God.*   God
rules the world by a body of intermediate agencies.   To these
angelic patrons of the nations an almost inconceivable liberty of
initiative is accorded.   The action of most of them is represented as contrary to the fulfilment of the Divine Will.   By
means of this conception the writer explains the national
reverses, and likewise the delay in the establishment of the
Messianic kingdom.

   (d) *Dualism and determinism in Daniel's conception of the world.*
The conflict between the kingdoms of this world and of Israel
springs essentially from their irreconcilable religious and ethical
aims.   But this moral conflict did not originate on this earth
but in the supernatural background.   Thus Persia has its
angelic guardian (10¹³), and likewise Greece (10²⁰), while the
patron angel of Israel is Michael (10²¹, 12¹).   Our author uses
the dualistic conception of the world to explain Israel's reverses,
and likewise the delay in the advent of the Kingdom of God,
as we have already pointed out.   It is difficult to reconcile this
conception with that of the triumphant kingdom of the Saints
and the final judgement executed by God in 7²⁶, ²⁷.   Since the
efforts of the angelic guardians of the nations are expressly
directed against God's chosen people, the dualism of our author's
world view cannot be questioned.   It is true, however, that he
avoids entering into details, and that he teaches that the world
of evil is doomed from the outset.

   That inconsistencies in the thought of the writer should exist
is inevitable.   The O.T. prophets dealt with the destinies of
this nation or of that, but took no comprehensive view of the
history of the world as a whole.   No more did any of the Greek
or Roman historians.   Hence Daniel was the first to teach the
unity of all human history, and that every fresh phase of this

history was a further stage in the development of God's purposes. One world empire succeeds another, each transcending its predecessors in wickedness, till at last wickedness reaches its final development and is impersonated in the God-opposing Antiochus, who blasphemously called himself 'God manifest', and made it his express aim to destroy the true religion, that is, the religion of Judaism. Never before had any of the world powers made this their aim. But Antiochus assumes the role of what was subsequently known as the Antichrist. Now in this inevitable strife the faithful bear their part, but at the best they can render but 'a little help' (11^{34}), seeing that the real victory of the righteous is secured in advance by their patron angel. Our author has no consistent theology.

The element of determinism manifests itself frequently. The most obvious instance is to be found in $4^{14(17)}$, where it is declared that Nebuchadnezzar's destiny is settled by the decree of the Watchers. In the attempt to determine at what exact date the end should come the element of determinism again comes to the front. It is not a question of the growth of character in man fitting him for the advent of the kingdom, but the problem is mechanically conceived, and the kingdom is to be realized on the lapse of a certain definite period of time, which comes at last to be declared to be three and a half years. There are other mechanical elements in the theology of Daniel, but it could not well be otherwise, since the prophetic era had passed and apocalyptic had begun its attempt to grapple with the world problems which confronted it—a struggle for which it was not sufficiently equipped.

(e) Attention might be called to the following points : The frequent condemnation of idolatry in chapters 3 and 5, the rules as to clean and unclean food (1^{8-16}), the giving of alms and good works ($4^{24(27)}$), the Bath-Ḳol, or voice from heaven ($4^{28(31)}$), the three hours of prayer ($6^{11(10)}$).

Finally it is noteworthy that neither Daniel nor his three friends show any consciousness of sin. Only in the interpolated prayer (9^{4-19}) and the clumsy verse 9^{20}, which was added to connect 9^{4-19} with its new context, is there any confession of sin on Daniel's part. Daniel is convinced of his possessing a conscience void of offence before God and man $6^{23(24)}$.

§ 25. *A Fragment of the pre-Theodotion Version*—Dan. 7⁹⁻²⁸.

In the course of my study of the versions I passed from one conclusion to another. At last I arrived at the conviction that in Justin Martyr (*Dial.* 31) we have a genuine fragment of the lost pre-Theodotion version, i. e. Dan. 7⁹⁻²⁸. In the earlier stages of my studies I had no consciousness of the direction in which I was moving, since the studies were often unconnected, and the problems dealt with in a piecemeal fashion. All I sought was to give to each isolated fact its full value. At last the above conclusion flashed suddenly upon me. Some of the grounds for this conclusion I will now give.

1. First of all I accept by virtue of my own studies as valid the inference already drawn by Salmon, Gwynn, Swete, Burkitt, and Thackeray that there were two pre-Christian Greek versions of Daniel. For this conclusion sufficient evidence is given in the Introd., § 13 c.

2. The above conclusion is confirmed by the fact that the same type of text, independent alike of the LXX and Th., is found in the Old Latin (see Burkitt, *Old Latin*, p. 22 seq.). Happily in Tertullian (*Adv. Marc.* iii. 7) we have a quotation from Dan. 7¹³⁻¹⁴ which I shall quote here over against the Greek in Justin.

Justin (*Dial.* 31).

7¹³. Καὶ ἰδοὺ μετὰ τῶν νεφελῶν τοῦ οὐρανοῦ, ὡς υἱὸς ἀνθρώπου ἐρχόμενος· καὶ ἦλθεν ἕως τοῦ παλαιοῦ τῶν ἡμερῶν, καὶ παρῆν ἐνώπιον αὐτοῦ καὶ οἱ παρεστηκότες προσήγαγον αὐτόν. 7¹⁴. καὶ ἐδόθη αὐτῷ ἐξουσία καὶ τιμὴ βασιλική, καὶ πάντα τὰ ἔθνη τῆς γῆς κατὰ γένη καὶ πᾶσα δόξα λατρεύουσα· καὶ ἡ ἐξουσία αὐτοῦ ἐξουσία αἰώνιος ἥτις οὐ μὴ ἀρθῇ, καὶ ἡ βασιλεία αὐτοῦ οὐ μὴ φθαρῇ.

Tert. *Adv.Marc.*iii.7(Oehlerii.130).

Et ecce cum nubibus caeli, tanquam filius hominis [1]veniens, venit[1] usque ad veterem dierum, et aderat in conspectu ejus et qui adsistebant adduxerunt illum. et data est ei potestas regia, et omnes nationes terrae secundum genera et omnis gloria famulabunda et potestas ejus usque in aevum quae non auferetur, et regnum ejus quod non vitiabitur.

Here observe that Justin and Tertullian agree against LXX and Th. in l. 3, save that Justin inserts καί before ἦλθεν : in l. 4

---

[1] So Cypr. *Test.* ii. 10.

καὶ παρῆν . . . αὐτοῦ : in l. 5 προσήγαγον αὐτόν. Next observe that
Justin and Tert. agree with LXX in l. 5 οἱ παρεστηκότες against
Th. : in l. 7 seq. πάντα τὰ ἔθνη τῆς γῆς κατὰ γένη καὶ πᾶσα δόξα . . .
λατρεύουσα : in l. 10 ἥτις οὐ μὴ ἀρθῇ : in l. 11 φθαρῇ. Thirdly
observe that Justin and Tert. agree in only two readings with
Th. against LXX, i. e. l. 1 μετά : in l. 3 ἕως τοῦ παλαίου τῶν. In
both these readings it reproduces the MT.
Again where Justin and Tertullian agree with the LXX, Th.
agrees with the MT. Thus Th. 7¹⁴ καὶ αὐτῷ ἐδόθη ἡ ἀρχὴ καὶ ἡ τιμὴ
καὶ ἡ βασιλεία, καὶ πάντες οἱ λαοί, φυλαί, καὶ γλῶσσαι δουλεύουσιν αὐτῷ is
an exact translation of the MT.

From this comparison it follows that Justin and Tertullian
are here making use of a pre-Christian version of Daniel, which
is closely allied to the LXX, but only in a very minute degree
to Th. The most reasonable explanation of these facts is that
the LXX is the older version. The second version, i. e. the
pre-Theodotion, was made at a much later date—say provi-
sionally 50 B. C.

3. We conclude, therefore, that there were two Greek versions
which were used by the Christian Church down to A. D. 150 and
later—the LXX (145 B. C.), and the pre-Theodotion (c. 50 B. C.) :
that Justin quoted from the second of these, and that Theodotion
used this second in making his version, i. e. Th., Justin and
Theodotion being contemporaries. The former was martyred
in A. D. 163.[1] The version of the latter is attributed to different
dates between A. D. 140 and 184.

4. The conclusion that (in *Dial.* 31) Justin quotes twenty verses,
not from the LXX but from a *later* version is confirmed by the
fact that in reproducing Dan. 7¹⁵ he uses as in Th. the non-
Semitic phrase αἱ ὁράσεις τῆς κεφαλῆς (see p. 42 : notes on 2¹⁹, ²⁸ᶜ
Transl.) : also that in 7¹³ he quotes the phrase †μετὰ† τῶν νεφελῶν,
as does the pre-Theod. and Th., where עם is a corruption of על, and
not as ἐπὶ τ. νεφελῶν as the LXX. It is to be observed that elsewhere
Justin always quotes this phrase in the form ἐπάνω τ. νεφελῶν (*Dial.*
14, 120; *Apol.* i, 1, 51). Justin may have found ἐπάνω instead
of ἐπί in his copy of the LXX, since the translator of the
LXX uses ἐπάνω as a synonym of ἐπί = 'upon' (i. e. על) in 7⁶.

---

[1] Justin's *Dial.* is assigned by Hort. to A.D. 142-8, and by Volkmar to A.D. 155.

Again the LXX in 7¹³ καὶ ὡς παλαιὸς ἡμερῶν παρῆν· καὶ οἱ παρεστηκότες †παρησαν αὐτὸν† (rd. παρέστησαν αὐτόν) represents an older text
וּבְעַתִּיק יוֹמִין תַּמָּה וְקָאמַיָּא קְדָמוֹהִי הַקְרְבוּהִי 'and one like an ancient of
days was there, and they that stood before him presented him '.
The translator of the LXX never uses ὡς as a preposition but
always ἕως. Possibly תמה was first corrupted into מטה. This
would naturally lead to the change of בעתיק יומין into עד עתיק יותיא
in the revised text.

5. From the above facts coupled with those that follow,
I conclude that the pre-Theodotion version was based on the
Semitic text of Daniel (c. 50 B.C.) but that it borrowed its
renderings largely from the LXX where the Semitic text allowed
of its doing so.

6. In the *Fragment of the pre-Theodotion Version*, which now
follows, most of the words and phrases, wherein this version
differs from the LXX, agree with the MT. The obvious conclusion is that the Semitic text of Daniel had undergone considerable revision and corruption between 145 B.C. and 50 B.C.
or thereabouts.

7. General conclusion. Justin never uses Th. but a pre-
Theodotion text. When he quotes short phrases or clauses he
apparently uses the LXX. Thus in *Dial.* 70, 76, 114 he quotes
ἐτμήθη (Dan. 2³⁴) from the LXX, where Th. has ἀπεσχίσθη. Again
in *Dial.* 110 he derives ἔξαλλα from the LXX where Th. has
ὑπέρογκα. But when he quotes an unbroken passage of twenty
verses as in *Dial.* 31, he diverges from the LXX though he has
always elsewhere followed it. The natural conclusion is that,
though he did not possess Th., he had before him the pre-
Theodotion version and in all probability the LXX. The latter
probability is practically a certainty.

In the text of Justin that follows, containing a fragment of
the pre-Theodotion version, words and phrases common to it
with the LXX are printed in thick type : those common to it with
Th. are underlined. Synonyms or even loose though equivalent
renderings are not underlined, save in a few passages where
the words are doubly underlined. Where Justin's text contains
additions these are enclosed in round brackets.

JUSTIN.

Dial. c. Tryphone 31 (Otto ed.).

Dan. 7[9]. Ἐθεώρουν ἕως ὅτου[1] θρόνοι ἐτέθησαν, καὶ ὁ παλαιὸς ἡμερῶν
ἐκάθητο, [2]ἔχων περιβολὴν ὡσεὶ χιόνα λευκήν, καὶ τὸ τρίχωμα τῆς
κεφαλῆς αὐτοῦ ὡσεὶ ἔριον καθαρόν,[2] ὁ θρόνος αὐτοῦ[3] ὡσεὶ φλὸξ πυρός,
[4]οἱ τροχοὶ αὐτοῦ πῦρ φλέγον.[4]

7[10]. [5]Ποταμὸς πυρὸς εἷλκεν ἐκπορευόμενος ἐκ προσώπου αὐτοῦ·[5] χίλιαι
χιλιάδες [6]ἐλειτούργουν αὐτῷ[6] καὶ μύριαι μυριάδες παρειστήκεισαν αὐτῷ.
[7]Βίβλοι ἀνεῴχθησαν, καὶ κριτήριον ἐκάθισεν.[7]

7[11]. Ἐθεώρουν τότε [8]τὴν φωνὴν[8] τῶν [9]μεγάλων λόγων[9] ὧν τὸ κέρας[10]
λαλεῖ,[11] [12]καὶ ἀπετυμπανίσθη[12] τὸ θηρίον, καὶ ἀπώλετο τὸ σῶμα αὐτοῦ καὶ[13]
ἐδόθη εἰς καῦσιν πυρός.

7[12]. Καὶ[14] τὰ λοιπὰ θηρία μετεστάθη τῆς ἀρχῆς αὐτῶν[14] καὶ χρόνος[15] ζωῆς
τοῖς θηρίοις ἐδόθη[16] ἕως[17]καιροῦ καὶ χρόνου.[17]

7[13]. ἐθεώρουν ἐν ὁράματι τῆς νυκτός, καὶ ἰδοὺ μετὰ[18] τῶν νεφελῶν τοῦ
οὐρανοῦ ὡς υἱὸς ἀνθρώπου ἐρχόμενος·[19] καὶ ἦλθεν[20] [21]ἕως τοῦ παλαιοῦ τῶν
ἡμερῶν, (καὶ) παρῆν[21] (ἐνώπιον αὐτοῦ) καὶ[22] οἱ παρεστηκότες[22] προσήγαγον
αὐτόν.[23]

[1] LXX οτε.
[2] So also LXX save that it rightly reads λευκον after εριον and not after χιονα
as pre-Theod. and Th. wrongly do. Th. Και το ενδυμα αυτου ωσει χιων λευκον
και η θριξ τῆς κεφαλης ωσει εριον καθαρον.
[3] >LXX.   [4] LXX ※τροχοι αυτου πυρ καιομενον ✕.
[5] LXX ελκων και εξεπορευετο κατα προσωπον αυτου ποταμος πυρος. Th. ειλκεν
εμπροσθεν αυτου.
[6] So Th. but LXX εθεραπευον αυτον.
[7] Justin inverts order of these two clauses in LXX and Th.
[8] Th. απο φωνης.   [9] LXX and Th. λογ. τ. μεγαλων.
[10] + εκεινο Th.   [11] ελαλει ※θεωρων ημην LXX ✕.
[12] So LXX but Th. εως ανηρεθη.   [13] Th. trs. bef. το σωμα.
[14] Justin agrees here with Th. or Pre-Theod. save that he adds αυτων with LXX.
Th. των λοιπων θηριων η αρχη μετασταθη. LXX τους κυκλωι αυτου απεστησε της
εξουσιας αυτων.   [15] Th. μακροτης.
[16] + αυτοις LXX, Th. but Justin gives τ. θηριος bef. εδοθη.
[17] LXX trs. the two nouns. Th. καιρου κ. καιρου.
[18] LXX επι. But Justin at beginning of *Dial.* 31 has επανω νεφελων.
[19] LXX ηρχετο.   [20] Th. εφθασε wh. it reads after ημερων. >LXX.
[21] LXX ὡς παλαιος ημερων παρην.   [22] >Th.
[23] LXX παρησαν αυτωι. Th. προσηχθη αυτωι.

7¹⁴. Καὶ ἐδόθη αὐτῷ ¹ ἐξουσία καὶ τιμὴ βασιλική, καὶ πάντα τὰ ἔθνη τῆς γῆς κατὰ γένη καὶ πᾶσα δόξα λατρεύουσα· καὶ ¹ ἡ ἐξουσία αὐτοῦ ἐξουσία αἰώνιος, ἥτις οὐ ² μὴ ἀρθῇ,² καὶ ἡ βασιλεία αὐτοῦ ³ οὐ ⁴ μὴ φθαρῇ.⁴

7¹⁵. ⁵(Καὶ) ἔφριξε τὸ πνεῦμά μου ἐν τῇ ἕξει μου, κ‹ιὶ› αἱ ὁράσεις τῆς κεφαλῆς μου ἐτάρασσόν με.⁵

7¹⁶. Καὶ ⁶ προσῆλθον ⁷ πρὸς ἕνα τῶν ἑστώτων,⁸ καὶ τὴν ἀκρίβειαν ἐζήτουν παρ' αὐτοῦ ὑπὲρ ⁹ πάντων τούτων. ¹⁰ Ἀποκριθεὶς δὲ λέγει μοι καὶ τὴν κρίσιν ¹⁰ τῶν λόγων ἐδήλωσέ ¹¹ μοι.

7¹⁷. Ταῦτα τὰ θηρία τὰ ¹² μεγάλα εἰσὶ ¹² τέσσαρες βασιλεῖαι, ¹³ αἳ ἀπολοῦνται ἀπὸ τῆς γῆς· ¹³

7¹⁸. Καὶ (οὐ) παραλήψονται τὴν βασιλείαν ¹⁴ ἕως (αἰῶνος καὶ ἕως) τοῦ αἰῶνος τῶν αἰώνων.

7¹⁹. ¹⁵ Τότε ἤθελον ἐξακριβώσασθαι ὑπὲρ ¹⁵ τοῦ τετάρτου θηρίου, ¹⁶ τοῦ καταφθείροντος πάντα καὶ ὑπερφόβου, καὶ ¹⁶ οἱ ὀδόντες αὐτοῦ σιδηροῖ καὶ οἱ ὄνυχες αὐτοῦ χαλκοῖ, ¹⁷ ἐσθίον καὶ λεπτύνον καὶ τὰ ἐπίλοιπα ¹⁷ αὐτοῦ ¹⁸ τοῖς ποσὶ κατεπάτει.¹⁹

7²⁰. ²⁰ Καὶ περὶ τῶν δέκα κεράτων αὐτοῦ ἐπὶ τῆς κεφαλῆς, καὶ (ἐκ) τοῦ ἑνὸς τοῦ προσφυέντος, καὶ ἐξέπεσον (ἐκ τῶν προτέρων) διὰ αὐτοῦ τρία, καὶ τὸ κέρας ἐκεῖνο εἶχεν ὀφθαλμοὺς καὶ στόμα λαλοῦν μεγάλα, καὶ ἡ πρόσοψις αὐτοῦ ὑπερέφερε τὰ ἄλλα.²⁰

¹ Th. η αρχη και η τιμη και η βασιλεια και παντες οι λαοι, φυλαι, και γλωσσαι δουλευουσιν αυτωι. In the LXX και τιμη βασιλικη is preceded by an asterisk and followed by a metobelus. Also after δοξα LXX inserts αυτωι.
² Th. παρελευσεται.   ³ + ητις LXX.   ⁴ Th. διαφθαρησεται.
⁵ So Th. save that it inserts εγω Δανιηλ after εξει μου. LXX και ακηδιασας εγω Δανιηλ εν τουτοις ἐν τωι οραματι της νυκτος.
⁶ >LXX.   ⁷ Th. ενι.   ⁸ Th. εστηκοτων.
⁹ Th. περι.   ¹⁰ Th. και ειπεν μοι την ακριβειαν και την συγκρισιν.
¹¹ Th. εγνωρισεν.   ¹² Th. τεσσαρα Β : μεγαλα τα τεσσερα Α.
¹³ Th. αναστησονται επι τ. γης αι αρθησονται.
¹⁴ This verse is corrupt in Justin owing first to the loss of αγιοι υψιστου και καθεξουσι την βασιλειαν (for τ. βασιλειαν Th. reads αυτην) LXX, Th. through hmt. and the subsequent insertion of ου before παραληψονται in order to give some meaning to the text.
¹⁶ Th. και εζητουν ακριβως.   ¹⁵ LXX, Th. περι.
¹⁶ LXX του διαφθειροντος παντα κ. υπερφοβον κ. ιδου. Th. οτι ην διαφερον παρα παν θηριον φοβερον περισσως.
¹⁷ LXX κατεσθιοντες παντας κυκλοθεν και.   ¹⁸ >LXX, Th.
¹⁹ LXX και περιπατουντες. Th. συνέπατει.
²⁰ So also LXX, save that after αυτου ιᵒ it adds των and του αλλου after ενος. Here Th. differs greatly : κ. περι τ. κερατων αυτου τ. δεκα τ. εν τη κεφαληι αυτου, κ. τ. ετερου τ. αναβαντος κ. εκτιναξαντος τ. πρωτων, ωι οι οφθαλμοι και στομα λαλουν μεγαλα κ. η ορασις αυτου μειζων τ. λοιπων.

§ 25 INTRODUCTION cxxi

7²¹. ¹ Καὶ κατενόουν τὸ κέρας ἐκεῖνο πόλεμον συνιστάμενον πρὸς τοὺς ἁγίους καὶ τροπούμενον αὐτούς.¹

7²². Ἕως ² οὗ ἦλθεν ὁ παλαιὸς ² ἡμερῶν, καὶ ³ τὴν κρίσιν ἔδωκε τοῖς ἁγίοις τοῦ ὑψίστου,³ καὶ ὁ καιρὸς ἐνέστη,⁴ καὶ ⁵ τὸ βασίλειον ⁵ κατέσχον ⁶ ἅγιοι (ὑψίστου).

7²³. ⁷ Καὶ ἐρρέθη μοι περὶ τοῦ τετάρτου θηρίου· ⁷ Βασιλεία τετάρτη ἔσται ⁸ ἐπὶ τῆς γῆς,⁸ ἥτις ⁹ διοίσει παρὰ ⁹ ¹⁰ πάσας τὰς βασιλείας ¹⁰ (ταύτας), ¹¹ καὶ καταφάγεται πᾶσαν τὴν γῆν ¹¹ καὶ ¹² ἀναστατώσει αὐτὴν καὶ καταλεανεῖ αὐτήν.¹²

7²⁴. Καὶ τὰ δέκα κέρατα,¹³ δέκα βασιλεῖς ἀναστήσονται,¹⁴ καὶ ¹⁵ ἕτερος ἀναστήσεται (μετ᾽ αὐτούς),¹⁵ ¹⁶ καὶ οὗτος διοίσει κακοῖς ὑπὲρ τοὺς πρώτους,¹⁶ καὶ τρεῖς βασιλεῖς ταπεινώσει.

7²⁵. Καὶ ῥήματα ¹⁷ πρὸς ¹⁸ τὸν ὕψιστον λαλήσει, καὶ ἑτέρους ¹⁹ ἁγίους τοῦ ²⁰ ὑψίστου καταστρέψει,²¹ καὶ προσδέξεται ²² ἀλλοιῶσαι καιροὺς καὶ χρόνους,²³ καὶ παραδοθήσεται ²⁴ ²⁵ εἰς χεῖρας ²⁵ αὐτοῦ ἕως καιροῦ καὶ καιρῶν καὶ ἥμισυ ²⁶ καιροῦ.

7²⁶. Καὶ ²⁷ ἡ κρίσις²⁷ ἐκάθισε,²⁸ καὶ τὴν ²⁹ ἀρχὴν μεταστήσουσι τοῦ ἀφανίσαι²⁹ καὶ τοῦ ³⁰ ἀπολέσαι ἕως τέλους.

---

¹ Th. ἐθεωρουν και το κερας εκεινο. εποιει πολεμον μετα των αγιων, κ. ισχυσεν προς αυτους.
² LXX του ελθειν τ. παλαιον.Th. ου ηλθεν ο παλαιος.
³ Th. το κριμα εδωκε αγιοις υψιστου.
⁴ LXX †εδοθη†. Th. εφθασεν. ⁵ Th. την βασιλειαν.
⁶ LXX, Th. add οι.
⁷ Th. και ειπεν το θηριον το τεταρτον. For τεταρτου θηριου LXX reads θηριου του τεταρτου, οτι.
⁸ Th. εν τηι γηι. ⁹ Th. υπερεξει.
¹⁰ LXX πασαν την γην. ¹¹ >LXX.
¹² Th. συνπατησει αυτην και κατακοψει.
¹³ + της βασιλειας LXX. + αυτου Th. ¹⁴ LXX στησονται.
¹⁵ LXX ο αλλος βασιλευς μετα τουτους στησεται. Th. οπισω αυτων αναστησεται.
¹⁶ Th. ος υπεροισει κακοις παντας τους εμπροσθεν. For ουτος LXX reads αυτος.
¹⁷ Th. λογους. ¹⁸ LXX εις. ¹⁹ LXX, Th. τους.
²⁰ >Th. ²¹ LXX κατατριψει. Th. παλαιωσει.
²² Th. υπονοησει του. ²³ LXX, Th. νομον.
²⁴ Th. δοθησεται. ²⁵ LXX παντα εις τας χειρας. Th. εν χειρι.
²⁶ Th. γε ημισυ. LXX εως ημισους. ²⁷ Th. το κριτηριον.
²⁸ LXX καθισεται.
²⁹ LXX. εξουσιαν απολουσι και βουλευσονται μιαναι.
³⁰ >LXX.

7²⁷. Καὶ ¹ἡ βασιλεία καὶ ἡ ἐξουσία¹ καὶ ²ἡ μεγαλειότης (τῶν τόπων)² τῶν ³ὑπὸ τὸν οὐρανὸν βασιλειῶν³ ἐδόθη ⁴ ⁵λαῷ ἁγίῳ ὑψίστου⁵ ⁶βασιλεῦσαι βασιλείαν αἰώνιον.⁶ καὶ πᾶσαι ⁷ἐξουσίαι ὑποταγήσονται αὐτῷ καὶ πειθαρχήσουσιν αὐτῷ.⁷ Ἕως ⁸ὧδε τὸ τέλος⁸ τοῦ λόγου.

7²⁸. Ἐγὼ Δανιὴλ ⁹ἐκστάσει περιειχόμην σφόδρα,⁹ καὶ ἡ ¹⁰ἕξις διήνεγκεν ἐμοί,¹⁰ καὶ τὸ ῥῆμα ἐν τῇ καρδίᾳ μου ἐτήρησα.¹¹

§ 26. Annalistic Tablet of Cyrus.

(Selections from Hagen's German translation—'Keilschrifturkunden zur Geschichte des König's Cyrus' in Delitzsch and Haupt's *Beiträge zur Assyriologie*, 1894, 215-23, rendered into English.)

The 'Annalistic Tablet' describes, year by year, the events of Nabu-na'id's reign. The top of the tablet is mutilated. The Babylonian forces in the second year were in the land of Hamath. In the third year the king mustered his forces and marched to the west. In the sixth year of Nabu-na'id (549 B. C.) 'Kûrash (i. e. Cyrus), king of Anshan' (a district in the south or south-west of Elam), is at war with Ishtuvegu (Astyages); but the troops of Ishtuvegu revolted, and surrendered their king into the hands of Cyprus, who thereupon attacked and made himself master of his capital, Agamtânu (Ecbatana). In the seventh year (548 B.C.) Nabu-na'id was in Temâ, and did not visit Babylon, so that the great annual ceremonies of Bel and Nebo on New Year's Day could not take place. In the meantime '*the king's son*,'¹² his nobles, and his soldiers were in the country of Akkad' (North Babylonia). The ninth year still

¹ LXX την βασιλειαν και την εξουσιαν.
² LXX την μεγαλειοτητα αυτων και την αρχην πασων. Th. η μεγαλωσυνη των βασιλεων.
³ Th. υποκατω παντος του ουρανου.   ⁴ LXX εδωκε.
⁵ Syr. Vers. but reads LXX υψιστωι. Th. αγιοις υψιστου.
⁶ Th. και η βασιλεια αυτου βασιλεια αιωνιος.
⁷ Th. αι αρχαι αυτωι δουλευσουσιν και υπακουσονται. LXX trs. αυτωι 1° after εξουσιαι.
⁸ LXX καταστροφης. Th. ωδε το περας.
⁹ Th. οι διαλογισμοι μου επι πολυ συνεταρασσον με.
¹⁰ So LXX, but it adds μου after εξις. Th. μορφη μου ηλλοιωθη.
¹¹ LXX †εσтηριξα†. Corrupt for ετηρησα. Th. διετηρησα.
¹² The 'king's son' is none other than Belshazzar, who acted as his father's general.

finds Nabu-na'id in Temâ[1] and his son and the troops in Akkad. In this year the king's mother died at Sippar on the banks of the Euphrates. In the month Nisan (March) Cyrus, 'king of Persia', mustered his forces and crossed the Tigris below Arbela ; and in Iyyar (April) made conquest of a country, the name of which has not been preserved.

Passing over the tenth and eleventh years in which similar statements respecting the king and 'the king's son' are repeated, we now come to the reverse side of the tablet, of which the part recounting the events of the twelfth to the sixteenth year is lost. In the seventeenth year (538 B. c.) the conquest of Babylon is recorded :

'(12) In the month Tammuz (June),[2] when Cyrus, in (the city of) Upê (Opis),[3] on the banks of (13) the Zalzallat, had delivered battle against the troops of Akkad, he subdued the inhabitants of Akkad. (14) Wherever they gathered themselves together, he smote them. On the 14th Sippar[4] was taken without fighting. (15) Nabu-na'id fled. On the 16th Gubaru, governor of the country of Guti,[5] and the soldiers of Cyrus, without striking a blow (16) marched into Babylon. Owing to delaying Nabu-na'id was made a captive in Babylon. To the end of the month the shield-(bearers), (17) of the country of Guti guarded the gates of E-sagil.[6] No one's spear approached E-sagil, or the sanctuaries, (18) nor was any standard brought therein. On the third day of Marcheshvan (October), Cyrus entered Babylon. (19) Dissensions (?) disappeared (?) before him. The city was secured against damage : peace to all Babylon (20) did Cyrus proclaim. Gubaru, his governor, appointed governors in Babylon. (21) From Kislev (November) to Adar (February, i.e. in 537 B.C.), the gods of Akkad, whom Nabu-na'id had brought down to Babylon, (22) returned to their own cities. On the 11th of Marcheshvan, during the night, Gubaru made an assault(?), and slew (23) the king's son (?). From the 27th of Adar (February) to the third of Nisan (March) there was lamentation in Akkad : all the people smote their heads.'

The rest of the Annalistic Tablet is mutilated, only occasional words and phrases being decipherable.

---

[1] A suburb of Babylon, or a favourite residence of the king in the country.

[2] Scholars differ in identifying the months. Tammuz (see Comm., p. 112) appears to be an error of the engraver for Tishri. In the *Encycl. Bibl.* iii. 3194, Marti identifies Tammuz with July, Marcheshwan with November, Kislev with December, and Adar with March, as also does Driver in his *Comm.*, p. xxix seq.

[3] On the Tigris 110 miles north of Babylon.

[4] Near the Euphrates, about 70 miles north-west of Babylon.

[5] A land and people in the north of Babylonia.

[6] The temple of Marduk in Babylon.

The Cyrus Cylinder.

(*Op. cit.*, pp. 209–213.)

' (7) The daily offerings he (Nabu-na'id) suspended . . . . he made in the cities . . . . The honour of Marduk the (8) King of the gods . . . . (9) On account of their (the Babylonians') complaints, the lord of the gods (Marduk) was very wroth, and [forsook] their province ; the gods dwelling among them left their abodes (10) in anger, because he had brought them to Babylon. Marduk . . . . (11) . . . . . took compassion. In all lands he made a survey and a quest throughout, (12) and sought a righteous prince, after his heart, to take him by his hand. Cyrus, king of Anshan, he called by name, proclaimed his name for universal sovereignty. (13) Kutu (Gutium), the whole of the Ummân-manda, he subdued under his feet ; the black-headed ones, whom he (Marduk) had given into his hands to conquer, (14) he cared for with judgement and right. Marduk, the great lord, saw with joy the protection (?) extended to his peoples, his (Cyrus') beneficent deeds, and his righteous heart ; (15) to his city Babylon he commanded him to march, and made him take the way to Babylon ; _ like a friend and a comrade going at his side .́ . . . . . (17) Without fighting or battle, he secured his entrance into Babylon. His city Babylon he spared distress. Nabu-na'id, the king, who did not fear him, he delivered into his hand. (18) All the inhabitants of Babylon, the whole of Sumer and Akkad, nobles and governors, bowed themselves before him, and kissed his feet : they rejoiced that he had become king . . . . . (20) I am Cyrus, king of the universe, the great king, the mighty king, king of Babylon, king of Sumer and Akkad, king of the four quarters of the heaven . . . . (22) . . . . . whose rule Bel and Nebo love, whose dominion they desired for the gladness of their heart . . . . (24) My far-flung armies marched peaceably into Babylon ; the whole of [Sumer and] Akkad I delivered from trouble (?) : (25) the needs of Babylon and all its cities I rightly took upon myself . . . . (26) Their sighing I stilled, freed (them) from their troubles. On account of my . . . . . deeds, Marduk, the great lord, rejoiced, and blessed me Cyrus the king who honoured him, and Cambyses, son of my body . . . . (33) And the gods of Sumer and Akkad whom Nabu-na'id, to the displeasure of the lord of the gods, had brought to Babylon, by the command of Marduk, the great lord, (34) I caused to take up their abode safely in their shrines in gladness of heart. (35) May all the deities whom I have restored to their cities pray daily before Bel and Nebo for length of years for me, ... and to Marduk, my lord, speak : &c.'

§ 27. Bibliography.

During the first eighteen centuries of the Christian era the authenticity and integrity of the Book of Daniel were assumed as a matter of course, except in the twelfth of Porphyry's fifteen books *against the Christians* (Κατὰ Χριστιανῶν). Porphyry was a neo-Platonic philosopher, and lived about the years A.D. 233–304. This book was intended to prove that the Book of Daniel was written by a Palestinian Jew in the time of Antiochus Epiphanes. He pointed out that the prophecies of Daniel are a correct record of events till the time of Antiochus Epiphanes, but from that time onwards they were simply guesses. This theory of Porphyry was in the opinion of his contemporaries and of subsequent generations so successfully refuted by the counter-treatises of Jerome, *In Daniel prophetam*, ed. Vallarsi, 1768, Methodius, Eusebius of Caesarea, and Apollinaris, that it was not fully revived till the nineteenth century. In the eighteenth century Sir Isaac Newton in a work on Daniel and Revelation expressly states that to reject Daniel's prophecies 'is to reject the Christian religion' (ed. Whitla, 1922, p. 155). It is true, however, that Collins (*The Scheme of Literal Prophecy considered, 1726*) argued for the Maccabean date of the book, but apparently for the time without result.

The first serious work to do justice to the historical problems of the book was that of Bertholdt (*Daniel neu übersetzt und erklärt, 1806*). His hypothesis, however, of several distinct authors drew upon him the adverse criticism of Gesenius, Bleek, and De Wette, who, however, accepted the Maccabean date.

Since the time of the above-mentioned works practically all the foremost scholars have maintained the unity of the work, and at the same time its Maccabean date. The upholders, of course, of ecclesiastical tradition laboured hard to maintain the asserted early date of the work. The chief writers of this class during the nineteenth century were Hengstenberg, Hävernick, Auberlen, and in our own country Pusey. These and subsequent scholars, not only of this school but of that of their opponents, laboured under a complete misapprehension of the nature of Apocalyptic. This appears in all their works, as the following passage from Pusey typical of the orthodox school amply proves :

'The Book of Daniel... is either divine or an imposture. To write any book under the name of another, and to give it out to be his, is, in any case, a forgery, dishonest in itself, and destructive of all trustworthiness. But the case as to the Book of Daniel, if it were not his, would go far even beyond this. The writer, were he not Daniel, must have lied on a most frightful scale, ascribing to God prophecies which were never uttered ... In a word, the whole book would be one lie in the name of God.' *Lectures on Daniel,* p. 1.

But the ultra-conservative standpoint of Pusey was not maintained by all the so-called defenders of Daniel, and a whole series of writers adopted an intermediate course, and sought to reconcile the statements of the text with the results of historical criticism. The latest representative of this school has been C. H. H. Wright.

The chief Commentaries for the last seventy years including Bonwetsch's Edition of the early Commentary of Hippolytus, i.e. *Hippolyts Comm. zum Buche Daniel,* 1897, and that of Jerome already mentioned, are as follows : F. Hitzig (in the *Kgf. Handb.*), 1850; H. Ewald in *Die Proph. d. Alten Bundes* (1868), iii. 298 ff. (Eng. transl., v. 152 ff.) ; E. B. Pusey, *Lectures on Daniel*[6], 1880; Keil, 1869; O. Zöckler, 1870; Fuller in the *Speaker's Commentary,* 1876 ; Meinhold, 1889; A. A. Bevan, *Book of Daniel,* 1892; Behrmann, 1894; Farrar *(Expositor's Bible),* 1895 ; Thompson, ' Daniel ' in the *Pulpit Commentary,* 1897 : Prince, *Book of Daniel,* Leipzig, 1899 ; Driver *(Cambridge Bible),* 1900; Marti, 'Das Buch Daniel ' in *Kurzer Hand-Commentar,* 1901 ; Jahn, *Das Buch Daniel nach der Septuaginta hergestellt,* 1904 ; C. H. H. Wright, *Daniel and its Critics and Daniel and his Prophecies,* 1906, ᵌ2 vols ; Charles, in the *Century Bible,* 1912 ; Boutflower, *In and Around the Book of Daniel,* 1923 ; Montgomery, *Book of Daniel,* 1927.

Special Studies : Bevan, E., *House of Seleucus,* 2 vols, 1902 ; Bludau, *Die Alexandrinische Uebersetzung des Buches Daniel,* 1897 : Graetz, ' Beiträge zur Sach- und Wörtererklärung d. Buches Daniel', *MGWJ.* vol. 20 (1871), 339-52, 385-406, 433-449; Hölscher, ' Entstehung d. Buches Dan.' *Theol. Stud. Krit.,* 1919, 113 : Mahaffy, *Empire of the Ptolemies,* 1896 ; Preiswerk, *Der Sprachenwechsel im Buche Daniel,* 1902 ; Riessler, *Das Buch Daniel,* 1899 ; Swete, *Introd. to O.T. in Greek,* 1900 ; Torrey, C. C., ' Notes on the Aramaic Part of Daniel ' in the *Transactions of the Conn. Academy of Arts,* 15 (1909) ; *Journal of Amer. Oriental Soc.,* 43 (1923), 229 ; Von Gall, *Die Einheitlichkeit des Buches Daniel,* 1895 ; Wilson, 'Aramaic of Daniel ' in *Bibl. and Theol. Studies* 'Scribner) (1912), 261-305.

Grammars, Inscriptions, Texts, and Versions:

Bauer und Leander, Gramm. d. Biblisch-Aramäischen, 2 vols., 1927.

Baumgartner, 'Das Arämaische im Buche Daniel', ZfAW, Band 4, 1927, pp. 81-133.

Corpus Inscriptionum Semiticarum, 1881 sqq.

Cooke, North-Semitic Inscriptions, 1903.

Cowley, Aramaic Papyri of the Fifth Century B.C., 1923—a book indispensable to serious students of Daniel.

Dalman, Gramm. d. Jüd.-Palaestinischen Aramäisch, 1894 : 2nd. ed. 1905.

Duval, Grammaire Syriaque, 1881.

Driver, Hebrew Tenses[3], 1892.

Field, Origenis hexaplorum quae supersunt, 1875.

Gesenius, Hebrew Grammar : Enlarged by Kautzsch[28], 1909 : Eng. Translation by Cowley[2], 1910.

Ginsburg, Kethubim, 1926, 631-682 (Text of Daniel).

Kamphausen 'Text of Daniel' in Haupt's Sacred Books of the O.T., 1896.

Kautzsch, Gramm. d. Biblisch-Aramäischen, 1884.

Lidzbarski, Handbuch der nordsemitischen Epigraphik, 1898.

Ephemeris für semitische Epigraphik, 3 vols. 1902-15.

Löhr, Daniel in Kittel's Bible : Pars II. 1160-84.

Marti, Gramm. d. Biblisch-Aramäischen Sprache[3], 1925.

Nöldeke, Compendious Syriac Grammar, London, 1904.

Sachau, Aramäische Papyrus und Ostraka, 2 vols., 1911.

Stevenson, Grammar of Palestinian Jewish Aramaic, 1824.

Strack, Gramm. des Biblisch-Aramäischen[6], 1921.

Swete, O. T. in Gk. 3 vols. 1887-1894 : 2nd ed. 1895 sqq.

Thackeray, Gramm. of the O.T. in Greek, vol. i., 1909.

Besides the above works the reader will find valuable material in the O. T. introductions of Driver, Cornill, König, &c. A very full bibliography is to be found in C. C. H. Wright, Daniel and its critics, pp. xviii-xxxvii, and Montgomery, Book of Daniel, pp. xv-xxvi.

§ 28. Abbreviations and Brackets.

(a) Abbreviations.

Aq. : version of Aquila.

Baumgartner : Das Aramäische im Buche Daniel. See above.

Bevan (i.e. A. A.) : Comm. on Bk. of Daniel, 1892.

Bevan, E. : House of Seleucus, 2 vols., 1902.

CIS : Corpus inscriptionum Semiticarum, 1881 seqq.

Clem. Alex. : Clement of Alexandria.

Cooke (G. A.) : North Semitic Inscriptions, 1903.

Cowley (A.) : Aramaic Papyri of the Fifth Century B.C., 1923.

Dalman : Gramm. d. Jud.-Palaestinischen Aramäisch. See above.

Dan. or even D. where the context is clear for Daniel.
DCB: *Dictionary of Christian Biography.*
Driver: *Comm.*, see p. cxvii.
E.: for Ezra where the context is clear.
Ges.-Kautzsch: *Hebrew Grammar.* See Gesenius, p. cxviii.
Ginsburg: Hebrew Bible, i.e. *Kethubim.* See p. cxviii.
JAOS: *Journal of the American Oriental Society.*
JBL: *Journal of Biblical Literature.*
KAT: *Keilinschriften u. das A.T.*³, Zimmern and Winckler, 1905 (earlier editions by Schrader).
KB.: *Keilinschriftliche Bibliothek*, Schrader, 1889–1900.
Kautzsch: *Gramm. d. Biblisch-Aramäischen*, 1884.
Löhr: Critical Notes in Kittel's *Biblia Hebraica*, pp. 1160–1184.
LXX; Septuagint Version.
Lidz. or Lidzbarski: *Handbuch d. nordsem. Epig.* See p. cxviii.
    ,,   *Eph.*   ,,   See p. cxviii.
MT: Massoretic.
MGWJ: *Monatschrift für Gesch. u. Wissenschaft d. Judenth.*
NHWB, Levy, *Neuhebräisches u. Chaldäisches Wörterbuch*, 1876–1889.
Pesh.: Peshiṭto Version.
SBOT: Haupt's *Sacred Books of the O.T.*
Schürer: *Gesch. d. Jüdischen Volkes*, vol. 1³ ᵘⁿᵈ ⁴, 1901, vols. 2–3³, 1898.
Sym.: Version of Symmachus.
Tert.: Tertullian.
Th.: Version of Theodotion.
Vulg.: Vulgate Version.
ZA: *Zeitschrift f. Assyriologie.*
ZATW: *Zeitschrift f. d. ATliche Wissenschaft.*
Zimmern: see under *KAT.*
ZNTW: *Zeitschrift f. d. NTliche Wissenschaft.*
ZWT: *Zeitschrift f. wissenschaftliche Theologie.*

(*b*) *Brackets.*

Words or phrases enclosed thus † † are corrupt.
Words or phrases enclosed in brackets ( ) are supplied by the editor and do not belong to the original.
Words or phrases enclosed in brackets ⌐ ⌐ are restored from the LXX or Th., Pesh., individually or from a combination of them.
Words or phrases enclosed in brackets ⟨ ⟩ are restorations of lost original clauses.
Words printed in thick type are emendations.

COMMENTARY

SECTION I

i. e. Chapter 1[1-19], in the third year of Jehoiakim.

§ 1. *The Object of this chapter.*

To enforce loyalty to the Law: to set forth the principles of a right education, i. e. obedience to the prescripts of the Law. The young so educated will prove to be best alike in body (ver. 15), and in mind (ver. 17), and also best fitted to face the evils of their time. And, even when they are called to face death by torture in obedience to their faith, as in 3, they will be able to do so with a calm and resolute spirit and fearlessly withal. And yet the emphasis is laid expressly on that element in Judaism which is the least valuable and least essential in true religion—the law of clean and unclean meats. But to the Jews in the days of Antiochus the eating of meats from the kings table appeared as sinful as idolatry itself. See note on 1[8-10].

This chapter (1[1-19]) deals with the discipline of the religious life and its fruitfulness—spiritual and other—for those who adopt it in their private relations.

§ 2. *Unhistorical statements in* 1[1, 2]. See note *in loc.*

§ 3. *The Hebrew of* 1-2[4a] *and of* 8-12 *from different translators.*

It will be seen later that the translator of 11 did not translate 8-10, 12.

Characteristic differences between the Hebrew of 1-2[4a] *and* 8-12.

(a) In 1[2, 18, 20], we find *vav* apodosis, whereas in 8-12 (containing 133 verses) this rare classical Hebrew idiom does not occur once. The three verbs are וַיְבִיאֵם 1[2], וַיְבִיאֵם 1[18], וַיִּמְצָאֵם 1[20] In the first and third passages the *vav* apodosis with the imperf. follows after a *casus pendens*, in the second passage after a time determination. This fact in itself points to a different translator. Again in 8-12, i.e. as 10[4, 9], we have the *vav* apodosis with the personal pronoun followed by the perf. Now this *vav* apodosis simply introduces the predicate after a *casus pendens* or time determination. There were two excellent opportunities for the translator of 1-2⁴ᵃ to use this simple *vav* apodosis in 1¹⁵, ¹⁷ as the translator of 8-10, 12 did in 10⁴,⁹, but he did not avail himself of it. Thus the translators diverge alike in the idioms they use and those they do not use.

(b) The translator of 1-2⁴ uses twice the *oratio obliqua* instead of the *oratio directa*—a sign of late Hebrew: i. e. in 1³ · · · ויאמר להביא, and in 2² ··· ויאמר לקרא. Now in 8-12 אמר is never followed by ל with the infinitive. The *oratio obliqua* is not used in 8-12 but the *oratio directa*: cf. 8¹³, ¹⁴, ¹⁷, ¹⁹, 10¹¹, ¹², ¹⁹, ²⁰, 12⁸, ⁹. It is noteworthy that this use of the former is a real Aramaism, occurring as it does in 2¹², ⁴⁶, 3¹³, ¹⁹, ²⁰, 4²³, 5², 6²⁴, though the *oratio directa* is used just as frequently. The fact, however, that this late Hebrew and Aramaic idiom never occurs in 8-12, differentiates 1-2⁴ᵃ very markedly from 8-12.

(c) In 1⁴ ספר ולשון כשדים = 'the literature and language of the Chaldeans'. This is bad Hebrew, being only found twice elsewhere in the O.T. See note *in loc.*

(d) In 1⁵, ¹⁹ עמד לפני = 'to serve'. It never bears this meaning in 8-12, where in 8⁴, ⁷, 11¹⁶ it = 'to withstand'. This of course may be accidental and apart from (a) and (b) would have no weight.

(e) In 1² the translator uses אדני—not found in 8-12.

(f) In 1¹³ the translator uses עשה עם as in 2 Chron. 2², whereas the translator in 11⁷ uses עשה ב (cf. Jer. 18²³) to express mainly the same idea. The two constructions are only found once elsewhere in the O.T.

(g) Strange fondness of this translator for singular forms which have apparently plural suffixes: Cf. משתיהם 1¹⁶ and analogous forms in 1⁵, ⁸, ¹⁰, ¹⁵. None such in 8-12.

§ 4. *Late Hebrew.*

Use of כשדים as denoting a caste 1⁴, 2⁴ and not in its earlier ethnic meaning. See note on 1⁴. עשה עם 1¹³, only here and in 2 Chron. 2².

§ 5. *Dislocations of the text.*

These have, especially in the case of 1²⁰⁻²¹, introduced obscurity and unintelligibility into the text. On pp. 52-54, I have adduced the grounds for the restoration of 1²⁰⁻²¹ to their original context after 2⁴⁹ᵃ. By this restoration sanity is restored to the text. In 1^5 I follow Marti in restoring 1^{5b} before 1^{5a}. This makes the construction normal.

§ 6. *Date of the Hebrew Version.*

Since the dislocation of $1^{20, 21}$, after 2^{49a} was already a *fait accompli*, when the Hebrew translator undertook his task, and since this same disorder of the text persisted when the Greek translator set to work about 145 B. C., we have in this date the *terminus ad quem*. It is most probable, however, that the Hebrew version of $1-2^{4a}$, 8–12, was completed soon after the publication of the original work in Aramaic.

§ 7. *Aramaisms.*

1^3. רַב—an early loan-word in Hebrew = שַׂר which our trans-lator uses in $1^{7, 9, 10, 11, 18}$. See Cowley, p. 309.

$1^{5, 10}$. מְנָה. Late Hebrew but old Aramaic מַנִּי. See Cowley, 27^9, Aḥ. 37.

1^{10}. אֲשֶׁר לָמָּה = 'lest': a wholly un-Hebraic, literal translation of an Aramaic idiom.

חִיַּב. Good fifth-century Aramaic, but not elsewhere in O.T. (MT). גִּיל = Hebrew דּוֹר: a loan-word from the Aramaic (?).

1^{13}. תֵּרָאֶה—an Aramaic vocalization.

§ 8. *Lost words and phrases.*

1^2. ⟨זרע המלוכה והפרתמים ומקצת⟩—lost through hmt. See note *in loc.*

1^3. *The exiles of.* Restored by help of Th. (and LXX) and 2^{25}. See note *in loc.*

1^4. *And literature.* Restored by help of LXX and 1^{17} of our text. See note *in loc.*

§ 9. *Interpolations.*

1^2. MT, Th., Pesh., Vulg., insert 'to the house of his god' against Syr^h and the general sense of the context.

1^7. After 'unto Daniel' MT interpolates וַיָּשֶׂם against the LXX and Th.

§ 10. *Corruptions.*

1^{10}. זֹעֲפִים corrupt for צְעִירִים. See note *in loc.*

1^{11}. With LXX for "אשר מנה שר הסריסים על ד read שר הסריסים אשר מנָּה. אשר מנָּה על ד".

§ 11. *Hebrew rendering of Aramaic phrase.*

i.e. לְבוֹ ⋯ וַיָּשֶׂם 1^8 of שָׂם בָּל לְ as in 6^{15}.

1^1. *In the third year of the reign of Jehoiakim, &c.* This book is divided into ten sections, and each section is carefully dated, eight out of the ten containing the date in the first verse of the section. See Introd. § 4. According to 2 Kings 23[36] Jehoiakim reigned eleven years, i. e. 608–597 B. C. Now our text states that in the third year of his reign Nebuchadnezzar besieged Jerusalem and transported some of the vessels of the house of God to Babylon. The text also implies that Nebuchadnezzar carried away Jehoiakim to Babylon.

The above statements are inaccurate. 2 Kings knows of no siege of Jerusalem by the king of Babylon. It tells only of raiding bands of Chaldeans, Syrians, Moabites, and Ammonites that invaded Judah (24[2]). The statement that Jerusalem was captured and Jehoiakim carried off to Babylon by Nebuchadnezzar appears first in 2 Chron. 36[6]. But 2 Kings 24[6] states that Jehoiakim died in peace in Jerusalem, and the LXX of 2 Chron. 36[8] asserts that he was buried in the garden of Uzza. It is reasonable to conclude that this statement is trustworthy, seeing that it runs directly counter to the prophecy of Jeremiah who foretold for him a shameful end, i. e. that his body would be cast outside the gates of Jerusalem, exposed to the sun by day and the frost by night and, when at last buried, would be ' buried with the burial of an ass ' (Jer. 22[19], 36[30]). It is of course possible that, though the writer of Daniel does record the carrying into captivity of the Jewish princes and nobility (wholly or in part), it does not necessarily follow that Jehoiakim was amongst them. But the natural and unforced interpretation of the text is against this.

Again from Jer. 25[1] we learn that Nebuchadnezzar did not become king till the fourth year of the reign of Jehoiakim. He cannot, therefore, have been king when, according to the text, he took Jehoiakim captive in the third year of the latter. If he did so, he can have only been Crown prince at the time, as in fact he was, when he invaded Egypt in 605 B.C. and defeated the Egyptian forces at Carchemish (604 B.C., in which year Nabopolassar his father died). But the text of Jeremiah knows of no such invasion of Judah in the third year of Jehoiakim, and even in his fifth year this invasion is still in the indefinite future (36[6, 29]). Furthermore in Berosus's account of Nebuchadnezzar's campaign (c. 605 B. C., see Josephus, *Ant.* x. 11. 1) there is no mention of any siege of Jerusalem, though there is of some Jewish captives.

Berosus states that hardly had Nebuchadnezzar completed his victorious campaign against Egypt when he learnt of his father's death. Accordingly having settled the affairs of Egypt and the rest of the country (i. e. Coele-Syria and Phoenicia) he put certain of his friends in command of the heaviest part of his forces and bade them escort to Babylon the Jewish, Phoenician, and Syrian prisoners and those of the nations of Egypt, and having done so hurried back to Babylon with only a few attendants.

The statement that Nebuchadnezzar besieged Jerusalem in the third year of Jehoiakim seems, therefore, to be due to a wrong combination of 2 Kings 24[1, 2], and 2 Chron. 36[6, 7]. The former passage tells how Jehoiakim became subject to Nebuchadnezzar for three years and then rebelled—probably at the instigation of Apries-Hophra, the new king of Egypt—and how his rebellion brought upon him successive attacks of †Chaldeans†[a] Ammonites, Moabites, and Syrians, neighbouring nations that still maintained their allegiance to Babylon. The historian records (2 Kings 24[6]) that Jehoiakim still made good his independence, and that on his death Jehoiachin his son reigned in his stead, and that in his reign Nebuchadnezzar came up in person against Jerusalem and carried away captive to Babylon Jehoiachin and all his people (2 Kings 24[10–15]). On the other hand, 2 Chron. 36[6, 7] testifies to the currency of a tradition of an attack upon Jerusalem in the reign of Jehoiakim.

Nebuchadnezzar. This name is spelt differently in different documents. Here alone in Daniel, if the text is correct, it preserves the silent א, and is written נבוכדנאצר. Elsewhere throughout the book, as in Ezra, Nehemiah, and Esther, this silent א is not used, but otherwise this late and incorrect form with or without the ו appears. The older and more accurate form is Nebuchadrezzar (נבכדראצר = Nabu-kudurri-uṣur, 'Nebo protect the boundary'), as in Ezekiel and generally in Jeremiah. But the later and incorrect form has already secured an entrance into 2 Kings 24–25[11], a few passages in Jeremiah, and of course into Chronicles, Ezra, and Esther. See the Oxford Hebrew Lexicon. The same variation appears in the Greek—the older

---

[a] We should here read 'Edomites'. ארם is here obviously a corruption of אדם as Graetz, Klotz, Benzinger, Burney have already recognized. Hence for 'Chaldeans' read 'Edomites'.

form Ναβουκοδρόσορος in Strabo, and Ναβουχοδονόσορ in the LXX. Is the corruption due to Aramaic influence?

King of Babylon. Since Nabopolassar, the father of Nebuchadnezzar, did not die till the fourth year of Jehoiakim (Jer. 25[1], 46[2]) the title is here proleptic.

1[2]. This verse is corrupt. It has not been transmitted to us as it left the author's (or the translator's) hands. It is clumsy and inconsistent. It is true that it so stood in the second century A.D. as the MT gives it, for Th's. version supports it, but it read differently in the first century B. C., if we can trust Syr[h], i. e. the LXX.

The difficulties of discovering a reasonable sense in the MT are insuperable. First of all the text is wrong in stating that God gave Jehoiakim into the hands of Nebuchadnezzar, but only a part of the vessels of the Temple. If we assume with the writer the conquest of Jerusalem, God gave both Jehoiakim and his people and the entire Temple into the hands of the king of Babylon. But, though everything fell into his hands, Nebuchadnezzar took possession only of a part of the sacred vessels, and carried these and the best of the people—the seed royal and the nobles : see ver. 3 sq.—to Babylon. This is unquestionably the thought of the writer. Is it possible to find the *disjecta membra* of the true text in the transmitted text? The present writer is assured that it is. As for the MT it is in some respects defective : in others pleonastic. Before I state what I believe to be the true solution of this problem and thus recover the original form of the text, I will give the solutions offered by Marti, Behrmann, and myself in my small commentary.

(1) If the words 'to the house of his god' are interpolated, as Marti assumes, the text is defective; for though it states that the king carried a part of the vessels of the Temple into the land of Shinar, as the suffix of the verb informs us, it makes no reference to the captives. And yet if the suffix in ויביאם were restricted to the vessels of the Temple, then we cannot explain why the vessels should be definitely and emphatically mentioned at the beginning of the next clause—את הכלים 'the vessels', where any reasonable writer would simply put אותם 'them'. In this case the text would be pleonastic. Thus the last clause 'and the vessels he brought into the treasure house of his god', presupposes a reference to the captives in what has gone before,

and prescribes a special destination for the vessels in contra-distinction to that of the captives. Moreover, in ver. 3 sq. some of the captives are specially mentioned as 'of the seed royal and of the nobles'. It is true that Marti maintains that the suffix in וַיְבִיאֵם ('and he carried them') includes both the captives and the sacred vessels, but, since no captives have as yet been mentioned, save Jehoiakim, this interpretation is inadmissible.

(2) Behrmann, recognizing the difficulty of the text, omits the final clause of this verse, 'and he brought the vessels into the treasure house of his god,' and relates the suffix to the sacred vessels, the destination of which are 'the house of his god'. He further adds that ver. 3 naturally presupposes that the captives also are carried away. But we may ask where are these captives referred to in ver. 2? If they are there referred to, then their only destination is the temple of Nebuchadnezzar. But what have they to do with this temple? Behrmann fails to justify alike his retention of the phrase 'to the house of his god' and his rejection of the final clause of the verse. The text of ver. 2 according to Behrmann runs thus: 'And the Lord gave J. king of Judah into his hand and part of the vessels of the house of God, and he brought them into the land of Shinar into the house of his god'.

(3) For the third solution of the problem, which I gave in my little commentary, I was indebted to Syr^h, i. e. the LXX. This version omits the four words after Shinar in the Hebrew text. The translation then runs: 'And the Lord gave J. king of Judah into his hand and part of the vessels of the house of God; and he carried them into the land of Shinar, ⟨and⟩ he brought them into the treasure house of his god'. This gives a perfectly clear text, but it concerns itself only with taking Jehoiakim captive and transferring part of the sacred vessels to Babylon. Also it takes no account of the captives, whom the last clauses of ver. 2 and ver. 3 presuppose. Hence it, like the two former solutions must be rejected.

(4) Before I put forward the solution at which I have arrived, I should state clearly what the actual text presupposes. It presupposes, as we have already seen, that ver. 2 mentioned definitely the transportation of a body of captives to Babylon. But this is not all. The text, as it stands at present, wrongly states that God gave Jehoiakim into the hands of Nebuchad-

nezzar, and a part and only a part of the vessels of the Temple. But this is not so. God gave the king and all these vessels into the hands of Nebuchadnezzar, who, however, transported only part of them, and together with them some of the most important classes of the Jewish population to Babylon. This is clearly what the writer meant and what his text should record, if we had it in its original form.

In the next place, if we take 'the house of his god' as standing in apposition to 'the land of Shinar' and as defining more specifically the destination of the things signified by the suffix, then we cannot escape the conclusion that the things in question are the sacred vessels of the Temple; for the statement of old expositors that the Babylonians brought their prisoners to present them before their gods in token of their triumph has no evidence to support it. Hence his phrase 'the house of his god' is to be rejected as the early gloss of a scribe, who inter-preted the suffix as referring to the vessels of the Temple only, an interpretation given also by most Christian scholars of the past and by not a few of the present day.

What remains now is to supply the missing words referring to the captives and to account for their early loss. The original text appears on very strong grounds to have been as follows:

ויתן אדני בידו את יהויקים מלך יהודה ומקצת (זרע המלוכה והפרתמים ומקצת)

כלי בית האלהים ויביאם. ארץ שנער ואת הכלים הביא בית אוצר אלהיו.

Hence we should translate: 'And the Lord gave J. king of Judah into his hand. And part of ⟨the seed royal and of the nobles and part of⟩ the vessels of the house of God he carried into the land of Shinar; but the vessels he brought into the treasure house of his god'.

The words in brackets were early omitted by a scribe through homoioteleuton. They are indispensable to ver. 2 and explain ver. 3. In the next place the words 'and part of ⟨the seed royal and of the nobles and part of⟩ the vessels of the house of God' forms a *casus pendens* and the predicate is intro-duced by the *vav* apodosis followed by the imperf. i.e. וַיְבִיאֵם. This is good classical Hebrew. See Ges., *Heb. Gram.*, §§ 111 h, 143 d. The same idiom reappears in vv. 18, 20 of the present chapter. In the Aramaic of Daniel it occurs (?) once, i. e. in 7^{20}. But this is unlikely. It is true, indeed, that in very late Aramaic, when used to translate Hebrew, this *vav* apodosis of

the Hebrew is without exception reproduced. Thus the
ו in וחלך in Gen. 22[24] is reproduced in the Targums of Onk. and
Ps.-Jon. and the Syriac, but omitted by the LXX and Vulg.
The same is true of Num. 14[16], save that the Vulg. presupposes
a different text or is corrupt. In Num. 14[36-37] the Targums,
Syriac, and LXX reproduce this *vav*, only the Vulg. omitting
it. Again, in Exod. 38[24] the Targums follow the Hebrew
literally, while the LXX, Syriac, and Vulg. omit the *vav*. In
1 Sam. 14[19], 17[24], 2 Sam. 21[16], 1 Kings 9[20-21], 2 Kings 25[22] Targ.,
LXX reproduce the *vav*, the Vulgate always omits, while the
Syriac omits or follows a different text, save in the third
passage, where it reproduces the *vav*. In Jer. 6[19], 28[8], 33[24],
44[25] this *vav* is reproduced by Targ. in the four passages, by
the LXX in the three latter (in 33[24] אAQ), in the Vulg. and
Pesh. only in the first. Thus the Targums reproduce the *vav*
in all the above passages, the Pesh. in over 30 per cent., the
LXX in over 60 per cent., and the Vulg. in less than 10 per cent.

Now we know that the *vav* apodosis occurs in original Syriac,
and, further, from the above facts we conclude that the late
Aramaic of the Targums had no objection to reproducing this
vav apodosis. But in original Aramaic before 165 B. C. outside
Daniel there is not a single certain instance of this idiom.[a]
In the six chapters of the original Aramaic in Daniel it is
found (?) once, i. e. in 7[20]. These facts taken together lead to the
conclusion that the Aramaic of Daniel is not as old as that of
Ezra; and also to the further highly probable conclusion that
the three instances of this idiom in the Hebrew of Dan. 1[2,18,20],
where the *vav* with the imperf. introduces the predicate, are
due to the Hebrew translator and not to the Aramaic which he
was translating. In the remaining five Hebrew chapters (8-12)
this *vav* (*vav* apodosis with imperfect) does not occur once—a fact
which points to different translators at work.

The Lord, i. e. אדני. This designation of God is used here
only in Daniel. See note on 9[3]. On the solitary occurrence of

---

[a] Cowley, Ah. 160 (fifth cent.) by his restoration of a hopeless line presupposes
its occurrence. The same restoration presupposes עמד to be an Aramaic verb.
But there is no evidence for its being so. That the *vav* consecutive is found in
the eighth cent. B. C. Zakar Inscription proves nothing, since this inscription
is a conglomerate of Aramaic, Canaanitish and Hebrew expressions: Cf. *Eph.*
III, p. 3.

Yahweh in 9² see note. 'Part of'—מִקְצָת is so punctuated without *daghesh forte* in Neh. 7⁶⁹, קְצָת like קְצֵה from meaning the end or extremity of a thing came to be a condensed term for all that was included within the extremities, and hence to be 'the whole'. מִן־קְצָת = 'part of the whole' occurs 2⁴²—a common Aramaic idiom.

Part of the vessels. Nebuchadnezzar raided the Temple three times : first through his great officers in Jehoiakim's reign (see note on ver. 1) ; secondly, in Jehoiachin's reign (2 Chron. 36¹⁰), and finally in Zedekiah's reign (*ibid.* 36¹⁸⁻¹⁹). In 2 Kings 24 sq. there is no mention of the king taking the sacred vessels of the Temple in Jehoiakim's reign, whereas in 24¹²⁻¹⁶ it is told that in Jehoiachin's reign he carried off *all* the vessels of the Temple and of the king's house, as well as all the royal family, nobility, fighting-men, and craftsmen.

God. אלהים is always used in our author with the article of the one true God as opposed to Nebuchadnezzar's false god.

The house of God. This is the usual name for the Temple in post-exilic writers. In the earlier books it was always called the 'house of Yahweh'. Our author avoids the use of this divine name, as do other late writers. See note on 9².

Carried. If we retain the words 'the vessels' in the following clause, the suffix in וַיְבִיאֵם must embrace not only the vessels but the captives and all the booty taken by Nebuchadnezzar, or rather, as I have shown above, the suffix recapitulates in itself the persons and things captured and already mentioned in the text. If we refer the suffix only to the Temple vessels, as the MT appears to demand, we cannot explain the words 'the vessels' (את הכלים) ; for in that case we should expect only 'them' (אֹתָם), Moreover, these words are placed in the most emphatic position in the clause, 'and the vessels he brought, &c.' If then these words are original and in their original position, they clearly imply that not only the sacred vessels but also the two classes of captives were definitely mentioned in the preceding clause. Thus the text requires, as we have already shown, the restoration of two phrases in the preceding clause, which were lost through homoeoteleuton.

The land of Shinar. Shinar, or rather Shin'ar, is mentioned eight times : Gen. 10¹⁰, 11², 14¹,⁹, Joshua 7²¹, Isa. 11¹¹, Zech. 5¹¹, Dan. 1², and stands for Babylon in the O.T. The word has not, however, been found in the Inscriptions. For various attempts at its identification see the Bible Dictionaries. It is no archaism, although it occurs as we have seen in Isa. 11¹¹ and Zech. 5¹¹. In the LXX the words 'to Babylon' are inserted before 'the land of Shinar'. They are an explanatory gloss. In Exilic times and later, writers spoke of Babylonia as 'the land of Babylon', ארץ בבל (Jer. 51²⁹), or 'the land of the Chaldeans', ארץ כשדים (Ezek. 12¹³). Syrʰ omits 'the land of Shinar'.

[*To the house of his god.*] That this phrase must be rejected we have shown above under solution 4. Both Marti and Driver recognize that they are not genuine. They as well as the two words that follow them are omitted by Syrʰ, i. e. the LXX.

But the vessels, &c. The LXX has here καὶ ἀπηρείσατο αὐτά, 'and he set them up'. But since in Polybius, iii. 92. 9, and often in Plutarch this verb means 'to deposit in', it does not presuppose a text differing from the MT. The verb occurs three times in 1 Esdras 1⁴¹, 2¹⁰, 6¹⁸ in the same connexion. The parallel passages in the O.T. to these passages are respectively 2 Chron. 36⁷, Ezra 1⁷, 5¹⁴, but the Hebrew verbs differ, though in that connexion they are synonymous.

Into the treasure house of his god. The statement in our text is confirmed by Ezra 1⁷, 5¹⁴, 1 Esdras 1⁴¹, 2¹⁰, 6¹⁸. But the Oxford Hebrew Lexicon states that in 2 Chron. 36⁷ היכל is to be rendered 'palace' and not 'temple'. The LXX of 2 Chron. 36⁷, however, renders it ναός, and carries with it the entire tradition connected with the question.

1³⁻⁵. Nebuchadnezzar gives orders to Ashpenaz to have certain noble youths of the Jewish captivity educated for the king's service. The education even of the royal princes in Persia was superintended by eunuchs (Rawlinson, *Ancient Monarchies*, iii. 221). It does not, however, necessarily follow that Ashpenaz was a eunuch. See below.

1³. *Commanded . . . to bring in.* The construction ויאמר · · · להביא belongs to late Hebrew. Cf. 2 Chron. 14³, 29²¹, 31⁴, Esther 1¹⁰. Earlier writers used the *oratio recta*.

Ashpenaz. The word is corrupt, just as Osnappar is in Ezra 4¹⁰, אס[ר]נפר, i.e. Assurbanipal (Ἀσεννναφάρ LXX). Its meaning is unknown. The LXX has Ἀβιεσδρί: Th. Ἀσφανέζ, which is a reproduction of the form in the MT. In Ἀβιεσδρί the δ is parasitic as in Ἐσδράς. Hence 'Abiezer', which is preserved in

Syr[h], is the form which the LXX presupposes. But the problem is still further complicated by the corruption in I[11].

The master of his eunuchs. רב סריסיו is here the equivalent of שׂר הסריסים in ver. 7. This phrase sometimes denotes a great official, as in 2 Kings 18[17], Jer. 39[3,13], or the keeper of the royal harem, who was of course a eunuch. Thus סריס המלך is explained in Esther 2[3] as שׁמר הנשׁים. In our text the LXX, Th., Vulg. take it in the latter sense : the Pesh. in the former. רב is of course the Aramaic for the Hebrew שׂר. This Aramaic word is found in the titles of great Assyrian and Babylonian officials in 2 Kings and Jeremiah. Cf. Rabsaris in 2 Kings 18[17]. See Oxford Hebr. Lex. *in loc.* סרים does not always mean eunuch. Potiphar, who bore this title, was married : cf. Gen. 37[36], 39[7].

Children of ⌜the exiles of⌝ Israel. Since the LXX inserts before τοῦ 'Ισραήλ the phrase τῶν μεγιστάνων, and Th. τῆς αἰχμαλωσίας, and seeing that as glosses they are needless, we conclude that the MT is defective here. Th. clearly presupposes בני גולת ישראל: cf. 2[25] בני גלותא די יהוד, where *both the LXX and Th.* render גלותא by τῆς αἰχμαλωσίας. For the Hebrew phrase cf. also Ezra 4[1], 6[19,20], 8[35], &c. We could then explain τῶν υἱῶν τῶν μεγιστάνων τοῦ 'Ισ. of the LXX as a rendering of בני גדולי ישראל, where גדולי is corrupt for גולת. This phrase, lost in the MT, limits the selection of the royal pages to the captives of Israel, independently of the further grounds for selection in I[4].

Children of ⟨the exiles⟩ of Israel, both of the seed royal and of the nobles. The phrase 'children of Israel' has a wider significance than 'the children of Judah' in ver. 7. According to 2 Chron. 11[16], it is true, the kingdom of Judah embraced members of all the tribes of Israel. But there was a tendency to identify the two expressions. Certainly in the latter half of the second century B.C. the Twelve Tribes were supposed to be living in Palestine : see the note in my Commentary on *Test. xii. Patr.*, p. 14. The same presupposition underlies the *Letter of Aristeas* (130–70 B.C. ?), according to which Eleazar the high priest sent six men from each of the Twelve Tribes to Ptolemy Lagus (322–285 B.C.). The older belief still persisted that the northern tribes were in captivity : see 1 Enoch 89[72] (*circa* 162 B.C.). Thus in the second century B.C. these two beliefs maintained themselves side by side. The idea of the apostasy and rejection of the Ten Tribes, which appears in the Mishna

(*Sanh.* xi. 3) was then unknown. All Jews came later to be
called Israelites, and all Israelites Jews, but our author appears
to have believed, as the author of the Testaments, that all the
Twelve Tribes had representatives in Palestine, but states that
the king limited his choice of royal pages to the captives of the
tribe of Judah.

Both . . . and. So וֹ—וֹ are to be translated as in 8¹³ Gen.
34²⁸, Josh. 9²³, Jer. 32²⁰. גַּם ' ' ' גַּם is more usual in this sense.

Nobles. The Hebrew פרתמים, found also in Esther 1³, 6⁹ is
a Persian loan-word: cf. *fratama* = 'first' (in the Achemenian
inscription) and the Sanskrit *prathama*. Philologically πρῶτος is
akin to these words. The LXX and Aq. agree in rendering it
respectively ἐπίλεκτοι and ἐκλεκτοί, but Sym. wrongly as Πάρθοι.

1⁴. *No blemish.* The perfection here asserted is physical, as
in Lev. 21¹⁷. Such perfection could not be asserted of eunuchs.
The Hebrew word מאום with א is found only here and in
Job 31⁷. Elsewhere it appears as מום as also in Aramaic.

Well favoured :טובי מראה. The youths were not only free
from any physical blemish but were of goodly appearance.

⌐*and literature*⌐: i. e. וספר, which with the LXX καὶ γραμματικούς
and 1¹⁷ of our text I have here restored.

Cunning. This is simply an archaism in the English Versions
for 'knowing', and may be retained. השכיל is only found in
Dan. with ב here and in 1¹⁷, 9¹³: elsewhere in the O.T. with
acc. אל or על), or ל, save in Joshua 1⁷, 1 Sam. 18¹⁴(?), Ps. 101².

Science. This word מַדָּע is borrowed from the Aramaic, but
it is found also in 2 Chron. 1¹⁰,¹¹,¹², and in the later work
Ecclesiastes.

The literature and the tongue, i. e. ספר ולשון בשדים—an un-
Hebraic idiom for ספר כשדים ולשונם. It is found, however, twice
elsewhere in the O.T., i. e. Ezek. 31¹⁶, Prov. 16¹¹. See *Ges.-
Kautzsch*, § 128 a. But it was current in late Maccabean times
as the inscription on the coins shows—ראש וחבר היהורים (Wellhausen, *Pharisäer*, 34). There is no room for doubting that the
language of the Chaldeans in Dan. 1⁴ means the non-Semitic
and Sumerian language in which the books on divination and
astrology were written, and not the Aramaic. The Jewish
youths were given time to master this language.

Chaldeans. This word has two meanings in Dan.

(1) *It has an ethnic significance*, in 5³⁰, 9¹. The word, which

is spelt Kaldu in Assyrian, in Greek Χαλδαῖοι, appears as כשדים in Hebrew. Before a dental, *l* is often changed into שׂ or שׁ. See C. H. H. Wright, *Daniel and his Critics*, p. 6.

The Chaldeans are believed to be alluded to in inscriptions already known as early as 1100 B.C. They are certainly referred to, and that frequently, in inscriptions from 880 B.C. onwards. The earliest mention of this nation is in the O.T. in Gen. 11[28.31], i.e. the name 'Ur of the Chaldees'. Here אור is the same as the Assyrian *urru* or *ûru* (F. Delitzsch, *Wörterbuch*). They lived originally to the south-east of Babylonia proper in the land of Kaldu, bordering on the Persian Gulf (Strabo, xvi. 1. 6). Being a vigorous nation they pressed steadily inland into Babylonia, and, despite their repeated defeats by the Assyrians, they so far gained the upper hand as to make a temporary conquest of Babylon under Merodach-Baladan in 721 B.C. For the next hundred years the Chaldeans and Assyrians were constantly at war, but it was not till the reign of Nabopolassar, 'king of the land of the Kaldu' (625–605), the father of Nebuchadnezzar, that the Chaldean dynasty was firmly established in Babylon, and the Chaldeans became the ruling caste in Babylonia. The Chaldean dynasty held the throne till the conquest of Babylon under Cyrus in 538. In the times of the New Babylonian Empire a Chaldean meant a member of the dominant race in Babylon.

For this ethnic use of the term 'Chaldeans', compare Isa. 43[14], 48[14.20], Jer. 21[9], Ezek. 23[14.15], 2 Chron. 36[17]. The king of Babylon is never called 'king of the Chaldeans' in the inscriptions (though the designation occurs in 2 Chron. 36[17]), but 'king of Babylon' or 'king of Babylon, Sumer, and Akkad'.

In Ezek. 23[23] the term 'Chaldeans' is more comprehensive than that of 'Babylonians', for they embrace Pekod, Shoa, and Koa. The term 'Babylonians', though frequent in later Jewish writings, is found in the O.T. only in Ezra 4[9].

(2) *The term Chaldeans denotes a caste of wise men* in 1[4], 2[2,4,5,10], 4[7], 5[7,11], and probably in 3[8]. This use of the word is unparalleled throughout the rest of the O.T., and there is no trace of it in the inscriptions. It cannot have arisen till the fall of the Babylonian empire, and, therefore, cannot have come into existence for one or more generations after the conquest of Babylon by the Persians in 538. It is idle to quote Herodotus,

i. 181, 183. For since Herodotus was born in 484, and died about 425, the earliest date we can assign to his history would be 445 B.C. Between 538 and 445 the term 'Chaldean' had ample time to acquire a new and distinct meaning, amply attested in Herodotus,[a] Strabo,[b] Diodorus Siculus,[c] Cicero, Suetonius, Tacitus, Juvenal, and other writers. The student will find an ample list of Latin authorities in Mayor's *Juvenal*, x. 94, xiv. 248 (vol. ii, pp. 104–5, 329–31).

But whereas in Diodorus Siculus the term 'Chaldeans' bears a generic sense, in Daniel it denotes a specific class in every case (1^{20}, $2^{2,4,5,10}$, 4^7, $5^{7,11}$), save in 1^4. But the several classes of men enumerated in Daniel, of whom the Chaldeans were one, find no real support in the inscriptions. Jastrow (*Religion of Babylonia and Assyria*, Boston, 1898, p. 656 sq.) mentions a number of classes of magicians and diviners, one of which —the *âshipu*—occurs in Dan. 1^{20}. But the list in Daniel falls far short of that which was current in Judah. Thus in Deut. 18 'no less than eleven classes of magic workers are enumerated'. Hence 'there can be little doubt but that the Pentateuchal opposition against the necromancers, sorcerers, soothsayers, and the like, is aimed chiefly against Babylonish customs' (Jastrow, *op. cit.*, p. 657).

But though this second meaning of the term 'Chaldean' was comparatively late, the practice of divination and astrology belongs to the earliest antiquity. King (*Hist. of Sumer and Akkad*, 1910, pp. 124, 266) has shown that the study of dreams and their interpretation was pursued as early as 3000 B.C. In 2800 B.C. divination by oil was practised. Zimmern (Hastings,

---

[a] i. 181: 'The Chaldeans being priests of this god' (i.e. Bel). In i. 183 the Chaldeans are thrice mentioned. In the second passage Herodotus definitely states that 'the Chaldeans consume also every year 1,000 talents of frankincense on the great altar'. The two other statements in this chapter are made on the authority of the Chaldeans (ὡς ἔλεγον οἱ Χαλδαῖοι and τὰ δὲ λέγεται ὑπὸ Χαλδαίων, ταῦτα λέγω).

[b] Strabo (born c. 63 B.C.), xvi. 1. 6, describes the Chaldeans as a class of savants in Babylon who directed their studies mainly to astronomy. He mentions also a tribe of Chaldeans who lived near the Arabian or Persian Gulf. Thus even in Strabo's time the two meanings of the word still persisted in the East.

[c] This writer (first century B.C.), speaks of the Chaldeans as forming a caste and possessing a fixed traditional lore. They were not only priests but magicians and astrologers. See ii. 29–31.

DRE 216 *b*) states that 'the texts relating to soothsaying and exorcism are so exceedingly numerous as to form the chief component of the whole Babylonian literature'. When the Chaldeans were subjugated by the Persians and reduced to a subject position, they took over the functions of the priestly diviners and astrologers, which had been practised in Babylonia from prehistoric times.

To return now to our author, we may reasonably conclude that he chose a number of terms denoting workers in magic, and traditionally associated with Babylon, and incorporated them in his work in such a way as to give a general view of the methods in which magical and kindred arts were pursued in Babylon.

1⁵. I adopt here Marti's proposal and transpose the latter half of this verse before the first half. The construction is thus regularized, and the latter half, which begins with the infinitive (ולגדלם), is thus a continuation of the infinitival constructions in vv. 3-4. Thus we have 'And the king commanded Ashpenaz... to bring (infin.)... and to teach... and to nourish them'. The sense also is improved.

Three years. According to Plato, *Alk.* i. 121 E, the education of chosen youths under the royal teachers began at the age of fourteen. For the previous seven years they had been trained to ride and hunt. At the age of seventeen they entered the king's service.

They should stand before the king. Cf. ver. 19, 1 Sam. 16²², 1 Kings 17¹, 18¹⁵, &c. The LXX presupposes יעמיד(ם) לפני המלך, i. e. 'to place ⟨them⟩ in the service of the king', as in Esther 4⁵. This would preserve the active construction through vv. 3, 4, and 5 *b*. Thus 5 *a* would close this part of the narrative. In chapter 1 עמד, whether it stands alone as in 1⁴ or is followed by לפני as in 1⁵,¹⁹, means 'to serve'. It never bears this meaning in 8-12. Thus עמד לפני means 'to withstand' in 8⁴,⁷, 11¹⁶, and has the same meaning when followed by לנגד in 10¹³. In 8¹⁵, 10¹⁶ this last phrase = 'to stand before' (locally).

At the end thereof. The מן in מקצתם has here, as in 1¹⁵,¹⁸, a different sense from what it bears in 1², i. e. 'after', 'after the lapse of'. See *Ges.-Kautzsch,* § 119 *y*, n³. The masc. suffix in מקצתם, where we should expect the fem., referring to the fem. noun שנים, occurs not infrequently in the O.T. See *op. cit.,*

§ 135 *o*. This anomaly recurs in 8[9] of our author, but many manuscripts emend the masc. suffix into the fem.

Appointed. מִנָּה 'to appoint', is poetical (Ps. 61[8]) and passed into the later prose (1 Chron. 9[29]). It recurs in 1[11] of our author, and in the Aramaic as מַנִּי in 2[24,49], 3[12]. But it is old Aramaic. See Cowley 27[9], Aḥ. 37.

A daily portion. דבר יום ביומו has already occurred in Jer. 52[34], 1 Chron. 16[37]. In 1 Kings 10[25], 2 Chron. 9[24] a yearly portion is mentioned.

The king's meat. פתבג (1[5,8,13,15,16], 11[26]—only in Daniel in O.T.) is a Persian loan-word, *patibaga*, signifying 'portion', 'offering' from the Sanskrit *prati-bhâga*. This word was transliterated into Greek as ποτίβαζις, which, according to a fragment of Dinon's *Persica* (*c.* 340 B.C.), preserved in Athenaeus, xi. 503, consisted of a meal of barley or wheaten cakes and wine: ἔστι δὲ ποτίβαζις ἄρτος κρίθινος καὶ πύρινος ὀπτὸς καὶ κυπαρίσσου στέφανος καὶ οἶνος κεκραμένος ἐν ᾧ χρυσῷ οὗ αὐτὸς βασιλεὺς πίνει. In Syriac the word means 'dainties'. But the LXX and Th. do not attempt to render the whole word. Their rendering of τράπεζα and δεῖπνον give the general meaning of the first half of the word in Hebrew, i. e. פת. See note on 11[26].

The wine which he drank. מִשְׁתָּיו (as in 1[8]) is sing. Cf. 1[10, 16; 15]. Cf. Nah. 2[5], Isa. 42[5], Ezek. 34[14]. See *Ges.-Kautzsch*, § 93 ss. These verses introduce the four young nobles of the tribe of Judah with whom the following narratives are mainly concerned.

1[6]. *Daniel.* There are three other Daniels mentioned in the O.T.: (1) the Patriarch (written דָּנִאֵל) in Ezek. 14[14,20], 28[3], who from his juxtaposition with Noah and Job cannot be the Daniel of our narrative, who was a mere boy at the time of the Exile; (2) a son of David, 1 Chron. 3[1]; (3) a certain Levite, Ezra 8[2], Neh. 10[6].

Mishael = 'Who is what God is?' Ass. form., cf. מתושאל. See Oxf. Heb. Lex. *in loc.* The names Mishael, Hananiah, and Azariah appear also among the contemporaries of Ezra: see Neh. 8[4], 10[3,24], which, as Bevan remarks, is 'probably accidental, since all three occur elsewhere, and we therefore have no proof that the author of Daniel intended to identify "them" with their namesakes in Nehemiah'.

1[7]. The practice of changing a person's name was common on the occasion of a change in his position, circumstances, or nationality.[1] See Gen. 41[45], Ruth 1[20], 2 Kings 23[34], 24[17], and especially Acts 13[9], where Saul's name is changed to that of Paul. As Driver remarks, the change of name 'has the effect in each case of obliterating the name of God: Daniel, "God is my judge"; Hananiah, "Yah is gracious"; Mishael, "Who is what God is?"; Azariah, "Yah hath holpen".' Seeing that in the age of our author Jews were discarding their Hebrew names and adopting Greek names, it is not improbable, as Marti and others suggest, that our text contains an intentional polemic against this custom.

Gave names unto them — וַיָּשֶׂם לָהֶם שֵׁמוֹת. This idiom is not found elsewhere in the O.T. exactly as it is here. Either שֵׂם is followed by אֵת, Judges 8[31], or without a preposition as in 2 Kings 17[34], Neh. 9[7], and even in the Aramaic of Dan. 5[12].

[*He gave.*] The second וַיָּשֶׂם is to be omitted with the LXX and Th.

Belteshazzar. This name, which recurs in 2[26], 4[5, 6, 15, 16(bis)], 5[12], 10[1] is not to be confounded with Belshazzar in 5[1] (where see note), as is done in the LXX, Th., and Vulg. Belteshazzar = *balāṭšu-uṣur*, 'protect his life'.

Shadrach. The derivation is uncertain. F. Delitzsch explains it as Shudur-Aku, 'the command of Aku', Aku being the Sumerian equivalent of Sin, the Semitic name of the Moon-God.

Meshach. F. Delitzsch explains this as equivalent to *Mî-sha-Aku*, 'Who is what Aku is?'.

Abed-nego. This is a corruption of Abed-nebo, 'servant of Nebo'—the deity mentioned in Isa. 46[1]. Proper names compounded with Nebo will be found in the Aramaic Papyri of the fifth century (Cowley, p. 298 seq.); a few also in the Palmyrene Inscriptions (see Cooke, 127[3], 134[2] 140 A[4]) of the first, second and third centuries A. D. Thus heathen Syrians (Cureton's *Ancient Syriac Documents*, p. 14, line 5, quoted by Bevan) long after the Christian era derived both names from Nebo. The actual name in our text occurs in a bilingual (Assyr. and Aram.) inscription (Schrader, *Cuneiform Inscr.*, p. 429), as Bevan states. The

---

[1] Psammetichus I, son of Necho, king of Memphis and Sais, had his name changed to Nabu-sizib-anni when he became subject to Assurbanipal, king of Assyria.

more usual form would be Amel-Nebo, 'servant of Nebo,' but 'Abed' or 'Abd' is frequently found in its stead. (See Schrader's *KAT*[3] Index, p. 654.)

1^{8-16}. Loyalty of Daniel and his companions to their religion and their consequent superiority physically to the other youths that were being educated with a view to the king's service.

1^{8-10}. This loyalty shown in their observance of the laws of their religion regarding clean and unclean meats. The need of this loyalty was felt to be of supreme moment in the time of Antiochus Epiphanes, who was doing his utmost to hellenize the Jews. To eat of unlawful food in such circumstances was as sinful as idolatry itself. Hence the faithful had to abstain from the food of the heathen, not only because the Levitical laws as to clean and unclean animals were not observed by the heathen in the selection and preparation of their food, but also because the food so prepared had generally been offered to idols (Exod. 34^{15}, Acts 15^{29}, 21^{25}, Deut. 32^{38}). Thus the observance of these laws, though seen later (Mark 7^{18-19}, Acts 10^{9-16}) to be only of temporary obligation, became an *articulus ecclesiae stantis aut cadentis* under Antiochus Epiphanes (1 Macc. $1^{47,48,62,63}$, 2 Macc. $6^{18\ sqq.}$, 7^{1}). Hence in our text Daniel and his friends confined themselves to vegetable products. But generally in heathen surroundings these laws were rigidly carried out by the faithful Jew; cf. Tobit $1^{10,11}$, 4 Macc. $5^{3,14}$, Judith $12^{1,2}$, *Vita Joseph.* 3. In this last passage it is recounted how certain priests that were sent to Rome limited their food on religious grounds to figs and nuts.

1^{8}. *Purposed in his heart.* שום על לב means 'to lay it to heart', 'to purpose'. It is found in Isa. 42^{25}, 47^{7}, $57^{1,11}$, and in Mal. 2^{2}. It is to be distinguished of course from שום לב על = 'to observe', 'pay attention to', Haggai $1^{5,7}$, Job 1^{8}. Probably שׂום על לב is here a rendering of the original Aramaic שׂום בל c. inf. Cf. 6^{15}.

Defile himself. The Hithpa'el of גאל is found only here. גאל is a later and weakened form of געל. The older Hebrew used חלל or טמא.

1^{9}. *Made Daniel to find favour, &c.* ויתן · · את־דניאל · · · לרחמים לפני שר הס״. Practically the same Hebrew construction is found in 1 Kings 8^{50}, Neh. 1^{11}, Ps. 106^{46}. An older form of this idiom is found in Gen. 43^{14}—יתן לכם רחמים לפני האיש.

1¹⁰. *Your drink.* מִשְׁתֵּיכֶם is sing. 'In a few instances, before
a suffix beginning with a consonant, the original *ăy* of the termination has been contracted to *ê*, and thus there arise forms
which have apparently *plural suffixes*' (*Ges.-Kautzsch*, § 93 *ss*).
There are other like formations in the sing. in Daniel : here
and in 1¹⁶ (משתיהם) and in 1¹⁵ (מראיהם). Cf. 1⁵,⁸ for a like
formation. See note on ver. 5 above.

Lest. אשר למה. This is not Hebrew, but the literal reproduction of an Aramaic idiom in unidiomatic Hebrew. Cf. שַׁלָּמָה
(in Cant. 1⁷) = 'lest'. The Hebrew for 'lest' is פֶּן. The
Aramaic idiom occurs in Ezra 7²³ דִּי לְמָה : in the Targums
דילמא : in the Syriac ܕܠܡܐ—all meaning 'lest'. In Ezra 4²²
למה practically = 'lest' = μήποτε (LXX), as also in *Aram. Pap.* :
Cowley, Aḥ. 126 יסנה · · · · למה 'lest . . . he come'.

Worse liking. The Hebrew word זעפים (which Aq. accepts
and renders by διεστραμμένα) is used elsewhere in the O.T. in the
sense of mental trouble—'to be out of humour'. In Gen. 40⁶
it = 'to fret against'; in Prov. 19³, 'the foolish man fretteth
against the Lord'; in 2 Chron. 26¹⁹, 'to be enraged'. Thus in
all these passages the word relates to a state of mind and not
to the outward appearance as in our text. This may be the
meaning attached to it by Th., who renders it by σκυθρωπά ; cf.
Matt. 6¹⁶, where the Pharisees bear a dejected look on account
of their fasting. But there are difficulties attaching to the
Hebrew word. The LXX has here διατετραμμένα καὶ ἀσθενῆ =
'alarmed and weak', which is most probably a double rendering
of what stood in the text. Now what did stand in the text ?
In Job 31³⁴ διατρέπομαι = 'stand in awe of' appears as a rendering of ערץ. If it is so here, then ערצים is a dittograph of צעירים,
of which ἀσθενῆ is a bad rendering. And yet διατετραμμένα is not
accidental ; for it recurs in ver. 13 in the LXX, where however
the MT and Th. have a different text. We fall back therefore
on צעירים = 'meaner looking'. Jos., *Ant.* x. 10. 2 supports this
text, as it reads εἰ δὲ μειωθέντας ἴδοι καὶ κακίον τῶν ἄλλων ἔχοντας.
ἀσθενῆ and μειωθέντας, then, both support צעירים. We should
therefore translate : 'lest he should see your faces meaner (or
worse-liking) than the youths of your own age'. In that case
we should reject זעפים as a corruption of the above word. It
is noteworthy that צעירה again underwent corruption in 8⁹, and
is there rendered both by the LXX and Th. as עריצה or עצומה ;
for they both translate the word by ἰσχυρόν.

To confirm the above conclusion we may compare 1[15], where the phrase בריאי בשר proves that it was only the physical fitness of the youths that was in question.

Age. The word ניל is borrowed from the Aramaic and corresponds to the Hebrew דור. It is found in the Samaritan of Gen. 6[9], 15[16], and in the Talmud.

Make . . . forfeit. חיב is a late Hebrew word, and does not occur elsewhere in the O.T.; for Cornill, followed by Bevan, rejects חוב in Ezek. 18[7]. The former takes it to be a corruption of שוב, the latter to be a dittography 'the first two letters of חבלתו having been repeated and a ו inserted afterwards'. In the fifth Century Papyri it is found with the same meaning as in our text. See Cowley 2[15], 18[3]. It is in fact a pure Aramaism.

1[11]. †*The Melzar*†. The word מלצר occurs only in this chapter. Friedr. Delitzsch thinks that it is derived from the Assyrian Maṣṣaru 'guardian', i. e. from the root נצר, the ל'ṣ indicating the resolution of the doubling of the ṣṣ as in בֹּשֶׂם and βάλσαμον. But the context is against the genuineness of the text. The Hebrew ignores the fact that Daniel has already been committed to the care of the chief of the eunuchs, who is expressly named in ver. 4. Furthermore, in this verse it is the prince of the eunuchs that Daniel must have addressed, as a comparison of 1[3,7–10,18] shows (Cheyne in *Encyc. Bib.* i. 334–335), and not a third person called Melzar or 'the Melzar'. The MT in 1[11,16] is therefore secondary. In fact all the forms אביעזרי (which the LXX presupposes in 1[3,11]), אשפנז (MT and Th. in 1[3]), המלצר (MT and Th. 1[11]), משיצר (? מניצר Pesh. 1[11]) are all corruptions of some word hitherto undiscovered, which may be called X. Cheyne believes the name to which all these corrupt forms point is בלשאצר 'Belshazzar'. But, though Cheyne's method is right, as Marti agrees, the conclusion at which he arrives is unconvincing.

†*The Melzar . . . appointed over Daniel*†. The LXX, which has rightly identified the chief of the eunuchs in 1[3,11] with the person here mentioned, has also preserved the true text. The LXX reads Ἀβιεσδρὶ τῷ ἀναδειχθέντι ἀρχιευνούχῳ ἐπὶ τὸν Δ. = שר הסריסים אשר מֻנֶּה על ד׳ = 'the prince of the eunuchs who was set over Daniel'.

1[12]. *Ten.* This is a round number. Cf. 1[20], 7[7], Gen. 24[55], 31[7], Amos 5[3], Haggai 2[16], Zach. 8[23]; 3, 4, and 7 are favourite numbers with our author. נֵם is the apocopated imperative for נֵפֵּה.

Let them give. The indefinite personal subject is frequently expressed in Hebrew by the 3rd plural masculine: see *Ges.-Kautzsch*, § 144 *f.*

Pulse. זֵרְעִים is a hapax-legomenon as also זֵרְעֹנִים in 1[16]. The form in the Talmud and in Syriac is זֵרְעֹנִים. Whether the forms in our text are genuine is questionable. On the other hand they may be current phonetic variations. For in our text there are different grammatical forms with no implication of a change of meaning, as Bevan points out p. 62 n.: ותחפעם 2[1] and ותפעם 2[3], תעמדנה and יעמדנה 8[22], הרשענו 9[5] and רשענו 9[15], בין and הבין, זרועות 11[15] and זרעים 11[31], חלקלקות 11[21,34], and חלקות 11[32]. But the latter variations in 11[21,34] in the MT are probably late corruptions. See note on 11[21].

1[13]. *Our countenances.* See note on 1[10] above.

Thou seest. תִּרְאֶה has the Aramaic vocalization: see *Ges.-Kautzsch.*, § 75 *hh.*

Deal with. עָשָׂה עָם. The treatment is to be favourable or unfavourable according to the results of the experiment. Only here and in 2 Chron. 2[2] is this construction found in the O.T., but in 2 Chron. the phrase is used in a favourable sense. Elsewhere this combination of עשה and עם requires an accusative such as הסד or אמת, &c.: cf. Gen. 19[19], 24[12], Joshua 2[14], Judges 9[19]. In 11[7] on the other hand עשה is followed by ב in a hostile sense, as in Jer. 18[23].

1[14]. *Hearkened . . . in this matter:* i. e. granted this request. The same construction is found in Gen. 19[21], 1 Sam. 30[24].

1[15]. *Fatter in flesh.* Cf. Gen. 41[2,18] בְּרִיאֹת בָּשָׂר for the same phrase used of the fat kine in Pharoah's dream. The plural בריאי is to be explained by reference to the suffix in מראיהם.

1[16]. †*The Melzar†.* See 1[11] note.

Was wont to take away . . . and give. The idea of duration is here conveyed by the combination of the substantive verb and the participle. See Driver[3], *Tenses*, § 135. 5.

1[17-19]. At the end of the three years Daniel and his three companions, who are found to be not only physically superior but also intellectually in knowledge and wisdom to the other youths that were educated with them, are appointed to serve in the court of the king.

The vegetarian diet is helpful also in the direction of spiritual development.

1[17]. *Knowledge.* The same word is rendered 'science' in 1[4].

All literature, i. e. all kinds of books. Cf. 1[4].

Wisdom. As Driver observes, 'Wisdom is used here, in a concrete sense, of an intelligently arranged body of principles, or, as we should now say, *science.* The term must be understood as representing the popular estimate of the subjects referred to : for the wisdom of the Chaldaean priests, except in so far as it took cognizance of the actual facts of astronomy, was in reality nothing but a systematized superstition.'

Daniel had understanding in all kinds of visions. These words serve to introduce the narrative that follows. They recall 2 Chron. 26[5] מבין בראות האל׳׳. They differentiate at the same time the unique gifts of Daniel even in relation to his three companions. This difference in spiritual endowment is observed in later passages, and, though Shadrach, Meshach, and Abed-nebo are ten times wiser than the sages of Babylon 1[20], yet Daniel possesses still higher gifts than theirs, and whereas at the close of chapter 2 the three companions are rewarded with high official appointments, Daniel is clearly set above all the wise men and governors of Babylon ; for he sits in the king's gate (2[49b]), i. e. is the Vizier or Prime Minister of the king, and so is not exposed to the risks that his three companions encounter in chapter 3.

1[18]. *Had commanded to bring them in.* A late Hebrew idiom. See 1[3] n.

וַיְבִיאֵם 'the prince of the eunuchs brought, &c.' We have here the *vav* apodosis with the imperf.—an idiom which has already occurred in ver. 2. See note.

1[19]. This verse closes the introduction to the book.

Stood before the king, i. e. became his personal servants : cf. 1[5].

SECTION II

i. e. Chapters 2[1-49a], 1[20,21], 2[49b], in the second year of the reign of Nebuchadnezzar.

§ 1. This chapter has a didactic purpose. As in chapter 1 the Jews are exhorted to be true to the Law, even to its ceremonial requirements, so in this chapter they are encouraged to hold fast to the national hope of the Messianic kingdom. To justify their belief in this expectation the superiority of the wisdom of the Jews to that of the heathen is shown in the incidents connected with the king's dream and its interpretation. This transcendent wisdom is shown to spring from the direct revelation of the God of the Jews (cp. Isa. 19[12]), and His supremacy above all gods is accordingly acknowledged by the king. In this dream the succession of the world empires is foreshadowed, and, as these had arisen in the order foreshadowed in his dream and its interpretation, the readers of Daniel were assured of the certainty of the coming kingdom.

The narrative in many respects recalls Gen. 41 (Stade, *Geschichte*, ii. 324). In both narratives a heathen king is visited by a dream which alarms him; in both he sends for his magicians, but they prove helpless; in both a youthful Israelite, who ascribed his wisdom wholly to the help of his God, gives the true interpretation, and is raised to the highest honours. For similarities in point of diction, cf. 2[1.2.30].

As the first chapter dealt with the discipline and fruitfulness of the religious life in its private relations, this chapter exhibits the same characteristics in the public activities of its true adherents, by recounting the triumph of Daniel and his three companions over the collective wisdom of the wise men of Babylon and Daniel's appointment as chief counsellor of the king and his three companions as great officials of the empire.

§ 2. (a) *Corruptions in the Hebrew of* 2[1–4a].

2[1]. For נהיתה read נדדה.

2[4]. For ארמית read ויאמרו. See note.

(b) *Corruptions in the Aramaic.*

2[5]. For עָנָה וְאָמַר read עֲנָה וְאָמַר. See note.

2[13]. For בְּעוֹ read בְּעוֹ, or else להתקטלה for לקטלה.

2[23]. For גבורתא (so MT, Pesh. and Vulg., due to a scribe's assimilation of the two adjoining phrases here to those in 2[20]) read with LXX שכלתנו.

2[35]. For 'the iron, the clay' with Th. read 'the clay, the iron' against the MT, LXX, Vulg. The context requires this change: also the order in 2[45] where LXX, Th., and Vulg. attest the right order. See note on 2[35].

2[40]. Here the MT is hopeless. See note *in loc.* I have restored the text in accordance with the claims of the context and that of 7^{23}, and with the help of the LXX of 2^{40}, though here very corrupt.

§ 3. *Interpolation.*

2^{24}. Excise אזל with LXX, Th. and Vulg.

2^{40}. Excise 'and as iron that crusheth all these' with LXX, Th., Pesh., and Vulg.

§ 4. *Lost phrases.*

2^{29}. Restore על לבך after סליקו since the language itself requires it.

2^{34}. Restore מטור with LXX, Th., Vulg., and Josephus. See note *in loc.*

2^{40}. See note *in loc.*

§ 5. *Dislocations.*

$1^{20,21}$. These must be transferred after 2^{49a}. See notes, pp. 52–54. The text absolutely demands this transference.

2^{28c} should be transferred after 2^{30}.

§ 6. *Hebraisms.*

2^{10}. יוכל (cf. תוכל 5^{10}). We should read יֻכַּל as in 3^{29}.

§ 7. *Late Semitic expressions.*

2^{28}. For חזוי ראשך the older language would have used חזוי לבבך: cf. Jer. 23^{16} חזון לב. In the *Aram. Papyri* the same holds true, though visions are not there referred to. See note on $2^{28\,b-29}$.

2^{33}. מנהון · · · מנהון seems to be late Aramaic.

§ 8. *Very late Aramaic order of words.*

2^{28}. מלכא נבוכדנצר. See note *in loc.*: and on 3^{9}. This order appears to be unknown before the time of our author.

§ 9. *Facts pointing to an Aramaic original.*

2^{11}. LXX renders יקיר by ἐπίδοξος (cf. Ezra 4^{10}) as well as by βαρύς. It has both meanings in Aramaic, but in Hebrew it means 'costly', precious.

2^{40}. πᾶν δένδρον = כל אילן where the אילן is corrupt for an ancient reading אלין.

2^{1-2}. Troubled by a dream Nebuchadnezzar summoned his wise men to make known to him the dream he had dreamed, and also its interpretation.

2^{1}. *In the second year.* This second section of the book begins, as in eight sections out of the ten, with the date of the events recorded. The events that follow are said to have occurred in the second year of Nebuchadnezzer's reign. In order to bring this statement into harmony with that of the 'three years' in 1[5,18] various hypotheses have been advanced. (1) Josephus (*Ant.* x. 10. 3) explains this second year as the second year after the sack of Egypt ' (μετὰ δὲ ἔτος δεύτερον τῆς Αἰγύπτου πορθή- σεως). (2) Hengstenberg, Hävernick, Zöckler, and others assume that in 1[1] and Jer. 25[1] Nebuchadnezzer was reigning conjointly with his father Nabopolassar, and that the second year in the text is the second year after Nabopolassar's death. (3) Ewald, Kamphausen, Marti, and others assume that עֶשְׂרֵה dropped out after שְׁתַּיִם (for a like loss, cf. Joshua 24[12]), and that the original text was 'in the twelfth year'. (4) Driver ingeniously defends the text. 'There is not, perhaps, necessarily a contradiction here with the "three years" of 1[5,18]. By Hebrew usage fractions of time were reckoned as full units : thus Samaria, which was besieged from the fourth to the sixth year of Hezekiah, is said to have been taken " at the end ". of three years (2 Kings 18[9,10]) ; and in Jer. 34[14] " at the end of seven years " means evidently when the seventh year has arrived (see also Mark 8[31] &c.). If, now, the author, following a custom which was certainly sometimes adopted by Jewish writers, and which was general in Assyria and Babylonia, "post-dated" the regnal years of a king, i. e. counted as his first year not the year of his accession but the first full year afterwards (see Art. *Chronology* in Hastings's *Dict. of the Bible,* i 400), and if further Nebuchadnezzar gave orders for the education of the Jewish youths in his accession year, the end of his "three years" of 1[5,18] might be reckoned as falling within the king's second year.'

Dreamed dreams. For the use of the plural i. e. 'visions' where a singular is meant we may compare 4[2 (5)], 7[1]. The LXX reproduces the plural, but Th. and Vulg. render it by the singular. On oneiromancy or divination by dreams see *Encyc. Bib.* i. 1118 ; Hastings, *DRE.* iv. 776.

His spirit was troubled. This phrase (רוחו ותתפעם) which recurs in 2[3] (ותפעם רוחו) appears to be suggested by Gen. 41[8].

His sleep †brake† from him. The Hebrew (נהיתה עליו שנתו) literally means ' his sleep was done for him ', i. e. ' left him ', and this text is supported by the LXX and Th., ὁ ὕπνος αὐτοῦ ἐγένετο

i. e. in 8[27] and Micah 2[4], but in both cases the text is doubtful. The same fact is expressed again in 6[19 (18)], שנתה נדת עלוהי, where Th. has ὁ ὕπνος ἀπέστη ἀπ' αὐτοῦ. Now, since Sym. renders the expression here in our text by the very same words, it is reason-able to suppose, with Behrmann, Marti, and others, that he found in 2[1] the exact Hebrew equivalent of the Aramaic in 6[19]. Hence for נהיתה we should read נִדְּרָה. We may then retain the rendering 'his sleep brake from him' as the English equivalent of the emended text. This is the usual verb in this connexion as in 6[19], Esther 6[1], Gen. 31[40]. With this use of עָלָיו, which expresses the dative of advantage or disadvantage, cf. 10[8], והורי נהפך עלי: also 5[9], 7[28], Jer. 8[18], &c.

2[2]. *Commanded to call.* See note on the construction on 1[3].

To call the magicians. The diction of Gen. 41[8] as in the pre-ceding sentence. Th. here supports the MT, but the LXX implies ויאמר · · להביא.

(1) *The magicians.* That the חרטמים stands first in the list of the six classes of diviners is due, as Bevan suggests, to Gen. 41[8]. The Hebrew word is probably derived from חֶרֶט = 'graving tool', 'stylus', with the formative termination -*om*. The word, therefore, would properly mean 'writers' originally. The sense in the O.T. would be secondary. This word is used once alone in our author, 4[6(9)], in a generic sense, where Daniel is called 'master of the magicians' (cf. 5[11]), and six (seven) times in conjunction with other terms, 1[20], 2[2,10,27], 4[6 (9)], ⌐5[7]⌐, 5[11].

(2) *The enchanters,* i.e. אשפים. Probably a Babylonian loan-word, Assyr. *ašipu*, which according to Zimmern (*KAT*[3]. 590, *n.* 1) means 'the purifier'. This word occurs in the Hebrew only here and in 1[20]: in the Aramaic in 2[10,27], 4[4], 5[7,11,15].

(3) *The sorcerers.* Only here in our author, but in the earlier books of the O.T. four times. Robertson-Smith derives מכשפים from כשף 'to cut'. Hence these were primarily persons who prepared magical drugs by shredding herbs into a magic brew (*Journ. Phil.,* xiv. 125, 126). Prince (*Book of Daniel,* p. 201) says that this theory has no foundation in fact, and that כשף is a well-known stem in Babylonian. i. e. Kašâpu, *to bewitch,* and that כֶּשֶׁף *incantation* and כַּשָּׁף *a conjuror* have exact equivalents in the Assyrian *kišpu* and *kaššapu*.

(4) *The Chaldeans.* This, as we have already seen, had an ethnic sense, and subsequently acquired the meaning it generally

bears in our text. See note on 1^4. It occurs five times alone 1^4 (in a general sense), $2^{4,5,10a}$, 3^8, and five times in conjunction with other terms, $2^{2,10b}$, $4^{4(7)}$, $5^{(7),11}$.

. (5) *Wise men* חכימין. Eleven times alone $2^{12,13,14,18,21,24}$ (*bis*),48, $4^{3(6),15(18)}$, $5^{7,8}$, and twice in conjunction with other terms 2^{27}, 5^{15}.

(6) *Determiners.* גזרין : four times 2^{27}, $4^{4(7)}$, $5^{7,11}$. These were probably astrologers or soothsayers. Probably from גזר, *to cut.* Words with this meaning often occur in the sense of determining. Hence we have גְּזֵרָה $4^{14,21}$, *decree* : later it meant *fate.* The determiners drew celestials, charts, and horoscopes, in which the position of the constellations were shown at the moment of one's birth. Cf. Isa. 47^{13}.

Of the above terms the magicians, enchanters, and Chaldeans occur most frequently together, $2^{2,10}$, $4^{4(7)}$, 5^{11}. A comparison of the passages in which the six classes of wise men are mentioned tends to show that they are used very vaguely. They do not correspond to any division found in the inscriptions,' and Lenormant's attempt (*La Magie*, p. 13 sq.) to identify them with certain classes of diviners in Babylon is a failure. For the literature of this subject, see Hastings's *DRE.* viii. 255.

2^{3-11}. The wise men are required to tell the dream and its interpretation. They reply that they are ready to interpret the dream if the king recounts it to them, but that they cannot meet both demands.

2^3. The king had not forgotten the dream, but had determined to test his wise men by requiring them to tell both the dream and its interpretation. Behrmann here mentions an exact parallel to our account in Ibn Hishâm's *Leben Mohammeds* (ed. Wüstenfeld, p. 9 sq.) : ' Rabîa son of Nasr, king of Yemen . . . saw a vision and could not understand it. Thereupon he assembled the diviners, magicians . . . and spake to them. I have had a dream which has terrified me ; tell me it and its interpretation. They replied : Tell us the dream and we will declare unto you its interpretation. Then said he : If I tell you the dream I cannot rely on your interpretation ; for he who knows not the dream, before I communicate it to him, does not know its interpretation.'

2^4. *Then spake . . .* †*in the Syrian language*†. If the text of the MT is retained, then it is better to render 'in Aramaic'.

which is said is given, אמר (= *said*) is almost universally used. It is true that in the MT דבר is used with the meaning apparently of אמר in Gen. 41[17], Exod. 32[7], 1 Kings 21[5], Ezek. 40[4]. Notwithstanding, this usage is abnormal, and the LXX and Vulg. either attest a truer text or emend the existing one in .Exod. 32[7] by presupposing לֵאמֹר, while the Syr. renders דבר in this passage, as if it were אמר. Again the LXX in Gen. 41[17] presupposes the addition of לֵאמֹר, while the Syr. again renders דבר as in Exod. 32[7]. Again in 1 Kings 21[5] the Syr. surmounts the difficulty in the same way, and in Ezek. 40[4] the LXX renders דבר by εἶπεν. Thus the text in Dan. 1[4] is abnormal, but the corrupt reading ארמית suggests the missing word. Hence Marti and Prince, following the suggestion of Haupt in Kamphausen, *Das Buch Daniel*, p. 11, hold that ויאמרו 'and said' should be restored after the words 'to the king', and that this expression was displaced by the corrupt reading ארמית *in Aramaic*. But it is more reasonable to suppose that ארמית is simply a misreading of ויאמרו, the misreading being suggested by the fact that Aramaic did follow.

In any case the words 'in Aramaic' cannot be accepted. Another explanation is offered by Oppert, Lenormant, and others. They suggest that 'in Aramaic' is a gloss, added as in Ezra 4[7] to designate the language of the chapters that follow; that this was the language in which 2[4 b]-7[28] were originally composed, and that this language was retained.

If the text meant to affirm (as it does in its present corrupt form) that Aramaic was used at court in official communications, the narrative in chap. 7 would have been resumed in Hebrew, whereas it is continued in Aramaic. Jerome in his Commentary on 2[4] ('Ab hoc loco usque ad visionem anni tertii regis Balthasar . . . lingua scribuntur Chaldaica) popularized this erroneous view that the wise men spake in Aramaic. Thence arose the false designation of Biblical Aramaic as Chaldee. Biblical Aramaic belongs to the North Semitic branch, which is usually subdivided into (1) Eastern Aramaic or Syriac, which was used by the Christian Syrians, and is found in modified forms in the Babylonian Talmud and the sacred books of the Chaldaeans. (2) Western or Palestinian Aramaic, which is found in Dan. 2[4]-7, Ezra 4[8]-6[18], 7[12-26], the Elphantine Papyri, the Jewish Targums, and the Palestinian Gemara. The nomenclature 'Eastern' and

'Western' is wrong, if taken literally; for, as I have shown in the Introduction, the so-called 'Western' was used by the Foreign Office in Babylon. Aramaic was long the *lingua franca* of the Oriental world. The wise men would have addressed the king in Babylonian or Assyrian, which is declared in Jer. 5^{15}, Isa. 28^{11}, 33^{19} to be unintelligible to a Jew. Assyria and Babylonia had a distinct Semitic language of their own, which maintained itself long after the fall of this empire. 'The latest connected Babylonian inscription is that of Antiochus Soter (280–260 B. c.). See Prince, p. 11 note. Aramaic had displaced Hebrew *as the popular language* long before the second century B.c.

O king, live for ever. The usual mode of saluting Oriental kings. Here as in $3^9, 5^{10}, 6^{6,22}$ the formula is in the second person : in 1 Kings 1^{31}, Neh. 2^3 in the third person—the older form. It had already been used at the Assyrian Court, and subsequently prevailed amongst the Sassanidae. As Prince (p. 66) remarks, this greeting was common in Babylonian times. Cf. *Beiträge zur Assyriologie*, i., p. 239 : 'May Nebo and Merodach give . . . everlasting years unto the king'.

We will show, נְחַוֵּא. So we read with Ginsburg unless with Marti, *Gram.*[3], § 65 c. we transform all the Pa'el forms into Haphel and read נַחֲוֵה. Bauer-Leander prefer the Pa'el.

2^5. *Answered and said.* The MT has here two participles עָנֵה וְאָמַר, but Nöldeke (*Göttingsche Gelehrte Anzeigen*, 1884, 1021) is most probably right in his suggestion that here and in $2^{8,15,20,26,27,47}$, $3^{14,19,24,25,26,28}$, $4^{16,27}$, $5^{7,13,17}$, $6^{13,17,21}$, 7^2, we should punctuate these words as עֲנָה וְאָמַר. For this is the Aramaic idiom where the consonants of the words are unmistakeable as in $2^{7,10}$. $3^{9,16}$, 6^{14}, where we have the finite verb followed by the participle עֲנוֹ · · · וְאָמְרִין. In 5^{10} these two verbs are in the perfect : and in 3^{24} we have two participles עָנַיִן וְאָמְרִין.

The thing †is gone† from me, i. e. the matter has left my memory. This misrendering, found already in Th. (ὁ λόγος ἀπ' ἐμοῦ ἀπέστη and the Vulgate), is now generally rejected. The clause was omitted in the original LXX, but in Origen's text it is supplied from Th. between an asterisk and a metobelus. This rendering originated in the view that אַזְדָּא was a dialectical variety of אֲזַל. Two explanations are given : (1) According to Nöldeke (*K A T*[2] 619), אזדא is a Persian word meaning 'sure', 'certain'. In this case we should render 'the word from me is sure', i. e. 'what I say shall certainly be carried out'. Cf. 3¹⁴ note. (2) According to Andreas (Marti's *Gram.*³, p. 58*) the word is Middle-Persian, and means 'news,' 'intelligence'. In this case we should render : 'the word from me is news', i. e. 'proclaimed'. *Its interpretation.* פשר appears in Eccles. 8¹ as a loan-word from Aramaic.

Ye shall be cut in pieces, הַדָּמִין תִּתְעַבְדוּן, i. e. 'dismembered limb from limb'. Cf. 3²⁹, where the same phrase recurs and the LXX has διαμελισθήσεται. In 2 Macc. 1¹⁶ we find μέλη ποιήσαντες, Jos., *Ant.* xv. 8, 4 μελιστὶ διελόντες προὔθεσαν κυσίν.

But the LXX seems to presuppose a different text here as it reads παραδειγματισθήσεσθε. Possibly it reads as in Ezra 6¹¹, where the punishment of hanging is referred to. It is noteworthy that in Num. 25⁴ παραδειγμάτισον is used to translate the Hebrew word הוֹקַע, where a public execution is meant : cf. ἐξηλιάζειν, 2 Sam. 21⁶·⁹·¹³, but what form the execution took is doubtful. Since the LXX, however, renders the same phrase in 3²⁹ of our text by διαμελισθήσεται, and the Pesh. renders the MT in 2⁵, 3²⁹ literally, it seems best to regard the LXX in 2⁵ as a free rendering, as Th. (εἰς ἀπωλίαν ἔσεσθε) and the Vulg. (peribitis vos) certainly are. Instead of the loose rendering παραδειγματισθήσεσθε 2⁵, the exact rendering would be, as in 3²⁹, διαμελισθήσεσθε. In 1 Esdras 6³¹ we have κρεμασθῆναι in a similar context. Hence the punishment may have been hanging followed by quartering. In Ezra 6¹¹ the punishment appears to be crucifixion.

To return to the MT, the word הַדָּם is the Persian *ändām*, in Zend *haṅdāma*. From the noun is derived the Aramaic verb הַדִּים (similarly in Syriac), 'to dismember'.

Your houses בָּתֵּיכוֹן. On the *daghesh forte* in ת and the *metheg* under the preceding letter, see Kautzsch, *Gram.,* §§ 63 : 12, 2, *e.*

Be made a dunghill. Cf. 3²⁹, Ezra 6¹¹. This was the greatest disgrace that could be inflicted on the memory of the persons executed. Here again the LXX presupposes quite a different text, for it reads ἀναληφθήσεται ὑμῶν τὰ ὑπάρχοντα εἰς τὸ βασιλικόν. This is the text presupposed in Ezra 6¹¹ by the Vulgate, 'domus autem ejus publicetur', and here (2⁵) 'domus vestrae publicabuntur'. See also 1 Esdras 6³¹, κρεμασθῆναι καὶ τὰ ὑπάρχοντα αὐτοῦ εἶναι βασιλικά.

2⁶. *Rewards.* נבזבה is said to be derived from the Persian by Andreas in Marti's *Gram.*³, p. 79*. It recurs in 5¹⁷ and later in the Palestinian Targ., Deut. 23²⁴.

Therefore. לְהֵן. On the various meanings of this word see note on 2¹¹.

2⁷. *Its interpretation* : i. e. וּפִשְׁרֵהּ. So Th., Pesh., and Vulg. The MT has 'the interpretation' as in ver. 4.

2⁸. *Of a certainty.* For the construction מִן־יַצִּיב, cf. מִן־קְשֹׁט in 2⁴⁷. יַצִּיבָה recurs in 3²⁴.

Would gain time. The LXX and Th. render καιρὸν ὑμεῖς ἐξαγοράζετε. The same phrase (verb in mid.) is found in Eph. 5¹⁶, Col. 4⁵. But the sense is different. In our text the object of the magicians is to temporize and defer the fatal moment : in St. Paul to utilize every present opportunity to the full.

Because. On כל־קבל־די see Introd., § 20. *ff,* where it is shown that a long development lies behind this later form. †*Is gone*†. See note on ver. 5.

2⁹. *The judgement upon you is inevitable*, literally, 'there is but one law for you '. Here חדה with the היא following is the same construction as in *Cant.* 6⁹ אחת היא יונתי 'my dove . . . is one ', i. e. 'the incomparable', as in our text it is 'the inevitable'. The word דת is derived from the Persian *dâta.* It occurs frequently in Hebrew and Aramaic of the Persian period—Esther, Ezra, and Daniel, but not found in any of the numerous law documents of the fifth-century Papyri B. c.

For lying and corrupt words. I have here as in the R.V. taken this clause as a ground for the king's forcible decision. But it could with Marti be taken as dependent on 'I know' in ver. 8.

Lying, כדבה. The word כדב occurs nine times in the *Aram. Pap. Fifth Cent.* It is of course the same as the Hebrew כזב.

Have concerted. The *Qr.* has here הִזְדְּמִנְתּוּן (Hithpa'el) : the *Kt.* הַזְמִנְתּוּן (Haph'el).

Know, אִנְדַּע. Here in the imperfect of ידע an epenthetic nun is inserted by way of compensation : Kautzsch, § 11. 2 ; § 43. 1 *b.* Cf. תנדע 2³⁰, ינדעון 4¹⁴, and אִנְבֵּהּ for אִבֵּהּ in 4⁹,¹¹,¹⁸. This is found also in the Targums.

2¹⁰. *The earth.* The Aram. is יבשתא = ἡ ξηρά, 'the dry land ', as in Gen. 1⁹, Jonah 1⁹, but here it is used generally of the earth.

Can יוכל *as* תוכל in 5¹⁶ are imperfect Hoph'als. Marti treats them as Hebraisms (*Gram.*[3], § 59 *b*. 2). The true Aramaic form occurs in 3[29] יִבַּל. In 2[10] the Massoretes allowed the false Hebraism to remain and in 5[16] corrected it wrongly into תכול.

No king, be he never so great and mighty, or *no great and mighty king.* 'Great King' was a title borne by the kings of Assyria: cf. 2 Kings 18[28]. The phrase in our text appears to be a reminiscence of the old Assyrian-Babylonian title.

King. מֶלֶךְ here, אֱבֶן 2[34], צְלֵם 3[5], קֶרֶן 7[8], חֲלֶם 4[2], are regarded as Hebraisms: Kautzsch, *Gram.*, § 54. 1, 2[a].

2[11]. *Difficult.* The LXX gives a duplicate rendering of the Aramaic word, βαρὺς καὶ ἐπίδοξος. יקיר has both these meanings in Aḥ. 93, 95, 111, 130 (see Cowley, pp. 215, 216, 217). יקיר means 'dear', 'costly', 'precious' in Hebrew, but not 'honourable'. In Ezra 4[10] it does mean 'honourable': cf. our text 2[37], 5[18,20], 7[14], where יְקָר means 'honour'. So far as it goes, this is an argument in favour of the LXX being made from an Aramaic original.

Except. So לָהֵן after a negative here and in 3[28], 6[6,8]. Cf. Cowley, 8[11], 13[12], 15[32], &c. In 2[30] it = 'but'. So also Cowley, 9[6,7,9]? In Ezra 5[12] it means 'however' without a preceding negative: cf. Cowley 34[6]. In 2[6,9], 4[24] it = 'therefore'.

2[12-16]. The king gives orders that all the wise men should be slain. At the request of Daniel the execution of this command is adjourned. Daniel, who with his companions was regarded as belonging to the guild of the wise men, promises to find an answer to the king's questions if he is granted time.

2[13]. *The decree went forth,* דתא נֶפְקַת. The rendering τὸ δόγμα ἐξῆλθε is almost identical with Luke 2[2] ἐξῆλθε δόγμα.

That the wise men should be slain. Literally, 'and the wise men were to be slain'. Here Th. followed by the Vulg. wrongly renders ἀπεκτέννυντο. The passive participle מתקטלין here does not express a completed act, as it generally does, but as in Hebrew (*Ges.-Kautzsch,* § 116 *e*) it has a gerundive or future meaning. Thus the LXX expresses, though freely, the thought of our author: ἐδογματίσθη πάντας ἀποκτεῖναι. See Kautzsch, *Gram.,* § 76, 3. The Aramaic idiom here represents, in a co-ordinate clause, what would naturally be represented in a dependent and final clause after a verb of commanding. Cf. Ezra 6[1].

†*Sought Daniel and his companions to be slain*†. The con-

struction here appears to be an illegitimate combination of two constructions. Hence it is reasonable to infer a corruption of the text. Moreover, the LXX and Vulg. represent one construction, while Th. and Syr. represent the other. Now the LXX has ἐζητήθη δὲ ὁ Δανιὴλ καὶ πάντες οἱ μετ' αὐτοῦ χάριν τοῦ συναπολέσθαι, i. e. 'Daniel and his companions were sought to be slain'. Th., on the other hand, ἐζήτησαν Δανιὴλ καὶ τ. φίλους αὐτοῦ ἀνελεῖν, i. e. 'they sought D. and his friends to slay (them)'. We have, therefore, either to change the vocalization of בְּעוֹ (= ἐζήτησαν) into בְּעוֹ, i. e. the passive of the Peal: cf. רְמִיו 3²¹— a suggestion of Marti's, who made it without noticing that it had the support of two Versions: or emend להתקטלה into לקטלה as in the next verse, and so arrive at the text presupposed by Th. and Pesh., i. e. 'they sought D. and his companions to slay (them)'.

2¹⁴. *Then.* בֵּאדַיִן is used by our author to introduce a new section or paragraph. Not so אדין of which it is compounded.

Returned answer with counsel and prudence. In Prov. 26¹⁶ the same phrase is found in Hebrew מְשִׁיבֵי טַעַם.

Arioch. An ancient Babylonian name—generally taken to be a corruption of Eri-aku, 'servant of the moon-god'. It is found in Gen. 14¹ as the name of an ancient king of Ellasar (in South Babylonia), whence it is probably borrowed both here and in Judith 1⁶. According to Sayce in Hastings's *B.D.* the name was of the Sumerian period, but not of the later—Nebuchadnezzar's.

Captain of the guard, רב טבחיא. This expression occurs in 2 Kings 25⁸ ˢqq·, Jer. 39⁹, 52¹² ˢqq·, and as שר־הטבחים in Gen. 37³⁶, 39¹, &c. The word טַבָּחַיָּא here rendered 'guard' originally meant 'slaughterers' or 'butchers' (of animals). Some trace of this may remain in 1 Sam. 9²³,²⁴, where, as in Arabic, it has the signification of 'cook'. The LXX and Th. in the present passage reproduce this meaning and render ἀρχιμάγειρος—a rendering found also in Jubilees 34¹¹, 39². In later times this official was the captain of the king's life guard.

2¹⁵. *Severe,* or 'harsh'. The LXX renders πικρῶς, Th. ἀναιδής. מְהַחְצְפָה contracted מַחְצְפָה 3²²—the Haphel participle of חצף.

2¹⁶. *Went in.* The Aram. verb is the equivalent of the Hebrew בוא. Hpp̄ʿīl יֵּרֶן Cf. תִּנְמוּ Ezra 7²⁰. This verb appears only in the Imperfect and the Infinitive. In 4¹⁴ of our text the ‌ is assimilated as in the Targums. Cf. אֶנְדַּע, ver. 9.

And (so) it would be his task to show the king the interpretation. This appears to be the only right rendering of לְהַחֲוָיָה וּפִשְׁרָא לְמַלְכָּא. The Versions vary. The Vulg. omits the ‌ and renders *ad solutionem indicandam regi.* But this is only shirking the difficulty. Syrʰ (i. e. LXX) and the Pesh. render καὶ δηλώσει (in Cod. 87 we have δηλώσῃ). Th. καὶ ... ἀναγγείλῃ. The last rendering is obviously wrong. Our author does not make such an absurd statement as ‘ Daniel implored the king to give him time that he (Daniel) would show the king, &c.’. Yet Kautzsch, § 102, and most scholars take it to be a final clause. But this seems wrong, and this last clause is co-ordinated with, and not subordinated to, the two preceding clauses ‘went in’ and ‘implored the king’. It does not represent Daniel’s request, but rather Daniel’s promise to the king—‘I will (it is my task to) show the king’. The same construction recurs in ver. 18, where it expresses the sense of obligation as in 5². Daniel said to his companions: ‘ You are to beseech compassion’, (אַתּוּן) רַחֲמִין לְמִבְעֵה. In the indirect this becomes literally, ‘ Daniel went and made known the matter to his companions, and so they undertook to beseech compassion’. On this construction in Hebrew and in Aramaic as early as Ezra, see Introd., § 20. *t.*

2¹⁷⁻²³. In answer to the prayers of Daniel and his companions the secret is revealed to him in a vision of the night, and thanksgiving is offered by him in a hymn for the mercy vouchsafed.

2¹⁸. *And (so) it was their task to implore compassion,* רַחֲמִין לְמִבְעֵה. It is impossible to render this idiom literally in English. The early Greek and Latin translators experienced exactly the same difficulty. The LXX attempts to render this idiom in half a dozen of different ways. The Vulg. evades the difficulty by rendering *ut quaererent*: so also the Pesh. The LXX presupposes a different text. Th. comes nearest the meaning of this idiom: καὶ οἰκτιρμοὺς ἐζήτουν. This idiom here and in 2¹⁶ may be a Hebraism in Aramaic : but see Introd., § 20. *t.* Also my Comm. on Revelation, i. 321-2.

The God of heaven. Cf. 2¹⁹,³⁷,⁴⁴; Ezra 1², 5¹¹,¹², 6⁹, Neh. 1⁴,⁵, 2⁴,²⁰, 1 Enoch 106⁵ (cf. 13⁴), Tob. 10¹¹, Judith 5⁸, 6¹⁹, Rev. 11¹³, 16¹¹. This phrase is found in Gen. 24⁷, but after the Exile it

became a favourite designation of God owing to the growing
transcendence of Jewish thought regarding God.   See note
on 4²⁶.

2¹⁹. *Secret.* רז is a Persian loan-word

Was . . . revealed. גְּלִי, so punctuated in 2³⁰, is the Peʿil, the
passive of the Peʿal.   It is here punctuated as גַּלִּי, and is to be
distinguished from the passive participle גְּלֵא.

The vision of the night. For the Hebrew form of this phrase,
see Isa. 29⁷: cf. Job 4¹³, 7¹⁴, 20⁸. חֶזְוָא an emphatic of חֵזוּ is
used, as the particular form in which the revelation was made
is definitely stated.

2²⁰⁻²³. *Daniel's hymn of praise consists of four stanzas of
tristichs and tetrastichs which alternate with each other.*

2²⁰. *Blessed be . . . God from everlasting to everlasting.*
Literally reproduced here in Aramaic from Ps. 41¹³.   But
Neh. 9⁵ may have been in the mind of the writer, 'Bless the
Lord your God from everlasting to everlasting, and let them
bless thy glorious name'.

The name of God.   This is equivalent to the Being of God—
as revealed or manifested in His dealings with men.   Scholars
in the past have referred to Cant. 3⁷ מִטָּתוֹ שֶׁלִּשְׁלֹמֹה: also 1⁶ as
pleonastic expressions of the genitive in illustration of שְׁמֵהּ דִּי
אֱלָהָא in our text.   The idiom in Cant. 3⁷ is an Aramaic one,
though approximations to it are found in Hebrew: see *Ges.-
Kautzsch*, § 129 *h* and § 135 *m* (foot-note). But that this pleonastic
method of expressing the genitive is as old as the fifth century
B. C. can now be proved from Cowley: see 30¹⁰, 46¹¹; Aḥ. 3, 47,
55: Beh. 2-3, 5, 13, 28.   It is found in an Aram. inscription of
fifth–fourth cent. B. C. in Cilicia: see Cooke 68². This idiom is
quite frequent in Syriac.   Since, however, it is not uncommon
also in Ethiopic (see Dillmann's *Gram. d. Aethiopischen Sprache*,
§ 186. δ (*b*): Praetorius, *Aethiopische Gram.*, § 133) it is not
impossible that it was a primitive Semitic idiom.

Wisdom and might are his.   This sentence is found in
Job 12¹³, save that our text connects with the first clause of
12¹³ the לֹ that belongs to the second clause.   The Targum of
Job reads almost letter for letter as our text חוכמתא וגבורתא דיליה,
though it rightly connects the last word with the clause that
follows.

The wisdom and the might of God are the theme of the

lines that follow. In 2²¹ᵃᵇ the exhibition of God's might is represented, and in 2²¹ᶜᵈ,²² examples of His wisdom. These attributes are in some measure delegated to Daniel in 2²³ to meet the present difficulty, though it is difficult to see how the divine might is exercised by Daniel here. The LXX relieves the text of this difficulty by reading σοφίαν καὶ φρόνησιν in 2²³, though herein it stands alone against the MT, Th., Pesh., Vulg. On the other hand in 2²⁰ Th. stands alone in reading ἡ σοφία καὶ ἡ σύνεσις, where σύνεσις is probably corrupt for δύναμις— the reading of Q.

2²¹. *The times of the world are in the hands of God, and all power and wisdom come from him.*

The seasons and the times (עדניא וזמניא). So LXX and Th. καιροὺς καὶ χρόνους. The 'seasons' are critical periods in the space of time as such, which are determined by God. Cf. Acts 17²⁶ᶜ ὁρίσας προτεταγμένους καιρούς. This distinction appears in Neh. 10³⁴ εἰς καιροὺς χρόνων. In 7¹² of our text the order of the Aramaic words is reversed זמן ועדן, and so the LXX χρόνου καὶ καιροῦ. The phrase has probably been borrowed in Acts 1⁷, 1 Thess. 5¹ from our text. But it should be observed that a definite distinction between these words cannot be established either on the ground of etymology or use. The Targums generally reproduce מועד by זמן and עת by עדן.

Removeth kings and setteth up kings. Though 'kings' (1) is omitted by LXX, Th., and Vulg., the number of beats require it. Cf. 2 Chron. 20⁶ 'Art not thou ruler over all the kingdoms of the nations?'

Giveth wisdom. Cf. Sir. 1¹ πᾶσα σοφία παρὰ κυρίου. Wisdom is given to him that already possesses it in some measure, and knowledge to them that study to have understanding. Cf. Prov. 4¹.

2²². *Revealeth the deep . . . things.* Cf. Job 12²², where this phrase is found.

נְהִירָא. So the *Kt.*, which the *Qr.* corrects into נְהוֹרָא, which is the ordinary form in the later Jewish Aramaic (cf. Dalman, *Gram.*, § 28. 6). The absolute form נַהִירוּ occurs in 5¹¹,¹⁴.

What. Here מה as in Ezra 6⁹ can be used as the equivalent of מה די, just as in the *Aram. Pap.* (see Cowley 38⁶,⁹, Aḥ. 79, 163, 177).

Dwelleth. שָׁרֵא is here a participle, passive in form but not

so in meaning. 'This use of the passive participle is frequent
in Syriac, e. g. ḳĕne "having obtained " . . . as contrasted with
ḳānē " obtaining "—similar is Hebrew לָבוּשׁ "having put on "'
(Bevan). Cf. Nöldeke, *Syr. Gram.*, § 280. The thought of the
clause is put conversely in 1 John 1⁷ αὐτός ἐστιν ἐν τῷ φωτί, and in
1 Tim. 6¹⁶.

2²³. *God of my fathers.* This phrase occurs in 2 Chron. 20⁶
as 'God of our fathers', and in Deut. 1²¹, 6³, 12¹, 26⁷, &c. as
'God of thy fathers'. Daniel closes his hymn with a thanksgiving to the God who, unchanged among all the changes and
chances of the world's history, had always been the Defender
and Saviour of His people. Daniel uses these words in
remembrance of the great deliverances Yahweh had wrought
for Israel in the past. Cf. 2 Chron. 20⁶⁻¹². אֲבָהָתִי, and not
the Hebraized אֲבֹתַי, is to be read.

Wisdom and insight. I have here followed the LXX, which
reads σοφίαν καὶ φρόνησιν. The corruption can be explained
through a scribe's assimilation of the phrase here to that in 2²⁰.
φρόνησις implies שָׂכְלְתָנוּ (cf. 1¹⁷ where it is a rendering of the
Hebrew השכל), which our author uses in 5¹¹,¹²,¹⁴. The MT
reads נבורתא.

Hast given. With the shortened form יְהַבְתְּ, which is given
by Ginsburg and Strack, we may compare תְּקֵפְתְּ 4¹⁹, עֲבַרְתְּ 4³²,
and הַשְׁפֵּלְתְּ 5²². Marti edits יְהַבְתְּ, and certainly the longer form
is more usual in Biblical Aramaic: cf. חֲוִיתָה *bis* in 2⁴¹.

Hast made known, i. e. הוֹדַעְתֶּנָא (so most editions). The MT
has הוֹדַעְתְּנָא, which Marti, *Gram.*³, § 50 *b* (foot-note) regards as
a Hebraism, but Kautzsch, § 37. 2, as a pausal form of הוֹדַעְתַּנָא
which gives the correct form of the first personal suffix with
pathach.

2²⁴⁻³⁰. *Daniel is brought at his own request by Arioch into the
king's presence, and declares his readiness to make known the dream
and its interpretations.*

2²⁴. *Went in.* According to Loehr 10 Hebrew MSS. omit
עַל, but he adds wrongly that the LXX and Th. do so also;
for the LXX, Th., and Vulg. support 'went in' by their
respective renderings εἰσῆλθε, ἦλθεν, and ingressus, but all three
omit אֲזַל, which is the ninth word later in the Aramaic text.
Marti agrees with Loehr, and treats the verb עַל as a dittograph
of the preposition עַל which follows. He further adds that אֲזַל

often stands at the close of the sentence in Aramaic. The last
argument is of no weight. Outside the present passage in
Biblical Aramaic אֲזַל stands at the beginning of three clauses.
D 6¹⁹, E 4²³, 5⁸, and at the close in two, D 2¹⁷, 6²⁰. But the
LXX, Th., and Vulg. are against the omission of עַל, as we have
just seen. Only the Pesh. supports the MT with both עַל and
אֲזַל. The MT cannot, so far as the Versions go, be older
than the Pesh. It should be noted also that the LXX renders
the neuter and active moods of עֲלַל by εἰσέρχεσθαι or εἰσάγειν, but
אֲזַל by ἀπέρχεσθαι or πορεύεσθαι. It is true that the Haph'el of עֲלַל
is followed by לְ with acc. of person in 2²⁵, or by acc. without לְ
6¹⁹. Hence the fact that the Pe'al is followed by עַל with person
is not surprising. This construction is found in the Targ. of
Isa. 54¹⁴, but not in the Fifth Cent. Papyri. This preposition
(= Hebrew אֶל) is used in 6⁷ in the same sense as it is used here.
Even in Hebrew עַל is used in a few passages after בּוֹא (of which
עֲלַל is the Aram. equivalent): cf. 2 Sam. 15⁴, 1 Chron. 12²³,²⁴,
and after הֲלַך in 1 Sam. 2¹¹. In Jer. 19¹⁵, 26¹⁵ עַל is used apparently interchangeably with אֶל in the Hebrew.

Had appointed. מַנִּי (cf. 2⁴⁹, 3¹²) is found in this sense in the
Aram. Pap. See Cowley 27⁹, Aḥ. 37, and also in the sense of
'to number' in 21⁴, as also in our text 5²⁶.

[*He went.*] See preceding note.

Bring me in. In הַעֲלֻנִי the suffix is added directly to the verb,
without the pathach which generally precedes the suffix. Cf.
יְשֵׁיזְבִנְכוֹן in 3¹⁵ and יִשְׁאֲלֶנְכוֹן in E 7²¹, which Marti (*Gram.*³, § 50 *b*,
note 2) calls energetic Haph'el imperfects with כוֹן־.

2²⁵. *Brought in*—הַנְעֵל. See note on 2⁹ on the epenthetic nun.

Said thus unto him. We should expect 'said thus before
him', but our author has used the phrase '*before* the king' in
the preceding clause: see notes on 3⁹, 6⁷⁽⁶⁾, and Introd.

I have found. הַשְׁכַּחַת. This form of the Haph'el is due to the
throwing back of the tone (as in הִתְמְוֹרֶת 2³⁴ for הִתְמְוֹרֶת) and the
influence of the guttural ח.

Children of the exiles. Cf. 1³, where the text has been restored
by the help of Th. (and the LXX), together with this passage.

Judah, i. e. Judaea. יְהוּד is found in the *Aram. Pap.*: see
Cowley 30¹, 31¹⁸. Bevan and Marti (*Gram.*³, § 68 *b*) take this
to be a secondary formation from יהודי, and to mean collectively
'the Jews'. But the *Aram. Pap.* are decisively in favour of its

being a territorial designation. So also the LXX, Th., and Vulg. in this passage.

The interpretation = the dream and its interpretation as in 2[16,24].

2[26]. *Able.* כהל has been taken by Bevan, Behrmann, and others to be a secondary formation from the Hebrew כול and יכל. Indeed Behrmann and Prince assert that it is peculiar to Daniel, its subsequent appearance in the Targums being due to Daniel. But this word is found nearly a score of times in the *Aram. Pap.* of the fifth century.

2[28]. *It is not wise men*, &c. The separation of the negative from the verb is done with an object. It is placed before 'wise men, enchanters, &c.' to emphasize that they cannot, but God can, make known what the king requires.

Determiners. See note on 2[2].

2[28 a]. *In the latter days* (באחרית יומיא = Hebrew באחרית הימים = in Targums בסוף יומיא), lit. 'in the end of the days'. The meaning of this phrase, which occurs fourteen times in the O.T., varies according to the outlook of the writer. In Gen. 49[1], Num. 24[14], Deut. 31[29] (4[30]), Dan. 10[14] it is used of various crises in Israel's history from the settlement in Canaan onwards down to the time of Antiochus Epiphanes. In other passages, as in Ezek. 38[16], Hos. 3[5], Isa. 2[2] (= Mic. 4[1]), Jer. 48[47], Dan. 2[28], &c., it refers to events and periods still in the future connected with the Messianic age. This biblical phrase recurs in the Zadokite Fragments 6[2], 8[10], 2 Bar. 10[3], 25[1]. It assumes many forms: 'the end of the ages', T. Lev. 14[1], 2 Bar. 59[8]; 'the last days', 4 Ezra 13[18]; 'the consummation of the time(s)', 2 Bar. 13[3], 19[5], 21[8], 27[15], 29[8], 30[3], 59[4]; 'the time of the end', Dan. 12[4]; 'the end', Dan. 7[26]; 'the end of the first age', 4 Ezra 6[7]; 'the end of this age', 4 Ezra 6[113]. For further forms of this phrase see the Index to my edition of the *Apoc. and Pseudep.*, vol. ii, under such headings as 'Consummated', 'Day', 'End', 'Hours', 'Times'.

The above phrases exhibit different nuances according to the contexts in which they occur, but they all agree in having an eschatological meaning. But there is another point to be remarked. The phrase in our text is an early Hebraism; for in all the passages in the O.T. where the Targums reproduce it they render אחרית by סוף.

King Nebuchadnezzar (so LXX and Th.). This order of the words is not found in Aramaic before the time of our author. In the *Aram. Papyri* of the fifth century B.C. the order is invariably 'N. the King'. So also in Ezra. Hence so far as our text gives the above order, it is unquestionably late. See note on 3[9], where it gives the right order: also Introd.

2[29]. *As for thee, O king.* These words follow naturally on 2[28b]: 2[28c] is clearly an intrusion in its present position, but full of significance if restored after 2[30].

Afterwards. אחרי דנה. אחרי used to be regarded as a Hebraism for באתר, but it is of frequent occurrence in the *Aram. Pap.*

2[30]. *But as for me.* These words following 'as for thee, O king', ver. 29, bring prominently before us the two chief actors in the scene.

Here, as Joseph in Gen. 41[16], Daniel declares that the power of interpretation comes not of his own wisdom but from God.

Is . . . revealed. גְּלִי. See note on 2[19].

To the intent that. על דברת די. Cf. Eccles. 3[18], 7[14], 8[2].

May be made known. יהודעון 'they shall make known'. The 3rd pers. pl. active is often used where in English we should use a 3rd sing. passive, and so LXX rightly renders ἕνεκεν τοῦ δηλωθῆναι τῷ βασιλεῖ. This use of the plural recurs in 3[4], 4[13],(16),22 (25),29(32), 5[20,29]. It is, as Bevan remarks, a favourite construction in the Mishnah.

2[28c]. I have restored this sentence to its most reasonable place after 2[30]. It forms an immediate introduction to 2[31 sqq]. The text underwent corruption early and likewise transposition. Thus the LXX omits through hmt. 2[28b–29a], i.e. what appears in MT, Th., Vulg. as τὸ ἐνύπνιόν σου . . . μετὰ ταῦτα. But happily it has been preserved in Syro-Hexaplar version of Paul of Tella. It is as follows: βασιλευ εις τον αιωνα ζηθι. το ενυπνιον και το οραμα της κεφαλης σου επι της κοιτης σου τουτο εστι· συ βασιλευ κατακλιθεις επι της κοιτης σου εωρακας παντα οσα δει γενεσθαι επι εσχατων των ημερων. Where the text has רעיונך על משכבך סליקו, Syr[h] has as its equivalent κατακλιθεὶς ἐπὶ τῆς κοίτης σου ἑώρακας. It seems impossible to recover the original here. It is noteworthy that the Vulgate translator experienced a difficulty here, since it reads as follows: 'cogitare coepisti in strato tuo'. In the midst of this confusion and doubt it will perhaps be most prudent to retain סליקו and regard it as defective, for the phrase we actually find in the Syr. Version of this passage—a well-known O.T. expression. Cf. על לבך ס״ Isa. 65[17], Jer. 3[16], Ezek. 38[10] (על לבך · · יעלו). The same phrase recurs in 4 Ezra 3[2], 'cogitationes meae ascendebant super cor meum': Acts 7[23]. The heart was regarded as the seat of thought by our author as by the Hebrew writers: cf. 2[30] 'thoughts of thy heart': also 7[28]. The seat of visions, however, was the head: cf. 2[28], 4[2,7,10], 7[1,15]. This expression I cannot find before Daniel. The older prophets would have spoken of חזון לב as Jer. 23[16]. In the *Aram. Pap.* לבב is used as the seat of emotion and thought: see Cowley, p. 294. ראש is never so used in the Papyri.

Thy dream and the visions of thy head . . . are these. These words can claim only here to be in their appropriate context. On grammatical grounds Marti raises the objection that דנה הוא can only refer to חלמך, But, as Kautzsch (§ 97. 1 (b)) points out, the connexion between the subject and predicate is at times so loose as to amount to an anacoluthon. On 7[1], where the same two phrases recur, Bevan regards 'the visions of thy head' as a further specification of the dream.

Visions of thy head. See close of first paragraph on 2[28c].

2[31-35]. The king's dream.

2[31]. *Behold.* אֲלוּ also in 4[7,10], 7[8]—and the form of ארו 7[2,5—7,13]. הלו is found in an inscription (4th cent. B.C.) on a fragment of pottery at Elephantine. See CIS. ii. 137. A¹, B⁴: Assyr. Lett. 9, 11, 13 (7th cent.): Cf. Lidz. *Eph.* ii. 230.

A. חד has here the meaning of the indefinite article as in Ezra 4[8]. But it has this meaning also in the *Aram. Pap.*: see Cowley 30[19,29], &c. The Hebrew אחד is similarly used in 1 Sam. 6[7], 24[15], 1 Kings 19[4].

Its brightness. זיו is believed to be a loan-word from the Assyrian 'zîmu'. See Oxford Heb. Lex.

2[32]. *As for this image.* Since הוא is not properly a demonstrative pronoun, its literal rendering would be 'it, the image', just as in 2[29] אנתה מלכא = 'thou the king'.

His breast. חדוהי from חדי found in the Syr., Targums, and New Hebrew. In Hebrew the form is חָזֶה, which is used only of sacrificial animals: Exod. 29[26], Lev. 7[30], &c.: so also in the Targums. The root occurs in Arabic. See Kautzsch, § 10. 1 (a).

His belly. מעוהי has the same meaning here as מעים in Cant. 5[14].

2³³. *Part . . . part.* *Qr.* reads here מנהין ‧ ‧ ‧ מנהין. This idiom is not found so far as I am aware in Earlier Aramaic. It is found exactly as here in the Syr. of 2 Tim. 2²⁰. In our text it recurs in 2⁴¹.

Clay. חסף is found in most of the Semitic languages.

2³⁴. *Was cut out.* הִתְגְּזֶרֶת as הַדְּקֶת, which follows in the next clause, and אֲמֶרֶת 5¹⁰ are segholate formations for הִתְגַּזְרַת, &c. Behrmann thinks that אבן is a Hebrew loan-word here. But it is found in the Aram. Pap. fifth cent. frequently.

From a mountain. After אֶבֶן we should restore the lost phrase מִטּוּר with the LXX, Th., and Joseph., *Ant.* x. 10. 4, all of which read here ἐξ ὄρους after λίθος. The Vulg. supports these Versions by reading 'de monte'. The Aramaic text 2⁴⁵ requires the above restoration; for there we find the emphatic form מִטּוּרָא, a fact which implies that *the mountain in question was previously mentioned.*

Smote. Ginsburg and Baer read מְחַת instead of מְחָת. The verb itself is found in the *Aram. Pap.*: Cowley, Aḥ. 82.

2³⁵. *The clay, the iron.* I have with Th. thus changed the order of these two expressions. I have followed Th. against the MT, LXX, Vulg. on the two following grounds. The first is that in 2⁴⁵, where the same text recurs, the LXX, Th., and Vulg. attest the order given in Th. in 2³⁵. The second is still stronger. If we look back to 2³²,³³ we see that the constituents of the image are mentioned in the following order (according to the MT and all the versions) as the narrator enumerates them from the head to the feet—head of gold, arms of silver, belly of brass, legs of iron, feet of iron and clay. Now, if the narrator wishes to enumerate afresh these substances, he would do so naturally, either in the order already given from the head downwards (as Joseph., *Ant.* x. 10. 4)— gold, silver, brass, iron, clay; or since the destruction began with the feet of clay, he would more fittingly enumerate them backwards, i. e. from the feet upwards. Thus we should have clay, iron, brass, silver, gold, as in Th. in 2³⁵, and in the LXX, Th., and Vulg. in 2⁴⁵. Accordingly both in 2³⁵ and likewise in 2⁴⁵ the order of the MT must be corrected as we have above seen. We may remark that the Pesh. follows the MT in both verses, and that Joseph., *Ant.* x. 10. 4, omits the clay constituent.

Broken in pieces—דְּקוּ to be so punctuated from דקק. See Kautzsch, § 46. 3: Marti, *Gram.*[3], § 66 c.

Together. כַּחֲדָה. This idiom is found in *Aram. Pap.*: Cowley 28[3]: also in late Hebrew כאחד—Ezra 2[64], 3[9], Eccles. 11[6], Isa. 65[25]. In the Classical Hebrew the phrase was יַחְדָּו. It is rendered by Th. by εἰς ἅπαξ, and by the LXX by ἅμα or ὁμοῦ, as also in Isa. 65[25]. It must not be confounded, as it has been by some scholars, with the Greek classical phrase καθ᾽ ἕνα or καθ᾽ ἕνα ἕκαστον = 'one by one'. The Hebrew for the latter would be לְאחד אחד Isa. 27[12]: cf. Eccles. 7[27].

Threshing-floors. אַדַּר occurs here for the first time, but it is of common occurrence in later Aramaic (Targums and Syr.).

Summer. קיט where Hebrew is קיץ, just as טור (=mountain) is the equivalent of the Hebrew צור.

No place was found for them. Reproduced exactly in Rev. 20[11] τόπος οὐχ εὑρέθη αὐτοῖς. Behrmann, followed by Marti, attaches to אתר the meaning of 'trace' by connecting it with an Arabic root. But אֲתַר does not admit of this meaning in Aramaic. In Aramaic it means 'place' as in Ezra 5[15], 6[3,5,7]. It is also found in *Aram. Pap.* fifth cent. The LXX has here ὥστε μηδὲν καταλειφθῆναι ἐξ αὐτῶν. Here the translator did not find אתר in his text. But there is a further anomaly. Seemingly the translator has rendered הִשְׁתְּכַח as if it were a Hebrew word, the Hithp. of שׁכח, which in Hebrew means 'to forget', but in Aramaic 'to find'. The Hebrew verb is twice rendered by καταλείπω in the LXX in Isa. 17[10], 23[15], just as in our text. This slip is strange, seeing that several times (cf. 2[25]) in this book the translator renders it correctly. Hence we are obliged to assume the other alternative, and this is that instead of השתכח the translator found the corrupt form השתביק.

Filled. מְלָאת (so Baer and Bevan): Ginsburg and Strack read מְלָאת.

A great mountain. This is a symbol of the Messianic kingdom: cf. Ezek. 17[22-24].

2[36-45]. The interpretation of the dream.

2[36]. *We will tell.* Daniel here acknowledges the spiritual help of his friends 2[13], just as in 2[17] he asks them to implore the help of God: in 2[23] he acknowledges that God has made known to them the thing they besought of Him. It follows naturally, therefore, that 1[20-21] should be restored to its right position after 2^{49a}; for in 1^{20-21} we are told that the king found Daniel and his three brethren ten times better than all the wise men of Babylon. The interpretation of the dream by Daniel with the help of his three brethren justifies this conclusion of the king.

2^{37}. *King of kings.* This was the usual title of the Persian kings: cf. Ezra 7^{12}. It is applied to Nebuchadnezzar in Ezek. 26^7, though 'Great king' was the usual title among the Assyrians: cf. Isa. 36^4. Bertholet and others doubt the genuineness of the title in Ezek.

Unto whom the God of heaven hath given. As already in 2^{21} our author declares that all kings owe their sovereignty to God. This was already the assured belief of Jeremiah, 25^9, 27^6, as well as of the later Isaiah, 44^{28}, 45^1.

2^{38}. *Wheresoever the children of men dwell . . . hath he given into thy hand.* The Aramaic of this clause was a source of difficulty to the Greek, Syriac, and Latin translators, as it has been some of our modern scholars. The Aramaic of the MT is as follows: בכל די דארין בני אנשא. The difficulty lies in בכל די. Pesh. and Vulg. presupposes כל אתר די דארין בה בני אנשא, save that the Vulg. omits אתר. But Th., which reads ἐν παντὶ τόπῳ ὅπου κατοικοῦσιν οἱ υἱοὶ τ. ἀνθρ., supports the Pesh. save that it does not omit ב before כל. The LXX renders freely ἐν πάσῃ τῇ οἰκουμένῃ ἀπὸ ἀνθρώπων. All these versions define the extent of the sphere over which the king rules. Hence it follows that the definition of this sphere is given in the phrase בכל די, which the English Bible has rendered by 'wheresoever'. But Marti questions this rendering, and both he and Behrmann maintain that we have here an anacolouthon. They explain this anacolouthon by suggesting that, when our author began with בכל די, he was intending to make these words the object of the second verb השלטך, but then, without thought of what he had already written, inserted יהב בידך. He then resumed the various things subject to the king's sway under the phrase בכלהון. But this explanation lands us in the following impossible text: 'Over all that dwell, the sons of men . . . he hath made thee to rule'. This gives no sense. The sphere of the king's rule is not defined. It is said to be 'men that dwell'. But where do they dwell? Hence we must find the note of locality in בכל די, and the whole clause that it introduces must be taken loosely as the object of

בכל די .יהב בידך is a difficult phrase, but it is not beyond explanation. די in Ezra 6³ = 'where', but the Hebrew relative
אשר never has this meaning. Hence when we find באשר
meaning 'where' in Hebrew (Ruth 1¹⁶,¹⁷, Job 39³⁰, Eccles. 8⁴),
it is due to the ב. In Hebrew we find an exact parallel to
בכל די, i.e. בכל אשר in Joshua 1⁷,⁹, Judges 2¹⁵, &c., but in every
passage this latter phrase means not 'where' but 'whither'.
Hence the Hebrew and the Aramaic phrases differ in meaning,
though each individual particle of the phrase in the one has the
same general meaning as in the other. Since the Pesh.
presupposes כל אתר די, and Th. and the LXX presuppose
בכל אתר די, it is not improbable that the text once read as בכל
אתר די—which would not however differ in meaning from the MT.

Dwell. 'Instead of the older דארין ּ ּ the *Qr.* has דירין, which
is the ordinary form in Syriac, cf. also קאמין (*Qr.* קימין) 3³, זאעין
(*Qr.* זיעין) 5¹⁹ . . . but in the stat. emph. of the Plural the א is
allowed to stand (קאמיא 7¹⁶).' Bevan. See Kautzsch, § 45. 3 *d*:
Marti, § 13 *b*. Formations without א appear to have maintained
themselves in use exclusively as nouns.

The beasts of the field. Derived from Jer. 27⁶, 28¹⁴.

The fowls of heaven. Cf. Judith 11⁷, 1 Bar. 3¹⁶,¹⁷. The latter
passage refers implicitly to Nebuchadnezzar and so to our text.

2³⁹. The second and third kingdoms, which are here briefly
referred to, are the Median and Persian. According to the
view of our author Darius 'the Mede' (5³¹, 9¹, 11¹) received the
kingdom on the overthrow of Belshazzar. How long he reigned
we are not told. Only his first year is referred to definitely in
7¹. On his death he was succeeded by Cyrus 'the Persian'
(6²⁸, 10¹). The Median kingdom is said in this verse to be
inferior to the Assyrian, and in 8³ to the Persian.

Another. אחרי the absol. stat. feminine of אחרן. The ת has
been lost as in מלכו for מַלְכוּת.

Inferior to thee, ארעא מנך. Cf. Targ. on Ruth 4⁴: also ארע מן
עֵלָּא מִן 6³ of our text.

2⁴⁰. Our author becomes more definite in his account of the
Fourth Empire—the Macedonian. This kingdom is symbolized
by iron in reference to its power under its founder Alexander.
Its division into several kingdoms and the relative strength and
weakness of these are symbolized by the mingling of iron and
clay.

Shall be strong as iron. By an oversight the LXX omitted ὡς ὁ σίδηρος, which was restored to it from Th. most probably.

Forasmuch as iron breaketh in pieces and shattereth all things : [*and as iron that crusheth*] *all these* (וכפרזלא די־מרעע) *shall it break in pieces and crush.* So the MT, which is obviously corrupt. The clause in brackets is either a dittograph of the preceding clause, or it is possibly a corruption of a phrase belonging to the close of the verse, the original of which is found only in the LXX. In any case the clause in brackets must be rejected. It has against it the united testimony of Th., Pesh., and Vulg., which in all other respects support the MT, save that they presuppose כן = 'so' before כל אלין.

When this bracketed clause is excised, we must connect כל אלין with the words that follow contrary to the accents, and we attain thereby a better text : 'Forasmuch as iron breaketh in pieces and shattereth all things, (so) all these shall it break in pieces and crush'.

But can this text be right ? It certainly was the accepted text from A. D. 150 to 300. But it is hard to explain the corrupt text of the LXX from it. And still more important, *it does not supply the conclusion that the context requires.* For what can the phrase 'all these' possibly mean ? It does not mean the preceding three world empires ; for the fourth has already taken their place. Instead of the vague and unmeaning phrase 'all these', *the preceding verses, with their clear definition of the extent of the sphere of rule exercised by the first and third empires, lead us to expect something equally clear and intelligible.* As 2[38] states that God had assigned the sovereignty over all men and beasts and birds under heaven to the first empire, and 2[39] that the third empire should bear 'rule over all the earth', so here 2[40], since the fourth empire is described as being as 'strong as iron that shattereth all things', we should expect to find in 2[40] two statements : (1) that the fourth empire would be a destructive power : (2) that it would exercise this power over all that came beneath its sway, i. e. *all the earth.* Such is the conclusion that we are led to expect by what precedes. Now to justify this conclusion we can appeal to the LXX, which in this verse is otherwise very corrupt.

The LXX reads as follows : ὥσπερ ὁ σίδηρος ὁ δαμάζων πάντα καὶ

*ὡς ὁ σίδηρος[1] πᾶν δένδρον ἐκκόπτων· καὶ σεισθήσεται πᾶσα ἡ γῆ. First of all, δένδρον = אֵילִין, which is obviously a corruption of אִלֵּין = 'these'. Now if we omit ὡς ὁ σίδηρος and the preceding καί, the LXX reads: ὥσπερ ὁ σίδηρος ὁ δαμάζων πάντα, πᾶν †δένδρον† ἐκκόπτων. How did the ἐκκόπτων originate? Since the corruption in the Aramaic (אֵילִין = δένδρον) made the text meaningless, it led to the false correction of מהדק which precedes into מגדר = ἐκκόπτων. Cf. 4[11] of our text, where the MT has actually this phrase גֹּדּוּ אִילָנָא (LXX ἐκκόψατε αὐτό, Th. ἐκκόψατε τὸ δένδρον). Thus to begin with the LXX presupposes כל די קבל פרזלא חשל כלא כל אלין תדק = 'Forasmuch as iron shattereth all things, all these shall it break in pieces'. Thus so far, the LXX presupposes a text agreeing word for word with the text presupposed by Th., Pesh., Vulg., save that it omits 'breaketh in pieces and', and agrees with the MT. in reading the unsatisfactory 'all these' or the equally unsatisfactory 'so all these' with the Pesh. and Vulg.

But the LXX adds the clause καὶ σεισθήσεται πᾶσα ἡ γῆ. Is this clause an interpolation or is it original? A comparison of this verse with 7[23] is in favour of the latter view. In both passages we have an interpretation of the fourth kingdom and its powers. In 7[23] this kingdom it is said 'shall consume the whole earth ... and break it in pieces' (ותאכל כל ארעא · · · ותדקנה). Surely this passage throws light on the last clause of this verse in the LXX καὶ σεισθήσεται πᾶσα ἡ γῆ. σεισθήσεται (= תְּזוּעַ: cf. Targ. Is. 24[19]) is here wholly unsuitable, and implies a corruption in the Aramaic. וּתְזוּעַ (intransitive), is an easy corruption of וְתֵרַע. But the reading of the MT πᾶσα ἡ γῆ in the LXX still calls for explanation. Since תֵּרַע is transitive we must read πᾶσαν τὴν γῆν. But how are we to account for כל ארעא (i. e. πᾶσα ἡ γῆ)? However it is to be explained, I accept it as the original text. The evidence of the LXX, where the translator was translating a corrupt and unintelligible text, and of the almost perfect parallel in 7[23] supporting the reading כל ארעא is sufficiently convincing. It is possible that even the MT preserves in the rejected clause די מרעע a corruption of the original text. Even the כל אלין (in the LXX כל אילן) which the MT has preserved may be a corruption of the original כל ארעא. It is a matter of demonstration that the Semitic MSS. of Daniel sometimes contained three

---

[1] Originally wanting in LXX and supplied from some version. The metabolus is wanting in the MS., but not the asterisk.

different forms of this same phrase, two of which were corrupt?
The translator of the LXX rendered literally the text he had
before him, however corrupt.

The conclusion of this long discussion then is that, whereas
די מרעע of the Mass. must be rejected either as a dittograph of
a preceding phrase or rather as a corruption of כל ארעא, we must
further excise כל אלין in MT, Th., Pesh., Vulg. as a corrupt
dittograph of the same phrase. The LXX alone preserves the
original phrase, but, as is frequently the case in this version, it
also contains in כל אילן another corruption of the same phrase.

We have thus arrived at the following satisfactory text : 'And
the fourth kingdom shall be strong as iron : forasmuch as iron
breaketh in pieces and shattereth all things, so shall it break in
pieces and crush the whole earth.'

2[41]. *Whereas.* So די also in 2[43], 4[20,23].

Part. On מנהון see 2[33] above, and 2[42] following.

A divided kingdom. These words refer to the dismemberment
of Alexander's kingdom among his Diadochi. See 11[5] note.

Strength. The dismembered kingdom shall still possess
elements of strength since together with clay iron forms a main
constituent of the feet. נצבתא 'strength': cf. the root in יציב,
2[45], 2[8], 6[13], 7[16]. This is the more likely meaning than that of
'root' as in Th., Pesh.

Miry clay. טינא is possibly a gloss. Th. omits. But the LXX,
Pesh., and Vulg. attest it.

2[42-43]. These two verses are omitted by Josephus, *Ant.* x. 10. 4.

2[42]. *Part.* מן־קצת. Cf. 1[2]. This expression is identical in
meaning with מנּה that follows. It is found in the *Aram. Pap.*,
Cowley, 29[3], 35[4].

2[43]. This verse refers to the marriages between the Seleucidae
(i. e. the iron) and the Ptolemies (i. e. the clay). For the details
see notes on 11[6,17].

They shall mingle themselves, i. e. by marriage alliances. The
kingdoms are here regarded as impersonated in their kings.
Hence the masculine.

On the form לֶהֱוֹן, see Introd., § 20. *s.*

Seed of men. The phrase זרע אנשא may be derived from
Jer. 31[27].

Even as. In הֵא־כְדִי we have a demonstrative particle prefixed
to כְ for greater definiteness. So Oxf. Heb. Lex.

2⁴⁴. *In the days* : i. e. of the Seleucidae, more particularly of Antiochus Epiphanes (175–164 B.C.) during whose reign the advent of the kingdom was expected.

Those. אֲנוּן. See Introd., § 20. *h.*

Shall . . . set up. יְקִים. Here as in 4¹⁴ we have the shorter form of this verb. Cf. תקים 6⁹ : in 5²¹, 6¹⁶ the fuller form יהקים (see Kautzsch, § 45. 4 *b*).

The kingdom : i. e. מַלְכוּתָה. The LXX has αὕτη ἡ βασιλεία, which supports the text and rendering. Th. reads ἡ βασιλεία αὐτοῦ, i. e. מַלְכוּתֵהּ. This is followed by the R.V. which renders ' the sovereignty thereof'.

Shall be left, i. e. תִּשְׁתְּבִק. Since the LXX reads ἐάσῃ it found תִּשְׁבֵק which has exactly this sense in Ezra 6⁷ and also in our author in 4²⁰⁽²³⁾, where Th. renders it by ἐᾶν, as the LXX does here.

2⁴⁵. *The clay, the iron, the brass.* So LXX, Th., and Vulg. MT. wrongly transposes 'the clay' after 'the brass'. See note on 2³⁵.

A great God. In the presence of a heathen monarch Daniel uses the indefinite expression of our text. The MT, Th., and the R.V. wrongly render it 'the great God'.

The dream is certain. Daniel concludes with a solemn affirmation of the truth of the dream and its interpretation after the manner of Apocalypses : cf. 8²⁶, 11², 10¹, Rev. 19⁹, 21⁵, 22⁶.

Sure. מְהֵימַן, which recurs in 6⁵ is the Haph'el participle of חֵימַן.

2⁴⁶. That the homage rendered to Daniel by the king was not simply such as was paid to Haman in Esther 3² is clear from his command 'to offer an oblation and sweet odours' to Daniel. As Bevan well remarks : 'We need not stop to inquire whether a strict monotheist would suffer himself to be thus worshipped, for the whole description is evidently ideal—Nebuchadnezzar at the feet of Daniel represents the Gentile power humbled before Israel (cf. Isa. 49²³, 60¹⁴)'. We have a good parallel in the legendary account of Josephus (*Ant.* xi. 8. 5), according to which Alexander prostrated himself before the Jewish high priest, and justified himself for doing so, when Parmenio, one of his generals, remonstrated with him, in the words : 'I did not adore (προσεκύνησα) him, but that God who had honoured him with his high priesthood'. Porphyry, according to Jerome (*In Dan.* 2⁴⁶),

attacked this passage on the ground that the proudest of kings
would not have worshipped one of his captives. Jerome supports the text by referring to the attempt of the Lycaonians to
worship Paul and Barnabas, and justifies the action of Nebuchadnezzar in practically similar terms to those he found in the
above passage of Josephus: 'Non tam Danielem quam in
Daniele adorat Deum, qui mysteria revelavit.' The word
'worshipped' is ambiguous in itself; but, as we have already
observed, the close of the verse represents Daniel as accepting,
or at all events as not refusing to accept, divine honours in
contrast to the Apostles in Acts 14¹³⁻¹⁸. And yet the king's
homage though ostensibly offered to Daniel was in reality paid
to Daniel's God, as 2⁴⁷ declares.

Fell on his face. 'A mark of respect—whether to God, as
Gen. 17³, or to man, 2 Sam. 9⁶, 14⁴' (Driver).

Worshipped. This word (סגד) is used also in 3⁵,⁶,⁷,¹⁰,¹¹, &c.
As Driver points out, it is used in the Targums 'of obeisance
done to a human superior (as 2 Sam. 14³³, 18²¹,²⁸, 24²⁰); so that
it does not necessarily imply the payment of divine honour'.

Sweet odours—Th. εὐωδίας. Only here and in Ezra 6¹⁰ is ניחחין
used absolutely instead of the usual sacrificial expression 'odour
of a sweet smell' (ὀσμὴν εὐωδίας ריח הניחח) as in Gen. 8²¹,
Lev. 1⁹, &c.

2⁴⁷. *Of a truth.* See note on 2⁸.

A God of gods and a Lord of kings. So the Aramaic here
אֱלָהּ אֱלָהִין is to be rendered and not 'The God of gods'. See
Kautzsch, § 80. 1. This indefinite title recurs in the Hebrew
in 11³⁶. The above English would imply אֱלָהּ אֱלָהַיָּא.

Lord. מָרֵא. This is the right orthography, and not מָרֵה.
See Cooke 63³: Cowley 30¹⁵.

2⁴⁸. *And to be chief governor.* רב סגנין must be regarded as
the accusative governed by the verb הַשְׁלְטֵהּ in the preceding
clause. Since the Aramaic has no real equivalent of the
Hebrew עשה, our author would possibly have used כַּנִּי יְתֵהּ (or יַחֲיֵהּ)
here, had he thought it necessary.

Governor. סגן is an Assyrian loan-word in Aramaic as well
as in Hebrew (only in plural). It is found five times in our
author and eight times in the *Aram. Pap.*

2⁴⁹ᵃ. Seeing that Daniel owed largely to the spiritual intercessions of Shadrach, Meshach, and Abed-nego his power both

to recall and interpret the king's dream, he naturally requests the king to reward them also. With this request the king complied by setting them over the affairs of the province of Babylon. The exact nature of their office is not defined by a special term in this passage, nor yet the still higher distinctions they received at the close of chapter 3, owing to their risking life and limb in defiance of the king's command, when they boldly declared that the God whom they served was able to deliver them and that He would deliver them out of the king's hand ; but that, even if He withheld such deliverance, they would not serve the king's god nor worship the image which he had set up.

1^{20}. We have here restored this verse to its original context. The dislocation of this verse occurred before the Hebrew translator set to work, as we shall find presently. We shall also find that 1^{21}, which I have bracketed as an interpolation, was an addition of the Hebrew translator. The Hebrew of that verse is very late and unclassical.

To begin with, let us treat 1^{20,21} as if both verses were original. What then do we find? First of all that they follow unnaturally after 1^{19}, which forms the true close to the introduction to the book : 'therefore stood they before the king'. Marti rejects both verses as an interpolation on the ground that 1^{20} ignores 1^{19b}, and resumes the subject matter of 1^{19a}. Next he points out that 1^{21} is parallel to 1^{19b} as 1^{20} to 1^{19a}. We might add that 1^{20} introduces to the detriment of the context a statement which is not justified till the close of chapter 2.

But 1^{20} is not an interpolation. It is simply an intrusion in its present context, having through some accident or misunderstanding been transposed from the close of 2^{49a}—to which context I have now restored it. 1^{20} is at variance with all that precedes it in chapter 1, and with all that follows it in chapter 2 down to 2^{49a}. If the king had found the Jewish youths *ten times wiser than all the sages of Babylon*, he would naturally have consulted them before these sages, and not have waited till in 2^{16} Daniel volunteered his help—a help dependent largely on that of his three companions. We ought to add further that, even if the king had consulted the Babylonian sages first, as a matter of policy, he would not, when they proved helpless, have failed to call in the Jewish youths, who according to the traditional order of the text were 'ten times better' than they. Hence our author, who represents the king as giving orders for the destruction of all the wise men of Babylon, in the number of whom Daniel and his three companions were included, 2^{12-13}, could not have inserted 1^{20} in its present position. Such an order could only have been issued after the failure of the chiefest of the wise men of Babylon.

1^{20} could not have stood after 1^{19}, or before chapter 2. But 1^{20} is not an interpolation. In the original text it follows with perfect fitness after $2^{49\,a}$,

When restored to its original context we have to assign to 1^{20} a new interpretation, and thereby recover the original meaning it was designed to convey by its author. In $2^{49\,a}$ Daniel, having himself received great gifts and the supreme authority in Babylon next to the king 2^{48}, makes a request of the king on behalf of his three companions to whom he was so deeply indebted (see note on 2^{36}), and so the king appointed them as great officials over the affairs of the province of Babylon. Hereon follows 1^{20}, *which concerns his three companions only and not Daniel.* In their new capacity as great officials these three companions were naturally brought into close relations with the king, who consulted them when the occasion demanded, and found these three ten times better than all the magicians and enchanters in all his realm. In the ancient monarchies no important step was taken without consulting the gods or the stars.

Wisdom and understanding. So the LXX, Th., Pesh., and Vulg. The MT reads 'wisdom of understanding'.

He found. Here for the third time in the Hebrew of the translator of $1-2^{4\,a}$ we have the *vav* apodosis, followed by the imperf. Cf. $1^{2,18}$. Since the Hebrew of 1^{20} is obviously from the same translator as 1^{1-19}, it follows that this translator found $1^{20\ulcorner-21\urcorner}$ already transposed from its original position after $2^{49\,a}$. The dislocation had already taken place when the Hebrew translator set to work on chapter 1.

Ten times. The plural of יד 'hand', is used in this sense in Gen. 43^{34}. The idiom is not found in Aramaic. See my reconstruction of the Aramaic of this verse below.

Than. על is used in this comparative sense in 11^{5}, Eccles. 1^{16}, Ps. 89^{8}, &c., and also in Aramaic. Cf. our text 3^{19}, 6^{4}.

Magicians and Enchanters. See note on 2^{2}. Nearly all the

Hebrew manuscripts omit the ' and ', but not so the LXX, Th., and Vulg. !

1²⁰ probably ran as follows in the original Aramaic : כל מלת חכמא ובינא די בעא מנהון מלכא ישכח להון חד עשרה על כל חרטמיא ואשפיא די בכל מלכותה. Five out of the first seven above Aramaic words occur in the *Aram. Pap.*, Cowley 38⁶ : מלה זי צחו יבעה מנכם 'the matter concerning which Zeḥo inquires of you '. But instead of מלת we should rather, perhaps, read פתגם : cp. our text 3¹⁶, 4¹⁴. See 3¹⁹ on חד שבעה.

1²¹. There is no justification for the presence of this verse at the close of the first chapter. Chapter 1 has already closed with 1¹⁹. If it had any justification it should be a link between 1¹⁹ and 2. But it has no reference of any kind to 2 which follows, nor has it any connexion with what precedes. In 1¹⁹ the pre-eminence of Daniel, Hananiah, Mishael, and Azariah over all the other youths of their race is emphasized. There seems, therefore, to be no reason for this fresh reference to Daniel in 1²¹, unless it mentioned some additional and distinctive merit on his part. In support of this verse it has been urged by Hengstenberg that Daniel lived to see the beginning of the new era initiated by Cyrus, who permitted the Jews to return to Palestine (Ezra 1¹, 5¹³, 6³). But, as Bevan rejoins : ' If the author of the book attached such importance to the Restoration in the first year of Cyrus, it must appear somewhat strange that he never alludes to the event, except indirectly in 9²⁵ '. He might have added also that, when we come to 9²⁵, Daniel learns that centuries must elapse before the restoration and building of Jerusalem. Hence 1²¹ cannot be *justified* on this ground. But it may come from the hand of our author from the wish to impress on the reader that Daniel actually lived through the period of persecution to the advent of Cyrus.

I have given it the benefit of the doubt. If it could appear in Daniel at all, its fitting place would be at the end of 2⁴⁹, and to this place I have relegated it, but enclosed it in brackets ⟨ ⟩ in order to make it clear that its originality is not beyond question, though it has the support of the Hebrew and all the Versions with slight variations.

And Daniel continued. These words must be interpreted in the sense that Daniel lived at the court until (עד) the first year of Cyrus, and that no notice is taken of the years he lived beyond that date. Cf. the use of עד in 1 Kings 11⁴⁰, 2 Chron. 5⁹. There is therefore no need to emend ויהי into ויחי.

The Hebrew of this verse is late. It is either a rendering of the Aramaic by the Hebrew translator of the rest of the chapter, or it is a gloss of this translator, or a Hebrew rendering of an Aramaic gloss. It is very pointless. It should be a link between 1¹⁻¹⁹ and 2. But this, we saw, 1²⁰⁻²¹ was not. Nor again, when 1²⁰ is rightly restored after 2⁴⁹ᵃ, does 1²¹ form a fitting sequel to 1¹⁹, which tells all that needs to be told as yet of the four Jewish youths serving as pages in the royal court. Nor does it serve as an introduction to chapter 2.

Continued. The use of היה to mean 'to exist' is unusual in Hebrew. In Classical Hebrew היה expresses the copula, or forms part of a compound tense, or is used with a note of place. When it means 'to continue', 'to exist', it is generally used in Hebrew with a word or phrase denoting locality. Cf. Deut. 22², 1 Kings 11⁴⁰, 2 Chron. 5⁹. Job 3¹⁶ and Isa. 23¹³ have been cited as supporting the usage in our text. But these passages are regarded by scholars as hopelessly corrupt—not to speak of the uncertainty of their dates. In Gen. 5⁵, 1 Sam. 1²⁸, Ps. 89³⁷, however, the verb connotes the idea of existence without any added note of place.

But though it can occur in Hebrew, it is unknown in this sense in the Aramaic of Ezra and of Daniel, and in about eighty passages where it occurs in the *Aram. Pap. Fifth Cent.* (save possibly an approach to it in 32⁸, where, however, הוה is a slip for בנה הוה as in 30²⁵, 32⁵, 33⁹) linguistic evidence is against the origination of the gloss in Aramaic.

The first year of Cyrus the king. The year designed here is the first year of Cyrus's reign as king of Babylon in 538 B. C., the seventieth year after the date of Daniel's captivity.

2⁴⁹ ᵇ. *But Daniel was in the gate of the king.* Cf. Esther 2¹⁹,²¹ These words define Daniel's position over against that of his three companions. They held high offices under the crown, but Daniel was, to use a later phrase, the Grand Vizier. Shadrach, Meshach, and Abed-nebo were of like rank with the satraps, deputies, governors, and other high officials, but Daniel stood alone and in a unique position of rank and authority next to the king himself—a position which serves in part to explain his immunity from the danger that his three companions had to

encounter in the next chapter. But this exalted position did
not carry with it immunity from danger, as we shall see in
chapter 4.

SECTION III

Chapter 3, in the eighteenth year of Nebuchadnezzar.

Condition of the Text, §§ 1-4.

§ 1. *In this as in the preceding chapters the MT is not wholly
trustworthy.*

This is apparent from the very first verse on several grounds.

(1) Our author's method of dating each section whether it
consist of narratives or visions is against the omission in the
MT of the date in this section. See Introd., pp. xxviii sqq.
But happily this date is preserved both in the LXX and Th.

(2) It being our author's practice to date each section, it
follows that he would not have left undated such an important
event as the consecration, if we may so use the term, of the
great golden image, a consecration which was clearly regarded
as an event of imperial significance, seeing that all the chief
officials of the empire were summoned together to worship it.

(3) If we go further and ask with what object the king erected
this golden image, we might reply that it was no doubt twofold:
the first to do honour to his god, and the second to celebrate his
victories. The erection of such pillars with either or both of
such objects was of not unfrequent occurrence under the
Assyrian or Babylonian monarchies. 'It was a common practice
of the Assyrian kings to erect images of themselves with laudatory
inscriptions in conquered cities, or provinces, as symbols of their
dominion, the usual expression in such cases being *ṣa-lam šarru-
ti-a* (*šur-ba-a*) *ipu-uš*, "a (great) image of my royalty I made".'
See *KB*. i. 69, l. 98 f. ; 73, l. 5 ; 99, l. 25 ; 133, l. 31 ; 135, l. 71 ;
141, l. 93 ; 143, l. 124 ; 147, l. 156 ; 155, l. 26, &c. (all from the
reigns of Asshur-naṣir-abal, b. c. 885–860, and Shalmaneṣar II,
b. c. 860–825.' (Driver, *Daniel*, p. 35). In our text the
object of Nebuchadnezzar was no doubt of this nature—to do
honour to his god and to celebrate his victories in the West.
Amongst these victories the Jew could not fail to remember was
the capture of Jerusalem on the 7th day of the 5th month

586 B. C., when Nebuchadnezzar had all but completed the eighteenth year of his reign.   We find this date actually given in
Josephus (*C. Apion.* i. 21), 'Nebuchadnezzar in the eighteenth
year of his reign laid our temple desolate '.[1]   This date is also
found in Jer. 32[1], 52[29] (MT), but the latter passage is not found
in the LXX.   Hence we accept the phrase 'in the 18th year'
as coming from the hand of our author.

(4) On the evidence advanced in (3) I have with some hesitation adopted into my translation the clause that is preserved in
the LXX, since it obviously gives the grounds for Nebuchadnezzar's erection of the golden image.

OBJECT OF CHAPTERS 3-4.

§ 5. The object of these chapters is to encourage the Jews not
to acknowledge any heathen religion, but to hold fast at all costs
to their own, the truth of which has been acknowledged in the
preceding chapter, and to prefer death to apostasy.   All true
Jews, therefore, are exhorted to be ready to make public confession of their faith, if necessary, as did the three Jewish
brethren, and to abide the consequences: 'There is a God,
whom we serve, who is able to deliver us . . . and He will
deliver us out of thy hand, O king : but if not . . . we will not
serve thy gods ' (3[17-18]).

§ 6. The lesson in § 5 is enforced by our author with all the
power at his command of vivid narrative and burning words.
Surely it is no mere coincidence that the year our author assigns
to these events, 586 B. C., is the very same year in which Jerusalem fell through its many years of disloyalty and vice and

---

[1] In the Babylonian Talmud, *Meg.* 11 *b*, there are very erroneous statements
as to the length of the reigns of the Babylonian kings.   To Nebuchadnezzar are
assigned 45 years; to Evil-merodach 23; to Belshazzar 2.   No other native Babylonian king is known to this rabbinical treatise.   It further states that Belshazzar
was acquainted with Jeremiah's prophecy of the 70 years exile (Jer. 29[10]), but
that he *wrongly began the calculation of the* 70 *years with the accession of Nebuchadnezzar.*   Adding to these 45 years the 23 of Evil-merodach, and the 2 of
his own reign that had already lapsed, Belshazzar according to these Rabbis
concluded that Jeremiah's prophecy of the 70 years' exile of Judah in Babylon
was mistaken, for the Jews had not yet returned to Palestine, and so were not
likely to return at all.   Emboldened by his erroneous miscalculation, Belshazzar
laid hands on the sacred vessels of the Temple and applied them to profane
uses at a royal feast.   Even Daniel is charged with a like miscalculation in
Meg. 12 *a.*

shame. The discerning eye cannot fail to recognize the implied contrast between the unfaithfulness and doom of Judah collec-tively as a nation in Palestine and the splendid faith and heroism of the three solitary youths and Daniel on the plains of Babylon. Sixteen years of unbroken prosperity have not cor-rupted or checked the moral and spiritual growth of the three Jewish brethren and Daniel in Babylon. Their manhood amid all the difficulties that beset success in an alien land has more than fulfilled its early promise. Now that they are called to face the supreme risks that their religion entails—either apostasy, or faithfulness to their people's God in scorn of consequence— they choose their part without hesitation, and so the three brethren are cast into the burning fiery furnace and Daniel into the lion's den. Faith must justify itself even at the cost of what to the heathen beholders appeared to be the supreme self-sacrifice and loss of everything.

§ 7. The difficulty that scholars have found in the fact that Daniel is not mentioned in chapter 3, and that his three com-panions are not mentioned in any subsequent chapter, does not really exist. This third chapter recounts the perils and triumph of the three Jewish brethren in the earlier part of 586 B.C., whereas chapter 4 recounts the triumph of Daniel in the later months of the same year. But obviously there is only one central figure in the book, and that is the Seer himself. With chapter 3 the significance of his three companions comes to a close. They have made their great confession, and willingly encountered the risks it entailed. Their history prepares us for the still greater achievements of Daniel, who henceforth alone occupies the stage as Judah's Seer.

§ 8. This chapter is evidently based on tradition. It is not a mere creation of our author. That individual Jews were committed to the flames we must infer from Jer. 29^{22}. Amongst the Jews death by fire was restricted to daughters of priests who had played the harlot (Lev. 21^9). The infliction of such a penalty on the Jews by the Babylonian authorities for refusal to acknowledge their national deities must have made a lasting impression on the nation. We may find a distant reference possibly to such a penalty in Isa. 43^2. Death by fire was a recognized punishment in Persia till quite a late date. It should, however, not be forgotten that Antiochus Epiphanes

resorted to this form of capital punishment when he was trying
to suppress Judaism. See 2 Macc. 7^{4-5}.

§ 8. *Corruptions.*

3^{12}. For לא שמו עליך מלכא טעם read with LXX, Th., and Vulg.
לא שמעו מלכא לטעמך. See 6^{14}, where the same corruption recurs.

3^{14}. For הצדא read האזדא with Bevan, &c. Cp. $2^{5,8}$.

3^{17}. For הן איתי" read די איתי אלה די אנחנא פלחין [די] יכל.

§ 9. *Interpolations.*

$3^{2,3}$. †Treasurers† appears to be a *vox nulla*. See Appendix,
p. 77 sqq.

3^{23}. This entire verse I have relegated to the foot-notes. It
is not found in the LXX. It is not supported either by what
precedes or what follows.

§ 10. *Omissions.*

3^1. This most important date, 'in the eighteenth year', which
has been preserved by both the LXX and Th., and is in keeping
with the practice of our author at the beginning of each section,
I have here restored in my translation.

In the same verse I have on the evidence of the LXX restored
a long clause. See note *in loc.*

§ 11. *Late Aramaic forms and order.*

(a) *Late forms.* 3^{28} שׁיזיב. In all earlier Aramaic as of the
fifth century B. C. this word was written שׁזב. Only in our author
and in Inscriptions after the Christian era and the Targum is
the form שׁיזב found. See note on 3^{28}.

3^7 (cf. 2^{43}, 5^{20}, $6^{11,15}$). We have the late Aramaic form כדי,
which in the fifth or fourth cent. Inscriptions B. C. is written כזי.

(b) *Late order.* 3^{16}. *King Nebuchadnezzar.* So LXX, Th. See notes on 2^{28},
$3^{1,9}$: and Introd., § 20. *dd.* This order is not attested earlier than
the second century B. C.

§ 12. *Late words.*

3^7. פסנטרין = $\psi\alpha\lambda\tau\acute{\eta}\rho\iota\sigma\nu$. This word shows the influence of the
Macedonian dialect which substituted ν for λ.

סמפניא. As the name of a musical instrument of very late
occurrence.

3^1. ⌈*In his eighteenth year.*⌉ So LXX and Th. ($\check{\epsilon}\tau\sigma\upsilon\varsigma$ $\grave{\sigma}\kappa\tau\omega\kappa\alpha\iota$-
$\delta\epsilon\kappa\acute{\alpha}\tau\sigma\upsilon$), but the MT and its dependent versions omit. See
Introd., § 4. The LXX uses the genitive of time, as also

does Th. The LXX uses also ἐν with the dat. 10¹, 11¹, or without it 9¹ to express a point or period of time.

⌜*When he had brought under his rule cities and provinces and all that dwell upon the earth from India to Ethiopia.*⌝ This clause is only found in the LXX, which runs as follows : διοικῶν πόλεις καὶ χώρας καὶ πάντας τοὺς κατοικοῦντας ἐπὶ τῆς γῆς ἀπὸ Ἰνδικῆς ἕως Αἰθιοπίας. It appears to be a rendering of the original Aramaic. It is generally regarded as an interpolation from Esther 1¹, 8⁹. But the only words in common—and they were most probably a popular expression designed to define the universal empire of these Oriental monarchs—are 'from India even to Ethiopia', מהדו ועד כוש. It is difficult to determine what the Aramaic word was, which is rendered by διοικῶν. διοικεῖν in Wisdom 8¹⁵, 12¹⁸, 15¹ means 'to rule'. Thus in the first of these passages we have διοικήσω λαούς. In Ezra 8³⁶ the noun διοικητής is used to render אחשדרפנים, i. e. satraps. Hence the original Aramaic may have been as follows : בְּמִשְׁלְטֵהּ בקרין ומדינן וכל דירין על ארעא מהנדיא ועד כוש.

Nebuchadnezzar the king. This is the *invariable* order, and never 'King Nebuchadnezzar' in the older Aramaic as in the *Eg. Pap.* : see Cowley 1¹, 2¹, 5¹, 6², 7¹, 8¹, 9¹, 10², 13¹, 14¹, 15¹, 20¹, 21³,¹⁰, 25¹, 27², 28¹, 29¹, 30²,⁴,¹⁹,²¹,³⁰, 31⁴,¹⁹, 32⁷, 35¹,⁶, 45¹ : Aḥ. 10, 27, 50, 51, 55, 60, 70, 76, 78 : Beh. 7, 12, 37 : in Ezra 4⁸,¹¹,²³, 5⁶,¹³,¹⁴,¹⁷, 6³(*bis*),¹³,¹⁵, 7²¹ : and often in *late* Hebrew: cf. Hag. 1¹,¹⁵, Neh. 2¹, 5¹⁴, Dan. 1²¹. But in seven passages out of twenty the MT forsakes older Aramaic order : cf. 2²⁸,⁴⁶, 3¹⁶, 4¹⁵, 5⁹,¹¹, 6¹⁰. But in 4¹⁵ Th., Pesh., Vulg., support the ancient order. In Classical Hebrew the order is almost invariably 'King David,' &c. Thus the older Aramaic order prevails invariably to 300 B. C., and possibly till early in the second century. In Nabataean Aramaic from 169 B.C. to A.D. 106 the usual order is for the personal name to precede the office. Thus for 'Maliku (or "Rebel") the King', see *CIS.* ii. 161, Col. iii, l. 3, 174, l. 3, 218, l. 4 : 'Maliku (or "Rebel," &c.) the King, King of the Nabataeans'. See Cooke 101¹⁰⁻¹¹, *CIS.* ii. 219, l. 7, 220, l. 3, 223, l. 5. On the other hand we find in *CIS.* ii. 195, l. 5, 'King Maliku, King of the Nabataeans'.

On the Maccabean coins the latter order is followed. In the N.T. we find 'King Herod', Matt. 2³, Mark 6¹⁴, Acts 12¹, and on the other hand 'Agrippa the King' 25¹³, 'Aretas the King' 2 Cor. 11³². When the king is directly addressed in Acts 25²⁶,

26², ¹⁹,²⁷but not in 25²⁴, the order is ' King Agrippa '. Lidzbarski (*Eph.* ii. 261) gives two Aramaic (Nabataean) inscriptions in this order הגרפס מלכא = ' King Agrippa '. Now in contrast to these varieties of order in later Aramaic the order in Aramaic before 303 B.C., perhaps before 200 B.C., was fixed. The proper name preceded the title. This fact in itself shows the lateness of the Aramaic in Daniel.

An image of gold . . threescore cubits. The image was not necessarily of solid gold. Even the golden altar in Exod. 39³⁸ was merely overlaid with gold (Exod. 30³). Such colossal statues were not unusual in the East. Herodotus (i. 183) speaks of a great golden statue of Zeus in the temple of Belus in Babylon.

Plain of Dura. This plain has not yet been identified, though three localities are mentioned in the tablets bearing the name Duru (Delitzsch, *Paradies*, p. 216), and several Babylonian cities had names compounded with Dur. Oppert (see Driver *in loc.*) suggests that one of the mounds—called Mounds of Dura—near a small river called the Dura, which falls into the Euphrates some six miles below Babylon, may have formed the pedestal of this colossal image. Jahn (*in loc.*) regards the text of the MT as corrupt, and follows the LXX here πεδίῳ τοῦ περιβόλου. Th. simply attempts a transliteration πεδίῳ Δεειρά.

3². *Satraps.* אחשדרפניא is from the Old Persian *Kshatra-pāwan*, 'protectors of the realm'. See Spiegel's, *Altpersische Keilinschriften*, p. 215. From this Old Persian form arise the Greek forms in inscriptions ἐξαιθράπης, ἐξατράπης, and in Greek writings σατράπης. The title is a Persian one (cf. Ezra 8³⁶, Esther 3¹², &c.), and not a Babylonian, and is accordingly an anachronism here.

Governors. פחה (pl. פחותא) is a loan-word from the Assyrian *paḥâti* abbreviated from *bel paḥâti*, 'lord of a district'. The form פחי which is found in the *Zinjirli Inscription* 745-727 B.C. (Cooke 62¹²) is probably from the same root. פחה occurs also in the Fifth Cent. Papyri (see Cowley 30¹, 31¹ : Beh. 18, 38). It is of frequent occurrence also in Hebrew, especially in the post-Exilic books.

Judges. אדרגזר is a Persian loan-word = *andaržaghar* Middle Iran. = Old Iran. *handarža* = counsellor, a title still in use under the Sassanian dynasty (Nöldeke, *Tabari*, p. 462 *n.*). But Ed. Meyer thinks it is a military title.

[*Treasurers.*] גדבריא. This is a highly doubtful word. It may be a textual corruption of גזבריא : see Ezra 1⁸, 7²¹ : or, as Graetz, Bevan, and others suggest, a mere error of the scribe, for הדבריא = ministers or counsellors : see 3²⁴,²⁷, 4³³, 6⁸ : or again it may be a dittograph for דתבריא that follows immediately. In favour of this last hypothesis is the fact that the LXX and Th. have each only seven names of officials, whereas our text has eight. See Appendix at close of this chapter, 77 sqq.

Counsellors. דתבריא a loan-word from *dâtabara*, law-bearer. This word has, as Driver observes, been found recently by Hilprecht in the Nippur inscriptions of the time of Artaxerxes I (465–425 B. C.) and Darius II (424–405 B. C.). With these officials we may compare the βασιλήϊοι δικασταί of Herod. iii. 14, 31, v. 25.

Sheriffs. תפתיא is found in the form of תיפתיא in Cowley 27⁹ between the words דיניא and גושכיא. The meaning assigned to this word is uncertain, but it denotes some kind of police or military official. The papyrus passage favours the former.

To come. לְמֵתֵא for לְמֵאתֵא without the א like לְמֵא 3¹⁹ and לְמֵמַר Ezra 5¹¹.

3³. The officials in this verse are the same as in ver. 2.

Stood. On קאמין see note on 'dwell' in 2³⁸.

3⁴. *Herald.* כָּרוֹזָא is according to Marti an Aramaic noun formed from כְּרַז, Haphel הַכְרִז 5²⁹. Cook's *Aramaic Glossary*, p. 66, gives כרוז = 'a herald', which is derived from inscription 86 in the *CIS.* ii. Of these inscriptions nos. 73–107 are of 'uncertain origin, ranging from the ninth to the fourth century B.C.' (p. 2). Cook (p. 66) infers from this inscription that the word 'herald . . . is not necessarily derived from κηρύσσειν'. But this inference is doubtful. The word there is rather to be taken as a proper name. The Oxford Heb. Lex. regards it as a loan-word from the Greek.

Cried aloud. קרא בחיל. So also in 4¹¹⁽¹⁴⁾, 5⁷. Its equivalent in Hebrew is קרא בחזקה Jonah 3⁸, or, as in Isa. 40⁹, בַּכֹּחַ. Cf. Rev. 18² ἔκραξεν ἐν ἰσχυρᾷ φωνῇ, which, however, is not from the hand of the Seer, who uses the form κράζειν φωνῇ μεγάλῃ 6¹⁰, 7²,¹⁰, 10³, &c.

It is commanded. Where we put the impers. passive, the Aramaic puts the 3rd plur. act. (part.) אמרין: cf. 4²²⁽²⁵⁾, where both the finite verb and participle are thus used.

Peoples, nations, and languages. This expression recurs :

$3^{7,29,31}$ (4^1), 5^{19}, 6^{26}, 7^{14}. Cf. Rev. 5^9, 7^9, 10^{11}, 11^9, 13^7, 14^6, 17^{15}. The various nationalities and races are represented by great officials.

3^5. In $3^{5,7,10,15}$ there are various kinds of musical instruments mentioned. Some of them bear Semitic names, others Greek. First of all the word for 'kind' זן is a Persian loan word = Middle Iran. *zan*, and has γένος as its etymological equivalent. It was adopted early into Aramaic, as it is found in the *Fifth Century Papyri* (Cowley, 17^3), and into late Hebrew: Ps. 144^{13}, 2 Chron. 16^{14}. Of the six instruments two are of Semitic origin—the horn and the pipe, and three of Greek—the harp, the psaltery, and the dulcimer. Whether the sackbut was originally Semitic or Greek is uncertain, but probably the former.

Cornet, lit. 'horn'. The word קַרְנָא is used here and in $3^{7,10,15}$, and in Syriac in the same sense as the Hebrew shophar שׁוֹפָר.

Pipe. מַשְׁרוֹקִיתָא from שׁרק Hebr. Isa. 5^{26}, 'to hiss, whistle'. The word שׁרק occurs in the *Fifth Century Papyri* (Cowley, *Ah.* 100) as an adjective meaning 'sharp'. But it is found in the Targums and in the Syr.

Harp. קִיתָרֹם (Kt.) should according to Kamphausen be punctuated קִיתָרֹם. *Qr.* reads קַתְרֹם, as also in the Targums. This word is borrowed from the Greek κίθαρις.

Sackbut. שַׂבְּכָא was a small triangular instrument with four strings. It is identical with the Greek σαμβύκη. According to Athenaeus iv. 175 *d*, *e* it was a Syrian invention, and *psaltriae* and *sambucistriae* were according to Livy xxxix. 6 introduced into Rome from the East in 187 B. C. Some scholars would connect the root of this word with that of the Hebrew שְׂבָכָה 'net, lattice-work'.

Psaltery. פְּסַנְתֵּרִין is derived from the Greek ψαλτήριον. For the transliteration of -ιον by ין- compare סַנְהֶדְרִין = συνέδριον. It will be observed that this loan-word is differently spelt in 3^7, i. e. פְּסַנְטֵרִין. The latter is more correct than the former; for in Aramaic and late Hebrew ת generally represents θ and ט = τ: cf. תֵּאטְרוֹן = θέατρον. The form פְּסַנְטֵרִין shows the influence of the Macedonian dialect, which substituted ν for λ. The psaltery was a stringed instrument, triangular in shape and like an inverted ∆. It had its sounding board above the strings, as the cithara had it below them (see Augustine, iv. 272 B, C.: 521 D, &c.).

Dulcimer, or rather 'bagpipe'. The Aramaic סומפניה 3[5,15], and סיפניא (Kt.) and סופניא (*Qr.*) in 3[10], is the Greek συμφωνία. This instrument is omitted in 3[7]. 'It was probably a goat-skin bag with two reed pipes, the one used as a mouthpiece to fill the bag . . . and the other employed as a chanter-flute with finger holes' (*Encyc. Bib.* iii. 3230). The word is first found with the meaning of 'a concord or unison of sound' in Plato and Aristotle, but not as denoting a musical instrument before the time of Polybius (204-122 B.C.). So far, therefore, as the literary evidence goes, the use of this Greek word is peculiar to late Greek. But the value of this evidence does not end here. It is surely an extraordinary coincidence that Polybius mentions this instrument as a favourite instrument of Antiochus Epiphanes. xxvi. 10, ὅτε δὲ τῶν νεωτέρων αἴσθοιτό τινας συνευωχουμένους ὅπου δή ποτε . . . παρῆν ἐπικωμάζων μετὰ κερατίου (a. l. κεραμίου, 'a jar of wine') καὶ συμφωνίας, ὥστε τοὺς πολλοὺς διὰ τὸ παράδοξον ἀνισταμένους φεύγειν. A later passage in the same historian (xxxi. 4) tells how Antiochus Epiphanes used to the shame of the onlookers to dance to the sound of this instrument: τῆς συμφωνίας προκαλουμένης, ἀναπηδήσας ὠρχεῖτο . . . ὥστε πάντας. αἰσχυνομένους φεύγειν.

3[6]. *The same hour.* בַּהּ שַׁעֲתָא. The MT has שׁ־ here where the Syriac has שׁ־. The suffix in בה is not pleonastic, but is used to give emphasis: cf. 3[7,8] and 4[30], 5[5] for a repetition of the preposition. Originally it meant any small period of time, and only later came to mean an 'hour'. שעה does not occur in Biblical Hebrew, but is found in the Targums and Syriac, New Hebrew, Ethiopic, and Arabic. Possibly it is a loan-word from the Assyrian.

Into the midst. לְגוֹא. גּוֹא or גּוֹ is the construct of גַּו, which has allied forms in Syriac and Arabic, גוא has final א in our author as in one Nabataean inscription: *CIS.* ii. 350[1].

Furnace. אַתּוּן is taken to be a loan-word from the Assyr. *atûna.* Since, however, the root is found in Arabic and Syriac, and the word እቶን፡ = 'furnace' is a common word in Ethiopic, it may be an old Aramaic word.

3[7]. *When.* כְּדִי has the same meaning in 5[20], 6[11,15], but in 2[43] it means 'according as'. This word has the former meaning in an Aramaic inscription (Cooke, 68[4], 5th-4th cent.), in *Aram. Pap.* (Cowley, 6[1], 8[24], 13[4], 27[2], 28[13], 40[2]); and the latter meaning in the *Aramaic Inscriptions (CIS.* ii. 145, C[3]). In these older documents the form is בּוּ. See Cowley also in 6⁷, 8²⁵, where it follows יִמָא 'to swear', with the meaning 'that'.

3⁸⁻¹². *The three young Jews accused of not falling down before the image.*

Observe how closely the charge in 3¹² brought against them resembles that brought against Daniel in 6¹⁴. The author's object is to encourage the Jews, who had 'set the king at nought' by refusing to forsake their religion. There is here a contemporary reference to Antiochus Epiphanes.

3⁸. *Certain Chaldaeans.* On the use of גֻּבְרִין (where the change from *a* to *u* is due to the following labial : cf. פֻּם, שֻׁם) here see Introd. Idiomatically, it = 'certain' as אנשים in certain passages, though the literal rendering is 'men, Chaldeans'.

Brought accusation. The phrase in the original אכלו קרציהון is peculiar : it literally means 'ate the pieces of'. It generally means in Aramaic *to slander, to accuse falsely*, as in Ps. 15³ (Targ.) : and in Luke 16¹ as a rendering of διαβάλλειν. Indeed the devil, i. e. ὁ διάβολος is ‎ܐܟܠܩܪܨܐ —the slanderer in chief. A variation of this idiom occurs in a fifth–fourth century B.C. inscription on the Carpentras Stele : *CIS.* ii. 141² כרצי איש לא אמרת, 'thou hast not calumniated any man'. Here the כ, as Nöldeke has shown, has been written instead of ק. But here and in 6²⁵ it has a different nuance : it means *to accuse maliciously*—not falsely. In the former meaning it occurs already in the Tel-el-Amarna Letters *akâlu-karṣi*, 44²⁵, &c., and later it is frequent in the Arabic. It was in use almost throughout the entire Semitic world. Lepsius (see Marti, *in loc.*) finds an allied phrase in the Persian ; *Der Christliche Orient*, 1897, p. 152.

3⁹. *Answered and said.* See note on 2⁵.

[*To Nebuchadnezzar the king.*] The LXX omits this addition : it reads simply ὑπολαβόντες εἶπον. From some later version ✳Ναβουχοδονοσὸρ τῷ βασιλεῖ has been supplied. It is true the MT reads אמרין לנבוכדנצר מלכא and is supported by Th. and the later versions. But this idiom is foreign to our author. If this phrase came from our author's hand we should have קֳדָם instead of לְ before the king's name. Only when the satraps and courtiers act with deliberate rudeness is the expression אֲמַר לְ used in our author when the person addressed is the king. See 6¹⁶ for an example of this nature. There is one exception

to this rule.   When קְדָם has just occurred with a preceding
verb, אֲמַר can be followed by לְ as in 2²⁵.

O king, live for ever!   See on 2⁴.

3¹⁰. *Hast made a decree.* שָׂמְתָּ טְעֵם. This idiom occurs in the
Aram. Pap. (see Cowley, 26²²,²³,²⁵). Contrast the meaning of this
phrase in the MT in 3¹².

3¹². *Whom.* יתהון · · · דִי. יתֿ- used here only in Biblical
Aramaic.   In the Targums it is very frequently used both with
and without pronominal suffixes. לְ is the particle used by
Aramaic normally in this sense. Like the Hebrew את־ it is
used before a definite object.   It occurs in the form ית with
suffix ותה in the eighth century Zinjirli Inscription.   See
Cooke, 61²⁸ : as ית in Nabat. and Palmyrene : see Lidz.,
N. E., 263.

† *Have not regarded thee†.* Corrupt : read 'have not obeyed
thy command'.   The Versions do not support the MT text
טעם · · · לֹא שָׂמוּ עֲלָיִךְ.   It is true that this same phrase recurs in
6¹⁴⁽¹³⁾.   In 3¹⁰,²⁹, 4³⁽⁶⁾, 6²⁷⁽²⁶⁾ we have שָׂם טְעֵם in its normal sense
of 'to command', as also in Ezra fourteen times. But in 3¹²,
6¹⁴⁽¹³⁾ quite a different sense is required in this phrase, if the MT
is correct—'to show deference' or 'respect'.   For this meaning
there is no authority outside these two passages in Daniel.
Elsewhere in Daniel טעם means 'decree' except in three passages.   In 5² it is used of the 'taste' of wine—an original
meaning of the word. In 2¹⁴ it has a secondary meaning derived
from the first, i. e. 'discretion' (as in Hebrew: cf. Prov. 26¹⁶),
while in 6³ it means 'report' : cf. Ezra 5⁵. This phrase שם טעם
(= 'to issue a command') occurs also in the Fifth Century Aram.
Pap., see Cowley, 26²²,²³,²⁵, 27²¹ : but never in the sense attributed to it in Dan. 3¹², 6¹⁴⁽¹³⁾.   I can find no occurrence of this
idiom in the Targums. The general usage of the word is thus
against the meaning universally assigned to the phrases in 3¹²,
6¹⁴.   Let us now turn to the Greek Versions and the Vulg., and
see if they support either this meaning or even the MT text.

3¹².	LXX.	Th.	Vulg.
	οὐκ ἐφοβήθησάν σου τὴν	οὐχ ὑπήκουσαν,	contempserunt,
		βασιλεῦ, τῷ	rex,
	ἐντολήν.	δόγματί σου	decretum tuum
6¹⁴	*missing*).	οὐχ ὑπετάγη τῷ	non curavit de
		δόγματί σου	lege tua

Now first of all in 3[12] we observe that all three Versions translate טעם as it is translated generally in Daniel, and especially in
the phrase שׂם טעם. In the next place the personal pronoun is
connected with this word. In other words, these three Versions
prove that the text before them was טעמך, and not עליך טעם.
Thirdly, Th. certainly read שמעו (cf. 7[27] where it renders ישׁתמעון
by ὑπακούσονται) and not שׂמו, which latter it renders in this connexion by τιθέναι or ἐκτιθέναι. Thus Th. presupposes לא שׁמעו · · ·
לטעמך 'they have not obeyed thy decree'. The LXX and the
Vulg. are loose but not inaccurate renderings of this text. On
the other hand Aquila supports the MT but the Pesh. omits
טעם. The present corrupt MT text existed therefore early
in the Christian era. Next in 6[14] Th. and the Vulg. are free
renderings of the text they presuppose in 3[12]. In N.T. Greek
ὑποτάσσεσθαι = ὑπακούειν constantly. Hence I read 'have not
obeyed thy command'. See also note on 6[14] on this idiom.

Thy god. Here I follow Qr. and read the singular, and not
'thy gods'. See 3[14,18], 4[5(8)].

3[13]. *Fury.* For חֲמָא we find חֱמָא in 3[19]. On other variations
in pointing see 2[19] and 7[4,5].

Were brought. הֵיתִיו (Hêphal, as Ginsburg, Marti, Kamphausen
read), has a passive meaning. Cf. הֵיתָיִת in 6[18]. But there is no
satisfactory explanation of this passive as Kautzsch (p. 67 *n.*)
declares. The active form Haph'el occurs in 5[3] הַיְתִיו.

3[14]. *Is it true?* The text reads הַצְדָא, which is generally
rendered 'Is it of purpose?' But to obtain this sense the
initial ה must be taken as an interrogative, and צדא, which is
not found elsewhere in Aramaic, would be a Hebraism from the
same root as צְדִיָּא (from צדה 'to lie in wait') found in Num. 35[20,22].
If so, Kautzsch, § 67. 2, says we should punctuate the word
הַצְדָא. But the explanation is far-fetched, and Bevan's conjecture
accepted by many scholars explains the corruption and gives
good sense. Thus for הצדא we should as in 2[5,8] read הַאֲזְדָא =
εἰ ἀληθῶς as in Th. and Pesh. אזדא is a Persian word and is
already found in the absolute state in the *Eg. Aram.* (Cowley,
27[8]). But Montgomery (p. 207) points out now that Lidz.,
Altaram. Urk., 1921, l. 12, cf. p. 12, has found הצדא (= 'true')
on an ostrakon.

My god. For לֵאלָהַי we should read with the Erfurt MS.
לֵאלָהִי 'my god,' i.e. Bel.

I have set up. הֲקֵימֶת. The usual form for the first person sing. ends in תְ–, but תֵ– is the normal ending in the Haph'el of ו״ע.

3¹⁵. *Well.* The construction is here elliptical. After the conditional sentence there is an aposiopesis. The missing word could be graphically replaced by a gesture. For similar aposiopesis in Hebrew and Greek, cf. Exod. 32³² : 1 Sam. 12¹⁴ ˢᵉ𐞥· : Luke 13⁹ : Iliad 1¹³⁶.

What god is there? מַן־הוּא אֱלָה. The הוּא simply strengthens the מַן, and the two are contracted in the Targums and Syriac into מַנּוּ. See Kautzsch, § 87. 3. The king's challenge recalls those of Sennacherib and Rabshakeh, Isa. 36¹⁹⁻²⁰, 37¹¹⁻¹², while the answer of the three Jews in the next verse recalls those of the seven brethren in 2 Macc. 7.

Shall deliver you. יְשֵׁיזְבִנְכוֹן׀ Probably a Shaph'el form derived from the Assyr. *šūzubu.* It is of frequent occurrence in our author whether as perfect, imperfect, infinitive, or participle. It was early adopted into Aramaic, as it is found in the *Eg. Aram.* See Cowley 38⁵, 54⁹, Aḥ. 46.

3¹⁶. The three Jews refuse to discuss a question which must be left to God.

No need. לָא חָשְׁחִין—the participle is to be preferred, though the MT favours the adjective חַשְׁחִין.

To answer thee in this matter. Cf. 1 Kings 12⁶,⁹ for a like construction.

3¹⁷. †*If it be so*† ... *to deliver us.* The king has asked : 'Is there any god who can deliver you ?' To this question this verse should supply the answer, but in such a way as to harmonize with 3¹⁶, where the three Jews have refused to debate the question. Hence 3¹⁷ should explain 3¹⁶ while answering 3¹⁵, and hence, further, we should expect 3¹⁷ to begin with 'for' or some such word. 'We have no need to answer thee in this matter ; for the God whom we serve either will or will not save us.' Deeds not words will answer the king's question. If this is the meaning of the context, it is clear that the words in the MT 'If it be so, our God whom we serve, &c.' cannot be right. Furthermore, that we have rightly interpreted the context follows from the four Versions—LXX, Th., Pesh., Vulg., all of which begin 3¹⁷ with 'for'.

But almost all modern scholars, following the Massoretic punctuation, give a different rendering of 3¹⁷ : 'If our God, whom we serve, be able to deliver us, &c.' But there are two insuperable objections to this form of the text. (1) It can hardly be that such strong champions of their God would for a moment admit that He was unable to deliver them, and that to a heathen king. They could admit the possibility of His not intervening to save them, but not His inability to save. (2) If we may infer our author's usage from other passages where he combines אִיתַי with a participle, we may learn that, when אִיתַי forms one idea with the participle, they should not be separated by any intervening word. Thus in:

2²⁶. הַאִיתָיךְ כָּהֵל 'Art thou able'.

3¹⁴. לָא אִיתֵיכוֹן פָּלְחִין 'Ye will not serve'.

3¹⁵. הֵן אִיתֵיכוֹן עֲתִידִין 'If ye are ready'.

3¹⁸. לָא־אִיתָנָא פָלְחִין 'We will not serve'.

This holds also in the Syriac: cf. Duval, *Grammaire Syriaque*, 323–5: and in the Hebrew with יֵשׁ and אֵין Cf. *Ges.-Kautzsch*, § 116 q. In the Eg. Aram. this usage does not occur save once in one emended passage: see Cowley, Aₕ. 159, where the two words are separated and the editor remarks on the unusual structure of the Aramaic. But our author's usage appears clearly to be against separating these two words if they express one idea. If this conclusion is right, then it is wrong to combine these words as do Kautzsch, § 67. 8, and Marti and others, and translate 'If our God, whom we serve, is able to deliver us'. The rendering should be: 'If our God, whom we serve, exists, He is able'. But this idea is highly unsatisfactory: contrast 2²⁸ 'There is a God'.

Since, therefore, the MT may be regarded as corrupt, let us turn to the Versions:

LXX. ἔστι γὰρ Θεὸς ἐν οὐρανοῖς εἷς κύριος ἡμῶν, ὃν φοβούμεθα, ὅς ἐστι δυνατός

Th. ἔστιν γὰρ Θεός, ᾧ ἡμεῖς λατρεύομεν, δυνατός.·

Pesh. = ἔστι γὰρ Θεὸς ἡμῶν, ᾧ ἡμεῖς λατρεύομεν, ὃς δυνατός ἐστι.

Vulg. 'Ecce enim Deus noster, quem colimus, potest.'

In these Versions we observe first that all agree in reading דִי = 'for' instead of הֵן = 'if', save the Vulgate 'ecce enim', which attests the conflate text דִי הֵן, but 'ecce' is a mistranslation of הֵן, or presupposes the variant הָא: cf. 3²⁵. For neither in Biblical nor earlier Aramaic can this word be so translated. It may, therefore, be regarded as conclusive that the הֵן of the

MT is a late corruption or correction. In the next place the
LXX and Th. require אֱלָהּ and not אלהנא as the MT (supported
by the Pesh. and Vulg.) reads. Thirdly, the LXX and Pesh.
read ὅς before δυνατός. Thus we are led to conclude that the
text originally stood as follows : (?די) די איתי אלה די אנחנא פלחין
יכל 'For there is a God, whom we serve, who is able to deliver
us'. This provides exactly the answer that the context requires. When the king asks, 'What god can deliver you out
of my hands ?' the three companions reply : 'We have no need
to discuss this question ; for there is a God, whom we serve,
who will deliver us, &c.' They answer first that there is such
a God, and next that it is the God whom they serve. See p. 354.

The φοβούμεθα in the LXX above = דחלין a corruption of פלחין
as in the MT.

3¹⁸. *But if not*: i. e. if He will not deliver us.

Thy god. Here read the singular לֵאלָהָךְ, as in v. 12, and not
the plural לאלהיך is to be read. Bel was the patron deity of the
king : cf. 4⁵⁽⁸⁾. The LXX has here τῷ εἰδώλῳ σου, but Th. and
Vulg. have reproduced the plural in the MT. The Pesh.
in all three cases rightly has the sing.

3¹⁹⁻²⁷. *The deliverance of the three faithful Jews from the burning
fiery furnace.*

3¹⁹. *Form.* צְלֵם (construct) which is elsewhere punctuated as
צֶלֶם. Strack (*Gram.*⁶, § 8 *c* : Marti, *Gram.*, § 71 Anm.) draws attention to the artificial forms introduced by the scribes to bring out
the difference between the use of צְלֵם (constr.) 3¹⁹ and צֶלֶם 3⁵
and טַעַם Ezra 6¹⁴, 7²³ and טְעֵם (three times) to distinguish the
idol (3⁶) from the form of the human face (3¹⁹), and God's will
from that of man.

Was changed. If we read אשתנו with Kautzsch § 47. 4,
Ginsburg, Strack, the plural is to be construed with אנפוהי : cf. 1
Sam. 2⁴, 2 Sam. 10⁹. Ges.-Kautzsch, § 146 *a*. The *Qr.* reads
the singular אֶשְׁתַּנִּי.

To heat. See 3² note. With the suffix at the close מֵזְיֵהּ.

Seven times, i.e. חד שבעה. With this peculiar Aramaic expression cf. *Aram. Pap.* (Cowley, 30³) חד אלף = ' a thousand
times '. It is a Syriac expression : cf. 11⁸,¹³, Exod. 22⁷ in Pesh ;
or it takes another form חד בשבעא Gen. 4²⁴ ; cf. Duval, *Gram.*,
p. 353 : Nöldeke *Syr. Gr.*, p. 166.

Wont. חֲזֵה (' wont ', ' fitting ') is frequent in this sense in the

later Aramaic, especially in the form חַיִּי. Cf. Onk., Lev. 5¹⁰,
9¹⁶, Num. 29⁶. See Driver, *in loc.* Later Hebrew was analo-
gously רעוי.

3²⁰. *And to cast.* The 'and' is not found in the MT, LXX,
or Th. Hence the infinitive לְמִרְמֵא is generally taken as dependent on the preceding infinitive. But Marti rightly suggests
that the ו has been lost after the preceding ו in גנו.

3²¹. On the perfect passive כְּפִתוּ and in the next clause רְמִיו
see note on 2¹⁹.

Their mantles. The meaning of סרבל is doubtful. The
authorities waver between 'mantles' and 'trousers'. It bears
the former sense in the Aramaic (Talmudic), whence it was
borrowed by Arabic in the form *sirbâl* (see Fränkel, *Aram.
Fremdwörter im Arab.*, 1886, p. 47: Levy, *NHBW.* iii. 584).
On the other hand the Versions support the latter meaning.
Thus LXX ἔχοντες τὰ ὑποδήματα αὐτῶν (but in 3²⁷⁽⁹⁴⁾ σαράβαρα) : Th.
σὺν τοῖς σαραβάροις αὐτῶν: Aq. τ. σαραβάροις: Sym. ἐν ταῖς ἀναξυρίσιν
αὐτῶν : the Pesh. and the Vulg. *cum braccis suis.* These σαράβαρα
were worn by the Persians and Scythians. The word appears
to have meant both *mantles* and *trousers* originally in Persian—in
Modern Persian still as Shalwar = *trousers*, Arabic *Sirwal*, Syr.
Sharbhala. See S. A. Cook, 'Articles of Dress mentioned in
Dan. 3²¹,' *Journ. of Philology*, xxvi. 306–13 (1899), who supports
the former meaning on the ground of the mantle being loose
and easily inflammable : cf. 3²⁷. On the other hand, Bevan,
Hitzig, and Ewald render the word by 'their trousers'.

Trousers. The exact meaning of פטישיהון is wholly uncertain.
The later Jews and Syrians had no certain tradition as to
whether it meant 'trousers' or 'tunic'. Payne Smith, *Thes.* 3098,
gives both meanings for the Syriac, and Levy, *NHWB.* iv. 34
the meaning 'trousers' in Talmudic Hebrew. If this meaning
is right, then the order in Th. τιάραις καὶ περικνημῖσι (so Vulg.
should be transposed into περικνημῖσι καὶ τιάραις. The Pesh. is
also out of order, and the LXX has ἐπὶ τῶν κεφαλῶν = בראשיהון,
which Montg. has plausibly recognized to be a corruption of
פטישיהון, which it then transposed to the third place to give the
sense 'hats on their heads', i. e. τιάρας ἐπὶ τ. κεφαλῶν αὐτῶν. Cook
regards this word as a later interpolation. Citations in the
Latin Fathers do not know of this article of attire : cf. Tertull.,
De Res. Carnis 58 ; but see Montg., *in loc.*

Hats. Following the conjecture in the last note as to the derangement of the order in Th., I identify τιάραις as the rendering of כרבלתהון. כרבלתא appears to mean 'hat' as in post-Biblical Hebrew: Levy, *NHWB.* ii. 395. Marti, *Gram.*[3], p. 75*, derives it from the Assyrian *Karballatu*, which according to the Persian translation on the inscription of Darius I (Naḳš-i-Rustam, l. 15) means 'helm' or 'hat'. In the later Jewish Aramaic and Syriac it 'signifies 'cock's comb'. The Gk. Vers. correctly renders כרבל by κυρβασία, which is likened to a cock's comb in Aristoph., *Av.* 487. Cf. Herod. v. 49; vii. 64. The RV. in assigning the meaning 'mantles' to this word has trusted too much to the doubtful connexion of the word with the Hebrew in 1 Chron. 15[27] מִכְרְבָּל.

Their garments. לבושיהון. This term is added to include all the rest of their garments.

3[22]. *Urgent.* On מחצפה see note on 2[15].

Exceeding. יַתִּירָה occurs as an adverb also in the *Eg. Pap.* (Cowley, Aḥ. 96).

Hot. The passive participle אֵזֵה is for אֲזֶה. Cf. Ezra 5[15], where אֵזֵל = אֲזֵל. See Kautzsch, § 15 e.

The flame of the fire. שביבא די נורא. Cf. 7[9], and see note in Bevan on this phrase in 3[22].

[[23]. I have bracketed this verse as a later interpolation, and relegated it to the foot-notes. Not a phrase of it is preserved in the LXX,[1] and, so far is it from contributing a single fresh fact to the narrative beyond what is already said in 3[21b], that it reproduces a weaker version of it. Nor, again, does it serve as an introduction to 3[24], which is perfectly intelligible without it. It is also noteworthy that in this verse נפל is used in the sense of 'to be cast down', whereas our author uses רמא ten times elsewhere, when it is necessary to express this idea. Finally the form תִּלָתְּהוֹן is unexampled in the Eg. Papyri as well as in Biblical Aramaic. It is, however, found in the Syriac *tᵉlâthaihôn*, which may have been formed on the anology of *tᵉraihôn*, 'they two'. On the other hand Cowley 38[8] restores the text by

---

[1] Seeing that both Tischendorf and Swete represent the LXX as containing this verse I will here print it for the sake of my readers : τοὺς μὲν οὖν ἄνδρας τοὺς συμποδίσαντας τοὺς περὶ τὸν Ἀζαρίαν ἐξελθοῦσα ἡ φλὸξ ἐκ τῆς καμίνου ἐνεπύρισε καὶ ἀπέκτεινεν, αὐτοὶ δὲ συνετηρήθησαν. This is beyond question a recasting of 3[22] and does not contain a single statement of 3[23].

reading לְ[תריה]ם = ' for both ', similarly as we have the Hebrew
שְׁנֵיהֶם. The construction is a well-known Hebrew one, and has
already occurred in our author 1¹⁷. Cf. 1 Sam. 20⁴².

But how are we to account for its interpolation? I know of
no satisfactory explanation. But that it is an interpolation,
the language, as I have just shown, seems to prove. The
context is also against it. In 3²¹ᵃ we are told the men were
'bound': in 3²¹ᵇ that they 'were cast into the midst of the
burning fiery furnace', a penalty which entails their immediate
destruction, as it did that of their executioners in 3²². After
this it would be the height of absurdity to say, as in 3²³, that
they 'fell down bound', seeing that they had been ' hurled ' into
the midst of the furnace. The use of נפל by our author implies
that the persons of which it is predicated had been standing
before they fell. So even in 7²⁰. Next to describe how fierce the
furnace was, as well as to suggest the speedy retribution that befel
the executioners, the writer diverges from his main theme for the
moment in 3²². But in 3²⁴ he resumes his theme, and in such
a way as to emphasize the antagonism existing between the
incidents just related in 3²¹ and their actual consequences in
3²⁴ so wholly contrary to all expectation. Moreover, in 3²⁴ the
king repeats the two most prominent phrases in 3²¹—the men
were 'bound' and 'cast . . . into the midst of the fire '.

Next, who was the interpolator? It was probably the
scribe, who interpolated the Prayer of Azariah and the Song
of Azariah and his two companions in the LXX, for the
LXX does not contain 3²³. We can only fall back on a
hypothetical account of the difficulties at issue. These two
additions written in Aramaic were inserted at an early date in
some manuscripts of Daniel, but not in others. Hence there
came to be current in the Jewish world two editions of Daniel,
the shorter of which was ultimately adopted into the Canon.
The Greek translation of these additions was made by some
other hand than that of the translator of the LXX. Somewhat
different forms of these Additions are reproduced in the LXX
and in Th.—the latter version being of course based on a much
older one, which was however much later than the LXX. But
in Th. 3²³ stands as it does in the MT. The progenitor of
Th. was made from an Aramaic text no less certainly than the
LXX, though it was main guided in its renderings by that

early version. This Aramaic text, as Th. testifies, contained 3^{23}. There were thus variations and alternatives in the larger text of Daniel.

In my small commentary I accepted the suggestion of von Gall, Bludau, and Rothstein that vv. 46–50 originally stood in a Semitic form between 3^{23} and 3^{24}. But, even if this were true, it would only be partially so; for in 3^{46} the king's mighty men are still represented as busily engaged in supplying the furnace with naptha, pitch, tow, and wood, although according to 3^{22} they had already been destroyed by the furnace. In the present commentary I have abandoned the above suggestion on the following grounds. First of all the Prayer of Azariah and the Song of the Three Children are independent works. The Prayer of Azariah was not originally composed in connexion with the incident of the Three Children. If it had been so, the speaker would have been not Azariah but Hananiah, that is, Shadrach, who is always the foremost of the Three. Again, in the Prayer itself, there is nothing to connect it with the events in the Book of Daniel. Next, as regards the Song of the Three Children, it too has no direct allusion to the Book of Daniel or its events save in 3^{88}, which was introduced to connect the Song of the Three Children with the Book of Daniel. It will be observed that the interpolator changes the order of the Three Children—an order which like that of the Medes and Persians was immutable, and recites them as follows: Ananias, Azarias, and Misael. Furthermore with a view to adapting the interpolated 3^{88} to its new context, the interpolator introduces certain changes. The last few verses will provide sufficient evidence to prove that the interpolator of 3^{88} has rearranged 3^{82-7} in order to bring 3^{88} into harmony with its new context.

As a rule the original writer of the Song of the Three Children wrote it in couplets, and in such a way as to carry on the thought of the reader from one couplet to another. Let us examine 3^{82-7} from the standpoint of this fact. 3^{82-3} call first on the sons of men, and then, as the theme advances, on Israel 'to bless the Lord, praise Him, and magnify Him for ever'. In 3^{84-5} the priests of the Lord and next the servants of the Lord are called to do likewise, or rather first the servants of the Lord and then His priests. But however this may be as to 3^{84-5}, there can be no doubt as to 3^{86-7}. This couplet was unquestionably written originally as follows, since in 3[86] we arrive at the climax :

3[87]. O ye holy and humble men of heart, bless ye the Lord,
     Praise Him and magnify Him for ever.
3[86]. O ye spirits and souls of the righteous, bless ye the Lord,
     Praise Him and magnify Him for ever.

But when the interpolator wished to add 3[88] and to bring Ananias, Azarias, and Misael into the foremost ranks of the living among 'the holy and humble men of heart', he was obliged to invert the order of 3[86-7], and so destroy the growing order of thought, which rightly found its climax of praise amongst 'the spirits and souls of the righteous'.

If then we omit the interpolated 3[88] and restore the original order of the couplets in 3[86-7], we may feel very confident that we have in some measure recovered the original form of this noble song, which then rightly closes in the fine doxology of 3[89-90].

But this Song had no connexion of any kind with our author, any more than had the Prayer of Azariah. The insertion of these works in the text of our author is due to some unknown scribe, who most probably added 3[23] to preface his interpolations.

The details of these interpolations are. After 3[22] came first 3[23], which has survived in the MT. and the later Versions, but not in the LXX. Then follows sixty-seven verses, i. e. 24–90 : vv. 24–45 the Prayer of Azarias : a descriptive passage recounting the destruction of the executioners, the descent of the angel, the doxology pronounced by the Three Children, and the hymn known as the *Benedicite*, 57–90. Thereupon we return to 3[24] of our author's text.]

3[24]. The LXX in 3[91] resumes the long addition it contains with the words καὶ ἐγένετο ἐν τῷ ἀκοῦσαι τὸν βασιλέα ὑμνούντων αὐτῶν καὶ ἑστὼς ἐθεώρει αὐτοὺς ζῶντας· τότε Ναβουχοδονοσὸρ ὁ βασιλεὺς ἐθαύμασε. This is very Hebraistic. Th. adds only ἤκουσεν ὑμνούντων αὐτῶν καί.

Counsellors. הדברין is peculiar to Daniel ; 3[27], 4[33 (36)], 6[8 (7)]. The original form and meaning are alike doubtful.

They answered. ענין is most probably an ancient corruption of ענו. See note on 2[5].

3[25]. *Loose.* The fire had merely destroyed their bonds.

Walking. Here and in 4[34(37)] we should read the Pa'el מְהַלְּכִין instead of the Haph'el מַהְלְכִין (see Kautzsch, § 33. 2).

A son of the gods, i.e. an angel. Cf. Gen. 6², Job 1⁶. When the true God is designated the sing. אלה, and not the plural אלהין, is used.

3²⁶⁻³⁰. *The three men come forth unhurt from the fiery furnace, and the king thereupon recognizes them as servants of the Most High God, and issues a decree that any nation that speaks against the God of Shadrach, Meshach, and Abednego should be destroyed.*

3²⁶. *Most High God.* Cf. 3³² (4²), 5¹⁸,²¹. The title ' Most High ' is found in 4¹⁴,²¹,²²,²⁹,³¹, 7²⁵. It was used by Jewish as well as by heathen writers : cf. Isa. 14¹⁴, Tob. 1¹³, 1 Esdras 2³, 6³¹, Mark 5⁷, Acts 16¹⁷. It is of very frequent occurrence in 1 Enoch, Test. xii Patriarchs, Jubilees, Ass. Moses, Wisdom, 2 Baruch, 4 Ezra, Philo, and Josephus. אֱלָהָא עִלָּיָא is the equivalent of the Hebrew אֵל עֶלְיוֹן, θεὸς ὕψιστος. That עליון was a proper name is clear from the fact that it never has the article even after prepositions. In the quotation from Philo Biblius in Eus., *Praep. Evang.* i. 10, we are told that among the Phoenicians Ἐλιοῦν was used as a name for God : Ἐλιοῦν καλούμενος Ὕψιστος. In our text the king recognizes the God of the Jews, not as the only God, but as the supreme God : cf. 3²⁹. Cf. the Divine name עליונין 7¹⁸,²²,²⁵,²⁷.

3²⁷. The gradation is obvious : the hair is not singed, the flowing mantles not hurt, and even the smell of fire had not passed upon them.

Saw. Here חזין is a participle, as is also the word translated ' being gathered together '. Asyndeton is characteristic of Biblical Aramaic. Hence we could translate here : 'assembled together and saw': cf. 3⁷.

The fire had no power. Here and in 7⁹ נורא is construed as masc. but in 3⁶ as fem., as it usually is, as in Syriac.

Bodies. ' The Western MSS. have נשמיהון (plur.) in the *Kt.*, but גשמהון (sing.) in the *Qr.*, while the Eastern MSS., have the latter rendering in both *Kt.* and *Qr.*' (Wright, *Daniel and his Critics*, p. 63). The *Qr.* has changed גשמיהון (*Kt.*) into גשמהון apparently because of the following ראשהון.

Passed. In עדת we have another anomaly. ריח its subject is never fem. in Hebrew or Syriac, though it is treated as so here.

3²⁸. *Doxology of the king.*

Sent his angel and delivered his servants. These two clauses are quoted in T. Sym. 2⁸ ἀπέστειλε τὸν ἄγγελον αὐτοῦ καὶ ἐρρύσατο αὐτόν: also in Acts 12¹¹.

Delivered. שֵׁיְזִב probably Shaph. as a loan-word from Assyr. *šûzub(u).* The earlier form of this borrowed word in Aram. is שׁוֺב: cf. Cowley 38⁵, 54⁹, Aḥ. 46: also *CIS.* ii. 113 in the proper name צלמשׁוֺב. These are fifth cent. B.C. But in later Aram., as in our author and in the Imtân Inscription (A.D. 93) Cooke 101¹²⁻¹³, we have the form שׁיוֺב as well as in the Targums. This fuller form appears in the Syr. as ܫܘܙܒ.

Trusted in him. רחץ על is frequent in the Targums and in the Christian Palestinian Aramaic. It is derived from the Ass. *raḥâṣu.* There is no evidence of its existence in the older Aram.

Set at nought, i. e. שַׁנִּיו. Cf. the Haph'el of this verb with the same meaning in Ezra 6¹¹.

Have given their bodies (to the fire). I have restored 'to the fire' with the LXX and Th. παρέδωκαν τὰ σώματα αὐτῶν εἰς ἐμπυρισμόν (Th. εἰς πῦρ). This passage seems to have suggested the form of words in 1 Cor. 13³, which Montg. compares καὶ ἐὰν παραδῶ τὸ σῶμά μου ἵνα καυθήσωμαι.

3²⁹. *Decree of the king.*

Anything amiss. So *Qr.* שָׁלוּ as in 6⁵. But since the *Kt.* reads שׁלה, this is probably with Hitzig to be punctuated שָׁלָה, i.e. שְׁאָלָה = דבר = 'word', 'thing': cf. 1 Sam. 1¹⁷ and 4¹⁴⁽¹⁷⁾ in our text. In Cowley 7⁶, 76⁴ it retains the meaning of 'request'.

Shall be cut in pieces, &c. See note on 2⁵.

Shall be made. ישׁתוה. In 2⁵ the verb is יתשׂמון.

3³⁰. *Caused . . . to prosper.* הצלח: that is, he caused them to prosper in the offices they already held in the province of Babylon: cf. LXX 6⁴: also pp. 151–2.

Appendix to Verses 3²,³.

The Eight (?) Classes of Royal Officials.

In 3²,³ the Aramaic gives a list of eight classes of royal officials in both verses. Since several distinguished scholars have maintained on various grounds that originally there were only seven, and appealed to the LXX and Th. in support of this view, some examination of the Versions on this question is necessary. For a full examination see Bludau, *Alexandrinische Uebersetzung des Buches Daniel*, pp. 99 seq.

1. First of all we observe that the Pesh. supports the Aramaic text both in respect of the order and number of the eight classes.

But the evidence of the LXX, Th., and Vulg. diverge here. In 3^2 these three Versions give only seven classes, while in 3^3 Th. gives apparently only six, while the Vulg. gives seven.

Let us compare the three Versions with regard to the fifth and sixth classes, remembering however that the LXX is borrowed from Th. by Origen in 3^3.

LXX	Th.	Vulg.
3^2. διοικητὰς καὶ τοὺς ἐπ' ἐξουσιῶν κατὰ χώραν	2. τυράννους καὶ τοὺς ἐπ' ἐξουσιῶν	2. tyrannos et praefectos
3^* τύραννοι μεγάλοι ἐπ' ἐξουσιῶν	3. τύραννοι μεγάλοι οἱ ἐπ' ἐξουσιῶν	3. tyranni et optimates qui erant in potestatibus constituti

Here we observe that μεγάλοι occurs in ver. 3 in the LXX and Th., which in these Versions is only an epithet, but that in the Vulg. it represents a distinct class. It is only reasonable to infer that the Versions are here corrupt and have compressed two classes into one, if we compare ver. 3 with ver. 2 in each Version, even if we fail to consider the presence of μεγάλοι. But, if we take it into account and the optimates in the Vulg., we may go further and infer that Th. in 3^3 has compressed *three* classes into one. But it is to be observed that these officials 3^3 were omitted in the LXX and borrowed by Origen from Th.

The renderings are loose and divergent: yet it is possible to identify them with the Aramaic which they profess to translate. The third of these classes οἱ ἐπ' ἐξουσιῶν (Th.) appearing only as ἐπ' ἐξουσιῶν in the LXX and qui erant in potestatibus constituti in the Vulg. are clearly the תפתיא 'sheriffs'; since in all three versions they correspond in order. Next the τύραννοι, μεγάλοι, οἱ ἐπ' ἐξουσιῶν are most probably renderings of דתבריא, הדבריא, תפתיא. The absence of the conjunctions in the Greek reflects the characteristic absence of conjunctions in the Aramaic.

Thus it is highly probable that there were originally seven

names in ver. 3. But the evidence is not conclusive. Symmachus gives really eight names in 3², and transliterates three
of the Aramaic words thus: τοὺς γαβδαρηνούς, τοὺς θαβδαρηνούς, τοὺς
θαβθαιούς.

SECTION IV

i. e. Chapter 4, in the eighteenth year of the reign of Nebuchadnezzar.

§ 1. *There are two forms of this Chapter.*

Both cannot be right. There is of course the possibility that
the order of both texts is wrong. An examination, however,
of the conflicting orders and texts will show that the LXX has
in the main preserved the true order of the text and its original
character, although it is very inaccurate in details and exhibits
frequent mistranslations and dittographies. In fact, though it
omits the later additions from the hand of a reviser, yet through
its frequent dittographies it contains nearly 40 per cent. more
words than the MT and the Versions dependent upon it.
In this estimate no account is taken of the three well-known
additions, *Susanna and the Elders*, the *Prayer of Azariah*, and
the *Song of the Three Children*. This great lengthening of the
text in chapter 4 is unique in the LXX of Daniel. In the next
chapter the LXX text is 30 per cent. shorter. Let us now
compare the two conflicting texts.

(a) *The Massoretic text.* In this text, which is followed by
Th., Pesh., Vulg., the entire narrative is given *in the form of
a prescript or imperial pronouncement which Nebuchadnezzar
issues to all his subjects.* It begins with a greeting to 'all the
peoples, nations, and languages that dwell in all the earth', and
proceeds to state the king's desire to make known to them 'the
signs and wonders that the Most High God had wrought
upon him, and that His kingdom is a kingdom for everlasting'
(3^{31-33}). He then recounts a dream which had troubled him,
and tells how he had summoned the magicians, enchanters,
Chaldeans, and soothsayers to make known its interpretation
(4^{1-4}); and how on their failure Daniel was brought before him
(4^{5-6}). Thereupon the king set forth his dream (4^{7-15}), which
Daniel forthwith interpreted (4^{16-24}). Within a year Daniel's
interpretation of the dream was fulfilled, and the king driven

forth to live with the beasts of the field (4^{25-30}). At the end of seven times the king's reason returned to him, and he was restored unto his kingdom, and so he praised and honoured and extolled the God of heaven (4^{31-4}).

(b) *The LXX.* Turning now to the LXX we observe first of all that it omits the first three verses in the MT, which transform the next thirty-four into an imperial prescript. This chapter begins simply, in the LXX, with the words $4^{1-2\,(4-5)}$: ' In the eighteenth year of his reign Nebuchadnezzar said : I Nebuchadnezzar was at rest in mine house . . .'. Then follows *in the same narrative form* $4^{7\,b-34\,(10\,b-37)}$, in which the king is represented as the speaker; $4^{3-7\,a\,(4-10\,a)}$ it rightly omits as we shall see presently, and gives quite a different version of $4^{15(18)}$. At the close of $4^{34\,(37)}$ comes the equivalent of the royal prescript, which in the Massoretic is placed at the beginning of the section, 3^{31-3} (4^{1-3}). It must be confessed that the order and contents of the prescript in the LXX are confused beyond conception, as we shall see presently. Notwithstanding, we shall discover that the LXX, and not the MT followed by the versions of Th., Pesh., and Vulg., has preserved the true character of this chapter and the right order of thought in the main, as it left the hands of our author. In this chapter as in chaps. 3 and 6 the king issues his prescript as a result of his spiritual and psychical experiences. Thus the same order of thought is observed by the LXX in chaps. 3, 4, and 6.

Let us summarize the evidence in support of the order of the text as preserved in the LXX.

(a) The order of the text in 4 follows the analogy of 3 and 6. Chap. 3, gives an account of Nebuchadnezzar's experiences in relation to the three young Hebrews, and then appends, as their natural sequel, the king's edict in which the king acknowledges the God of the Hebrews as the Most High God, and commends the faithfulness and heroism of His servants in worshipping Him at all costs, and secures by a decree (3^{29}) their right to do so without let or hindrance henceforth. 6^{1-24} tells of the plot of the satraps and presidents against Daniel, in the course of which they persuade the king to issue a decree, forbidding anyone to ask a petition of God or man for thirty days. Daniel refused obedience to this decree, he was cast into the den of lions, but delivered uninjured the next morning.

Thereupon (6^{25-8}) Darius issued a decree enjoining all his subjects to stand in awe of the God of Daniel. *The analogies of chaps. 3 and 6, therefore, support the order into which the matter is cast in the LXX in chap. 4. First comes the king's psychical experiences, and thereupon follows his royal prescript in the LXX but not in the MT.*

(β) But not only is the order in the LXX the more reasonable in itself and also confirmed by the analogy of chaps. 3 and 6, but traces still survive in the MT, which show that it is a secondary form or recast of a text which observed the same order as the LXX, that is, a narrative of thirty-four verses followed by a royal prescript; for in vv. 16, 25–30 (19, 28 sqq.) the narrative form persists in which the king is spoken of *in the third person. The redactor has here forgotten to transform these features of the narrative form in the third person into that of the prescript form in the first.*

(γ) The LXX alone of all the authorities preserves the date of Section IV (recalled in 4^{19}), and that, as is our author's all but universal method, in its opening sentence. Here Th., which alone supported the LXX in 3^1, fails us. And the explanation is not far to seek. When once the wrong and fatal step of transposing the royal prescript from the end of chap. 4 to the beginning was made by a reviser of the MT, the next step of omitting the date in $4^{1(4)}$ followed naturally. On their author's practice of dating each Section, see Introd., § 4.

(δ) The LXX shows its superior text in omitting vv. $4^{3-7\,a}$ $^{(6-10\,a)}$, which recount the assembling together of the wise men at the king's command to interpret his dream, their failure to do so, and finally Daniel's appearance before the king, who asks Daniel to interpret his dream. The relative positions of Daniel and the wise men during Nebuchadnezzar's reign[1] were settled once and for all in chap. 2. There was, therefore, no occasion to summon the wise men when Daniel was at the king's right hand; for Daniel was ruler over the whole province of Babylon and chief governor of all its wise men (2^{48}). The LXX, by thus omitting all mention of the wise men and representing the king as at once consulting Daniel in $4^{15\,(18)}$, puts the action of the king in a reasonable light. It would have been wholly in-

---

[1] The situation is quite different in 5^8. Nebuchadnezzar had died more than twenty years before the time of chap. 5.

congruous to summon Daniel's subordinates apart from himself, where the use of gifts was called for, in the possession of which gifts Daniel was absolutely unique, as alike the king and people knew only too well.

$4^{3-7a \, (6-10a)}$, then, appears to be an early addition made by a scribe, who, though he knew the text of the book, was not a master of its thought, nor yet of its phraseology. And the more the book is studied, the more convinced the student becomes of the clear and masterful mind of its author. 4^{3-7a} is composed of a variety of phrases drawn from the other Aramaic chapters in Daniel, but there are three misuses of the author's style in $4^{4,5,6}$ $^{(7,8,9)}$. There is only one phrase לא אנס 4^6 which is not found elsewhere in our author. Observe also that the four classes of wise men are drawn from 5^{11}. Again we find in $4^{31(34)c-32(35)}$ another addition of the reviser, in which the unity of the text is broken up as before, and where again the reviser betrays his ignorance of our author's phraseology (see 4^{31} sqq. note)). Thus the evidence of the text and that of the context agree in rejecting these additions of the reviser, and both conspire to prove that here our author is pursuing the order he observes in chaps. 3 and 6.

§ 2. *The source of the historical statements in this chapter.*

It is now generally agreed that there is nothing to be found in the inscriptions or in ancient history relating to Nebuchadnezzar's insanity. On the other hand, it is no less certain that the author of this chapter was following a popular tradition, another form of which is preserved by Eusebius (*Praeparatio Evangelica*, ix. 41) from the Assyrian history of Abydenus, who lived about 200 B.C. 'I found also the following statements concerning Nebuchadnezzar in the work of Abydenus, *Concerning the Assyrians* :

"Now Megasthenes (*floruit* 300 B.C.) says that Nebuchadnezzar was braver than Hercules, and made an expedition against Libya and Iberia, and, having subdued them, settled a part of their inhabitants on the right shore of Pontus. And afterwards, the Chaldeans say, he went up to his palace, and being possessed by some god or other uttered the following speech: 'O men of Babylon, I Nebuchadnezzar here foretell to you the coming calamity, which neither Belus my ancestor nor queen Beltis is able to persuade the Fates to avert. There will come a Persian mule, aided by the alliance of your own deities, and will bring you into slavery. And the joint author of this will be ⟨the son⟩[1] of a Median woman, in whom the Assyrians glory. O would that before he gave up my citizens some Charybdis or sea might swallow him utterly out of sight; or that, turning in other directions, he might be carried across the desert, where there are neither cities nor foot of man, but where wild beasts have pasture and birds their haunts, that he might wander alone among rocks and ravines; and that before he took such thoughts into his mind, I myself had found a better end.'

"He after uttering this prediction immediately disappeared, and his son Amil-Marudocus became king. But he was slain by his kinsman Iglisar, who left a son Labassoarask. And when he died by a violent death, Nabannidochus, who was not at all related to him (προσήκοντά οἱ οὐδέν) was appointed king. But after the capture of Babylon, Cyrus presents him with the principality of Carmania "' (Gifford's edition III. i. 484–5).

We have here clearly a legend of Babylonian origin referring to the overthrow of the Babylonian empire by Cyrus 'the mule', and the part borne therein by Nabu-na'id, the last of the Babylonian kings.

I have quoted the above passage in order to show on the one hand certain small points of contact between the history in Daniel and that in Abydenus, and on the other their hopeless divergence on the question of historical truth.

First as regards the resemblances, Nebuchadnezzar is represented in both as being on the roof of his palace: in both a divine voice makes itself heard (in the former work to the king, in the latter through him): and finally the doom pronounced in both is similar though its object differs. But neither form of the story is borrowed from the other, though that of Abydenus is more primitive, while that in Daniel has been transformed to serve a didactic aim.

Next as regards the divergence between these two lines of tradition. The popular tradition made the last Babylonian king a son of Nebuchadnezzar, whose wife, according to Berossus in

---

[1] I have here, after Schrader, Bevan, and others' example, introduced von Gutschmid's conjecture of υἱὸς Μήδης for Μήδης—son of a Median woman, e.g. Nabu-nâ'id.

Joseph., *C. Apion.* i. 19, had been brought up in Media, and so may (?) have been a Median (τὴν γυναῖκα αὐτοῦ . . . τεθραμμένην ἐν τοῖς κατὰ τὴν Μηδίαν τόποις). Herodotus apparently identifies Labynetus II with Nabūnā'id (i. 77), and makes the latter the son of Labynetus I, i. e. Nebuchadnezzar (i. 188). In our author this same tradition is reproduced : see 5² note. But Abydenus whom I have just quoted and Berossus (Joseph., *C. Apion.* i. 19) give the list of Nebuchadnezzar's four Baby-lonian successors ending with Nabūnā'id, and definitely state that the Nabūnā'id was not the son of Nebuchadnezzar ; nay more Abydenus states that he was not in any way related to him (προσήκοντά οἱ οὐδέν). If Nabūnā'id had married the widow of Nebuchadnezzar, such a union, with all the rights it entailed, would have made Abydenus's statement impossible.

§ 3. *The object of Chapter 4.*

The object of chapter 4 is not, as 3 is in part, to admonish the Jews against idolatry, but to show the sheer helplessness of the heathen powers over against the true God. However irresistible the power of Antiochus might seem to the Jews, our author teaches through the lips of the great king of Babylon, that the mightiest monarch, who resists the will of God, has no more power than the meanest of mankind, and can in one moment be reduced, not merely to the position of the latter, but even to that of the brute. The obvious lesson involved is that the Jews are not to fear the power of Antiochus Epiphanes ; for that God rules, and nothing can fall out but what He permits. As the pride of Nebuchad-nezzar was humbled, so would be that of the Syrian king. As the king learnt the lesson of religious toleration through the faithfulness of the three Jewish Confessors in iii, so now through that of Daniel he learns that the God of Israel is the supreme God.

§ 4. *The text.*

It may be at once confessed that it is impossible to recover the text in the form in which it left the author's hand. We have already recognized in § 1 that this chapter has been trans-mitted in two quite distinct forms, the more original being that in the LXX, seeing that the order of events in the LXX corre-sponds with that in chaps. 3 and 6. In other words the author observed a special order in developing his theme, and this order has been preserved in the LXX, but not in the MT, in this chapter. But, when we have necessarily conceded the greater originality of the LXX in this respect, we cannot but confess that the text of the individual passages in the LXX is often hopeless. A minute comparison of the LXX, which in many respects goes back to 145 B.C., with the MT, leads the student to conclude that the reviser or editor found this chapter in an appalling state of corruption, and that he acted drastically, reconstructing it from start to finish so far as its primitive character went, and making additions of his own, which it is not difficult to detect, as he was not wholly familiar with his author's style.

(a) *Omissions.*

4^1. 'In the eighteenth year of his reign.' Preserved in the LXX. This note of time is characteristic of our author at the beginning of each section.

(b) *Interpolations.*

$4^{3-7a\,(6-10a)}$. See note *in loc.*

$4^{15\,(18)}$. The reviser has excised the original $4^{15(18)}$ (preserved in LXX) and replaced it by a verse of his own composition in order to justify the large interpolation of $4^{3-7a\,(6-10a)}$. It begins with a construction unexampled in our author. Next, if the phrase 'king Nebuchadnezzar' is faithfully transmitted, then this order of the words is rare in Daniel and apparently unknown before Daniel.

4^{31c-32}. These verses are not found in the LXX. The two closing lines of 4^{31} are contrary to our author's mode of quoting them. See note *in loc.* Again in $4^{32\,e}$ יֵאמַר לֵהּ is wholly at variance with our author's usage, who would here have said יאמר קדמוהי. See note *in loc.* and Introd., § 20. *w.*

(c) *Late Aramaic.*

$4^{5\,(8)}$. דִּי שְׁמֵהּ בּ". Not (?) in Aramaic before 200 B.C.

$4^{23\,(26)}$. שמיא = God. Not in O.T. outside Daniel, but in Apocrypha and late Hebrew.

$4^{16\,(19)}$. אשתמם. The א is late for ה.

(d) Jussive forms (3rd plur.) lost unless in 4^{16}, 5^{10} after אל. I am convinced that in Ezra the jussive forms without final *nun*, even when not preceded by אל, occurred in $6^{5,7}$, but that they were subsequently assimilated to the ordinary 3rd plur. imperfect by scribes. In our author these forms have survived in three passages owing to the fact that they were preceded by אל. But it is probable that in the Aramaic of our author these forms had disappeared unless after the negative. Thus the 3rd plural imperf. ending in *nun* had to fulfil the double function, i.e. of a jussive, as in 4[13(16), 22(25),29(32)], and of an ordinary imperfect or future indicative elsewhere.

4[1,2,(4,5),7b—14(10b—17)],. *The king recounts his dream in his royal pronouncement.*

4[1(4)]. ⌜In the eighteenth year of his reign Nebuchadnezzar said⌝. In the introduction to this chapter I have shown that both the external evidence of the LXX, the internal inconsistencies of the MT, and the method· pursued by our author in 4 require us to transfer 3[31—33] (4[1—3]) to the close of the chapter. The words which I have introduced in brackets at the beginning of 4[1] are from the LXX. When the original order of the text was altered by the reviser, who sought to give the entire chapter the form of a royal prescript with the grounds on which it was based, the sentence in brackets being in the *third* person was obviously out of place amongst a succession of sentences in the *first*. Moreover, the retention of the date in this transformed context would have been incongruous.

At rest—contented and at ease—in a good or in a bad sense according to the context: Ps. 122[6], 73[12].

Flourishing. The word רענן, which is properly used of a tree, was possibly suggested by Ps. 92[11,15], where, as here, it is used figuratively of persons. It is used indifferently of the prosperity of the righteous, Ps. 52[10], or of the wicked, Ps. 37[35].

4[2(5)]. *Which made me afraid.* וידחלנני. The use of the imperfect for the perfect as here is rare in Biblical Aram. (cf. 4[17,33], 5[6], 6[20], 7[16]), and not in the Targums according to Bevan. The LXX adds here καὶ φόβος μοι ἐπέπεσεν, which appears to be a loose duplicate rendering of וידחלנני.

And thoughts upon my bed and the visions of my head troubled me. These two clauses were lost in the Aramaic MS. from which the LXX was translated, and the loss was caused by homoioteleuton יבהלנני · · · · · · · · · וידחלנני. All the words are those of our author (save הרהרין), and the phrases are used as our author uses them.

Thoughts or imaginations, i. e. הרהרין—derivatives of which occur in the Targums, Syr., and late Hebrew. Since Th. renders ἐταράχθην Bertholdt conjectures that he had הִרְהֵרֵת from הִרְהֵר, i. e. *I had evil fancies* or *thoughts*.

Visions of my head. Cf. 2²⁸, 4⁷⁽¹⁰⁾, ¹⁰⁽¹³⁾, 7¹,¹⁵.

[4⁰⁻¹⁰ᵃ. This passage I have relegated to the foot of the page in my translation, as an addition of the reviser who transformed this chapter from being a narrative, in which the king is spoken of in the third person followed by an edict, into a royal pronouncement in which it was the intention of the reviser to make the king speak throughout in the first person, but failed to transform the text thoroughly in this respect. See Introd. to this chapter, § 1 (δ), p. 81 sq.

4³⁽⁶⁾. *Made I a decree.* Cf. 3¹⁰,²⁹, 6²⁷⁽²⁶⁾.

To bring in, i. e. להנעלה, Haph'el inf. of עלל. This is the form of the Haph'el always found in the Fifth Cent. Pap. (see Cowley 15⁶,⁷,²⁴, 42¹²). In 5⁷ we find הֵעָלָה. In 2²⁵ we have the perfect הַנְעֵל.

To bring in all the wise men of Babylon. Though Daniel was the chief of all the wise men, he was not summoned along with them. The reviser who added 4³⁻⁷ᵃ is not conscious of this inconsistency, though in 4⁶ he makes the king address Daniel as 'master of the magicians'.

All the wise men of Babylon. The same phrase in 2¹²,⁴⁸, cf. 5⁷,⁸.

That they might make known, &c. Cp. 2³⁰ for the same phrase.

4⁴⁽⁷⁾. *Came in.* עללין Kt., Qr. עָלִּין. On the latter form see Marti, *Gram.,* § 66 e. The participle is found in 5⁸ in the same connexion.

The magicians, the enchanters, the Chaldeans, and the soothsayers. These four classes are enumerated in 5¹¹ and there only.

I told the dream before them. The phrase 'tell the dream' is found in 2⁴,⁷. The whole clause is אמר אנה קדמיהון. Now this use of קדם before any person less than God or the king, as again in the next verse קדמוהי אמרת, where it replaces ל, is against the usage of our author. The interpolator should have used ל after אמר here. קדם is found after אמר or some other verb when God or a king or a dynasty is spoken of or is addressed. See Introd., § 20. w.

4⁵⁽⁸⁾. †*At the last*†. This rendering of עד אחרין is doubtful. Michaelis and Bevan, adopting the Qr., read עַד אָחֳרָן, 'yet another'. See Kautzsch, § 69. 10 ; Marti, §§ 87 c, 94ᵇ, 98.

Whose name was B. This idiom "בּ שְׁמֵהּ דִּי is found also in
2²⁶, 4¹⁶. It is unknown, so far as I can discover, in earlier
Aramaic. In the *Aram. Pap.* (Cowley, 28⁴,⁹,¹³, 33¹⁻⁵, Aḥ. 1, 4–5,
18, Beh. 2, 7, &c.) the די is always omitted. See Introd.,
§ 20. z.

According to the name of my god, i. e. Bel. This is a mistake.
The name Belteshazzar is not derived from Bel. See note on
1⁷. This statement is a development of what is said in the
revised text in 5¹², where we read 'Daniel, whom the king
named Belteshazzar'. But according to 1⁷ it was not the king
but the prince of the eunuchs who gave this name to Daniel,
and apparently Nebuchadnezzar had no personal knowledge of
Daniel at all until after he had been trained by the prince of the
eunuchs for the king's service. The LXX knows nothing of
the false etymology here recorded, nor in 5¹² does it know
anything of the false statement that the king had named Daniel
Belteshazzar.

In whom is the spirit of the holy gods. This clause here as
also in 4⁶,¹⁵ is borrowed from 5¹¹,¹⁴. Cf. 6⁴⁽³⁾.

I told the dream before him. See note on 4⁴ on the interpo-
later's misuse of קדם.

Th. omits חלמא 'the dream'. We should then translate 'I
said before him'. This omission, it is true, removes the inconsistency between this verse and the next, where the king
according to the Aramaic *requires Daniel to tell him the dream,*
though according to the clause, with which we are immediately
dealing, the king has just declared 'I told the dream before him'.
Now either this statement or the statement in the next verse is
false. But the first statement is evidently that of the reviser;
for according to 4⁴ the king has already told the dream to the
wise men. The corruption, therefore, lies in the latter half of 4⁶.

4⁶⁽⁹⁾. *Master of the magicians.* Here again the reviser has
borrowed a phrase from 5¹¹, רב חרטמיא, where alone it is used
to designate Daniel beyond the present borrowed phrase. In
2⁴⁸ the king makes Daniel 'chief governor over all the wise
men' רב סגנין על כל חכימי בבל.

No secret troubleth thee. Behrmann observes that these words
כל רז לא אנס לך read almost like an Aramaic version of Ezek. 28³,
where Ezekiel says of the prince of Tyre: 'Behold thou art
wiser than Daniel: there is no secret that they can hide from

thee'—כל סתום לא עממוך. The Targum on Ezek. here gives כל רז לא יתכסא מנך.

⌜Hear⌝ the visions of my dream ... and tell the interpretation thereof. Here I follow Th., who inserts ἄκουσον. The Aramaic reads as follows: 'Tell the visions of mỳ dream ... and the interpretation thereof'. This is clearly corrupt. Even the reviser could not have been guilty of such an obvious self-contradiction as this text would create between this statement and the two different statements in 4⁴,⁵. Hence on the strength of Th. we assume the loss of שְׁמַע in the Aramaic, as Marti has done in his translation in Kautzsch's Die Heilige Schrift². In his commentary Marti abandons this emendation of the text, and, rejecting חזוי as the slip of a scribe, regards the resulting expression 'my dream and its interpretation' as a hendiadys. This would restore consistency to the text, but the method requires too many suppositions. It would be simpler with Giese-brecht (GGA. 1. 895, 598) to take חזוי as a corruption of אֲחַוֵּה 'I will recount my dream and do thou tell me its interpretation'.

Visions of my dream. This expression is not found elsewhere in the Aramaic of Daniel. Partly on this ground Giesebrecht, whom I have quoted in the preceding note, would emend it. But, since on other grounds we have concluded that 4³⁻⁷ᵃ is the addition of a reviser, who borrows all his phrases save one from our author, but misuses some of them, it is best to regard this phrase as persisting in the form in which it left the reviser's hand. This phrase, which both the Aram., Th., and Vulg. preserve, is contrary to the usage of our author, who speaks of ח" די ליליא 2¹⁹, 7², and ח" ראשי 2²⁸, 4²,⁷,¹⁰, 7¹,¹⁵, but never of ח" חלמי. The Pesh. = בחזוי חלמי חזית חזוי ראשי ופשרה אמר לי, which shows another attempt to emend the Aramaic.

4⁷ᵃ⁽¹⁰ ᵃ⁾. And the visions of my head. These words though not found in Th. appear in the Aramaic, as the close of the addition made by the reviser. They have already occurred in the beginning of the interpolation in 4², and thus resume that narrative where the addition broke off. We might compare his additions in 4³⁴ᶜ⁻³⁵,³⁶ᵃ.

4⁷ᵇ⁻¹⁴ ⁽¹⁰ᵇ⁻¹⁷⁾. In this dream of the king the imagery is clearly borrowed to a great extent from Ezek. 31³⁻¹⁴, where the glory of the Assyrian is likened to that of a cedar in Lebanon, in the boughs of which all the fowls of heaven made their nests, and under the branches of which all the beasts of the field brought forth their young, and under the shadow of which dwelt all great nations.　This great tree, like that in the king's vision, was suddenly destroyed.　Behrmann and Driver compare the dream of Xerxes recorded in Herod. vii. 19, in which he saw himself crowned with a shoot of an olive tree, the boughs of which cover the whole earth.

4⁷ᵃ⁽¹⁰ᵃ⁾. *Upon my bed I saw.*　So Th. and MT, though the Massoretes connect the word 'upon my bed' with the clause that precedes 'Thus were the visions of my head'.　In some form and most probably in this form these words belong to the original text, since the LXX also has corresponding words, though probably corrupt, ἐπὶ τῆς κοίτης μου ἐκάθευδον.

4⁷ᵇ⁻⁹. These verses form, as Marti has recognized, two stanzas of four lines each.　But in the first stanza the second line is bracketed as a dittograph of line 4, and in the second stanza the second line is a dittograph of line 5.

4⁸⁽¹¹⁾. *Began to reach.*　Here the imperfect follows the perfect as in 4²,³¹.

The sight thereof.　The form of חֲזוֹתֵהּ is difficult.　Kautzsch (§ 61. 4 Anm.) and Bevan think that it may be a mistake for חֲזוּתֵהּ.　The sense also not satisfactory.　It should mean not 'height' but 'extent' as the renderings of the LXX and Th. τὸ κύτος αὐτοῦ suggest.

4⁹⁽¹²⁾. *The leaves thereof.*　With עָפְיֵהּ compare עֳפָאִים Ps. 104¹². On the form of אִנְבֵּהּ see note on 2⁹.　Prince (*in loc.*) thinks that this is the original form of the word, and compares the Assyr. *inbu*, 'fruit'.

Meat, i. e. מָזוֹן.　Also in Heb. Cf. Gen. 45²³, 2 Chron. 11²³ (of Aramaic origin).　The long syllable in the preformative of this word, as also in the same word in Syriac, is not found elsewhere in Aramaic.　Yet Nöldeke (*Mand. Gram.*, § 110. 3) regards this as the ancient form.

For all.　לְכֹלָּא־בַהּ.　On the daghesh forte see Kautzsch, § 12. 2 *d*: 17. 1.

Were sheltering … dwelling … was being fed.　As Driver remarks, these tenses 'denote what was habitual, and therefore might be observed as taking place at the time of his dream'.

Were sheltering. תַּטְלֵל is a rare example of verb ע״ע not being

contracted in the Haph'el. Cf. Kautzsch, § 46. 3 : Marti, § 66 *a*.
Contrast תַּדִּק 2⁴⁰,⁴⁴.

Dwellmg. For יְדְרוּן the *Qr.* substitutes יְדְרַן, since the nom. "צ
is usually feminine. Cf. 4¹⁸.

4¹⁰⁽¹³⁾. *Saw* : literally 'was seeing', as in 4⁷⁽¹⁰⁾, 7⁴,⁷,⁹,¹¹,¹³,²¹.

A watcher. Cf. 4¹⁴⁽¹⁷⁾,²⁰⁽²³⁾. The word עיר is transliterated as
εἴρ by Th., and translated by the LXX by ἄγγελος, and by the other
versions by ἐγρήγορος. This last word appears frequently in the
Greek version of 1 Enoch. See 1⁵ n., 6², 10⁷,⁹,¹⁵, &c., where it
designates two classes of angels : (1) archangels (unfallen) ;
(2) fallen angels. The distinction of the Watchers into these
two classes seems to be already implied in our text ; for there
are not two heavenly beings who are referred to here but only
one. Hence the compound phrase 'the watcher and that a holy
one' (so also in 4²⁰⁽²³⁾) = 'a holy watcher'. Bevan seeks to
discount this conclusion by comparing it with the phrase
גֵּר וְתוֹשָׁב. But even in this phrase the second noun qualifies
the meaning of the first. The גר had civil rights. The תושב
had apparently none. Hence the second noun minimizes the
force of the first. It is used in the sense of 'angel' also in
Syriac. It is not impossible that the word originally occurred
in Ps. 82⁷, and that for שָׂרִים 'princes' we should read עירים.
Aramaic words are of not infrequent occurrence in the Psalms.
We should then translate :

> 'I have said, ye are gods
> And ye are all the sons of the Most High ;
> Nevertheless ye shall die like common men
> And perish like one of the Watchers.'

In Isa. 24²¹,²² the heavenly patrons of the nations are punished
for their offences : cf. Ps. 58¹ : in 1 Enoch 10¹¹⁻¹³, 14–16, 88¹,
Jubilees 5¹⁰, the punishment of the faithless Watchers is recorded. They shall be cast down into 'an abyss '.

The term 'Watcher' recalls the words שֹׁמְרִים = 'watchmen'
in Isa. 62⁶. These 'watchmen' are not prophets but heavenly
beings commissioned by God to put him in remembrance of the
walls of Zion.

An holy one. This designation denoting an angel—cf. 8¹³,
Job 5¹, 15¹⁵ ; Ps. 89⁶,⁸, &c.—is very frequent in 1 Enoch, where
see the note on 1⁹ in my edition.

Came down. With נְחָת where the primitive *ĭ* is retained cf. יְכִל 3[17], נְוָק 6[3], דְלִק 7[9].

Cried aloud. See note on 3[4].

4[11(14)]. The words of the watcher form a stanza of four lines.

From under it. For תְּחֹתוֹהִי (a Hebraistic pointing) read תְּחֹתוֹהִי as in 4[9].

4[12(15)]. *Stump.* עִקַּר should here as well as in 4[20,23] be punctuated עִקַּר (Kautzsch, § 59 *c*, who draws attention to the long vowel in the Syriac).

With a band of iron and brass. The meaning is somewhat obscure. A hope of restoration remained since the stump was left in the ground, but the band of iron and brass seems to be ‘ a figure of speech for the stern and crushing sentence under which the king is to live ’ (Bevan), so long as his punishment was to last. The words refer to the king only, as the next verse shows, and not to the second and third world powers, as has been suggested. Otherwise the clause may be a figure for the restraint which the king would have to endure during his malady (Prince).

4[13(16)]. *Let his heart be changed from man's,* &c. That is, ‘ let him receive the understanding of a beast (imagine himself an animal)’ (Driver). The heart here denotes of course ‘ the intellect ’. The heart, in Hebrew psychology, is the seat of the intellect : cf. Jer. 5[21], ‘ foolish people and without understanding ’ (וְאֵין לֵב) : Hos. 7[11].

Man's. Here and in the next verse the *Kt.* reads אנושא (a Hebraism—not in the Fifth Cent. Pap., nor in the Zinjirli Inscription eighth cent. (see Cooke, 62[23]), but the *Qr.* אנשא as in 2[38,43], 4[22,20]. On the construction מן אנושא for מן לבב א״ cf. 1[10]. Cf. the use of מן in 1 Kings 15[13].

Seven times : i. e. seven years as the LXX renders it. Cf. 7[25], 12[7]. So also Joseph., *Ant.* x. 10. 6.

Changed. In Hebrew (cf. 1 Sam. 21[14]), Assyr. and Syriac the verb שנא is used of mental derangement. See Prince *in loc.* יְשַׁנּוֹן—an active verb is used impersonally to express the passive as in 3[4].

4[14(17)]. *The decree of the watchers,* i. e. עירין for עיריא in imitation of poetical style. In 4[21,24] it is said to be ‘ the decree of the Most High ’. In the OT. the angels form a kind of heavenly council (Ps. 89[6,8] כהל and סוד קדשים). Job 1[6,12], 2[1,6]

Jer. 23[18]. This idea was developed in later Judaism to an extravagant and even blasphemous degree, in accordance with which God was represented as doing nothing without consulting this council (Sanh. 38[6], where this statement is made and this passage of Daniel quoted). When God wished to make Hezekiah the Messiah His council successfully resisted Him (Sanh. 94[a]), and when He purposed to admit the descendants of Nebuchadnezzar into the Jewish Community, the angels of service would not suffer it. See Weber, *Jüdische Theologie*, 175 sq.

By the word. Here the preposition is to be repeated from the preceding clause : cf. Ges.-Kautzsch, § 119 *hh*, as Michaelis pointed out,

Decision. שְׁאֵלְתָא is found in the *Fifth Cent. Pap.* (Cowley, 7[6]) in the sense of 'petition'. It also means 'question'. But, as Montg. *in loc.* has shown, it bears here the above meaning.

Men, i. e. אנשים, is pure Hebrew due to a thoughtless scribe. Read אנשא. Cf. the *Kt.* אלפים in 7[10] and מלכים in Ezra 4[13].

4[15(18)]. I have here given the translation of the LXX in the text, since it alone admits of a consistent view of the entire chapter, though the last clause seems corrupt. The LXX runs as follows :

σφόδρα ἐθαύμασα ἐπὶ τούτοις, καὶ ὁ ὕπνος μου ἀπέστη ἀπὸ τῶν ὀφθαλμῶν μου. καὶ ἀναστὰς τὸ πρωὶ ἐκ τῆς κοίτης μου ἐκάλεσα τὸν Δανιὴλ τὸν ἄρχοντα τῶν σοφιστῶν καὶ τὸν ἡγούμενον τῶν κρινόντων τὰ ἐνύπνια, καὶ διηγησάμην αὐτῷ τὸ ἐνύπνιον, καὶ ὑπέδειξέ μοι πᾶσαν τὴν σύγκρισιν αὐτοῦ.

The form and the contents of the Aramaic here calls for attention. (1) As regards the form דנה חלמא, if we are to translate it 'this dream', this is against the usage of our author in the other eleven passages where this pronoun occurs. It should follow not precede its noun. See Introd., § 20. *h*. Again the order 'king Nebuchadnezzar' is rare in our author. Out of nineteen instances the Aram. observes this order only in seven, one of which is the present passage. But the LXX supports the Aram. in only three out of these seven passages. Its text differs in the rest. Thus in addition to the overwhelming difficulties of the context, the text itself is not wholly free from difficulty, though outside the points criticized the idioms are quite those of our author. (2) The contents of the Aramaic stand or fall with 4[3(6)]⁻⁷[(10a)]. Since both the LXX omits this latter passage, and the context itself is against it, the present form of the Aramaic of 4[15] must be rejected as the work of the reviser who added 4[3-7 a], and the LXX accepted in default of a better.

I was alarmed, i. e. תְּוֵית. Cf. 3[24]. *My sleep departed*, &c., i. e. שְׁנתי נדת. Cf. 6[19]. *Arose early*, i. e. קמת בשפרפרא: cf. 6[20]. *Chief of the wise men*, i. e. רב חכימיא: cf. 2[48], 5[11]. *The master* (? סגן: cf. 2[48]). *Interpreters of dreams*, i. e. די מפשרין חלמין: cf. 5[12]. *Told him the dream*, i. e. אמרת לה חלמא: cf. 2[4,7].

And he made known to me all its interpretation = והודע לי כל פשרה. We should expect τοῦ ὑποδεῖξαι = להודעתני 'in order that he should make known'. Or else ἠρώτησα αὐτὸν ὑποδεῖξαι = שאל אנה לה".

[*Text of the above verse in the Massoretic.* This verse is mainly composed of phrases drawn from the rest of our author. But the reviser was not fully acquainted with our author's style. Thus he says דנה חלמא 'this dream', whereas our author always put the demonstrative after the noun. See Introd., § 20. *h.* Again the reviser writes מלכא נבוכנצר 'king Nebuchadnezzar', whereas our author barely once in three times uses this late order. He usually puts the personal name before the official, i.e. ' N. the king'. This latter argument would in itself be wholly uncertain, but that it occurs in connexion with the former which is certain. On the other hand since Th., Pesh., and Vulg. reverse the order of the Aramaic in this verse, it follows that our author used the later order only in six out of nineteen instances in the original text.

4[16(19)]. Observe that in this verse there is still a survival of the name.

Was appalled. אֶשְׁתּוֹמַם. Hebraism (Kautzsch § 36), cf. 8[27], and the only instance of such a form in Biblical Aramaic. But Nöldeke, *ZDMG*, 1876, p. 326, holds it to be a true Aramaic form.

For a while. In כשעה חדה, חדה (as in 2[31], 6[18]) has an indefinite meaning. So also in the Fifth Cent. Pap. (Cowley, 30[29], &c.) אחד has the same indefinite meaning in Hebrew: cf. 8[13], Exod. 33[5], רגע אחד. The phrase may mean 'for a moment'. Later it came to mean 'for an hour'.

The king answered . . . trouble thee. Both the LXX and Th. omit—probably through hmt.

Let . . . not trouble thee. Here and in 5[10 d] the jussive יְבַהֲלָךְ has maintained itself after אל with a suffix and in 5[10 e] without a suffix אל־יבהלונך. See Marti *Gram.* § 52[a], 32[b]. The jussive is distinguished from the usual imperfect through the non-insertion of the *-in* before the suffix here, and in $5^{10\,d}$ and in $5^{10\,b}$ without the final *nun* where no suffix follows. In the Eighth Cent. B.C. *Zinjirli Inscription* (Cooke, $61^{4,7,12}$) the third pl. imperf. ends also without the *nun*. Cooke holds that these are not jussive in meaning, but they appear to be jussives. In the Seventh Cent. B.C. *Nerab Inscriptions* (Cooke, $64^{9,11}$, 65^{9} the 3rd pl. imperf. without the final *nun* has a jussive force: יסחו 'let them pluck': יכטלוך ויהאבדו 'let them kill thee and destroy': יהבאשו 'let them make wretched'. Thus in the seventh century this distinction is observed in the Nerab Inscriptions (in North Arabia). In the inscriptions of the fifth the jussives are well attested. In a Tema (N. Arabia) inscription Fifth Cent. B.C. (Cooke, 69^{14} : *CIS.* ii. 113) ינסחוהי 'let them pluck him', and יהנ[פקו] (69^{21}) is also a jussive. In the fifth century papyri and documents, the 3rd pl. imperf. without final *nun has a jussive force*. Thus in *Eg. Pap.* (Cowley, 30^{8}, 31^{7}) ינדשו = 'let them destroy': (30^{6}, 31^{6}) יהעדו = 'let them remove': (26^{5}) יעבדו = 'let them make': (26^{6}) ינתנו = 'let them give'. In 30^{25} and 32^{9} יקרבון should have a jussive meaning, but in each passage the word is written over an erasure. יומיך יארכון in Beh. 58 is to be construed simply as an indicative. In another Elephantine papyrus (Cooke, $73\,B^{3}$ = *CIS.* ii. 137 : 4th cent. B.C.) we have יאכלו = 'let them eat'. In Jer. 10^{11} we have יֵאבַדוּ 'they shall perish'.

This jussive form was, therefore, in use from the seventh (if not from the eighth) century B.C. down to the fourth or third. In Ezra $6^{5,7}$—an old Aramaic fifth century document—however, we have יהתיבון and יבנון where we should expect jussive forms without the final *nun*. It may be reasonably concluded that the present forms are not original but adapted to later usage ; for this distinction was lost in later Aramaic (Stevenson, *Gram. of Palestine Jewish Aramaic*, § 29. 10: 38). Also in Ezra 4^{12} יחיטו may with many scholars be taken as corrupt for יהיטון. In respect of this old Aramaic idiom the text of Ezra seems untrustworthy; for not in a single passage does it preserve this ancient distinction of form and meaning. In Daniel, as we have already seen, this jussive form has been preserved in three passages 4^{16}, $5^{10\,(bis)}$, but only after אל, and no doubt owed its preservation to this prohibitive particle, which does not occur in Ezra. This tends to show that the later language was losing its knowledge of the jussive forms, and the imperf. indicative ending in *nun* had to serve both as an indicative and a jussive. If the Aramaic of our author were sixth or fifth century Aramaic, we should expect יִשְׁנּוֹ in 4[13], יַחְלְפוּ in 4[22,29], יטעמו in 4[22,29]; perhaps also יְקוּמוּ in 7[24] and יקבלו in 7[18], יהעדו, וישתמעו and יפלחו in 7[26,27]. This distinction is lost in later Aramaic.

My lord. מראי. So *Kt.* *Qr.* has מרי. But see note on 2[47]. The retention of the א shows that it still possessed its consonantal sound, as in the Fifth Cent. Pap. (Cowley, 16[8], 37[17], 38[2], &c.).

4[17−18(20−21)]. Repeated with remarkable effect from 8,9.

4 [18(21)]. *Were dwelling.* תדור corresponding to 'were sheltering', תטלל in 9, as in the next clause יִשְׁכְּנָן to יְדוּרָן.

4[19(22)]. *Art grown,* i. e. רְבִיתָ. *Qr.* reads רְבַית—a 3rd fem. form. *Is grown and hath reached,* i. e. רְבַת וּמְטָת.

The LXX makes a large addition to this verse, part of which appears to be original. The part, which contains a reference to the date of the chapter, i. e. the eighteenth year of the king's reign, when he destroyed Jerusalem—the head and front of his offending from a Jewish standpoint, I subjoin here: ὑψώθη σου ἡ καρδία ὑπερηφανία . . . καθότι ἐξερήμωσας τὸν οἶκον τοῦ θεοῦ τοῦ ζῶντος— 'thy heart is uplifted with pride . . . forasmuch as thou hast laid desolate the house of the Living God'.

4[20(23)]. See 4[10−13(13−16)].

4[21(24)]. *Has come,* i e. מְטָת (*Qr.*). The *Kt.* has מטית—a scribal error.

4[22(25)]. *Thou shalt be driven . . . shalt be wet.* טרדין · · · מצבעין. Here active participles are used where in English we use the passive verb. Intermingled with the participles are two futures 'shall be' (להוה) and 'they shall make (thee) to eat' (יטעמון)— a strange medley. See note on 3[4]. On להוה, which has here generally a future sense, as its context shows, see Introd., p. xcv. The dream is of the nature of a prophecy, and the disasters foretold may be escaped through reformation of life: cf. 4[24].

As oxen. תור occurs in *Aram. Pap.* (Cowley 33[10]).

4[23(26)]. *Commandment was given*: lit. 'they commanded'. אמרו. Plural here used as in the preceding verse.

The heavens. This term is best taken with Bevan and Driver as a synonym for God—a meaning not found in the O.T., but in the Apocrypha, 1 Macc. 3¹⁸,¹⁹, 4¹⁰,²⁴ ; 2 Macc. 9²⁰ ; Aboth (ed. Taylor) 1³,¹², 2²,¹⁶, 4¹⁷ ; Mark 11³⁰ ; Luke 15¹⁸ ; John 3²⁷. Behrmann and Marti less justly identify it with the inhabitants of the heaven, i. e. the watchers : cf. 4¹⁴⁽¹⁷⁾.

4²⁴⁽²⁷⁾. *My counsel.* מלכי is used in Assyrian *milku*, ‘counsel’: also in late Hebrew as a loan-word : Neh. 5⁷ יִמָּלֵךְ: in the Syriac, and Targums.

Be acceptable unto thee. Here שפר is followed by על, but in 3³² by קדם.

Break off, or ‘redeem’. This meaning is found in the kindred root פרק in Hebrew in Ps. 136²⁴ ; Lam. 5⁸. The metaphor is taken from the breaking of a yoke : cf. Gen. 27⁴⁰ and Aboth 3⁸, הפרק ממנו עול תורה ‘he who breaks off from him the yoke of Thorah’. The counsel here given agrees with that of Sir. 3³⁰⁻³¹, Tob. 4⁷⁻¹¹ and that of Aboth 4¹⁵, ‘ He who performs one precept has gotten himself one advocate, and he who commits one transgression has gotten to himself one accuser ’. But Sir. 3³⁰ which reads צדקה תכפר חטאת shows no dependence on, or knowledge of, our text here. Rabbi Aqiba said (Baba Bathra 10ᵃ) that God left the feeding of the poor to the faithful in order that the latter might be saved from the judgement of hell thereby.

Righteousness. This word means here ‘good works’, and at this date almsgiving was the chief of these. In Deut. 6²⁵, 24¹³ ; Isa. 1²⁷, 59¹⁶ ; Dan. 4²⁴, 9¹⁶ ; Ps. 24⁵, 33⁵, 103⁶, צדקה is rendered by ἐλεημοσύνη. In Prov. 10² צדקה תציל ממות ‘righteousness delivereth from death’, is reproduced in Tob. 4¹⁰, 12⁹ by ἐλεημοσύνη ἐκ θανάτου ῥύεται. This perversion of the original meaning is found in late Hebrew, in Aramaic, in Targums, Syriac, and Talmud. Cf. Aboth 5¹⁹, where נותני צדקה means ‘almsgivers’. Even in Matt. 6¹ δικαιοσύνη came to be interpreted, as ‘almsgiving’. Nay more the original δικαιοσύνη was dislodged by ἐλεημοσύνη ‘alms’, in many of the later MSS. It is significant that, as the chief Hebrew virtue ‘righteousness’ degenerated in course of time into the mere act of almsgiving, so the chief Christian grace, ἀγάπη, *caritas*, ‘charity’, incurred the same fate. Contrast the meaning of צדקה in 9¹⁶, where it means God’s righteousness exhibited in his dealings with Israel, and where the LXX rightly renders it by δικαιοσύνη, but Th. wrongly by ἐλεημοσύνη.

Thine iniquities. The absolute sing. עֲוָיה does not occur. The text is variously written עֲוָיָתָךְ and עֲוָיָתָךְ.

By shewing mercy to the poor. Cf. Prov. 14²¹ מְחוֹנֵן עֲנִיִּים. Marti derives עֲנָיִן with tone on penult from עֲנָא = Hebrew עָנִי, as נְקָא 7⁹ = Hebr. נְקִי. But see Bevan. The mercy here designed would include other works of mercy, such as lending to the indigent, visiting the sick, &c., which were in later times described גְּמִילוּת חֲסִידִים. See Weber (*Jud. Theol.*²) 285.

A lengthening of thy tranquillity. שְׁלוֹתָךְ presupposes שְׁלֵוָא. Cf. the adjective שְׁלֵה in 4¹. But the rendering of this word in Th. (παραπτώμασιν), Vulg. (delictis), suggested to Ewald that for לִשְׁלֵוָתָךְ we should read לִשְׁלוּתָךְ, and for אַרְכָה read אֲרֻכָה (cf. Isa. 58⁸). Thus we should have the text presupposed by the A.V. *marg.* and the R.V. *marg.*, 'an healing of thine error'. There is some support for the assignment of this meaning to ארכה in the LXX, which gives ἐπιείκεια δοθῇ σοι. But in 7¹² we have אַרְכָה 'length', 'duration'.

All this. The emphatic state כֹּלָּא has the force of a demonstrative here.

4²⁶⁽²⁹⁾. *On (the roof of) the royal palace.* Cf. 2 Sam. 11², where the word גַּג = 'roof' (Aram. אַגַּר) is expressed in the text.

4²⁷⁽³⁰⁾. *Is not this great Babylon, which I have built.* In these words of the king there is a large element of historical fact. Nebuchadnezzar was a great builder. He did not rebuild Babylon literally, but he restored its walls, temples, and palaces. 'Nearly every cuneiform document now extant dating from this monarch's reign treats, not of conquest and warfare, like those of his Assyrian predecessors, but of the building and restoration of the walls, temples, and palaces of his beloved city of Babylon' (Prince, p. 31). Cf. *KB* iii. 2, p. 39: 'Then built I my palace, the seat of my royalty': and vii. 34, p. 35: 'In Babylon my dear city which I love'. See Koldewey's *Das wieder erstehende Babylon* (Eng. tr. *Excavations at Babylon*, 1915: King's *History of Babylon*, 1915; ch. ii.

Great Babylon. Cf. Rev. 14⁸, 16¹⁹ in a figurative sense.

Have built. We have here the singular form בֱּנַיְתַהּ. Kautzsch, § 15 e, holds that we should read בְּנִ״ת, and Strack has found the latter in two manuscripts.

A royal dwelling place. Cf. Amos 7¹³ בֵּית מַמְלָכָה.

By the might. For בִּתְקַף we should expect בְּתָקֳף. Bevan suggests that the former is due to assimilation to the following לִיקָר.

4²⁸⁽³¹⁾. *Fell a voice from heaven.* This voice, called by the later Jews a Bath-kol, 'daughter of a voice', is referred to in T. Lev. 18⁶; T. Jud. 24²; 2 Baruch 13¹, 22¹; Matt. 3¹⁷; Mark 1¹¹; Luke 3²². With this phrase 'fell a voice' we might compare Isa. 9⁷. See Weber, *Jud. Theol.*², 194 sq.; *Jew. Encyc.* ii. 588–92.

4²⁹⁽³²⁾. This verse is a repetition of 4²²⁽²⁵⁾, save that one of its clauses is omitted.

4³⁰⁽³³⁾. The king's outward form and actions are adapted to his inward transformation.

Like eagle's feathers. כְּנִשְׁרִין is elliptical, as is also the next phrase. Cf. מִן־אֲנָשָׁא in 4¹³ for the same elliptical phrasing.

4³¹⁻³⁴⁽³⁴⁻³⁷⁾, 3³¹⁻³³, (4¹⁻³). At the close of the appointed time Nebuchadnezzar recovers his reason and acknowledges the sovereignty of the Most High (4³¹). He is restored to all his former greatness (4³³), and, in grateful recognition of His power (4³⁴), he issues a proclamation to all the nations of the earth in which he sets forth the power and goodness of God, and the everlastingness of His dominion (3³¹⁻³³).

4³¹⁻³³⁽³⁴⁻³⁶⁾. The LXX gives quite a different text here, which is most probably more original than the normalized text of the MT. In the LXX there is a considerable section to which there is no parallel in the MT, yet in the main the clauses and idioms of this section are those of our author. They are more idiomatic than those of the MT. But towards the close of this chapter before the Edict there are many clauses repeated (?) apparently from 2²¹,²³,⁴⁷, 4³, &c.

4³¹⁽³⁴⁾. *The days,* i. e. the 'seven times' in 4¹³,²⁰,²²,²⁹.

Lifted up mine eyes to heaven. Bevan draws attention to the interesting parallel in the *Bacchae* of Euripides (1265 seqq.): where Agave on looking up to heaven in her madness has her reason restored. The female Bacchants like Nebuchadnezzar are, in some measure, assimilated to animals : they wear their skins and suckle young fawns. In Susanna 9, the downward look of the Elders is associated with an ethical perversion :

διέστρεψαν τὸν νοῦν αὐτῶν καὶ ἐξέκλιναν τοὺς ὀφθαλμοὺς αὐτῶν τοῦ μὴ βλέπειν εἰς τὸν οὐρανόν.

Him that liveth for ever. Cf. 12[7]; Sir. 18[1] ; 1 Enoch 5[1].

His dominion is an everlasting dominion and his kingdom is with generation and generation (עָם דר ודר). This doxology is framed on that in Ps. 145[13], 'His kingdom is an everlasting kingdom (מלכות כל עלמים) and his dominion endureth throughout all generations' (בכל דור ודר). But it is noteworthy that the order of the nouns is reversed, and that עם is used instead of ב. But it is still more noteworthy that Ps. 145[13] is literally repro- duced save for the use of עם instead of ב in 3[33]. Hence since the Aramaic in 3[33] is supported both by the LXX and Th., we may reasonably conclude that the order of the words 3[33] is that which came from our author's hand, and, since the order in 4[31] contravenes both the order of the text in 3[33] and Ps. 145[13], and since the LXX omits 4[31], we may regard the variation of Ps. 145[13] in 4[31] as well as in other clauses as an interpolation from another hand. Yet see note on Transl. 4[31(35)] and cf. 7[14].

Again in 4[32] in the original of the clause 'none . . . can say unto him' (לה): our author's usage would require קדמוהי. See Introd., § 20. *w.* Hence 4[31c-32] are not a parenthesis as Bevan suggests, but an interpolation, which conflicts both with the order of the context and the linguistic usage of the author. Marti suggests that יתוב עלי · · · · ליקר should be excised and הדרי וזיוי be taken as the subject of the verb. But if we make this excision, we must go further, and excise 'and mine under- standing returned unto me' in 4[33], since this clause has already occurred in 4[31]. We should then take מלכות הדרי וזיוי as the subject of the following יתוב : cf. LXX 4[34], ἐν ἐκείνῳ τῷ καιρῷ ἀπο- κατεστάθη ἡ βασιλεία μου ἐμοὶ καὶ ἡ δόξα μου ἀπεδόθη μοι, and 4[34 b] ἐν τῷ λαῷ μου ἐκράτησα καὶ ἡ μεγαλοσύνη μου ἀποκατεστάθη μοι, which supports in the main the above suggestions. Thus instead of the text as it stands now in 4[31-33] we should read : ' And at the end of the· days I Nebuchadnezzar lifted up mine eyes unto heaven, | And mine understanding returned unto me, | And at the same time my kingdom and my majesty | And my splendour returned unto me, | And my lords sought unto me, | And I was established in my kingdom, | And excellent greatness was added unto me.'

4[32(35)]. *As persons of no account.* כלה חשיבין. But Th. renders ὡς οὐδὲν ἐλογίσθησαν. So also the Jewish expositors. In that case לה (elsewhere written לא) would be taken as 'nothingness'. But there is no authority for taking לא as a substantive. Hence

it is best with Bevan to take לא חשיבין as a single conception,
as לא יכלין in 4¹⁵. Bevan compares Isa. 55² לוא לחם 'that which
is not bread', and the Targ. on Isa. 63³ לא חשיבין 'not
respected'. The Targums use כלמה 'as nothing' to render
the Hebrew כאין : cf. Isa. 40¹⁷,²³.

[*And among the inhabitants of the earth*]. This, as Marti has
remarked, is a repetition of the phrase in the first line by a
scribe who thought by this addition to make the thought of this
second line complete, but did not observe that all that it implied
was already conveyed in the first.

Army of heaven. חיל שמיא, the Aramaic equivalent of the
Hebrew 'host of heaven', צבא השמים, i. e. the angels or the
stars : cf. צבא המרום, Isa. 24²¹ ; 1 Kings 22¹⁹. The phrase was
equivalent to both. The stars were regarded as conscious : cf.
1 Enoch 41⁵, 18¹³⁻¹⁶, 21¹⁻⁶.

None can stay his hand or say unto him, What doest thou?
These words refer to the judgment of the heavenly powers by
God. In 1 Enoch 18¹⁴ 'a prison for the stars and host of heaven'
is mentioned. The entire line is found in the Targum of
Eccles. 8⁴, מן הוא גברא דמחי בידיה וימר ליה מה עבדתא, as two alternative renderings of מִי יֹאמַר־לוֹ מַה־תַּעֲשֶׂה. Behrmann thinks that
the words in our author are borrowed from this passage in
Eccles., but Driver takes the opposite view. If, however, 4³¹ ᶜ⁻³²
is a later addition then Behrmann may be right. In any case
the combination in our text of the two phrases which are dittographic renderings in the Targ. of Eccles. 8⁴ of one and the
same phrase is strange. This idiomatic phrase recurs in the
Mishna (*Pesach* iv. 8), and is common in later literature (Dalman,
Dialectproben, p. 5).

Stay his hand, lit. 'smite his hand'. מחא is here Pa'el, in
2³⁴,³⁵ Pe'al.

None can . . . say unto him. לא אתי די ‥‥ יאמר לה. Instead
of לה our author would have written קדמוהי.

What doest thou? Cf. Isa. 45⁹ ; Job 9¹² ; Eccles. 8⁴. The
words are literally found in Job and Eccles.

4³³(³⁶). *Mine understanding returned unto me.* This clause is to
be omitted. See note on 4³¹. Its repetition is due to the interpolator of 31c-32 (34c-35). We must also excise וליקר 'and
for the glory' as Marti has already suggested. It is omitted in
the LXX.

My majesty, i. e. הדרי. Th. here read הֲדְרַת, i. e. ἦλθον. Hence his rendering is εἰς τὴν τιμὴν τῆς βασιλείας μου ἦλθον.

My splendour, i. e. זִיו. A loan-word from the Assyrian, used chiefly of the countenance. Cf. 7²⁸, 5⁶,⁹.

Sought. Since the Pa'el of this verb does not occur elsewhere, Bevan and Marti would read יְבְעוֹן.

I was established, i. e. הָתְקְנַת. Hoph'al 1st pers. sing. But the better attested reading is הָתְקְנַת (3rd pers. fem.). If this reading is adopted, then, as Marti states, עַל must be emended into עֲלִי and the text rendered 'and on me (i. e. for me) was my kingdom established'. See Bauer-Leander, *Gram.* 115 seq.

Other Hoph'al forms are הוּסְפַת which follows immediately and in 5¹³,¹⁵,²⁰, 6²⁴, 7⁴,¹¹.

4³⁴(³⁷). *Extol.* מְרוֹמֵם, a Hebraism. But it is found also in the Targums—Ps. 34⁴, 37³⁴, 75⁸, &c., and in the Chr. Pal. See Schultess, *Lex.* 191. The Hithpa'lel occurs in 5²³ of our text.

Truth. קשט is the Aramaic equivalent of the Hebrew אמת, though the stem is found in Prov. 22²¹ (where, however, it is said by some scholars to be an Aramaic gloss).

Walk. Rd. מְהַלְּכִין. See 3²⁵.

LXX iv. 34-34ᵃ (*First form*).
English Numbering.

τῷ ὑψίστῳ ἀνθομολογοῦμαι καὶ αἰνῶ ... ὅτι αὐτός ἐστι θεὸς τῶν θεῶν καὶ κύριος τῶν κυρίων καὶ βασιλεὺς τῶν βασιλέων, ὅτι
iv. 2 αὐτὸς ποιεῖ σημεῖα καὶ τέρατα ... οἱ γὰρ θεοὶ τῶν ἐθνῶν οὐκ ἔχουσιν ἐν ἑαυτοῖς ἰσχὺν ...
3 ποιῆσαι σημεῖα καὶ θαυμάσια
2 μεγάλα καὶ φοβερά ... καθὼς ἐποίησεν ἐν ἐμοὶ ὁ θεὸς τοῦ οὐρανοῦ ... ὅσοι [ἐλάλησαν εἰς τὸν θεὸν τοῦ οὐρανοῦ καὶ]¹ ὅσοι ἂν καταληφθῶσι λαλοῦντές τι, τούτους κατακρινῶ θανάτῳ.

¹ A doublet of the next clause.

LXX iv. 34ᵇ (*Second form*).
English Numbering.

iv. 1 Ἔγραψε δὲ ὁ βασιλεὺς Ναβουχοδονοσὸρ¹ ἐπιστολὴν ἐγκύκλιον πᾶσι τοῖς κατὰ τόπον ἔθνεσι καὶ χώραις καὶ γλώσσαις πάσαις ταῖς οἰκούσαις ἐν πάσαις ταῖς χώραις, γενεαῖς καὶ γενεαῖς. Κυρίῳ τῷ θεῷ τοῦ οὐρανοῦ αἰνεῖτε ... Ἐγὼ βασιλεὺς βασιλέων ἀνθομολογοῦμαι αὐτῷ ἐνδόξως, ὅτι οὕτως
2 ἐποίησε μετ' ἐμοῦ.

¹ The order Βασ. Ναβ. occurs four times or thereabouts out of eighteen in the LXX. Elsewhere Ναβ. βασ. In Th. once out of every three times.

Able to humiliate. לְהַשְׁפָּלָה. The same verb recurs in connexion with Belshazzar in 5²², where it is rendered ' to humble '. Here the sense is different : it clearly means 'to humiliate'. The adjective occurs in 4¹⁴ with again a different nuance— ' humble ' or ' low in station of life '.

The Edict of the King.

3³¹⁻³³ (4¹⁻³) (its three forms in the LXX and its form in the MT). Having recounted his experiences, the king now issues his proclamation, as at the close of chap. 3, and as Darius does at the end of 6. This proclamation has been wrongly transposed to the beginning of this chapter by the reviser of the Aramaic and the verses dependent upon it. But the LXX, though its text is almost incredibly confused, corrupt, defective (especially in the first and second forms), and interpolated, preserves the right order of events. After a series of additions, drawn in part from 2²¹,²³,⁴⁷, 3²⁹, 5¹⁹, it gives the proclamation in practically three forms, the first two of which are defective in part. I shall give these and that of Th. side by side, and number them as they are in Swete's edition. *Where the Greek is a rendering of words in the Aramaic it is underlined.*

LXX iv. 34ᶜ. (*Third form.*)
English Numbering.

1 Ναβουχοδονοσὸρ βασιλεὺς πᾶσι τοῖς ἔθνεσι καὶ πάσαις ταῖς χώραις καὶ πᾶσι τοῖς οἰκοῦσιν αὐταῖς· Εἰρήνη ὑμῖν πληθυνθείη ἐν παντὶ
2 καιρῷ. [καὶ νῦν ὑποδείξω ὑμῖν]¹ τὰς πράξεις ἃς ἐποίησεν μετ' ἐμοῦ ὁ θεὸς ὁ μέγας· ἔδοξε δέ μοι ἀποδεῖξαι ὑμῖν καὶ τοῖς σο-
3 φισταῖς ὑμῶν ὅτι ἔστι θεός, καὶ τὰ θαυμάσια αὐτοῦ μεγάλα· τὸ βασίλειον αὐτοῦ βασίλειον εἰς τὸν αἰῶνα, ἡ ἐξουσία αὐτοῦ ἀπὸ γενεῶν εἰς γενεάς. καὶ ἀπέστειλεν ἐπιστολὰς περὶ πάντων τῶν γενηθέντων αὐτῷ ἐν τῇ βασιλείᾳ αὐτοῦ πᾶσι τοῖς ἔθνεσι τοῖς οὖσιν ὑπὸ τὴν βασιλείαν αὐτοῦ.

Th. iii. 98-100.   MT
English Numbering.

iv. 1 Ναβουχοδονοσὸρ ὁ βασιλεὺς πᾶσι   iii. 31
τοῖς λαοῖς, φυλαῖς, καὶ γλώσ-
σαις, τοῖς οἰκοῦσιν ἐν πάσῃ τῇ
2 γῇ Εἰρήνη ὑμῖν πληθυνθείη. τὰ   32
σημεῖα καὶ τὰ τέρατα ἃ ἐποίησεν
μετ' ἐμοῦ ὁ θεὸς ὁ ὕψιστος
ἤρεσεν ἐναντίον ἐμοῦ¹ ἀναγγεῖλαι
3 ὑμῖν. ὡς μεγάλα καὶ ἰσχυρά·   33
ἡ βασιλεία αὐτοῦ βασιλεία αἰώνιος, ἡ ἐξουσία αὐτοῦ εἰς γενεὰν
καὶ γενεάν.

¹ A right rendering of קֳדָמַי.

---

¹ We have here a dittograph of what follows : ἔδοξε δέ μοι ἀποδεῖξαι.

The Edict of the King.

The reader will observe that in the LXX the king's proclamation is preserved in three different forms. The third of
these I have quoted in its entirety. At its close there is a statement to the effect that the king sent to his subjects with the
proclamation a complete account of *all that had befallen him.*
This implies that chap. iv in its entirety was sent by the king to
all his people. The second form of the proclamation is very
fragmentary. It preserves nothing of value, save that it confirms the clause γλώσσαις τοῖς οἰκοῦσιν ἐν πάσῃ τῇ γῇ of the MT
and Th. 3^{31} (4^1), though with a slightly different rendering, and
the clause ἐποίησεν μετ' ἐμοῦ. The first form is fuller than the
second, and supports other clauses of the MT and Th. though
with different renderings. It concludes with the punishment
that is to be visited on any of the king's subjects who speak
against the God of heaven—a passage which recalls 3^{29}.

From the above comparison we may reasonably conclude that
the text of the MT and its translations are trustworthy so far
as they go. But it appears to be defective in two respects.
(1) When the king's edict, which followed on the close of the
narrative of his experiences was mistakenly transposed from
the end of this chapter to its beginning by a reviser, the reviser
naturally omitted such an ending as is given in the first form of
the edict in the LXX or in its third form, since either would
have been out of place in its new context. Which of these two
endings is the original? The ending in the first form is questionable, since it is unsupported by any other version of this
passage, and also recalls 3^{29} too closely—which may be its
source. On the other hand, the explanatory addition at the
close of the third form from καὶ ἀπέστειλεν ἐπιστολὰς κτλ. comes
naturally from the hand of our author at the close of the section.
Besides it receives confirmation from the statement in form two
that the king sent an 'encyclical letter' to all his subjects (ἔγραψε
δὲ ὁ βασιλεὺς . . . ἐπιστολὴν ἐγκύκλιον πᾶσι τοῖς κατὰ τόπον ἔθνεσιν).
(2) Twice in chap. 4 it is definitely stated that the penalty
inflicted on the king was inflicted with solely one end in view,
i. e. 'to the intent that the living may know that the Most High
ruleth in the kingdom of men' ($4^{14(17)}$); and this penalty was to
be in force 'till thou know that the Most High ruleth in the

kingdom of men' (4²²⁽²⁵⁾). Now it is strange that no reference
is made to this fact in the proclamation as it appears in the
MT and its versions. On the other hand, in the third form of
the LXX this fact is referred to shortly: ἔδοξε δέ μοι ἀποδείξαι
ὑμῖν . . . ὅτι ἔστι θεός, καὶ τὰ θαυμάσια αὐτοῦ μεγάλα. But here the
first defective form supplies what we should expect—namely,
an acknowledgement from Nebuchadnezzar of the fact that 'the
Most High ruleth in the kingdom of men' (4²²). Thus it ends:
'I thank and praise the Most High . . . for He is the God of
gods, and Lord of lords, and King of kings; for He doeth signs
and wonders. For the gods of the nations have no power in
themselves . . . to do signs and marvels great and terrible . . .
as the God of heaven hath done unto me.'

3³¹⁻³³ (4¹⁻³). On the defectiveness of the text see above.

3³¹ (4¹). With the first words of the edict, cf. the first words of
the edict of Darius in 6²⁶⁽²⁵⁾.

Dwell. On דארין see note on 2³⁸.

Peace be multiplied unto you (שלמכון ישגא). Cf. 6²⁶⁽²⁵⁾, 1 Pet. 1²,
2 Pet. 1². In Ezra 5⁷ we have the formula 'all peace'. In
Cowley (17¹⁻²) we find the earlier equivalent of this phrase:
שלם מראן אלהין [ישאלו שגיא] = 'may the gods see to our lord's
peace abundantly': cf. 30², 31².

3³² (4²). *It hath seemed good unto me.* שפר קדמי. On this
phrase see technical use of קדם, cf. 6² and Introd.

Signs and wonders. So also in the decree of Darius 6²⁸⁽²⁷⁾.
With אתיא ותמהיא cf. אתות ומפתים in Deut. 4³⁴, 6²², Isa. 8¹⁸, *Sir.*
36⁶ אות׳ ׳׳׳ ומופת, and σημεῖα καὶ τέρατα in Mark 13²², Rom. 15¹⁹.

Most High God. Rather 'God the Most High'; see note
on 3²⁶.

3³²⁻³³ (4²⁻³). The Aramaic appears to be defective here. As
I have shown on p. 104 the sole end of God's visitations on
Nebuchadnezzar was that he and all men living might know
that 'the Most High ruleth in the kingdom of men'. An
acknowledgment of this fact is to be looked for. Now the
insertion which the reviser has made in 4³¹ᶜ⁻³²,³³ᵃᵃ meets this
expectation to some extent, but there are three objections to
this insertion. (1) It has no support from the LXX; (2) its
form is awkward—the bulk of it being of the nature of a parenthesis, as its strongest supporters must allow; (3) some of its
phrasing, which is intended to express the same thought that

is elsewhere expressed in our author, is not that of our author. Hence we conclude that the original of 3^{32} contained some such statement as the LXX in 4^{34} attests. It is possible also that $4^{32(35)}$ originally followed, which is omitted by the LXX and was, if original, recast and inserted in the long parenthesis in the Aramaic in $4^{31a-33a}$ by a reviser. It is of course *impossible* to recover the exact form or even substance of the original, seeing that, even where the Aramaic, the three forms of the LXX and Th. agree more or less in substance, they differ verbally. The following verses from the LXX and Aram. contain possibly the substance in some degree of what the author wrote.

2. 'I thank and praise . . . the Most High, for he is the God of gods and Lord of lords and King of kings; for he doeth signs and wonders (from LXX 4^{34}). It hath seemed good before me to declare the signs and wonders that God the Most High hath wrought toward me. How great are his signs! | And how mighty are his wonders! | His kingdom is an everlasting kingdom, | For his dominion is from generation to generation (from Aram. 3^{32}). 3^{a}. And all the inhabitants of the earth are as persons of no account, | And he doeth according to his will in the army of heaven, and among the inhabitants of the earth. | And none can stay his hand, | Or say before him What doest thou? (Aram. 4^{32}). 3^{b}. And he sent letters regarding all the things that had befallen him in his kingdom to all the nations that were under his sovereignty' (from LXX 4^{34c}).

$3^{33}(4^{3})$. *His kingdom is an everlasting kingdom.* This is the form in which our author reproduces Ps. 145^{13}, and not that in the interpolation in 4^{31} (4^{34}). Yet see 7^{14}.

SECTION V

i.e. Chapter 5^{1-30}, in the last year of Belshazzar[1]. The year is not mentioned, as it was in all probability unknown to the author, as well as any real knowledge of that person.

---

[1] Our author may have known of three kings of Babylon—Nebuchadnezzar, Evil-Merodach, and Belshazzar. But if so, he does not mention the second. The Talmud (*Meg.* 11^{b} seq.) knows nothing about Nergalsharezer, Labashi Marduk or Nabuna'id, but like Daniel confuses Belshazzar with his father Nabu-na'id. The Talmud (*op. cit.*) limits Belshazzar's reign to two years. As we know from the inscriptions and independent historians, Nabuna'id, with whom Belshazzar is often confused, reigned seventeen years,

The events of this section take place within twenty-four hours.

INTRODUCTION.

Historical inconsistencies. This chapter is notable for its historical inconsistencies. But before we enter on an account of these, we must devote a few words to the character of the Aramaic text under § 1, while the larger question of the historical misconceptions of our author will be dealt with under § 2.

§ 1. (*a*) *Dislocations.*

There is a *dislocation* of the text in 5^{7-9}. The true order of events is preserved in Josephus, who had access to a more trustworthy form of the LXX than is accessible to us. Even in the solitary manuscript of the LXX the true order of events is with the exception of some details rightly preserved. The Aramaic is altogether confused. See notes *in loc.*

(*b*) *Omissions.*

5^3. After 'the golden' restore with Th. and Vulg. 'and the silver'.

5^{11}. After 'in thy kingdom' restore 'whose name is Daniel' on the ground of the context of the LXX and Josephus. See note *in loc.*

(*c*) *Interpolations.*

5^{10}. The clause 'by reason of the words of the king and of his lords' is an interpolation. The form of the text of the LXX and Josephus cannot admit this clause: Th. omits it. The context is really against it, and further the very grammar makes it more than doubtful. The word לקבל elsewhere in Daniel does not mean 'by reason of' but 'before'. Hence I regard the clause as an interpolation of the reviser.

5^{12}. The clause 'whom the king named Belteshazzar' is an interpolation. The king did not give Daniel this name. See note *in loc.*

(*d*) *Corruptions.*

The inscription as given in the Aramaic in 5^{25} is without the support of the most ancient versions and Josephus. Furthermore the interpretation of the inscription in 5^{26-28} presupposes

a shorter inscription, and lends no support to the form transmitted in the Aramaic in 5^{25}.

§ 2. *Historical misconceptions of our author in this chapter.*

(a) *Who was Belshazzar in the view of our author?* According
to 5^2 Nebuchadnezzar was his father. In 5^{11} the same statement is made by the queen-mother three times, one of which is
no doubt an interpolation of the reviser. If this were not
enough, Belshazzar reiterates it in 5^{12}, and Daniel himself confirms it twice in the presence of Belshazzar $5^{18,22}$.

It appears to be impossible, therefore, to conclude otherwise
than that our author regarded Belshazzar as the son (or grandson) of Nebuchadnezzar.

Much controversy has raged round this personage. Before
the discovery of the Cyrus Cylinder, his name was unknown
as the last king of the Babylonian dynasty save in Daniel
and in 1 Bar. 1^{11}, and other late authorities dependent on
Daniel. Our author, however, accords him the title of king,
and represents him as the son (or grandson) of Nebuchadnezzar.
But from all the inscriptions discovered and published till the
year 1924, the only conclusions that could be drawn were that
Belshazzar was the eldest son of Nabuna'id, that he was as such
the crown prince and commander-in-chief of the armies of the
Babylonian empire, but *never king of Babylon.* Furthermore, it
was reasonably concluded that no tie of blood existed between
Belshazzar and Nebuchadnezzar.

But a new Persian verse account of Nabuna'id, which was
published in 1924 by Sidney Smith in the *Babylonian Historical
Texts*, 84 sqq., provides us with fresh information, which in
large measure justifies the account of Daniel in regard to Belshazzar. This text (Sidney Smith, *Bab. Hist. Texts*, p. 88)
Col. II, ll. 18–21 reads as follows:

'18. One camp he (Nabuna'id) put into the charge of his
eldest child (Belshazzar).

19. The troops he sent through the land with himself.

20. He struck his (Belshazzar's) hands, he entrusted the
kingship to him.

21. While he himself set out on a far journey.'

The words 'struck his hands' denotes a symbolic investiture.
Notwithstanding Nabuna'id retained the supreme power in his

own hands, and with the bulk of the forces made in 552 his expedition against Tema', i. e.. the Teima in Arabia Felix in the third year of his reign. It was in this year that Belshazzar was invested with royal authority, most probably, as king of Babylon.

That the kingship of Belshazzar is not recognized in the Cyrus Cylinder may be explained from the fact that Cyrus regarded himself naturally as the successor of Nabuna'id, the supreme sovereign of the Babylonian empire, and not of the vassal king, Belshazzar.

Belshazzar, then, was the son of Nabuna'id, and also the (vassal) king of Babylon. *How then does our author represent him to be the son of Nebuchadnezzar?* That he was not the son of Nebuchadnezzar we have already remarked above. That he may have been the grandson through the marriage of his father Nabuna'id with a daughter of Nebuchadnezzar is possible, but there is no evidence of this marriage, and the fact that the usurper Nabuna'id never made such a claim in any existing record, where such a claim would have been natural as justifying his position as the successor of Nebuchadnezzar, relegates this hypothesis into the limbo of unwarrantable conjectures. On the other hand about 140–150 years after the extinction of the dynasty of Nebuchadnezzar we find Herodotus (i. 188) representing Nabuna'id, whom he calls Labynetus, as the son of Nebuchadnezzar (i. 74, 77), whom also he designates as Labynetus. This relationship of Nabuna'id to Nebuchadnezzar is flatly denied by Abydenus in his *History of Assyria* (Euseb., *Praep.* ix. 41), and herein Abydenus has the support of the ancient texts.

How in the face of these facts are we to regard the historical statements in Daniel, who, as we have shown at the beginning of this section, obviously regarded Belshazzar as the actual son or grandson of Nebuchadnezzar?

We must therefore leave this question as one of the unsolved problems of history.

This difficulty is not a modern one. It was evidently discussed in the first century of our era. At all events Josephus, the most learned Jewish historian of earlier days, found himself in the same dilemma as our modern Fundamentalists. He found that the Book of Daniel required him to represent Bel-

shazzar as an ἔγγονος ('grandson' or 'descendant') of Nebuchadnezzar, and so in his *Ant.* x. 11. 4 he honestly describes him as
such.   But Josephus was not wholly dependent on Daniel ; for
he quotes at least twenty non-Jewish authorities, some of whom
were Greek and, some Babylonian historians.   We have not yet
done with Josephus's solution of his difficulties.   We shall
return to them after a brief consideration of the quotation he
makes from Berosus, a Babylonian historian (*c.* 250 B.C.), in his
Contra Apion. i. 20.   This quotation gives a short but trustworthy account of the kings of Babylon who succeeded Nebuchadnezzar.   Nebuchadnezzar was succeeded by his son Evil
Merodach, who after a reign of two years was murdered by his
brother-in-law, Neriglissar.   Neriglissar reigned four years, and
was succeeded by his son Laborosoardochus, who was assassinated by a body of conspirators, one of whom was Nabonnedus,
who in the seventeenth year of his reign was defeated and
dethroned as the last native king of Babylon by Cyrus.   So far
for Berosus, whom Josephus quotes, and accepts as an authority.
That Josephus was familiar with this statement when a few
years previously he wrote his *Antiquities* is unquestionable ; for
it led him to attempt an unhistorical reconciliation between
Berosus and Daniel.   According to the former Nabonnedus was
the last independent king of Babylon : according to Daniel it
was Belshazzar.   Josephus accordingly surmounts the difficulty
by a hypothesis for which he could advance no evidence, and
identifies Belshazzar with Nabonnedus, i.e. Nabuna'id of the
inscriptions.   Josephus (x. 11. 2) thus writes : 'The succession
. . . passed to Belshazzar, who was called Nebo-andelus by the
Babylonians . . .' (x. 11. 4) 'under whom Babylon was taken
when he had reigned seventeen years'.   But Josephus may not
have been the first to identify Belshazzar and Nabuna'id ; he
may therein only have been giving a larger currency to traditions that had been accepted by the best educated classes in
Judaea.

   We conclude, therefore, that, though Josephus and his predecessors (?) were wrong in identifying Belshazzar with his
father Nabuna'id, Josephus interpreted accurately *the belief of
our author* as to Belshazzar being a son (or grandson) of Nebuchadnezzar, and also as to his being the last king of the Babylonian dynasty.   Cf. 1 Bar. 1[11], where Belshazzar is said to be

the son of Nebuchadnezzar. Thus the traditions on which our author was dependent were in some respects trustworthy from an historical standpoint.

(b) *Was Belshazzar an absolute sovereign in the view of our author?* We have already seen that Josephus took this to be the only natural interpretation of the text of Daniel. In fact we can hardly doubt that the author of Daniel regarded Belshazzar as the last native and absolute king of Babylon. If the author of Daniel was acquainted at all with Nabuna'id's name his identification of Belshazzar with Nabuna'id was inevitable— an identification attested in *Ant.* x 11. 2. But Josephus had not sufficient historical data. To prove that Belshazzar was the supreme ruler in the eyes of our author, it is sufficient to state that he dates documents by the year of Belshazzar's accession in 7^1, 8^1—a practice that could not be reconciled with the hypothesis that our author knew that his father was alive and held the place of sovereign authority, as we know he did from the tablet recording the events of Nabuna'id's reign of seventeen years.[1] Certain apologists seek to evade this argument by the plea that, since Belshazzar invests Daniel with *the third place* in the kingdom 5^{29}, it follows that Belshazzar is himself not the supreme ruler but the second. But such an argument involves a self-contradiction ; for the man ' who can of his own authority make any one he pleases "third ruler in the kingdom" must obviously be supreme in the state ' (Bevan, p. 19).

§ 3. *Did the author of Daniel know that Nebuchadnezzar was succeeded by his son Evil Merodach?*

Our author may have been acquainted with this fact, since it is recorded *once* in the part of the O.T. that was accessible to him, i. e. 2 Kings 25^{27}.[2] *But it is quite possible that this single reference escaped him, and that he knew only of Nebuchadnezzar through the O.T. and of Belshazzar through tradition, and regarded the latter as the actual son of the former.* For there are certain statements in this chapter which show that our author was

---

[1] See pp. 108 sq.; also Introd., § 26, for an account of the inscriptions regarding Nabuna'id and Belshazzar.

[2] This king is also mentioned in Jer. 52^{31}, but this chapter of Jeremiah was not added to this book till after 200 B.C. ; for it is not found in the LXX and is merely an appendix added late to the work, consisting of 2 Kings 25.

drawing his materials from tradition, which agree in some slight measure with the inscriptions and records of Babylon. The main facts recorded in the inscriptions can be summarized shortly as follows. Cyrus, who became king of Anshan in 549, and was called 'king of Persia' in 546 or earlier, in the year 538 attacked Babylon. He defeated Nabuna'id at Opis (Babylonian Upê on the Tigris in Tishri = October (so with Meyer, *ZATW.*, 1898, p. 340 sq., we must read and not Tammuz, i. e. July, since September has already been reached two lines earlier), captured Sippar on the Euphrates on Tishri 14, and on the 16th his general Gubaru entered Babylon without striking a blow, and made Nabuna'id prisoner. On Marchesvan 3 (= Oct. 27) Cyrus made his entry into Babylon, and on the 11th (= Nov. 4) Gubaru slew the king's son (? the text is here defective) in a night assault.

Further, in the inscriptions of the first eleven years of Nabuna'id's reign, Belšaruṣur (= 'Bel protect the king'), of which Belshazzar is a corruption, is definitely named as 'the king's son' several times. *Later* 'the king's son' is mentioned, but no proper name attached. Whether 'the king's son' so mentioned is Belšaruṣur cannot be determined, since Nabuna'id may have had another son named Nebuchadnezzar. At all events there was an early tradition that there was such a son. But this tradition did not reach our author.

Amongst the historians who recount details reproduced (?) by our author is Herodotus (i. 188 : cf. i. 74, 77), who names the last king Labynetus (Λαβύνητος = Nabuna'id), and seems to have regarded him as the son of Nebuchadnezzar (see *KAT.*[3], p. 288).[1] He represents (i. 191) Cyrus as diverting the waters of the Euphrates and entering Babylon by the river bed, while the inhabitants were celebrating a festival. In Xenophon's *Cyropaedia* (vii. 5. 15-31) a similar account is given, though here the city is surprised by Gobryas and Gadates.

§ 4. *Conflict between the statements in our author and in the inscriptions and the historians.*

Now, if we compare the account in our text with those we have drawn from the Babylonian inscriptions and the Greek

---

[1] But according to Abydenus (Eus., *Praep. Evang.*, ix. 41), Nabuna'id was not related to Nebuchadnezzar in any way (προσήκοντά οἱ οὐδέν).

historians, it is clear at a glance that it agrees most with the latter. With the former it has nothing in common but the name Belshazzar. In the inscriptions Belshazzar is not the son of Nebuchadnezzar, but is only the son of the last king Nabuna'id, a usurper, and not descended from Nebuchadnezzar. Belshazzar as a vassal king of Babylon under Nabuna'id is represented as making a desperate resistance in some fastness of the city, after the city as a whole had been surrendered and Nabuna'id taken prisoner. In a night attack shortly after Cyrus's arrival this fastness was stormed and apparently Belshazzar was slain. But in Daniel Nabuna'id is not mentioned, and Belshazzar is represented as the sole and supreme authority, and that for at least three years (cf. 5, 7¹, 8¹). There is nothing to suggest in 5 that the greater part of the city was already in the hands of the enemy. On the contrary Belshazzar made a great feast, summoned to it 1,000 of his lords, called for the services of the magicians, enchanters, Chaldeans, and soothsayers, and made Daniel ruler of one third of the kingdom, though according to the inscriptions not a single city of that kingdom was any longer subject to him, and his authority did not extend beyond the palace or arsenal in Babylon in which the feast was given. Further, whereas our text represents Babylon as being captured by force, the inscriptions state that it was surrendered peaceably to the generals of Cyrus.

On the other hand our text agrees with the tradition, recorded both in Herodotus and Xenophon, that Babylon was taken *in the night, while the inhabitants were celebrating a feast.*[1] Further, if, as it seems, Herodotus believed Labynetus (i. e. Nabuna'id) to have been a son of Nebuchadnezzar, we have here an approximation to the statement in our text that Belshazzar was the son of Nebuchadnezzar, though Abydenus, as we have already seen, flatly denies this.

(5) *The purpose of our author is didactic.* The unhistorical statements made by our author *were made in perfectly good faith. His book is not fiction.* He made the best use of the traditional

---

[1] This idea in the popular account may have arisen from a misinterpretation of the joy with which the Babylonians received Cyrus as Marti suggests. On the 'Annalistic Tablet' of Cyrus it is stated that when Cyrus entered Babylon 'Dissensions (?) were allayed (?) before him. Peace for the city he established: peace to all Babylon did Cyrus proclaim'.

materials accessible to him. His purpose with regard to Belshazzar was didactic. And yet even the Jewish Rabbis (*Meg.*
12 *a*) thought that Daniel had misinterpreted certain facts contained in chap. 5. But, though they wrote centuries after our
author and with opportunities of learning the facts not available
to our author, they made no use of them, and are almost as
much at sea as our author ; for they recognized only three
Babylonian kings, Nebuchadnezzar, Evil Merodach, and Belshazzar. Our author's purpose was as we have stated didactic.
If Belshazzar was overthrown, in part at all events, for his profanation of the vessels brought to Babylon from the Temple—
as also the Talmud in *Meg.* 11 *b* teaches—what would befall the
king who (like Antiochus Epiphanes) offered heathen sacrifices
on the very altar of God in the Temple ?

§ 5. *Omissions in the MT.*

5³. 'And silver.' Restored in accordance with Th. and
Vulg.

5¹¹. 'Whose name is Daniel.' Restored in accordance with
the requirements of the context : implied by the LXX and found
in Josephus.

§ 6. *Interpolations in the MT.*

5⁷. 'And the king said to the wise men of Babylon.' LXX
does not admit of this addition and it is not found in
Josephus.

5¹⁰. 'By reason of the words of the king and of his lords.'

5¹¹. 'The king thy father.' Not found in the LXX, Th., or
Josephus.

5¹². 'Whom the king named Belteshazzar.' This is a false
gloss. It is not found in the LXX or in Josephus. This clause
is Hebraic in character "בל שְׁמֵהּ שֹׁם מלכא די. Cf. 2 Kings 17³⁴
for this idiom.

§ 7. *Corruptions in the MT.*

5⁶. For שׁנוהי עלוהי read שׁגו עלוהי with Bevan.
5⁷⁻⁹. MT corrupt, defective, interpolated, and confused as
to order. See notes *in loc.*

5¹². For מִפְשַׁר and מְשָׁרֵא read מִפְשַׁר and מִשְׁרֵא.

5²³. For 'silver and gold' read 'gold and silver'.

5²⁵. For MENE MENE TEKEL UPHARSIN read MENE TEKEL PERES—with LXX, Th., Vulg., and Josephus.

5¹. *Belshazzar* = the Babylonian Bel-šar-uṣur, 'Bel, protect the king', just as נרגל שראצר (Jer. 39³,¹³) = Nergal-šar-uṣur, 'Nergal, protect the king'.

The king. From one of the inscriptions Belshazzar appears to have been a vassal king of Babylon (see Introd. to this chap., p. 108). It is a matter of inference and not of demonstration that in the inscriptions Belshazzar was slain after the capture of Babylon.

Made a . . feast. With עבד לחם cf. the Hebrew עשׂה לחם Eccles. 10¹⁹, and the N.T. expression ἐσθίειν ἄρτον. עשׂת, משתה = 'to give a drinking bout' or 'feast' is the usual Hebrew ex‐pression: cf. Gen. 19³, 21⁸, 26³⁰, &c., and the Greek συμπόσιον κατασκευάζειν. The συμπόσιον, however, properly followed the δεῖπνον.

Drank wine before the thousand. Our author appears to lay emphasis on the evil example of Belshazzar. As Driver writes, 'we have little or no information respecting the custom of the king at state-banquets in Babylon ; but something similar is reported . . . of royal banquets among the Persians (*Athen.* iv. 26, p. 145 *c* . . .) and Parthians (*Athen.* iv. 38, p. 153 *a–b*)'.

5². *While he tasted the wine*: i. e. in the midst of the revel. This is the usual rendering, and if it is right, then טעם, though occurring about thirty times in Biblical Aramaic, is used here only in a literal sense. Hence Prince takes it in a metaphorical sense and renders it 'under the influence of wine', and adduces the rendering of the LXX ἐννψούμενος (*sic* for ἀν-) ἀπὸ τοῦ οἴνου, Vulg. 'iam temulentus', and Ibn Ezra 'at the bidding of wine'. The king is well on in his cups before he orders the sacred vessels to be used at the feast.

The golden and silver vessels. See 1² note. The word מאניא (= 'vessels') is Old Aramaic. Cp. Cowley 20⁵, 72⁴, Ah. 109 of the Fifth Century: and Cooke 65⁶ (Nerab II) Seventh Century.

Nebuchadnezzar his father. If we compare this statement with its threefold reiteration in 5[11,13,22] we cannot escape inferring that our author took Belshazzar to be an actual son (or grandson) of Nebuchadnezzar. But Belshazzar's father was Nabuna'id, the son of Nabu-balâtsu-ikbi, who was a usurper, and wholly unconnected by blood with Nebuchadnezzar. Since, however, according to Hebrew usage, the word 'father' could be used in the sense of grandfather (Gen. 28[13], 32[9]), or of great-grandfather (Num. 18[1,2]), or great-great-grandfather (1 Kings 15[11]), it is of course possible that Nabuna'id married a daughter of Nebuchadnezzar in order to strengthen his position, and in such a case Belshazzar would have been a grandson of the great king. But, if Nabuna'id really made such an alliance, there would surely have been some reference to it in one or more of the several inscriptions relating to Nabuna'id. But there is not even the shadow of an allusion to such an alliance. See Introd. to this chapter, p. 108 sqq.

That . . . might drink. וְיִשְׁתּוֹן. Cf. 2[13], 6[2] for the same idiomatic use of וֹ. See Introduction.

His wives and concubines. Th. here and in 5[23] reverses the order of these two phrases. LXX omits both. According to Curtius, v. 1. 38 women were admitted to such feasts as that in our text amongst the Babylonians in the time of Alexander: Babylonii maxime in vinum et quae ebrietatem sequuntur effusi sunt. As regards the Persians the accounts differ. Herodotus, v. 18 states that it was customary for the concubines and wives to sit side by side with the men at great feasts. Plutarch (*Sympos.* i. 1) and Macrobius (vii. 1), on the other hand, assert definitely that the Persians allowed their concubines but not their wives to be present on such occasions (μὴ ταῖς γαμε-ταῖς ἀλλὰ ταῖς παλλακίσι συμμεθύσκεσθαι). Aelian (*Var. Hist.* xii. 1) relates that μετὰ . . . τὸ ἐμπλησθῆναι τροφῆς οἱ Πέρσαι τῷ τε οἴνῳ . . . ἀπο-σχολάζουσι. During one of these feasts four Greek virgins were brought to Cyrus, three of whom had been thoroughly trained in the ἑταιρικὰ . . . ἔργα. The narrative in Josephus (*Ant.* xi. 6. 1) supports the latter view; for it states that Vashti out of regard to the laws of the Persians (φυλακῇ τῶν παρὰ Πέρσαις νόμων) refused to go to the king at the feast. It is worth observing that the LXX omits this phrase both here and in 5[3,23].

Wives. The word שֵׁגַל is rare, occurring in the O.T. only in

Neh. 2⁶, where the wife of Artaxerxes is spoken of, and in
Ps. 45⁹. It is not found in the Targums, and, in the few passages
in which it occurs in Rabbinic Hebrew, it does not preserve the
honourable meaning of wife. *Concubines,* לחנתא is found in the
Aramaic of the Targums in the same sense as in our text. In
Cant. 6⁸ queens and concubines are mentioned together.

5³. ⌜*And silver.*⌝ Restored in accordance with Th. and
Vulg.

5⁴. For 'the gods of gold . . . and of stone' the LXX reads
simply τὰ εἴδωλα τὰ χειροποίητα αὐτῶν, but adds καὶ τὸν θεὸν τοῦ αἰῶνος
οὐκ εὐλόγησαν τὸν ἔχοντα τὴν ἐξουσίαν τοῦ πνεύματος αὐτῶν. The substance
of these words recurs in 5²³ in the Aramaic and all the versions,
though here again the LXX diverges from all the other authorities in charging alike the king and his nobles with this offence,
whereas the Aramaic and the versions other than the LXX
name the king only as being the chief offender. This repetition
is a Semitic characteristic. Hence the words in the LXX may
be original. It is to be observed that the LXX πνεῦμα presupposes נִשְׁמָא here as in 5²³, just as in 10¹⁷ it renders the Hebrew
נְשָׁמָה. The LXX in this verse is in no way derived from 5²³,
where we have καὶ τὸ πνεῦμά σου ἐν τῇ χειρὶ αὐτοῦ, though here (5⁴)
the LXX seems to give a free and different rendering of the
same Aramaic clause which occurs in 5²³, save for the difference
of suffixes. Such varieties in rendering are characteristic of the
LXX. τὸν ἔχοντα τὴν ἐξουσίαν τοῦ πνεύματος αὐτῶν presupposes די
נשמתהון בידה, or possibly די שׁליט בנשׁמתהון.

5⁵. *In the same hour,* בַּהּ־שַׁעֲתָא. The suffix preceding the noun
used in the sense of a demonstrative pronoun: Kautzsch, § 88.
Cf. 3⁶,⁷,⁸, 4³⁰,³³, 7²⁴: also in 5¹² (cf. 5³⁰) with the repetition of the
preposition בֵּהּ בְּדָנִיֵּאל. The same idiom is found in connexion
with מִן 7²⁴ and עַל Ezra 4¹¹. See Stevenson, § 5. 14, where
a repetition of the preposition ל is given in the Palestinian
Aramaic. See Introd. § 20. q.

Came forth, נפקו. Qr. corrects into נְפַקָה on the ground of
gender, just as in 7²⁰ it corrects נפלו into נפלה. There is a like
correction in 7⁸. But the Kt. may be the original. There seems
to be no example of the 3rd pl. fem. in the Eg. Pap. with fem.
nouns as their subject. Yet in the Targums and occasionally
in the Palestinian Talmud and Midrashim the 3rd pl. fem. of the
perf. ends in א or ן. See Stevenson, § 17.3. Kautzsch (§ 23. 2) is

of opinion that the Massoretes introduced the distinction of the
3rd fem. pl., which was familiar to them in the Targums.   In
any case, as the participle כתבן which is co-ordinated with נפקו
shows, the latter form is used as a feminine.

Candlestick, i.e. נברשתא: in Syr. *nabreshtâ* and in the Targums—a foreign word of unknown origin.

The plaister, lit. *the chalk.*   This word (ניר) appears once in
Biblical Hebrew, Isa. 27⁹, where it is probably borrowed from
the Aramaic.   It is found in the Syr.   The walls of the Babylonian palaces were probably as the Assyrian, lined with white
alabaster for several feet from the ground, as Driver remarks,
appealing to Layard, *Nineveh and its Remains*⁵, i. 254-7,
262 sq.

Palm of the hand.   The hand appeared above the couch where
the king was reclining (Bevan).   In Hebrew in which it occurs
five times in one phrase it means either the *palm* of the hand or
the *sole* of the foot.   It is also used in the Targums in the same
connexion.

5⁶. *Countenance.*   זיו is taken to be a loan-word from the
Assyrian *zimu,* pronounced later as *ziwu* in Middle Iran.

Was changed.   As Kautzsch (§ 89. 2) points out, there is an
incorrect use of the verbal suffix here in שנוהי עלוהי.   He
proposes that we should read שנין עלוהי as in 5⁹.   But it is better
with Bevan to read שנו עלוהי.   Other forms of the phrase are
found in 5¹⁰ ישתנו and in 7²⁸ ישתנון עלי.   'Was changed' is a more
idiomatic English rendering of the phrase than 'was changed in
him'.   Similarly in 7²⁸.   The phrase is found in Job 14²⁰ משנה
פניו, but in a different sense, i. e. of changing the face in death.   The
עלוהי in 5⁶ (7²⁸), if translated at all, should perhaps be rendered
to his cost' : i. e. 'was changed for the worse', as in Gen. 48⁷,
Rachel died to my cost' (מתה עלי) or simply 'Rachel died'.
The Targum reproduces this idiom, and also the Pesh.   An
Irish peasant says at the present day 'my wife died on me'
where we have exactly the same idiom as in Gen. 48⁷,

Alarmed.   Cf. 4¹⁹.

The joints of his loins, lit. *the joints of his loin.*   קטרי חרצה.
This phrase is found in the Targ. Jon. on Gen. 50¹¹.   We
should have expected חרצוהי.   חרצא is the same word as the
Hebrew חלצים.   It is uncertain whether the *r* or the *l* is the

older; for the Arabic supports the Aramaic, as Bevan observes, though with a transposition of the last two consonants. We might compare the frequent Homeric phrase αὐτοῦ λύτο γούνατα, *Od.* iv. 703, *Il.* xxi. 114.

Were loosed, i. e. מִשְׁתָּרַיִן. As Bevan observes we should expect מִשְׁתְּרַיִן, since in Bibl. Aram. שְׁרִי (Ezra 5²) means 'to begin'. But in Syr. both the Ethpa'el and the Ithpe'al have this meaning: see Brockelmann, *Lex. in loc.* In Syro-Pal. Syr. only the latter tense appears to occur. Schulthess, *Lex.*, p. 215.

His knees smote, &c. Cf. Nah. 2¹¹⁽¹⁰⁾ It is noteworthy that for ארכבתה we have ברכוהי in 6¹¹.

5⁷⁻⁹. The text of these verses is in certain details uncertain. The MT (with its versions), the LXX, and Josephus differ from each other, but the LXX supported by Josephus gives clearly the right order of events, though its text is very corrupt. As the MT stands, the wise men appear twice on no intelligible grounds before the king. Thus in 5⁷ the king summons them and *on their coming before him* he tells them the gifts that he would give to the successful interpreter of the mysterious writing. But 5⁸ begins as though no such event had taken place, and reads 'Then came in all the king's wise men'. In the LXX and Josephus there is no such incoherency. According to both these authorities (LXX 5⁷ᵃ) the king first of all summoned the wise men to interpret the writing. These came in due course, but were unable to do so. Then were King Belshazzar and his companions greatly alarmed (this last sentence has been wrongly transferred into 5⁶ by the LXX but not by Josephus, whereas the MT has relegated it to 5⁹). *Then and not till then* (5⁸ᵇ) the king issued a proclamation setting forth the rewards that would be conferred on the man, whosoever he might be, who should make known the writing to the king (5⁸ᶜ). The wise men are not summoned again; for they had failed. The invitation is now general, but, tempted by the great rewards, the wise men presented themselves before the king in the hope of discovering the interpretation of the writing, but again failed.

It is obvious that we have here in the LXX (followed by Josephus) the rational order of events. But, though the order is that of our author, the text of the LXX is very corrupt.

Notwithstanding, we must here follow the LXX, though not necessarily its corruptions.

Before I give the full textual evidence, I must mention a clever suggestion by Loehr. He proposes the transposition of the first clause of 5[8] 'Then came in all the king's wise men' before 5[7b]. This certainly provides us with a smooth text: 5[7a] 'The king cried aloud to bring in the enchanters, the Chaldeans, and the soothsayers. 5[8a] Then came in all the king's wise men. 5[7b] The king spake and said to the wise men of Babylon, Whosoever shall read ... in the kingdom. 5[8b] But they could not read the writing, &c.' But the order of events in the LXX and Josephus furnishes conclusive evidence against this proposal. The MT and Th. attest a text that is not only dislocated but defective as well. Besides, this account is not at all in keeping with the high-handed action of a Babylonian despot, even when reduced to the plight of Belshazzar. It was the duty of the wise men to solve the enigma, and purely a matter of grace on the king's part to reward the successful. Hence the offer of such extrava-

Th. and the MT.

5[6] Τότε τοῦ βασιλέως ἡ μορφὴ ἠλλοιώθη, καὶ οἱ διαλογισμοὶ αὐτοῦ συνετάρασσον αὐτόν, καὶ οἱ σύνδεσμοι τῆς ὀσφύος διελύοντο καὶ τὰ γόνατα αὐτοῦ συνεκροτοῦντο.

5[7a] Καὶ ἐβόησεν ὁ βασιλεὺς ἐν ἰσχύι τοῦ εἰσαγαγεῖν μάγους,
5[7b] Χαλδαίους, γαζαρηνούς, [+ ἀπεκρίθη MT] καὶ εἶπεν τοῖς σο-
5[7c] φοῖς Βαβυλῶνος ° Ὃς ἂν ἀναγνῷ τὴν γραφὴν ταύτην καὶ τὴν σύγκρισιν γνωρίσῃ μοι, πορφύραν ἐνδύσεται, καὶ ὁ μανιάκης ὁ χρυσοῦς ἐπὶ τὸν τράχηλον αὐτοῦ, καὶ τρίτος ἐν τῇ
5[8] βασιλείᾳ μου ἄρξει. Καὶ εἰσε-

LXX

(the order of the words is that of the MS., the numbering is mine—not Swete's.)

5[6] Καὶ ἡ ὅρασις αὐτοῦ ἠλλοιώθη [καὶ φόβοι] καὶ ὑπόνοιαι αὐτὸν κατέ-
(5[6c][d]°) σπευδον. ἔσπευσεν οὖν ὁ βασιλεύς'
= Th.[9]) [καὶ ἐξανέστη καὶ ἑώρα τὴν γραφὴν ἐκείνην], καὶ οἱ †συνεταῖροι† κύκλῳ αὐτοῦ †ἐκαυχῶντο†.

5[7a] Καὶ ὁ βασιλεὺς ἐφώνησε φωνῇ μεγάλῃ καλέσαι τοὺς ἐπαοιδοὺς καὶ φαρμακοὺς καὶ Χαλδαίους καὶ γαζαρηνούς, ἀπαγγεῖλαι τὸ σύγ-
5[8a] κριμα τῆς γραφῆς. καὶ εἰσεπορεύοντο ἐπὶ [θεωρίαν] ἰδεῖν τὴν γραφήν, καὶ τὸ σύγκριμα τῆς γραφῆς οὐκ ἐδύναντο συγκρῖναι τῷ βασιλεῖ.
5[8b] τότε ὁ βασιλεὺς ἐξέθηκε πρόσ-
5[8c] (= ταγμα λέγων Πᾶς ἀνὴρ ὃς ἂν
Th.[7c]) ὑποδείξῃ τὸ σύγκριμα τῆς γραφῆς,

gant rewards could only naturally be made when, as in the LXX and Josephus, the wise men really failed to read and interpret the writing. Then it was that the king and his nobles were confounded and that the time had come to offer a guerdon beyond the dreams of avarice. Cf. the failure of the wise men in Gen. 41[8] to interpret Pharaoh's dream, and the wrath of Nebuchadnezzar with the wise men of Babylon and his edict for their destruction on a like occasion in our text 2[3—12].

With a view to clearness I shall treat 5[7—9] first *in regard to the order of events* in the text, and with a view to the discovery of the original order of events in the text, I shall arrange Th. (i.e. the MT), the LXX and Josephus accounts in parallel columns. This will be followed by a translation of the restored text. Secondly, I shall treat 5[7—9] afresh as regards some textual difficulties and their interpretation, though many of these must necessarily be dealt with under (i).

5[7—9]. (i) *The order of events:*

Josephus, *Ant.* x. 11. 2.

Ταραχθεὶς δὲ ὑπὸ τῆς ὄψεως συνεκάλεσε τοὺς μάγους καὶ τοὺς Χαλδαίους ... ὡς ἂν αὐτῷ δηλώσωσι τὰ γεγραμμένα. τῶν δὲ μάγων οὐδὲν εὑρίσκειν δυναμένων οὐδὲ συνιέναι λεγόντων, ὑπ᾽ ἀγωνίας ὁ βασιλεὺς καὶ πολλῆς τῆς ἐπὶ τῷ παραδόξῳ λύπης κατὰ πᾶσαν ἐκήρυξε τὴν χώραν τῷ τὰ γράμματα καὶ τὴν ὑπ᾽ αὐτῶν δηλουμένην διάνοιαν σαφῆ ποιήσαντι δώσειν ὑπισχνούμενος στρεπτὸν περιαυχένιον χρύσεον καὶ πορφυρᾶν ἐσθῆτα φορεῖν ... καὶ τὸ τρίτον μέρος τῆς ἰδίας ἀρχῆς. τούτου γενομένου τοῦ κηρύγματος ἔτι μᾶλλον οἱ μάγοι συνδραμόντες ... πρὸς τὴν εὕρεσιν τῶν γραμμάτων οὐδὲν ἔλαττον ἠπόρησαν. ἀθυμοῦντα

Order of events in Josephus.

(a) The king's alarm at the vision (ταραχθεὶς ... ὑπὸ τῆς ὄψεως) = LXX 5[6 a, b]: Th. 5[6].

(b) The king summons the wise men to interpret the writing (συνεκάλεσε ... ὡς ἂν .. δηλώσωσι τὰ γεγραμμένα) = LXX 5[7 a]: Th. 5[7a].

(c) The wise men come but are unable to interpret (τῶν δὲ μάγων οὐδὲν εὑρίσκειν δυναμένων οὐδὲ συνιέναι λεγόντων) = LXX 5[8a]: Th. 5[8].

(d) The king moved with anguish and trouble causes the proclamation to be made that the interpreter of the mysterious writing will be rewarded with a chain of gold, a purple robe, and a third part of his kingdom (ὑπ᾽ ἀγωνίας ...

Th. and the MT.

πορεύοντο πάντες οἱ σοφοὶ τοῦ
βασιλέως, καὶ οὐκ ἠδύναντο τὴν
γραφὴν ἀναγνῶναι οὐδὲ τὴν σύγκρισιν γνωρίσαι τῷ βασιλεῖ.
5⁹ καὶ ὁ βασιλεὺς Βαλτασὰρ ἐταράχθη, καὶ ἡ μορφὴ αὐτοῦ ἠλλοιώθη ἐν αὐτῷ, καὶ οἱ μεγιστᾶνες αὐτοῦ συνεταράσσαντο.
5¹⁰ καὶ εἰσῆλθεν ἡ βασίλισσα.

LXX.

στολιεῖ αὐτὸν πορφύραν, καὶ μανιά-
κην χρυσοῦν περιθήσει αὐτῷ καὶ
δοθήσεται αὐτῷ ἐξουσία τοῦ τρίτου
5⁸ᶜ μέρους τῆς βασιλείας. καὶ εἰσεπορεύοντο οἱ ἐπαοιδοὶ καὶ φαρμακοὶ
καὶ γαζαρηνοί, καὶ οὐκ ἠδύνατο
οὐδεὶς τὸ σύγκριμα τῆς γραφῆς
5¹⁰ ἀπαγγεῖλαι. τότε ὁ βασιλεὺς ἐκάλεσε τὴν βασίλισσαν.

The order of the events in the above three authorities has been preserved rightly by Josephus throughout but in a com-pressed form. His text is obviously based on the LXX. The solitary LXX manuscript has also preserved the order of the original version of the LXX, save that it has through some accident transferred two clauses which originally followed 5⁸ᵃ ἔσπευσεν ... †ἐκαυχῶντο† to the close of 5⁶. Josephus clearly used a manuscript in which this dislocation in the text of the LXX or of the Aramaic had not occurred. These two clauses should be restored after 5⁸ᵃ. The last half of 5⁶ of the LXX has not only two clauses which originally followed 8ᵃ and a clause also which belonged originally to 5⁵. This last (5ᵈ) is καὶ ἐξανέστη καὶ ἑώρα τὴν γραφὴν ἐκείνην. The first two words (καὶ ἐξανέστη) look like a mis-taken addition by a scribe who did not understand the meaning that ἔσπευσεν had here, i.e. that it was a rendering of מתבהל which Th. renders ἐταράχθη. That ἔσπευσεν is a legitimate rendering we shall show presently. Now as to the remaining five words καὶ ἑώρα τὴν γραφὴν ἐκείνην, these are a rendering of וחזה כתבה דנה, which

Josephus, *Ant.* x. II. 2.

δ' ἐπὶ τούτῳ θεασαμένη τὸν βασιλέα
ἡ μάμμη αὐτοῦ παραθαρσύνειν
ἤρξατο.

Order of events in Josephus.

ἐκήρυξε . . . τῷ τὰ γράμματα . . .
σαφῆ ποιήσαντι δώσειν ὑπισχνούμενος . . .) = LXX 5⁶ᶜ,ᵈ which
has been wrongly transposed
from its original position after
5⁸ᵃ, and in Th. i.e. the MT has
been transposed after 5⁸ and is
numbered 5⁹. The LXX should
be read thus: 5⁸ᵃ, 6ᶜ,ᵉ, 8ᵇ and
Th. 5⁹, ⁷ᶜ, but it omits before
5⁷ᶜ the indispensable clause
given in LXX 5⁸ᵇ.

(e) When this proclamation was
made, the wise men rushed
hastily to make another attempt
to decipher the enigma, but were
no more successful than before
(τούτου τοῦ κηρύγματος . . . οἱ μάγοι
συνδραμόντες . . . οὐδὲν ἔλαττον ἠπόρησαν) = LXX 5⁸ᶜ: Th. i.e. the
MT wanting.

is an abbreviation and corruption of the clause in 5⁵ i.e. ‏וחזה‎ · · ·
‏ירא‎ · · · ‏כתבה‎ which the translator found as ‏וחזה כתבה דנא‎. It is
thus a dittograph from 5⁵, and should be excised.

Let us now return to the two clauses 5⁶ᶜ, ᵉ which should be
restored after 5⁸ᵃ and which are identical with 5⁹ of Th. (i.e. the
MT), save that 5⁹ contains an additional clause. The two
clauses are ἔσπευσεν οὖν ὁ βασιλεὺς καὶ οἱ †συνεταῖροι† κύκλῳ αὐτοῦ
†ἐκαυχῶντο†. First of all ἔσπευσεν is the normal rendering of the
Aramaic ‏בהל‎: cf. 3²⁴ where σπεύσας = ‏בהתבהלה‎, though here
it has a different sense. But κατασπεύδω is used in 4¹⁶ to
render the Pa'el of ‏בהל‎ where Th. uses συνταράσσω. Th. never
uses either σπεύδω or κατασπεύδω as renderings of ‏בהל‎ in the
sense of causing alarm or being alarmed. But the LXX so uses it in
this sense in Exod. 15¹⁵, Judges 20⁴¹, I Sam. 28²¹. Next συνεταῖροι
= ‏חברוהי‎ (as in 2¹⁷), which may be a corruption of ‏הדברוהי‎.
If so, the latter as in Th. 3²⁴ could be rendered οἱ μεγιστᾶνες αὐτοῦ.
But if the versions can be trusted then ‏חברוהי‎ is a corruption of

רברבנוהי since μεγιστᾶνες is the rendering of this word in 5²³, 6¹⁷ of the LXX and in 5¹,²,³,⁹,²³ of Th. Once more it is clear that ἐκαυχῶντο is corrupt. By retroversion the source of the corruption is discoverable. This word = משבחין. The Targum on Jer. 9²³⁻²⁴ renders התבהל five times by שבח where the LXX has καυχᾶσθαι. But משבחין is impossible here, and is evidently a corruption of משתבשין, which stands in the MT and is rightly rendered by Th. by συνεταράσσοντο.

We have now proved that 5⁶ ᶜ, ᵉ of the LXX points back to the present text of the Aramaic, save that it has lost one of its clauses. We have further seen that these clauses have been dislocated from their original position after 5⁸ᵃ both in the LXX and in the MT and the versions dependent on it.

Again in Th. (i.e. the MT), 5⁷ᵇ ('The king answered and said to the wise men of Babylon') is clearly an interpolation. There is no place for it in the original text.

The list of the classes of the wise men in the MT. and Theodotion in 5⁷ᵃ seems to be imperfect. These should give four classes as the LXX does and as the MT and Th do in 5¹¹.

We are now in a position to give a translation of a text superior to that of the MT, and also to that presupposed by any individual version. In the translation that follows, which is that of the Aramaic, passages enclosed in ⌐ ¬ are restored from the LXX : passages enclosed in ⌐ ¬ are not found in the LXX.

5⁷ᵃ. 'The king cried aloud to bring in the ⌐magicians¬, enchanters, Chaldeans, and soothsayers ⌐that they should make known the interpretation of the writing¬.   5⁸ᵃ. Then came in all the king's wise men : but they could ⌐not read¬ the writing, ⌐nor¬ make known to the king the interpretation. 5⁹. Then was King Belshazzar greatly alarmed ⌐and his countenance was changed¬, and his lords were confounded. 5⁸ᵇ. ⌐Then the king made a decree, saying :¬ 5⁸ ᶜ. Whosoever shall ⌐read¬ this writing ⌐and¬ declare to me the interpretation thereof, shall be clothed with purple, and have a chain of gold about his neck and shall rule as one of three in my kingdom. ⌐And the magicians, and enchanters and soothsayers came in, but none could make known the interpretation of the writing¬.'

The preceding narrative is at once intelligible and vivid. Only one clause of the Aramaic is omitted i.e. 5⁷ᵇ 'and the king answered and said to the wise men of Babylon'. The LXX does not admit of it and Josephus omits it. In 5⁷ᵃ the clause restored from the LXX is supported by its repetition in the next verses in all the authorities. The words in 5⁸ᵃ 'not read' and 'nor' (LXX) are probably original; for in ver. 5¹⁷ (in all authorities) Daniel 'reads' the writing which the wise men could not. It is true that this clause is omitted in ver. 5⁸ ᶜ in the LXX. Probably at close of verse 8ᶜ we should read 'none could read nor make known', instead of 'none could make known'.

5⁷⁻⁹. (ii) *Some textual difficulties and their interpretation.*

5⁷ᵃ. *To bring in*, i. e. הֶעָלָה : in 4³ הנעלה.

⌐*The magicians*⌐. Since the LXX so reads, and since in 5¹¹ the same four orders of wise men are mentioned, we may reasonably infer that the phrase belongs to our author's original text.

5⁸ᵃ. ⌐*Read . . . and*⌐ The MT and Th. are no doubt right in this reading. Though the solitary manuscript of the LXX omits it (save in 5¹⁷ i. e. 5²⁵), it appears to be referred to in the text of Josephus τῶν δὲ μάγων οὐδὲν εὑρίσκειν δυναμένων οὐδὲ συνιέναι λεγόντων. These words imply that the wise men could neither make out the script nor interpret it. 5¹⁷ confirms this view, where Daniel undertakes to decipher the script and interpret it. The 'reading' of the script is referred to also in 5¹⁵, ¹⁶.

5⁹. On the position of this verse in the text the Aram., LXX, and Josephus disagree. The LXX is clearly wrong in making it a part of 5⁶. Josephus appears to be right in describing the consternation of the king as following on the first failure of the wise men. Thereupon the king issues a proclamation of the great reward to be won by any one who could interpret the writing.

Purple. The successful wise man was to be clothed with purple—a privilege which gave him a royal dignity among the Persians (Esth. 8¹⁵) and the right of being called the king's friend (1 Macc. 10²⁰, ⁶², ⁶⁴ 11⁵⁸, &c.). The Aramaic ארגון is the same word as the Hebrew ארגמן Num. 4¹³, Judges 8²⁶, and the Assyrian *Argamannu.* We find the Aramaic form in 2 Chron. 2⁶ ארגון. The derivation is doubtful.

Chain of gold. הַמְנִיכָא (*Qr.*), המוניכא (*Kt.*). The *Qr.* is according to Marti a later Aramaic form. The word is either borrowed from the Greek μανιάκης (Kautzsch, § 64⁴), or, according to Andreas (see Marti, *Glossar* 67*) from the Persian *hamyânak,* diminutive from *hamyân* (in Aram. הֵמְיָן), *girdle,* whence it was borrowed by

the Greeks. It should be punctuated הַמְיִנְכָא. But the change
of meaning is difficult. It is found in Syr. in the same form:
in the Targums in the abbreviated form מניכא. Pharaoh presents
the same gift to Joseph (Gen. 41[42]): and Cambyses to the
Ethiopians (Herod. iii. 20), and the younger Cyrus to Syennesis
(Xen. *Anab.* i. 2. 27). According to the last writer (*Cyr.* xiii.
5. 18) such chains could only be worn when presented by the
king. Thus they were distinctive of a certain royal order.
Polybius (ii. 31) explains the μανιάκης as χρυσοῦν ψέλλιον, ὃ φοροῦσι
περὶ τὰς χεῖρας καὶ τὸν τράχηλον οἱ Γαλάται.

Rule as one of three (?). The A.V. and the R.V. 'be the third
ruler' is inaccurate here as in 5[16,29]. Neither the word תַּלְתִּי
translated 'third' nor תַּלְתָּא in 5[16,29] is found elsewhere as an
ordinal. The ordinal for 'third' in our author, the Targums
and the Aramaic parts of the Talmud is תליתי, though only the
feminine of this numeral occurs in our author, i. e. תליתיא 2[39].
Hence we cannot give the meaning of 'third' to the MT forms
תַּלְתִּי or תַּלְתָּא. It is true that Th. in the second century A. D. in
5[7,16] renders the text τρίτος ἐν τῇ βασιλείᾳ μου. But Josephus (*Ant.*
x. 11. 2) in the first century paraphrases the text thus: δώσειν ...
τὸ τρίτον μέρος τῆς ἰδίας ἀρχῆς—a phrase which is repeated in x. 11.
3, and which was possibly influenced by the second century B. C.
paraphrase of the LXX: δοθήσεται αὐτῷ ἐξουσία τοῦ τρίτου μέρους τῆς
βασιλείας (5[9]. Cf. 5[16,29]).

How then is this perplexing clause to be translated? The
most satisfactory explanation appears to be that of Driver. He
takes תלתי or rather תלתא to be the same as תִּלְתָּא or תַּלְתָּא, which
both in the Targums and the Syriac means 'a third part'. Cf.
2 Kings 11[5, 6] 'a third part of you' תִּלְתָּא מִנְּכוֹן: 2 Sam. 18[2].
'Hence', he concludes, 'the literal rendering appears to be
"shall rule as a third part in the kingdom", i. e. ... be one of
the three chief ministers, "rule as one of three".' Now this
rendering of תלתא certainly receives support from the oldest
version. The Pesh. also gives in the three passages 'rule as
a third part in the kingdom'. Thus the LXX and the Pesh.
presuppose תלתא in all three passages.

Loehr suggests that we should emend תַּלְתִּי into תְּלִתִּי = 'third'.
But Bevan objects to the disappearance of the long *i* in the
emphatic state.

If the rendering 'be third ruler in the kingdom' were possible,

Driver's explanation then would be that the successful interpreter would 'have a third part of the supreme authority
in the country' as one of his three chief ministers, With this
we might compare 1 Esdras 3⁹ οἱ τρεῖς μεγιστᾶνες τῆς Περσίδος. Now
in 6³ of our text the institution of three supreme officers is mentioned, and as Daniel is presupposed to be one of them, the
explanation of Driver seems good.

On the other hand Marti regards תַּלְתִּי as = *triumvir*, being
derived from תלת *a third*. In this case he would regard Daniel
as coming third after the king and the queen-mother. Prince
and others explain Daniel as the third after Nabuna'id, but, as
Marti rightly rejoins, Prince herein forgets that in vv. 2 and 13
of this same chapter Nebuchadnezzar is definitely said to be the
father of Belshazzar. See my note on 5².

תַּלְתִּי is a unique word if it is a genuine word. But probably
it is a corruption of תַּלְתִּי or תַּלְתָּא : cf. 5¹⁶,²⁹. Apparently the
early translators found one and the same word in 5⁷,¹⁶,²⁹. At
any rate they recognize no such difference as the present text
presents. Kautzsch (§ 65. 1. Anm. 3), it is true, regards תַּלְתָּא
as an abnormal emphatic state of תַּלְתִּי—a view which Bevan
condemns as still more inaccurate than the view of Gesenius.
Gesenius regarded תַּלְתָּא as the emphatic state of a form תְּלַת,
third rank—a view which Kautzsch brands as undoubtedly
wrong.

5⁸ᵇ. Wanting in the MT and Th.

5¹⁰. The text of the MT 'the queen by reason of the words of
the king and his lords came' is more than doubtful. Th. omits
'by reason of the words of the king and his lords'; the LXX
does not admit of this phrase. Moreover לקבל which occurs
four times elsewhere in our author, means 'before' and not 'by
reason of' as here. It has this meaning once in the Aramaic of
Ezra, but not in our author, as we may reasonably conclude on
many grounds. See Introd., § 20. *ff.* The text of the MT is
here very difficult. It represents the queen as coming into the
banqueting chamber purely on her own initiative owing to the
exclamations of alarm on the part of the king and his lords that
had penetrated the rest of the palace. The LXX on the other
hand represents the king as at once summoning the queen on
his second failure to secure an interpretation of the writing—
τότε ὁ βασιλεὺς ἐκάλεσε τὴν βασίλισσαν περὶ τοῦ σημείου. Still another

version is given by Josephus (*Ant.* x. 11. 2), who represents the king's grandmother (or mother) (μάμμη) as a guest(?) at the banquet. We should observe that Josephus, *Ant.* x. 11. 2, identifies Belshazzar with Nabuna'id (Βαλτασάρην τὸν καλούμενον Ναβοάνδηλον παρὰ τοῖς Βαβυλωνίοις), and in x. 11. 4 as an ἔγγονος of Nebuchadnezzar. Recognizing the deep dejection of the king she encouraged him by her account of Daniel.

Since the oldest authorities are thus in conflict with each other, it is difficult to determine what exactly the original text was, though clearly the LXX preserves the essence of the original ; the king sent for the queen. We have seen how Josephus took this queen to be the grandmother of Belshazzar, that is the mother of Nabuna'id. But according to the Annalistic Tablet ii. 13 (*KB.* iii. 2, p. 131 ; *R.P.*² v. 160) this lady died eight years previously at Sippara in the ninth year of Nabuna'id. Origen takes her to be the mother of Belshazzar. The text of the LXX could admit of this view, though it does not necessarily involve it. See end of note. Porphyry accepts this view, but he refuses to take the question seriously, and, ridiculing the whole story, says that Belshazzar's wife knew more about the matter than her husband ('illudit plus scire quam maritum '— Jerome *in loc.* See vol. v. 520). Boutflower (*In and around the Book of Daniel*, p. 117) thinks that the queen in question was the widow of Nebuchadnezzar, whom Nabuna'id had married in order to strengthen his position, as he was not of the blood royal. Other writers maintain that this queen was the daughter of Nebuchadnezzar. But in the absence of all evidence as to any such alliance of Nabuna'id with either a daughter or widow of Nebuchadnezzar in the tablets dealing with Nabuna'id, where there was every reason for emphasizing it if it existed, the hypothesis has no foundation. See note on p. 108 sqq.

That this queen was the queen-mother is certainly to be inferred from the Aramaic text. She is not included among the wives of the king ($5^{2,3}$), and in the next place she speaks apparently from personal knowledge of the events of Nebuchadnezzar's reign (5^{11}). Furthermore the LXX does not proscribe this view, nor yet that she was the king's wife. Its text admits of either view. In Israel and Judah the queen-mother enjoyed great influence : see 1 Kings 15^{13}, 2 Kings 10^{13}, 24^{12}. Herodotus (ix. 109) speaks of the influence exerted in this respect by

Amestris, the wife of Xerxes, and also of Nitocris, the wife of Nebuchadnezzar, i. 185–8.

Let not . . . alarm thee. On the jussive forms יְבַהֲלוּךְ and יִשְׁתַּנּוֹ see note on 4¹⁶⁽¹⁹⁾.

In the days of thy father. These words, though in a slightly different connexion, occur also in the LXX and also in the other versions.

⌜5¹¹⌝. *Whose name is Daniel.* Some such words (= דִּי שְׁמֵהּ דָּנִיאֵל, cf. 2²⁶, 4⁵,¹⁶) must be supplied, since the phrase 'in the same Daniel' in the next verse implies that Daniel's name had just been mentioned. The LXX is corrupt in some respects, but it preserves the beginning of the queen's address to the king in the indirect narrative, ἡ βασίλισσα ἐμνήσθη πρὸς αὐτὸν περὶ τοῦ Δανιήλ, ὃς ἦν ἐκ τῆς αἰχμαλωσίας τῆς Ἰουδαίας; Josephus (*Ant.* x. 11. 2) confirms this reading, but gives it in the direct: ἔστι τις ἀπὸ τῆς Ἰουδαίας αἰχμάλωτος . . . Δανίηλος ὄνομα, σοφὸς ἀνὴρ κτλ. It is not improbable that after the addition I have already made to the text on the authority of the LXX and Josephus we should add the further clause from the LXX ⌜'who was one of the exiles of Judaea'⌝ (ὃς ἦν [indirect for ὅς ἐστι] ἐκ τῆς αἰχμαλωσίας τῆς Ἰουδαίας = דִּי מִן גָּלוּתָא דִּי יְהוּד. See ver. 13.

In whom is the spirit of the holy gods. This phrase here and in 5¹⁴ is the immediate source whence it was borrowed by the reviser and utilized in 4⁵⁽⁸⁾, ⁶⁽⁹⁾, ¹⁵⁽¹⁸⁾. The clause is most probably suggested by Gen. 41³⁸, 'A man in whom the spirit of the gods is'. Its equivalent, though in a non-polytheistic sense, is found in the LXX and Th. on the present passage.

The holy gods. The queen speaks as an idolater. Contrast Joshua 24¹⁹.

Holy gods. It has been urged by Lidzbarski (*Ephem.* iii. 255) that, since in Aḥ 126 (Cowley: Pap. 56¹ in Sachau) אלהיא is construed with a singular verb, the plural should be construed in the sing. as 'God', and that in Aḥikar אלהן always bears this meaning. But in Aḥ 115 and 124 it is construed with a plural verb. Hence Cowley and Perles are no doubt right in considering the singular verb as merely an error. In 34⁷ (Cowley: *c.* 407 B.C.), 56¹ (Cowley), אלהיא is followed by a plural verb. In 30²,²⁷, 31², 32³, 38³⁵, 40¹ the sing. אלה or אלה שמיא is used of Ya'u or Yahweh, the God of Israel. On the other hand when the heathen gods are referred to we find אֱלֹהֵי מצרים used as a plural in 71[8,26] (Cowley). See also 30[14], 31[13].

[*The king, thy father.*] An intrusion. It is not found in Th. nor any first-class authority such as the LXX or Josephus. But the intrusion may be due to the reviser, who would thus emphasize this idea of our author as to Belshazzar being the son or grandson of Nebuchadnezzar: cf. 5[2,11] (*bis*),[13].

Master of the magicians. This phrase is the source whence the reviser borrowed his in 4[6(9)].

Magicians, enchanters, Chaldeans, and soothsayers. Here as in 5[7a] (LXX) four orders of wise men are mentioned. From this chapter the reviser borrowed this clause to insert in 4[4(7)].

5[12]. *Interpreting . . . loosing.* These two participles in the text מְפַשַּׁר and מְשָׁרֵא are undoubtedly corrupt for מִפְשַׁר and מְשָׁרֵא respectively, as most scholars now admit.

Solving of riddles. אֲחַוָיַת אחידן. אחוית is here the construct of אחויה (Inf. Aph'el: Kautzsch, § 60. 1). This phrase is drawn from Judges 14[14,15,19]. The Hebrew in 14[14] is להגיד החידה = 'to solve the riddle', which the Targum renders לחואה חודיתא, which is practically the same phrase as in our text. The Hebrew synonym, which is etymologically the same, means 'riddle', Num. 12[8], or 'hard question', 1 Kings 10[1], or 'problem' or 'enigma of life', Ps. 49[5]. That the Aramaic word originally maintained itself in the Hebrew version of 12[8] I have given reasons for believing.

Loosing of spells. The A.V. and R.V. wrongly render 'dis-solving of doubts'. Bevan rightly recognized that קטרין meant 'magic knots', although unaware of the parallel in 1 Enoch 8[3], where we have the Greek equivalent, i. e. ἐπαοιδῶν λυτήριον = 'the resolving of enchantments'. In the same work 95[4] we have 'anathemas which cannot be reversed'. Th.'s rendering of our text confirms this view—λύων συνδέσμους.

Were found in the same Daniel. The Aramaic בֵּהּ בְּדָנִיֵּאל implies that Daniel's name had already been mentioned by the queen, but owing to the faulty text has been lost. I have restored it in 5[11]. This use of the pronominal suffixes before a noun serves as the equivalent of a demonstrative pronoun to emphasize the noun, *the previous mention of which it presupposes* (Kautzsch, § 88).

[Whom the king named Belteshazzar, i. e. די מלכא שׂם שׁמה ב׳.] This is a false gloss. It was the prince of the Eunuchs who gave

this name to Daniel before the king was personally acquainted
with him. There is no hint of this clause either in the LXX or
in Josephus. It may come from the hand of the reviser, or a
scribe. The right form of such a clause is given in 10¹ in Hebrew,
and in Aramaic would be "בל שְׁמֵהּ דִי as in 2²⁶, 4⁵⁽⁸⁾,¹⁶⁽¹⁹⁾ according to our author, and not "בל שְׁמֵהּ שָׁם מלכא דִי as here,
seeing that the statement itself is not true. The idiom itself is
certainly word for word Hebraic. Cf. 2 Kings 17³⁴ אשר שׂם שמו
ישׂראל. Possibly the idiomatic Aramaic would be קרא מלכא דִי
שׁוּי or "שׁמה ב instead of קרא. Pesh., however, reproduces this
idiom literally.

5¹³. *Art thou Daniel?* Daniel, though retained in the service
of the state (see 8²⁷) was personally unknown to Belshazzar.
The rendering 'that Daniel' (R.V.) is wrong. The הוא here
serves only to emphasize the אנתא that precedes it: 'Art *thou*
Daniel?' (Kautzsch, § 87. 3). The interrogative ה readily falls
away before a guttural as here according to Kautzsch, § 67. 2.
But it is retained in 2²⁶. The ground for such omission was
alleged to be considerations of euphony. But in Ges.-Kautzsch,
§ 150 *rem.*, this statement is contradicted, seeing that הֲ or הַ
occurs before a guttural 118 times. So in Aramaic the interrogative is not necessary, where the natural emphasis is enough
to indicate an interrogative sentence.

Art thou Daniel . . . whom the king my father brought, &c.
Nebuchadnezzar is clearly here implied to be Belshazzar's
father. Had our author taken him to be the grandfather or
great-grandfather of Belshazzar, he would naturally have represented Belshazzar as saying 'Nebuchadnezzar my father' in
order to distinguish him from his actual father.

5¹⁵. *That they should read . . . and they undertook to make known.*
Here דִי = ἵνα expressing purpose. But the second clause is not
subordinate to the דִי as in 6¹⁶, but is parallel to the principal
clause, 'the wise men were brought in'. Cf. 2¹⁸, where this
idiom expresses the idea of purpose or obligation without any preceding דִי. In 2¹⁶ this idiom—ל *c.* Inf.—is, as here, to be taken as
a finite verb, not as dependent on the preceding דִי but as parallel
to the principal verb that precedes, i. e. בעא, 'Daniel implored
the King . . . and undertook to show.' See Gen. Introd., § 20. *t.*

5¹⁶. *Interpretations,* i. e. פשׁרין. In 5¹² the text has חלמין, but
the reading in 5¹⁶ has the support of the LXX and Th.

K 2

As one of three. See note on 5[7].

5[17–24]. Before interpreting the writing, Daniel reminds the king of the pride of Nebuchadnezzar his father, and recalls the fact that, nowithstanding the nemesis of such pride, he went on his way, and giving free reins to his pride challenged the power of the God of heaven by the profanation of the sacred vessels of the Temple.

5[17]. *Let . . . be.* On לֶהֱוְיָן see Gen. Introd. *in loc.*

Rewards. On נבזביתך see note on 2[6].

5[18]. *Thou O king* is a Nominativus pendens and is resumed in the suffix in אבוך. Cf. 2[29] for a similar construction. This construction emphasizes the relation in which Belshazzar stands to Nebuchadnezzar. To him the Most High God gave all the glory he possessed and yet though all this glory was taken from him because of his pride, yet thou 'his son Belshazzar' (5[22]), hast not humbled thyself, though thou knewest all this.

5[19]. *Trembled.* זָאֲעִין : with א from זוּע. See note on 2[38].

Whom he would he slew. For like expressions cf. 1 Sam. 2[7], Ps. 75[7], Sir. 7[11], Tob. 4[19].

Kept alive, i.e. מַחֵא Aph'el part. of חיה. Some versions and editions wrongly punctuate מָחֵא = 'striking'. So Th. *ἔτυπτεν* and Vulg. *percutiebat*. But the parallelism is against the latter. See Bauer-Leander, § 49, k. This verb belongs to the ע″ע class.

5[20]. *Was lifted up.* Kautzsch, § 45. 1. d takes רָם here as a participle as שׂים in 3[29] 4[3(6)]. But Marti, following Bevan, and so Strack § 24, regards it as a perfect with intransitive vocalization. Cf. Hebrew מֵת, Syriac ܡܝܬ.

Was deposed. With the Hoph'al הָנְחַת, cf. 4[36], Kautzsch, § 42. 1 ; Marti, § 58 c.

Throne. כָּרְסֵא. This form is found in the Zinjirli inscription (Cooke 63[7]), in the *Aram. Pap.* (Cowley 6[2], Aḥ 133). But the Assyr. has *kussu* and the Hebrew כִּסֵּא. The word is thought to be an Akkadian loan-word according to Schrader (Bevan).

His glory. For וִיקָרָה 'the glory' read with Pesh. as Rosenmüller (followed by other scholars) suggests : וִיקָרֵהּ.

They took. The Aramaic uses the 3rd m.pl. Haph'al הֶעְדִּיו (cf. הֶחְסְנוּ 7[22]) where we should expect הֶעְדִּיו. Cf. Bauer-Leander, § 39, f.

5[21]. This verse summarizes statements made in 4[22 (25)], 29(32), 30(33).

From the sons of men. We have here מן בני אנשא replacing מן אנשא in 4²²⁽²⁵⁾, ²⁹⁽³²⁾, ³⁰⁽³³⁾, but Th. renders ἀπὸ τῶν ἀνθρώπων in all cases.

Was made: literally 'they made' שַׁוִּיו (*Qr.*). But the *Kt.* has שׂוי. Th. has certainly the passive ἐδόθη here, but in the next clause we find again the 3 pl. impersonal. *Kt.* has שׂוי which may be read as שַׁוִּיו or שַׁוִּיַ. See Bauer-Leander, § 47, s.

Like the beasts. On the elliptical construction here, cf. מן אנשא 4¹³⁽¹⁶⁾ and in note on 1¹⁰.

The wild asses. These animals are specially named here because they are the wildest and shyest of creatures (Job 39⁵⁻⁸). The king was to avoid all contact with mankind as much as they. Five manuscripts read אדריא 'flocks' instead of ארדיא 'wild asses', and are followed by Haupt and Prince.

Until he knew, &c. Cf. 4²²⁽²⁵⁾.

5²². *Thou his son.* Cf. 5¹¹, ¹⁸.

Though. Only here has כל קבל די in Biblical or earlier Aramaic this meaning.

5²³. *Hast lifted up thyself.* With הִתְרוֹמַמְתָּ, cf. the other Hebraistic form of this verb in 4³⁴.

The vessels. See note on 5².

Gold and silver. With Th. and the Pesh. I have transposed the order of these words. Unfortunately the LXX is defective here; but in 5² where all the authorities exist, the order is as it is here in Th. and Pesh.

Which see not, &c. The unreasonableness of idolatry is elsewhere dwelt on: cf. Deut. 4²⁸, Isa. 44⁹, Ps. 115⁵, ⁶, 135¹⁶, Rev. 9²⁰, &c.

Him hast thou not glorified. The MT has here connected לֵהּ with the דִּי which precedes, so that the English would run as follows: 'in whose hand thy breath is, and whose are all thy ways'. Cf. Jer. 10²³ 'O Lord I know that the way of man is not in himself'. But the Th. and the LXX (though it gives a somewhat different text) rightly regard the לֵהּ here as emphatic and as the object of the verb that follows. So Kautzsch, § 84. 1.

5²⁵⁻²⁸. *The writing and its interpretation.*

The writing may have consisted of ideograms; for according to the text even expert Babylonian scholars could not decipher it. The inscription therefore had to be read or translated into ordinary symbols of speech. This seems the obvious deduction from 5[7], where it is said that the wise men could neither 'read' the writing nor make known its interpretation, whereas in 5[17] Daniel declares that he will both read and interpret it[1]: cf. also 5[15, 16]. The text of the LXX is confused, and less trustworthy than the MT and Th. Thus 5[17] is clearly transposed from its original context in 5[25-8] as a duplicate interpretation of the words Μανή, φαρές, θεκέλ. 5[25] of the LXX which contained these words has unfortunately not been preserved in the solitary manuscript of the LXX. But that the LXX originally contained the equivalent of 5[25] is indubitable; for at the close of the title (or table of contents) of this chapter we read as follows: Μανή, φαρές, θεκέλ. (Did the translator understand these words as weights as Prince suggests, and accordingly transpose them?) ἔστι δὲ ἑρμηνεία αὐτῶν· μανή, ἠρίθμηται· φαρές, ἐξῆρται· θεκέλ, ἔστα ται. The interpretation 'numbered ... taken away ... weighed' admits of explanation even as to its order.

The title, therefore, of this chapter of the LXX agrees with, and confirms, the text of Th. in 5[25] though in a different order. Similarly, Josephus, *Ant.* x. 11. 3 has Μανή ... θεκέλ ... φαρές. Since Josephus has in the earlier verses followed the LXX, we may reasonably conclude that here also he was following a more trustworthy form of the LXX than that which has come down to us. Furthermore, Josephus in the interpretation of μανή uses the words χρόνον ... ἠρίθμηκεν ὁ θεός. See ἠρίθμηται in the title of this chapter given above on the LXX. Since Th. uses ἐμέτρησεν ὁ Θεός, Josephus was here obviously using the LXX.

The above facts throw serious doubt on the originality of the words *Mene, Mene, Tekel, Upharsin.* Let us first deal with the

---

[1] 5[17] (i. e. 5[25]), of the LXX preserves a reference to Daniel's reading in the inscription: τότε Δανιὴλ ἔστη, κατέναντι τῆς γραφῆς, καὶ ἀνέγνω, καὶ οὕτως ἀπεκρίθη τῷ βασιλεῖ Αὕτη ἡ γραφή Ἠρίθμηται, κατελογίσθη, ἐξῆρται. There are two points to be observed here. First the actual transliteration of the inscription is not given but only a translation of it, and this translation is defective; for ἠρίθμηται and κατελογίσθη are duplicate renderings of מנא, and there is no rendering at all of תקל, although even the table of contents at the beginning of this chapter contains the three enigmatical words. Again in 5[26, 28] there is no mention of תקל. 5[26] contains ἠρίθμηται a rendering of מנא: ἀπολήγει and συντετέλεσται are dittographic renderings of השלמה: whereas συντέτμηται, which is wrongly inserted between the last two verbs is a rendering of פריסת and should be transposed to the beginning of 5[28]. We should then read φαρές, συντέτμηται ἡ βασιλεία σου ... Μ. καὶ Ʈ. 11. δίδοται.

repetition of the first words. Against such a repetition we have
the authority of the LXX, Th., Vulgate, and Josephus, and
finally we observe that the interpretation in 5²⁶⁻⁷ takes no
account of such a repetition. Furthermore, Jerome here states
definitely: Tria tantum verba in pariete scriptura (scripta — so
Erasmus) signaverat: Mane, Thecel, Phares. Next as regards
the fourth word, we discover that the same authorities are
unaware of the form וּפַרְסִין and undoubtedly read פְּרַס.

Let us first take the words as they stand מְנֵא מְנֵא תְּקֵל וּפַרְסִין
and see what can be made of them.

(1) The usual interpretation is 'counted, counted, weighed and
pieces'. But though מְנֵא as passive participle of מנא might mean
'counted' תְּקֵל cannot mean 'weighed' (i.e. תקיל), and פְּרַס cannot
mean 'divided' (i.e. פריס) as the interpretation in 5²⁷⁻⁸ demands.
Moreover, the interpretation takes account of פרס and not really
of פרסין. These words תְּקֵל (the absolute of תִּקְלָא = Heb. שֶׁקֶל) and
פְּרַס as at present vocalized are not participles but substantives.
From these facts it has been inferred that no close connexion
exists between the inscription and its interpretation, and that
therefore the words themselves were not arbitrarily invented by
our author but borrowed from some other source. In that source
they appear to have stood in some relation to the events in the
text, else our author would hardly have incorporated them in his
account, since the interpretation in 5²⁶⁻⁸ is a real *tour de force*,
resorted to in order to give them a meaning in regard to the
present crisis.

But the interpretation in 5²⁶⁻⁸ cannot, as we have seen, be
adopted, since the translation does not admit of it. If we may
anticipate we might with Haupt and Prince render: 'There is
counted (מְנֵא) a mina (מְנֵה), a shekel and two half minas'. The
mina would refer to Nebuchadnezzar, the shekel (=one sixtieth
(or later one fiftieth) part of a mina) to Belshazzar and the half-
minas probably to the Medes and Persians. See Prince *in loc.*
To a modification of this interpretation we shall return.

(2) Owing to the difficulties of the text and its interpretation
many modern scholars, including Nöldeke, Bevan, Driver, Prince,
and Marti, have accepted the explanation put forward by Clermont-
Ganneau (*Journal Asiatique*, Mane, Thecal, Phares, 1886), who
pointed out that mᵉnê is the Aramaic equavalent of the Hebrew
מָנֶה, which was borrowed by the Greeks and written μνᾶ, by the

Latins *mina*. פרס he recognized to be the equivalent of פרש which he found on half-mina weights,[1] and which therefore he concluded must mean a half-mina. As regards the term תקל he was undecided, but Nöldeke (*Zeitschr. f. Assyr.*, i. 414–18) rightly identified it with the shekel. In a fifth century Pap. B.C. (Cowley 10[5]) תקל is used as the equivalent of שקל.

Thus the inscription runs: *a mina, a mina, a shekel, and two half-minas.* Here מנה can mean 'mina' but also 'numbered'. So Daniel shows his skill in interpreting it as meaning that Belshazzar's days are numbered. תְּקֵל (= shekel) might be written תקיל (= weighed): hence 'Thou art weighed': and פְּרַס or rather פְּרַס could suggest פרים = 'divided' as well as פרס 'a Persian'. But this interpretation does not account for פרסין.

(3) So far we have kept to the MT in 5[25]. But as we have shown at the beginning of the note, the MT of 5[25] is not supported by the LXX, Th., Vulg., Josephus, or Jerome or even by the interpretation given in 5[26–8] of our text. These six authorities agree in the main in one and the same text— מנא תקל פרס—or as in Th., LXX, Josephus, Μανή, θεκέλ, φαρές.

The MT. ופרסין (i. e. 'and half minas' or 'and Persians') would then be understood as an explanatory marginal gloss, which simply meant 'Persians' but which subsequently displaced the original פרס.

There would then be two ways of taking these words, following the guidance of [27–8], or a third if we considered the probable meaning of the proverbial saying by itself.

(a) Let us take the third first. The three words duly punctuated would mean 'a mina, a shekel, half a mina' and these three weights would contain a veiled allusion (as a proverb originating in later Persian circles and passing subsequently into Jewish) respectively to Nebuchadnezzar, Belshazzar, and the Persians —the relative values of the two monarchs being exhibited by the comparison of the mina and shekel, and the sequence in time of the Persian on the great Babylonian Empire.

[1] In the eighth century B.C., Zinjirli Aramaic inscription (Cooke, 62[6]) פרס is found with the meaning of half a mina: Cf. *CIS.* II. i. 10, where פרש in the Assyrian version is explained as 'a half mina'. In Eduy. III. 3; Yoma, iv. 4; Peâ, viii. 5 מנה ופרס = *a mina and a half.* פרס is found in this sense in an Egyptian papyrus. See Cowley 45[8] where it means 'half'.

(b) But, if this existed as an early proverb with the meaning suggested in (a), it would of course assume fresh significance in its new context without wholly losing its old. *Mane* (so Versions, though it should be read *mana* מְנָא) would mean 'mina', but would suggest mᵉnē (מְנָא) 'numbered'. Hence Belshazzar's days are numbered. *tekēl* (תְּקֵל) means 'shekel' but could be interpreted as pointing to תְּקִיל 'weighed'. Hence 'thou art weighed, &c.'. *Pares* or rather pᵉras (='half') could suggest pᵉrês (פְּרִים) 'divided' and also פָּרֵם = 'Persian'. Hence 'thy kingdom is divided and given to the Persians'. There is thus a double play on the word in 5²⁸.

(c) It is also possible that the text of the Versions is wrongly punctuated for מְנָא תְּקֵל פְּרֵם, i.e. 'a mina, a shekel, half a mina', where 'half a mina' would be a comment on Belshazzar as a worthless son of a great father. This use of weights to denote the value of persons is attested in the Talmud. It may have originated before the time of our author, and been borrowed from Persian sources. Thus in Ta'an. 21 b we have : מוטב יבא מנה בן פרס אצל מנה בן מנה ואל יבא מנה בן מנה אצל מנה בן פרס.

'It is more fitting that a mina son of a half-mina should come to a mina son of a mina, rather than that a mina son of a mina should come to a mina son of a half-mina.'

The text of the inscription cannot, therefore, be determined with certainty. The textual evidence, however, is decidedly in favour of its consisting simply of the three words given under (c). It was most probably an ancient proverb referring to the events with which our author was dealing and which he incorporated in his text and interpreted as he thought right.[1]

5²⁷. *In the balances.* מֹאזַנְיָא so some editors : others write מֹאוַנְיָא.

5²⁸. *Divided . . . given.* פְּרִיסַת . . . יְהִיבַת—both 3rd pers. fem. sing. Peʻil.

The Medes and Persians. The Jews regarded the Medes and Persians as closely associated. Hence we have our author speaking three times of the 'laws of the Medes and Persians' (6⁹ (8), 13 (12), 16 (15)). From the Greek standpoint their conflicts with Darius and his successors were indifferently designated as τὰ Μηδικά or τὰ Περσικά.

5²⁹. *Made proclamation.* הכריזו. See note on 3⁴.

[1] The student should consult Clermont-Ganneau, *Journal Asiatique*, 1886, pp. 36 sqq., Nöldeke, *Z. f. Assyr.* i. 414 sqq.

5[30]. The story closes here summarily with the mention of the murder of Belshazzar, and 5[31] properly belongs to the next narrative.

SECTION VI

i. e. 6[1-29] (5[31]–6[28]), dating from the first year of the reign of Darius, and giving an account of the events that followed immediately on the conquest of Babylon.

1. *Unhistorical character of this chapter.*

The historical difficulties of this chapter are all but incredible. Those connected with Belshazzar we found very great, but they are trivial and immaterial when compared with our author's records regarding ' Darius the Mede '.

We have here to investigate briefly the historical sources contemporary with the years preceding and succeeding the capture of Babylon by Cyrus in 538 B. C. in order to discover the identity of ' Darius the Mede ', whom our author represents as being appointed king of Babylon in 538 B. C., and to come to a definite conclusion as to whether such a person existed. Next, if we conclude that no such person was known to history, we must account for the origin of this mythical personage.

(a) *Short sketch of the history of Media down to its conquest by Cyrus the Persian, and his subsequent conquest of Babylon.* The Medes lived in the mountainous regions north and north-east of Babylon and south-west of the Caspian. Four of their kings are mentioned by Herodotus (i. 96–130), the first of whom is Deioces 699-646, who may have been an individual or a dynasty. The real founder of the monarchy was Phraortes, 646-624. The Medes were organized by his son Cyaxares (624–584) into a strong power. The latter sought to avenge the defeats of his father by the Assyrians. In his first attempt to do so in 614 he was unsuccessful, but in his second campaign in 612 against the Babylonians and Scythians [1] he destroyed the Assyrian capital, Nineveh. Cyaxares was succeeded by Astyages (584–550), who was betrayed by his own troops into the hands of Cyrus. Cyrus had been a vassal of Astyages.

---

[1] See Gadd, *The Fall of Nineveh*, 1923, based on the recently discovered 'Chronicle of Nabopolassar.'

(*b*) *The historical outlook of the author of Daniel in regard to the Median and Persian empires, and particularly in regard to Darius and Cyrus.* The empire of the Medes, thus absorbed into that of the Persians, became the Medo-Persian empire, the supreme factor of which was henceforth the Persian, which had hitherto been a subordinate power. Cyrus became the king of the united monarchies in 538 when he effected the conquest of Babylon.[1]

In our author the two peoples are sometimes represented as united (5[28], 6[9(8),13(12),16(15)] ; cf. 8[20]), but in other passages the distinctness of the two nationalities is emphasized, and this especially in regard to the heads of the empire. Thus on the fall of Babylon Darius the Mede (6[1], 5[(31)], 9[1], 11[1]) 'received the kingdom' and the title of *a supreme, not of a delegated, kingship* (6[3,4,7,8,9,13,14 (2,3,6,7,8,12,13)] &c.); exercised all the functions of a plenary and paramount jurisdiction (6[2,3,16,26,27 (1,2,15,25,26)]); as sole ruler divided his vast empire into 120 satrapies, 6[2(1)] ; which empire embraced all the peoples, nations, and languages, that dwell upon the earth (6[26 (25)]); as absolute despot sentenced to death the rulers of such satrapies as had accused Daniel 6[25(24)] ; and at the close of his reign—it does not say his death except in the LXX (6[29(28)]—was succeeded by Cyrus 'the Persian' (6[29(28)]: cf. 10[1]). And yet, though prerogative after prerogative and every divine right that marks and hedges in a king are piled on Darius, the Median empire is felt to be a kind of unintelligible episode in the history of Babylon—even by those whose historical knowledge is limited to the O.T. Our author though a convinced believer in this tradition of a Median Empire is perfectly aware that it is weaker, 8[3], than the Persian which he held succeeded it, 2[39].

(*c*) *Our author presupposes that the Medes conquered Babylon and that 'Darius the Mede' immediately succeeded to the throne of Babylon.* One underlying presupposition of the entire Book of Daniel is that Babylon was stormed and captured mainly by the Medes (5[28], 7[5], 8[3]), though in 5[28] Medes and Persians are

---

[1] Thus Cyrus, who was 'the King of Countries', i.e. of the entire empire, and who *appointed* apparently only for one year his son Cambyses as 'King of Babylon', leaves no room for Darius. Yet the traditionalists would identify Darius *this mythical ruler of the whole earth* with this temporary king of one of the lands over all of which Cyrus ruled. See *Introduction*.

mentioned together. Cyrus 'the Persian' has, so far as the narrative goes, no part in its overthrow. It is, therefore, perfectly in keeping with the positive statements of our author, as well as with the general implications of his work, that a Median prince should be appointed the first king of conquered Babylon. It is noteworthy that there is not a hint that he received the kingdom from the joint victors : much less is there the slightest foundation for the statement that the words 'Darius the Mede received the Kingdom' mean or imply that Darius was appointed by a superior.   The LXX and Th. here render παρέλαβε(ν) τὴν βασιλείαν.   This merely means that he received the kingdom in accordance with the will of God, the Ruler of all.   The very same phrase is used of Cyrus in the LXX in $6^{29(28)}$, where it diverges from the MT, and where it records that, on the death of Darius, Κῦρος ὁ Πέρσης παρέλαβε τὴν βασιλείαν αὐτοῦ. Cf. 5^{31} for the same phrase.   In Bel and the Dragon (ver. 1) the same phrase recurs in the version of Th. in connexion with Cyrus, and in 2 Macc. 4^7 (παραλαβόντος τ. βασιλείαν), 10^{11} with Antiochus Epiphanes and his son respectively.   Josephus uses it (βασιλείαν παραλαμβάνει) of Evil Merodach and of Neriglissar (*Ant.* x. 11. 2). In Bernstein's *Chrestomathia Syriaca*, p. 110, ' Ex Bar Hebraei Chron.' Dyn. x. 491 we have this phrase used of the accession of Ucataeus ܦܘܕ̈ܝܐܦ. Hoffmann, *Julianos der Abtrünnige*, p. 5 (see Bevan, p. 20) has found the same phrase קבל מלכותא used by a Syriac author in describing the accession of Julian the Apostate.

From the above it is simply incontestable that our author honestly believed that Darius was the sole and independent sovereign of the Babylonian empire after its conquest by Cyrus. The figure of Darius, a sovereign unknown, outside our author, to sacred or profane history, whether the latter be Greek or oriental, dominates the thought of our author ; for a whole chapter, i. e. 6, is devoted to one episode in his life, while, outside that chapter, he is mentioned three times (6^1 (5^{31}), 9^1, 11^1), whereas the great historical figure Cyrus, who from 558 to 529 dominated in growing measure the fortunes of eastern kingdoms, alike large and small, is only mentioned twice, i. e. $6^{29(28)}$, 10^1; for $1^{21\,b}$ appears to be a later addition.   But, if outside our author Darius is unknown to the O.T., Cyrus is mentioned by prophet and historian nineteen times—though the passages in

which it occurs are conflicting at times.   See *Encyc. Bib.* i.
978-982.

(*d*) *It is also incontestable that our author believed that a Median empire succeeded immediately on that of Babylon and preceded the Persian empire.*   Of such a Median sovereignty after the fall of Babylon neither Berosus nor any ancient writer oriental or Greek knows anything, and recent research has shown that in the annals of Nabuna'id and the Cyrus Cylinder, Cyrus is the immediate successor of Nabuna'id on the throne of Babylon. No more does the O.T. outside Daniel know anything of a Median empire after the fall of Babylon.   In the post-Exile Isaiah 40-48 Cyrus is represented as being expressly called to execute the divine judgements on Babylon, to set the Jewish captives free, and to restore Jerusalem and the Temple (48^{14,15}, 44^{28}, 45^{13}).

(*e*) *How then did this mythical king and this mythical empire gain a footing in history?*   Is it possible to explain this strange phenomenon in O.T. history, or rather on O.T. Apocalyptic? It is perfectly easy for those who have made a study of Jewish Apocalyptic.   Scholars have recognized the fact that O.T. prophecy foretold the conquest of Babylon by the Medes (Isa. 13^{17}, 21^2; Jer. 51^{11,28}), and have (see Bevan, p. 109) suggested that such prophecies may have given rise to the tradition that the Medes had in fact conquered Babylon.   But what these scholars have failed to see is that this is not one out of the many possible explanations, but that it is *the explanation.* In my Jowett Lectures on *Eschatology*, 1899, pp. 168 sqq.; I pointed out that one main source of Apocalyptic was to be found in prophecy, or rather indeed in unfulfilled prophecy, and developed this principle further in the second edition in 1913, pp. 184 sqq.   Since study and reflection entered largely into the life of the apocalyptist, and his chief studies were confined to the sacred books of Israel, it follows that a not unimportant element in apocalyptic is that of unfulfilled prophecy.   Unfulfilled prophecy was, as we know, a matter of religious difficulty to the prophets themselves as early as the Exile, and so such unfulfilled prophecies of the older prophets came to be re-edited by the later.   The first notable reinterpretation is due to Ezekiel.   Jeremiah 4-6[1] had foretold the invasion of Judah by

Cf. Isa. 10$^{5-34}$, 17^{12} sqq.; Mic. 5^{11}; Zeph. 3^8.

a mighty people from the north. But this northern foe failed to appear. And since inspired prophecy in his view could not remain unfulfilled, Ezekiel re-edits this prophecy and adjourns its fulfilment, and declares that the host, of whose coming the earlier prophets had foretold, was Gog : 'Thou art he of whom I spake by my servants the prophets of Israel, which prophesied . . . for (many) years that I would bring thee against them ' [1] (Ezek. 38^{17}).

In the same work I have shown that the non-fulfilment of prophecies as to the date of the Messianic Kingdom was a predominant source of apocalyptic. Thus Jeremiah prophesied that after seventy years (25^{11}, 29^{10}) Israel would be restored to its own land (24^{5,6}) and there enjoy the blessings of the Messianic Kingdom under the Messianic King (23^{5,6}), but this period passed by, and things remained as of old. Ezekiel cherished a similar expectation, but this no more than that of Jeremiah reached fulfilment. The same theme was dealt with afresh by Haggai and Zachariah, but their prophecies no more than those of their greater forerunners attained realization. In chapter ix of our author we shall return to this theme and discuss the fresh reinterpretation by our author of this old prophecy of Jeremiah, and recount subsequent attempts of other writers.

In this belief on the part of our author that unfulfilled prophecy must yet be fulfilled we have the means of solving the otherwise inexplicable problems of chapters 5–6. According to the two greatest prophets of the past, Isaiah and Jeremiah, the Medes were to overthrow Babylon. This prophecy could not be falsified. Hence round these prophecies the thoughts of Judah's seers revolved, till gradually there was evolved a tradition resembling no doubt in its main features Dan. 6, but assuredly recast by our author to suit the main purpose of his work.

Here we have the explanation of the thought underlying the greater part of the work of our author, i. e. his belief that Babylon was conquered by the Medes in 538, and that a Median prince became king of that great empire.

So far the solution of the problem holds good. There must have been, according to apocalyptic, a *Median conquest* of Babylon

---

[1] So LXX and Vulg. which omit the interrogative in this verse.

in 538, and following thereon a *Median empire*. That these were as truly historical facts as the most assured events in the past, the O.T. seers were convinced, starting from the same axiom as Ezekiel and subsequent prophets, the axiom that every prophecy of the past was inspired and must therefore be fulfilled. To them such a statement was a self-evident proposition. We have here, therefore, not free invention but rather logical inferences from an unquestioned axiom. The seers may have been long in arriving at such conclusions, but sooner or later such conclusions under the circumstances were inevitable, and the more so as their knowledge of the actual events of history was meagre and uncertain. In our author these conclusions have won a place in sacred literature.

(*f*) *But how is it that Darius came to be named as the king of this Median Empire?* There was no oracle of the past that foretold not only the conquest of Babylon by the Medes, but also the name of the Median prince who led them. Since, therefore, ancient prophecy failed to provide the name of this prince, these seers had to fall back on the history contained in their sacred books and probably in the Behistun Inscription of Darius Hystaspes, which was broadcasted in several languages throughout the Persian empire from India to Ethiopia. An Aramaic translation of this inscription, belonging to the fifth century B.C., has recently been found far up the Nile in Elephantine (see Cowley, *Aramaic Papyri*, 248 seqq.). In this inscription Darius, the son of Hystaspes[1], recounts his victories—especially over the provinces that had rebelled against him, and amongst them he twice reduced Babylon. Here then were both the conqueror of Babylon and his name ready at hand. That his date (521–495) did not tally with the conquest of Babylon in 538 was no real difficulty to men with very elementary ideas of dates and chronology in general. That they called this Darius 'Darius the Mede' was only a further development of their reconstruction of the history of the conquest of Babylon in 538.[2] The very

[1] The origin of 'Darius the Mede' in Darius Hystaspes was first suggested by Marianus Scotus, a Benedictine monk in the eleventh century of our era. See Berthold, *Dan.*, p. 844, quoted by Prince, p. 54.

[2] Names are sometimes used loosely in ancient authorities. Thus Tomyris queen of the Massagetae (according to Herod. i. 206) in rejecting Cyrus' proposal of marriage addresses him thus : ὦ βασιλεῦ Μήδων.

acts attributed to this mythical Darius recall the later Darius, the son of Hystaspes.

Thus our author tells us that this Darius set 120 satraps over the kngdom, which Josephus (*Ant.* x. 11. 4) says consisted of 360 provinces. Herodotus (iii. 89 sqq.) records that Darius, son of Hystaspes, divided the kingdom into twenty satrapies, and that this was first done under this king. In Esther 1¹, 8⁹; Esdras 3²; Add. to Esther 2¹, 5¹ there are said to have been 127 provinces.

The source then of the *name* of the mythical Darius appears undeniable. This Darius is a reflexion into the past of Darius, the son of Hystaspes. In 9¹ of our author this 'Darius the Mede' is said to have been the son of Ahasuerus (אחשורש) mentioned in Ezra 4⁶ and Esther *passim*. This is the Hebrew form of the Persian Khshayārshā, the Greek Xerxes, the Aramaic חשיארש (see Cowley 5¹), and חשירש (*op. cit.* 2¹). But Darius, the son of Hystaspes, was the father and not the son of Ahasuerus.

Finally the author of this myth *not knowing any real Median names gives two Persian names* to his two kings; for not only is Ahasuerus of Persian origin, but so also is Darius = Hebrew דריוש, Old Persian Darayava'ush.

Josephus is fully aware how the accounts in Daniel conflict with some non-Jewish authorities as to this Darius. We have in an earlier page (109 sqq.) found him identifying Belshazzar with his father Nabuna'id in an attempt to reconcile the statements of Greek and Oriental historians with conflicting statements in Daniel. Here again he shuffles, and writes (*Ant.* x. 11. 4); 'When Darius with the help of his kinsman Cyrus put an end to the hegemony of the Babylonians, he was sixty-two years old . . . but he was called by another name among the Greeks' (ἕτερον δὲ παρὰ τοῖς Ἕλλησιν ἐκαλεῖτο ὄνομα). This no doubt was Gobryas (Old Pers. Gaubaruva, Bab. Gubara), governor of Gutium, whom Cyrus, immediately after the fall of Babylon, made viceroy over the province of Babylon. But the father of Gobryas, however, was named Mardonius and not Xerxes. This Gobryas, or Gubaru, according to the Annalistic Tablet of Cyrus appointed governors in Babylon as the mythical Darius is said to have done. Shortly after he was superseded, as viceroy, by Cambyses, the Persian. That Cambyses is the 'other name' implied by Josephus is hardly worth consideration.

With Cambyses *the Persian* Josephus could not have identified
'Darius the Mede ',[1] though he might have identified him with
Gobryas, but thought it unnecessary to mention him.

With Cambyses Josephus deals later on with his succession
to the throne of Cyrus (*Ant.* xi. 1. 2).

Winckler, the learned Assyriologist (*KAT.*[3], p. 287), and those
who accept his identification of ' Darius the Mede ' with Cambyses, fail to recognize one of the main contentions of our author,
and this is that a *Median,* and not a Persian, became king of
Babylon immediately after its conquest in 538, and that this
Median king was the ruler of a Median empire before Cyrus the
Persian and the Persian empire came into power. It was owing
to Winckler's ignorance of one of the essential elements of
apocalyptic that this blunder of his is due. One of the aims of
our author is to show that the unfulfilled prophecy of Isaiah
and Jeremiah, that the Babylonian empire would be overthrown
by the Medes, was in very deed fulfilled. Hence Cambyses *the
Persian* cannot be identified with 'Darius the Mede '. Something might be said for the partial identification of Gobryas with
this mythical king, as we shall see in the next paragraph.

(*g*) *The mythical Darius is derived from the blending together of
historical facts associated with three* (?) *distinct persons—Darius,
son of Hystaspes, Gobryas, and Cambyses*(?). Under (*f*) we have
shown how to this mythical personage the name of Darius was
given in the course of tradition. In the same section we have mentioned the fact that Gobryas was made viceroy of Babylon immediately after its capture in 538 B.C., and that according to the
Annalistic Tablet of Cyrus he appointed governors in Babylon
as the mythical Darius is said to have done. The acts of
Gobryas were thus in the course of tradition transferred to this
mythical Darius. Again the fact that statements in our author
which seemingly assign only one year to the reign of the mythical
Darius over Babylon may (?) be due to the fact (transmitted

---

[1] Ctesias, it is true, in his *Persica* (excerpts 2 and 10) relates that Cyrus
after defeating Astyages and making himself master of Ecbatana, the capital of
Media, married Amytis, the daughter of Astyages, and that Cambyses was the
fruit of this marriage. It has been urged that Cambyses could be called
a Median on the ground of the nationality of his mother, but his nationality
would naturally be that of his father, Cyrus the Persian. Further Cyrus'
sovereignty over the Medes was not due to a marriage alliance but to conquest
by force.

through tradition) that Cambyses was made king of Babylon for only one year during the life of Cyrus, and that the year immediately following its conquest.

There is still another feature in this tradition calling for treatment. Whether we follow the MT or the LXX, it is clear that Darius is conceived as a man in the sixties if not older. This feature in the tradition cannot be derived from Darius, son of Hystaspes, who after his accession reigned for thirty-six years. Nor yet can it be derived from Cambyses, who even when he fell by his own hand can hardly have reached the sixties. It may, therefore, be derived from Gobryas or Gubaru who is mentioned in the Annalistic Tablet of Cyrus as the supreme governor in Babylon after Cyrus' conquest of that city.

§ 2. *Our author's aim in this chapter as distinguished from his aim in chapter 3.*

In 3¹⁻³⁰ the aim of our author was to direct his people how to act in their relations to *heathen religions* and to admonish them not to acknowledge or share in their worship, but rather to prefer death to apostasy. In this chapter it is his aim to enforce the duty of observing *their own religion.* And since during the exile this observance could not extend beyond acts of *private and personal* worship, it is just this side of the Jewish religion that has to be brought forward here, and it is the necessity of emphasizing this side that obliged our author to introduce certain unlikely or incredible features into his story, such as the king's issuing such a preposterous edict as that in the text in order to render Daniel's acts of private devotion a capital offence, and his failure to consult the chiefest and wisest of his great officers before issuing such an edict. These and other such features, however, appear no longer unreasonable when they serve to manifest Daniel's faithful observance of his religion *in private.* By such a story or parable our author sought to encourage his countrymen, who under the persecution of Antiochus Epiphanes were precluded in the main from all acts of public worship, to be true to their national faith and hold fast to the life of private devotion, even as Daniel had done.

§ 3.   (a) *Corruptions of the MT.*

6¹ᵇ⁻²ᵇ (5³¹ᵇ⁻6¹ᵇ).   See notes *in loc.*

6⁷⁽⁶⁾, ¹²⁽¹¹⁾, ¹⁶⁽¹⁵⁾. In these three passages the MT reads הרגשו,

and modern scholars render it in all three passages 'came tumultuously' and wrongly in all. The LXX, Th., Pesh., and Josephus require קרבו in 6⁷⁽⁶⁾. The context also is against הרגשו having been originally in the text. In 6¹²⁽¹¹⁾ the MT is right and was rightly rendered by the LXX, Th., Pesh., and Vulg., as 'kept watch'—a meaning attested in Aramaic and late Hebrew but not earlier than the 2nd cent. B.C. Daniel's enemies were spying upon him in order to discover him in the act of breaking the law. In 6¹⁶⁽¹⁵⁾ this verb is an interpolation. Both the LXX and Th. omit it. Furthermore, the context itself makes its presence impossible. Daniel's enemies did not leave the king's presence the entire day, while the king was striving to save Daniel.

6¹³⁽¹²⁾. For לא שם עליך מלכא טעם (='regardeth (?) not thee, O king') we should read לא שמע על טעמך ='obeyeth not thy decree'. No ancient authority supports the MT. See notes on 6¹³⁽¹²⁾ and 3¹².

6¹⁹⁽¹⁸⁾. See note *in loc.*

6²⁵⁽²⁴⁾. For הַיְתִיו read הֵיתַיִו and for רְמוֹ read וּרְמִיו. See note *in loc.*

6²⁹⁽²⁸⁾. The Massoretes or a reviser replaced the original הֲקֵים =LXX κατεστάθη) by הצלח, and so framed a conflate text from two independent texts. See notes on 6⁴, ²⁹.

(*b*) *Interpolations.*

6⁵⁽⁴⁾. 'Neither was there any error or fault found in him.' LXX and Th. om.

6⁸⁽⁷⁾, ¹³⁽¹²⁾. 'or man'.

6¹³⁽¹²⁾. 'Concerning the edict of the king.' Omitted by LXX, Th., and Pesh.

6¹⁶⁽¹⁵⁾. 'Came tumultuously to the king and.' LXX, Th. omit. Context against its presence absolutely.

(*c*) *Dislocations of the text.*

6¹⁹⁽¹⁸⁾. See note *in loc.*

(*d*) *Omissions.*

6¹⁴⁽¹³⁾. 'Before his God'. So LXX and Th.

(*e*) The Massoretes or individual revisers have dealt summarily with the original text of this chapter. Thus they appear to have introduced הרגשו in 6⁷⁽⁶⁾ instead of קרבו: to have added it against the early versions and the context in 6¹⁶⁽¹⁵⁾: to have conflated two distinct types of text in 6⁴, ²⁹.

6¹(5³¹). *Darius the Mede received the kingdom.* The origin of this mythical personage, Darius the Mede, was due as we have shown in the introduction to this chapter (see § 1 *c, e*) to a fundamental article in the creed of post-Exilic writers—especially of apocalyptic writers—that non-fulfilled prophecy must in due time be fulfilled : hence the prophecy of the overthrow of Babylon by the Medes, as foretold by Isaiah and Jeremiah, is in part recounted and everywhere presupposed by our author (see Introd. to this chapter, § 1 *e*). But, since the reinterpretation of such unfulfilled prophecies began more than 300 years before our author's time, the rewriting of history in order to bring it into accord with such prophecies followed soon and inevitably on the heels of this earlier practice, especially when the dates of the fulfilment of such prophecies had long expired. Since the Medes had lost all their influence centuries before our author's time, the fulfilment of Isaiah and Jeremiah's prophecies with regard to them must, if they were fulfilled at all, have been fulfilled in the past. The rewriting of history to authenticate these prophecies was naturally in most cases a slow process, and, when our author sat down to write, he most probably found the myth—as to Darius the Mede and the kingdom of the Medes following immediately after that of Babylon—already fully developed and at his disposal. The myth is composite and reflects features that in part belong to Gobryas, to Cambyses, and to Darius Hystaspes, as we have shown in the Introd. to this chapter § 1 (*g*).

Received the kingdom. The attempt to show that this phrase implies an authority delegated to a subordinate prince by a supreme prince completely breaks down : see evidence as to its real meaning in the Introd. to this chap. § 1 (*c*).

†*Being about threescore and two years old.* 6²⁽¹⁾. *It pleased Darius*†. As far back as the eleventh century of our era these words have been a source of difficulty to Jewish scholars (Rashi, &c.), since they imply that the father of Darius must have been a contemporary of Nebuchadnezzar, when he plundered the Temple. Besides the mention of the exact age of Darius is without a parallel in the rest of the book. Further, these words do not appear in the LXX, which in their stead reads καὶ Δαρεῖος πλήρης τῶν ἡμερῶν καὶ ἔνδοξος ἐν γήρει = ודריוש סבע יומין ושפיר בסיבו. From this text we might hypothetically explain the MT. Thus

סב may have been misunderstood as expressing a number
(so Behrmann) i. e. 62 and so came to be expanded into
שתין ותרתין. This once done, יומין could easily have been
changed into שנין, since in Aramaic and Hebrew they are in
such a connexion synonyms. We have then to suppose that
the corrector rewrote ודריוש סבע . . . ושפיר as ושפר קדם דריוש,[1]
modelling his correction on 3^{32} (4^2) where this phrase occurs.
This is of course quite hypothetical. But if we are to reach
some explanation, we must apparently begin with the expansion
of סב. If such an expansion did take place, the text had
necessarily to be rewritten. What it was originally must be
left as an unsolved problem. This, it will be said, is a complicated explanation of the text: but so is the textual problem.
Since the difficulties of the Aramaic and Th. are so great I propose to follow the LXX instead, though itself uncertain : ' And
Darius was full of days (or rather "years") and glorious in
old age '.

The attempt to explain πλήρης τῶν ἡμερῶν καὶ ἔνδοξος ἐν γήρει as
a doublet by retroversion into Hebrew is open to manifold
objections. The evidence for an Aramaic as against a Hebrew
original is overwhelming. In any case such a solution is not
open to a scholar who presupposes an Aramaic original. But,
even if we accepted the hypothesis of a Hebrew original, the
solution offered is improbable—to most minds incredible. This
solution is that ἔνδοξος is a rendering of כַּבִּר : but the LXX never
so renders it save in a single doubtful passage in Job 34^{24} : and
that πλήρης is a rendering of כָּבֵד on the ground that the LXX so
renders it once out of nearly a hundred passages, where its
rendering is different.

$6^{2(1)}$. *An hundred and twenty satraps.* On ' satraps ' see note
on 3^2. Some sort of division of Babylon is recorded on the
Annalistic Tablet of Cyrus, where it is said that Gubaru,
governor of Babylon under Cyrus, ' appointed governors in
Babylon '. But the division *into 20 satrapies* of the whole
empire is attributed to Darius Hystaspes by Herodotus iii, 89 sqq.
In Esther 1^1 and 8^9, 1 Esdras 3^2, Add. to Esther 2^1, 3^1 the number
of satrapies is increased to 127. But these numbers are in-

---

[1] In 6^3 Daniel is said to be ἔνδοξος ἔναντι Δαρείου = שפיר קדם דריוש. This
appears to be a dittograph of the first clause in 6^1 MT. שפר קדם דריוש = ' it
pleased Darius '.

accurate according to the inscriptions of Darius, which ascribe his division of his empire successively into 21, 23, and 29 satrapies. Our text does not literally assert that ‘Darius the Mede’ was the first to institute the 120 satrapies.

Over them עֲלָּא מִנְּהוֹן. This phrase does not occur in the Aram. Pap. Possibly the Old Aram. would have been עֲלֹוי: cf. Cowley 5⁶, ⁹. מִן עלֹא occurs as an adverb: *op. cit.*, 5¹⁰, ¹³, 25⁶, 48². The phrase in our text occurs in the Targ. on Isa. 14¹⁴.

Three presidents. סרכין is generally taken to be a loan-word from the Persian sâr, *head, chief.* It is found also in the Targums סרכא as a rendering of שֹׁטֵר, &c. With this triumvirate we might compare 5⁷ (note).

Give account—יהבין · · · טעמא, a phrase only here in Biblical Aramaic. For this meaning of the noun, cf. Ezra 5⁵, and for a parallel to the whole phrase the Targ. on Prov. 26¹⁶ יהבי טעמא, though with a different nuance.

Should have no damage = לֹא · · · נְזִק. The Haph‘el of נזק occurs three times in Ezra 4¹³, ¹⁵, ²² : the noun once in Hebrew in Esther 7⁴ and occasionally in the Targums. The Pa‘el(?) is found in the *Aram. Pap.* (Cowley, 37¹⁴): also in Assyrian.

6⁴(³). *Was distinguished*, i.e. מתנצח. This word is found in Hebrew : also in the *Aram. Pap.*, Beh. 60, exactly in the same sense as in our text. See Cowley, p. 254.

Thought, i.e. עֲשִׁית. 3rd masc. perf. but according to Nöldeke part. pass. with an active meaning as in Syriac. In the Ethpa‘el it has this meaning : cf. *Aram. Pap.* (Cowley, 30²³). This Aramaic verb has been adopted in the Hithpa‘el into Hebrew in Jonah 1⁶.

⌜*And he prospered in the king's business which he carried out*⌝. I have restored this clause to the text from the LXX, which reads καὶ εὐοδούμενος ἐν ταῖς πραγματείαις τοῦ βασιλέως αἷς ἔπρασσε. Since the LXX *uses* εὐοδοῦν *six times out of seven, more or less, as a translation of* צלח taking the Hebrew and Aramaic together, we may safely conclude that εὐοδούμενος is here a rendering of הצלח (or Hebrew הצליח). For the rendering in this word by εὐοδοῦν in the Aramaic passages, cf. Ezra 5⁸ and in the Hebrew of Daniel in 8¹², ²⁴, ²⁵, 11²⁷, ³⁶. Th., on the other hand, renders the Aramaic הצלח by κατευθύνειν in 3³⁰, 6²⁸, and, similarly, the Hebrew הצליח in 8²⁴, ²⁵, 11²⁷, ³⁶. Only in 8¹² has Th. been influenced by the LXX and rendered it by εὐωδώθη. From this investigation it follows that εὐοδούμενος in the LXX here is a rendering of הצלח.

From this verse, where its occurrence is justified in every respect, it was borrowed by an early reviser of the text, whose revision is here at all events represented by Th., and who transferred it to 6²⁹ where he replaced by it the original verb הקים. Thus not only has a false text been established in 6²⁹ ⁽²⁸⁾ but a conflate type of text introduced thereby. *6²⁹ should represent the king's realization of his intention which is expressed in 6⁴.* See next note.

Thought to set him over the whole realm. The text is doubtful. At all events there are two readings. The above text is supported by the LXX, Pesh., and Vulg. Only Th. is opposed to it with the reading κατέστησεν αὐτόν. At first sight this seems to be a simple error for ἐβουλεύσατο καταστῆσαι αὐτὸν ἐπὶ πάσης τῆς βασιλείας αὐτοῦ (LXX and other Versions as well as the Aram.). But a further study of the entire chapter—especially 6⁴, ²⁹ (6³, ²⁸) reveals the fact that either the LXX as a whole is right, or Th. as a whole is right, and that the MT (with Pesh. and Vulg.) is a confused medley of the two types of text. (1) First of all the LXX in 6⁴ records that the king 'thought to set Daniel over the whole realm', and repeating this clause in 6⁴ (ὅτε δὲ ἐβουλεύσατο ὁ βασιλεὺς καταστῆσαι τὸν Δανιὴλ ἐπὶ πάσης τῆς βασιλείας αὐτοῦ) dwells on the fact that this intention of the king was due to Daniel's successful dispatch of the king's business and at the same time brought about a plot against Daniel. Then, when we pass on to 6²⁹ ⁽²⁸⁾ after the plot was defeated and Daniel's enemies destroyed, we read as we should expect: καὶ Δανιὴλ κατεστάθη ἐπὶ τῆς βασιλείας Δαρείου. Here the LXX stands alone against Th. (and the rest) which reads καὶ Δανιὴλ κατεύθυνεν ἐν τῇ βασιλείᾳ Δαρείου. (2) The second consistent type of text is that of Th. Instead of ἐβουλεύσατο καταστῆσαι (LXX = MT, Pesh., Vulg.), Th. reads κατέστησεν. Here the king's intention is represented as an accomplished fact. In 6²⁹ ⁽²⁸⁾ it therefore consistently records that after the plot was defeated 'Daniel prospered in the reign of Darius' (see the text above). (3) Passing from these two consistent types of text we come to the third—that of the MT followed by the Pesh. and Vulg. Here, it is stated in 6⁴ ⁽³⁾ that the king 'intended to set Daniel over the whole realm', and accordingly we expect to find after the shipwreck of the conspiracy, a clause in 6²⁹ to the effect that the king *did carry out his intention* and set Daniel over the kingdom as in the LXX, but we find no such clause but only this rather colourless statement that 'Daniel prospered in the reign of Darius', a statement which is in itself a conflation of a clause in 6³ of the LXX though differently worded καὶ εὐοδούμενος ἐν ταῖς πραγματείαις τοῦ βασιλέως αἶς ἔπρασσε (=והצלח בעבידת מלכא די עבד) and the original text in 6²⁸ ודניאל הקים על מלכות דריוש. The reviser has borrowed הצלח from this clause in the original Aramaic behind the LXX of 6⁴ ⁽³⁾ and replaced הקים in 6²⁹ ⁽²⁸⁾ by it. In 6⁴ the clause restored from the LXX is given as one of the reasons for the king's determination to set Daniel above all the rest. 6²⁹ ⁽²⁸⁾ represents the king as carrying this determination into effect.

From the above facts it follows that we must adopt either (1) or (2). Since, however, the documentary evidence for (1) is so strong and since Th. not only stands alone but has the appearance of being a late emendation, we must adopt (1) and accordingly in 6²⁹ ⁽²⁸⁾ read καὶ Δανιὴλ κατεστάθη ἐπὶ τῆς βασιλείας Δαρείου i.e. ודניאל הֳקִים על מלכות דריוש instead of ודניאל דנה הצלח במלכות דריוש.

An excellent spirit. Cf. 5¹².

6⁵ ⁽⁴⁾. *Find . . . against Daniel.* "להשכחה לד. For this meaning of ל, cf. Cowley 27² מנדעם מחבל ⟨לא⟩ אשתכח לן = 'nothing disloyal was found against us'. In the next verse we find על in the same construction.

Fault. i. e. שחיתה. Cf. 2⁹. *Faithful,* i. e. מהימן. See 2⁴⁵. *Error,* i. e. שלו. See 3²⁹.

[*Neither was there any error or fault found in him*]. Since both the LXX and Th. omit these words, I have with Behrmann relegated them to a foot-note as a marginal gloss on the preceding words.

6⁶ ⁽⁵⁾. *Shall . . . find any occasion.* Here עֳלָה is to be understood—after השכחנא.

Except, i. e. לָהֵן. The perfect (הַשְׁכַּחְנָא) here and in 7²⁷ only in Biblical Aramaic has the sense of a future just as after כִּי אִם in Hebrew: cf. Gen. 32²⁶.

Law. Here as in Ezra 7¹²,¹⁴ sq. דָּת denotes the Jewish religion at the period when law constituted the chief element in religion.

6⁷ ⁽⁶⁾. *Drew near to.* So the LXX προσήλθοσαν ¹, Th. παρέστησαν 'presented themselves'; but Hippolytus who follows Th. reads προσῆλθον; Pesh. ܩܪܒܘ. These two or rather three versions imply קָרִבוּ and not הרגשו in the text. The Vulg. *surripuerunt*

---

¹ קרב is rendered by the LXX by προσέρχεσθαι in 3⁸, ²⁶, 7¹⁶, and by Th. in 3⁸, ²⁶, 6¹³, 7¹⁶; by ἐγγίζειν by the LXX (Syr. mg.) in 7¹⁶, and by Th. in 6²¹. Once elsewhere the LXX renders it by ἐντυγχάνειν 6¹³, and Th. by προσάγεσθαι 7¹³.

which is either corrupt or an alternative form[1] for *surrepse-runt* supports קרבו; though it describes the approach of the nobles to the king as furtive and underground, in order to ensnare him into their conspiracy against Daniel. Jerome approves of the rendering : ' pulchre dixit *surripuerunt* (i. e. surre-pserunt). Non enim hoc locuti sunt quod agere cogitabant, sed per honorem regis, inimico moliuntur insidias.' Jos. (*Ant.* x. 11. 5) supports the LXX πρὸς τὸν Δαρεῖον ἐλθόντες ἀπήγγειλον αὐτῷ.

Thus no version or other authority from the second century B. C. to the fourth A. D. supports הרגישו in this passage in any sense that can be assigned to it. The context is also against it. Hence we reject it as a late introduction into the Aramaic text by some Jewish scribe or reviser in the place of the original word קרבו.

But הרגשו recurs in 6¹²⁽¹¹⁾,¹⁶⁽¹⁵⁾, where it cannot be translated as ' came tumultuously ' with the main body of scholars, nor as ' assembled '[2] with the R.V.—which last meaning does not appear to belong to the verb in any case. Here the context is against this meaning ' to come tumultuously ', and may be accordingly disregarded. The courtiers have succeeded in getting a law enacted against Daniel. Their next object is obviously to discover Daniel in the act of breaking this law. What sane writer, let us ask, would in such a case represent them as ' coming tumultuously '[3] to Daniel's house in order to *detect* Daniel in the act of transgressing the law? Thus the context itself exposes the absurdity of this rendering. But not only does the context come to our help, but also the versions. The latter attach the meaning of ' to keep watch upon ', ' to spy upon ' to הרגשו. Thus the LXX reads ἐτήρησαν, Th. παρετήρησαν, Pesh. ܣܟܝܘ (= Th.), Vulg. ' curiosius inquirentes '. Now this meaning of הרגש is actually found in the Jer. Targ. on Exod. 2³ מַרְגְּשִׁין עלה = ' watched her ', ' perceived her ' : Nidda 13ª ; Shabb. 129ª, Aph'el ארגיש ' he observed '. Cf. also late Hebrew in Meg. 15 b ירגיש ' will observe ' : Shabb. 13 b : Ned. 13 a. This is a common

---

[1] Cf. Plautus, *Mil.* 2. 3. 62, where the converse change is found i. e. surrepsit for surripuerit.

[2] I can find no authority for the meaning ' assembled ', assigned to this word in the R.V. The word has two established meanings, the later of which only is found in 6¹²⁽¹¹⁾, the other meaning not occurring.

[3] In the Targ. on Ruth 1¹⁹ this meaning is found ארגישו כל יתבי קרתא עלויהן ' All the inhabitants of the city were stirred up about them '.

meaning of the word in Syriac, and also in Mishnaic Hebrew:
cf. J. Tal. *Ber.* v. 9 *a*. Erub. i. 19^b. It is implied also in Josephus, *Ant.* x. 11. 6: διὰ τὴν φυλακὴν καὶ διατήρησιν. Hence I have
rendered the text in 6¹²⁽¹¹⁾ 'Then these men kept watch and found
Daniel '.

In *Aram. Pap.* (Cowley, Aḥ. 29) we have שניא ירגש 'will be
greatly enraged ', where the verb may be in the Haph'el so far
as the form goes. In Hebrew it occurs in Ps. 2¹ רגשו = ' are
enraged ', or ' are in a tumult '. Thus, the meaning of הרגשו in
6¹²⁽¹¹⁾ = ' kept watch ' is not attested earlier than the date of our
text, whereas the other meaning is attested in the fifth cent. B.C.

There remains now the third passage, i. e. 6¹⁶⁽¹⁵⁾. Here both
the LXX and Th. omit הרגשו. The Vulg., however, reads
' intelligentes ', which implies this reading, while the Pesh. gives
the other meaning ܐܘܪܒܘ = *tumultuati sunt.* The latter meaning
is in part suitable to the context. The enemies of Daniel have
secured evidence of his breach of the law, and this breach must
lead to his destruction.

But there is a difficulty. Th. omits¹ the words ' came tumultuously to the king and '. The LXX differs throughout in
details, but it and Jos., *Ant.* x. 11. 6, *presuppose the presence of
the satraps and presidents throughout the whole interview,* 6¹¹⁻¹⁵.
The omission in Th., to which we have just referred, involves
the same presupposition. Furthermore even 6¹⁵⁽¹⁴⁾ of the MT
cannot be interpreted apart from this presupposition ; for it
implies the presence and active exertions of Daniel's adversaries
throughout the entire day. This being so, 6¹⁶⁽¹⁵⁾ cannot begin
' Then those men came tumultuously to the king and said '. In
fact neither possible meaning of this verb is admissible in this
context. Hence I have excised the clause ' came tumultuously
unto the king and ' as an interpolation, which has no support
before the fourth century A. D., and is also against the context.

Said before him. Thus with the LXX εἶπαν ἐναντίον τοῦ βασιλέως
we must emend אמרין לה into אמרין קדמוהי. When subjects
address the king the idiom always (twenty-three times) is as
I have emended, save in 6¹⁶⁽¹⁵⁾, where the adversaries of Daniel are
deliberately rude to Darius, and in 2²⁵ where our author having
used קדם in the clause immediately preceding does not repeat

¹ A few MSS. of this version add as in Aramaic παρετηρήσαντο ἐπὶ τὸν βασιλέα
καί.

it after אמר. In 3⁹ 'said to Nebuchadnezzar' אמרין לנב", the
text is corrupt. See § 20. w.

6⁸⁽⁷⁾. *All the presidents.* Is this misrepresentation made deliberately in order to lead the king to believe that Daniel had taken
part in this appeal to the king? But according to the LXX 6⁴
only the two colleagues of Daniel conspire against him; for
according to 6³ (LXX) the fact that they are specially mentioned
as being put under Daniel made them naturally hostile to Daniel.
Accordingly in 6²⁵⁽²⁴⁾ it is only these two men that are cast into the
den of lions. This is a much more reasonable form of the story,
but Josephus (*Ant.* x. 11. 6) here follows our text.

The deputies and satraps. See note on 3².

That the king should establish a statute. So Rosenmüller,
Hitzig, Marti, and others (following the MT punctuation). This
the king does in 6¹⁰ ⁽⁹⁾. מלכא stands at the end, as Marti observes, in order not to separate לקימה קים, which corresponds to
לתקפה אסר. Compare a similar construction in Hebrew in
Isa. 5²⁴, 20¹, &c., where the object follows immediately after the
infinitive and then the nominative of the subject. Another rendering is 'to establish a royal statute'. So Th. στῆσαι στάσει
βασιλικῇ. This rendering is supported by Ewald, Bevan, Behrmann, and others: cf. 6¹³ אסר מלכא 'the king's interdict'. But
this second rendering ignores the emphatic מלכא, whereas we
have the emphatic form in 6¹³.

Make a strong interdict. תקף occurs in Hebrew, Job 14²⁰, 15²⁴,
Eccles. 4¹², as a loan-word from Aramaic. אֱסָר is practically the
same word as the Hebrew אִסָּר in Num. 30³,⁴, &c.

Any god. Aramaic adds here 'or man'. But since בְּעָא can
be used not only of prayer but of any sort of petition, the statement that no man should be allowed for thirty days to make
a single request of any of his neighbours is too extravagant to
be taken seriously. The text is concerned only with prayer
directed to a god. This does not include requests directed to
the king, who was regarded as a demi-god. Moreover Daniel's
enemies admit that they can find no occasion against him save
in respect to his worship of his God. Finally we remark that the
LXX and Josephus omit this phrase. The text of the LXX thus
flatters Darius by implicitly ranking him with the gods. Antiochus
Epiphanes regarded himself as a god. Josephus (*Ant.* x. 11. 5),
however, states that the decree forbade requests to the king.

Den of lions. The Assyrian and Persian kings kept lions in enclosures for hunting purposes. But 6¹⁸⁽¹⁷⁾ where the mouth of the גֹּב is said to be covered by a stone, and the stone, sealed with the signet of the king and of his lords, suggests that the writer is here thinking not of a fenced-in enclosure but of a *pit* which is its proper meaning: cf. Targ. on Gen. 37²², Jer. 38⁶,⁷, where it is a rendering of בור. But in such pits animals could not have lived save for a very short time. The tradition which our author was using probably contained no definite conception of the 'den' or 'pit' in question.

Lions. אַרְיָוָתָא, pl. of אריא 'exactly agrees with the Syriac form as vocalized by the East Syrians (Nestorians); the West Syrians pronounce *aryawâthâ* with short *a* in the second syllable' (Bevan). The former punctuates ָ for ַ before a *vav*: cf. כָּרְסְוָן 7⁹ from כרסא.

6⁹ ⁽⁸⁾. *Establish the interdict and sign the writing.* Here two distinct actions are mentioned. First the king gives his sanction to the interdict: next the interdict is issued in written form with the royal signature. In 6¹⁰ ⁽⁹⁾ 'the writing and the interdict' means the writing which contains the interdict; cf. Jer. 36²⁷ ('the roll and the words', i.e. the roll which contained the words).

That it be not changed. On the construction די לא להשניא see Introd., § 20. *t.*

Which altereth not. Cf. Esther 1¹⁹, 8⁸.

6¹¹ ⁽¹⁰⁾. *Now his windows,* &c. This clause is parenthetical. Literally it runs: 'now he had in his chamber windows opening'. כַּוִּין pl. of כַּוָּה : Targ. כַּוְּתָא (emphatic state). The windows were of the nature of lattices: cf. Prov. 7⁶: 2 Kings 1², opposed to closed windows Ezek. 41²⁶.

His chamber, i.e. עִלִּיתֵהּ = Heb. עֲלִיָּה —a roof-chamber: see *Enc. Bib.* I. 509. Cf. LXX and Th. ὑπερῷον. This chamber was constructed on the flat roof of the house: cf. Acts 10⁹ ἐπὶ τὸ δῶμα. Such a chamber was specially used for prayer, mourning, and acts of devotion: cf. Isa. 22¹, Ps. 102⁸, Acts 10⁹, Judith 8⁵. It was such a chamber (עֲלִיָּה) that was built on the roof for Elisha by the Shunammite, 2 Kings 4¹⁰. But this latticed chamber may have been over the gateway: see *Enc. Bib.* II. 2131, or rather 'a room attached to the wall by a separate stair' as the Press Reader suggests.

Toward Jerusalem. The custom of turning to Jerusalem became usual, no doubt, from the Exile onwards. Cf. Tob. 3¹¹, 1 Esdras 4⁵⁸. The practice is referred to in the Mishnah—Berakh. iv. 5, 6. Authority for turning to Jerusalem was to be found in 1 Kings 8⁴⁴, towards the Temple in 8³⁸,⁴⁸. Cf. Ezek. 8¹⁶ ˢqq·, Ps. 5⁷, 28². See Schürer, *GJV.*³ ii. 453.

Was wont to kneel, i. e. הֲוָא בָּרֵךְ. So Baer, Bevan, Marti, &c., with eleven manuscripts. But most manuscripts read הוא ברך. Cf. 1 Kings 8⁵⁴, Ezra 9⁵—the posture for prayer, but it was usual later to stand when praying: cf. Matt. 6⁵, Mark 11²⁵, Luke 18¹¹, Berakh. v. 1.

Three times a day. Cf. Ps. 55¹⁷, 'at evening and at morning and at noonday': 2 Enoch 51⁴. In later times the hours of prayer were not, as it has been wrongly inferred from Acts 2¹⁵, 3¹, 10³,⁹,³⁰, the third, sixth, and ninth hours of the day, but the three actual hours of prayer were (1) the early morning at the time of the morning offering תפלת שחר ; (2) in the afternoon—the ninth hour (our 3 p.m.) at the time of the evening meal offering תפלת מנחה; cf. 9³¹: (3) in the evening at sunset תפלת הערב: cf. Berakh. iii. 3, iv. 1. See Schürer, *GJV.*³ ii. 293. Yet in 1 Chron. 23³⁰ only morning and evening prayer are prescribed. See *Jewish Encyc.* x. 164 sqq.

Prayed and gave thanks. On מצלא cf. Cowley 30¹⁵ : on מודא see 2²³ of our text.

Before his God. On our author's use of קדם see note on 6⁷⁽⁶⁾ : and Introd., § 20. w.

As he did aforetime. This can also be translated 'forasmuch as he had been wont to do aforetime'. The king's interdict did not affect the fulfilment of Daniel's religious duties.

6¹²⁽¹¹⁾. *Kept watch.* That this is the right translation of הרגשו here, see the evidence given in the note on 6⁷⁽⁶⁾. This is the later meaning of this verb. Its earlier meaning is inadmissible in this context.

6¹³⁽¹²⁾–18⁽¹⁷⁾. The adversaries of Daniel arraign him before the king for his breach of the royal interdict. Notwithstanding the reluctance of the king, he is obliged in accordance with the law to condemn Daniel to the den of lions. The text clearly implies that the struggle between the king and the adversaries of Daniel *continued without break throughout the entire day.* There is no withdrawal of the latter from the palace after they have made

their charge and no subsequent return as the corrupt text of the
MT represents. These six verses represent *a single scene* in
the drama of this narrative.

6¹³ ⁽¹²⁾. *Concerning the king's interdict ; hast thou not.* This
text is very doubtful. The LXX reads simply ' Darius
(> Th.) O king hast thou not'. Th. 'O king': the Pesh.
'O king live for ever: hast thou not ?' Only the Vulg. supports the words but not their connexion : *super edicto : Rex,
numquid non.* We should best read with the LXX, ' Darius
O king, hast thou not'. The order of the words ' Darius the
king' is the older one : see Introd., § 20. *dd.*

Any god. Here as in 6⁸ ⁽⁷⁾ the Aramaic wrongly interpolates
'or man'. LXX omits. See note on 6⁸⁽⁷⁾.

6¹⁴ ⁽¹³⁾. *Hearkeneth not, O king, to thy decree.* In the note on
3¹² I have dealt with this corrupt passage and shown that for the
corrupt MT לאשמעליבמלכבאמטעם = ('regardeth not thee, O king' ?)
we should read לאישמעלטמעמך 'hearkeneth not to thy decree'. Since
the LXX omits this clause, and Th. and Vulg. omit מלכא, and
and none of these authorities recognizes the MT, we must mark
it as corrupt and read as above suggested. The Pesh. pursues
a different course in each passage, but agrees with no other
authority. Josephus, *Ant.* x. 11. 6, twice supports the above
restoration. Thus he states that the nobles accused Daniel of
being 'the only person that transgressed the decrees' : παρα-
βαίνοντος μόνου τοῦ Δανιήλου τὰ προστεταγμένα, and again in the next
clause καταφρονήσαντι τῶν ἐκείνου προσταγμάτων. All the other subjects
of the king took care τὰ προστεταγμένα μὴ παραβῆναι.

In the Biblical Aramaic only the Hithpaʻel 7²⁷ ישתמעון is used
in the sense of *obeying.* But the evidence of the Greek versions
gces to prove that the Peʻal of שמע had also this meaning. In
Hebrew שמע is followed by על 2 Kings 22¹³, &c., or ל 1 Sam. 8⁷,
&c., with a noun = 'to obey'.

⌜*Before his God.*⌝ We should with the LXX δεόμενον τοῦ προσώπου τοῦ θεοῦ αὐτοῦ and Th. αἰτεῖ παρὰ τοῦ θεοῦ αὐτοῦ τὰ αἰτήματα αὐτοῦ
restore קדם אֱלָהֵהּ. The words, 'before his God', are important
here. Daniel is accused—not of making vague but of making
definite petitions to his God in direct contravention of the law.
Now since in 6¹¹⁽¹⁰⁾, ¹²⁽¹¹⁾ this phrase is found in thisconnexion,
and since the LXX and Th. support this full form of the text,
we have restored it as above.

6¹⁵⁽¹⁴⁾. *Was sore displeased*, i. e. שׂגיא באש עלוהי = Hebrew רעע
לו רעה גדולה : cf. Neh. 2¹⁰, Jon. 4¹ (רעע אל). For the expression
of the opposite emotion see 6²⁴⁽²³⁾ note.

Set his heart. Here only in Biblical Aramaic is בָּל found
meaning 'heart'. But it occurs in the *Aram. Pap.* (Cowley,
Aḥ. 97) and in the later Syriac and Palestinian Aramaic. In
Hebrew cf. שׂים לב in 1 Sam. 9²⁰, where it has the same meaning
as the phrase in our text.

Till the going down of the sun. עד מֶעָלֵי שׁמשׁא is the exact equivalent of the Hebrew עד־בוא השׁמשׁ.

6¹⁶⁽¹⁵⁾. *These men.* The MT adds an impossible clause here—
'came tumultuously unto the king'. For the grounds on which
I have excised this clause see note on 6⁷ ⁽⁶⁾.

Said unto the king, i. e. אמרין למלכא. This phrase expresses the
discourteous attitude of the courtiers to the king. See note on
6⁷ ⁽⁶⁾. At the beginning of the interview, which lasted all day,
their attitude was different : see 6¹³⁽¹²⁾ 'said *before* the king'. See
notes on 2²⁵, 3⁹.

Know, O king, &c. This is a very discourteous reminder to
the king that he is bound by his own law, which has the tradition
of the past behind it.

No interdict ... may be changed. On the idiom לא להשׁניא see
Introd., § 20. *t.*

6¹⁷⁽¹⁶⁾. *Continually.* בתדירא is used in the Targums without the
ב in the same sense. Also we find עלת תדירא = ' the daily sacrifice' the equivalent of the Hebrew תמיד.

6¹⁸⁽¹⁷⁾. *Was brought*—הֵיתָיַת. Passive perfect Haph'el—in
reality a Hoph'al. See 3¹³ note.

Laid upon. שְׂמַת is abnormal, and should with Kautzsch
(§ 45. 1 *d*), Kamphausen, Bevan, &c., be punctuated שֻׂמַת.

Signets. עִזְקָת pl. construct according to the best manuscripts
with Baer and with the LXX. But inferior manuscripts and Th.
have the singular.

Nothing. לא ... צְבוּ This word, which originally meant
' purpose', is here used in the sense of 'thing'—a sense in
which it is current in Syriac and also in the Palmyrene Aramaic.
For similar weakenings in the significance of words cf. שׁאלתא
4¹⁴ ⁽¹⁷⁾ (?) : in Hebrew חֵפֶץ Eccles. 3¹, 5⁷. In the *Aram. Pap.*
(Cowley 15²⁵,²⁹, and frequently) the verb צבי occurs in the full
sense of ' to wish '.

6[19(18)]. *Fasting.* טְוָת is taken to be a feminine noun in the absolute state used adverbially.   It occurs in Syriac.

Neither were †instruments of music†.   The meaning of the text here is uncertain.   It is also most probably corrupt.   The meaning of דַחֲוָן here rendered 'instruments of music' is really unknown.   Th. renders it by ἐδέσματα (as also the Pesh.): Ibn Ezra, 'instruments of music': Saadi, 'dancing girls': Berthold and others 'concubines'.   It is perhaps best with Bevan, Marti, and Prince to emend the word into לְחֵנָן = 'concubines': cf. 5[2,3,23].   These were usually present in oriental courts.

But the entire text may be corrupt.   When the Aramaic text (followed by Th., Syr., and Vulg.) states that 'the king passed the night fasting' and that 'neither were *dachavan* brought to him, and his sleep fled from him', the text is inconsistent with itself.   Surely if a man passes the night fasting, it follows as a matter of course that he was awake throughout the night.   It would be absurd to say that a man who slept throughout the night spent the night in fasting.   Hence the clause 'and his sleep fled from him' is either an interpolation, or it should precede the clause 'and passed the night fasting'.   In the latter case we should have the natural order of events and language: the king spent a sleepless night, but he had no recourse to food or women. But against this restoration of the text we have the MT, Th., Pesh., Vulg.   On the other hand the LXX omits this disturbing clause and reads ηὐλίσθη νῆστις καὶ ἦν λυπούμενος περὶ τοῦ Δανιήλ. Josephus (*Ant.* x. 11. 6) was clearly acquainted with both texts since he combines them together: δι' ὅλης δ' ἄσιτος τῆς νυκτὸς καὶ ἄυπνος διῆγεν ἀγωνιῶν περὶ τοῦ Δανιήλου.   The last four words here are a reproduction of the last four in the LXX.   We have, therefore, to choose between the two forms of text of which these are renderings:

LXX.	MT with the final clause restored to its right place.
'Then the king went to his palace, and he kept grieving about Daniel.'	'(*a*) Then the king went to his palace, and (*d*) his sleep fled from him, (*b*) and he passed the night in fasting, (*c*) and dancing girls were not brought before him.'

And his sleep fled from him. Cf. 2¹ for the same clause in Hebrew. Baer reads שְׁנָתֵּה, Ginsburg שְׁנָתֵּה. עֲלוֹהִי is not used here for מֵעֲלוֹהִי, but constitutes the dative of disadvantage as in 2¹ : 'his sleep fled upon him ', i. e. to his hurt.

6²¹⁽²⁰⁾. *When he drew near,* i. e. כְּמִקְרְבֵהּ. כ is here used of a point of time. לְ is used with the infinitive in the same way in the *Aram. Pap.* (Cowley, Beh. 8. 12) לממטה = 'when he arrived '. Is this latter use correct Aramaic ? Since it is a Hebrew idiom (cf. Isa. 7¹⁵ לְדַעְתּוֹ = 'when he knoweth ' : 2 Sam. 18²⁹, Gen. 24⁶³, it may be a true Aramaism. Th. omits 'to Daniel' and 'the king spake and said to Daniel'.

The living God. Cf. Deut. 5²⁶, Josh. 3¹⁰, 1 Sam. 17²⁶, &c.

6²²⁽²¹⁾. *Spake Daniel unto the king.* Here the Aram. is עִם מַלְכָּא מַלִּל = the Hebrew דִּבֶּר אֶל. Generally עם with pers. follows מלל in the Targums and Syriac. It is followed by עַל c. pers. in the *Aram. Pap.* (Cowley 69²). The rule relating to אמר לְ and אמר קדם does not hold in the case of this verb. See note on 3⁹.

6²⁴⁽²³⁾. *Was . . . exceeding glad.* Contrast this phrase with שְׂגִיא בְּאֵשׁ עֲלוֹהִי in 6¹⁵⁽¹⁴⁾. The phrase used in the *Aram. Pap.,* equivalent to that in our text, is טִיב לִבַּב (Cowley 2⁹, 14⁶, 15¹⁵, &c.). 'The perfect טאב seems ', as Bevan remarks, 'to have been formed on the analogy of בְּאֵשׁ, since in the former word the א does not properly belong to the root'. In the *Aram. Pap.,* though of frequent occurrence, the form is either טיב or טב : in Hebrew טוב. See also Cooke 65³.

Should take up. Haph. inf. הַנְסָקָה for הַסָּקָה, where the n is assimilated. Cf. הַנְעָלָה 4³⁽⁶⁾. In 3²² we have הַסִּקוּ : in 6²⁴⁽²³⁾ הֻסַּק the Hoph'al as though from a form נסק. See Bauer-Leander § 43, a–h.

6²⁵⁽²⁴⁾. The destruction of Daniel's enemies with their children and wives in conformity with the primitive conception of the solidarity of the family : cf. Josh. 7²⁴⁻²⁵ : 2 Sam. 21⁵⁻⁹. Note the reaction against this rough method of justice in Deut. 24¹⁶, Jer. 31²⁹⁻³⁰.

†*They cast them*†. Seeing that the LXX (αὐτοὶ . . . ἐρρίφησαν), Jos., *Ant.* x. 11. 6 βληθῆναι, Th. (ἐβλήθησαν αὐτοί), and the Vulg. (' missi sunt ') agree in taking the Aramaic here as a passive, we should no doubt emend רְמוֹ into רְמִיו = they were cast. אִנּוּן, moreover, which the MT represents as an accusative = αὐτούς, is not found either in Ezra or elsewhere in Daniel in the accusative, and should accordingly be taken as the subject of the

verb = αὐτοί. As Marti suggests, for הַיְתִיו we should read the
passive הֵיתָיוּ. This suggestion, though Marti did not observe it,
has the support of the Vulg. *adducti sunt.* Thus we should
render 'and those men were brought and were cast . . . they,
their children and their wives'.

Their children and their wives. So MT and Th. But the
LXX, Pesh., and Vulg. give the reverse order, and perhaps
rightly in accordance with the O.T. usage—over seven times out
of ten. The MT order is Greek.

Had the mastery of them. Another rendering of שׁלטו is 'fell
upon them', which is the meaning more in keeping with the
context. This meaning belongs to בְּ שְׁלֵט in the Targ. on Judges
8²¹, 15¹²; 2 Sam. 1¹⁵; 1 Sam. 22¹⁷,¹⁸, as a rendering of the
Hebrew פָּגַע. It occurs in other Targums with the same
meaning.

Or ever, &c., lit. 'they did not come to the bottom of the
den until' (עד די). So עד זי in *Aram. Pap.* (Cowley 30²⁷, Aḥ
52. 95).

6²⁶⁻²⁹. Just as at the close of chapter 3 Nebuchadnezzar
issues a decree forbidding any people, nation, or language to
speak against the God of Shadrach, Meshach, and Abednego,
for that no other god could be set beside Him, and at the close
of 4 (through a necessary transposition of the text) makes a
proclamation to all the peoples of the world to the effect that
His power has been manifested in signs and wonders, and that
His kingdom is unto everlasting, so here Darius[1] issues a further
decree requiring all men that dwell upon the earth to worship
the God of Daniel, in that He is the living and eternal God, and
His sovereignty one that endureth for ever. This edict is expressed in terms and phrases already used by our author : cf. 2⁴⁴,
3³¹⁻³³ (4¹⁻³), 5¹⁹.

6²⁶ ⁽²⁵⁾. *Peoples, nations, and languages.* Cf. 3²⁹ and 3³¹,
which latter forms the conclusion of 4.

Dwell. On דאריָן see 2³³, n. 3³¹.

6²⁷ ⁽²⁶⁾. *I make a decree.* Cf. 3²⁹.

---

[1] With the words of this decree of Darius : 'King Darius . . . unto all the
peoples, nations, and languages that dwell on the earth' we might compare
the following expressions in the Susian or Elamite version of the Behistun
Inscription of Darius Hystaspes : 'By the grace of Auramazda I made inscriptions . . . and sent those inscriptions into all lands'. See Cowley, p. 248 sq.

Tremble and fear. The same words are used of the relation of the subjects of Nebuchadnezzar to their king. Just as Nebuchadnezzar was supreme in all matters affecting the lives of his subjects, so the God of Daniel was to be regarded as the Supreme Being alike in heaven and earth. It is not unnatural that the essential character of the historical incidents recorded in the preceding chapters is here at their close set forth in verse.

Steadfast, i. e. קַיָּם. In the Targums it is used often as a rendering of חַי 'living'; cf. Joshua 3¹⁰; and in the phrase קִים יי הוא 'as Yahweh liveth', Judges 8¹⁹.

His kingdom. Cf. 2⁴⁴, 3³³, 4³¹, 7¹⁴,²⁷. Before די לא we must understand מַלְכוּ.

Unto everlasting, i. e. עַד סוֹפָא, literally 'unto the end', but essentially means 'for ever'. Cf. 7²⁶.

6²⁸ ⁽²⁷⁾. *He delivereth and rescueth* : and not any earthly prince. Cf. 3²⁸, ²⁹.

Signs and wonders. Cf. 3³²,³³ (4²,³).

From the power, &c. This expression (מִיד אַרְיָוָתָא) recalls 1 Sam. 17³⁷, 'from the paw of the lion'.

6²⁹ ⁽²⁸ ᵇ⁾. *So Daniel was **set over the kingdom of Darius**.* Thus Darius succeeded in realizing the purpose expressed in 6⁴ ⁽³⁾. That this was the original text I have sought to prove in the note on 6⁴⁽³⁾. In that note I have given the text of the LXX, of which the above is a rendering. I have there shown the defectiveness of the MT text, which, instead of the above clause reads : 'So that Daniel prospered in the reign of Darius' Here the MT is conflated from two clauses, one in 6⁽³⁾ and the other in 6²⁹⁽²⁸⁾, i. e. והצלח בעבידת מלכא די עבד and הקים על מלכות דריוש.

6²⁹ ⁽²⁸ ᵃ⁾. ⌐*And King Darius was gathered to his people.*⌐ This clause, which I have restored from the LXX, is wrongly set at the beginning of the verse in that version.

⌐*And Cyrus the Persian received his kingdom.*⌐ So the LXX. The revised text first appears in Th., and then in the MT, Pesh., and Vulg. The LXX presupposes the following Aramaic original—ודניאל הָקִים עַל מלכות דריוש ומלכא דריוש אִתְכְּנֵשׁ לְעַמֵּהּ וכורש פרסיא קבל מלכותה.

SECTIONS VII–X. THE VISIONS OF DANIEL.
CHAPTERS 7–12

SECTION VII

i.e. Chapter 7, being a Vision of Daniel in the first year of the reign of Belshazzar.

§ 1. The MT is interpolated, defective, and corrupt, but can be corrected in almost every passage by means of the versions and in a few by the imperative demands of its own context.

(a) *Interpolations.* In 7^1 'he told' (אמר) must be rejected with the LXX and Th. Daniel does not first write down and then tell his visions. See note *in loc.*

In 7^2 'Daniel answered and said' is to be excised as an interpolation with LXX, Th., and Vulg.

In 7^5 'a second' is to be excised with LXX and Vulg.

In 7^{10} 'and went forth' (ונפק) is to be excised as a marginal explanation of נגד, which apparently occurs here for the first time in literature. The LXX and Th. have only one verb : but the MT, Pesh., and Vulg. are conflate and have two.

In 7^{11} the second 'I beheld' is to be excised with LXX and Th. against MT, Pesh., and Vulg.

In 7^{18} 'For ever and' is to be excised with LXX and Th. against MT, Pesh., and Vulg.

(b) *Omissions.* The MT is defective. It omits 'beast' in 7^6 against LXX, Th., Pesh. At the close of 7^9 we should restore 'and he made war with the saints' with LXX and the like statements in 7^{21}, and a parallel one in 7^{25}. In 7^9 for 'the ancient of days' we must in conformity with the custom of Apocalyptic in such matters emend this irreverent and impossible designation of God into '⟨one like⟩ an ancient of days': i.e. כ(עתיק). There is no version or other documentary evidence in support of this restoration, but none the less it should be made. See note *in loc.* Finally in 7^{22} for 'judgement was given' we should with Ewald, and other scholars, &c. read 'judgement ⟨was set and dominion⟩ was given'. There is no authority for this emendation but the requirements of the context.

(c) *Corruptions.* Some of these corruptions are very serious and mislead the reader of the text on important questions :

others are only important from the standpoint of a correct text and do not essentially affect its sense. I shall enumerate them in the order of their occurrence. The evidence bearing on these corruptions is given in adequate fulness in the notes.

In 7² for 'in my vision in (עם) the night' we should with LXX, Th., and Pesh. read 'in my visions of the night'.

In 7⁹, by the wrong (probably accidental) transposition of the word 'white' (חִוָּר) from its right place at the close of the stichos to the third place, we arrive at the corrupt text 'His raiment was white as snow and the hair of his head like spotless wool'. This rendering based on the Massoretic accentuation is now abandoned by most scholars, who render the second clause 'was spotless as wool' in accordance with Th. (Pesh. and Vulg.). But the sense is wholly unsatisfactory. Wool is not of necessity either 'spotless' or 'white'. Hence we should with the LXX restore 'white' to the close of the clause. Thus we recover the original text and a wholly satisfactory meaning: 'His raiment was as snow, and the hair of his head was spotless as white snow'. Cf. 1 Enoch 46¹, Rev. 1¹⁴.

In 7¹³ the MT 'with (עם) the clouds of heaven' appears corrupt for 'on (על) the clouds of heaven'. So LXX and Pesh. The clouds are the chariot of the supernatural figure and *not his companions*, just as they form the chariot of God in Ps. 104³. There is no evidence for the existence of this unsatisfactory text of the MT before the beginning of the Christian era. Unhappily both the corrupt text has found its way into the N.T. as well as the original. See note *in loc.*

In 7¹⁵ I have rendered 'therewith' in accordance with the LXX and Vulg. i.e. בגו דנה which was subsequently corrupted into בגו נדנה which is rendered 'in the midst of the sheath' or 'its sheath' by a change of vocalization. As Marti observes, this is unintelligible. See my note *in loc* for the emendation I have made, which is supported by earlier and later Aramaic usage.

7¹⁷. In this same verse we have the most disastrous corruption of all in this chapter. The MT reads 'these great beasts . . . which shall arise out of the earth'. This is a radical misstatement of Jewish tradition, according to which these monsters arose out of the sea (see my note *in loc.*), and so our author asserts plainly in 7³. How this corruption in the MT arose is as mysterious as many other corruptions in the same text. We must here undubitably follow the LXX here 'which shall be destroyed from the earth'. Th. is conflate and gives a rendering of the original and also of the corrupt text.

§ 2. *Evidence of an Aramaic original.*

In 7⁶, though the sole LXX MS. (11th cent. A.D.) has lost the last clause of this verse, happily it has been preserved by the Syriac version of it made in the beginning of the seventh century. It presupposes γλῶσσα ἐδόθη αὐτῷ. The MT, however, has here שלטן which Th. rightly renders ἐξουσία. γλῶσσα is the rendering of a corruption of שלטן, i.e. לשן. This corruption could not be explained on the hypothesis of a Hebrew original.

In 7⁷ ὁ φόβος αὐτοῦ ὑπερφέρων ἰσχύι is due to a corruption in the Aramaic : see note *in loc.*

On the other hand in 7⁸ Jahn urges that the corruption in ἐξηράνθησαν could easily be explained on the ground of a Hebrew original : see my note *in loc.* This is quite true. But it is not necessary to go back to the Hebrew. As it has already been pointed out, it could be explained as a corruption of ἐξήρθησαν. Now ἐξαίρω is used at least four times as a rendering of עקר.

§ 3. *Peculiarities of Syntax and Vocabulary.*

In 7²⁰ it is said that we have *vav* apodosis in ועינין לה, an idiom not elsewhere found in Biblical Aramaic, nor (?) in the *Aram. Pap.* See note *in loc.*

§ 4. The vision in this chapter is parallel with that in chapter 2. The four world kingdoms followed by a fifth—that of the Saints—are the subject of both, the four kingdoms being symbolized by the four parts of the great image in 2 and the four beasts in 7.

Three questions call for consideration. These are (1) The four world empires; (2) The ten horns; (3) The horns plucked up.

(1) *The Four World Empires.* Only the two interpretations that gained the suffrages of the centuries immediately following the publication of Daniel have real claims to consideration here, though I mention a third that appears in 1 Enoch. The first, of which only a few, but indubitable, traces survive, identified the fourth kingdom with the Greek empire, the other,

which is attested in the first century of the Christian era, but probably originated earlier, identified it with the Roman empire. *It goes without saying that if the latter had been first in the field, it would never have gained a hearing after the close of the second century B. C.* ; for then the Roman and not the Greek empire was all powerful in the East. This first interpretation, which is also the true one, passed out of currency just because history had failed to confirm it. In this as in other instances of unfulfilled prophecy, the believers in the infallibility of verbal inspiration applied themselves anew, as they do now, to study the prophecy in question, and so a fresh interpretation of the four kingdoms was issued, which discovered in the fourth kingdom the empire of Rome.

Since this is a simple statement of historical fact, it will be unnecessary to enter here on the vagaries of medieval and modern hermeneutics on this chapter. It will be sufficient to give briefly the evidence for the above statements.

(*a*) According to the older and true interpretation the four kingdoms were (1) the Babylonian, (2) the Median, (3) the Persian, (4) the Greek or Macedonian. The identification of the Seleucidae or Greek rulers of Syria with the fourth kingdom first appears, though in a veiled form, as befits the character of the work, in the Sibylline Oracles, iii. 388–400. This portion of the book, which was written not later than 140 B. C., refers to the ten horns of our text.

III. 388   ἥξει καί ποτ' ἄπιστος ἐς Ἀσίδος ὄλβιον οὖδας
         ἀνὴρ πορφυρέην λώπην ἐπιειμένος ὤμοις
         ἄγριος ἀλλοδίκης φλογόεις· ἤγειρε γὰρ αὐτοῦ
         πρόσθε κεραυνὸς φῶτα· κακὸν δ' Ἀσίη ζυγὸν ἕξει
         πᾶσα, πολὺν δὲ χθὼν πίεται φόνον ὀμβρηθεῖσα.
         ἀλλὰ καὶ ὣς πανάιστον ἅπαντ' Ἀίδης θεραπεύσει·
         ὧν δήπερ γενεὴν αὐτὸς θελει ἐξαπολέσσαι,
   395 ἐκ τῶν δὴ γενεῆς κείνου γένος ἐξαπολεῖται·
         ῥίζαν ἴαν γε διδούς ἣν καὶ κόψει βροτολοιγός
         ἐκ δέκα δὴ κεράτων, παρὰ δὴ φυτὸν ἄλλο φυτεύσει,
         κόψει πορφυρέης γενεῆς γενετῆρα μαχητὴν
         καὐτὸς ὑφ' υἱῶν ὧν ἐς ὁμόφρονα αἴσιον ἄρρης
   400 φθεῖται· καὶ τότε δὴ παραφυόμενον κέρας ἄρξει.

I have here followed Geffcken's text, which is uncertain in

III. 399. But the uncertainty of the text here does not affect
the interpretation as a whole.

In these verses we have the interpretation *that was put on the
ten horns in the fourth kingdom* about 140 B.C. and the interpretation takes the passage in Daniel as referring to the Greek
empire beyond the possibility of doubt. It may not, it is true,
agree exactly with any modern identification of the ten 'horns'
or kings, but it is at one with them in regarding the 'horns' as
kings of the Greek empire. In the Sibyllines 'the man clad
with the purple cloak' is Antiochus Epiphanes. The race,
which Antiochus Epiphanes wished to destroy, was that of his
brother Seleucus IV, Philopator (187–175 B.C.). But the son of
the latter i. e. Demetrius I (162–150 B.C.) shall put to death the
' one root' (ῥίζαν ἴαν) which Antiochus left, i. e. Antiochus V,
Eupator (164–162 B.C.), or, in the words of the Sibyl, 'shall cut
(him) off from among ten horns'. Demetrius I was in turn
slain by 'the side shoot' (φυτὸν ἄλλο), i. e. Alexander Balas, who
claimed to be a son of Antiochus Epiphanes, and reigned from
150 to 146 B.C. He was attacked and defeated by Demetrius II
and Ptolemy VI, Philometor, and afterwards murdered (1 Macc.
11⁸⁻¹⁹, Josephus, *Ant.* xiii. 4. 8) by an Arabian prince named
Zabdiel. The horn growing alongside (παρὰ δὴ φυτόν) is Trypho
who had his ward Antiochus VI removed and reigned in his
stead from 142 to 137 B.C. The text of the Sibyllines is not free
from corruption.

(*b*) A second and very different interpretation was apparently
given to the fourth kingdom in Dan. 7, by the author of 1 Enoch
37–70. This section of Enoch (written before 64 B.C.) knows
nothing of the Romans. The last oppressors of the Jews are the
later Maccabean princes (see my note on 38⁵). The writer does
not attempt a detailed exposition of the text of Dan. 7, but he
uses and even quotes it as in 46¹, ² 'And there I saw One who
had a head of days | And His head was like white wool [1] | And
with Him was another being whose countenance was as the
appearance of a man, | And his face was full of graciousness like
one of the holy angels. And I asked the angel who went with
me . . . concerning that Son of Man . . . why he went with the
Head of Days?' The judgement will ensue immediately and

_____

[1] So it should be translated and not as in my Commentary 'Was white like
wool'. The latter is possible grammatically.

'the kings and the mighty', i. e. the later Maccabean princes will be judged according to their deeds (cf. $48^{5, \, 8-9}$, 53^{3-5}, $62^{3, \, 11}$). The same right interpretation of the fourth kingdom as referring to the Greek empire (though it is not spoken of as 'the fourth') is quite definitely set forth in Josephus, *Ant.* x. 11. 7 ταῦτα ἡμῶν συνέβη παθεῖν τῷ ἔθνει ὑπὸ 'Αντιόχου τοῦ 'Επιφανοῦς, καθὼς εἶδεν ὁ Δανίηλος. Antiochus Epiphanes thus fulfills the prophecies of Daniel in chap. 8. There follows a statement in Josephus' text that Daniel wrote also about Rome as the destroyer of his country, but this sentence is excised by Niese. Again, the Syriac Version of Daniel actually identifies in 7^7 the fourth kingdom with that of the Greeks.

Next in 4 Ezra 12^{10-12} (A. D. 80–120), we turn to a very different document. This work *interprets the fourth kingdom of the Roman empire*, but states quite definitely that *this interpretation is not the interpretation which the angel gave to Daniel*, i. e. *that which identified the Greek empire with the fourth kingdom, and which till Rome became mistress of the East had been the accepted one.* The passage in Ezra runs: 12^{10} 'And he said unto me: This is the interpretation of the vision which thou hast seen. 11. The eagle which thou sawest come up from the sea is the fourth kingdom, which appeared in vision to thy brother Daniel. 12. But it was not interpreted unto him as I now interpret it unto thee or have interpreted it'. To this passage I shall return later. In 4 Ezra 11^1 the eagle comes up from the sea, i. e. the Roman Empire.

This interpretation was still prevalent in the third century A.D.; for it was recognized by Porphyry (A. D. 233–304), and in the fourth by Ephrem Syrus (A. D. 300–350).

According, therefore, to the authentic interpretation of Daniel 2, 7, and 8, the symbols are to be identified as follows:

Chapter 2. *The great image.*	Chapter 7. *The four beasts.*	Chapter 8.	
The golden head =	Lion with eagle's wings =		} Babylonian empire
Silver breast and arms =	Bear with three ribs in its mouth =	First and shorter horn of ram	} Median empire
Brass belly and thighs =	Leopard with four wings =	Second and longer horn of ram	} Persian empire
Iron legs, feet, and toes, partly iron, partly clay =	Beast with iron teeth and ten horns, among which arose a little horn =	Goat with one horn followed by four horns out of one of which arose a little horn	Greek empire (Alexander and his successors)

(c) The third interpretation which thus arose on the failure of the first (for the second interpretation never gained the public ear), and identified the Roman empire with the fourth kingdom is found in the New Testament. But it probably originated in the 1st cent. B.C.; for with the assertion of the power of Rome in the East this reinterpretation was inevitable. Probably from Pompey's time onward Rome came in certain circles in Palestine to be identified with the fourth kingdom. Thus in the *Psalms of Solomon* 2²⁹: τοῦ εἰπεῖν τὴν ὑπερηφανίαν τοῦ δράκοντος ἐν ἀτιμίᾳ,[1] Pompey is called 'the dragon'—a term associated with the Antichrist. He impersonated the power of Rome, as Nebuchadnezzar did that of Babylon. In the LXX of Jer. 28³⁴ (Hebr. 51³⁴) the latter is compared to a dragon.

The way was thus prepared for the almost universal reinterpretation of the four kingdoms in the 1st cent. A.D. The oldest work of that century where this reinterpretation appears is the Assumption of Moses (A.D. 7-30). In chapters 8-9 of this work there is an account of the calamities endured under Antiochus Epiphanes. But that period is past so far as the author of the Assumption is concerned, and his gaze is fixed on the immediate future and on the power that threatens his own people. That this power is the Roman empire, there is no room for doubt. Thus in 10⁸ we have the following passage, the reference of which, even though corrupt, cannot be mistaken. It predicts the overthrow of Rome symbolized as 'the Eagle':

'Then thou, O Israel, shalt be happy
And thou shalt †mount upon the necks and wings of the eagle
And they shall be ended†.'

Here the phrase *cervices et alas* (i. e. *alae*) have been accidentally transposed from the third to the second line: by restoring them we shall have:

'And thou shalt go up against the eagle
And its necks and wings shall be destroyed.'[2]

In the passage just dealt with, Rome (or the fourth empire) is referred to under the symbol of the eagle, instead of that used

---

[1] τοῦ εἰπεῖν = לאמר corrupt for להמיר. Hence the clause = 'to turn the pride of the dragon into dishonour' (Wellhausen).

[2] See details in my edition of the *Apocrypha and Pseudepigrapha* for the Oxford University Press, vol. ii. 422.

by our author, i.e. 'a beast dreadful and terrible'. He has herein followed Ezekiel in symbolizing this fourth world empire by 'a great eagle with great wings' (17³), though in Ezekiel it is a symbol of Nebuchadnezzar.

The reason for the adoption of the definite symbol of the eagle instead of the indefinite one of our author 'a beast dreadful and terrible' (7⁷) is due to the fact that the military emblem of Rome was the eagle. The indefinite symbol in Daniel has now become definite through the reinterpretation of the fourth kingdom and its identification with Rome, whose symbol was that of the eagle.

We shall next quote 2 Bar. 39³,⁴ (before A.D. 70) where the text is definitely based on Daniel and the new interpretation of the fourth kingdom set forth.

'Behold the days come and this kingdom (i.e. Babylon) will be destroyed which once destroyed Zion, and it will be subjected to that which comes after it (i.e. the Persian or Medo-Persian). Moreover, that also again after a time will be destroyed, and another, a third (i.e. the Greek), will arise, and that also will have dominion for its time and will be destroyed. And after these things a fourth kingdom (i.e. the Roman) will arise, whose power will be harsh and evil far beyond those which were before it.'

In a slightly later work (already referred to above) 4 Ezra 12¹¹⁻¹⁴ (A.D. 69-79 or A.D. 96-97) this reinterpretation is not only given but it is distinctly stated that *the angel, that instructed Daniel as to the fourth kingdom being Greek, was wrong*:

'The eagle which thou sawest come up from the sea is the fourth kingdom which appeared in vision to thy brother Daniel. But it was not interpreted unto him as I now interpret it unto thee. Behold the days come when there shall arise a kingdom upon the earth and it shall be more terrible than all the kingdoms that were before it.'

If we advance to later Jewish writings, we find that Rome was taken by them to be the fourth kingdom. This is definitely stated in the Aboda zara 2ᵇ. Rome is here plainly identified with the fourth kingdom. See also Cant. rab. ii. 12; Gen. rab. xliv. 20; Lev. rab. xiii.; Midr. Teh. Ps. 80¹⁴ (*Jewish Encyc.* x. 394).

Turning now to the Christian Church, we find the first identification of the Roman empire with the fourth kingdom in Daniel in the Little Apocalypse in Mark 13 (=Matt. 24=Luke 21) as it is edited by Luke 21²⁰ ; for, whereas Mark 13¹⁴, Matt. 24¹⁵ take the phrase τὸ βδέλυγμα τῆς ἐρημώσεως as referring to the profanation of the Temple by the Antichrist, Luke interprets it as referring to the destruction of Jerusalem by the Romans— ὅταν δὲ ἴδητε κυκλουμένην ὑπὸ στρατοπέδων Ἰερουσαλήμ. Thus the role of the fourth kingdom is connected by Luke with Rome. The date of this reinterpretation is probably between A.D. 70 and 80 In Rev. 13¹, sqq. this reinterpretation is reinforced in terms drawn from our author. The first monster, which emerges from the sea with seven heads and ten horns is the Roman empire. The same view is to be found in *Ep. Barn.* iv. 4 (c .A. D. 100–120) and in Hippolytus ix. (c. A. D. 220).

Some modern scholars have advocated this view, but it is wholly untenable. The former view is now accepted by the whole world of scholarship.

(2) *The ten horns.* The 'ten horns' represent ten kings (cf. *v.* 24), and not ten kingdoms as in 8⁸, where the four horns stand for kingdoms. Now, since after these ten horns there arises another horn, the 'little horn', and since this little horn is Antiochus Epiphanes, it follows that the ten preceding horns are kings. But owing to the paucity of our information it has not yet been determined definitely who these ten kings are. They have been taken to represent the successors of Alexander by many scholars ; and so we have (1) Seleucus I, Nicator (312–280 B.C.) ; (2) Antiochus I, Soter (279–261) ; (3) Antiochus II, Theos (261–246) ; (4) Seleucus II, Callinicus (246–226) ; (5) Seleucus III, Ceraunus (226–223) ; (6) Antiochus III, the Great (222–187) ; (7) Seleucus IV, Philopator (186–176) ; (8) Heliodorus ; (9) Ptolemy VII, Philometor (182–146) ; (10) Demetrius I, Soter. These last three had all stood in the way of Antiochus Epiphanes and had either directly or indirectly suffered at his hands in his efforts to secure the throne and establish his power. But as Hitzig, Kuenen, Bevan, and others urge, the list should begin with Alexander, since the fourth beast represented the Greek supremacy. Hence they begin the list with Alexander the Great and reckon the last three as (8) Seleucus IV, Philopator ; (9) Heliodorus ; (10) Demetrius I, Soter.

(3) *The three horns plucked up.* Of the ten horns three were to be 'plucked up' (*v.* 8), overthrown (*v.* 20), or 'put down'

(*v.* 24), by the eleventh horn, i.e. Antiochus Epiphanes. These were most probably the last three in the list of ten just given.

Antiochus Epiphanes would appear to the Jews, as may be inferred from our text, to have instigated the removal of Seleucus Philopator by Heliodorus. The latter, we know, he crushed through the help of his friends Attalus and Eumenes of Pergamum. The grounds are less cogent with regard to Demetrius Soter. It is true that he was the rightful heir to the kingdom, but he was kept out of his inheritance by Antiochus. He could hardly, therefore, be said to have reigned before Antiochus or to have been slain by him. On these grounds it has been objected that Demetrius Soter cannot be rightly included in the above list. Instead of Demetrius Soter it has been suggested by Gutschmidt that the last of the three horns was not this Demetrius but a brother of his, who was executed by the orders of Antiochus according to John of Antioch (Müller, *Frag. Hist. Graec.*, iv. 558, quoted by Bevan). If we accept this suggestion the last three princes satisfy fairly the conditions of the problem.

SECTION VII

i.e. Chapter 7.

7[1]. *In the first year of Belshazzar.* The narratives came to a close with the last chapter. A series of four visions begin herewith, the first two of which are assigned to the reign of Belshazzar, and recounted in 7–8.

Daniel saw. As in 10[1] the author here begins in the third person in accordance with his practice in the narrative sections, but forthwith represents Daniel as speaking in the first person. In 1 Enoch 1[1,3] and in 92[1], 91[1] we shall find these sections introduced by the author speaking in the third person and then going on to speak in the first. So also in 2 Bar. 1[1 sqq.], 78[1 sqq.] : Test. xii Patr., Test. Reub. 1[1 sqq.], &c.

Even visions of his head upon his bed. This phrase defines the nature of the dream. It has already occurred in 2[28c], which I have restored after 2[30] as the context requires.

He wrote the dream. From 7[2] onwards to the end of the book Daniel speaks in the first person except in 10[1], as already

observed. But the words are important here. At the beginning
of this new section of his book Daniel is represented like other
members of the apocalyptic school as writing down his visions.
Thus in 1 Enoch 14[1], which belongs to the oldest part of this
book, i. e. before 170 B. C., we find 'The book of the words of
righteousness', and in 15[1], 12[3] Enoch is called 'the scribe of
righteousness'. Again in 82[1] the text runs: 'And now my son,
Methuselah, all these things *I am recounting to thee and writing
down for thee*, and I have revealed to thee everything, and given
thee books concerning all these; so preserve, my son Methuselah, the books from thy father's hands and (see) that thou
deliver them to the generations of the world'. In 81[6] Enoch is
bidden 'to write down' the visions he had seen, but according
to 1[2] these were 'not for this generation but for a remote one
which is for to come'. With these directions from 1 Enoch we
might compare 8[26] in our author: 'Shut thou up the vision; for
it belongeth to many days to come', and similarly 12[4], 'But
thou, O Daniel, shut up the words and seal the book, even unto
the time of the end'. It is presupposed throughout our author,
as we infer from the last quotation, that he committed his visions
and teachings to writing.

(*Even*) *a complete account.* The Aramaic text ראש מלין אמר
cannot be right, and the interpretation assigned to it is just as
inadmissible. First of all as to the text. Daniel does not first
'write down' his vision and then recount it *orally.* The word
אמר has always the meaning of speaking orally and presupposes
generally, and certainly always in our author the presence of a
hearer or hearers: cf. 2[4,7,9,36] [4[4(7),5(8)] 5[7], 6[13], 7[16]. It is, therefore,
an intrusion here. If, however, we retain it we should invert
the order of the verbs and read: 'he told the dream, and wrote
down a complete account'. Cf. the passage from 1 Enoch 82[1]
(quoted in the preceding note). But there is no ground for
supposing that Daniel is addressing any one. Hence אמר is an
intrusion, and this hypothesis is confirmed by the LXX and Th.
Th. omits the entire clause 'told a complete account'. But the
LXX is, no doubt, right in omitting only 'told'. It reads τὸ
ὅραμα ὃ εἶδεν ἔγραψεν εἰς κεφάλαια λόγων. Hence we must retain
ראש מלין as original, while we excise אמר as an interpolation.

The phrase, therefore, ראש מלין is original. The next question
is: what does it mean? Bevan, followed by Marti, renders with

the English version '"the sum of the matters", that is, the essential import of the revelation', and compares Ps. 119¹⁶⁰. ראש דברך = 'the essence of Thy word'. But would not this rendering and interpretation require ראש מליא? Hence, since מלין is undetermined, the meaning seems to be 'a summary of matters' or 'a complete account' (so Behrmann).

7². The MT begins this verse with a gloss 'Daniel answered and said'. Both the LXX, Th., and Vulg. omit them. Jerome takes no account of them, nor yet does Hippolytus in their commentaries on Daniel. Only the Pesh. supports the MT. I find that Bludau and Marti have recognized this gloss.

I saw: literally 'was seeing'. LXX and Th. ἐθεώρουν. See note on 4¹³.

†*In my vision by night*† : i. e. בחזוי עם ליליא. Here LXX, Th., and Pesh. presuppose בחזוא די ליליא. Since this latter phrase recurs twice in this chapter, i. e. in 7⁷,¹³, it appears to be the original one here. I cannot find any such temporal use of עם in the *Aram. Papyri* nor yet in the inscriptions. The parallels that have been cited in our text 3³³, 4³¹ are not quite of the same nature as in this passage. In the Talmud it has a temporal meaning, i. e. 'towards' but not 'in': Shabb. ii. 7: Joma 87 *b*: see Levy, *Ch. W.*, p. 222.

Four winds of heaven. Cp. 8⁸, 11⁴ ; Zech. 2⁶, 6⁵ ; 4 Ezra 13⁵.

Stirred up the great sea. This, as Levy (*Ch. W.*, p. 136) and others have already shown, appears to be the truer rendering of מגיחן לימא רבא. The other rendering 'brake forth upon, &c.' would require עַל or בְּ instead of לְ. Although 'the great sea' here recalls Num. 34⁶,⁷, Joshua 9¹ הים הגדול, i. e. the Mediterranean—elsewhere called the הים האחרון Deut. 11²⁴, 34², &c., yet this sea is not referred to in its geographical but in its mythological character, as in Isa. 51¹⁰, Ps. 74¹³ ˢᑫ. As Marti here rightly suggests, 'the whole representation from 7² onwards points to the elements of the old mythological cosmogony, which from the earliest times was known not only in Babylonia but also in the west of Asia'. In 1 Enoch 18² the 'four winds which bear the firmament' are mentioned.

7³. *Four great beasts.* The symbolism here goes back to ancient mythology, according to which beasts came up originally from the sea, which was the seat of evil: cf. Isa. 27¹, ; 1 Enoch 60⁷ ; 2 Bar. 29⁴ ; Rev. 13¹ ; 4 Ezra 6⁴⁹,⁵⁰, 11¹, 12¹¹. In 4 Ezra 13³ the text seems conflate ; for it represents the Messiah ' which flew with the clouds of heaven ' as arising from the heart of the sea.   The Latin version rightly omits this statement, though the Syriac, Arabic, and Armenian versions support it.   It seems to be due to an early scribe, who did not understand the Antichrist tradition.

7⁴. *The first was like a lion and had eagle's wings.*   The first and greatest empire is that of Babylon which appears as a lion with eagle's wings—the lion being the noblest of animals, the eagle the greatest of birds.   In 2³²,³⁸ it is symbolized by gold, the most precious of metals.   The symbol of the winged lion is a fitting one for the empire of Nebuchadnezzar.   Such sculptured figures were familiar to these ancient empires.   But of the mythological meaning or origin of these symbols it is probable that our author knew nothing.   The symbol came to him from tradition with its own associations.   He could find materials for its construction in the prophets of the past.   Nebuchadnezzar was compared by them to a lion Jer. 4⁷, 49¹⁹, 50¹⁷, and his armies to an eagle because of the extraordinary swiftness of their marches, Jer. 49²², Hab. 1⁸, Ezek. 17³.   Its distinguishing characteristics belong naturally to the animal world.   But after a time these animal characteristics disappear.   Its wings—which figure its brutal swiftness—are taken from it, and so its speed of conquest is checked : nevertheless it is raised from the earth and made to stand erect like a man, and a man's heart is given to it.   Hitzig, Ewald, Keil, Driver, Prince, &c., recognize in these changes the growing humanization of the Babylonian kingdom in the person of its head, i. e. Nebuchadnezzar.   In this symbolism these scholars think they can detect a reference to the experiences of this king in chap. 4, Nebuchadnezzar being here, as in 2³⁸, identified with the kingdom of Babylon.   By the loss of his reason the powers of Babylon were maimed. Throughout the king's illness he is described as having a beast's heart, 4¹³ ⁽¹⁶⁾, which in due time was removed from him.   Thereupon his reason returned unto him, 4³¹ ⁽³⁴⁾, and a man's heart was given unto him, 7⁴, and he glorified the God of heaven, 4³¹,³⁴. But the comparison of the two passages is in this respect irreconcilable.   In 7⁴ Babylon has the heart of a beast during its career of conquest : it is not given a man's heart till this is over and it is made to stand erect upon its feet, 7⁴.   But in 4¹³ ⁽¹⁶⁾

Nebuchadnezzar is not deprived of his man's heart till his career of conquest and statesmanlike achievements is over. Then and not till then is the beast's heart given unto him. When a period of seven times is passed his understanding is restored, 4[31 (34)]. From this insurmountable conflict of ideas it follows that it is idle to attempt to combine things that are really incompatible. So far as 7[4] refers to the growing humanization of Babylon, it has no point of contact with the temporary illness of Nebuchadnezzar in 4[13(16)]. Moreover in 7[4] we are dealing with symbols relating to the empire of Babylon: in 4[13 (16)] with a concrete fact in the life of Nebuchadnezzar.

Made to stand. הֳקִימַת is a passive perfect Hoph'al—not a Hebraism.

Two feet. רַגְלִין is here a dual as elsewhere in our author.

7[5]. The Median empire, which is referred to here as succeeding the Babylonian, is, as we have seen, a mythical one. (See p. 141 (d): also Introd. to this chapter, § 4, pp. 166 sqq.). Our author has drawn his history from tradition. There was of course a great Median empire, but it was the forerunner, not the successor, of the Babylonian.

This empire appears in the form of a bear. As the bear is inferior in strength to the lion, so the Median empire, which in 2[30] is symbolized by silver, 2[32,39], was inferior to that of Babylon, which is symbolized by gold, 2[32,38]. This statement holds true of the actual Median empire, which preceded the Babylonian.

[*A second.*] This word I have bracketed as a gloss on the word 'other' which precedes it. It is omitted by the LXX, which reads μετὰ ταύτην ἄλλο = אחריה אחרי (a mere dittograph), and Vulg. The text in 7[6] 'and lo another' supports the LXX. Th. (Hippol. εἰς τ. Δαν. iv. 1) and the Pesh., on the other hand, omit 'another', and read 'a second one'. The MT is conflate and gives both readings. But for the strong documentary evidence of the LXX and the text in 7[6] we might have accepted the reading of Th. Cf. 7[7.]

It was raised up, i. e. הֳקִמַת with some manuscripts, LXX and Th. The MT reads הֳקִמַת 'it had raised up'. The difference is immaterial so far as the meaning goes, which is far from obvious. Perhaps the words point to its inferiority in respect to the first kingdom, 2[39].

On one side, i. e. לְשִׂטַר־חַד. The rendering of the A.V. and

R.V. ᵐᵍ· follows the corrupt reading of a few manuscripts
לְשִׁטַר־חַד = 'raised up one dominion'.

Three ribs were in its mouth. These words point to the
ravenous nature of the beast—an idea suggested by those passages of the prophets in which the Medes are summoned to
ravage Babylon (Isa. 13¹⁷, Jer. 51¹¹, ²⁸). This interpretation is
confirmed by the words with which this symbolic account of this
kingdom closes: 'Arise, devour much flesh'. The later interpretation, which was unknown till the first century of our era
(see Introd. to this chapter, § 4. (1)), and which regarded the
bear as symbolizing the Medo-Persian empire, took the three
ribs to denote Lydia, Babylonia, and Egypt—the first two of
which were conquered by Cyrus and the third by Cambyses.
But this interpretation is merely one in the long line of reinterpretations of unfulfilled prophecy. It has nothing to do with
the original thought of our author.

It was said. The Aramaic idiom here אָמְרִין 'they say'.

7⁶. *Another ⌜beast⌝.* I have here with the LXX, Th., and the
Pesh. restored חֵיוָה before אחרי. The last word always follows
its noun in our author. Hence here ἕτερον θηρίον (Th.) as in 2³⁹
is wrong as to order, whereas the LXX has θηρίον ἄλλο.

Upon the back of it, i. e. גַּבַּהּ the *Qr.* For this meaning of גב
compare the Hebrew גַּב. The *Kt.* reads גַּבַּיהּ which Bevan,
Behrmann, and Driver derive from גנב, Syr. ܓܒܐ, and render
'on its sides'. The four wings are regarded as indicating the
might of the Persian empire as extending to the four quarters of
the earth, and the four heads as symbolizing the four Persian
kings, 11².

In על נבה is rendered by LXX ἐπάνω αὐτοῦ and in Th. by
ὑπεράνω αὐτῆς. This meaning על גב bears in the Targ. Jon. ii on
Lev. 1¹⁷.

And dominion was given to it. Cf. 2³⁹, where Persia is described as ruling 'over all the earth'. The LXX is here defective, but a corrupt equivalent of the clause is preserved in the
Tellan Syr. = καὶ γλῶσσα ἐδόθη αὐτῷ. This clause of the original
LXX is interesting. γλῶσσα = לְשֵׁן, which is a corruption of שָׁלְטָן,
as Bludau has observed. This corruption is not explicable from
a Hebrew original.

7⁷⁻⁸. *A fourth beast,* i. e. the Greek empire—'too fearful to
be likened to any known creature; both in strength and fierce-

ness it far surpasses its predecessors' (Bevan).   No creature or combination of creatures (as in 7[4]) could adequately express them.

7[7]. *Terrible* (אֵימְתָנִי) *and strong exceedingly.*   The LXX has a strange rendering here ὁ φόβος αὐτοῦ ὑπερφέρων ἰσχύι, which, however, can be easily explained, as due to a corruption of the Aramaic text.   Thus it=יתירה בְּתָקְפָא אֵימָתַהּ which is a corruption of אימתני וחקיפא יתירה.   אימתא (emphatic state of אימא) is found in the Aramaic of the Talmud and the Targums.   For 'terrible' the R.V. has 'powerful', which is a rendering of אֵמְתָנִי—a ἅπαξ λεγ. or rather a corrupt reading.

It was diverse from all.   These words give the impression created in the oriental mind by the conquests of Alexander. While the preceding empires had left local traditions and customs untouched, the Greek empire overthrew the older civilizations and transformed them.   It did its task with thoroughness, 'it devoured and brake in pieces and trod the residue with its feet'.

It had ten horns.   These are ten kings (cf. 7[24])—most probably successors of Alexander on the throne of Antioch.   In Jewish apocalyptic the horn is used as a symbol of a king 7[24], 8[5, 8a, 9, 21], or a dynasty of kings 8[3, 6, 7, 8b, 20, 22].   In 1 Enoch 90[9] 'the great horn' denotes Judas Maccabaeus.   1 Enoch 83-90 was written while Judas was still warring.

7[8]. *Came up.*   For סִלְקָת read סְלִקַת as in 7[20].

Among them i. e. בֵּינֵיהוֹן which the *Qr.* corrects into בֵּינֵיהֵן on the ground of the gender of קרן.   See 5[5] for like changes.

Another horn, a little one.   The 'little horn' is Antiochus Epiphanes here as in 8[9].   He was 'little' to begin with.   His success was due to his seizing the crown by treachery (11[21]).

Three of the first horns.   On the identification of these three horns see Introd. to this chapter, § 4 (2).   These three were probably (1) Seleucus IV (Philopator) murdered by his minister Heliodorus; (2) Heliodorus who was soon removed after his usurpation by Attalus and Eumenes of Pergamum; (3) Demetrius I (Soter), who was the son and lawful heir of Seleucus IV (Philopator).

Were plucked up by the roots, i.e. אתעקרו.   Here the LXX has ἐξηράνθησαν.   This is adduced as a proof that the original was Hebrew; for this word=נֻשְּׁתוּ, which could be an easy corruption of נְחִשׁ. But, unless numerous examples of this nature could be produced, it can only be regarded as a coincidence. ◦ For ἐξηράν-θησαν can be most easily explained as a corruption of ἐξήρθησαν, which latter is a rendering of נתש in Deut. 29[28], Jer. 12[17], 18[7], 2 Chron. 7[20]. Moreover, we find this corruption elsewhere in the LXX. Thus in ἐξήρανα τὸν κάρπον Amos 2[9] the verb is un-doubtedly corrupt for ἐξῆρα (ואשמיר). The same corruption is found in Joel 1[16], Zech. 10[2], Sir. 10[17], Jer. 28[36] (51[36]) in one or all the Greek MSS. This corruption was first explained by Scharfenberg : see Nestle, *Marg.* 40, who has recognized Jer. 28[36], Zech. 10[2] of the above.

Eyes like the eyes of a man. These symbolize his intelligence and shrewdness. In 8[23], 11[21], the use he made of such powers is represented ; he was double dealing, 8[23], and a flatterer when it served him, 11[21]. עַיְנִי is here a dual though a plural in form. The dual construct is עֵינֵי and with the suffix עֵינַי 4[34 (31)].

A mouth speaking great things. Cf. Ps. 12[3] 'the tongue that speaketh great things', Obad. 12, Rev. 13[5], 2 Bar. 67[7]. These words are especially appropriate to Antiochus Epiphanes. In 1 Macc. 1[24] it is recounted that he and his followers 'spake very presumptuously' (ἐλάλησαν ὑπερηφανίαν μεγάλην) after they had robbed the Temple of all its treasures. His conduct is described in analogous terms in 2 Macc. 5[17, 21]. In our text he is described in 11[36] as one who would ' Speak marvellous things against the God of gods '.

⌜*And he made war with the saints*⌝. I have with the LXX (καὶ ἐποίει πόλεμον πρὸς τοὺς ἁγίους) restored this clause to the text, as Rothstein has already proposed. This war upon the saints forms the crowning sin of the little horn, and the context requires it. For where the description of the little horn recurs in 7[21, 25], in addition to the mention of the mouth speaking presumptuous things, there is mentioned the fact that he 'made war with the saints and prevailed against them ', 7[21], or ' wore down the saints ', 7[25]. Hence at the close of this verse we should add the following Aramaic clause : ועבדה קרב עם קדישׁיא ; cf. Rev.11[7], 12[17], 19[19] on the violent measures taken by Antiochus Epiphanes against the Jews, cf. 8[10—14, 24, 25].

7[9—14]. *Divine judgement of the heathen powers.* As in 7[1-8] Daniel saw in a vision on the earth in the first year of Belshazzar the four kingdoms that would successively hold the world in thrall, so here at their close his vision is carried from earth to heaven, and he learns in the final judgement of God the right explanation of the course of the world's empires and their history. At this judgement, which he foresees in his vision, the thrones are set for the heavenly powers, the assessors of the Judge, and the Almighty Himself appears seated on a throne of fire and encompassed with myriads of angelic beings. The books are opened and the fourth beast is slain because of the horn that spoke great things, and the power of the other three beasts is taken away, though their lives are prolonged for a time. Then there comes on the clouds of heaven a being like a son of man and to him is given an everlasting dominion and a kingdom that cannot be destroyed.

7⁹. *Thrones were placed*, i.e. for the angelic assessors. On the expression cf. Ps. 122⁵ 'thrones for judgement'. Here as in 4¹⁷ the heavenly powers take part with God in the judgement. With רמיו 'were set' we may compare יריתי 'I have set', Gen. 31⁵¹. Cf. 1 Enoch 90²⁰ ' I saw till a throne was erected . . . and the Lord of his sheep sat thereon'. The Ethiopic here = ᾠκοδομήθη. But our text may have suggested the passage in Enoch.

⟨*One like*⟩ *an ancient of days*. As the texts stands עתיק יומין means literally ' one aged in days '—an aged being. In the Syriac version of Wisdom 2¹⁰ we find a close approach to the phrase in our text ܣܒܐ ܤܓܝܐܝ ܝܘܡܬܐ which is a rendering of πρεσβύτου . . . πολιὰς πολυχρονίους. Cf. Gen. 24¹ בָּא בַּיָּמִים. But there is an essential difference. In our text there is no reference to a *human* being but simply to a being. The emphasis, moreover, lies on the time element in the expression. Hence it *suggests but is not equivalent to* such expressions as 'the first and the last ', Isa. 44⁶, ' He that is enthroned of old ' (ישב קדם) Ps. 55¹⁹, and ' the Eternal One ' (ὁ αἰώνιος), 1 Bar. 4¹⁰, ¹⁴, ²⁰. But the expression in our text does not contain the element of eternity. It emphasizes the idea of longevity, while its context presupposes but does not express the idea of eternal existence. Hence it is an extraordinary expression to apply to God, and accordingly, if we take into account the fact that, throughout this and all other Jewish apocalypses, every reference to or description of God is couched in terms of the utmost reverence, we find it impossible to accept this irreverent designation of God as original in its present form. If this be so, it is more than probable that, instead of ' an ancient

of days' the text originally read 'one like an ancient of days'.
This would be the true apocalyptic form of expression, resembling that in Ezek. 1²⁶. In this latter passage, it is true, the idea
of humanity is present 'the likeness as it were the appearance
of a man' (רמות כמראה אדם) but not in our author. On the above
grounds I suggest that כעתיק יומין 'one like an ancient of days',
was an apocalyptic designation of God in Aramaic. Clem. Alex.
Paed. ii. 10 alone attests this expression : ὡσεὶ παλαιὸς ἡμερῶν and
LXX 7¹³ of our text. When this designation was once accepted,
the next stage in its development was possible, i.e. to drop the
comparative particle and therewith to transform the *indefinite
apocalyptic* form of expression into a *definite non-apocalyptic* i. e.
instead of 'like an ancient of days' we have 'the Ancient of Days'
(7¹³, ²²) i. e. עתיק יומיא. We have an exactly similar development
in the case of 'like a son of man' (7¹³) and 'the Son of Man'
(1 Enoch 46², &c.). The latter has no meaning apart from its
development out of 'like a son of man'. The phrase 'an ancient
of days' denotes simply, as above said, *an aged being.* But the
apocalyptic phrase 'like an ancient of days' affirms at once
a likeness and an unlikeness. The likeness consists in the
longevity and probably the dignity that goes therewith, the unlikeness in the fact that the Being so described is not one whose
age is measured by years but one who is at once 'the first' and 'the
last', the Everlasting. I have accordingly inserted כ before עתיק,
and so brought the expression into conformity with its context.

*His raiment was as snow and the hair of his head was spotless
as white wool.* There are three ways of dealing with the text.
(1) The Massoretic : ' His raiment was as white snow and the
hair of his head like spotless wool '. This is practically abandoned by scholars. (2) 'His raiment was white as snow and
the hair of his head was as spotless wool'. This departure from
the Massoretic accentuation has the support of Th. (Vulg., and
Pesh.) τὸ ἔνδυμα αὐτοῦ ὡσεὶ χιὼν λευκόν καὶ ἡ θρὶξ τῆς κεφαλῆς ὡς ἔριον
καθαρόν. But, though this rendering is preferable to (1) in the
first clause, it is most unsatisfactory in the second. For wool is
neither necessarily spotless or white. Hence we must fall back
on (3), which has the support of the LXX. (3) 'His raiment
was as snow and the hair of his head was spotless as white
wool ': or 'as white spotless wool '. Since the LXX reads ἔχων
περιβολὴν ὡσεὶ χιόνα (*al.* χιών) καὶ τὸ τρίχωμα τῆς κεφαλῆς αὐτοῦ ὡσεὶ ἔριον

λευκὸν καθαρόν, it is clear that in the Aramaic it presupposes the חִוָּר (= λευκός) as belonging to the second clause and not to the first and as following immediately after כעמר. This is, we may justly conclude, the original text. It has the support, moreover, of Rev. 1¹⁴ ἡ κεφαλὴ αὐτοῦ καὶ αἱ τρίχες λευκαὶ ὡς ἔριον λευκόν—a free rendering of the Aramaic text presupposed by the LXX. There is a still earlier testimony in 1 Enoch 46¹ which = ἡ κεφαλὴ αὐτοῦ ὡς ἔριον λευκόν (or λευκή). Both renderings are possible, but in my translation of 1 Enoch I ought undoubtedly to have adopted the first. The Aramaic therefore should be read כעמר חור נקא = 'spotless as white wool'. נקא means 'cleansed', 'free from spot', but not 'white'. Hence, since wool may have two or more colours, it requires the epithet 'white', i.e. חִוָּר.

His throne was fiery flames. We might compare 1 Enoch 14¹⁸⁻²² (pre-Maccabean in date) with 7⁹⁻¹⁰ of our text.

18. 'And I looked and saw therein a lofty throne:
     Its appearance was as crystal,
     And the wheels thereof as the shining sun,
     And there was the vision of cherubim.
19. And from underneath the throne came streams of flaming fire,
     So that I could not look thereon.
20. And the Great Glory sat thereon,
     And His raiment shone more brightly than the sun,
     And was whiter than any snow . . .
22. The flaming fire was round about Him,
     And a great fire was near unto Him . . .
     Ten thousand times ten thousand were before Him :
     Yet He needed no counsellor.'

The wheels thereof burning fire. Cf. 1 Enoch 14¹⁸ quoted above and Ezek. 1¹⁵ sqq., 10².

7¹⁰. *A fiery stream . . . [went forth] from before Him.* Cf. 1 Enoch 14¹⁹ ὑποκάτω τοῦ θρόνου ἐξεπορεύοντο ποταμοὶ πυρὸς φλεγομένου.

Flowed [and went forth]. It is a question whether the original text was נְגֵד וְנָפֵק; for the LXX has only ἐξεπορεύετο=נפק and Th. only εἷλκεν (Hippol. εἰς τ. Δαν. iv. 1) = נגד. Pesh. and Vulg. incorporate both readings as does the MT, while Justin Martyr (*Dial. c. Tryph*, 51) reads εἷλκεν ἐκπορευόμενος. Since the Pesh. and Vulg. are confessedly the latest of these authorities and the MT in its present form often very late, the natural conclusion is that

they contain here a conflate text. Which of the two readings is
then the original? Since נגד is a late word and appears here
apparently for the first time in Aramaic, though it occurs in
many senses, as well as in that which it bears here, and in the
Targums and Syriac, it appears most reasonable to regard נפק
as an explanatory marginal gloss upon נגד. נפק is found in a
fifth century inscription B.C. (CIS. ii. 113. 21) and very frequently
in the fifth century *Aram. Pap.* (Cowley, 30⁵, 31⁴, &c.) though
not in exactly the same connexion as in our text. Hence I have
relegated 'and went forth' to a foot-note, though with some
hesitation.

Thousand thousands . . . stood before him. Possibly derived
from 1 Enoch 14²² (before 170 B.C.) μύριαι μυριάδες ἐστήκασιν ἐνώπιον
αὐτοῦ. On the other hand the phrases 'thousand thousands . . .
yea ten thousand times ten thousand' seem to have been the
source of 1 Enoch 40¹ (before 64 B.C.) 'thousands of thousands
and ten thousand times ten thousand', 71⁸, ¹³, Rev. 5¹¹, though
in this last passage the order of the phrases is reversed. Cf.
Deut. 33², 1 Enoch 1⁹, 40¹, 71⁸, ¹³, Jude 14, 15. For the *Kt.* רבון
read רִבְּוָן. The *Qr.* רִבְבָן is a Hebraism. See Kautzsch § 65. 4.

The judgement was set. The judgement here = 'those who
judge', just as in Jer. 23¹⁸, ²², Ps. 89⁸, Job 15⁸ 'council' (i.e.
סוד) = 'those who deliberate'.

The books were opened. There are several kinds of books in
the Old Testament and later Jewish Literature.

(1) The book of life (or its equivalents ' God's book' in Exod.
32³² ˢᵠ· ' Blot me I pray thee out of thy book'; 'book of the
living ', Ps. 69²⁸) was a register of the citizens of the Theocratic
community. To have one's name written in this book implied
the privilege of participating in the *temporal* blessings of the
Theocracy, Isa. 4³, while to be blotted out of this book meant
exclusion therefrom. In the O. T. this expression was originally confined to *temporal* blessings only, but in our author 12¹
it is transformed through the influence of the new conception of
the Kingdom, and distinctly refers to an immortality of blessedness. This meaning it has in 1 Enoch 104¹, 47³, Jub. 30²⁰ ˢᵠᵠ·
In the N.T. the phrase is of frequent recurrence, Phil. 4³, Rev.
3⁵, 13⁸, &c.

(2) Books in which the deeds of men were recorded. For
those wherein good deeds were recorded, cf. Ps. 56⁸, Mal. 3¹⁶,

Jubilees 30^{22}; wherein evil deeds were recorded, cf. Isa. 65^6, 1 Enoch 81^4, 89$^{61-64,\,68,\,70,\,71}$, &c., 2 Bar. 24^1; wherein both good and evil deeds were recorded, cf. 7^{10} of our author, Rev. 20^{12} (βιβλία ἠνοίχθησαν), Asc. Is. 9^{22}, Aboth 2^1. For a completer treat.ment of this question see the note on my edition of 1 Enoch 47^3; Dalman, *Worte Jesu*, i. 169 seq; *KAT.*^{3} ii. 405; Bousset, *Rel. d. Judenthums*, 247; Weber, *Jüd. Theol.*^{2} 242, 282 seqq.; Volz, *Jüd. Eschatologie*, 93 seq., 266, 316.

7^{11}. The fourth beast, i. e. the Greek Empire, is destroyed once and for all because of the blasphemies of Antiochus Epiphanes (7^8); for the measure of its guilt has now become full (8^{23}).

I beheld at that time, i. e. חזה הוית באדין. This order is without a parallel in Daniel or Ezra. באדין or אדין occur taken together fifty-one times elsewhere in Daniel and always at the beginning of the clause and not as here after the verb. But both the LXX and Th. support this abnormal order—ἐθεώρουν τότε: so also does Justin Mart., *Dial. c. Tryph.* 31 who in the main follows the LXX here. But the Vulg. omits 'at that time' and the Syr. the entire first clause but through *hmt.* But I retain the above order, since I find in 1 Enoch 83–90 (a vision written before 161 B.C. and that by a seer acquainted with the work of our author) that the order 'after that I saw' occurs four times 89$^{19,\,30,\,72}$, 90^2, and 'I saw at that time' only in 90^{26}; similarly, 'again I saw' 86$^{1,\,3}$ 87^1, 89$^{2,\,7}$, but 'I saw again' in 89$^{3,\,51}$.

Because of the voice, &c. These words give the reason for the destruction of the beast which is mentioned in the dependent clause. They would more naturally have followed in that clause.

Horn spake. The MT. here adds 'I beheld' חזה הוית, but it is clearly uncalled for. It is omitted both by the LXX (as the Syr^h. proves) and Th. and Justin Mart. (*Dial. c. Tryph.* 31). On the other hand the MT has the support of the Pesh. and Vulg. It is thus a late insertion.

Destroyed. הובד Hoph'al from אבד.

He was given to be burned by fire. This is the final place of punishment—a place of fire as in 1 Enoch 10^6, 18^{11}, 21$^{7-10}$. These passages are older than our text. Cf. 91$^{24-27}$, which belongs to a Maccabean section.

7^{12}. The apparent meaning of this verse is that the three remaining beasts are not destroyed forthwith as the fourth beast. In 2$^{32-35}$ the four empires are destroyed simultaneously, but

there owing to the *nature of the vision* their destruction is represented as taking place contemporaneously, though in reality it
was not so. The great image representing in itself the four
kingdoms falls all at once, and so implies a simultaneous destruction. But here the first three heathen powers survive the loss
of their dominion as *nations*; as empires, they cease to be : as
for the fourth empire it was to be utterly destroyed. The
remaining Gentile nations are not doomed to this annihilation,
but are to exist for an indefinite time and to become subject to
the kingdom of the saints ($7^{14,27}$).

The rest of the beasts. The LXX has here τοὺς κύκλῳ αὐτοῦ,
where the MT has שאר חיותא. This is not an isolated anomaly;
for in 7^7 and 7^{19}, where we have κύκλῳ and κυκλόθεν respectively,
the MT has simply שארא. Possibly κύκλῳ αὐτοῦ in 7^{12} is a rendering of שַׁחֲרָנוֹהִי, which may be a corruption of שאר חיותא.
I am writing שׁ for ס. It is wholly impossible to explain the
corruption from the hypothesis of a Hebrew original.

$7^{13,14}$. *The eternal kingdom of the saints.*

7^{13}. *Came on the clouds of heaven.* Here I follow the LXX
ἐπὶ τῶν νεφελῶν . . . ἤρχετο, and not Th. which has μετὰ τῶν νεφελῶν . . .
ἐρχόμενος. The LXX and Pesh. preserve here the original text.
The ʻone like a son of manʼ comes not ʻwithʼ but ʻon the
cloudsʼ. The clouds are not his companions (μετά), but the
chariot as it were on which he approaches the Ancient of Days.
The figure is suggested by the O.T., Ps. 104^3, ʻWho maketh the
clouds his chariotʼ: cf. Is. 19^1. But עַל (=ʻonʼ) which the LXX
attests was corrupted—*perhaps not earlier than the beginning of the
Christian era* into עם (ʻwithʼ). The text presupposed by the
LXX is followed by the Pesh., also by Matt. 24^{30}, 26^{64} (in both
cases ἐπί); Rev. $14^{14,16}$, Justin, *Ap.* i. 51, *Dial.* 120 (ἐπάνω in
both); Didache 16^8 (ἐπάνω). Mark 13^{26} (ἐρχόμενον ἐν νεφέλαις μετὰ
δυνάμεως) and Cyprian, *Test.* ii. 26, are doubtful, but should
probably be classed here. The reading of the MT עם = μετά
is followed by Th., Mark 14^{62}, Rev. 1^7, 4 Ezra 13^3, Justin,
Dial. 31, Tert., *Adv. Marc.* iii. 7, and also by the Vulg. Thus
the corrupt reading had established itself in Mark, Rev., 4 Ezra
within the first century in our era, but Matt. (*bis*), Justin (*bis*),
the Pesh., and the Didache (authorities of the first three centuries) still attest the primitive text first found in the second century version B.C.; i.e. the LXX. Cf. Dalman, *Worte Jesu*, p. 198

One like unto a son of man, i. e. כבר אנש. On the subsequent
history of this phrase in Jewish Apocalyptic see my edition of
1 *Enoch*[2] 46[2], n. 48[2] n., pp. lxiii.—vi, 306-9. In apocalyptic
visions where men are symbolized by beasts, angels and other
supernatural beings are symbolized by men. This symbolism
will be found on a large scale in 1 Enoch 89-90. If, therefore,
the expression is to be taken strictly, it undoubtedly suggests
a supernatural being or a body of such beings. Since the beings
thus referred to are, according to the interpretation of the
angel, the people of ‘ the Saints of the Most High ’ (7[18,22,25,27]), we
are to infer that the faithful remnant of Israel are to be transformed into heavenly or supernatural beings as in 1 Enoch 90[38]
(161 B.C.) and in later apocalypses, which expect an everlasting
kingdom upon earth, whose members will be clad with garments
of light: cf. 1 Enoch 62[15,16], 108[12]. The peculiar expression
קדישי עליונין, 7[18], confirms the above view. See note *in loc.*

They brought him near before him. This is the reading of the
MT, Th., Pesh., and Vulg. The LXX οἱ παρεστηκότες παρῆσαν αὐτῷ
presupposes a different text, i. e. קאמיא קרבו קדמוהי ‘ They that
stood by drew near before him ’. These, i. e. ‘ they that stood
by ’, are mentioned again in 7[16]. This reading is supported by
Tertullian, *Adv. Marc.* iii. 7, ‘ qui adsistebant ’, and Cyprian,
Test. ii. 26, ‘ qui adsistebant ei ’. In 7[16] there is apparently an
order of angels in immediate attendance on the Ancient of Days.
If we might insert קאמיא before קדמוהי in the MT, we could interpret this class of angels as a like order in attendance on ‘ the one
like unto a son of man ’. This use of קום קדם has already occurred
in 7[10]. The text then would run ‘ they that stood before him
(i. e. the Son of Man) brought him near to him (the Ancient of
Days) ’. So at all events Justin understood the text. Thus
these attendants are angels of the Son of Man, *Apol.* i. 31,
ὡς υἱὸς ἀνθρώπου ἔρχεται ἐπάνω τῶν νεφελῶν τοῦ οὐρανοῦ καὶ οἱ ἄγγελοι αὐτοῦ
σὺν αὐτῷ. These, as his escort, present him to the Ancient of
Days: *Dial.* 31 οἱ παρεστηκότες προσήγαγον. The text is uncertain.

7[14]. The sovereignty of the Saints (7[18,22,27]) is described as
everlasting and in terms used elsewhere of the sovereignty of
God: cf. 3[33] (4[3]), 6[27(26)]. There is no personal Messiah. The
writer of the Parables of 1 Enoch 37-71 was the first student of
our text, so far as existing literature goes, to interpret ‘ one
like a son of man ’ in this passage as relating to an individual.

The moment he did so he rose to the conception of a super-
human Messiah, by following the natural method of interpreting
the vision.   See second note on preceding verse.

7[15]. *And my spirit . . . even of me Daniel.* The original רוּחִי
אֲנָה דָנִיֵּאל is literally 'the spirit of me Daniel'. This construction of the pronoun with the suffix is common to both Aramaic
and Hebrew. For the former cf. Ezra 7[21] מִנִּי אֲנָה אַרְתַּחְשַׁסְתָּא,
and for the latter in 8[1] of our author and 1 Sam. 25[24] בִּי אֲנִי
'on me'. Cf. Cowley 81[14] where אנה = 'of me'.

Was distressed. In אֶתְכְּרִיַּת the daghesh in the *yodh* is to call
attention to its being a consonant here. The Hebrew rendering
of this verb combined with רוּחִ' occurs in 2[3] וַתִּפָּעֶם רוּחִי—a phrase
which occurs in Gen. 41[8]. In 2[1] of our text the translator uses
the Hithpaʿel וַתִּתְפָּעֶם רוחי.

Therewith. So the LXX ἐν τούτοις. Here the MT reads בגו
נדנה, which is rendered 'in the midst of the sheath' if we
punctuate נִדְנֶה, or 'in the midst of its sheath' if we punctuate
נִדְנַהּ or נִדְנָהּ. The word is of Persian origin *nidāna* (Bevan).
It is found in later Hebrew—1 Chron. 21[27], where it bears the
meaning of the 'scabbard' or 'sheath' of a sword. It is strange
that, when it means the sheath of a sword in the Targums, it is
written לְדָנָא or לִדְנָא: cf. 2 Sam. 20[8]; Ezek. 21[3,4,5]; Jer. 47[6];
Ezek. 21[3,4,5]; except in 1 Sam. 17[51]; Ezek. 21[30]. In the former
of the last two passages according to Levy, *Ch. W.* i. 403:
ii. 93 both readings are found: in my copy of the Targum נדנא
is given. The latter seems a corruption of the former. We
may reasonably conclude that לדנא was always used to mean
sheath of a sword. Turning to the use of נדנא we find that Levy
gives only two passages where it occurs in the same connexion
as in our text, i. e. Sanh. 108[a] (לנדנה ·· שלא = 'that their soul
should not return to it sheath') and Ber. rabba, § 26, which, as
Driver recognizes, are in all likelihood based on our text. But
if our text is itself corrupt, these two passages are as worthless
as their original.

Noting the singular character of this phrase, Weiss, Buhl, Marti,
and Driver emend בגו נדנה into בְּנִין דְּנָה 'on this account'. But
Driver recognizes that בנין occurs only in the Jerusalem Targums.
To this we may add the further fact that it is unknown in the
Aramaic inscriptions and the *Aram. Papyri.* Hence I conclude
that this attractive suggestion is of doubtful worth, and suggest

in its stead that בגונדנה is to be taken as a corruption of בגודנה,
of which the LXX ἐν τούτοις and Vulg. *in his* would be exact renderings. The corruption lies, therefore, in נדנה and not in the
בגו, which occurs *as a preposition* in our text in 3²⁵, 7¹⁵, but in
4⁷ and in Ezra in 4¹⁵ in the form בנוא. Furthermore it occurs
in the *Aram. Pap.* frequently *as an adverb* = 'therein' or
'therewith', and in a connexion exactly similar to that in our
text. Thus in 2⁹ טיב לבבן בגו 'our heart is content therewith':
as also in 15⁶,¹⁵, 20⁹. It is thus a familiar phrase, and בגו
was thus used for the first time in Aramaic hitherto known
as a preposition in Ezra 4¹⁵, 6² (with suffixes and also in
the Persian period) with nouns, Lidzbarski, *Eph.*, p. 211, b²
בגו בירתא = 'in the fortress', as in our author, later in the
Targums). Thus on the basis of the LXX supported by the
usage of the phrase in older Aramaic and the grammatical use
of בגו in our author I have emended as above, and therefore
translate 'therewith' or 'in this matter'. Is נדנה a real
Aramaic word? It is found once in late Hebrew in the O.T.,
i. e. 1 Chron. 21²⁷.

7¹⁶. *One of them that stood by.* This appears to be one of the
angels in attendance on God (7¹³). The angel gives at first a
short and summary answer (7¹⁷⁻¹⁸), and afterwards a full interpretation in answer to Daniel's request for further information.
In the visions of the earlier prophets God Himself spake to the
prophets (Amos 7, 8; Isa. 6; Jer. 1, &c.) but in the later prophets
the part of the interpreter is discharged by an angel in Zech.
1⁷⁻6⁸; Daniel 1; Enoch; Test. xii Patriarchs; Jubilees; 2 Baruch;
4 Ezra. In Ezek. 40–48 we have a combination of both methods,
and this section accordingly marks the period of transition from
the one method to the other.

7¹⁷⁻¹⁸. *The angel's interpretation of the vision in 7¹¹⁻¹⁴.*

7¹⁷. *Kings.* Here the LXX, Th. (βασιλεῖαι), and Vulg. read
'kingdoms'. But this is only an interpretation and not a
translation, seeing that in 8²⁰ 'kings' are used as synonymous
with kingdoms.

[*Which are four.*] This phrase is omitted by the LXX. It is
certainly unnecessary; for the seer knows perfectly well the
number of the kingdoms. It may be due to a corruption of the
original text attested by the LXX. See next note.

⌐*Which shall be destroyed from the earth*⌐. So the LXX αἱ

ἀπολοῦνται ἀπὸ τῆς γῆς. So also Justin, *Dial.* 31. Here the LXX is certainly right and the MT hopelessly wrong. To say that these kingdoms 'arise from the earth' is contrary to the traditional idea as to the origin of these kingdoms; for as we know from Jewish tradition these kingdoms arose from the sea; cf. Rev. 13[1] ἐκ τῆς θαλάσσης θηρίον ἀναβαῖνον; 4 Ezra 11[1] 'ascendebat de mari aquila'; cf. 12[10-11];[1] also Rev. 11[7], 17[8], where the beast comes from the abyss, or 13[11] where it denotes the priesthood of the imperial cultus. But it is not only contrary to tradition but to the belief of our author himself. For in 7[3] we read that 'four great beasts came up from the sea'. But this is not all. Even Th. preserves in its conflate text the earlier reading, as we shall see presently, and the later redactional addition.

Again let us observe how wholly incongruous is the text of the MT. The angel interprets the vision in 7[17-18], and tells Daniel that these kingdoms 'shall arise' out of the earth. But it cannot be said of the Babylonian empire, even from the assumed date of the Seer (i.e. 6th cent. B.C.), that it 'shall arise'; for it has already arisen and is fast nearing its end. But this is not all. Immediately after this incorrect statement as to the *future* rise of the heathen empires, the angel proceeds to declare, without a single allusion to their subsequent destruction, that the Saints of the Most High shall receive the kingdom. Yet in the vision itself an entire section 7[11-14], prior to the setting up of the Messianic kingdom, is devoted first to the destruction of the *power* of the beasts, and then to that of the beasts themselves.

Now the way out of the above *impasse* lies before us in the LXX: 'These great beasts are four kingdoms, which shall be destroyed from off the earth', the relative clause of which is a translation of מן ארעא (or יהובדון, cf. 7[11]) די יאבדון. Of the correctness of this retroversion we may feel reasonably confident, seeing that in 2[24], 7[11, 26] ἀπολλύναι is a rendering of אבד.

If this was the original text, we ought to be able to explain some of the corruptions in the other versions. With the Vulg. we need not concern ourselves, since it is almost a reproduction of the MT. The Pesh. follows the MT closely but it does not admit that the beasts arose 'from the earth': it changes this

---

[1] 4 Ezra 13[3] which represents the Messiah as arising from the sea is against Jewish tradition and should be excised as an interpolation. All the versions except the Latin contain this interpolation.

intô 'on the earth' and so escapes creating a violent contradiction with the statement in 7³. We have now to deal with Th. (reproduced by Hippolytus in his commentary on Daniel (c. 210–230) iv. 10 ταῦτα τὰ θηρία τὰ τέσσαρα, τέσσαρες βασιλεῖαι ἀναστήσονται ἐπὶ τῆς γῆς αἱ ἀρθήσονται. ἀναστήσονται is a rendering of יקומון, but, as the Pesh., Th. has changed 'from the earth' to 'on the earth'. As we have already observed, Th. is conflate, as the relative clause αἱ ἀρθήσονται proves. It has all the appearance of the addition of a later hand. At all events αἴρω is not used by Th. elsewhere with the meaning it clearly bears here; for this clause = 'which shall be destroyed' (= יאבדון) or 'pass away' (= יעדון). The LXX renders די לא יערה by ἥτις οὐ μὴ ἀρθῇ in 7¹⁴, and תֵּאַבֵּר by ἦρας in Isa. 26¹⁴. This addition to Th. was made by a scribe who was acquainted with another form of the Aramaic text than that which Th. reproduces. This text preserved יאבדון, which the LXX presupposes, or possibly יעדון a corruption of it. Thus Th. in its present form reproduces the meaningless text of the reviser ἀναστήσονται, but a later scribe adds the original reading in a relative clause. We can now rewrite the text which not only Jewish tradition on this question, but also the actual text of our author in 7³ and the LXX and even Th. require, and this text was אלין חיותא רברבתא אנין ערבעה מלכין די יאבדון מן ארעא 'These great beasts are four kings which shall be destroyed from off the earth'.

7¹⁸. *Saints of the Most High.* Cf. 7²²ᵃ,²⁵,²⁷. קדישי עליונין (rendered by the LXX and Th. by ἅγιοι ὑψίστου) is a peculiar designation for the Saints; for in 4¹⁰ קדיש is used of an angel. This phrase is entirely different from הסידי עליונין. In the Psalms (30⁴, 31²³, &c.) the Saints are the חסידים. But our author has chosen the phrase in our text to express the divine or supernatural character of God's people as contrasted with the other peoples of the earth. In 7²¹,²²ᵇ 'the Saints of the Most High' are spoken of simply as 'saints'. See note on 7¹³. עליונין may here, as Hitzig and other scholars explain it, be due to the plural preceding. Cf. בָּתֵּי כְלָאִים as the plural of בית כלא (Isa. 42⁷,²². Other scholars with Driver take עליונים as plural of majesty, and compare the use of קדושים for God in Prov. 9¹⁰, also Joshua 24¹⁹. עליון is not Aramaic but Hebrew. The Aramaic equivalent for it is עֶלָּיָא, עֶלָּאָה, 4¹⁴ ⁽¹⁷⁾, ²¹⁽²⁴⁾.

The kingdom. Though the phrase 'kingdom of God' is not

found in Daniel, we have here substantially the thought for which it stands. The thought here is not 'the divine sovereignty'—the meaning it bears all but universally in the N.T. and Rabbinic writings, but 'a divinely organized community'. This is clear from 7¹⁴, where the rule of the saints is described in terms that are elsewhere used of the rule of God Himself: cf. 4³¹ ⁽³⁴⁾, 6²⁶.

Possess. החסן is found often in the *Arm. Pap.* (Cowley, 7², 8², &c.). The Hebrew also has nouns and adjectives derived from this Aramaic (?) root. As Cowley remarks (p. 20) it is the regular word for 'holding property'.

The kingdom. MT, Pesh., and Vulg. add 'for ever and' against LXX and Th.

7¹⁹. *To know the truth.* לְיַצָּבָא is the Pa'el inf. of יצב. We have the adjective יַצִּיב = 'certain', 'true' in 2⁸,⁴⁵, and a substantive יְצִיבָא in 7¹⁶.

Nails of brass. The absence of this phrase in 7⁷ is strange.

7²⁰. *That had eyes.* In וְעַיְנִין לַהּ it is said that we have the solitary instance of *vav* apodosis in Biblical Aramaic. But in Cowley's edition of the *Aram. Pap.* Aḥ. 160 we have a fifth century B.C. example of this idiom in Aramaic, if his restoration of the passage is valid, which is doubtful. In the Hebrew in 8¹⁰ we have another use of *vav*, i.e. *vav* explicative. See Ges.-Kautzsch, § 154 *a*, n. *b*.

Appearance was more stout, &c. The small horn (7⁸) grew quickly to a great size (8⁹).

7²¹⁻²². *A recapitulation of* 7⁸⁻¹², ¹³⁻¹⁴. The only addition is the clause 'and prevailed against them'. This is repeated in another form in 7²⁵, where the little horn is to 'wear down the saints'. The clause 'made war with the saints' has already occurred according to the original text.

7²¹. *Prevailed against them*: till the intervention of the Most High.

7²². *The Ancient of Days*, i.e. עַתִּיק יוֹמַיָּא. Here the apocalyptic form of the expression (see 7⁹ note) is dropped as in 7¹³.

Judgement ⟨*sat and dominion*⟩ *was given.* I here follow Ewald and other scholars in restoring יְתִב וְשָׁלְטָנָא before יְהַב. Cf. 7¹⁰ ᵇ, ¹⁴, ²⁶, ²⁷. Otherwise a different meaning must be assigned to דִּינָא here (i.e. 'judgement', i.e. 'justice') from that which belongs to it in 7¹⁰,²⁶, i.e. 'judgement was given in favour of the saints'.

The saints do not judge, but God alone. They are His assessors.

The time came, i. e. the time fixed by God as the limit of heathen rule. Cf. Luke 21[8] ὁ καιρὸς ἤγγικεν.

Take possession of. On this meaning of החסן see note on 7[18].

7[23]. *A fourth kingdom . . . diverse from all the kingdoms.* This kingdom was different in the eyes of the Seer from all the kingdoms that went before, and more terrible in its destructive activities.

The whole earth. This is to be understood rhetorically as in 2[39].

7[24]. *Shall be diverse, &c.* The eleventh king shall be diverse from the ten not only in removing his three predecessors, but in his blasphemies against the Most High and his persecution of the saints.

7[25]. *Speak words against* (לצד) *the Most High.* Cf. 11[36] 'Speak marvellous things against (על) the God of gods'.

Against. Though לצד is derived from the Hebrew צד, it bears a meaning which has no parallel in the Hebrew. In the sense of 'against' the Hebrew would be לנגד as in 10[13], Prov. 21[30], ל after certain verbs (Gen. 27[42]; 2 Kings 5[7], &c.), or על as in the parallel passage in our author in 11[36]. Nor in the Targums does לצד appear ever to be used in a hostile sense. Hence the word may be simply a corruption of על, which bears a hostile sense in 3[19,29] (על · · ויאמר), 6[5]. By this word the Pesh. renders the preposition that stood in the text and the Vulg. by *contra*. The LXX and Th. have here respectively εἰς and πρός, which show no sign of the presence of such a peculiar word as לצד. In 3[19] Th. has ἐπί, 3[29] κατά, as renderings of על. In 3[29] the LXX renders על (= 'against') by εἰς, in 3[19] by ἐπί.

Wear out. The Pe'al of בלא occurs in the sense of 'to be worn out' in the *Aram. Pap.* (Cowley 26[1]). Here it is the Pa'el, and 'shall wear out' expresses the meaning well. Cf. LXX κατα-τρίψει, Th. παλαιώσει. There is no ground, therefore, for taking it to mean 'shall afflict', as Bevan suggests, who compares 1 Chron. 17[9] where לבלתו is substituted for לענותו, cf. 2 Sam. 7[10]. Driver compares the Targ. on Isa. 3[15], 'the faces of the poor ye wear away' (מְבַלְּיִן).

Shall think: i. e. יסבר. This word occurs in the *Aram. Pap.* (Cowley, 37[7]).

The times and the law. Antiochus attempted to suppress the religious festivals of the Jews and the law: cf. 1 Macc. 1⁴⁴⁻⁹. The law (דת = Hebrew תורה) here is the Mosaic law as in 6⁶⁽⁵⁾, and the times are the set times for all the Jewish religious observances, as well as their great festivals. Antiochus interfered also with the heathen cults: cf. 1 Macc. 1⁴¹,⁴², a passage which is confirmed by our text in 11³⁷.

A time and times and half a time. The same expression in its Hebrew form recurs in 12⁷ and in Greek in Rev. 12¹⁴ καιρὸν καὶ καιροὺς καὶ ἥμισυ καιροῦ. A time here means a year as in 4¹⁶ (see note). Hence this period during which the Jewish religion was to be suppressed was three and a half years. This was the traditional limit assigned to the kingdom of the Antichrist. Here this period began with the legation of Apollonius about June, 168, 1 Macc. 1²⁰,²⁹, and terminated in 165 B.C. on the 25th of Chislev (i.e. Dec.) on the rededication of the Temple (1 Macc. 4⁵²,⁵³). The edict of Antiochus (1 Macc. 1⁴¹ seqq.) was issued contemporaneously with or later than the legation of Apollonius and was enforced on Chislev (Dec.) 15, 168 (1 Macc. 1⁵⁴). If we assume that the edict of Antiochus followed immediately on the legation of Apollonius, then the rededication of the Temple occurred exactly three years after its desecration. In any case this prediction was fulfilled with reasonable accuracy. For like predictions cf. that of Jeremiah relating to Hananiah in Jer. 28¹⁶⁻¹⁷, or of Isaiah in relation to Damascus, Isa. 8⁴, which was fulfilled within three years or so (Montg.). See note on 8¹⁴, where another suggestion as to the beginning of this period is given.

Times. עִדָּנִין has here a dual sense, cf. עֵינִין in 7⁸.

7²⁶⁻²⁷. *At the close of the three and a half years the judgement will take place, and the kingdom of the Saints be established, which is to embrace every country under heaven and not merely the fourth kingdom.*

7²⁶. *The judgement shall sit.* Cf. 7¹⁰ᵇ,¹¹ᵇ,²². יִתִּב Imperfect of יְתִב.

His dominion shall be taken away. Literally 'they shall take away his dominion'. Cf. 7

So that it may be consumed, &c. לְהַשְׁמָדָה, Active to be rendered passively in English.

Unto everlasting. עַד סוֹפָא ('unto the end') as in 6²⁶.

7²⁷. *Of the kingdoms,* i.e. מַלְכְוָת which is in the construct before the preposition תחות and the following words—all which are treated as a substantive—in Aramaic a unique construction. In Hebrew we find the construct case frequently before prepositions : before בְּ in Isa. 9² שִׂמְחַת בקציר 'the joy in the harvest' ; 2 Sam. 1²¹ ; also before לְ, אֶל, מִן, עַל. See Ges.-Kautzsch, § 130 a. This construction is frequent in Syr.

Under the whole heaven. Cf. 9¹² and Deut. 2²⁵, 4¹⁹, &c., whence this phrase is derived.

Shall be given. The perfect יְהִיבַת is used for the future to express certainty. Cf. 6⁵ השכחנא and 11³⁶ נעשׂתה.

Its kingdom is an everlasting kingdom. The kingdom is that of the Saints. °On this phrase see note on 4³¹. The same terms are applied to the kingdom of the Saints as to the kingdom of God. They ultimately come to be one and the same.

7²⁸. *Here,* lit. 'hitherto'=Hebrew עַד־כֹּה Exod. 7¹⁶ ; Josh. 17¹⁴

My thoughts, &c. Cf. 4¹⁶ ⁽¹⁹⁾, 5⁶, ¹⁰.

Changed upon me. Or, since 'upon me' is a *dativus ethicus* simply read 'changed'. Cf. 5⁶, ⁹.

Kept the matter in my heart. Cf. LXX 4²⁵ (τοὺς λόγους ἐν τῇ καρδίᾳ συνετήρησε) : Gen. 37¹¹, T. Lev. 6², 8¹⁹ ; Luke 2¹⁹.

SECTION VIII

i. e. Chapter 8, the Vision of the Seer in the third year of Belshazzar.

The introduction to this chapter deals wholly with the MT, the LXX, and other Versions. and the help rendered by the versions towards the recovery of the original Hebrew version or even of the Aramaic original.

§ 1. *Hebrew renderings in the MT of Aramaic phrases which have already occurred in* 2⁴⁻⁷.

8⁵. הייתי מבין והנה a rendering of משתכל הוית ואלו in 7⁸.

8⁷. ירמסהו ,,   ,, ברגליה רפסה 7⁷,¹⁹. In these two passages exactly the same events are recorded of Antiochus.

8⁹. קרן אחרת צעירה (emended) a rendering of קרן אחרי זעירה 7⁸.

יתר   ,,   ,, יתירה 3²², 7⁷,¹⁹.

8¹⁵. ואבקשה בינה   ,,   ,, צבית ליצבה 7¹⁹.

§ 2. *Interpolations in the MT.*

8². ויהי בראתי where it has a different meaning from that which it has in 8¹⁵ and usually. See note *in loc.*

8². ואראה בחזון. See note *in loc.*

8²¹. השעיר interpolated after הצפיר. First appeared as a marginal gloss, explaining the Aramaism.

8²⁴. ולא בכחו.

§ 3. *Corruptions in the MT emended by means of the LXX and other versions.*

8⁵. צפיר [ה]עזים, LXX, Th. τράγος αἰγῶν.

8⁸. חזות corrupt for אחרות, LXX ἕτερα.

8¹¹⁻¹³. MT very corrupt. Read ועד שר הצבא הגדילה וממנה הורם התמיד ותשלך מקום ומקדש יצרה. 12. ויתן על ⌐מזבח⌐ התמיד הפשע וַתִּשְׁלַ֔ךְ אמת אַ֥רצה ועשתה והצליחה. ... 13ᵇ. התמיד ⌐מורם⌐ והפשע השמם נָתָ֫ן וקרש יצדה מרמס.

LXX ἐξήρθη θυσία καὶ ἐρράχθη ὁ τόπος [αὐτῶν] ... καὶ τὸ ἅγιον ἐρημωθή-σεται. 12. ἐγενήθησαν ἐπὶ τῇ θυσίᾳ αἱ ἁμαρτίαι ... 13. ... ἡ θυσία [ἡ] ἀρθεῖσα καὶ ἡ ἁμαρτία ἐρημώσεως [ἡ] δοθεῖσα καὶ τὰ ἅγια ἐρημωθή-σεται εἰς καταπάτημα. So the LXX, save that I have reversed the order of the first two verbs in ver. 11, and transposed θυσία καὶ before ἐρράχθη as καὶ θυσία. See notes *in loc.*

8¹⁴. אלי corrupt for אליו (so LXX, Th., Pesh., and Vulg.).

8²². מגוי corrupt for מגויו (so LXX, Th., and the context).

8²³. כְּהָתֵם הַפּשְׁעִים corrupt for כְּתֹם פִּשְׁעֵיהֶם (LXX and Th. (Pesh. and Vulg.)). Here there were three variants in the Hebrew version. כהתם could be retained in an intransitive sense. But this would be against the translator's usage.

8²⁴. נפלאות ישחית corrupt (?) for נ׳ יחשב. This corruption has already occurred in the MT. in 2 Sam. 20¹⁵ ; it is equally possible in the Aramaic ; see note *in loc.*

§ 4. *Words lost in MT restored.*

8⁸. קרנים (with LXX, Th., Vulg.).

8¹², ¹³. See under § 3.

8¹⁷. ויעמד before אצל (with LXX and Th.).

§ 5. *Dittographs in the original Hebrew Version, before the translator of the LXX, some of which may be duplicate renderings of the original Aramaic text.*

8⁷. συνέτριψεν in the LXX = ירססהו (an Aramaic word) where the true reading is attested by the MT. ירמסהו = Th. συνεπάτησεν. The original Aram. verb was most probably רפס : cf. 7⁷,¹⁹.

8¹¹. LXX has ἕως ὁ ἀρχιστράτηγος ῥύσεται τὴν αἰχμαλωσίαν = עד שר

הצבא הציל השבי. Here the MT has עד שר הצבא הגדיל. This doublet may have arisen within the Hebrew version, in which case השבי would be a dittograph of הצבא and הציל of הגדיל.

8[11]. LXX here implies dittographs in the Hebrew: τὰ ὄρη τὰ ἀπ' αἰῶνος = הרי התמיד and ἐξήρθη θυσία = הורם תמיד.

8[11–12]. LXX εὐωδώθησαν καὶ ἐγενήθη . . . ἐποίησε καὶ εὐωδώθη (= MT) והצליחו ונעשתה and MT והצליחה ועשתה. These are variants inside the Hebrew version.

8[16]. See note *in loc.* where the Hebrew presupposed by the LXX and the MT are given together. It is possible that these two may be due to an internal corruption in the Aramaic original. LXX ὁ ἄνθρωπος· ἐπὶ τὸ πρόσταγμα = נברא לדברא, MT = נבריאל הסבר גבריאל הסבר, The entire last clause of 8[16] in the LXX is a doublet of the preceding nine words. The preceding nine words are an exact translation of the MT.

8[24c–25a]. See notes *in loc.*

§ 6. *Aramaisms in the MT or the Hebrew presupposed by the LXX.*

8[2]. אבול (so LXX, Pesh., Vulg.) = 'gate' where the MT has אובל = 'river'.

8[5]. צפיר is really an Aramaism.

8[7]. συνέτριψεν (LXX) presupposes an Aramaic verb. See § 5 above.

8[1]. *Unto me Daniel*, i. e. אלי אני דניאל. This idiom is both Hebrew and Aramaic. See 7[15] note.

After that which appeared. In הַנִּרְאָה the Massoretes regarded הַ (before the perfect Niph'al) as the equivalent of אשר as in Joshua 10[24]; 1 Kings 11[9]; 1 Chron. 26[28], &c.: but Ges.-Kautzsch (§ 138 *i, h*) regards הַנִּרְאָה (the participle) as the most probable reading.

Aforetime, i. e. בתחלה 'at the first', first in a series : cf. 9[21], Gen. 13[3], 4[21], 43[18,20].

8[2]. The seer is carried in a vision to Shushan, as Ezekiel was carried to Jerusalem, Ezek. 8[3]–11[24], 40[2 sqq.].

And I was in Shushan. Here the MT inserts before these words the clause וַיְהִי בִּרְאֹתִי (drawn from 8[15]). Hence we may translate '[Now it was so when I saw] that I was in Shushan'. But I have omitted the bracketed words since they are not to be found in the LXX, Th., Pesh., or Vulgate, nor in Hippolytus' Commentary on the text of Th. Moreover the interpolated clause adds nothing to the text. It is a mere tautology. This interpolation must have been made not earlier than the third or fourth century A.D. according to the evidence of the Versions. It is found in a few late Greek MSS. and in Chrysostom and Theodoret.

The idiom ויהי בראתי ‥‥ ואני is good Hebrew, though the action or event introduced by the *vav* clause is here contemporaneous with that expressed by בראתי: cf. Gen. 19²⁹ ויהי בשחת ‥‥ ויזכר. This, so far as I am aware, is a very rare usage. The action or event introduced in the second clause is almost always subsequent to that expressed by ב with the inf. after יהי: cf. Gen. 4⁸, 11²; 1 Sam. 30¹; 2 Sam. 1²; 1 Kings 8¹⁰, 18⁴; 1 Chron. 15²⁶; Esther 2⁸, 3⁴, and 8¹⁵ in our text. But in the present passage it seems justifiable to regard this construction with its exceptional meaning as due to an accidental interpolation, and not as one authenticating this exceptional idiom.

Shushan the palace or 'castle'. This is the regular description of Shushan in the O.T.: Neh. 1¹; Esther 1²,⁵, 2³,⁵, &c. The word for 'castle' or 'citadel' is בירה—late Hebrew, and probably a loan-word from the Assyrian bîrtu, 'fortress' (Delitzsch, *Ass. H.*, p. 185: quoted by Driver), and found elsewhere only in 1 Chron. 29¹,¹⁹; Ezra 6²; Neh. 2⁸, 7². This citadel of Shushan, i.e. Susa, was celebrated for its strength in ancient times (Herod. v. 49). As the citadel, it is distinguished from the city in Esther 3¹⁵. Shushan was in later times probably the capital of Elam. The first Susa with its palace was destroyed by Assur-bani-pal (668-626 B.C.). See *K. B.* ii. 203 seqq. To this Susa there is no reference in the O.T. It was refounded by Darius Hystaspes (521-485 B.C.), and according to Xenophon (*Cyrop.* viii. 6. 22) 'was the winter residence of the Persian kings, the rest of the year being spent by them at Babylon and Ecbatana' (*Encyc. Bib.*, IV. 4499 sq.).

Elam. Shushan is here said to be in Elam, but in Ezra 4⁹ it is distinguished from it.

After Elam the MT adds 'and I saw in the vision'. This clause appears to be a dittograph of the opening clause, and the fact that the LXX (according to Syr ʰ) and Th. and Hippolytus (*Comment. in Dan.* xxv) omit it transforms this possibility into a practical certainty.   ₐ

The †river† Ulai. The versions here diverge from the MT.

Th. omits Ulai and reads simply Οὐβάλ here and in vv. 3, 6. So far as it goes, however, it supports the MT אובל, which is merely a phonetic variation of יובל in Jer. 17⁸. But the LXX (πρὸς τῇ πύλῃ), Pesh., and Vulg. presuppose not אובל but אבול = 'gate' here and in vv. 3, 6 (Vulg. not in ver. 3, where it reads 'paludem'). The latter is an Aramaic word (J. Aram., Syr. ܐܒܘܠܐ, Assyrian *abullu*), and it is possible that it was originally in the text. The phrase would then mean the 'water gate of the Ulai'. The Ulai flowed close to Shushan. This reading would suit in ver. 3; for the ram representing Media and Persia would then be standing in front of the water gate that commanded the entrance to Shushan, while ver. 6 represents the he-goat (i. e. Alexander the Great) as attacking the ram who stood in front of the water gate. We know that Nearchus brought reinforcements up this river to Alexander.

Ulai. This is the Eulaeus on which, according to Pliny (*H.N.* vi. 27), Susa was situated, though Herodotus (i. 188, v. 49, 52) places it on the Choaspes. Three rivers flow from the north near Susa into the Persian Gulf: the Kerkha (= the ancient Choaspes); the Abdizful (= the Coprates) which falls into the Karun = the Pasitigris); and the Eulaeus, 'a large artificial canal . . . which left the Choaspes at Pai Pul, about twenty miles NW. of Susa, passed close by the town of Susa on the N. or NE., and afterwards joined the Coprates' (Driver).

8³. *I lifted up my eyes and saw*, i. e. in the vision: cf. Gen. 31¹⁰, Zech. 2¹, 5¹,⁹, 6¹.

†*River*†. See note on ver. 2.

A single ram, i. e. איל אחד. So the words should be rendered. The אחד is here a definite numeral as on 10⁵: cf. König, *Syntax*, § 291 *d*.

Ram. The ram was a well-known symbol of might and dominion: cf. Ezek. 17¹³, 39¹⁸; 1 Enoch 89⁴³⁻⁴⁹, 90¹³,¹⁴,¹⁶,³¹ (before 161 B. c.). But though a single ram is a symbol of the kingdoms of Media and Persia in our text, since they are regarded as akin to each other, their diversity is brought forward. The ram has two horns, the stronger which comes up later represents Persia, while the earlier and weaker represents Media. Cf. 2³⁹ for a like distinction.

Horns. קְרָנַיִם and קַרְנָיו ver. 7 are duals, but the vocalization follows the analogy of the plural. Elsewhere we find always קְרָנַיִם, קַרְנָיו: see Ges.-Kautzsch, § 93 *n*.

8⁴. The conquests of Cyrus and Cambyses.

The eastern conquests of the Achaemenidae were of no interest to the Jew, and it is urged that on this ground they are not mentioned. Seeing, however, that the LXX reads πρὸς ἀνατολάς before πρὸς βορρᾶν καὶ πρὸς δυσμὰς καὶ μεσημβρίαν, the phrase may belong to the original text, since the Seer is represented as seeing in vision the actual conquests of the Persians, which of course extended to the east as well as to the other quarters of the earth.

Thrusting, i. e. butting : used of animals Exod. 21²⁸, and then applied figuratively to nations 11⁴⁰—symbolized as animals : cf. Deut. 33¹⁷ ; Ps. 44⁵.

No beasts could stand before him. For this idom יעמדו לפני cf. Judges 2¹⁴; 2 Kings 10⁴ : also in our author 8⁷, 11¹⁶. For this idiom with quite a different meaning cf. 1⁵.

Neither was there any that could deliver, i. e. וְאֵין מַצִּיל. In ver. 7 there is an equivalent phrase. But the LXX and Th. presuppose 'neither was there the one that could deliver', i.e. הַמַּצִיל.

According to his will, i. e. his caprice. Cf. 11³,¹⁶,³⁶, Esther 9⁵.

Magnified himself. Cf. vv. 8, 11, 25. There is a nuance of arrogance and insolence to the word: cf. Ps. 55¹², Jer. 48²⁶.

8⁵⁻⁷. An he-goat (= the Greek empire) attacks the ram and overcomes it, especially in the two great conflicts at Issus and Arbela. The goat had a notable horn between its eyes, i. e. Alexander the Great (8²¹).

8⁵. *Was observing and behold.* Here הייתי מבין והנה is the Hebrew equivalent, and no doubt the rendering of the Aramaic מִשְׂתַּכַּל הֲוֵית וַאֲלוּ—a phrase which has already occurred in 7⁸ in a like connexion.

An he-goat. Since the LXX and Th. have here τράγος αἰγῶν, and further since in apocalyptic visions significant terms and phrases are on their first occurrence mentioned without the article, but on their recurrence with the article, we should correct צפיר העזים into צפיר עזים (2 Chr. 29²¹). In proof of the usage just mentioned many illustrations could be quoted from 1 Enoch and other Jewish Apocalypses, but the reader can verify this usage in Rev. 4⁶⁻⁸ τέσσαρα ζῷα ... τὰ τέσσαρα ζῷα : 5⁶⁻⁸ ἀρνίον ... τοῦ ἀρνίου : 15²ᵃ ᵇ θάλασσαν ὑαλίνην ... τ. θαλ. τ. ὑαλ., &c. Marti wrongly observes that the article in the Hebrew is due to the fact that the beast here is the well-known beast. Apocalyptic usage is against this statement, no matter how important the thing may be. When this expression recurs in ver. 8 it necessarily has the article. Even in this verse we have a further illustration of this usage, i.e. 'a notable horn'. Now as to the antiquity of this phrase, צפיר or צפיר עזים occurs only in late Hebrew such as Ezra 8³⁵; 2 Chron. 29²¹; in Biblical Aramaic Ezra 6¹⁷; in the Targums, in Talmudic Hebrew, and in Syriac. צפיר, therefore, appears in Hebrew to be a loan-word from Aramaic. The classical Hebrew word for he-goat is עתוד, which, however, is only used in the plural. As the word in our text, it is used figuratively of princes and leaders: cf. Isa. 14⁹, Ezek. 34¹⁷.

And touched not the ground. Here וְאֵין נֹגֵעַ should be taken as וְאֵינֶנּוּ נוֹגֵעַ, which is Classical Hebrew. Cf. ver. 27 for a like phrase, and 12⁸ for the idea. The words themselves recall the swift march of Cyrus in Isa. 41³, 'with his feet he treadeth not the road'.

A †notable† horn. קֶרֶן חָזוּת = 'a horn of conspicuousness'. In vv. 8 and 21 it is called 'the great horn'. We have somewhat analogous expressions in 2 Sam. 23²¹, 'a goodly man' (lit. 'a man of appearance' (אִישׁ מַרְאֶה): 1 Chron. 11²³ אִישׁ מַרְאֶה = 'a man of great stature'. For חָזוּת, which Th. omits, the LXX reads ἓν = אחת. There is no early attestation of חזות. The Vulg. supports it: 'cornu insigne'·; the LXX θεωρητόν is asterisked as a later addition: in Th. it appears in the manuscripts A Γ. Hence I have marked this reading as doubtful. Perhaps we should read with the LXX 'a horn'.

This notable horn is Alexander the Great, who crossed the Hellespont in 334 B.C., overthrew Darius Codomannus at Issus in 333, traversed Palestine, reduced Egypt, and finally crushed Persia at Arbela in 331. After further victorious campaigns in the far East and in India, he died of fever in 323 B.C.

8⁷. *Come close unto.* אֵצֶל after a verb of motion, denotes closer proximity than does עד in the preceding verse. אצל is not used after verbs of motion save in this verse, in ver. 17, and 2 Chron. 28¹⁵. Levy (*NHWB.*) cites no instance of the use of this preposition after verbs of motion from the Talmudic writings. It seems, therefore, to have been of late origin and confined to a limited area.

Was moved with choler, i.e. יתמרמר. The Hithpalpal of מרר is not found elsewhere in Biblical Hebrew save here and in 11¹¹.

It is used seldom in late Hebrew. Th.'s rendering ἐξηγριάνθη here (cf. 11[11]) is good.

Trod upon him. רמס, which is used in 2 Kings 14[9] allegorically of a wild beast 'treading down' its enemy, is here and in ver. 10, it can hardly be doubted, a Hebrew rendering of the Aramaic רפס, which is used in 7[7, 19] in describing exactly the same action on the part of Alexander the Great. I have, therefore, in all four passages rendered these two verbs by the same English verb. Since the LXX has συνέτριψε in this verse, and καταπατεῖν in 8[10], 7[7], it possibly found יִרְסָחֻ instead of ירמסהו. But the former is an Aramaic verb = the Hebrew רצץ.

8[8]. Death of Alexander and the division of his empire into four kingdoms.

The great horn was broken. Alexander was struck down by a fever when he had reached the summit of his power.

Others, (*even*) *four ⌜horns⌝*. The MT reads חָזוּת ארבע which Hitzig and others render 'four conspicuous (horns)', and Ewald 'as it were four horns'. But Graetz, Bevan, Kamphausen, Loehr, Driver, &c., rightly reject both renderings. Both are questionable renderings, and as a matter of fact the former is at variance with our author's own statement in ver. 22, where they are described as lacking in the power of Alexander. But the LXX with its rendering ἔτερα τέσσαρα κέρατα enabled Graetz, followed (herein) by most recent scholars, to emend חזות into אֲחֵרוֹת. Hence the above rendering. Further, since the LXX, Th., and Vulg. include 'horns' in their renderings I have restored it. Th. and Vulg. give no equivalent for חזות. The corruption in the MT arose probably from ver. 5. The אחרות must be taken as standing in apposition to the number that follows, as in my rendering. Otherwise we should expect ארבע קרנים אחרות: cf. 12[5], Ezra 1[10], &c. But in 8[13] we have a like construction.

On the death of Alexander his empire became the cause of endless rivalries and wars amongst his generals, which raged over twenty years before a final settlement was arrived at through the battle of Ipsus in Phrygia in 301. By this settlement Egypt was confirmed to Ptolemy in the south; Asia Minor including Paphlagonia and Pontus to Lysimachus in the north; Seleucus received Syria, Babylonia, and other eastern provinces as far as the Indus in the east; Cassander, Macedonia, and Greece in the west. These four new kingdoms rose on the ruins of Alexander's empire and are symbolized by the 'four horns'.

8⁹⁻¹⁴. The 'little horn', i.e. Antiochus IV (Epiphanes), 175–164 B.C. Cf. 1 Macc. 1¹⁰, Josephus, *Ant.* x. 11. 7.

8⁹. Our author passes over without mention all the Seleucidae from 301–175 B.C. His sole concern is with Antiochus Epiphanes, whom he regarded as the last and greatest enemy of the Jews and of their faith.

Of them, i.e. מהם where the suffix is masc. though 'horns' are fem. See Ges.-Kautzsch, § 135 *o* : also note on 1⁵ of our text, Some manuscripts read מהן.

Came forth. With יָצָא before a feminine subject. Cf. 1 Kings 22³⁶.

Another *horn, a little one,* i.e. קֶרֶן אַחֶרֶת צְעִירָה—being Bevan's emendation of the MT קֶרֶן אַחַת מִצְּעִירָה. Here we have the Hebrew rendering of the Aramaic phrase קֶרֶן אָחֳרִי זְעֵירָה 7⁸, just as in 8⁵ above we have another Hebrew rendering of a clause in the Aramaic of 7⁸. Bevan's restoration of the text is accepted, or regarded as the best as yet proposed, by Marti, Kamphausen, Loehr, and others. The MT is generally regarded as corrupt. Ewald emends מִצְּעִירָה into מַצְּעִירָה='showing smallness'. Graetz would excise the initial מ. König's explanation (*Syntax,* § 352 z) of the MT as 'a horn less than small' is unsatisfactory. Bevan's restoration is a real recovery of the original. Even the LXX and Th. which represent a corrupt original support Bevan's restoration : i. e. κέρας ἰσχυρὸν ἕν (Th. ἕν ἰσχ.) ; for ἰσχυρόν = עצומה an easier corruption of צעירה than of מצעירה.

Waxed exceeding great. With תגדל יתר cf. Isa. 56¹² and the use of יַתִּירָה (Aram.) in 3²², 7⁷,¹⁹ in our author. The LXX has καὶ ἐπάταξεν = וַתַּךְ corrupt for יתר.

Toward the south, i.e. Egypt, cf. 11²⁵, 1 Macc. 1¹⁶⁻¹⁹.

Toward the east, i.e. Elymais in Persia, invaded by Antiochus in the last year of his life. Cf. 11²⁵ sq·, 1 Macc. 3³¹,³⁷, 6¹⁻⁴. But how can the Seer from his vantage ground in Susa refer to Persia and Media as the east? It lay to the east of Syria. In 1 Macc. 6¹ Elymais is described as 'a city renowned for riches' : in Josephus, *Ant.* xii. 9. 1 as 'a very rich city in Persia'.

Towards the glorious land. Cf. 11¹⁶,⁴¹. In Ezek. 20⁶,¹⁵ Palestine is called 'the glory of all lands' (צבי היא לכל הארצות) : in Zach. 7¹⁴ 'the pleasant land' (ארץ חמדה) ; in 1 Enoch 89⁴⁰ 'a pleasant and glorious land'. Cf. Jer. 3¹⁹. The text before the LXX had צפון i.e. βορρᾶν, and Th. had הצבא i.e. τὴν δύναμιν— both corruptions of הַצֶּבִי.

8¹⁰. 'The host of heaven' in this verse represents the people of God. The *heavenly* character and destiny of Israel as distinguished from those of the nations is here accentuated as elsewhere in our author (see 7¹³,¹⁸ nn.). The phrase 'the stars of heaven' is a definition ot 'the host of heaven', and the *vav* that introduces it is the *vav* explicative (cf. 7²⁰). This is not infrequent in Hebrew, cf. Gen. 4⁴; Exod. 24¹², 25¹²; Isa. 1¹ 'Judah and (= and particularly) Jerusalem'), 2¹: see Ges.- Kautzsch, § 154 a. n. b. In 1 Enoch 46⁷ 'the stars of heaven' denote the righteous Jews. Elsewhere in the O. T. 'the host of heaven' means the stars or the celestial beings in attendance on God. See Driver in Hastings, *DB*. ii. 429 seq.

Our text here refers to the persecution of the Jews by Antiochus Epiphanes and possibly to the murder of the high priest Onias III, who is referred to more definitely in 1 Enoch 90⁸.

8¹¹⁻¹³. These verses form one of the most difficult passages in Daniel owing to the corruptions of the text. Some of the foremost scholars regard the text as impossible. Bevan is of opinion that 'no plausible emendation has been suggested'. But this hopeless view of the text, if corrected and restored by the help of the LXX and Th., does not appear to be well founded. It is true that these two versions are themselves very corrupt— the LXX being 'hopelessly confused' according to Bevan—but it is possible in the opinion of the present writer to recover the original text in the main. In doing so the accounts of the same incidents in 1 Macc. are decidedly helpful.

Let us study the LXX and Th. of 8¹¹, ¹²ª side by side with the MT.

MT	LXX	Th.
ועד שר הצבא הגדיל	ἕως ὁ ἀρχιστράτηγος †ῥύσεται† [τὴν αἰχμαλω- σίαν] καὶ δι' αὐτὸν [τὰ ὄρη τὰ ἀπ' αἰῶνος] ἐρράχ- θη, καὶ ἐξήρθη ὁ τόπος αὐ- τῶν καὶ θυσία, [καὶ ἔθηκεν αὐτὴν ἕως χαμαὶ ἐπὶ τὴν γῆν] [καὶ εὐωδώθησαν καὶ ἐγενήθη]· καὶ τὸ ἅγιον ἐρημωθήσεται.	καὶ ἕως ὁ ἀρχιστράτη- γος †ῥύσηται† [τὴν αἰχ- μαλωσίαν], καὶ δι' αὐτὸν θυσία ἐράχθη, [καὶ κα- τευοδώθη αὐτῷ]· καὶ τὸ ἅγιον ἐρημωθήσεται.
וממנו הורם התמיד		
והשלך מכון מקדשו		
וצבא 12.		

There are *in ver. 11* of the LXX many dittographs of phrases and clauses *belonging to ver. 12* and even two in Th., as we shall show herewith. These (with the exception of the first) were originally alternative renderings of the translator which he placed in the margin, but which a subsequent copyist incorporated in the text and *in the wrong verse*. First of all τὴν αἰχμαλωσίαν in the LXX and Th. = השבי which must be a dittograph of הצבא. ὁ ἀρχιστράτηγος = שר הצבא. שר in this sense is never translated in the LXX or Th. by ἀρχιστράτηγος unless צבא follows it. The insertion of this dittograph in the Hebrew led to the emendation of הגדיל into הציל: cf. LXX 8⁴, ⁷ where ὁ ῥυόμενος is a rendering of מציל. We thus see that in the first clause these three authorities agree.

The next dittograph τὰ ὄρη τὰ ἀπ᾽ αἰῶνος = הרי התמיד, which is a dittograph of הורם התמיד.

There are two other dittographs, the first καὶ ἔθηκεν αὐτὴν ἕως χαμαὶ ἐπὶ τὴν γῆν contains a dittograph within itself; for ἕως χαμαί and ἐπὶ τὴν γῆν are duplicate renderings of ארצה. ἔθηκεν αὐτήν seems a loose rendering of וַתִּשְׁלֵחָהָ. In other words we have in ver. 11 a duplicate rendering of ותשלר · · · ארצה which belongs to ver. 12. Finally καὶ εὐωδώθησαν καὶ ἐγενήθη as another dittograph of the last words in ver. 12, ועשתה והצליחה, though the order is reversed and other changes made.

But the LXX still presents a confused text, and the confusion may have originated in the LXX. Thus we can make nothing of δι᾽ αὐτὸν ἐρράχθη καὶ ἐξήρθη ὁ τόπος αὐτῶν καὶ θυσία as it stands. But the solution of the difficulty is obvious. There is a transposition of the two verbs. ἐξήρθη should be connected immediately with θυσία; for in 8¹³ we have ἡ θυσία ἡ ἀρθεῖσα. Hence as in the MT the LXX should be read καὶ δι᾽ αὐτὸν θυσία ἐξήρθη καὶ ἐρράχθη ὁ τόπος αὐτῶν.

Thus the Hebrew presupposed by the original text of the LXX = ‡מקומם‡ והשלך התמיד הורם ¹וממנה ¹הגדילה הצבא שר ועד ומקדש יצדה= ‘ Even unto the prince of the host it magnified itself, and by it the continual burnt offering was taken away and ‡their‡ place cast down and the sanctuary laid desolate ’.

This I am convinced was almost to the letter the original text of ver. 11 save in the case of מקומם. But we have still to justify the last two clauses; for in their stead the MT has והשלך מכון

---

¹ Emended from הגדיל and ממנו as קרן is feminine.

מקדשו וצבא =‎ 'and the foundation of his sanctuary was cast down.
12. And the host'.   Instead of מכון מקרשו the LXX presupposes
מקומם ומקדש.   מקום has the support of two MSS. of the MT.,
the Vulgate, and of 2 Macc. 5[16, 17, 19, 20], where Jerusalem is called
ὁ τόπος in connexion with the attacks of Antiochus on Jerusalem.
In 1 Macc. 1[31] it is recorded that Antiochus had the houses and
the walls thrown down ; καθεῖλεν τοὺς οἴκους αὐτῆς καὶ τὰ τείχη αὐτῆς.
I conclude then first of all that מכון (never elsewhere translated
by τόπος in the LXX) of the MT is a corruption of מקום.
Secondly, that the original was מקומומקדש which through the
transposition of the two underlined letters became the text presupposed by the LXX מקוממוקדש and by the loss of the first of
them and further corruption became the present MT מכון. מקרש.
Thirdly, the LXX and Th., both of which read καὶ τὸ ἅγιον ἐρημωθή-
σεται as the final clause of this verse, enables us to recover the
Hebrew before them, i.e. ומקדש יֻצָּדֶה (or יצדא).   This verb[1] is
really Aramaic, but this is no solid objection in a Hebrew translation of an Aramaic original.   Besides it had already been adopted
once into Hebrew, cf. Zeph. 3[6]. It corresponds constantly in the
Targum on Ezek. to ἐρημοῦν in the LXX.   But since LXX and
Th. omit וצבא at the beginning of the next verse, they seem
to have read יצדא in its stead.[2]   Now in support of the LXX
and Th. we may quote the remarkable parallel in 1 Macc. 1[39]
τὸ ἁγίασμα αὐτῆς ἠρημώθη.   This is an exact equivalent of the clause
in the LXX and Th.   Again in 4[38] of the same book it is said
that Judas and his companions found τὸ ἁγίασμα . . . ἠρημωμένον.
Finally in the LXX of our author in 8[13] practically the same
clause recurs τὰ ἅγια ἐρημωθήσεται.

Hence if the corruption arose in the Hebrew, the Hebrew of 8[11]
originally was [3] ‎ועד שר הצבא הגדילה וממנה הורם התמיד וְהֻשְׁלַךְ מקום ומקדש
יצדא 'Even unto the prince of the host it magnified itself, and by

---

[1] So Bludau ; but the corruption may have arisen through a dittograph in the
Aramaic.   Thus ומקדשאיחול (So LXX καὶ ἅγιον ἐρημωθήσεται) was rewritten (?)
ומקדשא וחילא, whence the MT.   For חלל = 'to destroy' cf. Cowley Ah 168—
a secondary meaning, it is true — and not the original or ordinary one.   The LXX
presupposes the Hebrew ומקדשיׁשׁם.

[2] So Irenaeus De Antichristo, xxv, et sanctum desolabitur ; (12) et datum est
in sacrificium peccatum.

[3] The MT read ומקדשו 'and his sanctuary'; LXX and Th. 'and the
sanctuary'.   Perhaps the article should be restored before the last two nouns
'place' and 'sanctuary'.

it the daily burnt offering was taken away and (the) place cast down and (the) sanctuary laid desolate'.

Prince of the host, i.e. God. The host is the host of heaven.

Took away (הֵרִים the *Kt.*), but the *Qr.* reads הֻרַם 'was taken away'.

The daily burnt-offering. The full expression was עולת התמיד as in Exod. 29⁴², Ezek. 46¹⁵, &c., but owing to familiar use it came to be spoken of simply as התמיד 'the continual' or 'the daily' in later Judaism — in the Mishna, as in Daniel, but not elsewhere in the O.T.

Cast down. So וְהֻשְׁלַךְ of MT with LXX and Th.

. *The sanctuary laid desolate.* On this text which we owe to the LXX and Th. see notes above.

8¹². In our criticism of ver. 11 we arrived at the conclusion that the oldest authorities did not read וצבא at the beginning of this verse but read יצדא or צרה instead and connected it with the preceding verse.

The MT calls for further correction, but before we proceed to do so, let us compare the attempts of the chief Hebraists to make sense of the MT as it stands. Von Lengerke renders: 'And an host is delivered over together with the continual burnt offering on account of iniquity'. Here צבא is construed as a feminine noun. The verb could of course be emended. But there is another difficulty. על is here apparently against all Hebrew usage rendered 'together with'. There are passages indeed where על has this meaning; but in such passages there is a community of nature between the things linked together by the על; cf. Exod. 35²² האנשים על הנשים='men together with women', i.e. both man and woman; see also 1 Kings 15²⁰; Jer. 3¹⁸; Gen. 32¹²; Lev. 2², ¹⁶, 3⁴, &c. Hence we must reject this rendering of Von Lengerke. There is no natural community between a warlike host and a burnt offering. Hitzig and Driver: 'And a warfare was undertaken against the continual burnt offering with transgression'. Ewald (and so practically the second marginal rendering of the R.V.) : 'And armed force is imposed upon the daily sacrifice through transgression.' Here Hitzig, Driver, and Ewald attach a meaning to צבא in ver. 12 different from that which it bears in ver. 11. But further, the meaning they wrest from these renderings is unsatisfactory. They are explained to mean that Antiochus had recourse to violent

measures and established a garrison in Jerusalem to suppress
the sacred rights of the Jews. But the words are not adapted
to convey this sense. The armed force is directed against one
specific detail of Jewish worship, whereas they should mean
that it was directed against every detail of Jewish worship. The
R.V. has : 'And the host was given over (to it) together with the
continual burnt offering through transgression.' The R.V. is in
one respect, as we have already shown in our criticism of Von
Lengerke, impossible, and in another worse.

As Bevan and Marti remark, the text as it stands admits of
no satisfactory rendering. Bevan abandons the attempt to emend
it in despair. Von Gall, Marti, Moore, and Loehr reject וצבא
as impossible, and propose its excision, and cite the LXX and
Th. as omitting it. But, as we have seen in the notes on the
preceding verse, these two versions attest a reading which
I take to be original text, of which וצבא is merely a corruption,
and rightly assign it to the close of ver. 11.

The MT, however, is still corrupt, but the task of emendation
is easy, and has already in part been achieved by Von Gall and
Marti in dependence on the LXX and Th. Thus for תִּנָּתֵן
עַל־התמיד בְּפשע וְתַשְׁלֵךְ אמת we should read with the LXX and Th.
וַיִּנָּתֵן עַל־הַתָּמִיד הַפֶּשַׁע וְתַשְׁלֵךְ אמת = 'and the transgression was
placed on the daily burnt offering and truth cast down to the
ground'. Th. καὶ ἐδόθη ἐπὶ τὴν θυσίαν ἁμαρτία καὶ ἐρίφη χαμαὶ ἡ δικαιοσύνη. The text seems to refer to the facts recorded in 1 Macc.
1⁵⁴ ᾠκοδόμησαν βδέλυγμα ἐρημώσεως ἐπὶ τὸ θυσιαστήριον, and in 1⁵⁹
where the Syrians are described as θυσιάζοντες ἐπὶ τὸν βωμὸν ὃς ἦν
ἐπὶ τοῦ θυσιαστηρίου.

But what sense can we assign to the words ' the transgression
was placed on the daily burnt offering'? 'The daily burnt
offering' was not a place. Hence, if the text is so far correct,
it must be recognized as defective, and we must restore מזבח
before התמיד [1], i. e. 'and the transgression was offered on the
(altar of the) daily burnt offering': or else assume an original
corruption of עַל in the Aramaic original such as חלף = 'instead
of', of which תחת would be the Hebrew rendering. We should
then have 'and the transgression was offered **in place of** the

[1] The Aramaic would then be מדבחא די תמידא. The loss of the first word
would then be accidental. The lost (i. e. the first) word contains three letters in
common with the second.

daily burnt offering'. The context requires emendation, and
either of these suggestions would harmonize the text with the
facts of history. But the former is much to be preferred. It
provides us with a text that is satisfactory—grammatically, con-
textually, and historically.

The transgression : i. e. הפשע emended in accordance with the
LXX (αἱ ἁμαρτίαι) and Th. (ἡ ἁμαρτία) from בפשע. 'The transgression' is, in all probability, the offering of heathen sacrifices
and specially of swine upon the altar: cf. 1 Macc. 1⁴⁴,⁴⁶,⁴⁷ καὶ
ἀπέστειλεν ὁ βασιλεὺς βιβλία ἐν χειρὶ ἀγγέλων . . . μιᾶναι ἁγίασμα . . . καὶ
θύειν ὕεια. But if this reconstruction of the text under the
guidance of the LXX and Th. is right, it follows that it is hardly
justifiable to identify 'the transgression' with 'the abomination
that maketh desolate' in 11³¹, 12¹¹ as do some scholars. The
latter appears to be the heathen altar that was built on the
altar of burnt offering. See notes *in loc.* The Seer does not
necessarily give a complete record of the series of events in
each case—as for instance the profanation or desolation of the
sanctuary (8¹¹, 11³¹), the building of the heathen altar on the
altar of burnt offering (11³¹, 12¹¹) and the offering thereon of
abominable sacrifices 8¹².

Did its pleasure *and prospered.* It acted with effect. Cf.
ver. 24 : 2 Chron. 31²¹. See note on 11³².

8¹³⁻¹⁴. Dialogue between two angels overheard by the Seer,
through which he receives information as does the Seer in
Zech. 1¹². What the first angel said is not recorded, but the
answer by the second to his unrecorded question is given.

8¹³. Here as in Zech. 1⁹⁻¹² the Seer receives information from
an angel.

I heard. The form וָאֶשְׁמְעָה is due to the influence of the
guttural ע : see Ges.-Kautzsch, § 10 *h.* The cohortative form
with *vav* consecutive 'occurs only at rare intervals except in
two or three of the later writers, some ninety instances of its
use being cited altogether. . . . It is principally found in . . .
Daniel, Ezra, and Nehemiah, where the narrative is told in the
first person. . . . In Dan. 8-12 there occur ten cases with *-ah*
against eight without it (verbs ל״ה of course not reckoned)'
(Driver, *Tenses*³, § 69).

A holy one, i. e. אחד קדוש. This un-Hebraic order is according
to König (*Syntax,* § 310 *b*) caused probably by the antithesis

'one . . . another'. In 10⁵ אִישׁ אֶחָד represents the Hebrew order, but the addition of the אֶחָד to אִישׁ makes it 'expressly indeterminate', as Ges.-Kautzsch, § 125 b, observes, and gives it the sense of our indefinite article 'a man'—a rare idiom in the O.T. See also 8³ above. It is always postpositive when it bears this meaning in Hebrew, but not so‚in the Mishnah as Bevan (p. 30) points out. On the other hand in the present verse where the אֶחָד is prepositive, it is in apposition to קָדוֹשׁ— 'one, an holy one'. Cf. the emended passage in 8⁸, where אַחֲרוֹת stands in apposition to the number that follows.

That certain one. The Hebrew פַּלְמוֹנִי, which is found here and nowhere else, is taken to be a contraction or conflation of פְּלֹנִי and אַלְמֹנִי, which words occur only together as in Ruth 4¹; 1 Sam. 21³; 2 Kings 6⁸. The LXX, Th., and Pesh. transliterate the word, as they do not understand it. The Vulg. renders 'alteri nescio cui' : Symmachus τινί ποτε.

How long (shall be) the vision ? The words which follow are to be taken in apposition, as Driver points out, to indicate the contents of the vision, and to this we must add its duration.

While the daily burnt offering is taken away. Here the MT is defective, as most scholars recognize, and we must with the LXX and Th. ἡ θυσία ἡ ἀρθεῖσα insert מוּרָם after הֻפְשַׁע. So Bevan, von Gall, Moore. Here the second article may be disregarded, as the LXX and Th. are very arbitrary in inserting or omitting the article.

And the transgression that appalleth set up. Here again we have to fall back upon the LXX and Th. ἡ ἁμαρτία ἐρημώσεως ἡ δοθεῖσα. The second article may be disregarded as in the preceding clause. In that case δοθεῖσα implies נִתָּן. Cf. 11³¹, 12¹¹. Hence we should read with Von Gall, Marti, Loehr, and others, though they omit the article, הֻפְשַׁע הַשֹּׁמֵם נתן. שֹׁמֵם is the abbreviated Po'el participle for מִשׁוֹמֵם. For examples of the Pu'al participle without the preformative see Ges.-Kautzsch, §§ 52 s, 55 c. Bevan led the way in this reconstruction of the text by restoring מוּרָם and emending שמם into שִׂים. Hence he rendered 'while the daily sacrifice is taken away and the Iniquity is set up'. But the former reconstruction seems preferable.

And the sanctuary laid waste to be trodden under foot. I have here (with some hesitation and yet with a conviction that, if either represents the original, it is the LXX and not the MT)

followed the LXX καὶ τὰ ἅγια ἐρημωθήσεται εἰς καταπάτημα, i. e. וקדש
יצדא מרמס, instead of the MT וצבא מרמס ק". This expression
is found in 1 Macc. 3⁴⁵ καὶ τὸ ἁγίασμα καταπατούμενον. This is the
second time that the LXX has ἐρημωθήσεται where the MT has
וצבא. See note on ver. 11 above. קדש as representing the only
sanctuary can dispense with the article as עיר stands for Jerusalem. If we do not accept the LXX here, there are two other
possible texts.

(1) The MT which = 'and the sanctuary and host (וצבא) to
be trodden under foot'. As to the meaning of 'host' here
scholars are divided. Some take it to be 'the host of heaven'
as in ver. 10: others to be the army of the Israelites. Others
again (including Bevan and Oxford Hebr. Lex.) render צבא by
'service',¹ i. e. of the temple. As the MT stands צבא occurs
five times in 8¹⁰⁻¹³ and with different meanings. In ver. 10 it
appears twice to mean Israel, the heavenly people as distinguished from the nations of the earth. In ver. 11 to mean
'the angels', though it could be interpreted in the same sense
as in ver. 10. In ver. 12 some scholars take it to mean the
army of the Israelites (as in R.V.) given over into the power of
the enemy: others, doing more justice to the context, as the
Syrian force established in Jerusalem against the Jews. With
the different meanings assigned to it in ver. 13 we have dealt
above. But if we accept the LXX, we escape these difficulties.
It attests צבא in the first three passages in vv. 10-11, where the
same meaning can be assigned to it in all three, and for וצבא
reads יצדא in the last two, in the former of which it is supported
by Th. In any case it attests an ancient text of the second
century B.C., which bears just such a meaning as the context
requires and 1 Macc. supports, whereas there is no external
authority earlier than the second century A.D. which supports the
text of the MT. No scholar is satisfied with the MT, and
few scholars agree as to its exact meaning.

8¹⁴. *Unto him.* So the LXX, Th., Pesh., and Vulg. read
אליו. The MT incorrectly reads אֵלַי 'to me'.

¹ In the sense of 'religious service' the Aramaic חילא is used as a translation
of צבא in the Targ. on Lev. 4³, ²³, ³⁰, ³⁵, but this use of it is not acknowledged
in Levy's *NHWB*. It is also used twice as a translation of צבא in the sense of
'military service' or rather 'the hard service' of life, in Job 7¹, 40². But these
meanings are in all probability due to the word חילא renders and not to itself.

Two thousand and three hundred evenings and mornings. The phrase ערב בקר is to be explained in accordance with ver. 26. It is not the equivalent of νυχθήμερον and so to be taken as a unit of time, i. e. a period of twenty-four hours (Gen. 1⁵,⁸, &c., but as in ver. 26 ערב ובקר are to be reckoned as 'successive evenings and mornings' (Ewald, Hitzig, Bevan, &c.). This peculiar mode of reckoning 1,150 days is due to the fact that the Seer regards the suppression of the evening and morning sacrifices as the chief of the many outrages offered by Antiochus to religions. Accordingly he counts up the omitted sacrifices, i. e. 2,300 = 1,150 days.

This time determination is of importance in settling the date of our author's work. It is clear from the preceding two verses that he wrote after 'the transgression had been offered "on the ⟨altar of the⟩ daily burnt offering" (8¹²)' or after the erection of the heathen altar (11³¹, 12¹¹) on the 15th of Chisleu, 168 B.C. (12¹¹), and *before* the dedication of the new altar on the 25th of Chisleu (= Dec.), 165 B.C. (see 1 Macc. 1⁵⁴, 4⁵² seq.); for the period between these two amounts only to three years and ten days. Now, if we reckon the year at 360, 364, or 365 days, three years and ten days will amount to 1,090, 1,102 or 1,105 days respectively, i. e. in all cases less than the predicted 1,150 days. Hence we conclude that the book was written before the dedication of the new altar, since otherwise the period of 1,150 days would be unintelligible. This is the view of Wellhausen, Bevan, Driver, and most scholars. The 1,150 is therefore a *bona fide* prediction.

With this period of the suspension of the daily sacrifice we are not to confound the three and a half years (7²⁵, 12⁷) during which the entire persecution was to last. See note on 9²⁷.

Then shall the sanctuary be justified: i. e. ונצדק. The Jewish sanctuary after the lapse of the above period will be vindicated and restored. Here only in O.T. Hebrew is צדק found in the Niph'al.

8¹⁵⁻¹⁹. *The appearance of Gabriel.*

Sought to understand (it). This expression has its equivalent in the Aramaic in 7¹⁹ צבית ליצבא ' I desire to know the truth '.

Stood before me: i. e. עֹמֵד לְנֶגְדִּי. Cf. 10¹⁶ ; Joshua 5¹³. See note on 1⁵.

As the appearance of a man. We have in ' as the appearance of' the apocalyptic form of expression already found in Ezek. 1¹³,¹⁴,²⁶,²⁷,²⁸, 8², &c. He is called 'the man Gabriel' in 9²¹. With the phrase here כמראה גבר we should compare כמראה אדם in 10¹⁸ and in Ezek. 1²⁶. The word used for man גבר (= ἀνήρ, *vir*) is apparently chosen as a play on the name Gabriel = גבריאל 'man of God'. But it is worth observing that גבר is an old Aramaic word, whereas אדם (= ἄνθρωπος, *homo*) is rare in later Aramaic and the Targums, and does not occur at all in the older (or any?) Aramaic inscriptions, nor in the *Aram. Papyri*. Did the name originate in Aramaic? The Hebrew גֶּבֶר, mainly poetical, occurs over sixty times in the O.T., but the Aramaic גְּבַר nearly forty times in the few Aramaic chapters in the O.T. Gabriel is mentioned only here and in 9²¹ in the O.T. In 1 Enoch 9¹, 10⁹ (before 170 B. C., and originally written in Aramaic) the name of Gabriel is found, and in the later Parables of Enoch 40⁹, 54⁶ written originally in Hebrew in the first century B.C. In the Targ. of Jonathan on Gen. 37¹⁵ Gabriel is said to have guided Joseph when looking for his brethren. Here the same play on words recurs : גבריאל בדמות גברא. In the Targ. on Job 25² he is said to stand on God's left hand, Michael on His right.

The LXX carelessly renders the phrase in our text by ὡς ὅρασις ἀνθρώπου. Instead of ἀνθρώπου Th. has the exact rendering ἀνδρός. It is worth noticing that in 1 Enoch 'the Son of Man' in the Ethiopic = 'filius viri' 62⁵, 69²⁹, 71¹⁴, and 'filius hominis' in 46², ³, ⁴, 48².

8¹⁶. *A man's voice.* Since the voice so described is heard in a vision, it is not improbable that the words signify 'an angelic voice'; for in a vision an angel is described as a man : cf. 10⁵. Marti compares 2 Sam. 7¹⁴, where God is spoken of as chastening men 'with the rod of men' שבט אנשים.

Between the banks of *the Ulai.* The LXX rightly renders ἀνὰ μέσον τοῦ Οὐλαί. The voice was heard above the river : cf. 12⁶ sq.

Gabriel. Gabriel is mentioned in. 1 Enoch 9¹, 20⁷ as one of the four and seven archangels respectively. This section of Enoch is older than the book of Daniel. See note above.

This man, i. e. הַלָּז, abbreviated as in Judges 6²⁰ ; 1 Sam. 17²⁶, &c. from הַלָּזֶה : cf. Ges.-Kautzsch, § 34 *f.*

At the close of this verse in the LXX we have a dittographic rendering of the preceding clause : καὶ ἀναβοήσας εἶπεν ὁ ἄνθρωπος Ἐπὶ τὸ πρόσταγμα ἐκεῖνο ἡ ὅρασις. In the first rendering of the Hebrew Th. follows the LXX : καὶ ἐκάλεσε καὶ εἶπεν Γαβριήλ, συνέτισον ἐκεῖνον τὴν ὅρασιν. This first rendering (1) is acknowledged by the Hexaplaric text as borrowed, and the second rendering (2) is no doubt the original version of the LXX. Here it chances that in rendering הבין the LXX uses (as does Th.) συνετίζειν, though its usual rendering of בין or הבין is διανοεῖσθαι (twelve times). But this is no reason for inferring that the rendering (1) in the LXX is a late interpolation from Th. The usual rendering of this Hebrew verb by Th. is συνιέναι (sixteen times). Yet the LXX once uses this rendering in 11[33], where there is no probability of the LXX being affected by Th. Both the LXX and Th. have other renderings of this verb.

Thus LXX (2) =

גברא לדברא = ויקרא ויאמר הגבר אל הדבר הלו המראה

MT (LXX (1), Th.)

גבריאל הסבר = ויקרא ויאמר גבריאל הבן להלו את־המראה

With the construction הָבֵן with לְ = 'make to understand' cf. 11[33]: it is usually found with את.

I have underlined the text of the two where they differ. Here again as in 8[11] we have a dittograph rendering from the hand of the original Greek translator of the Hebrew Version. But the *dittograph already existed in the Hebrew*; for the MT does not admit of these two Greek renderings. The Greek is that of the translator of the LXX. πρόσταγμα is his rendering of דבר in 9[2,12,23 (bis),25], but this Hebrew word is never so rendered by Th. But further the two Hebrew renderings may (?) be alternative renderings of a corrupt Aramaic original: read variously as גבריאל הסבר, where אסבר = 'make to understand' in the Targums. The Pa'el is used in the sense in the Targ. of Isa. 40[14]: or as גברא על דברא.

8[17]. *Came ⌐and stood⌐ near where I stood.* I have with the LXX, Th. (καὶ ἔστη), and Vulg. restored וַיַּעֲמֹד before אצל. Hippolytus xxv reproduces Th.

This combination of עָמַד and עֹמֵד is found twice elsewhere in our text, 8[18], 10[11], and 2 Chron. 30[16], 34[31], 35[10]; Neh. 13[11]. It is a late Hebrew expression. The Classical Hebrew for עמדי על in ver. 18 would be תֻּחְתִּי: cf. 1 Sam. 14⁹. It is strange that the translator uses the Classical Hebrew in 8⁸, ²².

Was affrighted. The Niph'al נִבְעַת is found only in late prose : 1 Chron. 21³⁰; Esther 7⁶.

Fell upon my face. On the appearance of the angelic visitant the Seer falls upon his face through fear : cf. Ezek. 1²⁸, 3²³, 43³ ; Rev. 1¹⁷.

Son of man. A natural designation of a human being by an angelic one : cf. Ezek. 2¹,³,⁶, &c. This designation has nothing in common with the Messianic one, 'Son of Man'.

For the vision belongeth to the time of the end. Cf. ver. 19 and Hab. 2³, 'For the vision is yet for the appointed time, and it hasteth toward the end'. Gabriel bids the Seer give heed to the vision, inasmuch as it dealt with no less a crisis than the final one of the world's history. For the writer this was the age of Antiochus. Time was then to give place to the kingdom of the Eternal, 7¹⁴,¹⁸,²²,²⁷, 12²,³. In our text we have 'time of the end' 8¹⁷, 11³⁵,⁴⁰, 12⁴,⁹ (cf. 2 Bar. 29⁸, 59⁴), 'the end' 9²⁶, 12¹³ (7²⁶), 'the appointed time of the end' 8¹⁹. The O.T. expression 'the end of the days' is the oldest eschatological expression. See note on p. 394.

8¹⁸. During the revelation of Gabriel to Daniel the latter loses consciousness: cf. 10⁹. Not till the angel touches him is his consciousness restored : cf. 10¹⁰,¹⁶,¹⁸, 1 Enoch 60³,⁴, 4 Ezra 5¹⁴,¹⁵; Rev. 1¹⁷.

Made me to stand. Instead of יעמידני the LXX found יְעִירֵנִי, which it rendered by ἤγειρε. Since the Seer had fallen into a deep sleep this word is very appropriate to the passage. It is noteworthy that in 10¹⁰, where the MT has וַתְּנִיעֵנִי, both the LXX and Th. have καὶ ἤγειρε = וַתְּעִירֵנִי, and the Pesh. and Vulg. 'et erexit' = ותעמידני. It is not improbable that, as Jahn suggests, the text here originally contained both these verbs. If so, we should render 'he waked me and made me stand where I had stood'.

Made me to stand where I had stood. See note on preceding verse on this late idiom.

8¹⁹⁻²⁶. *Gabriel's explanation of the vision.*

8¹⁹. *The latter time of the indignation,* or 'the last time'. The word 'indignation', i.e. זַעַם, is the technical term for the wrath of God, which Israel and Judah had incurred according to the teaching of the pre-Exilic prophets (cf. Isa. 5²⁵). This wrath had manifested itself in Israel's subjection to the nations. After the Exile it was expected to come to an end in the immediate future, but this consummation was ever deferred, till in the time of our author the faithful did not hope for its close till the final judgement, and the advent of the kingdom of the saints. According to our author the divine wrath was to be fully satisfied by the persecution Israel endured under Antiochus; for according to 11³⁶ Antiochus 'shall prosper till the indignation be accomplished'. Cf. Isa. 10²⁵. 'For yet a very little while and the indignation shall be accomplished'.

8²⁰. *The kings of Media and Persia.* Here 'kings' undoubtedly represent kingdoms as also in 7¹⁷. The same irregular use of symbols recurs in the next verse.

8²¹. *The he-goat.* צְפִיר הָעִזִּים. This is the reading required by the LXX, Th., Pesh., Vulg., and Hippolytus εἰς τ. Δαν. xxvii. as in ver. 8. In ver. 8 the LXX and Th. have ὁ τράγος τῶν αἰγῶν. Since צפיר is a loan-word from the Aramaic (cf. Ezra 6¹⁷ צפירי עזין), some scribe added the Hebrew synonym הַשָּׂעִיר (= 'the he-goat') in the margin as an explanatory gloss. This was incorporated by a later scribe after צפיר, but, so far as external testimony goes, not before the 4th cent. A.D. But some modern scholars have adopted this late conflate text and rendered it 'the rough he-goat', since שָׂעִר = 'hairy', cf. Gen. 27¹¹, ³³, and also 'he-goat', apart from the addition העזים.

King of Greece. Here מֶלֶךְ stands for 'kingdom' but in the next clause for 'king'. On Greece (Hebrew יָוָן) cf. 10²⁰, 11²; Zech. 9¹³. The Hebrew word is formed from the Greek Ἰάονες, originally Ἰάϝονες. This was the name by which the Greeks were known to the Assyrians, Old Persians, and Egyptians, since they dwelt on the west coast of Asia Minor and came through their advanced civilization and commerce early into contact with these empires.

The first king, i.e. Alexander the Great.

8²². *And as for that which was broken and, &c.* This is not a real example of the *casus pendens*, which indicates a condition, the occurrence of which involves further consequences, cf. Ges.-Kautzsch, § 116 w. It summarizes shortly 8⁸ᵇ in order to make its interpretation the clearer in this context.

Kingdoms, i.e. מַלְכֻיּוֹת. With this peculiar plural, cf. חֲנִיּוֹת, Jer. 37¹⁶, see Ges.-Kautsch, § 87 i.

Shall arise. Most manuscripts read יעמדנה, but since the correct form תעמדנה occurs in the preceding clause, this anomalous form should with two manuscripts be replaced by the correct one. עמד is only used in the later books in the sense of קום 'to arise': cf. 8[23], 11[2, 3, 4, 12]; Neh. 7[65] = Ezra 2[63]; Ecclus. 47[1, 12]. Cf. Ps. 27[3] תקום ‧ ‧ ‧ מלחמה with the later reproduction of exactly the same fact in 1 Chron. 20[4] תעמד מלחמה.

His nation, i.e. גויו. So LXX, Th., and Vulg. τοῦ ἔθνους αὐτοῦ. As Bevan remarks this restoration, first made by Graetz, is confirmed by the following phrase ולא בכחו. The suffix in each case refers to Alexander the Great. The MT wrongly reads גוי 'the nation'.

Not with his power. None of the four kingdoms (see note on 8[8]) which were to arise on the division of Alexander's empire would be of like power. The ב in בכחו is used similarly in 8[6]. As a standard of measurement ב is used in 2 Sam. 14[26]; Deut. 3[11].

8[23]. *Their kingdom,* i.e. מַלְכוּתָם where the suffix is masc. where it should be fem. Cf. מהם in 8[9]. The four kingdoms were to come to an end with the death of Antiochus.

When their transgressions are come to the full, i.e. כְּתֹם פִּשְׁעֵיהֶם as in the LXX and Th. πληρουμένων τῶν ἁμαρτιῶν αὐτῶν. The Pesh. and Vulg. support this text save that they omit the suffix. It is strange that Ewald, Bevan, Von Gall, Marti, &c., follow the later versions in omitting the suffix. But not only do the LXX, Th., and the context support the suffix, but also a doublet of this clause in Cod. of the LXX (see Field, ii, p. 924) which reads ὡς ἂν σφραγίσονται τὰ παραπτώματα αὐτῶν = כְּתָם פִּשְׁעֵיהֶם. פִּשְׁעֵיהֶם is we may safely conclude, the original text. The wrong text arose simply through the misplacement of the ה. Next on the basis of the LXX, Th., Pesh., and Vulg. we may accept כְּתֹם as also original, though the MT כהתם could stand, if we emend הַפִּשְׁעִים into פִּשְׁעֵיהֶם = 'when they had completed their transgressions'. From כהתם arose the variant כהתם above referred to, cf. 9[24]. In 9[24], and generally, the Hiph'il of תם is transitive and has its object expressed (save in 2 Sam. 20[18]; Isa. 33[1]). Thus, unless we read פשעיהם it is best to regard כהתם as secondary. Of course we might take התם as intransitive as in Isa. 33[1], but our author uses the Hiph'il transitively in 9[24] as it all but universally is used. Our text then will refer to the heathen whose sins had reached their climax under Antiochus.

If we follow the MT we should render 'when the sinners (הַפֹּשְׁעִים) fill up their measure'.

Insolent. עַז־פָּנִים seems to be borrowed from Deut. 28⁵⁰. The LXX and Th. render ἀναιδὴς προσώπῳ: cf. Prov. 7¹³ where the verb is used of the harlot.

Skilled in double dealing. So Bevan. The sense is that he was skilled in ambiguous expression, a master of intrigue: cf. 11²¹. The same idea is partly to be found in 11²¹, where he is said to have 'obtained the kingdom by flatteries'. Otherwise render literally 'skilled in dark sayings'.

8²⁴. [*But not by his own power*]. These words are interpolated after 'his power shall be mighty'. They imply, if rendered as they are here, that Antiochus would be strong by the permission of God. If the phrase belongs to the original it is best to render it 'but not by his power', i.e. but by his intrigues. But, as Bevan suggests and as Marti and others adopt the suggestion, the phrase should be excised as an intrusion from ver. 22. It is omitted by Th. The phrase, which in ver. 22 applies to all the successors of Alexander, is an idle repetition here.

Shall **devise** *presumptuous things.* The combination נפלאות ישׂחית is, as Marti observes, so astounding that we must recognize in ישׂחית a corruption due to השׁחית which follows a few words later. Job 37⁵ is quoted in support of נפלאות as an adverb, but Duhm, Driver, and Buchanan Gray and others rightly regard the text in Job as corrupt and take the word as a noun in the acc. So Bevan, Marti, and others do here. Bevan emends יַשְׂחִית into יָשִׂיחַ. This gives a good text: 'shall utter presumptuous things'. Bevan compares 11³⁶ ידבר נפלאות. We should compare also מְמַלֵּל רברבן 7⁸, ²⁰. But the word is purely poetical in this sense, and the construction before us does not occur with this meaning: cf. Ps. 105² = 1 Chron. 16⁹. Hence I propose to emend ישׂחית into יחשׁב, seeing that the very same corruption occurs in 2 Sam. 20¹⁵ of חשׁב into שׂחת, and furthermore that חשׁב is used twice in 11²⁴, ²⁵ in reference to the designs of Antiochus. Accordingly we render 'shall devise presumptuous things'. This corruption may have arisen even in the Aramaic original whence the Hebrew is translated; for שׂחת is found in Aramaic inscriptions of the 8th cent. B.C. and in *Aramaic Papyri*, and חשׁב is also Aramaic, cf. 4³² in our text and the *Aram. Pap.* 81¹, where we find a noun derived from it.

8²⁴ ᶜ⁻²⁵ ᵃ. This passage is corrupt as a number of the foremost scholars have recognized, but happily the LXX provides us with the means of emending it, though even the LXX includes two renderings of one and the same phrase. Where this dittograph in the text may have originated we shall consider later. The MT text והשחית עצומים ועם קדושים ועל שכלו והצליח מרמה בידו (which is generally rendered 'And he shall destroy the strong (or 'the many') and the people of the saints, and through his policy he shall cause fraud to prosper') Bevan flatly declares is impossible to translate grammatically. Let us here give the LXX and the Hebrew text it presupposes:

LXX

8²⁴ ᶜ. καὶ φθερεῖ δυνάστας καὶ δῆμον ἁγίων = והשחית ¹ עצומים ועם קדושים

8²⁵ ᵃ. καὶ ἐπὶ τοὺς ἁγίους τὸ διανόημα αὐτοῦ   ועל קדושים שכלו והצליח
καὶ εὐοδωθήσεται

By this retroversion of the LXX into Hebrew we can easily recognize that ועם קדושים and ועל קדושים are doublets in the Hebrew, or possibly duplicate renderings of the Aramaic ועם קדישין—one of them in the text and the other in the margin— where the עם in the second case was a corruption of על. The context requires the excision of עם קדושים and 11²⁸ supports על ק"ק 'his heart shall be against the holy covenant'. So Graetz, Bevan, Marti, &c. Our author could hardly say that Antiochus would 'destroy the holy people' and then weakly add that 'his policy would be directed against them'. When this doublet has been removed, the interpretation, as Bevan points out, is clear. The עצומים or 'mighty ones' are 'the political enemies of Antiochus, who, being a usurper, naturally had many opponents among the the upper classes (see 11²²⁻⁴). It was not until he was firmly established on the throne that his hatred of the Jewish religion began to show itself (Bevan)'. Thus the Hebrew text should be read as follows: והשחית עצומים ועל קדושים שכלו והצליח. It should be added here that Driver seeks to defend the MT and renders 'and on the basis of his understanding he will cause deceit to prosper'. This is rather forced, but he cannot do better with

¹ The ו before השחית and after על שכלו is very difficult of explanation, if it is at all explicable, and in his *Hebrew Tenses*, §123 γ, Driver mentions it as an example of the perfect with *vav* consecutive. But the true text does not attest this *vav*.

the MT. On the other hand he makes no attempt to reconcile
the fact that in 8²⁴ it is stated that Antiochus 'shall destroy the
holy people' and yet after a prosperous career of intrigue it is
said in 8²⁵ that he shall only succeed in causing the destruction
of some by taking them unawares. His objection also to Bevan's
acceptance of the reading of the LXX on the ground that שׂכל
does not signify διανόημα or 'mind' is of no weight; for though
Bevan so translates, it is not necessary for his emendation.
'Policy' or 'astuteness' will serve just as well. There can be
no doubt, moreover, that διανόημα is here the LXX's rendering
of שׂכל; for in 11³⁵ we find διανοηθήσονται as a rendering of ישׂבילו,
the original text of which the MT יכשלו is a corruption.

8²⁵. *And he shall cause . . . to prosper.* Having recovered
what we conclude to be the original text in the preceding notes,
we see that in והצליח we have no example of *vav* consecutive with
the perfect following after an adverbial phrase—as the corrupt
Massoretic text represents it and as Driver interprets it (*Tenses*,
§ 123 γ)—and therefore not admitting of translation. The *vav*
here is to be translated.

Magnify himself in his heart. . Cf. 8⁴, ⁸, ¹¹.

In their security shall he destroy many. Antiochus will attack
them when off their guard. But בשׁלוה can also be rendered
'unawares'. The text probably refers to the treacherous attack
on Jerusalem recounted in 1 Macc. 1²⁹, ³⁰, where the Greek word
ἐξάπινα is used, which Greek word is twice used in the LXX of
Dan. 11²¹, ²⁴ as a rendering of this very Hebrew expression.

Prince of princes, i.e. God. Cf. 8¹¹. The princes are the
angelic chiefs. Cf. 12¹ 'Michael, the great prince', also 10²⁰.

Broken without hand, i.e. by Divine intervention. Cf. 2³⁴.
According to Polybius xxxi. 11, Antiochus died suddenly of
madness (δαιμονήσας) at Tabae in Persia in 164 B.C., a few months
after the rededication of the Temple, 25 Chisleu, 165. See note
on 11⁴⁵. The term 'broken' which was applied to the horn in
8⁸ is used frequently in the O.T. of the destruction of a kingdom
(Jer. 48⁴), of an army (2 Chron. 14¹³), and of individuals (Jer.
17¹⁸, our text 11²⁶).

8²⁶⁻⁷. A solemn affirmation of the truth of the vision and the
conclusion, cf. 10¹, 11², 12⁷. In Rev. 21⁵ᶜ God's testimony to
John's book is given, in 22⁶ Christ's attestation of its truth, and
John's own in 22⁸.

8^{26}. *Vision of the evenings.* Cf. ver. 14.

Shut thou up the vision. This vision, which is placed by the Seer in the third year of Belshazzar, relates really to the time of Antiochus. It is to be 'sealed', i.e. kept secret. This command is intended to explain how this revelation made to Daniel was not made known till the days of Antiochus—in other words till the actual time of its author. Cf. $12^{4, 9}$. Besides, the Seer declares that only the wise of that period will be able to understand it, cf. 12^{10}. On this command to reserve the revelation for a distant age, the aim of which we have just explained, cf. 1 Enoch 1^{2}, 93^{10}, 104^{12-13}; 2 Enoch 33^{9-11}, 35^{3}; 2 Ezra 14^{46}; and contrast with it the command in the Christian Apocalypse 22^{10}: 'Seal not up the words of the prophecy of this book; for the time is at hand'. The Christian Seer was not obliged to use an ancient name to win confidence in his message.

Belongeth to many days, i.e. refers to a distant age. The same Hebrew phrase occurs in Ezek. 12^{27}: cf. $8^{17, 19}$, 10^{14} of our text.

8^{27}. *Was sick.* The MT reads נִהְיֵיתִי וְנֶחֱלֵיתִי. The first word here, which occurs in 2^{1} and Micah 2^{4} and is in both passages corrupt, I have excised as a dittograph of the second. It is omitted by the LXX.

None understood it. The vision was sealed up, i.e. withheld from Daniel's contemporaries, it cannot refer to them. But since it was fully explained to Daniel according to $8^{16, 19}$, it can hardly be said that he did not understand *the vision*. Marti, following Bevan, regards the phrase as defective for 'I did not understand', i.e. אֵינֶנִּי מֵבִין instead of אֵין מ". He further maintains that Daniel understood the vision; for its explanation made him ill, but that he could not understand why it should be kept secret for many days. This further knowledge is provided in 9^{24-7}, by Gabriel, who declares in 9^{22} that he had come to give Daniel complete understanding. Yet see 12^{8}.

SECTION IX

i.e. Chapter 9, being the explanation of Jeremiah's prophecy of the seventy years given to the Seer in the first year of Darius by the Angel Gabriel to the intent that the seventy years meant seventy weeks of years.

In this section a prayer in Hebrew (9^{4-19}), drawn mainly from existing liturgies, was unskilfully interpolated before 145 B.C., while the Aramaic was being translated into Hebrew, or after the translation was completed.

The introduction to this chapter deals almost exclusively with the MT, the LXX, and other versions, and the help rendered by these versions towards the recovery of the original Hebrew version or even of the Aramaic original, where such an original existed. In the case of 9^{4-19} there can be no question of an Aramaic original. This prayer consists mainly of extracts from existing Hebrew liturgies. A comparison of 9^{4-19} with Neh. $1^{5 \text{ sqq.}}$, $9^{6 \text{ sqq.}}$; 1 Baruch $1^{15}-2^{15}$ shows that these writers have not borrowed from each other but from existing liturgical forms. Thus observe that, though in Jer. $32^{20, 21}$ it is stated that God had gotten Him a name as at this day and brought forth his people out of Egypt, these two statements are reproduced literally, but in the reverse order in Dan. 9^{15} and 1 Baruch 2^{11}. This and other like evidence go to prove that such passages are drawn independently from existing liturgies. But the compiler of this prayer has also frequently drawn materials directly from the Old Testament, cf. 9^6 with Jer. 44^{21}.

§ 1. *The interpolated Hebrew prayer.*

In the note under 9^{4-19} I have given the grounds on which this passage must be treated as an addition made to the text, either when the Aramaic $9^{1-3, 21-27}$ was being translated into Hebrew or after this translation was completed. It was interpolated at latest before the version of the LXX was made about 145 B.C. 9^{20} was added to connect it with what follows.

In this prayer the prophets and the priests are deliberately excluded from the list of the unfaithful classes in Israel: not so in Jer. 2^{26}, 5^{31}, 13^{13}, 14^{14}, 26^{7-8} nor in Neh. 6^{14}; see note on 9^6. In Neh. 9^{34} the priests, but not the prophets, are declared to be as disobedient as the kings, princes, and fathers.

This prayer is a mosaic of passages from the O.T. Thus for instance 9^{6-7} are drawn almost verbally from Jer. 7^9, 44^{21}, 4^4, 25^{26}, 16^{15}; Lev. 26^{40} (Ezek. 17^{20}).

The prayer was compiled by a Jew resident in Judaea. See note on 9^{16} and the full note on the prayer as a whole on 9^{4-19} p. 226-7.

§ 2. *Hebrew renderings of Aramaic phrases which have already occurred in 2^{4-7}.*

It should be remembered that only $9^{1-3,\ 20-27}$ is translation Hebrew, the rest was Hebrew to begin with.

9^{23}. יצא דבר a rendering of מאמר נפק in 2^{13} (4^{14}).

9^{27}. See § 3.

§ 3. Emendation through retranslation into Aramaic.

9^{27}. והגביר כרית—a mistranslation of וקים יתקף. The Hebrew translator has here given the wrong of two possible renderings of קים. Earlier scholars have taken הגביר to be corrupt. But this verb has the support of the LXX, Th., Aq., Symm., Pesh. (?), and Vulg. Moreover, this documentary evidence is confirmed by the fact that this is really a Hebrew translation of an analogous Aramaic phrase found in 6^8 לתקפה אסר following immediately after לקימה קים.

§ 4. Corruptions in the MT emended by means of the LXX or of other versions.

9^{24}. לכפר עון. Here the LXX and Vulg. require למחות עון. The reading of the MT is not here a corruption but a deliberate change. There is no evidence for its existence before the 2nd cent. A.D.

9^{25-26}. For בצוק העתים 'in troublous times' read with LXX (in the main) בקץ ה״ 'at the end of the times'.

9^{26}. For עַם='people' with 1 MS. and LXX, Th., Pesh., Aq., Vulg. read עִם 'with'.

9^{27}. For ישבית 'cause to cease' read with LXX, Th., and Vulg. יִשְׁבּוּת 'shall cease'.

§ 5. Emendations demanded by the context.

9^{25}. For להשיב ולבנות read לשוב ולב״ 'to rebuild'.

9^{27}. For על כנף read על כנו 'in its stead'.

§ 6. Lost phrases restored through LXX or other versions.

9^{15}. See note in loc.

9^{21}. We should with the LXX, Th. (and Vulg.) restore והנה 'behold' before האיש גבריאל. This is the only passage in Dan. 8-12 where the vav apodosis occurs. Text is corrupt in 8^{25}, where it reads the perfect with vav consecutive after an adverbial phrase. In 9^{26a} we have vav explicative.

9^{23}. Insert with Th., Vulg., and Sym. איש before חמודות. Cf. $10^{11,\ 19}$.

§ 7. *Very late Hebrew.*

9⁵. עֲוֹנִי—only elsewhere in O.T. in Esther 1¹⁶ for the older
הֲעֲוֹנוּ : and הִרְשַׁעְנוּ : cf. also 11³², 12¹⁰ when used intransitively
for the older רִשַׁעְנוּ. Yet the interpolated prayer contains in 9¹⁵
the older form רָשַׁעְנוּ,—a fact which need not surprise us.

9¹. *Darius.* See Introd. to 6, § 1. *b–g* (pp. 139–146).

Son of Darius. Ahasuerus is a transliteration of the Hebrew
אֲחַשְׁוֵרוֹשׁ (cf. Ezra 4⁶ ; Esther 1 ˢᵠᵠ·, which in Greek took the form
of Xerxes. But, since the Persian word was *Khshayârshâ*, the
original was no doubt transliterated אֲחֲשִׁירֵשׁ. In the *Aram. Pap.*
(Cowley, 5¹, 64. 20, 29) it is found three times in its Aramaic
form as חשיארש, the first of which is dated 471 B.C., and as
חשירש in 2¹ (484 B.C.). Xerxes I, who reigned from 485 to
465 B.C. ,was the son of Darius Hystaspis (521–485 B.C.).

Was made king. הָמְלַךְ the Hoph'al of מלך occurs only here.
Just as it has been shown on 6¹ (also pp. 139–141) that קַבֵּל does
not imply a delegated authority, no more does המלך do so here.
The fount of the authority of Darius according to the Seer is
God ; as is clear from 5²⁸ 'Thy (i.e. Belshazzar's) kingdom is
divided and given to the Medes and Persians'.

9². Daniel is represented as reflecting on Jeremiah's prediction
of the seventy years' exile. The author of the book was pro-
foundly conscious that this prediction had not been fulfilled
except in a very minor degree. Since, however, no such prophecy
could fail (see Introd. to chap. 6, p. 141 sqq.), he necessarily concluded that it had been misinterpreted and therefore needed to
be interpreted afresh. This new interpretation is given in the
vision in 9²⁴⁻²⁷. The probability, that this reinterpretation was
suggested by a comparison of Lev. 26¹⁸ ˢᵠᵠ· (where it is said that
the Israelites are to be punished *seven times* for their sins) and
Jer. 29¹⁰, 25¹¹, does not invalidate the reality of the vision nor
the possibility that this reinterpretation was actually received in
a vision. For the mind of the Seer necessarily works with the
materials accessible to him, however he may draw from other
sources. The Seer has already pondered on the possibility of
this explanation. In his vision he is assured that he is right.

Understood. With the form בִּינוֹתִי cf. רִיבוֹת Job 33¹³. Ges.-
Kautzsch (§ 73 *a*) is inclined to take these as shortened forms of
the Hiph'il, but in a note this hypothesis is withdrawn in favour

of the view that it is ' a secondary formation ' from the Imperf.
Qal יבִין, which was wrongly taken as an Imperf. Hiph'il. Nöldeke
(*ZDMG*.xxxvi, pp. 525 sqq.) shows that it cannot be a shortened
form of the Hiph'il. We have, therefore, to regard בִּינוֹתִי here, as
בִּין in 10¹, as irregular forms of the Perf. Qal, or take it to be an
error for בַּנְתִּי.

The books. The books here are the sacred books, i. e. the
Scriptures. The phrase implies the formation of a definite collection of O.T. books, but how extensive this collection was
cannot be determined from the present statement. The immediate books referred to are no doubt Leviticus, i. e. 26¹⁸ sqq.
and Jeremiah, i. e. 29¹⁰, 25¹¹. That the threefold division of the
O.T., the Law, the Prophets, and the Hagiographa already
existed in some form we know from the Preface to Sirach.

The word of God, i. e. דבר אלהים. Since 9⁴⁻²⁰ did not belong
originally to the text, as we shall see presently, this would
be the only verse in our author where the Divine name
Yahweh is used. Von Gall excises it on this ground, and compares 9²³,²⁵ for the use of 'word' standing in this sense by itself.
Marti would retain it on the ground that the writer is using
a citation from Jeremiah. But, since the LXX reads ὅτε ἐγένετο
πρόσταγμα τῇ γῇ = אשר היה דבר לאדמה, it seems that לאדמה is
corrupt for לאדני, and that the Hebrew read אדני here as in 1²
and not יהוה. Th. renders the phrase by λόγος κυρίου, therein supporting the MT in 9². So the LXX and Th. render אדני in 1²⁰, &c.
Hence I read here דְּבַר אלהים or דָּבָר לאלהים. It is to be noted
that the phrase recurs in 9²³ where the LXX has πρόσταγμα παρὰ
κυρίου. But the παρὰ κυρίου is not found in the MT nor in the versions.

Came to Jeremiah . . . seventy years. Cf. Jer. 25¹¹⁻¹², 29¹⁰.

*Which according to the word of the Lord . . . were to be accom-
plished:* lit. 'which, the word of the Lord came to Jeremiah the
prophet, were to be accomplished'. The אֲשֶׁר here is the subject
of לְמַלֹּאות; for this construction is in the Aramaic of our author
a familiar one: see notes on 2¹⁶,¹⁸, 5¹⁵, 6¹⁶ and Introd., p. § 20. *t.*
It is also a familiar construction in Hebrew. The words of
Jeremiah 25¹² בִּמְלֹאות שבעים שנה are clearly in the mind of the
writer. אשר is not therefore to be rendered as if it were an acc.
of limitation as in the RV., i. e. 'Whereof the word of the Lord
came to J. . . . for the accomplishing': and in Marti, Behrmann,
&c. The clause 'the word of the Lord came to J. the prophet'

are then parenthetical, if they are not a marginal gloss incorporated in the text, or a circumstantial clause. Deut. 5⁵ is such
a clause consisting of nineteen words, intervening between דִּבֶּר
and לֵאמֹר. See Driver, *Tenses*, § 161.

On the form לִמְלֹאות see Ges.-Kautzsch, § 74 *h*.

9³. *Set my face*, i. e. וָאֶתְּנָה אֶת פָּנַי as in 10¹⁵. For this phrase cf.
2 Chron. 20³. But observe שֶׂם פָּנִים in 11¹⁷.

God. Here the interpolator of 9⁴⁻²⁰ seems to have inserted
אדני before אלהים owing to the frequent occurrence of the former
in the interpolated prayer : i. e. 9⁴,⁷,⁸,⁹,¹⁵,¹⁶,¹⁹ (bis) and not elsewhere
in the book save in 1². In 6¹¹(¹⁰) where we have a parallel expression אלהים is used.

To seek by prayer: literally 'to seek prayer'. Cf. Zeph. 2³.

With fasting, i. e. as a preparation for the reception of a revelation ; cf. Exod. 34²⁸ ; Deut. 9⁹ ; Esther 4⁶.

Fasting and ˙sackcloth and ashes. As in Neh. 9¹ save in the
last phrase, where our author writes אפר where Neh. has אדמה.

9⁴⁻¹⁹. These verses, as Von Gall (123-6) and others have
recognized, are an interpolation. The interpolation was made
before the book was translated into Greek, but after it was
translated from Aramaic into Hebrew. Some of the grounds
for excising these verses as an interpolation are : (1) They
betray the hand of an interpolator since they are unnecessary
repetitions of 9³, ²⁰ sq. (2) The conclusion of the chapter *takes
no account of the subject of the prayer*, which supplicates for forgiveness and deliverance. Here a prayer for illumination and
not a liturgical confession is required by the context : cf. 9²¹ sqq.,
which proceeds to explain *the prophecy of Jeremiah.* (3) The
prayer contains clear evidence that it was written by one who
consciously expressed himself as a resident in Palestine—and
not in Babylon, as the author of the book as a whole represents
himself as being. Thus in 9⁷ it speaks of those 'that are near
and that are far off in all the countries whither thou hast driven
them'. Those 'that are near' are obviously the Jews in Palestine as opposed to those that are far off in all the countries
whither they had been carried into exile. Again in 9¹⁶ the
words 'because for our sins and for the iniquities of our fathers,
Jerusalem and thy people have become a reproach to all that
are *round about us*', betray the hand of a resident in Judaea,
especially those in italics. In 1 and 2 Baruch analogous pheno-

mena occur, as we shall discover as we advance. (4) The name
Yahweh is found in these verses, but not elsewhere in Daniel,
except in 9^2, where it is an interpolation, and where Adonai was
the original Hebrew as the corrupt text of the LXX shows. In
9^2 the divine name Yahweh owes its presence to a later scribe,
who was influenced by its occurrence five times in 9^{4-20}.

(5) In 9^{4-19} there are no Aramaisms. But Aramaisms are, as
we have seen, not infrequent throughout the rest of the Hebrew
sections in Daniel.

(6) The prayer asks for the immediate advent of the kingdom :
cf. 9^{17-19}. But, according to Jeremiah's prophecy, Daniel knew
that the deliverance of the Jews could not come for 'many days',
8^{26}, i. e. till some distant future.

(7) A critical comparison of 9^{4-19}, with Neh. $1^{5 \text{ sqq.}}$, $9^{6 \text{ sqq.}}$;
1 Bar. $1^{15 \text{ sqq.}}$, shows that repeatedly the verses in Daniel agree
word for word with those in the passages just mentioned, and that
the writers of these passages have not borrowed from each other
but from existing liturgical forms, which each writer adapted
more or less fully to his own requirements.

On the above grounds, which will be strengthened as we
advance, we conclude that 9^{4-19} is an addition to the text, 9^{20}
serving to connect it with what follows.

9^4. *Prayed . . . and made confession.* Cf. Neh. 1^6 'pray . . .
and confess'. הִתְוַדָּה stands here absolutely as in Ezra 10^1 ;
Neh. 9^3. It is only used in late Hebrew.

O Lord the great and dreadful God . . . commandments. These
clauses agree literally with Neh. 1^5. Cf. also 9^{32}. It was clearly
a current liturgical form. The words 'which keepeth covenant
and mercy with them . . . that keep his commandments' are
drawn word for word from Deut. 7^9 : cf. Exod. 20^6. The particle
אָנָּא rendered 'O' is a strong expression of entreaty, 'Ah, now'.
It is found in the same connexion in Neh. 1^5, where the R.V.
renders it 'I beseech thee'.

Love thee . . . thy commandments. So the LXX, Th., and
Vulg. The use of the second person is supported by the next
verse. The MT reads 'him' and 'his'.

9^5. *Have sinned . . . and done wickedly.* Our text חטאנו ועוינו
והרשענו has its equivalent in 1 Bar. 2^{12} ἡμάρτομεν, ἠσεβήσαμεν, ἠδικήσαμεν : and in Ps. 106^6 with an additional phrase. The ultimate
source is 1 Kings 8^{47} חטאנו והעוינו רשענו, where this confession

is commanded in Solomon's prayer exactly as in our text, save
that the writer of this confession in our text has replaced the
Hiph'il, which is the older form, העוינו ('dealt perversely') by the
Qal עוינו, which is late Hebrew—only once elsewhere in O.T.,
Esther 1[16], and רשענו by הרשענו, which is late Hebrew, when
used intransitively: cf. 11[32], 12[10]. Yet in 9[15] we find רשענו an
example of the classical use which has survived in this compila-
tion from ancient liturgies.

And turned aside, i. e. וָסוֹר. The infinitive absolute here
replaces the finite verb: cf. Ges.-Kautzsch, § 113 *z*. מצותך is
written defectively: see Ges.-Kautzsch, § 91 *n*.

9[6]. Two classes are distinguished, the nobility embracing the
kings, princes, and fathers, and the people of the land. This
latter phrase—עם הארץ—came in later Judaism to denote the
uncultured and ignorant laity. The term 'fathers' here denotes
not 'forefathers' but 'leaders'.

Neither have we hearkened unto thy servants the prophets. Cf.
Neh. 9[34] 'Neither have our kings, our princes . . . nor our
fathers . . . hearkened unto thy commandments'. Cf. Jer. 26[5]
'to hearken to . . . my servants the prophets': also 29[19], 35[15],
44[4], all of which include the phrases 'servants the prophets' and
'have not hearkened'.

*To our kings, our princes, and our fathers, and to all the people
of the land.* This clause is borrowed almost literally from Jer.
44[21] 'Your fathers, your kings and your princes, and the people
of the land'. In the confession in Neh. 9[32] there is a different
enumeration of the classes concerned : 'on our kings, on our
princes, and on our priests, and on our prophets, and on our
fathers, and on all thy people'. So again in Neh. 9[34], with the
omission of 'and on all this people', and in 1 Baruch 1[16] with
the same omission of 'and on all thy people'. Here clearly the
writer follows Jeremiah where he differs from later writers. It
is remarkable that the compiler of this prayer excludes the
prophets and the priests from the list of the unfaithful, and
represents the sin of Israel and Judah as originating in their
disobedience to the guidance of the prophets: cf. 9[6,10]. Not so
Jer. 14[14], and frequently Neh. 6[14]. In Neh. 9[34] the priests but
not the prophets are mentioned as guilty.

9[7]. *Righteousness belongeth unto thee, but unto us confusion of
face, as it is this day; to the men of Judah and to the inhabitants*

of Jerusalem. These words are found also in 1 Baruch 1[15]
τῷ κυρίῳ Θεῷ ἡμῶν ἡ δικαιοσύνη, ἡμῖν δὲ αἰσχύνη τῶν προσώπων ὡς ἡ ἡμέρα αὕτη,
ἀνθρώπῳ Ἰούδα καὶ τοῖς κατοικοῦσιν Ἰερουσαλήμ. The phrase 'confusion
of face' is found Jer. 7[19]; Ps. 44[15]; 2 Chron. 32[21]; Ezra 9[7].

To the men of Judah and to the inhabitants of Jerusalem. This
combination is peculiar to Jeremiah (eight times 4[4], &c.) and
2 Kings 23[2] (= 2 Chron. 34[30]) in the O.T. outside the present
passage. It is reproduced in 1 Baruch 1[15], as we have shown
in the preceding note just as in our text.

That are near and that are far off. Cf. 2 Chron. 6[36].

In all the countries whither thou hast driven them. From Jer.
16[15], 23[3,8], 32[37]. This clause is reproduced in 1 Baruch 2[4,13,29].

Their unfaithfulness wherein they have dealt unfaithfully. The
words connote treachery rather than trespass. They are found
in Lev. 26[40]; Ezek. 17[20], 18[24]; 1 Chron. 10[13].

9[8–9]. These two verses are expansions of the introductory
clauses in 9[7].

9[8]. *O Lord,* i. e. יהוה. So Ginsburg, Baer, with many manuscripts, but Kittel אדני.

To us . . . confusion of face. Cf. 9[7] note.

To our kings, &c. See 9[6] note.

9[9]. *Forgivenesses* Cf. Neh. 9[17] 'a God of forgivenesses'
(הַסְּלִיחוֹת as in our text).

9[10]. *Neither have we obeyed the voice . . . which he set before us.*
Almost word for word from Jer. 26[4 c–5 a]. The phrase 'law
which I set before you' is found in Deut. 4[8], 11[32]; Jer. 9[13], 44[10].

*To walk in his laws which he set before us by his servants the
prophets.* Here it is to be observed that the writer uses the
plural of תורה, i. e. תורתיו 'his laws'. When this word is used
in the plural it has a general meaning of instructions and
teachings, whether attributed to God directly or to the prophets
or priests. It occurs only about thirteen times in the plural,
and in the plural 'the laws' were never defined as 'the laws of
Moses'. When the Law of Moses or Deuteronomy, which was
ascribed to Moses, is referred to, the singular is always used as
in 9[11,13], in the words that follow. In Neh. 9[13, 14] we have
exactly the same succession of the plural 'laws' and 'a law by
the hand of Moses thy servant'. In Neh., however, the 'laws'
are not those made known by the prophets as in our text, but
are those which in conjunction with 'judgments', 'statutes', and

'commandments' God gave on Sinai. In 1 Baruch 1¹⁸, 2¹⁰ we find πορεύεσθαι τοῖς προστάγμασιν Κυρίου οἷς ἔδωκεν κατὰ πρόσωπον ἡμῶν, without any mention of the prophets in this passage, though they are referred to in 1²¹, 2²⁰, ²⁴. Moreover in 1²⁰, ²¹ the activities of Moses and the prophets are distinguished just as in our text.

The prophets occupy a high place in this prayer. They are never blamed. They are regarded as the leaders of the nation into fresh truth and higher obedience. Where the law of Moses is mentioned, the prayer deals mainly with the penalties that Israel has brought upon itself by disobedience to 'the law of Moses', though this law is identified with the law of God in 9¹¹.

To walk in his laws. But in Jer. 26⁴(32²³, 44¹⁰) the sing. 'law' and not 'laws' is used. The LXX, which reads κατακολουθῆσαι τῷ νόμῳ σου ᾧ ἔδωκας ἐνώπιον [Μωσῆ καὶ] ἡμῶν, is corrupt. Th. and the Pesh. support the MT, and therein these three agree rather with Neh. 9¹³, ¹⁴ (see preceding note) than with Jer. 26⁴.

9¹¹. *The curse . . . and the oath.* Cf. Num. 5²¹; Neh. 10²⁹.

The curse . . . that is written in the law of Moses. Cf. Deut. 29²⁰; 1 Baruch 1²⁰.

Hath . . . been poured out, i.e. וַתִּתַּךְ. Cf. 9²⁷; Jer. 42¹⁸, 44⁶; 2 Chron. 12⁷, 34²¹, ²⁵. The expression is Aramaic also. Cf. the *Zinjirli Inscription* (Cooke, 61²³) והדד חרה ליתכה 'Let Hadad pour out wrath upon him'. In Rev. 16¹ we have the same metaphor: ἐκχέετε τὰς ἑπτὰ φιάλας τοῦ θυμοῦ τοῦ θεοῦ.

Moses the servant of God. Cf. Neh. 10²⁹ and the form 'M. the servant of Yahweh', Deut. 34⁵; Josh. 1¹, ¹³, &c.

9¹²⁻¹³ᵃ. Cf. 1 Baruch 2¹⁻² καὶ ἔστησε Κύριος τὸν λόγον αὐτοῦ, ὃν ἐλάλησεν ἐφ' ἡμᾶς καὶ ἐπὶ τοὺς δικαστὰς ἡμῶν τοὺς δικάσαντας τὸν Ἰσραὴλ καὶ ἐπὶ τοὺς βασιλεῖς ἡμῶν καὶ ἐπὶ τοὺς ἄρχοντας ἡμῶν καὶ ἐπὶ ἄνθρωπον Ἰσραὴλ καὶ Ἰούδα, τοῦ ἀγαγεῖν ἐφ' ἡμᾶς κακὰ μεγάλα, ἃ οὐκ ἐποιήθη ὑποκάτω παντὸς τοῦ οὐρανοῦ καθὰ ἐποιήθη ἐν Ἰερουσαλήμ, κατὰ τὰ γεγραμμένα ἐν τῷ νόμῳ Μωυσῆ. Here we have several clauses which reproduce Dan. 7¹²⁻¹³ᵃ and clauses out of Dan. 9⁷, ⁸, and differ mainly in the order of their occurrence. Furthermore the Greek of Baruch differs both from that of the LXX and of Th. Here the writer of 1 Baruch, as does our author, appears to make use of the same liturgical source. 1 Baruch may be as old as the end of the 2nd cent. B.C., though scholars are divided on this question. They are as a whole agreed that 1 Baruch 1–3⁸ was written in Hebrew.

9¹². *Hath confirmed his words.* This clause is found also in Neh. 9⁸, Deut. 9⁵, as also in 1 Baruch 2¹, ²⁴.

Judges. A general term for rulers as in Amos 2^3; Ps. 2^{10}, but in the parallel passage in 1 Baruch 2^1 the term is used of the Judges in Israel that preceded the kings.

Bringing upon us a great evil. Cf. Jer. 35^{17}, 36^{31}.

For under the whole heaven hath not been done, &c. Cf. 1 Baruch 2^2 for the same clause, also Exod. 9^{18}, 10^6, 11^6.

9^{13}. *As it is written in the law of Moses.* This phrase occurs three times earlier in the O.T., i.e. 1 Kings 2^3, 2 Chron. 23^{18}, 35^{12}. Cf. 'book of law of Moses', Joshua 8^{31}, 23^6, &c.

All this evil is come upon us. The אֵת before כל הרעה had best be excised. Behrmann takes this clause as the acc. after לְהָבִיא. Bevan explains the את as due to the preceding passive כָּתוּב, and compares Num. 32^5; 1 Kings 2^{21}. But this explanation leaves difficulties in the text. Ges.-Kautzsch, § 117 *m* regards אֵת־ as here almost equivalent in sense to the Latin *quod attinet ad,* and so as introducing the noun with some emphasis.

Entreated the favour, i.e. חִלִּינוּ אֶת־פְּנֵי יי‎. A familiar phrase in O.T. Cf. Jer. 26^{19}; 1 Sam. 13^{12}; Exod. 32^{11}. With 9^{13} cf. 1 Baruch 2^{7-8} πάντα τὰ κακὰ ταῦτα . . ἦλθεν ἐφ' ἡμᾶς. Καὶ οὐκ ἐδεήθημεν τοῦ προσώπου Κυρίου τοῦ ἀποστρέψαι ἕκαστον ἀπὸ τῶν νοημάτων τῆς καρδίας αὐτῶν τῆς πονηρᾶς, which appears to be derived from the same liturgy as that on which our author drew.

To have discernment in thy truth, i.e. to gain insight into God's revealed will as Driver and Prince explain. Or it may be rendered 'to deal wisely through thy truth', that is, to become wise through God's truth; so Von Lengerke and Behrmann.

9^{14}. Found almost verbally in 1 Baruch 2^{9-10}, 1^{18}.

Watched over the evil and brought it upon us. Cf. Jer. 1^{12} 'I watch over my word to bring it to pass', שֹׁקֵד אֲנִי עַל דְּבָרִי לַעֲשֹׂתוֹ‎, see also 31^{28}, 44^{27}, and 1 Baruch 2^9 ἐγρηγόρησεν . . . ἐπὶ τοῖς κακοῖς καὶ ἐπήγαγε κτλ. This means that God is not mocked. His judgements are duly executed.

For the Lord our God is righteous in all his works, &c. Cf. Jer. 12^1; Ezra 9^{15}.

Righteous in all his works, i.e. in regard to all his works. Cf. Neh. 9^{33} where the same peculiar use, as Driver observes, of עַל is found. 'Thou art righteous in regard to all that is come upon us'. See also 1 Baruch 2^9.

9^{15-19}. *Prayer for deliverance* follows on the confession just made.

9^{15}. The first two clauses of this verse are borrowed ultimately

from Jer. 32²⁰, ²¹, but in reverse order. The first is from 32²¹
and the second from 32²⁰. 1 Baruch 2¹¹ reproduces Jer. 32²⁰,²¹
but inverts the order as does our text: ἐξήγαγες τὸν λαόν σου ἐκ γῆς
Αἰγύπτου ἐν χειρὶ κραταιᾷ . . , καὶ ἐποίησας σεαυτῷ ὄνομα, ὡς ἡ ἡμέρα αὕτη.

*Thou hast brought thy people forth out of the land of Egypt with
a mighty hand* ⌜*and a stretched out arm*⌝. Cf. Jer. 32²¹. I have
with the LXX added the clause in brackets, but the LXX omits
'with a mighty hand' which the MT, Th., and Pesh. attest.
Both phrases are found in Jer. 32²¹ and also in 1 Baruch 2¹¹
though separated from each other (ἐν χειρὶ κραταιᾷ . . . καὶ ἐν βραχίονι
ὑψηλῷ). It is hardly credible that the translator or a copyist of
the LXX would replace the one phrase by the other, though he
might inadvertently omit one or other of the two. Accordingly
I conclude that the text originally was ביד חזקה ובאזרוע נטויה.
The same combination is found in Deut. 26⁸, Jer. 32²¹ in the same
connexion. If 1 Baruch 1¹⁵-3⁸ is dependent on Daniel, then we
have an external testimony to the presence of these two phrases
in our text. If it is not dependent on Daniel, then it attests their
presence in the liturgy on which both Daniel and 1 Baruch drew.
In Deut. 6²¹, 9²⁶ only the first phrase occurs.

Gotten thee renown. Cf. Jer. 32²⁰; Neh. 9¹⁰; 1 Baruch 2¹¹;
also Isa. 63¹², ¹⁴; 2 Sam. 7²³ (here שׂום instead of עשׂה). The
remembrance of God's deliverances of Israel in the past was still
a strong factor in their faith during the Maccabean age.

We have done wickedly. On רשענו see note on 9⁵.

9¹⁶. *Thy righteous acts,* lit. 'righteousnesses' (צִדְקֹתֶךָ without י
of plural as מצותך in 9⁵), cf. Judges 5¹¹; 1 Sam. 12⁷; Mic. 6⁵;
Ps. 103⁶. The Seer implores Yahweh, as he calls to mind His
interventions on behalf of Israel in the past, to intervene now
on their behalf in their present sore distress, and to turn away
his anger from Israel who now confessed their sins and were
repentant. The turning away of His anger was synonymous
with the removal of their reproach in the sight of the heathen.
It was at once an act of mercy as well as of justice, and as such,
by virtue of His covenant with Israel, Israel claimed His help.
It is noteworthy that Th. and 1 Baruch 2¹² imply בכל־צדקתיך instead
of "בכל־צר and that the latter connects the phrase with the words
in the preceding verse, and so we have ἠδικήσαμεν . . . ἐπὶ πᾶσιν τοῖς
δικαιώμασίν σου. This forms a better parallel to the close of 9¹⁶.
Eleven Hebrew manuscripts read בכל instead of ככל. But רשע is

not followed by ב in the O.T. But ב could here be rendered 'despite'. If this is right then the first three words of this verse should be construed with the closing words of 9¹⁵ 'we have done wickedly, O Lord, despite all thy righteous acts'.

Let thine anger . . . be turned away. Cf. Num. 25⁴; Jer. 23²⁰, 30²⁴; 1 Baruch 2¹³.

Thy holy mountain. Cf. Isa. 2²ˢ⁹·; Ps. 2⁶, 15¹.

Iniquities of our fathers. Cf. Neh. 9²; 1 Baruch 3⁵· ⁷· ⁸. The phrase is found in the earlier books, cf. Jer. 11¹⁰; Lev. 26³⁹.

A reproach to all that are round about us. Cf. Ps. 44¹³, 79⁴. These words are spoken from the standpoint of a Jew resident in Judaea, see note on 9⁴⁻¹⁹. The taunts came from their heathen neighbours, the Edomites, Ammonites, and others. The same phrase is applied in 1 Baruch 2⁴ in the confession of the Palestinian Remnant 'round about *us*' (i.e. this remnant), whereas the phrase 'hath scattered *them*' refers to the exiles. Contrast the confession of the Exiles in Babylon 2¹³ 'We are but a few left among the heathen, where thou hast scattered *us*'; 3⁸ 'We are yet this day in our captivity, where thou hast scattered *us*'.

9¹⁷. *O our God.* So MT. The LXX and 1 Baruch 2¹⁴ (εἰσάκουσον, Κύριε, τῆς προσευχῆς ἡμῶν) read only אדני or יהוה 'O Lord', Th. 'O Lord our God'. If the latter is a conflation, which of the two texts is original?

Hearken unto the prayer. Cf. Neh. 1⁶; 1 Kings 8²⁸.

Cause thy face to shine upon. The LXX has ἐπιβλεψάτω τὸ πρόσωπόν σου ἐπί. But ἐπιβλεψάτω cannot be a rendering of הָאֵר. It appears to have read יֵרֶא. For the phrase in our text cf. Num. 6²⁵; Ps. 80¹⁹⁽²⁰⁾. This petition is the natural sequel to 'let thine anger . . . be turned away' in the preceding verse.

Desolate. שָׁמֵם is used of Mount Zion in Lam. 5¹⁸ and recalls שֹׁמֵם in 8¹³. Cf. 9²⁷, 11³¹, 12¹¹. The expression is probably chosen with reference to שִׁקּוּץ שֹׁמֵם 9²⁷, 12¹¹.

For the Lord's sake. This abrupt transition to the third person in the midst of a series of petitions in the second is very harsh, and suggests a corruption in the text. The evidence of the ancient versions turns this probability into a practical certainty. Accordingly we should either with the LXX ἕνεκεν τῶν δούλων σου, δέσποτα, read למען עֲבָדֶיךָ אדני 'for thy servants' sake, O Lord' (comparing Isa. 63¹⁷ 'return for thy servants' sake), so Bevan. Or with Th. and Vulg. למענך אדני 'for thine own sake, O Lord', so Kamphausen, Prince, &c. The latter, which recurs a few clauses later, has probably the support of 1 Baruch 2¹⁴ εἰσάκουσον, Κύριε, τῆς προσευχῆς ἡμῶν . . . καὶ ἐξελοῦ ἡμᾶς ἕνεκεν σοῦ.

9¹⁸. *O Lord . . . behold.* These clauses are borrowed literally from 2 Kings 19¹⁶ (= Isa. 37¹⁷). I have here followed the LXX and 1 Baruch 2¹⁶, which read Κύριε i.e. יהוה as does 2 Kings 19¹⁶. Th. of Dan. 9¹⁸ renders here κλῖνον, ὁ Θεός μου, τὸ οὖς σου καὶ ἄκουσον, where the LXX has πρόσχες, Κύριε, τὸ οὖς σου καὶ ἐπάκουσόν μου. The MT, which reads אלהי (Th. ὁ Θεός μου), thus seems to be secondary.

Open. פְּקָחָה *Kt.,* פְּקַח *Qr.* Perhaps we should punctuate (see Ges.-Kautzsch, § 48 *i*) פְּקָחָה as סְלָחָה and שְׁמָעָה in 9¹⁹.

Desolations. Cf. Isa. 61⁴.

The city over which thy name has been called. העיר אשר נקרא שמך עליה. It is best with Driver to render this idiom literally here. It implies that God has conquered it and made it His own: cf. 2 Sam. 12²⁸: also Deut. 28¹⁰; Isa. 4¹; Amos 9¹²; Jer. 7¹⁰. This expression recurs in the next verse. Cf. the rendering of the LXX and Th. as compared with that in 1 Baruch 2²⁶. Thus אשר ··· עליה is rendered by the LXX of Dan. 9¹⁸ by ἐφ' ἧς . . . ἐπ' αὐτῆς and in 1 Baruch 2²⁶ by οὗ . . . ἐπ' αὐτῷ.

Present our supplications before thee, i.e. מפילים תחנונינו לפניך. This idiom is found only in Jer. in the O.T., cf. 38²⁶, 42², ⁹, 36⁷, 37²⁰. The LXX renders freely δεόμεθα ἐν ταῖς προσευχαῖς ἡμῶν. Th. literally ῥιπτοῦμεν τὸν οἰκτειρμὸν ἡμῶν, 1 Baruch 2¹⁹ καταβάλλομεν τὸν ἔλεον—all independent renderings of the same Hebrew liturgical formula. I am quoting 1 Baruch to show that we have in it an independent witness to original liturgical formulae.

Thy great compassions. This expression is found in 1 Baruch 2²⁷; Neh. 9¹⁹, ²⁷, ³¹, and in the earlier books: Ps. 119¹⁵⁶; 2 Sam. 24¹⁴. It was thus a familiar formula in liturgical prayers.

8¹⁹. *Hear . . . forgive.* A reminiscence of 1 Kings 8³⁰, ³⁴, ³⁶.

Defer not. Cf. Ps. 40¹⁸⁽¹⁷⁾.

9²⁰. This verse serves to connect 9⁴⁻¹⁹ with its new context. 9³ was originally followed immediately by 9²¹. In 9²⁰ we have a summary of the interpolated prayer. It is composed of phrases which have already occurred in 9⁴⁻¹⁹. Thus for 'praying and confessing', cf. 9⁴; for 'my sin and the sin of my people Israel', cf. 9¹⁶; for 'presenting my supplication', cf. 9¹⁸; and for 'the holy mountain of my God', cf. 9¹⁶.

My sins and the sins. So LXX, Th., Pesh., Vulg. MT reads
'my sin and the sin'.

9²¹. Resumption of the original text.

In prayer, i.e. בִּתְפִלָּה. For this reading Ginsburg quotes
several witnesses, and, as Marti urges, it is to be preferred to
בַּתְּפִלָּה of the MT, which means that Daniel was 'repeating a
prayer learnt by heart'. The latter reading would suit, if 9⁴⁻¹⁹
belonged to the text. But the text does not include the prayer
which Daniel prayed from the depths of his heart with fasting
and sackcloth and ashes—the object of which was to learn the
true interpretation of the prophecy revealed to him (9³) and
which Gabriel assures him he had come to reveal to him. The
LXX also presupposes a good text ἐν τῇ προσευχῇ μου בתפלתי.

⌜Behold⌝. Since the LXX and Th. read καὶ ἰδού here and the
Vulg. *ecce*, I assume the loss of הנה in the Hebrew. In any case we
have the *vav* apodosis, three examples of which occur in chapter I,
but there before a verb, where it is also the *vav* consecutive.

The man Gabriel, האיש גבריאל. Cf. 8¹⁵ כמראה גבר.

†*Being sore wearied*†. This seems the only admissible
translation of מֻעָף בִּיעָף. The participle is thus the Hoph'al of יָעֵף.
But the sense is inappropriate as applied to an angel. On the
other hand this participle could be the Hoph'al of עוף and the
phrase rendered 'being caused to fly swiftly'. But בִּיעָף is in
this case incapable of explanation. It may possibly have originated as a dittograph of מעף. The above rendering, which ignores
ביעף, has the support of the ancient versions. LXX τάχει φερόμενος,
Vulg. *cito volans*, while Th. gives simply πετόμενος. On the other
hand, nowhere else in the O. T. are angels represented as having
wings. The first undoubted passage in Jewish literature which
bears on this question is I Enoch 61¹, and even there the angels
are not naturally winged but only adopt wings for a special purpose. The idea of wings was in due course taken from the winged
Seraphim and Cherubim and included in the conception of angels
generally.

If the text is right, then we must connect it with Daniel, as do
Meinhold and Keil, and render 'whom I had seen in the vision
aforetime when I was sore wearied'. In 8¹⁷, ¹⁸ Daniel was
affrighted, when Gabriel came to him, and lost consciousness.
It required the angel to touch him to restore him to consciousness and vigour. On this occasion also the touch of the angel

restores Daniel, who was no doubt overwearied by his prayer and fasting (9^3).

Touched me. נֹגֵעַ אֵלַי should naturally bear the same meaning here as in 8^{18}, 10^{16}, and so Th. renders ἥψατο. The touch of the angel strengthens Daniel. נגע can be used in a good sense as in these three passages. In 8^7, 12^{12} it has a neutral meaning 'to come near to' or 'to come to', which may be followed by unhappy or happy effects subsequently. As examples of the latter may be cited 12^{12}; of the former 8^7; Micah 1^9; Jer. 51^9; *Aram. Pap.* (Cowley) Aḥ. 165, 166. It could bear the meaning assigned to it in the LXX προσήγγισέ μοι, but that meaning does not suit the context, though Bevan, Behrmann, and Marti adopt it. By so doing, they are obliged to follow the text presupposed by the LXX at the beginning of the next verse.

The time of evening oblation. Cf. 2 Kings 16^{15}; Ezra $9^{4, 5}$, &c. See note on 6^{10}. The manuscripts vary between כ and ב before עת.

9^{22}. *Instructed me.* For וַיָּבֶן read ויבינני with Th. (συνέτισέν με) and Vulg. Cf. 8^{16}. The pronoun is all but necessary in the Hebrew. Otherwise with LXX (καὶ προσῆλθε) and Pesh. read ויבא or ויבו = וַיָּבֹא, as do Bevan and other scholars, comparing 1 King 12^{12}.

Gabriel's sole communication refers to the seventy weeks, but in no single respect to the subjects of the prayer in 9^{4-19}.

To make thee skilful of understanding, i.e. to make thee clear in understanding. The בינה in this phrase השכיל בינה serves to recall ואין מבין in 8^{27}, as Marti observes. בינה is here used adverbially; cf. Deut. $2^{9,24}$ אל תתגר בם מלחמה. ' Phrases of this kind form the transition from the use of the abstract verbal noun as the object of the verb (as in ויך בהם מכה גדולה 1 Sam. 19^8) to the so-called accusative of manner (as in ... Jer. 3^{15}).'— Bevan.

9^{23}. *A word went forth.* The 'word' here does not mean the command given to Gabriel to go to Daniel but refers to the Divine pronouncement made in 9^{24-7}. It is repeated in the closing words of this verse. יצא דבר would be the classical Hebrew equivalent (cf. Isa. 2^2; Mic. 4^2; later Hebrew Esther 1^{19}) of the Aramaic מאמר נפק: cf. 2^{13}, 4^{17}.

After 'went forth' it is possible that with the LXX παρὰ κυρίου we should add 'from the Lord'. מאדני could easily fall out before the next word ואני through homoioteleuton.

To tell (*thee*). After להגיד add לְךָ with two manuscripts and LXX, Th., Pesh., Vulg.

⌜*Man*⌝ *greatly beloved.* I have here with Th. (ἀνὴρ ἐπιθυμιῶν), Vulg., Sym. (ἀνὴρ ἐπιθυμητός) restored איש before חמודות. Thus we recover the full phrase which recurs in 10¹¹,¹⁹ (MT, LXX, Th., Vulg.). It is true that the plural by itself can be put as an emphatic predicate: cf. Cant. 5¹⁶ וכלו מחמדים 'he is altogether lovely'. With the use of the fem. plural חמודות as 'an object of desires': cf. Ps. 21⁷ ברכות as 'an object of blessings': 110³ 'thy people is freewillingnesses' נדבות: Ezek. 27³⁶ 'Thou art become terrors' בלהות: cf. Ges.-Kautzsch, § 141 c. But Driver (*Tenses*, § 189 (2)) states that it is 'unnecessary and wrong' to supply איש. It is true of course that the idiom in the MT is good Hebrew. Considering, however, the frequent corruptions of the MT of Daniel, and the fact that the full phrase occurs twice in the next chapter, and that in Daniel חמודות is used in our author only of *things* elsewhere (10³, 11³⁸, ⁴³), it is only reasonable to infer that חמודות needed to be more clearly defined, when applied to a man, by prefixing איש. With this phrase in our author we might compare Jer. 31²⁰ ילד שעשועים = 'a pleasant child'. Bevan explains the LXX ἐλεεινός (ἄνθρωπος ἐλεεινός 10¹¹, ¹⁶) as a rendering of חֲסָדוּת, and compares Jer. Sot. ix. 24ᶜ אנשי חסידות.

9²⁴ (1) *The criticism of the text.*

This is a most difficult verse. It is worth while devoting some attention to the versions in the hope of throwing some light on our text. First of all Th. makes no contribution. Some of the manuscripts indeed read ἕως τοῦ παλαιωθῆναι τὸ παράπτωμα, καὶ τοῦ συντελεσθῆναι ἁμαρτίαν, which presupposes לְבַלֵּא as a doublet of לבלא.[1] This variant is the only one with which Tertullian, *Adv. Jud.* viii, is acquainted, 'quoad usque inveteretur delictum'. When we remove καὶ ἀπαλεῖψαι τὰς ἀδικίας,[2] which is a borrowed phrase from the LXX, and which forms with καὶ τοῦ ἐξιλάσασθαι ἀδικίας a duplicate rendering of ולכפר עון, Th. has exactly the same number of clauses as in the MT. But τοῦ

---

[1] Read לְכַלּוֹת with Bevan, Kamphausen, and others. Yet לבלא may be an Aramaized form of it.

[2] Observe that all the infinitives in Th. in this verse are preceded by τοῦ except this borrowed one and also that in the LXX none of the infinitives is preceded by τοῦ.

σφραγίσαι ἁμαρτίας clearly goes back to לְחְתֹּם חַטָּאות, which is the
Kt. of the MT. The Qr. "ח להתם is supported by Aquila τοῦ
τελειῶσαι τὴν ἀθεσίαν.

Thus the Kt. and Qr. of the MT in this clause existed in the
second century A. D. The Vulg. diverges in two respects from
the MT : (1) '(ut) finem accipiat peccatum' = לְהָתֵם חַטָּאת, which
is the Qr.; (2) '(ut) deleatur[1] iniquitas' = לִמְחוֹת עוֹן and not
לכפר עון. The Pesh. supports the Qr. להתם חטאת.

We now turn to the LXX. It is very corrupt, yet it can give
some help towards the recovery of the original text. The first
clause τοῦ συντελεσθῆναι τὴν ἁμαρτίαν is obviously a rendering of
לכלות הפשע (i. e. לכלא). The second clause, καὶ †τὰς ἀδικίας σπανί-
σαι† is corrupt. The order of the words is wrong. In the other
six clauses in this verse the verb precedes the noun as it should
here. Next, since ἀδικία is never in the LXX used as a rendering
of חטאת, it follows that חטאת did not occur in the faulty Hebrew
manuscript used by the LXX translator. Finally, σπανίσαι—so
rendered also in the Syr[h]—appears to be best explained as a
corruption of σφραγίσαι (so Th.).[2] For Kt. חטאות (so also LXX,
Th., Pesh.) Qr. reads חטאת (so Aq., Vulg.).

The third clause is καὶ ἀπαλεῖψαι τὰς ἀδικίας. This corresponds
to the Hebrew לכפר עון. But neither ἀπαλείφω nor ἐξαλείφω is
ever used in the LXX as a rendering of כֵּפֶר, but of מחה. Hence
the LXX translator, like the translator of the Vulg. as we found
above had למחות עון (cf. Ps. 51[11], &c.) before him.

The next clause καὶ διανοηθῆναι τὸ ὅραμα is clearly wrong. There
could hardly be two references to the vision within six short
clauses. Moreover, the context is concerned with the various
stages of the fulfilment of the vision and cannot admit of an
otiose reference to the understanding of it in the midst of these.
The aim of the entire message is to make the Seer understand
the vision. Can this unmeaning phrase be explained? I can

---

[1] מחה occurs thirty-four times in the O.T. Of these it is rendered thirty
times in Vulg. by delere, especially in Ps. 51[3,11]; Isa. 43[25], 44[22], where it
expresses the full and free Divine forgiveness. Hence we justly conclude that
it occurred in Dan. 9[24].

[2] So Bevan. C. H. H. Wright says this is incorrect, and suggests that
σπανίσαι is a rendering of לכלא, but even the translator of the LXX could
hardly have been guilty of such a rendering. There seems to be no way of
explaining σπανίσαι through a corruption of the Hebrew or of the Aramaic
original.

only suggest mere possibilities. διανοηθῆναι = לֹהבן which may be a corruption of לֹהביא. The converse corruption we found in 9²². If this is the לֹהביא that follows in the next clause, then the intervening words τὸ ὅραμα καὶ δοθῆναι are an interpolation. But why were they interpolated? There is still another possibility. The LXX originally omitted προφήτην or according to the Syrʰ καὶ προφήτην καὶ εὐφρᾶναι. Is then לֹהביא חזון a dittograph of חזון ונביא which got displaced into this earlier clause and was then emended in order to give some seeming sense? If we could regard διανοηθῆναι (i. e. לֹהבן corrupt for לֹהביא) τὸ ὅραμα as a dittograph, then by its omission we should attain to a text full of meaning. For δοθῆναι δικαιοσύνην αἰώνιον (=לתת צדק ע״) would mean 'to set up everlasting righteousness', i. e. The kingdom of everlasting righteousness.

Next in the fifth clause συντελεσθῆναι = לֹהתם which is corrupt for לֹחתם—the converse corruption of what the translator of Th. found in the second clause.

Finally, in the sixth clause εὐφρᾶναι = לְשַׂמֵּחַ which is corrupt for לִמְשֹׁחַ. Hence read χρίσαι. The same error occurs probably in Hos. 7³.

Thus the recovered and emended text of the LXX would run thus: συντελεσθῆναι (rd. συντελέσαι) τὴν ἁμαρτίαν καὶ τὰς [ἀδικίας] †σφραγίσαι† (rd. πληρῶσαι) καὶ ἀπαλεῖψαι τὰς ἀδικίας καὶ δοθῆναι δικαιοσύνην αἰώνιον καὶ †συντελεσθῆναι† (rd. σφραγίσαι) τὸ ὅραμα καὶ ⟨προφήτην⟩ καὶ †εὐφρᾶναι† (rd. χρίσαι) ἅγιον ἁγίων. Thus the Hebrew text presupposed by the LXX and emended is to be translated as follows:

> 'Seventy weeks are decreed upon thy people and upon thy holy city
> To complete the transgression and bring sins to the full,
> And to blot out iniquity and to set up everlasting righteousness,
> And to seal vision and ⌐prophet⌐ and to anoint a most holy place.'

24 ᵇ ᶜ (restored text) לְכַלּוֹת הַפֶּשַׁע וּלְהָתֵם חַטָּאוֹת
וְלִמְחוֹת עָוֹן וְלָתֵת צֶדֶק עֹלָמִים.

As we have seen above the LXX together with the Vulg. in the third line diverges from the MT in reading 'to blot out' (cf. Ps. 51¹¹) where the MT has 'to make reconciliation for'. Again in the same line we have 'to set up'. Thus the text of the third

line is as old as 145 B.C. There is no external attestation of
the text of the MT for this line earlier than the 2nd cent. A.D.

(2) *The interpretation of the text.*

This verse lays down the principle that the seventy years
foretold by Jeremiah are to be understood as seventy weeks of
years, i.e. 490 years, and that these years concerned God's holy
people and city. This is clear from 9^2, where Daniel is said to
have observed in the Scriptures that the seventy years of
Jeremiah had reference to the desolations of Jerusalem. But
since the Seer did not understand why it should not be fulfilled
for so many days, he sought illumination through a vision 9^3.
In answer to his prayer Gabriel is sent, who explained the
years to mean weeks of years. The notion of a week of years
was already familiar to the Jews. But the word שָׁבוּעַ which in
$9^{24, 25, 26, 27}$ means a week of years, has not this meaning elsewhere
in the O.T. It occurs, however, with this meaning some
hundreds of times in the Book of Jubilees (bef. 100 B.C.) and in
the Mishna (Sanh. v. 1) and the Talmud. But the way had
been prepared for the statement in our text by 2 Chron. 36^{21}
'until the land had enjoyed her sabbaths; for so long as she lay
desolate she kept sabbath, to fulfil three score and ten years'
(cf. Lev. $26^{34, 35}$). Here the ideas of seventy years and of
sabbatical years are brought together.

Weeks. Our author uses the masc. plural שָׁבֻעִים six times,
whereas the rest of the O.T. uses שָׁבֻעוֹת.

The transgression, i.e. the heathen worship established in the
Temple: cf. $8^{12, 13, 23}$.

Are decreed, i.e. נֶחְתַּךְ, a ἅπ. λεγ. in the O.T. but found in the
Mishna and Talmud in the sense of 'to decide'. The singular
verb after the plural subject is to be explained on the ground
that the seventy weeks are regarded as a unit of time: cf. Gen.
35^{26} for a still stranger example of this idiom. When this period
of seventy weeks had passed, then all the blessings mentioned in
the next three lines were to be fulfilled.

To complete, i.e. לְכַלֵּא—an Aramaised form for לכלות. So Hitzig,
Marti, and others. Bevan, Driver, &c. render 'to make an end
of'. But see next clause.

The transgression, i.e. הפשע. Cf. $8^{12, 13, 23}$.

To bring sins to the full, להתם חטאות. So Hitzig, Marti, &c.
Cf. 8^{23} where the same Hebrew phrase recurs. Here again

Bevan, Driver, and others prefer to render 'to make an end of', and compare Num. 25[11] ; Ezek. 22[15]. But the meaning is determined by the correct text in 8[23].

*To **blot out** iniquity,* i.e. למחות עון. See above p. 237 sq. It is God who here 'blots out iniquity'. This is the oldest attested text according to the LXX. It is also supported by the Vulg. The phrase occurs in Ps. 51[11] : cf. 51[3] ; Isa. 43[25], 44[22]. It implies a full and free forgiveness. The Massoretic reading לכפר seems to be a late replacement of the earlier phrase. It has generally a propitiatory sense, unless in Deut. 21[8], 32[43] ; Ezek. 16[63] ; Jer. 18[23] ; Ps. 65[4], 78[38], 79[9], where it is used without any reference to a propitiatory rite. It is seldom used by the prophets—only once in Jer. 18[23], but Duhm and Cornill reject that verse as a later addition. The meaning of this verb differs, as Driver points out, 'according as the subject is the priest or God : in the former case the meaning is to . . . *screen* the sinner by means usually of a propitiatory sacrifice'. It is then generally rendered, as here in Th., by ἐξιλάσκεσθαι. When the priest is the subject, the object of the verb is never the *guilt* as in our text. If the guilt from which the offender is freed is mentioned it is preceded by מן (Lev. 4[26], 5[6, 10], &c.) or על (Lev. 4[35], 5[13], &c.). 'In the latter case it means to *treat as covered*, to pardon . . . without any reference to a propitiatory rite ' in relation to either the offender or the offence. See passages above referred to. Cf. Driver *in loc.* and *Deut.*, p. 425 sq. Again *kappēr* with a few exceptions (Lev. 5[20–26], 19[19–22] ; Num. 5[6–8]) was only used of the forgiveness of sins committed involuntarily and not deliberately. But the context requires the latter meaning. Hence the usual meaning of the word and the context reinforce the unquestionable evidence of the LXX and Vulg.

Though כפר can be used in the sense of a free forgiveness (cf. Lev. 16[30]), its implications are generally of a different nature in the distinctively priestly phraseology of the Priest's Code and Ezekiel. The present context is decidedly against any such thought, and, independently of the strong documentary evidence, favours למחות as the original reading. This latter, which appears to be the original reading, helps to determine the meaning of the next clause.

Everlasting righteousness. This expression is without a parallel in the O. T. But starting from the true reading in the preceding clause it may be defined as the eternal ethical righteousness of the Messianic kingdom If the MT. עון לכפר be retained there is much to be said on behalf of Bevan's suggestion that 'the words כפר and צדק are both legal terms, and that by the "atoning of sin" and the "bringing in of everlasting righteousness" is meant the termination of that controversy . . . (ריב) which God has with His people (see Isa. 27⁹ (וִיכַפֵּר עֲוֹן יַעֲקֹב)'.

To seal vision and prophet, i.e. to confirm the vision of the prophet, cf. John 3³³, 6²⁷. This is a sort of hendiadys. The metaphor is taken from affixing a seal to a document to attest its genuineness (1 Kings 21⁸; Jer. 32¹⁰, ¹¹, ⁴⁴).

A most holy place. The expression 'holy of holies' (קרש קרשׁים) is a priestly term and is applied to a great variety of objects but not to persons. Here it denotes apparently the Temple that was to be consecrated in the Messianic age. Cf. Isa. 60⁷; Ezek. 40 sqq. In Ezek. 43¹², 45³, 48¹² it is used of the temple in Ezekiel's vision. Elsewhere it is used of the altar of burnt-offering, Exod. 29³⁶, ³⁷, 30²⁹, 40¹⁰: of the altar of incense, Exod. 30¹⁰; of the tent of meeting, 30²⁶⁻⁹; of the sacred incense, 30³⁶; and of many other things connected with the sacrifices. See Driver *in loc.*

9²⁵⁻⁷. *The resolution of the 70 years into periods of 7, 62, and 1.*

9²⁵. First of the three periods, consisting of 7 weeks. In this verse as the preceding I will treat first the recovery of the text by critical methods and next its interpretation.

(1) *Criticism of the text.* The MT is decidedly corrupt in two passages of this verse. But in both passages we can recover the original text with the help of the versions backed by the requirements of the context.

To rebuild Jerusalem. I have here emended לְהָשִׁיב וְלִבְנוֹת with the Pesh. and Vulg. into לשוב ולבנות 'to rebuild'. But, even apart from these versions, we are obliged by the context to make this emendation. As Bevan rightly urges, the expressions להשיב ולבנת and תשוב ונבנתה are evidently intended to correspond to each other, that is, are intended to bear the same meaning. But they do not bear the same meaning as the MT stands. Hence 'most commentators translate the former "to restore and to build", and the latter "shall be built again", taking the first in a literal and afterwards in a derived sense' (so Ewald). Von Lengerke and Hitzig try to avoid the difficulty by translating תשוב 'shall be restored'. But Driver objects that השיב though used of restoring exiles is not used elsewhere of restoring, i. e. rebuilding a city. In support of Driver's objection I may add that no ancient version so renders it here. Bevan proposes (and Driver regards the emendation as plausible) to read לְהָשִׁיב וְלִבְנוֹת 'to people and to build', and to render the second clause 'shall be peopled and built', and cites Isa. 44[26]; Jer. 30[18]; Ezek. 36[10-11] in support of his emendation. But they are not true parallels. Isaiah declares that Jerusalem will be inhabited and the cities of Judah built: Ezekiel that the cities shall be inhabited and the waste places builded; while Jeremiah is distinctly against Bevan's emendation as it reads: 'the city shall be builded . . . and the palace be inhabited' (so Cornill, &c.). In itself the idea is so obvious as not to call for expression. It is a case of *cela va sans dire*. Some repopulation of Jerusalem must of course precede the rebuilding. We now pass on to the next proposal—that of Marti. He suggests on the ground of Jer. 29[10] that we should translate the first clause thus: 'to bring back Jerusalem and to build', and explains Jerusalem as meaning the people of Jerusalem and Judaea. This rendering does not meet Bevan's objection and incurs still greater disabilities of its own.

We are thus obliged to emend the MT להשיב, although it is as old as 145 B. c. or thereabouts, seeing that the LXX attests it. But neither the LXX nor Th. could give any intelligible meaning to it: they render it indeed by the word ἀποκριθῆναι—a rendering quite possible in itself but quite impossible in this context. I, therefore, emend this ancient corrupt form להשיב ולבנות into לשוב ולבנות, or לשוב לבנות. Cf. Deut. 24[4]; Jer. 44[14]. For להשיב may not be translated 'again'. Cf. also Ezek. 18[7] where the corrupt MT is emended by Cornill and others into שוב ישיב 'restores'.

With square and moat, i. e. רחוב וחרוץ. Bevan with the Pesh. emends this into רחוב וחוץ 'with public places and streets'. These two words are found in parallelism in Prov. 1[20], 7[12]; Isa. 15[3]; Jer. 5[1]. Bevan contends that חריץ, with which it is compared and which occurs in the Mishna and Talmud, does not mean 'trench' or 'moat', but only a ditch in a field or garden (cf. B. Talm., *Kil.* v. 3: ii. 8 : Jer. Talm., *Shabb.* iii. 5[c]), and never a trench used for the purpose of fortification. But this is not so. In the Zakar Inscription A. 10 (8th Cent. B. c.), which is in the main Aramaic, but contains Canaanitish and Hebrew elements, חרץ means a trench dug out for this very purpose : הרמו שר מן שר ⟨חזרך והעמקו חרץ מן חר⟨צה⟩ 'they raised a wall higher than the

wall of Chazrek and dug a trench deeper than its trench'.
Bevan's objection is that a city built on such uneven ground as
Jerusalem was could be very imperfectly defended by a moat
or trench. But a trench or even a moat is not necessarily constructed to be filled with water. Jerusalem was to be a strongly
entrenched city with large public spaces.

It may be added here that the word is found in the Assyrian
as ḥariṣu. The renderings of the LXX εἰς πλάτος καὶ μῆκος (in the
dittography in the first rendering the phrase is omitted) and Th.
πλατεία καὶ τεῖχος are simply guesses.

26ª. *And at the end of the times, even after.* Here the MT (so
Vulg.) has וּבְצוֹק הָעִתִּים, which = ' even in troublous times and'.
Th. has καὶ ἐκκενωθήσονται οἱ καιροί = הֻוקצצו העתים(?). These two
readings appear to be corruptions of בקץ העתים. So the LXX
κατὰ συντέλειαν καιρῶν, and also the Pesh. This phrase must be
transferred to the beginning of 9²⁶, and the וּ before אחרי should
not, as Bevan, followed by Von Gall, Marti, and others, proposes,
be omitted, but should be retained and rendered by 'even ' (i. e.
the *vav* explicative).

(2) *The interpretation.* With the emended text this is simple.
The going forth of the word. The text refers to the word of
God spoken by Jer. 30¹⁸, 31³⁸ ˢᑫ.

The date implied by these words should be 604 B. C. (i. e. from
Jer. 25¹¹ ˢᑫ. combined with 25¹), or 596 B. C. (from Jer. 29¹⁰).
But the writer does not think of these dates, but makes the
destruction of Jerusalem the point of departure, i. e. 586 B. C.

Unto an anointed one. The prince here referred to is, as
Eusebius, Graetz, Bevan, Marti, and others hold, the high
priest, Lev. 4³,⁵,¹⁶, 6²² ; 2 Macc. 1¹⁰—'the anointed priest '. The
word 'prince' is applied to the high priest in 9²⁶, 11²². The
first seven weeks, therefore, come to a close with the restoration
of the Jewish worship (*circa* 538 B. C.) under Jeshua, the son of
Jozadak (Ezra 3²), the first high priest after the return from the
Exile, Hag. 1¹ ; Zech. 3¹. Others think that Cyrus is meant,
but this is less likely.

Second of the three periods, consisting of sixty-two weeks.

9²⁶. *Three score and two weeks,* i. e. during this period. On
this period see note on 9²⁶⁻²⁷.

9²⁶⁻²⁷. *The seventh week—171–164 B.C.* Since the seventh
week must embrace the years 171–164, a difficulty arises as to

the *terminus a quo* of the sixty-two weeks. In the notes on the preceding verse we found that the first seven weeks came to a close in the year 538 B. C. But from 538 to 171 B. C. there is an interval, not of 434 years (i. e. sixty-two weeks of years), but only of 367. In other words there is an error of sixty-seven years. Some scholars have thought to surmount this difficulty by making the first seven weeks of the sixty-two weeks to run parallel with the first seven weeks of the seventy weeks, i. e. 586-538 B. C. But this interpretation fails to explain the anomaly. Of the other explanations offered the best is that supported by Graf, Nöldeke, and Bevan, which is that our author followed a wrong computation. The materials for an exact chronology from the destruction of Jerusalem, 586 B. C. to the establishment of the Seleucid period in 312 B. C., were not at the disposal of a Jew living in Palestine, nor apparently of any Jew. For Schürer (*Gesch. des Jüd. Volkes*³, III. 189 seq.: Engl. Transl., II. iii. 53 seq.) has shown that dates covering this period which are given by professed historians of Judaism, such as Josephus and the Egyptian Jew Demetrius (*floruit ante* 200 B. c.), are untrustworthy in the way of excess, as in our text and that the excess in Demetrius is almost exactly that in Daniel. Thus (1) in the *Bell. Jud.* vi. 4. 8 of Josephus he states that 639 years had elapsed between the second year of Cyrus and A. D. 70. In that case the second year of Cyrus would have been 569 B. C. (2) In *Ant.* xx. 10 he reckons 414 years as having elapsed between the return from the captivity in the first year of Cyrus and the time of Antiochus V Eupator (164-162): and (3) in *Ant.* xiii. 11. 1 he reckons 481 years between the first year of Cyrus and the time of Aristobulus (105-104). Thus according to these three time determinations, Cyrus became king respectively in the years 570 B. C., 578 and 586, whereas his accession to the throne was really in 538. These three statements of Josephus show that he was wrong in his chronology to the extent of forty to fifty years. Schürer *in loc.* and iii. 349-351 draws attention to the historian Demetrius as having made almost exactly the same miscalculation as our author. Thus he states that 573 years[1]

---

[1] See quotations from Demetrius in Clem. Alex. *Strom.* i. 21. 141: ἀφ' οὗ δὲ αἱ φυλαὶ αἱ δέκα ἐκ Σαμαρείας αἰχμάλωτοι γεγόνασιν ἕως Πτολεμαίου τετάρτου ἔτη πεντηκόσια ἑβδομήκοντα τρία μῆνας ἐννέα. But the figures are corrupt in the rest of this quotation. For in the same quotation he says that the interval between the captivity of Israel and that of Judah was 128 years and six months, and

elapsed between the exile of the Ten Tribes (722 B. C.) and the accession and the time of Ptolemy IV (222 B. C.), and thus like Daniel reckoned this interval by some seventy years too much. From these facts Schürer concludes that Daniel was following the chronology current in his time.

An anointed one be cut off. The anointed one is the high priest Onias III (son of Simon II), who was removed from the high priesthood in 175 B. C. by Antiochus for a bribe of 440 talents of silver offered by Jason, the brother of Onias (2 Macc. 4$^{7-9}$). After Jason had held the high priesthood for three years he was supplanted by a Benjaminite (cf. 4^{23} with 3^4) named Menelaus, whom he had sent with the 440 talents to the king. Menelaus betrayed his employer, and secured the high priesthood for himself by outbidding Jason by 300 talents. When, however, he failed to pay this money the king summoned him before him. On arriving at the court Menelaus found that the king had gone off to quell an insurrection in Cilicia, and had left Andronicus, one of his courtiers, to act as his deputy. Menelaus availed himself of this opportunity to secure the favour of Andronicus by the gift of golden vessels which he had stolen from the Temple. On learning this latter fact, Onias censured him sharply and withdrew for safety into the sanctuary of Daphne, close to Antioch. Resenting this rebuke Menelaus prevailed on Andronicus to assassinate Onias. Antiochus on his return was so indignant at this crime that he had Andronicus put to death on the very spot where he had murdered Onias. See 2 Macc. 4$^{7-9, 23-38}$.

This account of the death of Onias has been generally and rightly accepted by historians such as Ewald, v. 295, 355: Schürer^3, i. 196: Graetz, ii. 2, 203. But on the grounds that 2 Macc. (which undoubtedly contains unhistorical matter) alone records the murder of Onias, and that Josephus[1] gives a con-

that the interval between the Captivity of Judah and Ptolemy IV was 338 years and three months. Thus, according to this second computation the entire interval between the Captivity of Israel and Ptolemy would be 466 years and nine months, and the two computations for the same period would differ to the extent of 107 years.

[1] Josephus not only does not record the assassination of Onias, but in *Ant.* xii. 9. 7 : xiii. 3. 1–3 : xx. 10 speaks of the Onias the son of Onias—brother of the martyred Onias in xx. 10. 1—as fleeing into Egypt and building there a temple at Leontopolis ; whereas, in *Bell. Jud.* i. 1. 1, vii. 10. 2, 3, he states that Onias himself, after the capture of Jerusalem by Antiochus, fled to Egypt and founded a temple in the district of Heliopolis.

flicting account, Wellhausen (*Isr. und Jüd. Gesch.*[3], pp. 244–47 :
Willrich, *Jüden und Griechen*, pp. 86, 90, 120 sqq.) brands the
whole record of the assassination of Onias as apocryphal. But
the grounds are not valid. (1) Josephus' statements not only
conflict with those of 2 Macc. but with one another. If we
compare *Ant.* xii. 5. 1 with xv. 3. 1 : xix. 6. 2 : xx. 10. 3 we
learn that Menelaus was called Onias, and was also a brother of
Jason. Schürer rightly remarks that, if the first statement is
right, then the second is very improbable ; for in that case two
brothers would both have borne the name Onias. That Menelaus was not a brother of Jason but a Benjaminite, as 2 Macc.
(4[23], 3[4]) states, there is no justifiable ground for questioning.[1]
(2) But it is not true, as is apparently universally assumed, that
there is no other evidence than that of 2 Macc. for the assassination of a high priest under Antiochus Epiphanes. In
1 Enoch 90[8] the only valid interpretation of the words 'the
ravens flew upon those lambs, and took one of those lambs
and dashed the sheep in pieces ' is that 'the one ' here referred
to is Onias, the son of Simon. By general consent 'the ravens '
are the Syrians under Antiochus Epiphanes. 'The lamb '
cannot be interpreted of any one of the Maccabean princes,
since in that case he would, according to the usage of the writer,
have been symbolized by *a horned lamb* or *a ram*: cf. 90[9], which
refers to the Maccabees under the symbol of 'horned lambs '.
1 Enoch 83–90 was written before the death of Judas Maccabaeus, 161 B.C., and possibly before his purification of the
Temple in 165 B.C.

And he shall have no . . The MT is defective, it reads וְאֵין לוֹ.
This is sometimes rendered 'and shall have nothing '. But this
is the questionable rendering of an uncertain text. The
meaning also is unsatisfactory. The LXX καὶ οὐκ ἔσται implies
וְאֵינֶנּוּ 'and shall be no more': Th. καὶ κρίμα οὐκ ἔστι ἐν αὐτῷ =
וְאֵין דִּין לוֹ 'and that without judgement': Fell (*Theol. Quartal-
schrift*, 1892, 355–395) and Marti propose וְאֵין אָוֶן לוֹ 'though
guiltless': and Graetz וְאֵין עוֹזֵר לוֹ 'without a helper '.

*The city and the sanctuary shall be destroyed, together with a
prince.* Here with Bevan, Von Gall, and Marti I emend

---

[1] See also Büchler (*Die Tobiaden und die Oniaden*, 1899, pp. 106–124, 240 sq.
and Niese (*Kritik der beiden Makkabäerbücher* (1900), p. 96 seq.), who maintain
the accuracy of the record of Onias' death in 2 Macc.

יַשְׁחִית ('shall destroy') into יְשָׁחֵת 'shall be destroyed', and with one manuscript and five versions—LXX, Th., Pesh., Vulg., Aquila—עַם 'people' into עִם. The MT reads : 'And the people of the prince that shall come shall destroy the city and the sanctuary'. This would refer to the forces of Antiochus, who made a spoil of Jerusalem, setting it on fire and laying low its houses and walls (1 Macc. 1³¹,³²,³⁸). The word עַם in this case would mean 'soldiers' as in 2 Sam. 10¹³, &c. But this text obliges us to take נגיד 'prince' in a different sense from what it bears in the preceding verse, where it refers to the Jewish high priest. This is not an insurmountable difficulty. But the emended text is clearly preferable. But who is the prince referred to? Bevan says Jason, the brother and successor of Onias III. But Jason was the leader of the Hellenizers in Judea, and could not, therefore, be regarded with favour by the Seer. The description of his miserable death in Sparta (2 Macc. 5⁷⁻¹⁰) would fall in well with our text. It is best, therefore, with Marti to recognize in the indefinite נָגִיד a second reference to Onias III, though in that case we should normally expect הנגיד. With the removal and death of Onias III began the ruin of the city and sanctuary through the Hellenizers in Jerusalem.

9²⁶ᶜ⁻²⁷. The third of the three periods, consisting of 1 week.

And the end shall come. Here 1 accept the emendation of Von Gall, Marti, and others of הַבָּא וְקִצּוֹ into וּבָא הַקֵּץ, following in the main the LXX καὶ ἥξει ἡ συντέλεια αὐτοῦ. 'The end' is a technical expression for the last period of affliction : cf. 8¹⁷,¹⁹. Graetz (following the LXX exactly) reads ובא קצו 'and his end shall come'.

With a flood. Cf. Neh. 1⁸, 'with an overrunning flood (שֶׁטֶף) he will make a full end of the place': cf. Jer. 47². This metaphor recurs in 11²². It signifies overwhelming war. The war is that of Antiochus against the Saints.

That which is determined of desolations. In the phrase (נחרצת שׁממות) the first word is the Niph'al inf. construct. It is borrowed from Isa. 10²³, 28²², which contain the double phrase at the close of the next verse. The LXX has here καὶ ἀφαιρεθήσεται ἡ ἐρήμωσις = ונחרצה השממה. Th. had the words but not the syntax of the MT before him. For the desolations referred to see 1 Macc. 1³⁹, 3⁴⁵, 4³⁸, and cf. note on 8¹¹ of our text.

9²⁷. This verse describes the last of the seventy weeks beginning in the year 171 B. C.

9²⁷. *And a stringent statute shall be issued against the many.* Such appears to me the rendering of what was the original text, as I hope to show on many grounds. But first let us deal with the MT והגביר ברית לרבים, which is supported by Th.,[1] and is perforce rendered : 'And he shall make a firm covenant with the many.' If the interpretation of the preceding verses is correct, then Antiochus has not, so far, been definitely referred to, and yet this rendering presupposes him to be the subject of the verb. The text I propose gets rid of this difficulty. But there are other difficulties. Only once elsewhere does the Hiph'il הגביר occur in the sense of 'to make strong' or 'to confirm', i. e. in Ps. 12⁵. But this is not an insurmountable difficulty. The real difficulties lie in the second and third of the three words. Of these the second word 'covenant' (ברית) does not occur elsewhere in Daniel in this sense. It does occur in 11²²,²⁸,³⁰,³², where it practically means the religion of Israel alike as a creed and its expression in worship. Those who translate לָרַבִּים (so MT) 'with the many' are obliged to take ברית in the sense of 'covenant', and to recognize 'the many', with whom the covenant is made, as the Hellenizing Jews. Antiochus is in this case the subject of the verb, and he makes a covenant with the Hellenizers. But the Hellenizers and their converts are said to be πολλοί but not οἱ πολλοί in I Macc. 1¹¹, and are represented as saying in I Macc. 1¹¹, 'Let us go and make a covenant with the nations round about us' (πορευθῶμεν καὶ διαθώμεθα διαθήκην μετὰ τῶν ἐθνῶν τῶν κύκλῳ ἡμῶν). But since לָרַבִּים (if the Massoretic punctuation is right, and it is so accepted by scholars) should be translated 'the many' just as in 11³³, יבינו לָרַבִּים is to be translated 'shall instruct the many', and in 11³⁹ והמשילם בָּרַבִּים 'shall cause them to rule over the many', so here we should render the MT, 'shall make a firm covenant with the many'. Now who are 'the many'? This is clear from 12³, where the phrase recurs, and where מצדיקי הָרַבִּים is to be rendered 'they that turn the many to righteousness'. This last expression is clearly borrowed from

---

[1] δυναμώσει διαθήκην πολλοῖς. The LXX renders the Hiph'il intransitively καὶ δυναστεύσει ἡ διαθήκη εἰς πολλούς.

Isa. 53[11] לָרַבִּים · · · יצדיק 'shall make the many righteous'.[1]
'The many' then *were not the small body of Hellenizers but the main body of the people.*

If this conclusion is right, then it follows that והגביר ברית is corrupt. Antiochus did not make a covenant with the main body of the Jews but with a minority who were Hellenizers. Recognizing the corruptness of this expression—not on the last ground I have advanced but on the earlier, Bevan holds that 'covenant' should here retain the meaning it has in 11[22,28], &c., and that הגביר should be emended into הופר. This emended text would then be translated: 'And the covenant (i. e. the religion of Israel) shall be annulled for the many:' i.e. there shall be a period of general apostasy. הופר is unlike הגביר. Also Marti thinks that the construction with ל in this emended text is difficult, and proposes וְתֶעֱבֹר 'and religion shall come to an end for the many'.

But, whilst we acknowledge that these two scholars have recognized the impossible character of the MT, it does not follow that הגביר, which is really supported by the LXX and Th., is corrupt. The corruption appears to lie elsewhere. Since the mass of evidence points to the Hebrew of Daniel being a translation from the Aramaic, we may not improbably discover the source of this impossible text in a mistranslation of the Aramaic. והגביר ברית is the literal rendering of the Aramaic וקים יתקף. Now קְיָם has two meanings in Aramaic—i. e. 'covenant' and 'statute'—the former more frequently. The Hebrew translator wrongly rendered it by 'covenant', a rendering which הגביר and the context, as we have seen above, do not admit of. An analogous Aramaic phrase has already occurred in 6[8], לתקפה אסר 'to make a stringent interdict' immediately after לקימה קים 'to establish a statute'. Hence we conclude that the original Aramaic was וקים יתקף על [2] שניאיא. The Hebrew translator here punctuated the verb as a Pa'el instead of as a Qal. Hence his doubly wrong rendering. We should render, 'And a stringent statute shall be issued against the many', i. e. against the mass of faithful Jews. This statute is explained by what follows.

[1] Modern scholars regard this text as corrupt and emend it. It is at all events older than the book of Daniel.

[2] ל is used in Hebrew after many verbs denoting hostility. Hence I take it here as a rendering of the Aramaic על.

And so for the half, &c. This clause and the rest of the verse
deal with the second half of the last week, which embraces the
period from the 15th of Chisleu 168 to the 25th of Chisleu
165 B. C. (see 1 Macc. 1[54] and 4[52 sq.]), during which period (see
8[14]) the Temple services were suspended. But this period does
not coincide with the three and a half years referred to in 7[25],
12[7], during which the entire persecution was to last. This
period may have begun with the expedition of Apollonius against
Jerusalem earlier in 168 (1 Macc. 1[29]; 2 Macc. 5[24]). On the two
different periods given in 12[11,12] see notes *in loc.*

Shall cease. Here with the LXX, Th., and Vulg. ἀρθήσεται we
should correct the MT יַשְׁבִּית into יִשְׁבֹּת. The sacrifice and
meat offering include all kinds of sacrifice; cf. 1 Sam. 2[29], 3[14];
Ps. 40[7]. The latter was the proper accompaniment of the
former. Exod. 29[40,41].

In its stead. Here Van Lennep, Kuenen, Bevan, Kamphausen, Driver, Prince, and others emend the unintelligible
עַל כְּנַף 'on the wing' into עַל בְּנוֹ 'in its stead'. The LXX and
Th. have the equivalent of עַל הַקֹּדֶשׁ. The metaphor 'on the
wing of desolation' is wholly out of keeping with the context.
We have parallel passages in 8[13] and 11[31]. In the former,
'How long shall be the vision, while the daily burnt offering is
taken away and the transgression that maketh desolate set up?':
in the latter, 'They shall take away the daily burnt offering and
set up a horror that appalleth'.

It has been suggested by some earlier commentators (and this
suggestion has been revived by Montgomery: see his *Comm.*,
pp. 387[sq.]) that כְּנַף should be ̧ rendered 'pinnacle', i. e. τὸ
πτερύγιον τοῦ ἱεροῦ (Matt. 4[5] = Luke 4[9]). Lightfoot (ed. Pitman:
vol. xi, p. 83) is inclined to identify this pinnacle with the אולם
or porch of the Herodian temple in this passage. In the present
case the porch would of course belong to the earlier temple.
But, as Driver observes, 'there is no evidence that the Hebrew
or Aramaic כנף acquired this sense'.

Shall be a horror that appalleth. Here for שקוצים משמם we
should read שקוץ משמם: cf. 11[31]. The מ was by a slip wrongly
repeated, and then שקוצם was written fully as שקוצים: or rather
with 12[11] read שִׁקּוּץ שֹׁמֵם.

A horror that appalleth, i. e. the altar and image of Zeus.[1]

---

[1] Cf. Taanith iv. 6 העמיד צלם בהיכל : 28[b], 29[a]: also Jerome on Dan. 11[31]

Here שקוץ שמם, as Nestle (*ZATW*, 1884, p. 248) has shown, is a deliberate play or pun on בעל שמים, 'Baal of heaven', the title of the supreme heathen deity. It is found often in Phoenician, Palmyrene (*CIS.* I. 7, 132 B.C. שמם לבעל לאדן: I. 139: Lidzbarski, *Eph.* i. 248, n.: Euting, Nabatäische Insc. 4. 2), and Aramaic inscriptions: Nestle points out that the Syriac version of 2 Macc. 6² actually renders Ζεὺς 'Ολύμπιος by בעל שמין. In Eusebius, *Praep. Evang.* (ed. Gifford, 1903, vol. i. 46) i. 10, Philo of Byblus is quoted: Τοῦτον γάρ, φησί, θεὸν ἐνόμιζον μόνον οὐρανοῦ κύριον, Βεελσάμην καλοῦντες, ὅ ἐστι παρὰ Φοίνιξι κύριος οὐρανοῦ, Ζεὺς δὲ παρ' Ἕλλησι. Cf. Plaut., *Poen.* v. 2. 67: Balsamen = בעל שמן. Thus שקוץ is substituted for בעל, just as בּשֶׁת = 'shame' is substituted for בעל in Hos. 9¹⁰; Jer. 3²⁴, 11¹³; cf. Ishbosheth, 2 Sam. 2⁸, which is the equivalent of Eshbaal in 1 Chron. 7³³. Next, שֹׁמֵם 'causing horror' is likewise a pun on שמים or שמן. Thus the heathen Semitic 'god of heaven' or the Greek Olympian Zeus is for our writer merely 'a horror that appalleth'.

The LXX and Th. have here βδέλυγμα τῶν ἐρημώσεων (cf. 11³¹, 12¹¹; 1 Macc. 1⁵⁴)—an impossible rendering.

A consummation and strict decision. The phrase כלה ונחרצה is borrowed from Isa. 10²³, 28²². See 9²⁶, 11³⁶ also of our text. נחרצה and נחרצת are taken by Barth, *Nominalbildung* 90 (Oxf. Heb. Lex. 358) to be infinitives construct.

Shall be poured out, i. e. תִּתַּךְ is frequently used of the pouring out of anger or fury: see 9¹¹ above.

SECTION X

i. e. Chapters 10–12—the fourth vision of the Seer in the third year of Cyrus, King of Persia. For short summary, see below.

Chaps. 10–11¹. *Prologue to the vision of the Seer.*

This introduction to the Prologue is concerned wholly with the MT, the LXX, and other Versions, and the help rendered by the latter as well as by the MT towards the recovery of the

mentions this interpretation: 'ab Antiocho missi sunt . . . ut . . . in templo Jerusalem Jovis Olympii simulacrum . . . ponerent'.

original Hebrew version, or, in occasional passages, of the original Aramaic.

§ 1. *Hebrew renderings of the Aramaic :*

in 10[8] הודי נהפך עלי למשחית recalls in an intensified form זיוי ישתנון עלי in 7[28].

§ 2. *Aramaisms in the Hebrew Version:*

10[17]. הֵיךְ—only elsewhere in O.T. in 1 Chron. 13[12]. This is Palestinian Aramaic. The older Aramaic of the fifth century in Babylon and in Egypt was אֵיךְ just as in Hebrew.

10[21]. כְּתָב an Aramaism not earlier than 400 B.C.—found in Ezra, Chronicles, Esther. רָשׁים—a loan word from the Aramaic—here only in O.T.

§ 3.

10[12]. נָתַתָּ אֶת לִבָּךְ. Only in 1 and 2 Chron. and Eccles. The translator of chap. 1[8] uses quite a different and rare Classical Hebrew phrase שִׂים עַל לֵב to express the same idea.

10[16]. עצר כח—not earlier than 1 and 2 Chron.

10[21]. התחזק עם = 'holdeth with me': in this sense only in 1 Chron. 11[10] : cf. 2 Chron. 16[9].

§ 4. *Interpolations.*

10[4]. 'Which is Hiddekel'.

10[10]. ' Upon my knees and the palms of my hands.'

10[20]. The interrogative ה before יָדָעְתָּ.

§ 5. *Loss of particle.*

10[5]. כ is to be restored before אִישׁ.

§ 6. *Corruptions in the* MT.

10[10]. וַתְּנִיעֵנִי, 'caused me to totter,' should with LXX and Th. and the sense of the context be emended into ותעירני = 'waked me'.

10[5,13]. See notes *in loc.*

10[6]. כעין נחשת קלל. Based on Hebrew of Ezek. 1[7], which was already corrupt? See note *in loc.*

§ 7. *Dislocation of text.*

10[20]–11[1]. Here no words require to be emended or excised, but a clause needs to be restored to its original position. See notes *in loc.*

§ 8. *Use of vav apodosis.*

10[4]. וַאֲנִי.

10⁹ᵇ. The vav here before אני is to be rejected with the LXX, Th., Pesh., and Vulg.

Chapter 10 forms the Prologue of this section; the revelation itself (11²–12⁴) consisting of a survey of the world's history so far as it affected Israel from the beginning of the Persian period down to the later years of Antiochus Epiphanes. The Seer foretells the death of this king and the immediate advent of the kingdom of the Saints. This was to be accompanied by the resurrection of the pre-eminently righteous and the pre-eminently wicked Israelites that they might severally receive their due recompense of reward (12¹⁻⁴). Then follows the Epilogue in which the time of the advent of this kingdom was deferred in the hope that history might confirm the words of prophecy.

10–11¹. *Introduction or prologue to the revelation made to the Seer. His conversation with the angel.*

10¹. *In the third year of Cyrus.* This is the latest date in the book. The LXX reads 'in the first year of Cyrus'. See 1²¹, which is restored after 2⁴⁹ᵃ in this commentary.

King of Persia. This title was used of Cyrus only before his conquest of Babylon. After this event the title of Cyrus and the other reigning members of the Achaemenidae was 'king of Babylon', 'the king', 'the great king', 'the king of kings', or the personal name preceding the title king (as in Ezra 4⁸ 'Artaxerxes the king'), 'the king of countries'. If it so pleased the king, he might designate the Crown Prince as 'the king of Babylon', in which case he reserved for himself the title 'king of countries'. This holds true of Cambyses, who for nearly a year was named 'King of Babylon' by Cyrus, as well as of the earlier Belshazzar, as we have seen in ch. 5. After the fall of the Persian empire the title king of Persia was used of its kings to distinguish them from their Greek successors. See Driver, *Introd. LOT.*⁹, 545.

On this question I may quote the valuable notes of Driver (*Introd. LOT.*⁹), p. 546 *n*. 'In the extant royal inscriptions "King of Persia" . . . is used once . . . of Cyrus, where there is a reason for it, viz. after his conquest of Persia, when he had just before been called "King of Anshan." . . . In some 1,600 contracts of the Persian period, which have been examined, the

title, " King of Persia " (alone), occurs once only under Xerxes.'
And again on p. 554 *n.*: 'Out of some 1,560 contracts dated
under Cyrus, Cambyses, Darius, and Artaxerxes, known in
1904 (see statistics in R. D. Wilson, *Princeton Theol. Rev.* 1904,
266–9; cf. 1905, 565 *nn.*), all have one or other of these titles,
and not one has "king of Persia": only under Xerxes, out of
eleven known in 1905 (*ib.* 1905, 560 f.), and thirty-five known in
1908 (*ZDMG.* 1908, p. 642 f.), the king's name is followed *once*
(*ZDMG.* No. 23) by " King of Persia " (alone), and once (No. 9)
by "King of Persia (and) Media"; elsewhere his usual title is
" King of Babylon, King" (or "and King")of lands ", preceded
sometimes by " King of Persia and Media ".'

Unto Daniel. Daniel is here spoken of in the third person.
See note on 7¹, where the same usage occurs.

The thing or 'word': cf. 9²³. The LXX inserts before this
word 'the vision and '.

True, i. e. אמת as in 8²⁶.

And a hard service. On this use of צבא cf. Isa. 40²; Job 7¹,
10¹⁷, 14¹⁴.

Understood: i. e. בין perf. Qal. for בָּן. Cf. בִּינֹתִי in 9². בִּינָה,
which follows, is a substantive, i. e. 'understanding' as in 1²⁰,
8⁵, 9²². The LXX, though it mistranslates the latter half of
this verse, yet practically presupposes the text of the MT, with
slight variations.

10². The ground for Daniel's mourning is not mentioned, but
from 10¹⁴ it is clear that it was due to his concern as to what
should befall Israel in the latter days. The fasting prepares
him for the vision that follows just as did the fast in 9³.

Three whole weeks: lit. 'three weeks, days'. For this
pleonastic use of יָמִים cf. Deut. 21¹³; 2 Sam. 13²³, 14²⁸;
Jer. 28³,¹¹; and Ges.-Kautzsch, § 131 d. The reason for so
prolonged a fast is given in 10¹³.

Was mourning. Cf. T. Reub. 1¹⁰ ἤμην πενθῶν, which is derived
from our text as the next verse proves.

10³. *I ate no pleasant bread.* לחם חמדות as opposed to לחם עֹנִי
'bread of affliction', Deut. 16³. The whole phrase is quoted in
T. Reub. 1¹⁰ πάντα ἄρτον ἐπιθυμίας οὐκ ἔφαγον. The Seer did not
fast absolutely, but avoided all attractive food.

Neither came flesh . . . into my mouth. Quoted in T. Reub.

καὶ κρέας οὐκ εἰσῆλθεν ἐν τῷ στόματί μου. *Nor wine.* Cf. T. Reub. 1[10]
καὶ οἶνον . . . οὐκ ἔπιον.

Neither did I anoint myself. In fasting all pleasant food and self-indulgence were avoided. So anointing, which was of the nature of a luxury, was likewise shunned. The omission of anointing 'was a sign of mourning, the resumption of the practice a sign that mourning was over': 2 Sam. 12[20], 14[2]; Judith 10[3]: cf. Isa. 61[3]; Eccles. 9[8] (*Encyc. Bib.* i. 173).

10[4]. *The first month.* That is Nisan, Neh. 2[1], or as it was earlier called, Abib, Exod. 23[15]. Daniel, therefore, with his companions (10[7]) kept this fast in the month to which belonged the great festival of the Passover (i. e. the 14th day) and that of the Unleavened Bread (15th–21st)—during which the Law prescribed that 'bread of affliction' should be eaten, Deut. 16[3].

I was: i. e. ואני הייתי. We have here a form of the vav apodosis.

The great river [which is Hiddekel]. I have with Behrmann and Marti bracketed the explanatory clause as a mistaken gloss. The Hiddekel, i. e. the Tigris, is mentioned only here and in Gen. 2[14]. But 'the great river', according to Gen. 15[18], Josh. 1[4], and also 'the river', Gen. 31[21] (cf. Isa. 7[20], Jer. 2[18]), is without doubt the Euphrates, and not the Hiddekel. Furthermore Daniel's companions were with him in Babylon, and Babylon was on the banks of the Euphrates, whereas the Hiddekel was at least fifty miles distant. There is no question, therefore, of both Daniel and his companions *being translated* to a distant river of purely secondary importance such as the Hiddekel. This river is again referred to in 12[6,7], though not by name.

10[5–9]. The appearance of the heavenly messenger.

10[5]. The vision follows the fast, as in 2 Bar. 5[7] (see note in my edition), 9[2], 12[5], 21[1], 47[2]; 4 Ezra 5[20], 6[35], 9[26,27], 12[51].

Lifted up mine eyes. Cf. 8[3].

And looked, and behold. On this and kindred forms of apocalyptic expression see the note on 4[1] in my Commentary on Revelation.

⟨*One like unto*⟩ *a man.* The MT supported by the Versions here reads איש אחד, which means merely 'a man', some man or other. If we translate this apocalyptical symbol into ordinary speech it means 'an angel', some angel or other. But the magnificent description that follows is absolutely against this view. The being here referred to is not only a supernatural being, but one holding a pre-eminent dignity amongst such beings. He is not to be identified with Gabriel, though in the two preceding visions Gabriel had appeared to the Seer and instructed him: see 8^{16-18}, 9^{21-23}. In the latter Gabriel is called 'a man', just as in Ezekiel's visions $9^{2,3,11}$, 10^2. But, as I repeat, it is not Gabriel that appears to the Seer in this vision. Not only does the description of this unnamed angel transcend immeasurably that of Gabriel in chapters 8 and 9, but the effect of his appearance on the Seer is far more profound. In 8^{17}, when Gabriel appears, the Seer is affrighted and becomes unconscious, but recovers immediately on being touched by Gabriel. In the next vision the Seer is not affected at all by Gabriel's appearance, 9^{21}, whereas in this third vision, where we should expect him to be similarly unaffected, *if it were Gabriel who appeared*, the Seer is continually overcome and requires to be quickened three times, $10^{8,9,15,16,17}$.

But this is not all. The vision in this chapter is one vision, and mediated by one and the same being.[1] And yet when the Seer mentions this being he does not venture to name him. He designates him as 'one like the similitude of the sons of men', 10^{16}, and in 10^{18} as 'one like the appearance of a man'. Hence, since he is not the archangel Gabriel and yet one transcending Gabriel in majesty, I conclude that we should for איש אחד (= 'a man', cf. Exod. 16^{33}; 1 Kings 19^4, 22^9; 2 Kings 7^8, &c.) read כְּאִישׁ א". In the Aramaic the Hebrew translator found כנבר. The initial letter which has been preserved in $10^{16,18}$ was early lost here as in 7^9. Thus in the three passages, where this mysterious being is referred to, he is not named, but is described as 'one like unto a man', 'one like the similitude of the sons of men', and 'one like the appearance of a man'. In the Test. of XII Patriarchs there is also a nameless angel who is simply called 'the angel of peace', whose office is to 'strengthen Israel' (T. Dan. 6^5): to 'guide the soul' of the righteous man (T. Benj. 6^1), and at death 'to lead him into

---

[1] Thus, this being states that he has been sent in consequence of the Seer's prayers, $10^{11,12}$, to make him understand what should befall his people in the latter days 10^{14}. The Seer is again overwhelmed and again revived by his supernatural visitant $10^{17,18}$. It is one and the same being who quickened the Seer and came to tell him 'that which was inscribed in the writing of truth', 10^{19-21}.

eternal life' (T. Ash. 6⁶). Who is this mysterious being, who
is an angel and yet is carefully distinguished from both Gabriel
and Michael? In the Test. XII Patr. the nameless angel is
the guardian not only of Israel but of all the righteous. See
the note on T. Levi 5⁶.

A man clothed in linen. The phrase is suggested by Ezek.
9²,³, &c. As a man in apocalyptic technically denotes an angel,
so here the linen garment may represent the angelic body as
composed of light (cf. Ps. 104²): see Gressmann, *Ursprung d.
isr.-jüd. Eschatologie*, 344 sqq.

Fine gold of †Uphaz† : i. e. בֶּתֶם אוּפָז. The second of these
two words is borrowed from Jer. 10⁹, where it is generally
acknowledged to be a corruption of אוֹפִר. So Ewald conjec-
tured. The corruption in our text may, then, be due to the
corrupt text in Jer. 10⁹. But seeing that the LXX has in place
of these two words the meaningless phrase ἐκ μέσου αὐτοῦ φῶς =
מתוכו אור, and also that in מתוכו we have the word כתם though
the letters are disarranged, we may not unreasonably conclude
that אור points to אוֹפִר rather than to אופז.

10⁶. Cf. Rev. 1¹⁴ᵇ⁻¹⁵.

His body : וּגְוִיָּתוֹ. The word occurs in Ezekiel's vision in 1¹¹,²³.

Beryl. The LXX renders תרשׁישׁ by χρυσόλιθος in Exod. 28²⁾,
39¹³, and so also Josephus, *Ant.* iii. 7. 5.

As the appearance of lightning, and his eyes as torches of fire.
Cf. 2 Enoch 42¹ (B), 'their faces like extinguished lamps' is said
of the fallen angels, whereas of the righteous angels it is said,
1⁵, 'their eyes too were like a burning light'.

The words in our text were suggested by Ezek. 1¹³, 'The
living creatures . . . their appearance . . . like the appearance of
torches . . . and out of the fire went forth lightning'.

His feet like the gleam of burnished brass. From Ezek. 1⁷.
'Their feet . . . shone like the gleam of burnished brass'. Cf.
Rev. 1¹⁵, οἱ πόδες αὐτοῦ ὅμοιοι χαλκολιβάνῳ. But כעין נחושת קלל is
against the LXX and Latin, which require, as Cornill suggests,
כעין נחושת ‹וכנפיהם› קלות. In this case our text follows the corrupt
text of Ezekiel.

Voice of a multitude. Cf. Isa. 13⁴, 33³.

10⁷. *Daniel alone saw the vision:* cf. Acts 9⁷, where Paul alone
saw the vision which led to his conversion. Here the MT reads

מַרְאָה for 'vision' as in 10[16], but in 8[16,27], 9[23], 10[1] it uses מַרְאֶה in the same sense, while in 8[15], 10[6,18] it means 'appearance'.

Fled to hide themselves. The Hebrew בְּהֵחָבֵא is peculiar here. We should expect לְה" as in 1 Kings 22[25]. The LXX ἐν σπουδῇ and Th. ἐν φόβῳ presuppose בַּבֶּהָלָה as in Ps. 78[33] = 'in terror'.

10[8]. With the effect of the appearance of the angel on the Seer, cf. 8[17].

There was left no strength in me. Cf. 1 Sam. 28[20].

My comeliness was turned into corruption. The Hebrew literally = 'my comeliness was turned upon me (עָלַי) into corruption'. The words 'upon me' represent a dative of advantage or disadvantage, and cannot really be translated into English, unless in the way of paraphrase—'to my sorrow'. This idiom has already occurred in 2[1], 5[6,9], 7[28]. In some passages it can be translated as in 2[1]. This idiom is found frequently. Thus in Gen. 48[7] (cf. 33[13], Eccles. 2[17]) Jacob says, 'Rachel died upon me', i.e. 'to my loss'.

My comeliness, &c. The Hebrew הודי נהפך עלי למשחית recalls the Aramaic וְזִיוַי יִשְׁתַּנּוֹן עֲלַי in 7[28].

Corruption: i.e. משחית. In Isa. 52[14] we have the exact parallel to this use of the word כֵּן־מִשְׁחַת . . . מַרְאֵהוּ, 'his countenance was so marred'. The distich in which this expression in Isaiah occurs is however rejected as a later interpolation by some of the best modern scholars.

[*I retained no strength.*] I have with Behrmann and Marti excised this clause from the text, as a gloss drawn from 10[16] (where see note), as repeating in a weaker form what has already been said in this verse.

10[9]. *I fell into a deep sleep with my face to the ground.* With Th., Pesh., and Vulg. I omit ואני of the MT. The LXX omits the ו. If this expression (ואני) is retained, we should explain the whole clause with Bevan as circumstantial and inserted parenthetically. But 8[18] is against the MT and against this interpretation of it. The unconsciousness in both cases is a result of the appearance of the angel.

With (literally 'upon') *my face to the ground* (i.e. על־פני ארצה). So the MT save that with the LXX (ἐπὶ πρόσωπόν μου ἐπὶ τὴν γῆν) and Pesh. I have omitted וּפָנַי after עַל פני. The clause, when this phrase is omitted, corresponds exactly with that in 8[18]. Some copies of Th. contain the same reading, though the bulk of them

(= καί τὸ πρόσωπόν μου ἐπὶ τὴν γῆν) presuppose וּפני instead of על פני.
The MT is conflate.

10[10]. Some scholars identify the angel in 10[10 seqq.] with the
angel in 10[5-6]: others regard them as distinct. It is the same
being throughout.

Waked *me.* So I emend alike on the grounds of the context
and the attestation of the LXX and Th. the extraordinary text
of the MT: †'Set me tottering upon my knees and upon the
palms of my hands.'† This I take to be corrupt. The incident
here in 10[9-11] corresponds very closely and at times verbally
with that recorded in 8[17-18]. In 8[17] the Seer, on seeing the
angel, falls on his face to the ground, and while the angel talks
to him 8[18], the Seer falls into a deep sleep with his face to the
ground (נרדמתי על־פני ארצה). Thereupon the angel touches him
and causes him to stand upon his feet (ויעמידני על עמדי) : or possibly
'⟨waked him and⟩ caused him to stand upon his feet.'.

So much for 8[17-18]. Here we have evidently (or should have,
as becomes evident on a study of the context) a corresponding
series of events. In 10[9] the Seer, seeing and hearing an angel,
falls into a deep sleep with his face to the ground (הייתי נרדם
על פני ארצה). In 10[10] the angel touches him and †sets him
tottering (ותניעני) on his knees and the palms of his hands†, and
in 10[11] bids him to stand upon his feet (so MT). Now, save in
the words that I have bracketed as corrupt, the series of events
correspond exactly.

The context is thus against the words in brackets. Seeing
that the Seer is in a deep sleep with his face to the ground, we
should expect the angel to awake him 10[10] before he bids him
with his own powers to stand upon his feet, 10[11]. Hence
instead of ותניעני we should expect וַתְּעִירֵנִי 'and he waked me' (as
in 11[25]). And this is exactly what we find in the LXX and Th.,
i. e. ἤγειρέ με. Thus here we have three events, i. e. 'touched
me', 'waked me' (10[10]), and the command 'stand upon thy
feet' (10[11], עמד על עמדך), which the text in 8[18] compresses into
two, 'touched me and made me to stand upon my feet' (ויעמידני),
though even there it is possible that we should restore 'and
waked me' after 'touched me'. In Ezek. 1[28], 2[1] we have a good
parallel. On seeing the vision Ezekiel falls on his face. Whilst
prone on his face (though not asleep as in our text) the heavenly
being said unto him : 'Son of man, stand upon thy feet'. In

our text the Seer is first awaked and then bid to stand upon his feet.

Instead, therefore, of 'set me tottering'—a most grotesque result of supernatural intervention on the part of the angel, I restore the reading 'waked me'. Since this is evidently the original text, it is easy to explain the origin of the addition 'upon my knees and (upon) the palms of my hands'. When once תעירני was corrupted into תניעני, this word called for explanation. Hence על ברכי was a redactional addition or a gloss incorporated from the margin added by one scribe in the margin (LXX ἐπὶ τ. γονάτων : Th. ἐπὶ τὰ γονατά μου), and כפות ידי by another scribe—possibly in a different copy in the LXX. While Th. only recognizes the former addition, the LXX incorporates both, but without a conjunction ἐπὶ τ. γονάτων ἐπὶ τὰ ἴχνη τῶν ποδῶν μου. This is in itself a sign of conflation—the conflation of two glosses! The LXX omits also the first μου after γονάτων. The third stage in the corruption of the text appears in the MT (Aq. and Sym.), which inserts the copula between the two phrases, but does not repeat the על before כפות. The final stage is reached in the Pesh. and Vulg., which presupposes the על omitted by the MT. Various minor variations in these glosses appear in some of the Greek manuscripts and the Syr^h.

10^11. *Man greatly beloved.* See note on 9^23.

Stand where thou hast stood: i.e. stand as thou didst before. On this late Hebrew idiom see note on 8^17. Now that the Seer is waked he is bidden to stand upright by virtue of his own powers.

Trembling: i.e. מרעיד—intransitive as in Ezra 10^9.

10^12. *Set thine heart* (i.e. נתת את לבך)—a late idiom found only in 1 Chron. 22^19; 2 Chron. 11^16, and five times in Ecclesiastes. In 1^8 we have a different idiom to express the same meaning, i.e. שום על לב (which is classical Hebrew). Both Hebrew idioms are probably renderings of one and the same Aramaic phrase שום בל, c. inf., which occurs in 6^15. In 10^12 the LXX has ἔδωκας τὸ πρόσωπόν σου διανοηθῆναι = נתתָּ את פניך להבין—the same idiom that occurs in our text in 9^3, 10^15—solitary occurrences, so far as I am aware, in the OT. Is the MT in 10^12 an alternative rendering of the Aramaic or a substitution of a later synonymous idiom?

To understand, i.e. what was in store for Israel.

To humble thyself (להתענות)—i. e. by the various forms of mortification accompanying a fast as in Ezra 8²¹. The cognate noun תענית (Ezra 9⁵) may mean ' fasting '—a meaning it bears normally in the Mishna. The usual OT. expression is ' to afflict the soul ' : Lev. 16²⁹,³¹ ; Ps. 35¹³, &c.

10¹³. *Prince of the kingdom of Persia.* The doctrine of angelic patrons of the nations appears definitely in I Enoch 20 (which is pre-Maccabean), then in our text: cf. 10²⁰,²¹, 11¹, 12¹, and next in I Enoch 89⁵⁹ seqq. (where see my note). How the idea arose does not concern us here, as the reader can consult the art. ' Angel ' in the Encyc. Bib. and Hastings's *B.D.* It appears in Sir. 17¹⁷ ἑκάστῳ ἔθνει κατέστησεν ἡγούμενον : Deut. 32⁸ (LXX) ἔστησεν ὅρια ἐθνῶν κατὰ ἀριθμὸν ἀγγέλων θεοῦ. But whereas Sirach and Jubilees 15³² speak of God as the immediate ruler of Israel, contemporary and later authorities designate Michael as the patron of Israel. The destinies of these nations and their angelic patrons were closely interwoven, and no nation was punished before the fitting judgement was meted out to its angelic patron : cf. Isa. 24²¹ ; Jubilees 15³² (in my edition) ; Weber, *Jüd. Theol.*, p. 170.

Withstood me one and twenty days. This explains why the Seer received no answer for the three weeks during which he prayed and fasted. See 10².

Michael. This angel is the patron of Israel. So he is first described in I Enoch 20⁶ (yet only as yet of the saints of Israel), and towards the close of the second century B. C. in the T. Levi 5⁶ ; T. Dan. 6², though in the last two passages a still higher role is assigned to him. See also my note on Rev. 12⁷ for the later developments in the conception of Michael's functions, and Luecken, *Michael*, 23–30. See also Bible Dictionaries on this angel. On the phrase עמד לנגד see note on 12¹.

I left him alone there with ⌐*the prince of*¬ *the kings.* I have followed Meinhold, Behrmann, Marti, and Loehr with the LXX and Th. (αὐτὸν κατέλιπον [κατέλειπον Th.] ἐκεῖ) in emending נותרתי into הותרתיו, and restored שר after אצל with the same authorities. Since αὐτόν precedes the verb in LXX and Th. it may be best to emend ואני נותרתי into ואתו הותרתי. The guardian angel of Israel does not contend with the kings of Persia but with their guardian angel. The MT reads ' I remained there with the kings '. Bevan with some hesitation follows the traditional

text, and, taking ואני נותרתי וגו' 'as a circumstantial clause
describing the previous situation of the speaker', renders:
'whereas I had been left alone there (contending) with the kings
of Persia.' Driver objects, however, that this verb means not
to leave simply, but *to leave remaining*: 'so that it is doubtful
whether it would here be suitable.' If this objection is valid it
would be possible to take הותרתי as a corruption of הנחתיו. But
this seems unnecessary; cf. Gen. 32²⁵; Exod. 10¹⁵.

10¹⁴. *I am come.* Here the closing words of 10¹² are repeated:
cf. 9²³.

To make thee understand. Cf. 8¹⁶, 9²³.

What shall befall thy people in the latter days. Almost a
quotation from Gen. 49¹.

Yet a vision for the days: i. e. there is yet another vision
relating to the last days. The LXX by reading εἰς ἡμέρας supposes לְיָמִים: i. e. 'the vision is yet for days'—a distant period:
cf. 8²⁶.

10¹⁵. *Set my face toward the ground* (נתתי פני. See note on
10¹²). Daniel does not fall prostrate but fixes his eyes on the
ground and remains silent.

10¹⁵–11²ᵃ. *The Seer's conversation with the supernatural being.*

10¹⁶. *One like the similitude of the sons of men.* This is the
same supernatural being as that mentioned in 10⁵, where see
note. The LXX has here ὡς ὁμοίωσις χειρὸς ἀνθρώπου = כדמות יד
אדם. But the MT. is supported by 10¹⁸.

Touched my lips (i. e. נגע על שפתי). This phrase is suggested
partly by Isa. 6⁷, where a hot coal touches the prophet's lips
with a view to cleansing them, and Jer. 1⁹, where the Divine
hand touches the prophet's mouth and so inspires him to deliver
his message. Here the touch of the angel's hand restores to the
Seer his power of speech.

My pangs have come suddenly upon me: lit. 'turned upon me',
נהפכו צירי עלי. This expression is found in 1 Sam. 4¹⁹ (נהפכו
עליה צְרֶיהָ), though there it is used of the pangs of a woman in
childbirth. In Isa. 21³ the prophet adopts the phrase metaphorically as the Seer in our text: 'pangs (צירים) have taken
hold of me as the pangs of a woman in travail'.

Retain no strength. This idiom עצרתי כח is late, and does not
occur elsewhere in the O.T. save in 10⁽⁸⁾, 11⁶, and 1 Chron. 29¹⁴;
2 Chron. 2⁵, 13²⁰, 22⁹.

10¹⁷. *How:* i. e. הֵיךְ only in 1 Chron. 13¹² elsewhere in the O.T.   This form is Palestinian Aramaic: see Targums on Gen. 3⁹; Job 21³⁴.   The older Aramaic form is אֵיךְ: see *Aram.* *Pap.* (Cowley) 16⁷; Aḥ. 37; and אֵיךְ וְי Beh. 52—which is also Hebrew: cf. Gen. 44³⁴; 2 Sam. 1⁵,¹⁴, &c.

How can the servant, &c. ?   The first 'this' (זה) is to be taken with 'servant', where it has a contemptuous meaning as in 1 Sam. 10²⁷, and the second 'this' with 'lord' with an honorific meaning as in Gen. 5²⁹ (Behrmann).   The sense then is: 'How can so mean a servant of my lord talk with so great a one as my lord?'

For as for me †straightway† there remained no strength, &c. Since Daniel had already deplored his total lack of strength, he cannot well state that 'from now on' (מֵעַתָּה) he had no strength.   If we keep to the MT we should translate: 'from now there remained, &c.'[1]   Since the LXX reads ἠσθένησα καί, Bevan suggests that it found מעדתי in the text and adduces Ps. 18³⁷, where this rendering is found.   To this we may add Ps. 26¹.   If this is right, we may render: 'For I tottered: there remained, &c.'   Bevan prefers to take this verb to be a corruption of מִבְּעָתָה 'from terror', and compares 8¹⁷.   It is just as possible that מעדתי is a dittograph of יעמד which follows.   Both the Pesh. and Vulg. omit it.   If this was so, then the rendering would be: 'For as for me there remained no strength in me'.

10¹⁸. *Touched me again.*   Cf. 10¹⁰,¹⁶.

One like the appearance of a man.   Cf. 10¹⁶, 8¹⁵; Ezek. 1¹³,¹⁴, &c.   It is one and the same angel whom the Seer saw throughout this vision, and apparently this angel is not Gabriel.   It was Gabriel who instructed the Seer in 8¹⁶, and likewise Gabriel who gave him further instruction in the vision in 9²¹.   See note on 10⁵.

10¹⁹. *Greatly beloved.*   Cf. 10¹¹.

Be strong, and of a good courage : the MT reads חֲזַק וַחֲזָק = 'be strong, yea be strong'.   But the repetition of the imperative with a conjunction is exceptional.   When the imperative is repeated the conjunction is omitted: cf. Judges 5¹²; 2 Sam. 16⁷; Isa. 51⁹, 52¹,¹¹.   Since six Hebrew manuscripts read חֲזַק וֶאֱמָץ and the LXX and Th. read ἀνδρίζου καὶ ἴσχυσαι (ἴσχυε Th.), and the Pesh. and Vulg. support this reading, I have with Bevan and Buhl restored it in place of the MT, and accordingly translate:

'Be strong and of a good courage.' The latter expression is of
frequent occurrence: Deut. 31[7,23]; Joshua 1[6,7,9,18]; 1 Chron.
22[13], &c. Marti, on the other hand, points out that in Ps. 90[17]
the conjunction is used as in our text. But the cases are not
parallel.

10[20-21]. The text of this passage is confused, weak, and
illogical. It is very weak for the divine messenger to say
'Knowest thou wherefore I am come?' seeing that in 10[14] he
had definitely stated that he had come to make the Seer understand what should befall Israel in the latter days, and that his
coming had been due to the Seer's prayers, 10[12]. The Seer, it is
true, had prayed for three weeks without receiving an answer,
10[2]. The reason for this delay, the messenger tells him, was
the opposition of the prince of Persia for one and twenty
days, 10[13].

This passage, then, should deal with two leading facts:
(1) The coming of the messenger to instruct the Seer as to the
destinies of Israel. (2) The need of despatching this task with
all haste, seeing he had to return to his war with the prince of
Persia—a war which he had for the moment forsaken on the
Seer's account.

Now by dropping the foolish note of interrogation and by the
restoration of the words אגיד לך את־הרשום בכתב אמת immediately
after ועתה, and the relegation of אבל from the beginning to the
close of this clause, we can recover a sane and, I believe, the
original order of the text. Thus we have (10[20a]) 'Then said he,
Thou knowest wherefore I am come unto thee. And now (10[21a])
I will tell thee that which is inscribed in the writing of truth.
Howbeit (I must not linger). (10[20b]) I am returning to fight with
the prince of Persia : and when I have done with this task (lit.
"go forth"), lo, the prince of Greece shall come. (10[21b]) And
there is none that holdeth with me against these, but Michael
your prince.'

Marti had already recognized that 10[21b] should follow immediately on 10[20b]. But his and Behrmann's excision of 11[2a] as
an interpolation and their substitution of 10[21a] in its place seem
to me quite unnecessary and unjustifiable.

10[20]. The text reads: 'Knowest thou', &c. A rhetorical
question (cf. 1 Sam. 2[27]). But such a rhetorical question here
after the definite statements in 10[12,14] is so incredibly weak and

unlike our author that I have omitted the interrogative הֲ, and
rendered : 'Thou knowest wherefore,' &c.

10²⁰ᵃ. *And now* (10²¹ᵃ) *I will tell thee that which is inscribed in
the writing of truth.* Here 'inscribed' (רשום) is a loan-word from
the Aramaic. The Hebrew would be חקוק. The reference is
to the heavenly tablets. These tablets, which are mentioned in
1 Enoch 81¹,², and which Enoch read, contained an account of
coming events. They are constantly mentioned in Jubilees,
and their contents relate mostly to other than future events,
but according to 5¹³, 23³⁰⁻³², 30²¹⁻²² future events also are
recorded in them. See the notes in my editions of 1 Enoch 47³;
Jubilees 3¹⁰; T. Levi 5⁴; T. Ash. 2¹⁰, 7⁵. These tablets
according to Jubilees contained (1) Laws, Levitical and criminal;
(2) A contemporary heavenly record; (3) Predictions and pre-
destined events.

The writing of truth. כְּתָב is an Aramaism : cf. 5⁷,⁸,¹⁵, 6⁹,¹⁰,¹¹, &c.

Howbeit I am returning to fight : i. e. אבל אשוב להלחם. For
this restoration of the order of the text see note above. It is
just possible that אשוב is a weak rendering of the Aramaic
למתב = 'I must return', or 'I have to return'. This idiom
occurs in the Aramaic of Ezra 6⁸ and four times in the Aramaic
of Daniel. See Introd., § 20. *t.* It is also a Hebrew idiom.
With our text compare Rev. 12⁷, where τοῦ πολεμῆσαι = 'I must
fight'. This unnamed angel declares that he must return to
resume the conflict mentioned in 10¹³.

When I go forth, lo, the prince of Greece shall come, i. e. 'when
I have done with the war against Persia, that with Greece will
then begin'. The Hebrew verb יצא appears to be used here in
the sense of 'when I am free from' or 'done with' as in
1 Sam. 14⁴¹; Eccles. 7¹⁸. So Berthold, Hitzig, Bevan, &c.
Other scholars take it in its more usual sense 'when I go forth',
i. e. to fight with the angel of Persia : cf. Judges 9²⁹; 2 Sam.
11¹; 2 Kings 9²¹. The parallel verbs express the appearance
of the angel of Greece on the scene the moment that the nameless angel has triumphed over Persia. For the use of the
participles (יוצא and בא) in this 'idiomatic and forcible construction'
cf. Driver, *Tenses*, § 169.

10²¹ᵇ. *Holdeth with me :* i. e. התחזק עמי, as in 1 Chron. 11¹⁰;
2 Chron. 16⁹.

11¹. *And as for me.* The LXX omits אני, but it is attested

by Th. and the Vulg. The Pesh. also retains it, but connects
it with the close of 10²¹ ‏כי אם־מ׳ ״שרכם ואני‎.

In the first year of Darius the Mede. So Pesh. and Vulg. For
the last three words the LXX reads Κύρου τοῦ βασιλέως and Th.
simply Κύρου. It is hard to determine which is the older
reading. But several scholars, such as Robertson Smith,
Bevan, Behrmann, Marti, regard the whole phrase as 'the
fragment of a heading which was wrongly introduced here by
a scribe' after the analogy of 7¹, 8¹, 9¹, 10¹. Next it is urged
that the LXX and Pesh. represent the speaker as receiving
help and not as giving it—in other words, the latter half of 11¹
may read as 'standeth (emending ‏עמדי‎ into ‏עֹמֵד‎) as a strengthener
and a defence to me' (‏לי‎ instead of ‏לו‎).[1] It is further urged that
the date so given is unsuitable in an account of wars in heaven
among the angelic princes.

But the date may be original so far as these objections are
concerned. They do not appear to be justifiable. The fortunes
of any nation on earth were according to the beliefs of the
time the immediate reflection of what occurred in heaven.
Indeed every event on earth was either inscribed from of old in
the way of predestination or contemporaneously (see note on
10²⁰ᵃ) on the heavenly tablets. There is thus no objection of
any kind to the date on this ground. In the next place the
speaker, who is the nameless angel (see note on 10⁶), states that
in the first year of Darius (or Cyrus) he came forward to support
Michael. The implication is that it was through his intervention
that Darius (or Cyrus) became friendly henceforth in his relations
to Israel.

The evidence of the Jewish books of the 2nd cent. B.C., which
enforced strongly the immediate relations between each nation
and its patron angel, and which taught that the history of
nations was recorded in the heavenly books or else determined
in advance, justifies every clause in 11¹⁻², though a change of
a letter may be required in one or two words.

[1] Since the LXX renders εἶπέν μοι where the MT has ‏לו‎ . . ‏†עמדי†‎ Bevan
rightly concludes that ‏אמר‎ was a corruption of ‏עמד‎, but wrongly that the
‏לו‎ is a corruption of ‏לי‎. For, when once ‏עמד‎ was corrupted into ‏אמר‎
(= εἶπεν), the correction of the MT ‏לו‎ into ‏לי‎ followed inevitably, in order
to give sense to the passage. The reading ‏אמר‎ would account also for the
omission of ‏אני‎ in the phrase ‏ואני‎ at the beginning of the clause.

SECTION X (*continued*).

INTRODUCTION TO CHAPTER XI.

This is the most difficult of all the chapters in our author, so far as the text goes. The Hebrew throughout this book is late. But in this chapter it is not only late but bad. In former chapters we have remarked the absence of certain classical idioms and their replacement by those of late Hebrew and Aramaisms. In this chapter we recognize not only the absence of certain classical idioms but the actual misuse of certain others—a misuse which does not occur throughout the rest of the book. Finally the text is very corrupt.

I do not propose to deal with the historical questions involved in this chapter, seeing that they are for my purpose sufficiently dealt with in the notes that follow. My concern is rather with the text and its recovery from a study of the general method of apocalyptic writers and of our author in particular, next from a study of the context of the corrupt passages, and lastly by a critical study of the versions which repeatedly preserve the original text, or at all events an older text, where the MT is itself corrupt or meaningless.

§ 1. *Characteristics of the text of this chapter.*

(*a*) *Bad Hebrew.* Jussives are used as simple futures in 11[4,10,16,17,18,19,25,28,30] in this chapter, and not once throughout the remaining five Hebrew chapters of our author. The apparent example in 8[12] (see note) is absolutely discredited by the LXX and Th. These facts undoubtedly suggest the hypothesis of a Hebrew translator distinct from the translator or translators of the other five chapters.

(*b*) *Late Hebrew.*

(*a*) 11[7,20,21,38]. כנו על = 'in his stead' = class. Hebr. תחתיו. This phrase occurs only in this chapter in our author and not elsewhere in the OT. On many grounds (see notes *in loc.*) it would appear that the original Aramaic read תְּחֹתוֹהִי, which the Hebrew translator rendered by על כנו in 11[(7),21,38], but in 11[20] by לתחיה (where the LXX has εἰς ἀνάστασιν) owing to a corruption of the Aramaic into לתחיותא. Since Th. presupposes על מקומו we may conclude that על כנו was not the original rendering in all four passages 11[7,20,21,38], but that the text was normalized by the Massoretes.

11[8]. נְסִכֵיהֶם from נָסִיךְ 'a molten image' here only in this sense. It properly means 'a libation'. But possibly the word is a mis-punctuation for נְסִכֵיהֶם from נֶסֶךְ.

11[15]. עיר מבצרות = 'a fortified city'. But Class. Hebrew uses עיר מבצר to express this idea. Jer. 5[17] uses the plural masc. once in this expression. But the fem. plural is found here and here only with עיר to express this idea.

11[43]. בְּמִצְעָדָיו 'in his steps'. Here only literally used: in Ps. 37[23]; Prov. 20[24] used figuratively of course of life. In the older Hebrew בְּרַגְלָיו (Judges 4[10]) is used.

11[45]. ויטע אהלי. Here only in O.T. in this sense, which uses נטה 'to spread out' instead: cf. Gen. 12[8], 26[25], 35[21]; Judges 4[11], &c. The nearest use of נטע is in Isa. 51[16], where it is used of spreading out the heavens as a tent. But נטע means 'to plant'. Hence Duhm, Cheyne, Marti reject לִנְטֹעַ in Isa. 51[16], and rightly as a corruption of לִנְטֹת = 'to spread out the heavens'.

11[7]. עשה בהם 'to deal with in hostile fashion': cf. Jer. 18[23]. Contrast the Hebrew translator's phrase עשה עם 1[13] (cf. 2 Chron. 2[2]) 'in hostile fashion or otherwise'.

(β) 11[10,25]. התגרה = 'to wage war', only in Dan. 11[10,25] used absolutely in this sense. In Class. Hebrew 'to excite oneself against', Deut. 2[5,19].

11[24]. יבזור = 'shall scatter': only here and in Ps. 68[3].

11[32]. מרשיעי ברית = 'those who deal wickedly against the covenant'. This intransitive use of Hiph'il not earlier than 400 B.C.

(γ) 11[10,11]. ובא בוא. This idiom is used contrary to grammatical usage. When the inf. abs. follows the verb it implies repetition or continuance.

(δ) 11[21,32]. †בחלקלקות† = 'with flatteries'. On various grounds I regard this form as a *vox nulla* for בחלקות in this sense. See note on 11[21].

(c) Aramaisms.

11[11]. ונלחם עמו עם מלך—where the repetition of the עם is a pure Aramaism, exactly as in 5[12].

11[12]. רִבֹּאוֹת—an Aramaic form of the Hebrew רבבות.

11[16]. Here the LXX has τῆς θελήσεως = צבותא, where the Hebrew has הצבי. This passage as do many others show that there were alternative renderings of the original Aramaic.

11[17]. בתקף—an Aramaic phrase. About ten derivatives from this root are found in the Aramaic chapters: in late Hebrew it occurs as noun, verb, or adjective in Job 14[20], 15[24]; Esther 9[29], 10[2]; Eccles. 4[12], 6[10].

11[20]. LXX has εἰς ἀνάστασιν. On the implications involved see under I (b) (a) above.

11[24]. עד עת (= ἔως καιροῦ Th.). But the LXX has εἰς μάτην, which = לשׁוא, a manifest corruption of לשעה (cf. 3[6,15], 4[16,30], 5[5])— a pure Aramaism, but adopted in later Hebrew. The Masso-retes or rather earlier revisers of the text replaced this Aramaism by a Class. Hebr. phrase.

11[43]. מכמנים. This is from an Aramaic root.

§ 2. Emendation of the text of chap. 11.

(a) Restoration of the symbols which were used by the author for denoting individuals, nations, countries, but which the Hebrew translator in some passages and the translator of the LXX in many passages replaced by the individuals, nations, and countries so symbolized.

Thus in 11[8] where the MT reads 'into Egypt' we should restore the original text 'into the south': in 11[42] where the MT reads 'land of Egypt' we should restore 'land of the south', and in 11[43] where the MT reads 'things of Egypt' we should restore 'things of the south'. This use of definite geo-graphical terms is contrary to our author's usage: cf. 11[5,6,7,8,9,11(bis),13,14,15(bis),25,29,40(bis),44]. So also in the vision in 8[9].

In the LXX this replacement of symbols by the things which they symbolized has been much further developed as in 11[5,6,9,11,14,15,25(bis),29,40]. Th. in these passages reproduces the MT save that in 11[24] he too introduces ἐπ' Αἴγυπτον owing to his having found על מצרים in his manuscript instead of על מבצרים. See note on 11[8].

(b) National designations must be excised. If the nations so designated have any part in the vision, they could only appear under certain symbols: in the interpretations the symbols could be interpreted, but not in regard to recent history. See note on 11[8].

In 11[30] ציים כתים 'ships of Kittim' must be unhesitatingly rejected in its present form. In any case כתים—a gloss—as a national designation cannot appear in the vision. On the probable original text see note on 11³⁰. כתים was already in the text when the translator of the LXX did his task, but neither he nor Th. found ציים.

On like grounds we must reject 11⁴¹ᵈ, 'Edom and Moab, and the chief (or "rest") of the children of Ammon'. This interpolation, which was possibly a marginal gloss to begin with, makes nonsense of the entire verse. As they stand, they evidently define the peoples who were to be delivered out of Antiochus' hands. But Edom and Ammon were professed and loyal confederates of Antiochus.

For the same reason the final clause of 11⁴³ must be excised as an interpolation. It too may have originated in a marginal gloss. The object of such a gloss was to heighten the contrast between Antiochus with all the east and south at his feet and his wholly unexpected overthrow. But this passage belongs to the province of prediction and not of history.

A comparison of 1 Enoch 83-90 (before 161 B.C.) confirms the above rule. There the nations are symbolized by wolves, wild boars, foxes, and Israel by sheep.

(c) *Corruptions of the text.* These can be emended (1) by studying the requirements of their respective contexts, where both the MT and the versions are corrupt: or (2) by the help of LXX or the LXX with the further support of the other versions.

(1) 11⁴. For כעמדו with Graetz and other scholars read כעצמו as in 8⁸.

11⁶. For תנתן read תִּנָּתֵשׁ = 'shall be rooted up'. This reading harmonizes with the metaphor in the preceding clause.

For הַיִּלְדָה (MT) I read with Von Gall, Marti, and others יַלְדָּהּ 'her son'. This is indirectly supported by the Pesh. and Vulg. which presuppose 'her sons'.

11¹⁸. See note *in loc.*

11²²,²⁶. Read הַשָּׁטוֹף with Bevan for הַשֶּׁטֶף, and compare 11²⁶ where יְשָׁטוֹף is to be emended into יְשֶׁטֶף.

11³⁹. עִם should be emended into עַם.

11⁴⁰. בָּאֲרָצוֹת can hardly be right. See note *in loc.*

11⁴¹. For רַבּוֹת = 'many' of the countries, read with De Wette, Bevan, &c., רִבּוֹת 'tens of thousands'. The punctuation of the

MT is due to the corrupt reading בארצות in the preceding verse.

(2) (*a*) Emendation of the MT by means of the LXX.

11¹³. For בוא read בו with many manuscripts and the LXX. Cf. 11¹⁰.

11¹⁷. Omit לו with LXX.

11³⁴. With the LXX read ⟨בעיר ורבים⟩ אחד בחלקתו רבים. See note *in loc.*

(*b*) By the LXX and Th.

11²,¹⁵. See notes *in loc.*

(*c*) 11²⁶. By LXX, Th., Pesh., Vulg.

11¹⁷. Read מישרים instead of וישרים.

(*d*) By LXX, Th., Vulg.

11⁵. See note *in loc.*

§ 3. *Late revision of the text by the Massoretes or earlier scholars.*

Among such passages I would reckon 11¹⁸,²⁵⁻²⁶, 11³⁰ (ציים), and many others.

11¹. *The first year of Darius the Mede.* There appears to be no valid objection to the mention of a date in this connexion; for the events of human history are according to our author but reflections of what is occurring in heaven. We can now return to the question with which this note began, did the original speak of Darius the Mede (MT, Pesh., Vulg.) or of Cyrus (LXX, Th.)? The combination of the LXX and Th., when they are clearly independent of each other, is of equal, if not much greater, weight than the combined evidence of the MT, Pesh., and Vulg. That Aquila and Sym. support the MT is what is to be expected. In this conflict of documentary evidence we must fall back on the context and the chronological views of the time. The vision with its prologue and epilogue in Chapters 10-12 takes place in the third year of the reign of Cyrus (10¹). Now, in the view of our author, Cyrus is the successor of Darius on the throne. Hence, since the reference in 11¹ is obviously to a date anterior to this vision, which is ascribed to the third year of Cyrus, and, since further *in our author's view* the Jews first came into favour in the reign of Darius 6²⁵⁻²⁸, it was natural to conclude that this change was due to the intervention of the nameless angel, when he 'stood up . . . to strengthen' Michael, the prince of the Jews. On these grounds 'Darius the Mede' is to be regarded as the original reading. But the later reading

'Cyrus the king' (LXX) or 'Cyrus' (Th.) could hardly have failed to suggest itself to scribes well read in the earlier books of the O.T., which connected the return of the Jews to Palestine with Cyrus and none other. The reading 'Cyrus the king' is therefore secondary and 'Darius the Mede' original.

I stood up. For עמדי read עֹמֵד, of which אמר, which the LXX εἶπεν presupposes, is a corruption. Or read עמדתי (with Th. and Vulg.). If we read עֹמֵד we should restore אני after the *vav* at the beginning of the verse. See foot-note, p. 267).

To confirm and strengthen him. So also Th. (save that it omits 'him') and Vulg. The LXX implies להתחזק ולהתאמץ = 'to be strong and of a good courage'.

11²⁶–12⁴. *The revelation given to the Seer.*

11². *And now I will show thee the truth.* Here the heavenly being partially repeats what he had said in 10²¹ᵃ. But this is in keeping with his previous repetitions of 'unto thee am I now sent' 10¹¹, 'I am come for thy word's sake' 10¹², 'now I am come to make thee understand' 10¹⁴, 'thou knowest wherefore I am come' 10²⁰.

There shall stand up yet three kings. Who are the four kings? Since Cyrus is still reigning, he is necessarily included in the four. Cyrus (558–529) is, therefore, the first of the four. It is no less clear that the fourth referred to in this verse is Xerxes (485–465), who invaded Greece. But who are the second and third? The second should be Cambyses (529–522), and the third Darius Hystaspes[1] (522–485). But Bevan, Marti, and others are probably right in thinking that the four kings mentioned in Ezra 4⁵⁻⁷ are here referred to, but in the order Cyrus, Darius Hystaspes, Artaxerxes, Xerxes, since these are the only four names of Persian kings that occur in the O.T., and since the O.T. was at all events the principal source of information accessible to the writer. If this is right, the reckoning of Xerxes as the successor of Artaxerxes would be one of the historical errors of the book. The author would thus take account of five kings—the first being Darius, of whom we have already treated, and who is regarded by our author as the pre-

[1] Our author probably distinguished the Darius, whom he makes king after Belshazzar and before Cyrus, as 'Darius the Mede', 5³¹, 11¹, or as 'Darius .. of the seed of the Medes', 9¹, from 'Darius the Persian', Neh. 12²², or 'Darius king of Persia', Ezra 4⁵, ²⁴. Wright (*Dan. and his Prophecies*, p. 244) finds six Persian kings in the O.T.

decessor of Cyrus; for the visions are given in chronological order: the first and second being in the first and third years respectively of Belshazzar, 7^1, 8^1: the third and fourth being in the first year of Darius and the third year of Cyrus respectively, 9^1, 10^1.

When he is waxed strong: i.e. Xerxes. Cf. Herod. vii. 20-99 on the immense forces which Xerxes raised against Greece.

Shall stir up †all against the realm† of Greece. The expedition which terminated so disastrously for Xerxes at Salamis in 480 B.C.

Shall stir up †all against the realm†. The MT—את הכל יעיר מלכות יון—is here most unusual Hebrew, and is without the support of the versions. The LXX and Th. read ἐπαναστήσεται παντὶ βασιλεῖ (πάσαις βασιλείαις Th.) Ἑλλήνων. Here these two versions diverge from each other—the former implying מלך, the latter מלכיות (so also the Pesh.). Again ἐπαναστήσεται πάσαις βασιλείαις presupposes יָעוּר על כל מלכיות. The loss of על before כל, or possibly after יעור would explain the Pesh. יעיר כל מלכיות. This latter fact favours the originality of the LXX or Th., or at all events their greater antiquity, which of course cannot be disputed. In the next place since Greece in the age of Xerxes consisted of many independent states, the reading of Th. and the Pesh. 'kingdoms of Greece' is preferable to kingdom or realm of Greece (MT). But, if the text presupposed by Th. is original, it should help to explain the extraordinary Hebrew of the MT. Like the text presupposed by the Pesh. the MT has already lost על. The difficult את could be explained as a ditto-graphy of the closing letters of מלכיות, i.e. מלכיות את. which words were then transposed into את מלכיות, and כל read as הכל. If Th. is right, then we should render: 'When he is waxed strong through his riches, he shall rouse himself against all the kingdoms of Greece'.

But if we retain the MT we have to explain אֶת. Driver renders יעיר הכל את 'shall stir up all (in conflict) with', and refers to 11^{25}; Isa. 13^{17}; Jer. 50^9, but in these three passages יעיר is followed by the normal preposition על. Behrmann and Marti simply take את to be the equivalent of על, and quote Jer. 38^5 אין המלך יוכל אתכם דבר in support of their view. But even here אֶת has to be taken in a pregnant sense as meaning 'in dealing with', 'towards', as in Isa. 66^{14}; Ps. 67^2; Deut. 28^8,

or rather with the LXX אתכם has to be emended into אליכם.
Does אֶת ever mean 'against' unless after verbs of fighting?
Bevan conjectures יערך לקר[את 'he shall array (his armies)
against the kingdom of Greece', and compares 1 Sam. 4².

Hence we conclude that the MT is corrupt, and that the text
presupposed by Th. is the best we can get. Here Greece can be
mentioned definitely and not under a symbol at this early date.

11³. Alexander the Great (336–323 B. C.).

Do according to his will. Cf. 11¹⁶,³⁶, 8⁴.

11⁴. *When he is waxed strong.* I have here with Graetz,
Bevan, Marti, Driver, taken the MT כעמדו 'when he shall
stand up' to be a corruption of בעצמו, which has already
occurred in 88. The point of the writer is that the moment
Alexander achieved his greatest success he was cut off.

Toward the four winds of heaven. The same words are used
in 8⁸ regarding Alexander's empire and its division into four
kingdoms.

And shall be divided : i. e. וְתֵחָץ. We should here expect
וְתֵחָצֶה. The jussive (Niph'al of חצה) is used here 'without any
recollection of its distinctive signification' (Driver, *Tenses*³,
§§ 171, 175, *Obs.*). Other instances of this misuse of the jussive
are to be found in this chapter : 11¹⁰,²⁸ וְיָּשֵׁב : 11¹⁶ וְיַעַשׂ : 10¹⁷
וְיָשֵׂם, instead of וְיָשִׂים : 11¹⁸,¹⁹ וְיָשֵׁב : 11²⁵ וְיָעֵר (where however
see note): 11³⁰ וְיָּבֶן. On p. 218 (foot-note) Driver remarks : 'The
Hebrew of the book of Daniel is late; and in other respects
also the syntax of chap. 11 is much inferior to that of the usual
prophetic style.' Only one other example of the misuse of
this idiom occurs in our author : i. e. in 8¹², where, however,
וְתַשְׁלֵךְ is as the LXX and Th. show a mispunctuation for וְתֻשְׁלַךְ.

Not to his posterity : i.e. לֹא לאחריתו. But the LXX reads
οὐ κατὰ τὴν ἀλκὴν αυτοῦ = לֹא בכחו. Alexander, the posthumous
son of Alexander by Roxana his wife, and Herakles, his illegitimate son by his mistress Barsine, were both murdered some
thirteen years after the death of Alexander. It is to these facts
that the MT refers, if it is original. On the other hand the
reading of the LXX = 'not with his power' (i. e. לֹא בכחו) is
supported by the parallel expression which follows 'nor
according to his dominion wherewith he ruled'. Furthermore
the same phrase 'not with his power' is applied to Alexander's

successors in 8²². But there is no reason to suspect the MT, and I cannot explain the LXX.

For it shall be rooted up. These and the words that follow to the close of the verse I have restored to their original position after 'not to his posterity'. I have also transposed ו that follows מלכותו before it. Thus the text reads ולא לאחריתו כי תנתש מלכותו לאחרים מלבד אלה ולא כמשלו אשר משל instead of the confused order of the traditional text. But there are other grounds than the sense of the context which call for this restoration. נתש is used of the plucking up of individuals and nations, Jer. 12¹⁴, ¹⁵,¹⁷; 1 Kings 14¹⁵; Deut. 29²⁷, where the object is expressed, but not of the plucking up of an empire, unless where the object is understood. It is once used of the plucking up of a city, Ps. 9⁷. Hence it seems right to connect the verb here with the posterity of Alexander. After dealing with the fate of Alexander's posterity, the writer next tells of the destiny of his empire and its diminished glories : 'his kingdom shall be for others besides these, but not according to the dominion with which he ruled.' This restored order of the text corresponds exactly with the order of events in 8²², where the same subject is dealt with.

His kingdom shall be, &c. We must here understand היא or תהיה, as Bevan suggests, referring to 8¹⁹,²⁶; Ps. 16⁸.

For others besides these. The 'these', i. e. Alexander's generals, have been already implied in connexion with the previous clause 'his kingdom . . . shall be divided toward the four winds of heaven'. The 'others' are 'the dynasties which arose in Macedonia, Thrace and Asia Minor, Syria, and Egypt during the century and a half that followed upon the death of Alexander' (Bevan). Hitzig and Marti interpret the 'these' as referring to Alexander's posterity, and the others to be Alexander's generals. Hence they take מלבד to mean 'to the exclusion of', though it means elsewhere in the O.T. 'in addition to'. But could it mean 'apart from these', and be a rendering of the (Targum) Aramaic בַּר מִן, and so = 'irrespective of these', i. e. Alexander's children ?

11⁵⁻¹². The Ptolemies and the Seleucidae before the time of Antiochus Epiphanes. These two dynasties contended for the possession of Palestine, which was dominated mainly by the former during the third century B.C. In 198 B.C. it passed under the control of the Ptolemies at the battle of Panion.

11⁵. *King of the South* : i. e. the king of Egypt, Ptolemy I, son of Lagus, one of Alexander's ablest generals, who secured Egypt on the partition of Alexander's empire and ruled it as satrap from 322 to 306 B.C., when he assumed the royal title. He reigned as king from 306 to 285 B.C.

The South. In the O.T. the Negeb (נגב) generally means the southern part of Judah (Gen. 12⁹, 13¹). But in this chapter (11⁵,⁶,⁹,¹¹,¹⁴,¹⁵,²⁵,²⁹,⁴⁰) and in 8⁹ it denotes Egypt as opposed to Syria, with its capital Antioch, which is denoted by 'the north'. In 11⁸,⁴²,⁴³ the Hebrew translator or a subsequent scribe has interpreted this word by 'Egypt'.

But one of his princes shall be stronger than he. So I render with the LXX and Th. and Vulg., and for ויחזק read יחזק. There is here no *vav* apodosis as in 10⁴, where the LXX and Th. attest it. The *vav* is a dittograph. The Massoretic accentuation is here wrong : it requires us to render : 'And the king of the south shall be strong and one of his princes ; and he shall be stronger'. For על after חזק in the above sense cf. 1 Chron. 21⁴.

One of his princes : i. e. מן שריו. Cf. 11⁷ ; Gen. 28¹¹ ; Exod. 6²⁵ ; Jer. 41¹ ; Ruth 2²⁰ ; Neh. 13²⁸. This prince or captain is Seleucus Nicator, who was one of Alexander's companions and of Ptolemy, and at the convention of Triparadisus, 321 B.C., was rewarded with the satrapy of Babylon. When required to give an account of his administration in 316 by Antigonus (who in 323 had been placed over Phrygia and two adjoining provinces), he fled for refuge to Egypt, where Ptolemy made him a general and four years later helped him to win the battle of Gaza in 312. With this year, when he recovered also the satrapy of Babylon, begins the era of the Seleucidae (Oct. 1), by which the Jews in later times reckoned their historical events : cf. 1 Macc. 1¹⁰ ; Josephus, *Ant.* xiii. 6, 7.

His dominion shall be a great dominion. By his crowning victory over Antigonus at Ipsus (301 B.C.) Seleucus received vast accessions of territory stretching from Phrygia, Cappadocia, and Syria on the W. almost as far as the Indus on the E. His empire, with Antioch founded as its capital in 300 B.C., thus became the most powerful of those which had been formed out

out of the dominions of Alexander. He was the true heir of Alexander.

But in the redistribution of the provinces, Coele-Syria, Phoenicia, and Palestine, were long under the domination, now of this, now of that successor of Alexander. 'At Triparadisus, in 321, Syria was assigned to Laomedon; but Ptolemy got possession of it in 320, only to lose it again in 315 to Antigonus, to recover at least the S. part of it after the battle of Gaza in 312, and to relinquish it a second time to Antigonus in 311. After the battle of Ipsus in 301, Ptolemy, as a matter of fact, obtained Coele-Syria and Phoenicia; but his right to these provinces became a subject of protracted dispute between the later Ptolemies and Seleucidae. On the one hand, it was alleged that after the victory it had been distinctly agreed that Seleucus should have "the whole of Syria"; on the other, it was claimed that Ptolemy Lagi had only joined the coalition against Antigonus on the understanding that he should receive Coele-Syria and Phoenicia (*Polyb.* v. 67; cf. also the quotation from Diodorus in Mahaffy, *Empire of the Ptolemies*, p. 66). Upon the whole, during the period in question, Palestine remained, with short interruptions, in the hands of the Ptolemies till the battle of Paneion in 198, after which it was retained permanently by the kings of Syria' (Driver).

11⁶. Ptolemy II, Philadelphus, 285–247 B. c., and Antiochus II, Theos, 261–246 B. c. Antiochus I, Soter, 280–261 B. c., the son and successor of Seleucus I, is here left out of account.

About the year 249 B. c. Ptolemy II gave his daughter Berenice in marriage to Antiochus II on the condition that he should put away his wife Laodice and deprive his two sons, Seleucus and Antiochus, of the right of succession. On the death of Ptolemy two years later Antiochus II divorced Berenice, and took back Laodice. The latter, distrusting the constancy of Antiochus, poisoned him and procured the murder of Berenice, her child, and attendants.

At the end of some years, i. e. thirty-two years after the death of Seleucus I Nicator to the event described. For the phrase לקץ שנים cf. 2 Chron. 18².

To make an agreement. For מישרים = 'equity' (LXX and Th. συνθήκας) cf. Ps. 98⁹; 1 Chron. 29¹⁷, 'Thou hast pleasure in

equity' (מ" תרצה). Hence here it means an equitable arrangement, cf. 1 Macc. 7¹² for the use of δίκαια.

But she shall not retain the strength of her arm. This would
mean that Berenice would not ultimately prevail against Laodice.
Graetz and Bevan, observing that in the phrase עצר כח the word
כח is always in the absolute state, and that זרוע is employed
metaphorically in 11¹⁵,²²,³¹ and comparing 2 Chron. 13²⁰, would
render 'but this support shall not retain strength'.

Neither shall he stand nor his arm. Here Th., Sym., and Vulg.
read וְרֵעוֹ instead of וּזְרֹעוֹ. This gives excellent sense 'neither
shall his seed stand': i. e. endure. The reference then would
be to the children of Antiochus by Berenice.

She shall be rooted up. The MT reads here תנתן, and many
scholars assign to it the meaning of 'shall be given up to death'.
But the word without למות, as in Ezek. 31¹⁴, cannot bear this
meaning.

Hence I have (with the indirect help of the LXX—see below)
emended תנתן into תנתש 'she shall be plucked up'—a verb
which has already occurred in 11⁴. This harmonizes well with
the metaphor in the preceding clause. The same metaphor is
used in the verse that follows, 11⁷. But this is not all. The
LXX has here ναρκήσει = תנשת, which is an easy corruption of
תנתש—the original text. The converse corruption is found in
Jer. 18¹⁴, where for the MT ינתשו we must with Cornill, Giese-
brecht, &c., read ינשתו: cf. Isa. 19⁵. Again in Gen. 32³³, where
the MT has גיד הנשה (= 'the sinew of the thigh vein'), the LXX
has τὸ νεῦρον ὃ ἐνάρκησε, which presupposes הנגיד הַנָּשֵׁת.

They that brought her: i. e. her suite.

Her son. Here I follow Von Gall, Marti, and others in
reading יַלְדָהּ instead of the extraordinary הַיֹּלְדָהּ of the MT, 'he
that begat her'. There are a few sporadic examples of this
abnormal combination of the article with the participle when
the participle has a suffix. See Ges.-Kautzsch, § 116 *f*. Some
of these abnormalities have been removed by modern scholars.
The LXX unfortunately omits the word. Hence we must fall
back on the other versions. The Pesh. and Vulg. indirectly
support the above emendation, since they presuppose יַלְדֶיהָ
'her sons'. Furthermore, Berenice's father, Ptolemy II, died
an old man, possibly of shock at Berenice's fate in Egypt about

this time, and was succeeded by Ptolemy III. See Bevan, *House of Seleucus*, i. 183. Thus on every ground the text of the MT is impossible. On the mysterious disappearance or death of Berenice's son owing to the plots of Laodice see Bevan, i. 181–183.

He that obtained her : i. e. Antiochus II her husband : cf. 11²¹ for this use of the verb. If we render it ' he that supported her ' then we must interpret the phrase of Ptolemy III Euergetes.

11⁷⁻⁹. *Ptolemy III (Euergetes I), 247–222 B.C., and Seleucus II, Callinicus, 246–226 B.C.* Ptolemy III, with a view to his avenging of the murder of his sister Berenice, invaded the northern kingdom, seized Seleucia, the port of Antioch, overran the greater part of Syria and Babylonia, and returned to Egypt with an immense booty. But his return to Egypt was due to an insurrection there. See Bevan, *op. cit.* i. 189 sq. Two years later Seleucus II invaded Egypt, but sustained an overwhelming defeat and returned with only a handful of his troops (240 B.C.).

11⁷. The text of this verse is uncertain as the earliest versions show.

A shoot from her roots. Since the LXX reads φυτὸν ἐκ τῆς ῥίζης αὐτοῦ, Bevan, Behrmann, and Marti (comparing Isa. 11¹) read ' a shoot from her roots ', i. e. נֵצֶר מִשָּׁרְשֶׁיהָ instead of מִכֵּן שָׁרָשֶׁיהָ = ' out of a shoot from her roots '. But the MT could bear the same meaning as the LXX (cf. 11⁶).

A shoot : i. e. Ptolemy III, brother of Berenice.

In his place : i. e. כנו. Ptolemy Philadelphus is referred to by the suffix. Bevan and other scholars hold that כנו is here used adverbially with the same meaning as על־כנו 11²⁰,²¹,³⁸. But it does not appear that the translator of the LXX had this word before him. He renders καθ' ἑαυτόν = כָּמוֹהוּ, while Th. has ἐπὶ τῆς ἑτοιμασίας αὐτοῦ = על מכונו (as in Ezra 2⁶⁸, Ps. 88(89)¹⁴, and the Pesh. = על־כנו. Now the translator of the LXX knew how to translate על כנו, since he renders it ἐπὶ τὸν τόπον αὐτοῦ in 11²¹,³⁸, as also does Th. (ἐπὶ τόπον αὐτοῦ in 11³⁸).[1] If the LXX is right, we should render : ' And one of the shoots of her roots shall arise like unto him ', i. e. Ptolemy III, brother of Berenice was to be like her father, Ptolemy II. On the remarkable rendering

---

[1] But Th. has ἐπὶ [11⁷ om.] τῆς (τὴν) ἑτοιμασίας (-αν), in 11⁷, ²⁰⁻²¹. This points apparently to על מכונו in these passages and gives rise to the idea that the Massoretes have normalized the Hebrew considerably.

εἰς ἀνάστασιν of the LXX in 11²⁰, where the MT has על כנו,
see note *in loc.*

March against the (Syrian) army: not 'march unto the army',
i. e. his own army to place himself at its head. If there was any
thought of the latter it would be naturally expressed with his
army (בהחיל), as in 11¹³. Ptolemy marches against the Syrian
forces and the Syrian fortress. But Bevan, followed by Kamphausen, prefers וְיָבֵא חַיִל [ם] אֱלֵהֶן 'and he shall bring an army
against them' (i. e. the Syrians).

The fortress: i. e. Seleucia on the coast of the Mediterranean,
which remained long in the possession of the Ptolemies.

Deal with them: i. e. עשה בהם. In Jer. 18²³; Neh. 9²⁴ (לעשות
בהם כרצונם) the same phrase is employed with the same hostile
significance. In 1¹³ of our text the verb is followed by עם,
where the treatment is to be hostile or otherwise according to
the issues involved.

And shall prevail: i. e. והחזיק. Here only in O.T. used absolutely in this sense.

11⁸. According to Jerome (following Porphyry) Ptolemy
brought back to Egypt the statues of Egyptian gods carried off
by Cambyses 280 years before. On this ground his subjects
conferred on him the title Euergetes. In all he brought back
2,500 precious vessels including the images of the gods, and
40,000 talents of silver. For this and other services the title of
Benefactors was conferred on the king and queen. This statement is confirmed by the Decree of Canopus (238 B. c.) in which
Ptolemy and his consort are described as 'Benefactor Gods':
see Mahaffy, *Empire of the Ptolemies,* pp. 205, 230. In this
Decree, l. 7, the king and queen are designated as Θεοι Ευεργεται.

Molten images. Here only does נָסִיךְ mean a molten image,
unless נְסִכֵּיהֶם is simply a mispunctuation for נִסְכֵּיהֶם from נֶסֶךְ,
'a molten image', Isa. 41²⁹, 48⁴, &c.

Their goodly vessels: i. e. כְּלֵי חֶמְדָּתָם—the same phrase as in
2 Chron. 32²⁷, 36¹⁰; Hos. 13¹⁵.

Of silver and gold. Better with Bevan render 'in silver and
gold'—not in apposition, since this would require the articles,
but used as 'a term of specification'.

*The **south**.* The MT מצרים reads 'Egypt'. This is not a
translation of the original but an interpretation. On a variety
of grounds I have restored in its stead the phrase 'the south'.

In the apocalyptic visions of Daniel as in that of the contemporary writer of 1 Enoch 86-90 proper names whether of individuals, nations, countries, or empires are, as a rule, not mentioned. This rule holds rigidly in 1 Enoch 86-90, and also in the visions of Daniel, and even in the interpretations of these visions given by Gabriel or some other angel *especially when the interpretation is dealing with recent events.*

The vision in 7^{1-14} is interpreted by an angel, but the symbolic terms used in the vision are reproduced in the interpretation 7^{17-28}. The vision described in 8^{2-14} is interpreted by Gabriel in 8^{20-26}. When the symbols refer to ancient events Gabriel explains the symbols : thus the ram with the two horns is said to be kings of Media and Persia, 8^{20}, and the he-goat to be a king of Greece. *But when the vision deals with recent or contemporary events, the interpreter refrains from giving any definite information as to name or country ; for it was quite needless.* Though 8^{23-26} is highly symbolical, every Jew in Palestine knew the person to whom these verses referred. Again in 9^{22-27}, when Gabriel is solving Daniel's difficulties as to the seventy weeks of which Jeremiah prophesied, the strictest reticence is observed as regards the name and nationality of Antiochus, who is, as in former visions, the subject of these disclosures. And yet his ambitions and aims were a question of life and death for the Jews.

Naturally the use of symbols varies somewhat in the different visions. In 7^{4-7} the four empires are symbolized by animals— a lion, a bear, a leopard, and a monstrous beast : the ten kings by ten horns 7^7 : Alexander the Great by 'a notable horn', 8^5, and in 8^{21} by 'the great horn' : Antiochus Epiphanes by 'a little horn' 8^9.

Similarly in 1 Enoch 89^{55} the Assyrians and Babylonians are symbolized by lions and tigers, in $89^{16,55}$ the Egyptians by wolves, but in $90^{2,11,13}$ by vultures and kites, in $90^{8,9,12}$ the Syrians by wolves, while in $90^{2,4,13,16}$ the Macedonians are symbolized by eagles.

Passing on now to the disclosures in 11^{2-45} we observe that the same, if not greater, reticence is practised in regard to recent history. The kings of Persia are mentioned and the expedition of Xerxes against Greece in 480 B.C., 11^2. Now, though there is a survey of oriental history from this date to that of Antiochus.

Epiphanes, there is not a single name mentioned, nor, when we recover the original text, even a single country. Alexander the Great is described simply as 'a mighty king' 11³, and the Seleucid kings as kings of 'the north', while the Ptolemies are described as the kings of 'the south'. Wherever anything more definite appears, we can without hesitation brand it as an *interpretation* or else as an intrusion into the text. 'The south' 11⁸,²⁹, 'the land of the south' 11⁴², is of course Egypt: 'the king of the south' 11⁵,⁶,⁹,¹¹,¹⁴⌈¹⁵⌉,²⁵(bis),⁴⁰ is one of the Ptolemies: 'the king of the north' 11⁶,⁷,⁸,¹¹,¹³,¹⁵,⁴⁰ one of the Seleucidae.

Having now observed this practice of the period in regard to visions, and the interpretations of them in our author, let us now turn to breaches of this practice in this chapter. Here the interpreter is at work. As a rule, it is the Greek translator who has interpreted 'the south' by 'Egypt', but even the Hebrew translator had already intervened in the present verse and rendered הנגב by מצרים. It is no doubt he also that in 11⁴² renders the Aramaic ערע דרומא before him by ארץ מצרים 'land of Egypt', instead of by ארץ הנגב 'land of the south', and דרומא in 11⁴³ by מצרים. Again in the closing words of 11⁴¹ the use of the proper names 'Edom and Moab and the chief of the children of Ammon' is wholly against this convention of our author and of his time.¹ He would have used symbolic terms if he referred to these nations. Besides the clause is very meaningless in itself. Another similar interpolation occurs in 11⁴³. See notes *in loc.*

The practice thus begun by the Hebrew translator in 11⁸,⁴²,⁴³ was developed on an extensive scale by the LXX. Thus in addition to the three above interpretations which appear in the Hebrew Version, the translator of the LXX renders הנגב by Αἴγυπτος in 11⁵,⁶,⁹,¹¹,¹⁴,¹⁵,²⁹,⁴⁰. If we turn from the LXX to Th., we find that he reproduces the present Massoretic text, save that in 11²⁴ he evidently found על מצרים instead of על מבצרים, which he rendered by ἐπ' Αἴγυπτον.

Refrain some years from : יעמד ממלך, i. e. from attacking the king of the north. Cf. Gen. 29³⁵ ; 2 Kings 4⁶. Others render

---

¹ In Test. Joseph 19, 2 Bar. 53 there is a similar use of symbols and constantly in 4 Ezra, as well as in other Apocalypses—not to speak of The Apocalypse.

'continue alive longer than', and others 'continue stronger than'. The last rendering is that of Th. στήσεται ὑπὲρ βασιλέα.

11⁹. When Seleucus Callinicus re-established his power in Asia (242 B. C.) he invaded Egypt, but was forced to retire with only a remnant of his forces.

11¹⁰⁻¹⁹. The next ten verses deal mainly with the times of Antiochus III, the Great. Seleucus Callinicus left two sons, Seleucus III Ceraunos and Antiochus. The former after a reign of two years (226–223 B. C.) was murdered during a campaign in Asia Minor. He was succeeded by Antiochus III the Great, 223–187 B. C. Soon after his accession Antiochus attacked Palestine, which was then subject to Ptolemy Philopator, king of Egypt, and in the course of two campaigns conquered the greater part of it. But in 217 B. C. Ptolemy met Antiochus at Raphia and defeated him with great loss. Palestine was thereupon reannexed to the empire of the Ptolemies.

11¹⁰. *His son.* So the *Kt.* בנו, i. e. Antiochus. The LXX, as the *Kt.*, reads ὁ υἱὸς αὐτοῦ (though it reads καὶ before the verb that follows), and uses the singular throughout the verse, and herein I have followed its guidance. So Von Gall, Marti, and others. Does the καί ... καί = 'both ... and'. This is in keeping with the usage in 10¹¹,¹²,¹³ sqq., where the king is the subject, and not the army. Since the *Kt.* reads the plural יתגרו towards the end of the verse, the plural is explained by treating המון חילים, i. e. the army, as singular or plural as the uncertain MT text requires. This is very unsatisfactory. The Pesh. throughout uses the plural, whereas the MT, Th., and the Vulg. use sometimes the singular and sometimes the plural.

If we accept the *Qr.* בניו, then we must regard the campaign of Seleucus in Asia Minor as the first part of an organized attack of Syria on Egypt. Seleucus himself never invaded Egypt.

Shall war and shall assemble : i. e. יִתְגָּרֶה וְאָסַף. So the LXX, whereas the MT, Pesh., and Vulg. read יִתְגָּרוּ וְאָסְפוּ. In this sense התגרה is used absolutely only in this chapter of Daniel. Cf. 11²⁵.

And he shall come on. Antiochus attacks Egypt. Seleucus is already dead, having been assassinated by one of his officers during his campaign in Asia Minor. The text could also be taken of the great multitude just mentioned 'it shall come,' &c.,

but the context, as I have pointed out in the first note on this verse, is in favour of a single leader, i. e. Antiochus being the subject. For וּבָא בֹא thirteen manuscripts, and Pesh. read וּבָא בוֹ. So also the LXX though it erroneously reads κατ' αὐτήν for κατ' αὐτόν. The same phrase recurs in 11[13], where many manuscripts and the LXX again read בו for בוֹא. When the inf. absolute follows the verb it elsewhere implies continuance or repetition: cf. Num. 23[11], 24[10]. Hence בוֹ may be right here. In that case we should render: 'he (Antiochus) will attack him' (the king of Egypt).

Overwhelm and pass over: i. e. שטף ועבר, borrowed from Isa. 8[8]. Antiochus's first invasion of Egypt was in 219 B. C.

And he shall again carry the war even to his fortress. Here with the LXX, Th., and the *Qr.* I read יְתְגָּרֶה, where the *Kt.* has יתגרו, and take ישב in the sense of 'again'. There is a reference to Antiochus returning to complete the conquest, after having wintered in Ptolemais and left garrisons in Phoenicia and Coele-Syria (Polyb. v. 66). Some scholars take the subject of the last five verbs of this verse to be the army, which, accordingly as it is treated as a singular or plural, takes a singular or plural verb.

His fortress. Antiochus after rest in winter quarters marches his forces to the south. The fortress is taken by Driver to be Gaza, the strongest Palestinian fortress in the south. In favour of this view Driver recognizes a play on the name of Gaza, i. e. עזה, in the Hebrew word used here for fortress, i. e. מעזה. But this word is used in this chapter of different fortresses: cf. 11[1,10,19], [31,38]. Besides the verb יתגרה presupposes that the fortress in question is the objective of Antiochus's attack. But as Gaza belonged to Antiochus, we must take the fortress to be Raphia, which was Ptolemy's.

11[11]. *King of the south.* Ptolemy Philopator.

Shall be moved with choler (cf. 8[7], where the same verb is used of Ptolemy) *and go forth and fight with him* to resist the advancing forces of Antiochus. But according to Polybius (v. 68–69) a large Egyptian army led by Nicolaus was the first to take the field and march through Palestine, where between Lebanon and the sea it was completely defeated by Antiochus.

Fight with this same king of the north: i. e. נלחם עמו עם מלך הצפון. This is a pure Aramaism—in fact the customary idiom where

the following word is expressly emphasized.   See 5¹²; also
Kautzsch, *Gr. d. Bibl. Aram.*, § 81 *e* and § 88.   It is true that in
Joshua 1² we have להם לבני ישראל : cf. Num. 32³³ ; Judges 21⁷,
&c. (Ges.-Kautzsch, § 131 *n.*).   But most of these examples from
the standpoint of Hebrew are textually doubtful.   There are of
course in the later books several such Aramaisms.

He shall raise a great multitude, &c.   The subject of the verb
here is Antiochus.   Hitzig takes the subject to be Ptolemy.

But the multitude shall be given into his hand.   Here clearly
the same force is mentioned as in the preceding clause, since
ההמון must refer to המון רב.   This army is that of Antiochus
which was defeated by Ptolemy.   On the expression נתן בידו, cf.
1 Kings 20²⁸.

Another interpretation is given to the above clauses : ' And he
(Ptolemy) shall raise a great multitude and the multitude shall
be placed under his (Ptolemy's) command.'   In support of this
meaning of נתן ביד Gen. 39⁴, 2 Sam. 10¹⁰ are adduced.   But the
sense is very unsatisfactory.

11¹². *The multitude shall be swept away.*   Here as in the preceding verse the המון is the army of Antiochus.   For the use of
the verb נִשָּׂא cf. Isa. 40²⁴, 41¹⁶ ; Job 32²² ; also 2³⁵ in our text.
Hitzig, as in the preceding verse, interprets this verse of
Ptolemy: 'the multitude shall stand up (to fight), its (or
Ptolemy's) heart being uplifted.'   Here נִשָּׂא is used in the same
sense as in Isa. 33¹⁰, and the clause ירום לבבו is circumstantial.

And his heart shall be uplifted: i. e. Ptolemy's.   ירום לבבו can
be taken as a circumstantial clause, but it is best to read וְרָם with
the *Qr.*, LXX, Th., and Vulg.   On the Hebrew phrase, cf.
Deut. 8¹⁴, 17²⁰ : also 5²⁰ (Aram.) in our text.

Shall cast down: i. e. at Raphia, where, according to Polybius
(v. 86), Antiochus was defeated by Ptolemy with the loss of
almost 10,000 infantry, 300 cavalry, and more than 4,000
prisoners.

Tens of thousands.   רבאות is an Aramaic form instead of the
classical Hebrew רבבות.   Contrast the Hebraism proposed by
the *Qr.* in the Aramaic in 7¹⁰.

Shall not prevail.   After his victory at Raphia, Ptolemy IV
Philopator recovered Coele-Syria (Polyb. v. 86), but failed to
follow up his success.   Owing to his effeminate and dissolute

character he had not the energy to complete the overthrow of Antiochus. See Bevan, *House of Seleucus*, i. 318-320.

11¹³⁻¹⁶. Twelve years after the battle of Raphia, i. e. in 205 B.C., referred to in the preceding verses, Ptolemy IV Philopator died, leaving only one son, aged five years, who succeeded his father as Ptolemy V, Epiphanes, 205-181 B.C. Antiochus seized on this opportunity of attacking Egypt, and formed a league with Philip of Macedon for this purpose (Polyb. xv. 20). After varying fortunes Scopas (see Bevan, *House of Seleucus*, ii. 36-37), the general of Ptolemy, recovered possession of Judaea in 200 B.C., but two years later was utterly crushed at Panion (Josephus, *Ant.* xii. 33) i. e. Paneas, now named Banias, the Caesarea Philippi of the Gospels), and forced to take refuge in Sidon, where he was besieged and forced to surrender, but dismissed unhurt.[1] Antiochus invaded Phoenicia and Syria and captured Gaza (Polyb. xvi. 18, 40). On this battle of Panion, Bevan (*House of Seleucus*, ii. 37) rightly observes : ' The battle is the landmark denoting the final and definite substitution of Seleucid for Ptolemaic rule in Palestine '.

11¹³. *And again . . . shall raise.* Here והעמיד · · ושב is to be so rendered, as Bevan and Driver do, and not 'and . . . shall return and shall raise '. Antiochus does not return to the south and raise a huge army, but again he raises an army in order to take advantage of the weakness of Egypt.

Shall attack him. Here with many manuscripts and the LXX I read יבוא בו instead of the MT יבוא בוא. Cf. 11¹⁰. The MT = ' shall come on repeatedly '.

At the end of years. לקץ [העתים] שנים. The עתים is omitted as an intrusion from the next clause. The number of years was, as we otherwise know, twelve. The close of these is definitely referred to in 11¹⁴.

Great army. I have here followed the LXX in reading רב instead of גדול. See note on 11²⁵.

Substance. Apparently רְכוּש ' camp-baggage ' as in Gen. 14¹¹,¹² ; 2 Chron. 21¹⁴, &c.

11¹⁴. *There shall many stand up*, &c. These words refer to

---

[1] Antiochus besieged Scopas in Sidon, where he had taken refuge with 10,000 men ; Cum decem millibus armatorum obsedit clausum in Sidone . . . donec fame superatus Scopas manus dedit et nudus cum sociis dimissus est. Jerome, *Comm. on Dan.* 11¹⁵.

Antiochus, Philip of Macedon, and the many insurgents in Egypt itself owing to the oppressive measures of Agathocles, the chief minister of Ptolemy Philopator, whom Polybius designates ὁ ψευδεπίτροπος Πτολεμαίου (xv. 25). He was ultimately put to death by some soldiers, and thereby rescued from the far worse fate which befel his family (xv. 33).

The children of the violent among thy people. These constituted a faction amongst the Jews, i. e. Tobias and his followers. To Schlatter (*ZATW.*, 1894, 143–151) this identification is due as Marti points out. Ptolemy alienated the affections of the Jews by supporting Joseph, the head of the Tobiadae, by a garrison in Jerusalem. This family got hold of the high-priesthood and robbed the nation by their endless exactions and taxes. Without intending it they contributed by their conduct 'to establish the vision', i. e. to bring about the end foretold, while the result for themselves was no less unintentional, i. e. their own destruction. Bevan regards בני פריצים as impossible Hebrew, but this faction (בני הפריצים) was a corporate body, a troop of robbers, and Marti compares with this expression בני הנביאים. פריץ denotes a robber: hence in Jer. 7[11] 'den of robbers' מערת פריצים.

11[15]. *Earthworks* (lit. 'a mound').

A well fenced city. This is Sidon, where Scopas with 10,000 men, after his defeat by Antiochus at Paneas (Jerome, *Comm. on Dan.*, 11[15]: Polyb. xvi. 18; xxviii. 1), had taken refuge, and which Antiochus captured (198 B. C.). עיר מבצרות is late Hebrew: it is unique in the O.T. The proper Hebrew is עיר מבצר: cf. 1 Sam. 6[18]; 2 Kings 3[19], 10[2]; Jer. 1[18], &c. Only once, i. e. in Jer. 5[17], does the plural of מבצר follow עיר or ערי (the construct), and then it is the masculine plural and not the feminine as in our text here. The translator uses the plural masc. in 11[24,39], but not in the phrase we are dealing with.

11[15a—16]. *Complete overthrow of the Egyptian suzerainty over Syria.*

The forces (cf. 11[22,31]) *of the ⌜king of the⌝ south shall make a stand, even the élite of his troops, but the strength to make a stand shall be lacking.* The one assured conclusion to be drawn from a study of the MT and the LXX, Th., and Vulg. is that not one of them represents the original. The MT = 'the arms of the south shall not withstand, neither his chosen people, neither shall there be any strength to withstand.'. From a comparative

study of the MT and Versions it is possible to secure a more
ancient and authentic text. First of all we should restore מלך
הנגב with Th. (τοῦ βασιλέως τοῦ νότου) and the LXX (βασιλέως Αἰγύπτου). Next with the LXX, Th., and Pesh. (which is conflate)
we should omit the negative לא before יעמדו. Only the Vulg.
herein supports the MT. This negative, therefore, appears to
be a late intrusion. Omitting then this לא, what are we to make
of what remains? The last three words אין כח לעמד of the MT
may be taken as free from corruption (though possibly defective),
seeing that the LXX, Th., and Pesh. reproduce them, and also
the Vulg., though defectively. The LXX adds לו after כח, and
the Pesh. להם.

There remain therefore only the words וְעַם מִבְחָרָיו ׀. Here
the LXX (μετὰ τῶν δυναστῶν αὐτοῦ καί) read עִם בַּחוּרָיו ׀ : Th. (καὶ οἱ
ἐκλεκτοὶ αὐτοῦ καί) read ובחוריו ו. The Vulg. agrees with Th. save
that it omits the second καί. The Pesh. is conflate and corrupt
but has a phrase = מבחר העם. Thus Th. and the Vulg. omit
עם. But since this word appears in the LXX and MT, as a
preposition in the one case and a noun in the other, and since
it has thus the ancient testimony of the LXX, we may reasonably conclude that it was omitted by the late versions. The
text thus appears to have been וְעַם מִבְחָרָיו ׀, or regarding the מ
as a dittograph we may read וְעַם בַּחוּרָיו ׀. So practically Th.,
Pesh., and Vulg. In favour of the latter form is the fact that
מבחר is not found elsewhere in the plural in the O.T. It is
also possible that the LXX may be right: 'the arms of the king
of the south (Αἰγύπτου is an interpretation of הנגב, i.e. τοῦ νότου)
shall withstand with his strongest troops, but he shall have no
strength to withstand him'. Marti makes a good emendation.
He omits the מ and the ו before אין as dittographs, and thus
reads עם בחוריו אין 'but his best troops shall have no strength
to withstand'. The text I arrive at omits לא with the LXX and
Th. and takes the ו before עַם as explicative, and gives a good
sense with a minimum of change.

11¹⁶. *But he* (Antiochus) *that cometh against him* (Ptolemy).

None shall stand before him : אין עומד לפניו, i. e. 'be able to withstand him'. See note on 1⁵ on the different meanings of this
phrase in our author.

The glorious land : i. e. ארץ הַצְּבִי, Palestine. See note on 8⁹.

The LXX renders הצבי by τῆς θελήσεως here (Syr^h) and in 11^45, thus deriving it from the sense of the root in Aram. Cf. צבותא.

And in his hand shall be annihilation. Cf. 9^27 for כלה. Both the LXX and Th. (τελεσθήσεται) take כָּלָה as a verb = 'shall be destroyed', but there is a dittography in the LXX—τελεσθήσεται πάντα = וכלה כל. The destruction is directed against the Jews or the Egyptian garrisons in Palestine. If for כָּלָה we read כֻּלָּהּ the above clause would run: 'with all of it in his hand (Bertholdt)'.

11^17. *Set his face:* i.e. וְיָשֵׂם פָּנָיו 'make it his aim': cf. Gen. 31^21; 2 Kings 12^18; Jer. 42^15,17.

To come with the strength, &c. Antiochus will march with his entire forces against Ptolemy. Antiochus in 197 B.C. mustered his fleet and all his forces to attack the cities on the coast of Cilicia, Lycia, and Caria, which were in Ptolemy's possession. Driver (*in loc.*) quotes Livy, xxxiii. 19: 'omnibus regni viribus connixus, cum ingentes copias terrestres maritimasque comparasset.' He did not persist in this attack, but made a treaty instead with Ptolemy.

But shall (instead) make an agreement with him. The MT, which reads וִישָׁרִים עִמּוֹ וְעָשָׂה 'and the upright ones with him; and he shall do', is undoubtedly corrupt. We should with the LXX (καὶ συνθήκας μετ' αὐτοῦ ποιήσεται), Th. (καὶ εὐθεῖα πάντα μετ' αὐτοῦ ποιήσει), Vulg. read ומישרים עמו יעשה. For מישרים in the sense of 'agreement' or 'equitable conditions', cf. 11^6. It is possible that ישרים is the plural of יֹשֶׁר 'uprightness'.

With power: בתקף—an Aramaism: cf. 2^37, 4^27, &c.

Shall give him the daughter of women. בת הנשים is peculiar, if it is genuine. Can it mean 'the woman' *par excellence*, just as בר אנשא 'the man'? When Antiochus abandoned his designs on Egypt owing to the intervention of Rome, he made an alliance with Ptolemy Epiphanes and gave him his daughter Cleopatra in marriage, with the provinces, or rather the revenues of the provinces, of Coele-Syria, Phoenicia, and Palestine as a dowry. The Egyptians understood the dowry in the former sense, but Antiochus in the latter (Polyb. xxviii. 17). Mahaffy, however (*op. cit.* 306), upholds the claim of the Egyptians. This marriage took place 194–193 B.C. at Raphia (Livy, xxxv. 13).

To destroy it: i.e. Egypt. Antiochus' real motive in giving his daughter to Ptolemy was at once to protect himself against Roman interference and to gain a footing in Egypt, which he

could turn to his own purposes when the opportunity arose.
The rendering 'to corrupt her' (לְהַשְׁחִיתָהּ) gives no tolerable
sense. Cleopatra adopted the cause of her husband, advised
him to maintain an alliance with Rome, and lived happily
in Egypt. Ptolemy accordingly retained the friendship of
Rome, while Antiochus forfeited it wholly. Antiochus was
moved by no friendly spirit towards Egypt, but was simply
biding his time in the hope of securing it for himself.
Hearing at Lysimacheia a false rumour of Ptolemy's death,
he set out forthwith to make himself master of Egypt (Livy,
xxxiii. 41).

But it shall not stand neither shall it come to pass : i. e. לא תעמד
[ולא [לו] תהיה. Here we have the later Hebrew reproduction (cf.
Ps. 33[11]) of the same expression as in Isa. 7[7] לא תקום ולא תהיה :
cf. 14[24]. עמד is used as the equivalent of קום in the sense of ' to
be established ', 'to maintain itself' here and in Esther 3[4]. The
plan of Antiochus will not succeed. I have with the LXX
against the MT, Th., Pesh., and Vulg. omitted לו. It originated
most probably as a dittograph of לא, and then it won the support
of the Massoretes, Th., Pesh., and Vulg. owing to their wrongly
conceiving Cleopatra to be the subject of these two clauses,
whereas it is clearly the plan of Antiochus that is the subject.
Of course it is possible to incorporate לו into the second clause,
but it weakens the impressiveness of the old prophetic words,
and the author is not culpable in this respect.

11[18]. The historical facts behind this verse are, shortly, as
follows. In 197 B. c. Antiochus made an expedition into Asia
Minor. This expedition was attended with great success, and
most of the cities made their submission to him. In the same
year he made himself master of the Thracian Chersonese, and,
when he had consolidated these conquests, he effected a landing
in Greece in 192, and seized parts of Greece north of Corinth.
But here his successes came to an end. In 191 his forces
were routed by the Romans at Thermopylae, and in the following year his huge army of 80,000 men sustained such an
overwelming defeat at Magnesia by the Romans under Lucius
Cornelius Scipio (Livy, xxxvii. 39–44: Mommsen, *Hist. of
Rom.*, Book III, chap. ix, 270 seqq.) that he had to relinquish
his claims to all his European possessions or conquests as well
as to all parts of Asia Minor west of the Taurus. The latter

half of 11[18] deals with this catastrophe. On the events behind this verse see Bevan, *House of Seleucus*, ii. 88–112.

Turn his face : i. e. וְיָשֵׂב. Here the *Qr.* reads וְיָשֵׂם as in the LXX καὶ δώσει, and in 11[17] of our text. But, as Bevan remarks, the *Kt.* is to be retained, since here it is not a question of purpose but of actual movement as in 11[19], where we have the same phrase repeated. The expedition referred to here is that of Antiochus against Asia Minor. See preceding note.

To the †coast lands† : i. e. לְאִיִּים, the islands and coastlands of the Mediterranean. But the LXX here reads ἐπὶ τὴν θάλασσαν = לְיָם ('to the west'), which is either a corruption of לְאִיִּים or vice versa. If the LXX is right the 'many' that Antiochus captured would probably be prisoners. Both on sea and land Antiochus fought against Rome for the independence of the East. If the MT is right, then the 'many' would mean coast lands and provinces on the Mediterranean. But Antiochus' attempts ended in failure.

The two following clauses are very difficult. The foremost scholars turn down the MT absolutely. Their emendations fail, however, to account for the texts presupposed by the LXX and Th. I have attempted a fresh departure and offer two restorations of the text, both of which keep close to the MT and account in the main for the LXX and Th. The second appears the more justifiable.

But a chief shall put an end to his contumely : i. e. וְהִשְׁבִּת קָצִין חֶרְפָּתוֹ. On the Roman commander see first note on this verse. Antiochus offered hospitality to Hannibal, and told the Romans that they had no more business with his doings in the East than he had with theirs in the West : 'Asiam nihil ad populum Romanum pertinere : nec magis illis inquirendum esse, quid Antiochus, quam Antiocho, quid in Italia populus Romanus faciat' (Livy, xxxiii. 40).

So that he (Antiochus) *shall not requite his* (the Roman chief's) *contumely upon him.* The Roman victory was to be so overwhelming as to exclude the possibility of further resistance on the part of Antiochus. The above translation requires the omission of one letter in the MT, and indirectly it serves to explain the variants in the LXX and Th. The MT, LXX, Th., Vulg., and Pesh. run as follows :

MT. ‏והשבית קצין חרפתו לו בלתי חרפתו ישיב לו‏.

LXX. καὶ ἐπιστρέψει ὀργὴν ὀνειδισμοῦ αὐτῶν ἐν ὅρκῳ κατὰ τὸν ὀνειδισμὸν αὐτοῦ.

Th. καὶ καταπαύσει ἄρχοντας ὀνειδισμοῦ αὐτῶν· πλὴν ὀνειδισμὸς αὐτοῦ ἐπιστρέψει αὐτῷ.

Vulg. Et cessare faciet principem opprobrii sui et opprobrium eius convertetur in eum.

Pesh. = καὶ καταπαύσει τὸν ἄρχοντα τὸν ὀνειδίσαντα αὐτὸν καὶ ὀνειδισμὸν αὐτοῦ ἐπιστρέψει αὐτῷ.

(1) Now first of all we observe that חרפתו occurs in all the authorities in some form twice—in the Pesh. once as a participle.

(2) Next in the LXX ὀργήν = קצף, which is an obvious corruption of קצין.

(3) In all the authorities there are two verbs expressed or implied, i.e. השבית and ישיב, except in the LXX, which reads השיב for השבית, a⸗d omits ישיב. But, as Bevan suggests, ἐπιστρέψει αὐτῷ καί could have easily been lost through homoioteleuton before ἐπιστρέψει at the beginning of 11¹⁹.

(4) The LXX reads ἐν ὅρκῳ where the MT has לו בלתי and Th. πλήν, but the Vulg. and Pesh. have no equivalent. Now, it is generally assumed, but wrongly as I believe, that ἐν ὅρκῳ here presupposes בִּשְׁבֻעָה, which Bevan takes to be a corruption of שִׁבְעָתַיִם 'sevenfold'. Thus we have 'he shall requite his insults sevenfold'. Marti seeks to improve on Bevan. He reads והשיב (with the LXX), and omitting several words reads והשיב לו קצין חרפתו שבעתים. But this is rewriting the text and not emending it. Besides it furnishes no explanation of the genesis of the MT text. To return to Bevan's suggestion: how can we accept שבעתים as a corruption of לו בלתי, or how can it in any way account for it? Moreover there is not a trace of this proposed Hebrew word in any of the other versions. The conjecture is, I think, not only a counsel of despair, but impossible under the circumstances.

(1) My first proposal. What then does ἐν ὅρκῳ represent? Possibly באלה [1] (cf. Prov. 29²³; Gen. 24⁴¹, Lev. 5¹), which comes very close to בלתי. It also is a vain attempt to translate a corrupt original. The πλήν of Th., which = אֲבָל, is another emendation of בלתי and an attempt to make something of the

---

[1] When אלה and שְׁבֻעָה occur together as in Num. 5²¹; Neh. 10³⁰, the renderings are ἀρά and ὅρκος (ἐνόρκιον). But אלה is occasionally rendered (ὅρκος, ὁρκισμός) and it alone serves to explain the MT.

corrupt text.   For בלתי cannot be rendered 'only' with Ewald,
or 'certainly' with Hitzig or 'nothing but' with Drechsler.

What, then, are we to make of the MT באלה, בלתי (LXX), and
אבל (Th.)?   My first proposal is to read לְבִלְתִּי, of which לו בלתי
is a corruption.   This, though generally a preposition, is used
also as a final conjunction: cf. Exod. 20²⁰; 2 Sam. 14¹⁴ (cf. מן
in this sense in Deut. 33¹¹), and so also in the correct text in
Jer. 23¹⁴ (לבלתי ישבו), 27¹⁸ (לבלתי יבאו).   We should then translate:
'And a chief shall so put an end to his contumely that he shall
not requite his contumely upon him'.   The discomfiture of
Antiochus was to be crushing and complete.   The above
restoration keeps very close to the MT and is indirectly supported by the LXX and Th.   By thus keeping close to the
documentary authorities we are obliged to take the first חרפתו
as referring to Antiochus and the second to the Roman consul.

(2) My second proposal.   If it appears unsatisfactory to take
חרפתו as referring to two different persons, it is possible to make
the two refer to Antiochus alone by emending לו בלתי into
לְכְלָה[1] 'for annihilation' (cp. 9²⁷, 11¹⁶, Ezek. 13¹³).   לכלה would largely
explain the corrupt readings presupposed by the LXX (באלה)
and Th. (אבל) and give an excellent sense.   In 11¹⁶ Antiochus
was master of the situation.   He had in his hand כלה, i. e. 'the
annihilation' of Palestine, &c.   The tables are now turned.
The Romans shall effect the annihilation (כלה) of Antiochus.
We should then render: 'And a chief shall put an end to his
contumely (even) unto annihilation (לכלה): (yea) he shall requite
him with his own contumely.'   This emendation does more
justice to the context: the former is closer to the text of the MT.

The last three words וחרפתו ישיב לו are derived from Hos. 12¹⁴.

11¹⁹.   In order to meet the vast fine imposed upon him (Polyb.
xxi. 14: Livy, xxxvii. 45) Antiochus retired to the fortresses of
the East.   He had to levy contributions where it was possible,
and temples were not exempt from his exactions.   After plun-
dering the temple of Bel in Elymais he and his followers were
attacked by the inhabitants and slain in 187 B.C.   See Bevan,
House of Seleucus, ii. 120.

11²⁰.   Seleucus IV Philopator, 187–175 B.C.   This king im-

---

[1] Even possibly תכליִת which means 'utterly' Job. 11⁷, 28³, but it is not so
close to the MT form.

pressed himself on the memories of the Jews by his attempt to rob the Temple through the agency of Heliodorus. The full account is given in 2 Macc. 3[1-40]. With this we deal later in this verse. Driver, on the other hand, thinks 'the allusion may be of a general kind: Seleucus had to pay for nine years an annual sum of 1,000 talents to the Romans ... the reference may be to the "exactor" who visited Palestine regularly for this purpose'. An officer of Antiochus Epiphanes who had duties in Judaea was called ἄρχων φορολογίας (1 Macc. 1[29]).

Shall stand up in his place one that shall cause an exactor to pass through with royal splendour. The text is doubtful, and the versions of little or no help, save that they presuppose some form or other of the MT though diversely and corruptly. The LXX reads καὶ ἀναστήσεται ... εἰς ἀνάστασιν, ἀνὴρ τύπτων δόξαν βασιλέως = לעמד איש נגע הדר מלך ••• ועמד. Here we observe that the LXX omits עלכנו 'in his place', that לעמד replaces מעביר, and אישנגע replaces נגש. But על כנו of the MT is original. It is supported by Th., Pesh., and Vulg., as well as by the context. Hence this phrase must be retained. Th. reads ἀναστήσεται ... ἐπὶ τ. ἐτοιμασίαν αὐτοῦ παραβιβάζων, πράσσων δόξαν βασιλείας = ועמד ••• על מכונו מעביר נגש הדר מלכות, which, though rather meaningless, supports MT in the main. The Vulg. is hopeless, but the Pesh. is clearly based on an emendation of the current Hebrew text. It = ועמד על כנו מעביר זרוע והדר מלכיות 'there shall stand up in his place one that shall cause the strength and splendour of kingdoms to pass away'.

From the above examination we may reasonably conclude that the MT is trustworthy. All that remains to do is to determine its meaning. נוגש clearly means 'an exactor'. The difficulties lie in the last four words of the Hebrew, which are usually rendered 'one that shall cause an exactor to pass through the glory of the kingdom'. But in no other passage in the O.T. has this verb two accusatives. הדר should be preceded by a preposition על or ב. Furthermore the analogy of הוד מלכות in the next verse shows that we have here not a concrete conception 'the glory of the kingdom' but an abstract one. It can then be translated as an adverbial phrase 'with royal splendour', or with Bevan transpose מעביר and נוגש, and render 'Then shall stand up in his place an exactor who shall cause royal splendour to pass away'. Bevan attaches the same meaning (cf. 2 Sam. 12¹³; Esther 8³) to מֵעֲבִיר that the Pesh. does. He would take the 'exactor' to be 'Seleucus, who made himself unpopular by his avarice; Livy speaks of this king's reign as "otiosum, nullis admodum rebus gestis nobilitatum"' (xli. 19).

But the 'exactor' is clearly Heliodorus (2 Macc. 3¹⁻¹³,²²⁻³⁰). Simon, a Benjaminite, who was at variance with Onias the high priest, and had charge of the Temple, gave information to Apollonius, the governor of Coele-Syria and Phoenicia, that the treasury was full of untold sums of money, and that, as they were not assigned to the maintenance of the Temple sacrifices, the king could secure them. When Seleucus learnt this he at once sent Heliodorus his chancellor (τὸν ἐπὶ τῶν πραγμάτων) to seize these treasures. But, according to the writer, Heliodorus was prevented from carrying out his sacrilegious purpose through a supernatural appearance.

This account is confirmed by two inscriptions on the bases of two statues erected to Heliodorus before 175 B.C. Of these inscriptions a full account is given in Deissmann's *Bibelstudien*, Eng. transl., 303–307. In the second of these inscriptions Heliodorus is described as being a relative of this king (cf. l. 3 τὴν συγγένειαν αὐτοῦ), and in both of them as his foster-brother (σύντροφος). In both also he is called the chancellor or first minister of the crown (cf. 2 Macc. 10¹¹, 13²) in the phrase ἐπὶ τῶν πραγμάτων τεταγμένον, exactly as in 2 Macc. 3⁷.

Few days : twelve years—short in comparison with the longer reign of Antiochus III. Otherwise the 'few days' are to be reckoned from the mission of Heliodorus to the murder of the king, or from the inception of the plot to its execution.

Shall be destroyed : (lit. 'broken'). Seleucus is the first of the three horns mentioned in 7⁸ of our text. According to Appian, *Syr.* 45, Seleucus met his death owing to a conspiracy set on foot by Heliodorus (ἐξ ἐπιβουλῆς Ἡλιοδώρου). See Bevan, *House of Seleucus*, ii. 125.

In anger (i. e. בְאַפִּים). It is objected that we should expect בְאַף in this sense; but the dual is used in the sense of anger in such phrases as אֶרֶךְ אַפִּים : cf. Prov. 14²⁹, 15¹⁸, &c. : also in 30³³ מִיץ אַפַּיִם 'the forcing of wrath'. But, as Behrmann points out, 'not in anger' is not what we expect here. Hence he suggests that בְאַפִּים is used as בְאַנְפִּין in Aramaic (= the Hebrew פָּנִים, cf. Deut. 5⁴). Hence the phrase would mean 'not openly', 'not in a fair face to face encounter'. This would agree with the fact that Seleucus was the victim of a secret conspiracy.

11²¹⁻⁴⁵. Antiochus IV, Epiphanes, 175–164 B. C. This Antiochus was the son of Antiochus the Great and the brother of Seleucus Philopator. For fourteen years he had been a hostage at Rome in accordance with the treaty concluded by the Romans with his father, and was treated then, as he afterwards boasted, 'pro rege, non pro obside, omnibus ordinibus' (Liv. xlii. 6). At the request of Seleucus IV the Romans released Antiochus in his twelfth year and took in his stead Demetrius, Seleucus' own son. On his way back to Antioch Seleucus IV was murdered by Heliodorus (11²⁰), who sought to become king. But by the help of Eumenes, King of Pergamum, and Attalus, Antiochus seized the throne, which belonged legitimately to his nephew Demetrius.

11²¹. *A contemptible person.* These words express the Jewish verdict on Antiochus IV. The term may be applied to him in derision of the title he assumed, Θεὸς ἐπιφανής—'God manifest', of which Θεὸς ἐπιμανής is a fitting and well-deserved parody.

On whom had not been bestowed, &c. Here ולא נתנו עליו הוד מלכות is to be taken as a relative clause with אשר omitted. The same phrase is found in 1 Chron. 29²⁵ ; cf. Num. 27²⁰.

In time of security : i. e. shall take them unawares. Cf. 11²⁴, 8²⁵.

By flatteries : i. e. †בחלקלקות†. This word recurs in 11³⁴ with the same meaning, but in 11³² as בחלקות. The question arises : Were both these forms, bearing the same meaning, used by the Hebrew translator ? Th. either found one and the same form in all three passages, or else he identified the form in 11³² with that in 11²¹,³⁴ so far as the meaning is concerned. But the LXX, though corrupt, supplies evidence for the decision of this question. In 11²¹,³⁴ it renders ἐν κληροδοσίᾳ αὐτοῦ (αὐτοῦ omitted in 11³⁴) = בחלקה or בחלקתו 'in the (or "his") portion'. In 11³² its rendering is ἐν σκληρῷ λαῷ, which is a corruption of ἐν κληροδοσίᾳ through a confusion of Δ and Λ and a transposition of C: i. e. ΚΛΗΡΟΔΟΣΙΑΙ is a corruption of CΚΛΗΡΩΙΛΑΩΙ. Thus the LXX in all three passages attests the same Hebrew text. Th. does the same, but does not help to determine which of the two Hebrew forms חלקות or חלקלקות should be read in the three passages. But the LXX does. Its rendering was in the three passages בְּחֶלְקָה or בְּחֶלְקָתוֹ, which, since they are meaningless in

11²¹˒³², are corruptions of בַּחֲלַקְלַקּוֹת and not of בחלקלקות. Hence the latter word in the MT should in 11²¹ be corrected into בחלקות, and in 11³⁴ into בחלקתו (see note *in loc.*). There is thus no evidence that the longer Hebrew word ever bore the secondary meaning of 'flatteries' or 'fine promises'. It appears in the O.T. (Ps. 35⁶; Jer. 23¹²) only in its original sense of 'slipperiness', and, when the LXX of Daniel was translated, it had not yet displaced the shorter form בחלקות. חֲלַקּוֹת is an exceptional pointing for חֲלָקוֹת (Isa. 30¹⁰).

11²²⁻²⁴. *Events in Syria during the first five years of Antiochus' reign, 175–170 B.C.*

11²². *Armies shall be utterly swept away.* Here with Marti and others I follow Bevan's emendation of הַשֶּׁטֶף [1] into הָשְׁטֹף, an infinitive strengthening the finite verb which follows—יִשָּׁטֵפוּ. The armies in question were those of Heliodorus and other domestic enemies. The MT זרעות השטף 'the armies of the flood' (i. e. overwhelming forces) 'would be a singularly inappropriate designation for the armies defeated by Antiochus'. Some scholars interpret this verse of the forces of Egypt and of Ptolemy Philometor, the son and successor of Ptolemy Epiphanes. But there is no express reference to Egypt before 11²⁵.

And shall be broken; yea also the prince of the covenant. Marti proposes וישבר נם instead of וישברו וגם. This would connect the verb with the final clause: 'And the prince of the covenant also shall be broken'. The prince, as Theodoret observed, was the Jewish high priest Onias III, who was removed from his office by Antiochus in 175 B.C. and murdered at Antioch in 171. See note on 9²⁶, where Onias is described as 'an anointed one'. Cf. 1 Enoch 90⁸. The text of this verse is uncertain. Th. supports the MT save in respect of one phrase: see note below. The LXX—καὶ τοὺς βραχίονας τοὺς συντριβέντας συντρίψει ἀπὸ προσώπου αὐτοῦ καὶ μετὰ τῆς διαθήκης—presupposes והורעות הנשברות ישבר מלפניו ועם ברית. The first four words of this Hebrew when compared with those of the MT suggest independent renderings of a corrupt Aramaic text.

From before him: i. e. מלפניו—a rendering of the Aramaic מִן־קָדְמוֹחִי: cf. 7¹⁰.

---

[1] Th. (τοῦ κατακλύζοντος) punctuated this word as הַשּׁטֵף the participle: 'The armies of him that swept down'.

11²³. Antiochus outwitted all his friends and confederates.

From the time they shall make a league with him. מִן here used in the same sense as in 9²⁵. הִתְחַבְּרוּת is an Aramaized infinitive: see Ges.-Kautzsch, § 54 *k*: cf. הַשָּׁמֵעוּת in Ezek. 24²⁶. The subject is not expressed just as in Ps. 42⁴. Contrast 42¹¹.

We could also translate: 'by means of their league with him.' The first half of this verse refers to Antiochus over-reaching his friends—whether his allies in general, or Ptolemy Philometor, or Jason (see 9²⁶).

11²³ᵇ⁻²⁴ᵃ. *He shall take the field and become strong with a small force. And in time of security† he shall attack the fattest places of the province†.* So the MT, save that with Bevan, &c., I have removed the *vav* before במשמני and placed it before the preceding word. For עלה being used absolutely in the sense of ' to take the field' without a preposition or defining word following, cf. Isa. 21². The MT is uncertain, and, since the versions differ so much, it is quite impossible to be sure what the original was. However, as 8²⁴,²⁵ also refer to the earliest acts of Antiochus, these verses may be helpful. Thus in 8²⁴ we have והשחית עצומים and in 8²⁵ בשלוה ישחית רבים. These two phrases suggest that in our text we should find two statements: first, that Antiochus would destroy mighty ones; and secondly, that he would do it unexpectedly. Now the LXX reads καὶ ἐπὶ ἔθνος ἰσχυρὸν ἐν ὀλιγοστῷ ἔθνει (11²⁴) ἐξάπινα ἐρημώσει πόλιν. Here these two ideas are repro-duced. But עלה (= ἀναβήσεται) easily fell out before the succeeding על גוי עצום, as Jahn recognizes. The loss of עלה led next to the deliberate removal of the *vav* which either preceded or followed בשלוה. The LXX then presupposes ועלה על גוי עצום במעט גוי בשלוה ושמם מדינה 'and with a small force he shall take the field unexpectedly against a mighty force and lay waste a province'. In this case ושמם would either be the original or a corruption of משמני in the MT. But Th., Pesh., Vulg. support the MT. Here as in 8²⁴ we could interpret the first clause of Antiochus overcoming his political rivals, and the second of his onset on Palestine. The גוי עצום are the עצומים of 8²⁴. But for גוי we hould expect עם as Bevan remarks. Where the MT has ועצם and the LXX presupposes על גוי עצום, Th. presupposes ועצם מהם.

If we retain the MT we must at all events transpose the *vav* before בשלוה and translate: 'And in time of security he shall attack the fattest places ', &c.

Bevan prefers to render משמני מדינה by 'the mightiest men of (each) province', and compares Isa. 10¹⁶, Ps. 78³¹. The words וחשחית עצומים in 8²⁴ appear to support Bevan.

The MT is thus wholly uncertain. If the translator of the LXX had found במשמני מדינה יבוא, it is inconceivable that he should have left an easy word like יבוא untranslated, unless we regard him as incapable of translating משמני.

11²⁴ᵇ. *He shall do that which his fathers have not done,* &c. If these words stood alone, they could refer to Antiochus' attempts to Hellenize his subjects and to put down all religions but his own. But if they refer to what follows, they may be explained by Antiochus' prodigal generosity. Cf. 1 Macc. 3³⁰: 'He feared that he should not have enough, as at other times, for the charges and the gifts which he used to give aforetime with a liberal hand, and he was more lavish than the kings that were before him.' Cf. Livy, xli. 20: 'Spectaculorum quoque omnis generis magnificentia superiores reges vicit.' According to Polybius, xxvi. 10, he was for ever giving presents of all kinds, even to strangers. In one of his campaigns in Egypt he gave a piece of gold to every Greek in Naukratis (Polyb. xxviii. 17. 11). This characteristic is marked by Livy, xli. 20: 'vere regius erat animus in urbium donis et deorum cultu;' and Polyb. xxvi. 10: ἐν δὲ ταῖς πρὸς τὰς πόλεις θυσίαις καὶ ταῖς πρὸς τοὺς θεοὺς τιμαῖς, πάντας ὑπερέβαλε τοὺς βεβοσιλευκότας.

Among them: i. e. his adherents apparently. For this vague use of the plural, cf. 11⁷.

Shall scatter: יבזור. Only found elsewhere in the O.T. in Ps. 68³¹. The form is Aramaic, a synonym of the Hebrew פור. The usual form in Aramaic is בדר.

Prey, spoil, and substance. Cf. 1 Macc. 1¹⁹: ἔλαβεν τὰ σκῦλα γῆς Αἰγύπτου.

Devise his devices against, &c., i. e. against the strongholds of Egypt, such as Pelusium—'the gate of Egypt' (Claustra Aegypti, Livy, xlv. 11). Cf. 1 Macc. 1¹⁹: κατελάβοντο τὰς πόλεις τὰς ὀχυρὰς ἐν τῇ Αἰγύπτῳ. But Antiochus' ambition reached further; he sought to be king of Egypt: 1 Macc. 1¹⁶.

For a time: i. e. עד עת and Th. ἕως καιροῦ: i. e. the time fixed in the counsels of God. But the LXX has εἰς μάτην. How did this last rendering originate? It clearly is a rendering of לַשָּׁוְא (cf. Ps. 41⁶, 127¹⁻²⁽ᵗʳⁱˢ⁾; Jer. 2³⁰, 4³⁰), which cannot be other than a corruption of לְשֻׁעָה. The fact that this word is Aramaic (cf. 3⁶,¹⁵, 4¹⁶,³⁰, 5⁵) is not against it. It was used also in late Hebrew (Jer. Talmud). From this it follows that עַד־עֵת is a late replacement of an Aramaism by a classical Hebrew phrase. The time is that fixed in the counsels of God : cf. 11²⁷,³⁵.

11²⁵⁻²⁸. *Antiochus' first Egyptian campaign.* In this campaign Antiochus defeated Ptolemy Philometor near Mount Casius, captured Pelusium, the key of Egypt, and with Ptolemy in his suite proceeded to Memphis. Pretending to act in the interests of the latter, Antiochus made himself master of Egypt (1 Macc. 1¹⁸⁻²⁰). In the meantime the Alexandrians had made Ptolemy's brother king under the title of Ptolemy Physcon. Antiochus next besieged Alexandria, but, after many ineffectual efforts to capture it, withdrew to Syria on the approach of three Roman envoys, who had been appointed by the Senate to put an end to the war. On his return Antiochus plundered the Temple in Jerusalem : 1 Macc. 1²⁰⁻²⁴ ; 2 Macc. 5¹¹⁻²¹. Cf. Mahaffy, *Empire of the Ptolemies*, p. 333.

We have thus adopted the view of Wellhausen (*Israels- und Jüd. Gesch.³*, 1897, p. 246 *n*), who maintains that Antiochus made only two Egyptian campaigns, the third, that of 11⁴⁰⁻⁴¹, being an unfulfilled prediction. So also Mahaffy (*Empire of the Ptolemies*, p. 494 seq.), who contends that what are commonly regarded as the two distinct campaigns of 170 and 169 B. c. are really two stages in one and the same campaign. Driver favours this view, but points out that, since the persecuting edict belongs to the year 168 B. c., Antiochus' attack on Jerusalem must have taken place in 170 B. c. owing to 1 Macc. 1²⁰,²⁹,⁵⁴. Mahaffy (*op. cit.* 495) says that Antiochus 'paid his first hostile visitation to Jerusalem . . . in 169 B.c. at latest '.

King of the South : i. e. Ptolemy VI, Philometor.

11²⁵. *Shall stir up.* The MT reads יָעֵר, a jussive form wrongly used = יָעִיר. See note on 11⁴, where other examples of this misuse of the jussive in this chapter are given. But since the LXX (ἐγερθήσεται), Th., Pesh., and Vulg. presuppose יֵעוֹר, it is probable that this is a corruption of the older text יָעִיר.

With a great army. The LXX has the rendering ἐν ὄχλῳ πολλῷ here as in 11¹³, whereas Th. has ἐν δυνάμει μεγάλῃ in both passages. In the LXX we find that πολύς in twelve passages out of fifteen is a rendering of רַב (the exceptions being 11¹³,²⁵,

28,[1] where it seems to be a rendering of גדול if גדול is right. In Th. πολύς in this chapter is in every passage save two (11²⁸,⁴⁴) also a rendering of רב. On the other hand μέγας is always a rendering in Th. of גדול in the Hebrew of Daniel save in 11⁵, where it renders רב.

The all but universal usage, therefore, is clear. But why, then, have we ἐν ὄχλῳ πολλῷ καὶ ἐν χρήμασι πολλοῖς in 11¹³, where the MT has בחיל גדול וברכוש רב? How are we to explain the repetition of πολύς in two adjoining phrases, if there were different adjectives in the Hebrew? Since the translator of the LXX is to some extent a stylist and tends therefore to avoid the monotonous repetition of the same adjective rather than to perpetrate the contrary offence, i. e. of reproducing different Hebrew adjectives in adjoining clauses by one and the same Greek adjective, it seems reasonable to conclude that the Hebrew text before the translator of the LXX was בחיל רב וברכוש רב. If this is right, then it follows that the variation גדול ··· רב in the MT (followed herein by the Pesh. and Vulg.) was introduced subsequently for the sake of variety in the manuscript from which ultimately the MT was derived. Hence the rendering I have given.

But this is not all. Again in 11²⁸ the LXX has ἐν χρήμασι πολλοῖς and Th. ἐν ὑπάρξει πολλῇ. On the united attestation of the LXX and Th. here we emend ברכוש גדול into ברכוש רב.

Finally in 11²⁵, since the LXX reads ἐν ὄχλῳ πολλῷ (supported by the Pesh. = בחילא רבא), it appears that we should read בחיל רב. If these conclusions are right, it follows that where πολύς occurs in the LXX of Daniel (Hebrew section) it always represents רב, and that only once in Th. (i. e. 11⁴⁴) does πολύς represent גדול.

He shall not stand, for they shall devise, &c. Ptolemy Philometor could not maintain the contest owing to the treachery of his followers. Antiochus defeated him near Pelusium and got possession of the border fortress of Pelusium by dishonourable means.

11²⁶. *They that eat of his meat,* &c. Possibly Eulaeus and Lenaeus, whose ill-judged advice led to Ptolemy's attempt to reconquer Syria. Ptolemy fell under their influence after the

---

[1] In the latter part of this note I hope to prove that where πολύς occurs in the LXX of Daniel, רב stood before the translator.

death of his mother Cleopatra in 174 B.C. Cf. Bevan, *House of Seleucus*, ii. 134-136: Mahaffy, *Empire of the Ptolemies*, 332 seq. But the MT text is more than doubtful.

Let us place the MT, the LXX, and Th. in parallel columns:

MT.	LXX.	Th.
וְאֹכְלֵי פַּתְבָּגוֹ יִשְׁבְּרוּהוּ	καὶ καταναλώσουσιν αὐτὸν μέριμναι αὐτοῦ καὶ ἀποστρέψουσιν αὐτόν.	καὶ φάγονται τὰ δέοντα αὐτοῦ καὶ συντρίψουσιν αὐτόν.

First of all let us deal with the second clauses in the LXX and Th. Here ἀποστρέψουσιν (corrupt for ἀποτρίψουσιν) αὐτόν and συντρίψουσιν αὐτόν are legitimate renderings of יִשְׁבְּרוּהוּ. In the next place both the LXX and Th. read וְאָכְלֵהוּ and not וְאֹכְלֵי. But there is no connexion of any kind between פתבגו and the LXX and Th. renderings μέριμναι αὐτοῦ and τὰ δέοντα αὐτοῦ. On the other hand, it is possible to show a connexion between the originals of the Greek renderings. Thus the LXX is a free rendering of צעריו (Mishnaic Hebrew) or צָרֹתָיו (Classical Hebrew), while Th. = צְרָכָיו. It is, therefore, impossible to explain the MT from the two oldest Greek versions. We must, therefore, conclude that if the MT truly represents the original Aramaic, then the LXX and Th. attest a corruption as early as the middle of the second century.

In 1⁵,⁸,¹³,¹⁵,¹⁶ on the other hand the Greek translators of the LXX and Th. found פתבגו, and rendered it either by δεῖπνον or τράπεζα—that is, they gave what they regarded to be the general sense of the first part of the word, i.e. פַּת = 'morsel' of bread, and ignored the rest of the word. Since there is no like attempt to render פתבג or anything like it here, it seems conclusive that they did not find it in their Hebrew manu-scripts. The MT reading פתבגו appears, therefore, to have been suggested by אכלי. The Massoretes found a very corrupt text, and tried to make something out of it. Here then the guidance of the LXX and Th. should be followed. In the original text this and the preceding verse were taken closely together. We should then have 'For they shall devise devices against him; (11²⁶) ואכלוהו צרתיו ושברוהו and his anxieties shall wear him away and work his ruin'. After the defeat of Ptolemy Philo-metor's army on Mount Casius 'all was given up for lost. The young king was hurriedly packed on board ship to escape,

if he could, to the sacred island of Samothrace.[1] It was a foolish
step. Ptolemy was intercepted by the Syrian vessels, and fell
into the hands of Antiochus.' (Bevan, *House of Seleucus*, ii. 136.)

Shall be swept away. For יִשְׁטוֹף (cf. 11[22]) 'shall overflow', we
should with Bevan and others read יִשָּׁטֵף 'shall be swept
away', i. e. Ptolemy's army. The MT would naturally refer to
that of Antiochus.

Many shall fall down slain. In 1 Macc. 1[18] practically the
same words are used of the same events : ἔπεσαν τραυματίαι πολλοί.

11[27]. *Their hearts shall be to do mischief*, &c. When Antiochus
conquered Ptolemy Philometor, the Alexandrians raised his
brother, under the title of Ptolemy Physcon, to the throne.
Antiochus, thereupon, took Philometor under his protection,
Antiochus on the one side professing that he did so solely in the
interest of Philometor (Livy, xlv. 11 : 'cui regnum quaeri suis
viribus simulabat'), and Philometor, on the other hand, professing that he believed in his uncle's disinterestedness.

Mischief : i. e. מֵרַע in pause from מֵרַע, Hiph'il part. treated as
a substantive. Cf. מַשְׁחִית in 10[8].

It shall not prosper : i. e. his subjugation of Egypt, which shall
not take place until 'the time appointed'. See 11[43]. But 'the
end' in the verse may refer not to this matter but to Antiochus'
death.

11[28]. Antiochus' attack on Jerusalem at the close of his first
Egyptian campaign on his way back to Antioch. See Mahaffy,
Empire of the Ptolemies, p. 495.

With great substance : i. e. 'the spoils of Egypt', τὰ σκῦλα γῆς
Αἰγύπτου, 1 Macc. 1[19] : Sibyll. iii. 614 seq.,

> ῥίψει δ' Αἰγύπτου βασιλήιον· ἐκ δέ τε πάντα
> κτήμαθ' ἑλὼν ἐποχεῖται κτλ.

The holy covenant : i. e. the Jewish religion. Cf. 9[27] note.
Return to his own land. Cf. 1 Macc. 1[24]; 2 Macc. 5[21].

11[29–39]. *Antiochus' second Egyptian campaign 168 B. C. and
his persecution of the Jews.* This campaign was directed against
the two brothers Ptolemy Philometor and Ptolemy Physcon,
who were now reconciled.

11[29]. *At the time appointed :* i. e. in the counsels of God.
Cf. 11[27].

But it shall not be in the latter time, &c. This campaign shall have a very different issue from the former. On the Hebrew idiom כבראשנה וכאחרונה, cf. Josh. 14[11]; 1 Sam. 30[24]; Ezek. 18[4].

11[30]. **Those who go forth from the west:** i. e. היצאים מים. This is an emendation of the MT which here reads ציים כתים 'ships of Kittim'. There are several objections to the MT. The chief is that individuals and nations are not mentioned in a vision. They are denoted by some symbol taken from the animal world as in chapters 8–9, or by some geographical description as king of the north, king of the south, &c. The second is that כתים is used as an adjective only here in the O.T. It seems to have arisen as a marginal gloss. The third is from the Versions.

The LXX reads Ῥωμαῖοι καὶ ἐξώσουσιν: Th. οἱ ἐκπορευόμενοι Κίτιοι: Pesh. = 'acies Chittorum': Vulg. 'trieres et Romani'. We should observe that the LXX in 11[18] presupposes לְיָמָּה = ἐπὶ τὴν θάλασσαν, where the MT has לאיים. The text, therefore, cannot be discovered by textual means alone. We shall see reason presently to infer that the Greek translator found מִיָּם instead of ציים. But, if we bear in mind that proper names in such visions are either later interpretations or interpolations, the possibility of recovering the original is not so hopeless. The interpretation as to the quarter from whence the fresh attack on Antiochus comes is no doubt right: it is from the west, and it emanates from Rome; but כתים is not used of Rome in any 2nd cent. B.C. authority. See later on. We may, therefore, dispense wholly with the Pesh. and Vulg., and confine our attention to the MT, LXX, and Th. Since our author is constantly using the geographical designation in order to symbolize the individuals and nations appearing in this vision, we may reasonably conclude that 'the west' was part of the designation of our text: they were 'from the west', מִיָּם: cf. 8[4–5]. Next Th. with his οἱ ἐκπορευόμενοι = היצאים completes the needed phrase—היצאים מים 'those who go forth from the west'. This phrase was rightly interpreted of the Romans by the LXX and Vulg. As regards the proper name כתים it has nothing to do with the original text. It is a late attempt to emend it. For its existence there is no evidence before the 2nd cent. A.D. This emendation of the MT is possibly to be traced to Num. 24[24], וצים מיד כתים. It is noteworthy that here the LXX, Vulg., Pesh. imply ויצאו instead of וצים. Again, the LXX rendering of our text καὶ ἐξώσουσιν could be a rendering of והוציאו, which is closely allied to the text presupposed by Th.

In further confirmation of the above restoration of the text, there is no evidence that a Roman fleet invaded the east. There was simply an embassage composed of C. Popilius Laenas and his suite—who may have come in a single ship. When Antiochus demurred to the demands of the Roman envoy, the latter summarily required Antiochus to leave Egypt. On this notable meeting of Antiochus with Popilius Laenas, see Polyb. xxix. 11; Appian, *Syr.*, 66; Livy, xlv. 12;[1] Velleius Paterculus, i. 10.

Finally, it is rather far-fetched to identify the 'Kittim' with the Romans. This word originally denoted a town in Cyprus, then generally the inhabitants of Cyprus (Gen. 10⁴; Isa. 23¹'¹²), and later the isles and coasts of the Mediterranean (Jer. 2¹⁰; Ezek. 27⁶). In 1 Macc. 1¹, 8⁵; Jubilees 24²⁸'²⁹, 37¹⁰; Josephus (*Ant.* 1.6.1) it is used of the Macedonians. Even 1 Macc. and Jubilees late 2nd cent. B. C. books do not use this word of the Romans. If the above restoration of the text is rejected, possibly we should read צירים מים 'envoys from the west', herein adopting Michaelis' suggestion of צירים.

And he shall be cowed: i. e. ונכאה. Cf. Ps. 109¹⁶; Ezek. 13²². The words of Polybius, xxix. 27, form a remarkable parallel to the MT. When Antiochus accepted the ultimatum of Popilius Laenas after the expiration of the time appointed for the withdrawal of his troops, according to this historian he did so in the following manner: ἀπῆγε τὰς δυνάμεις εἰς τὴν Συρίαν, βαρυνόμενος μὲν καὶ στένων, εἴκων δὲ τοῖς καιροῖς κατὰ τὸ παρόν.[2] See foot-note also. The LXX, however, reads καὶ ἐμβριμήσονται = 'and shall threaten him' = והכיחהו. The Pesh. = והכוהו: Vulg. reads 'et percutietur' = והכה. It seems therefore that there were different readings here from the 2nd cent. B. C. onwards.

And he shall return. This is the second occurrence of this verb in this verse. The first refers to the retirement of Antiochus from Egypt to Judaea. The present to his march from Judaea to Antioch.

And have regard (וְיָבֶן jussive wrongly used for imperfect) *unto*

---

them that forsake the holy covenant. On his return to Antioch, Antiochus kept up communication with the apostate Jews. It was not Antiochus that took the initiative in the attempt to Hellenize the nation. Before his time a party had arisen among the Jews who, under the renegade Jason, subsequently high priest, had made this their object, and, after the accession of Antiochus, these approached the king and obtained his sanction to construct a gymnasium in Jerusalem and introduce Hellenic customs. 'They had themselves uncircumcised and they forsook the holy covenant' (ἐποίησαν ἑαυτοῖς ἀκροβυστίαν καὶ ἀπέστησαν ἀπὸ διαθήκης ἁγίας: 1 Macc. 1^{15}): cf. 2 Macc. 4$^{7-17}$: Assumpt. of Moses 8$^{1-5}$.

11^{31}. *Armies:* i.e. זרעים with masc. plural ending: contrast זרעות 11^{15}. On the forces brought by the chief collector of Antiochus (i.e. Apollonius, 2 Macc. 5^{24}), see 1 Macc. 1^{29}.

Profane the sanctuary. On the profanation of the temple, see 8^{11}. Cf. 1 Macc. 1^{37} ἐμόλυναν τὸ ἁγίασμα.

The fortress. The Temple is so designated in 1 Chron. 29^{1,19} הַבִּירָה. Cf. Neh. 2^8, 7^2 on the use of this word for a fortress near the Temple. It had fortifications at this period as we may infer from their being afterwards rebuilt according to 1 Macc. 4^{60}, 6^7. See 1 Macc. 1$^{29 sqq}$.

And shall take away: i.e. וְהֵסִירוּ הַתָּמִיד. Cf. 12^{11} הוסר התמיד. A similar statement is made in 8^{11}, where, however, instead of הסירו, the Hebrew is הורם התמיד. These may be alternative renderings of one and the same Aramaic verb, העדי (Haph'el), which is used in the *Aram. Papyri* (Cowley, 30^6, 31^6) in a like connexion as well as in later Aramaic: cf. Targ. on 2 Kings 18^4. In 1 Macc. 1$^{41-53}$ there is an enumeration of the religious rites and usages of the Jews, the observance of which was henceforth forbidden by Antiochus.

Shall set up a horror that appalleth: i.e. the heathen altar that was built on the altar of burnt offering. This was done according to 1 Macc. 1^{54} on the fifteenth day of Chislev (December) 168 B.C., and on the twenty-fifth of the same month they offered heathen sacrifices on this altar which had been built on the altar of God (cf. 1 Macc. 1^{59}: θυσιάζοντες ἐπὶ τὸν βωμὸν ὃς ἦν ἐπὶ τοῦ θυσιαστηρίου). In 1^{54} of the same book we have almost the same words as in our text—ᾠκοδόμησαν βδέλυγμα ἐρημώσεως ἐπὶ τὸ θυσιαστήριον. With regard to the peculiar expression 'a horror that appalleth', see note on 9^{27}.

X 2

This phrase, which also appears in 1 Macc. 1[54] as βδέλυγμα ἐρημώσεως, was first applied to the heathen altar and then probably to the image of the Olympian Zeus beside it. For according to Taanith iv. 6 (העמיד צלם בהיכל) a statue of Zeus was set up.[1] The Greek rendering in the LXX and in 1 Macc. 1[54], βδέλυγμα ἐρημώσεως, is at once an incorrect rendering of the Hebrew, and proves that the translator failed to recognize the grim jest designed by our author.

The prophetical writings of the O.T. and many of the Jewish Apocalypse are full of puns. Bevan quotes one on שמים in the Ber. rabba (Sect. 4), where the sky is called שמים 'because the people are *astonished* at it' (שהבריות משתוממים עליהן).

With regard to the grammar of the phrase, we have already corrected הפשע שמם into הפשע השמם in 8[13]; in 9[27] שקוצים משמם into שקוץ משמם (see *in loc.*). Here in 11[31] השקוץ משמם should be corrected into "הש השמם or "הש המשמם, or else the article should be excised in 11[31] since it is not found in 12[11], which is a continuation of the same vision.

11[32]. *Such as do wickedly against the covenant*: i. e. מרשיעי ברית (cf. 9[5], 12[10]). This intransitive use of the Hiph'il of רשע is not earlier than 400 B. C. or thereabouts. Contrast מצדיקי הרבים in 12[3]. These offenders are the apostates mentioned in 11[30]. Bevan prefers to take the Hiph'il transitively and renders 'those who bring guilt upon the covenant' (i. e. the covenanted people), and contrasts it with מצדיקי הרבים in 12[3].

Shall he pervert: i. e. (יחניף) into still more evil ways, into sheer irreligion: cf. Jer. 3[9], where the Hiph'il should be read 'shall pervert the land'. These are the apostates referred to in 11[30]. The expression here, therefore, would imply the degradation of character that follows upon the deliberate abandonment of high religious principles. It is out of keeping with the context to render the verb 'make apostates' (Bevan and Driver), seeing that these men were such already.

By flatteries (i. e. בחלקות: see note on 11[21]). Cf. 1 Macc. 2[18] which enumerates the advantages to be won by those who

---

[1] Cf. the quotation from Philo of Byblos in Eusebius, *Praep. Evangel.* I. 10. τοῦτον γάρ, φησίν, θεὸν ἐνόμιζον μόνον οὐρανοῦ κύριον, Βεελσάμην καλοῦντες, ὅ ἐστι παρὰ Φοίνιξι κύριος οὐρανοῦ, Ζεὺς δὲ παρ᾿ Ἕλλησι. Also Plautus *Poenulus*, v. ii. 67. Gunebel balsamen (ed. C. H. Weis). The speaker is Hanno, the Carthaginian, whose words are here transliterated into Latin.

renounced Judaism. But these perverts have already done so. Antiochus by his flatteries seeks to make them his mere tools, and members of a religion of which he is himself one with the chief deity.

The people that know their God shall be strong (i. e. יַחְזִקוּ). Cf. 1 Macc. 1⁶²: 'Many in Israel were fully resolved (ἐκραταιώθησαν ℵ V) and exerted their strength (ὀχυρώθησαν ἐν αὑτοῖς probably = התחזקו בנפשותיהם)... so as not to profane the holy covenant'.

And do. This absolute use of the Hebrew verb has already occurred in 8¹²,²⁴, 9¹⁹, 11²⁸,³⁰. This meaning is found occasionally in the O.T., 2 Chron. 31²¹; Jer. 14⁷; Ezek. 20⁹.

11³³. *They that be wise.* These are not the teachers, but the godly—the Chasidim. They were strongly opposed to the Hellenizing party, and constituted the Hasidaeans referred to in 1 Macc. 7¹³; 2 Macc. 14⁵. Around them were gathered the soundest elements in the nation. On this party and its attitude to the Maccabeans, see 1 Enoch 90⁶⁻⁹. Cf. 1 Macc. 2⁴²⁻⁴³, συνήχθησαν πρὸς αὐτοὺς (the Maccabeans) συναγωγὴ Ἀσιδαίων, ἰσχυρὰ δυνάμει ἀπὸ Ἰσραήλ, πᾶς ὁ ἑκουσιαζόμενος τῷ νόμῳ. καὶ πάντες οἱ φυγαδεύοντες ἀπὸ τῶν κακῶν προσετέθησαν αὐτοῖς.

Shall instruct the many (i. e. יבינו לרבים): i. e. 'cause them to understand alike by their teaching and example'. Here the ל with the acc. is a mark of late Aramaized Hebrew: cf. 2 Chron. 35³.

Shall fall by the sword, &c. See 1 Macc. 1⁶⁰,⁶³, 2³¹⁻³⁸, 3⁴¹, 5¹³; 2 Macc. 6¹⁰,¹¹,¹⁸⁻³¹, 7. These persecutions are referred to later in Heb. 11³⁶⁻³⁸.

11³⁴. *A little help.* The help here referred to is that of the Maccabees. The rising of Mattathias and his sons assisted by the faithful in growing numbers, and their early victories, are described in 1 Macc. 2⁴²⁻⁴⁸, 3¹¹,¹²,²³⁻²⁶, 4¹²⁻¹⁵, but to our author the greatest victories won by the arm of man are only 'a little help'. He looks for deliverance not from this source but from the Lord.

In 1 Enoch 83–90 (written before 161 B.C.) the rise of the Chasidim and from amongst them the Maccabees is thus described symbolically in a dream vision, 90⁶⁻¹², 'But behold lambs (i. e. the Chasidim) were borne by those white sheep (i. e. the faithful adherents of the Theocracy), and they began to open their eyes and to see and to cry to the sheep. Yea, they cried

to them, but they did not hearken to what they said to them. . . .
And I saw in the vision how the ravens (i. e. the Syrians) flew
upon those lambs, and took one of those lambs (i. e. Onias III),
and dashed the sheep in pieces and devoured them. And I saw
till horns grew upon those lambs (i. e. the rise of the Maccabees—the horned lambs) and the ravens cast down their horns,
and I saw till there sprouted a great horn on one of those
sheep (i. e. Judas Maccabaeus). . . . And it cried to the sheep,
and the rams saw it and all ran to it. . . . And those ravens
fought and battled with it and sought to lay low its horn, but
they had no power over it.'

The writer of 1 Enoch 83-90 loosely includes Onias III
among the Chasidim, and also the Maccabean family. The
Chasidim are distinguished from the Maccabees and their
immediate followers in 1 Macc. 3¹³. They formed an organized
body before the Maccabean outbreak, 1 Macc. 2⁴², 3¹³. They
generally supported Judas, but were at times antagonistic on
legal grounds, 1 Macc. 7¹³⁻¹⁴. It was only after much indecision
that they cast in their lot with the Maccabean party, because
this movement brought them into opposition with the high-priest
of the time, the legitimate and religious head of the nation.

And there shall join them many ⌈in the city and many⌉ in ⌈their
several⌉ homesteads. The MT reads 'and many shall join themselves unto them with flatteries'. These words are taken to
indicate that many joined the national cause from sheer terror,
because of the ruthless severities practised by Judas and his
party. See 1 Macc. 2⁴⁴, 3⁵⁻⁸, 6¹⁹,²¹,²⁴, 7⁶,⁷,²⁴⁻³² (where Judas
takes vengeance on those who had deserted), 9²³. But the
context, as the following verses show, is against the idea, that
the Maccabees had as yet attained much power. In 11³⁵ of
our text it speaks only of martyrdoms on the part of the faithful,
and in 11³⁶ the successes of Antiochus during the time allotted
to him. The same conclusion follows from the almost contemporary account (before 161 B. C.) in 1 Enoch 90¹⁶ : 'All the eagles
and vultures and ravens and kites (i. e. Ammonites, Edomites,
Syrians) . . . came together and helped each other to break that
horn of the ram' (i. e. Judas Maccabaeus). It would not, therefore, be natural to pay court to a cause struggling for a very
doubtful victory. The MT is, therefore, corrupt. Th. is of no
assistance here as it is a literal reproduction of the MT. But

the LXX appears to have preserved the original text. It supplies the right thought, and it explains how the corruption in the MT arose. It reads as follows: καὶ ἐπισυναχθήσονται ἐπ' αὐτοὺς πολλοὶ ἐπὶ πόλεως καὶ πολλοὶ †ὡς† ἐν κληροδοσίᾳ = וְנִלְווּ עֲלֵיהֶם רבים ובעיר ורבים⌐ אחר בְּחֶלְקָתוֹ. Here בעיר רבים was lost through homoioteleuton. Next ὡς is a corruption of εἰς = אחד. The corruption of εἰς into ὡς led inevitably to the excision of αὐτοῦ after κληροδοσίᾳ. Finally בחלקות is as we found (see note on 11²¹) a corruption for בחלקות or rather בְּחֶלְקָתוֹ = ἐν κληροδοσίᾳ ⟨αὐτοῦ⟩. Jahn suggests that ὡς ἐν κληροδοσίᾳ = כבחלקות, where the כ is a dittograph of the following ב. We should then have: 'and there shall join them many in the city and many in the fields'. In my restoration the חֶלְקָתוֹ ('his portion') is the definite portion of ground assigned to each individual: cf. Deut. 33²¹.

11³⁵. *Some of them that be wise*, i. e. the faithful. This phrase rendered 'the wise' (cf. 11³³, 12³,¹⁰) could just as well be rendered 'the teachers', i. e. those that make wise, as in 9²² and possibly in 12³.

†*Shall fall*† : i. e. יַבְשִׁלוּ. According to the MT (followed by Th., Pesh., and Vulg.) some of the teachers or wise should fall, but that was to be no excuse for despair—their martyrdom would have as its effect the disciplining and perfecting of the faithful wherever found.

But the text of the LXX διανοηθήσανται presupposes יַשְׂכִּילוּ: We should then translate 'some of them that be wise shall be wise'. The words that follow in the LXX refer not to the faithful generally but to this pre-eminently faithful minority— εἰς τὸ καθαρίσαι ἑαυτοὺς καὶ τὸ ἐκλεγῆναι [καὶ εἰς τὸ καθαρισθῆναι]. The pre-eminent among the wise will take special measures 'to refine and make themselves pure'—until the time of the end. Thus the LXX presupposes יַשְׂכִּילוּ לְצָרוּף אֹתָם וּלְהִתְבָּרֵר. The rendering ἐκλεγῆναι is only justifiable in the chronicler's use of ברר 'to choose', 'to select'. Now though Th. presupposes the יכשלו of the MT, yet it supports the LXX in two out of the three verbs that follow: τοῦ πυρῶσαι αὐτοὺς (ed. αὐτοὺς) καὶ τοῦ ἐκλέξασθαι [καὶ τοῦ ἀποκαλυφθῆναι (corrupt for ἀπολευκανθῆναι)]. For ἐκλέξασθαι we should expect ἐκλεγῆναι. It is noteworthy that these two verbs recur in 12¹⁰ in the passive, and there also it is the wise who are the subjects of the three verbs—the personalities who are spiritually disciplined. Hence I suggest that with the LXX (and in part with Th.) we should render as follows : ' And some of the wise shall be wise so as to refine and make themselves pure.' Cf. 12¹⁰.

So as to refine and make themselves pure : i. e. לצרוף אותם ולהתברר. This, I am convinced, was the original text. The MT is very late לצרוף בהם ולברר ולללבן = 'to refine amongst them and to purify and to make white'. The grounds for the above conclusion are as follows. The LXX reads εἰς τὸ καθαρίσαι ἑαυτοὺς καὶ εἰς τὸ ἐκλεγῆναι [καὶ εἰς τὸ καθαρισθῆναι]. Now it is obvious that τὸ καθαρίσαι and τὸ καθαρισθῆναι are here duplicate renderings of one and the same Hebrew phrase. To confirm this conclusion we have only to turn to the MT (12¹⁰) where the same combination of three Hebrew verbs recurs but in a different and corrupt order. But the LXX in 12¹⁰ has only two verbs ἕως ἂν †πειρασθῶσι† καὶ ἁγιασθῶσι. Here πειρασθῶσι is an obvious corruption for πυρωθῶσι as we see in Th., and thus the LXX pre-supposes עַד יִצָּרְפוּ : cf. 12¹⁰. Next ἁγιασθῶσι in 12¹⁰ (LXX) is a rendering of יתבררו. Thus according to the LXX there were *only two verbs* in each passage. It is to be noted that the Pesh. also presupposes only two Hebrew verbs in 11³⁵.

It is not till we come down to Th. that we find three Hebrew verbs presupposed as in the MT. In 11³⁵ Th. reads τοῦ πυρῶσαι ἑαυτούς καὶ τοῦ ἐκλέξασθαι καὶ τοῦ †ἀποκαλυφθῆναι† (corrupt for ἀπολευκανθῆναι : some manuscripts have ἐκλευκανθῆναι). In 12¹⁰ Th. has ἐκλεγῶσιν καὶ ἐκλευκανθῶσιν καὶ πυρωθῶσιν; B^{ab} A add καὶ ἁγιασθῶσιν which is an alternative rendering of יתבררו and may be borrowed from the LXX. In both passages Th. supports the MT. But the oldest authority is against the MT and Th. in three respects. (1) It has only two verbs, and these two are closely connected with each other. צרף means 'to smelt', 'to refine', so as to get rid of the dross (cf. Isa. 1²⁵). The metaphor is taken from one who works in metals and is used of God in Zech. 13⁹, Ps. 66¹⁰. In many passages of the prophets God is the Refiner (cf. Mal. 3², where the refining is done with fire). When men are so refined in the fire of affliction ' they are made pure ' יתבררו, and the change is an inward one. (2) The LXX retains the right order in both passages : first comes the smelting away of man's impurities, then comes his purity. But, though the MT and Th. preserve the right order in 11³⁵, it is wholly con-fused in 12¹⁰, where the many are to purify themselves, make

themselves white and refine themselves (i. e. undergo the pre-
liminary spiritual smelting—last of all !). (3) The LXX is free
from the weaker expression 'make themselves white'. הלבין is
used metaphorically in the O.T. of the outward whiteness that
follows on inward cleansing. The other two verbs deal with the
spiritual transformations of the faithful. Moreover this outward
'whiteness' follows on the internal smelting, rightly, in 11[35], but
precedes it in 12[10] ! The metaphor originates with the smelting of
metals. Has this external whiteness any real *raison d'être* here ?

In both passages 11[35], 12[10] the LXX alone appears to attest
the original Hebrew version. I may add here that צרף is good
Aramaic as well as good Hebrew : cf. Cowley 5[7], 28[11], 38[3].

To refine them (i. e. לצרוף בהם). Here ב in בהם, if we hold fast
to the MT, is to be taken in the sense of ' among ' : cf. Exod. 14[28].
But we must emend into אֹתָם : see preceding note.

[*To make white.*] For the contracted Hiph'il לַלְבֵּן (i. e. לְהַלְבִּן)
Hitzig and other scholars read לְלַבֵּן. The Pi'el does not not
occur in the O.T., but is frequent in post-Biblical Hebrew.
This verb, however, is omitted by the LXX, and appears to be
a late gloss.

To purify : i. e. לְבָרֵר. Read להתברר with the LXX.

To the time of the end. According to the MT the martyrdoms
were to persist to the time of the end : according to the Hebrew
text presupposed by the LXX the sense would be : they that
endure to the end—the same shall be saved.

End . . . time appointed, קֵץ · · · מוֹעֵד. These words are found
in the Hebrew of Sir. 36[8]. They have already occurred in our
text in 11[27]. In Sir. 37[7] we have possibly an echo of Dan. 11[36 e]
'Wake up indignation and pour out wrath' (העיר אף ושפך חמה).

When the Jews took this ultimate measure of sacrificing
everything to their religious ideals, it was clearly a moment of
transcendent importance in their spiritual life, and Bevan (*House
of Seleucus*, ii. 174) rightly emphasizes it: ' Under the stress of
those days numbers of Jews conformed ; those who held fast
generally forsook their homes and gathered in wandering com-
panies in desolate places. But there also shone out in that
intense moment the sterner and sublimer qualities . . . of uncom-
promising fidelity to an ideal, endurance raised to the pitch of
utter self-devotion, a passionate clinging to purity. . . . It was
an epoch in history.'

11[36-39]. These verses characterize Antiochus, his measureless arrogance and impiety, and show how he set at naught the various national religions, in order to establish the cult of his own god—with whom he identified himself.

11[36]. *According to his will.* This phrase has been used in 8[4] of the Persian empire, in 11[3] of Alexander, and in 11[16] also of Antiochus.

Exalt himself (i. e. יתרמם). The LXX reads παροργισθήσεται = יתמרמר as in 11[11]. In Hos. 12[15(14)] καὶ παρώργισεν implies וּמררני of which the MT תמרורים is a corruption (Marti).

Magnify himself. Again in 11[37]. Cf. Isa. 10[15].

Above every god. Cf. 5[23], where Belshazzar lifts himself up against the Lord of heaven. On the coins of the early years of the reign of Antiochus the inscription was simply βασιλεως Αντιοχου with representation of Apollo. Later a star appears on his forehead, which betokens his claim to divine honours, but Apollo is not represented. Still later the star disappears from the coins; but these now bear the inscription βασιλεως Αντιοχου Θεου Επιφανους, or else represent his head as surrounded by a diadem of rays in attestation of his divine dignity. During the closing period Zeus is represented on the coins and not Apollo, and the inscription claims the honours of Zeus himself: Βασιλεως Αντιοχου Θεου Επιφανους Νικηφορου, the last epithet being peculiar to Zeus Olympius. See Driver *in loc.*, whence I have drawn these facts, and the Catalogue of Coins in the National Library in Paris (Babelon, *Les Rois de Syrie*, 1891, pp. xcii–iv). Nestle (*Marginalien*, p. 42) calls attention to the fact that Babelon in the work just mentioned (p. xlviii) states without any consciousness of this passage in Daniel : 'Apollon assis sur l'omphalos disparait presque complètement de la série des monnaies Séleucides après le règne d'Antiochus IV Épiphane ; il se trouve supplanté, à partir de ce moment, *par le type de Zeus Olympien*'. See also Gardner's *Coins of the Seleucid kings of Syria*, xi. 2, xii. 13, xi. 9, xii. 11. But to return to Nestle (*op. cit.* p. 42) who further cites Babelon : 'Der olympische Zeus hatte sich schon auf den Münzen der 3 ersten Seleuciden gefunden ; aber—um wieder Babelon reden zu lassen : "à partir d'Antiochus ce type disparaît pour ne faire sa réapparition que sous Antiochus IV Épiphane à l'occasion sans doute de l'inauguration de la statue colossale de Zeus Olympien à Daphne." Man sehe nur die wun-

dervollen Tafeln bei Babelon; erst auf der zwölften, eben unter
Antiochus Epiphanes, erscheint wieder der olympische Zeus, und
es sollte eigentlich keinen Daniel-Kommentar geben, der nicht
von diesen Münzen aus eine Abbildung des "Greuels der Ver-
wüstung" bringen würde.'

Bevan (*House of Seleucus*, ii. 156 seq.) emphasizes the fact
that Antiochus identified himself with Zeus and turned this
claim to practical purposes. For as Zeus Olympius whom he
identified with the God of the Jews (2 Macc. 6²) he naturally
appropriated the treasures of the Temple (1 Macc. 1²¹ ˢᵉ۹·), while
'at Hierapolis where the deity was feminine, but identified with
Hera (Lucian, *De Syria Dea*), he claimed the temple treasures
as his wife's dowry'. The entire chapter ii. 148–161 should be
read. Polybius (xxxi. 4, 10) states that 'he plundered most
temples' (τὰ πλεῖστα τῶν ἱερῶν), and his death was due to an unsuccessful attempt to plunder a temple in Persia (1 Macc. 6¹,⁴).

Speak marvellous things. Cf. 7⁸, 'a mouth speaking great
things': 7²⁵, 8²⁴.

Against the God of gods: i. e. אֵל אֵלִים, the God of Israel: cf.
2⁴⁷ אֱלָהּ אֱלָהִין, where the phrase is used by an idolator. Contrast
the full form in Deut. 10¹⁷ אלהי האלהים.

The indignation be accomplished (i. e. כלה זעם). Cf. 8¹⁹ and Isa.
10²⁵, whence the phrase is derived. Since both the LXX and Th.
have ἡ ὀργή we should perhaps correct זעם into הזעם. In Isa. 10²⁵
the word should probably be read זעמי or הזעם (with the LXX).

That which is determined shall be done (i. e. נחרצה נעשתה). The
first word is borrowed, as in 9²⁷, from Isa. 10²³ and 28²². The
divine will must be carried out.

11³⁷. The efforts of Antiochus to bring about uniformity in
religion and custom throughout the empire (cf. 1 Macc. 1⁴¹,⁴² :
καὶ ἔγραψεν ὁ βασιλεὺς πάσῃ τῇ βασιλείᾳ αὐτοῦ εἶναι πάντας εἰς λαὸν ἕνα, καὶ
ἐγκαταλείπειν ἕκαστον τὰ νόμιμα αὐτοῦ), and his supreme devotion to
the Olympian Zeus—no less than his identification of himself
with this god in his later years—led him to discredit the local
deities, even those whom his fathers and he himself had worshipped. Amongst these was the Greek Apollo, whose form,
represented on the coins of his fathers, and on his own coins at
the beginning of his reign, was subsequently wholly displaced
by that of the Olympian Zeus.

Nor the desire of women. Probably the Phoenician deity

Tammuz, the equivalent of the Greek Adonis, whose cult had been popular in Syria for centuries, especially among women (Ezek. 8[14], where the prophet beheld within the precincts of the Temple 'the women weeping for Tammuz'). The XV Idyll of Theocritus is entitled Ἀδωνιάζουσαι, 'Women keeping the festival to Adonis'—τὰ Ἀδώνια. According to Hippolytus, *Refut. Haer.* v. 9, the Assyrians called Adonis the thrice desired, τριπόθητος.

Nor any god. Since Antiochus identified himself more or less with Zeus Olympius, he was superior to all other gods and their treasures were his. It is true that he erected great temples to some gods. They shared with him the rights of divinity. The LXX omits ועל כל אלוה.

11[38]. *The god of fortresses.* This is apparently Jupiter Capitolinus, to whom Antiochus erected a magnificent temple in Antioch: cf. Livy, xli. 20, 'Antiochiae Jovis Capitolini magnificum templum, non laqueatum auro tantum, sed parietibus totis laminâ inauratum'. According to Livy, xlii. 6, Antiochus sent to Rome golden vessels of 500 pounds in weight, which were distributed amongst such temples as the Quaestors thought fitting.

A god whom his fathers knew not: i. e. Zeus Capitolinus. The preceding Seleucidae recognized Zeus Olympius, indeed as their coins prove. But Zeus in Antiochus' conception of him claimed all the attributes of the Roman Jupiter Capitolinus. This seems to be the most reasonable explanation of the text.

11[39]. *He shall †deal with the strongest fortresses by the help† of a strange god.* The beginning of this verse in the MT is, as Bevan declares, unintelligible. Besides the meaning extracted is unsatisfactory. Hence Meinhold, Hitzig, Bevan, Marti, and others change עָם into עַם and render: 'he shall procure for the strong fortresses the people of a strange god'. The reference would be here to the heathen colonists and soldiers settled by Antiochus in the fortified cities of Judaea and in Jerusalem: 1 Macc. 1[33], 3[36,45]. Driver regards the rendering 'procure' for עשׂה very questionable here, and objects that the parallels quoted in support of it in 2 Sam. 15[1]; 1 Kings 1[5] are hardly parallel. If Driver's objection is valid, we can find in 1 Sam. 8[16] (ועשׂה למלאכתו = 'will use for his service'); Exod. 38[24] excellent parallels to the idiom in our text and an idiom that is also suitable to the context: 'He shall use for the strongest fortresses the people of a strange god': i. e. as their garrisons, as 1 Macc. 3[36,45] state.

People of a strange god. With this emended text compare עַם כְּמוֹשׁ Num. 21²⁹.

Strange god. Cf. Deut. 32¹² אל נכר as here.

Whomsoever he recognizes, he shall honour highly. הִכִּיר (which after אשר does not need to be changed into יַכִּיר with *Qr.*, cf. Deut. 15¹⁴ אשר ברכך יהוה אלהיך תתן לו) bears the same meaning as in Ruth 2¹⁰,¹⁹. But the same words could also be translated: 'Whosoever acknowledgeth him, he shall honour highly'.

Cause them to rule over the many and divide the land for a price. The chief offices and confiscated lands were divided amongst the king's adherents, as in 1 Macc. 9²⁵, καὶ ἐξέλεξεν Βακχίδης τοὺς ἀσεβεῖς ἄνδρας, καὶ κατέστησεν αὐτοὺς κυρίους τῆς χώρας. Jason purchased the high priesthood, and he was soon displaced by Menelaus, who offered a higher price, 2 Macc. 4⁸⁻¹⁰,²⁴.

11⁴⁰⁻⁴⁵. Transition from history of the past in disguised language to actual prediction of the future. Three different interpretations have been given to these verses. (1) They have been regarded as a recapitulation, and as giving a brief sketch of the course of events from about 171 B.C. to the death of Antiochus. But the introductory words, 'at the time of the end', exclude the assumption that we have here a recapitulation. The present belongs to the time of the writer. The time of consummation referred to in 11³⁵, with a view to which the faithful would make preparation (so text of LXX), had now actually begun. (2) They have been taken as relating to historical events following on those already mentioned, i. e. after the year 168 B.C. But our historical authorities know nothing of an expedition against Egypt after this date.[1] The chief events of the reign of Antiochus in 167 B.C. are his institution at Daphne of a great series of games lasting thirty days and rivalling in magnificence those just celebrated by Aurelius Paullus in Macedonia, and his reception of the envoy of the Roman Senate, whose suspicions he succeeded

[1] In dealing with 11⁴⁰⁻⁴¹ Jerome speaks of another expedition against Egypt on the authority of Porphyry : 'Et haec Porphyrius ad Antiochum refert : quod undecimo anno regni sui rursus contra sororis filium Ptolemaeum Philometorem dimicaverit.' Further on Jerome says that the clauses in question refer not to Antiochus but to the Antichrist. Returning to the exposition of Porphyry he writes : '(Antiochus) festinans contra Ptolemaeum regem Austri, Idumaeos, et Moabitas, et Ammonitas qui ex latere Judaeae erant, non tetigit : ne occupatus alio praelio, Ptolemaeum redderet fortiorem.' But there is no foundation in history for Porphyry's view.

in placating.[1]   In the following year, 166 B.C., he started on an expedition in the course of which he perished.   It is true that Porphyry, according to Jerome, does speak of another expedition to Egypt, but the incidents recorded by Porphyry, apart from one or two details, could all have been drawn from the text of Daniel, and the mention of Antiochus pitching his tent at Apedno is due evidently to a misunderstanding of the Hebrew word אָפַּדְנוֹ in 11[45].   (3) Hence the third hypothesis alone is tenable that this passage is not a description of the past but a forecast of the future.   As Driver (p. 197) writes, 'the author draws here an imaginative picture of the end of the tyrant king, similar to the ideal one of the ruin of Sennacherib in Isa. 10[28–32]: he depicts him as successful where he had previously failed, viz. in Egypt; while reaping the spoils of his victories, he is called away by rumours from a distance; and then, just after he has set out on a further career of conquest and plunder, as he is approaching with sinister purpose the Holy City, he meets his doom'.

11[40]. *At the time of the end.*   The period spoken of in 11[35] has now come to its close.   The author clearly expected another invasion of Egypt after 168 B.C.   See last note.

The king of the south: i. e. Ptolemy Philometor.   There was no third invasion of Egypt.   See Mahaffy, *Empire of the Ptolemies*, pp. 494 seq.

Make a thrust against him: i. e. יִתְנַגַּח עִמּוֹ.   עִם = 'against' when it is used with verbs such as רִיב, נִלְחַם, &c.   In 8[4] it is used of the butting of the ram in the vision, where the ram is a symbol of the Medo-Persian empire.   Here the king of the south is the ram.   The very same symbol is used to denote the Chasidim in 1 Enoch 90[10,11] and Judas Maccabaeus in 90[13,14,16]—an almost contemporary apocalypse.

---

[1] At the close of the games Tiberius Gracchus with a suite was sent from Rome to determine the attitude of Antiochus and his alleged ambitions.   But as Polyb. xxxi. 5, states, Antiochus received them with such an extraordinary display of friendliness as not only wholly to disarm Tiberius of all his suspicions, but to cause the latter to visit with his disapprobation the persons who had set such suspicions on foot: Οἶς (i. e. the envoys) οὕτως ἐπιδεξίως ἀπήντησεν Ἀντίοχος καὶ φιλοφρόνως, ὥστε μὴ οἷον τοὺς περὶ τὸν Τιβέριον ὑποπτεῦσαί τι περὶ αὐτοῦ πραγματικόν, ἢ παρατριβῆς ἔμφασιν ἔχον ἐκ τῶν κατὰ τὴν Ἀλεξάνδρειαν ἀλλὰ καὶ τῶν λεγόντων τι τοιοῦτον καταγινώσκειν, διὰ τὴν ὑπερβολὴν τῆς κατὰ τὴν ἀπάντησιν φιλανθρωπίας. And yet Polybius adds that Antiochus was ἀλλοτριώτατα διακείμενος πρὸς Ῥωμαίους.   Antiochus was a past master in the worst forms of diplomacy.

Storm against him (i. e. יִשְׂתָּעֵר). Antiochus will advance like a whirlwind against Ptolemy. For this use of the kindred verb סער, cf. Hab. 3[14].

Come into the countries. This is taken to mean the countries that lay between him and Egypt. If the text which is supported by the Vulg. is right, then this clause summarizes proleptically what is expressed in detail in 11[41-43]. But the LXX, Th., and Pesh. read בארץ here and not בארצות, the LXX and Pesh. omitting ושטף ועבר. In 11[10], where the same three verbs ובא ושטף ועבר ‧ ‧ occur, the textual authorities differ as to what followed ובא. Taking together the uncertainty of the text and the unsatisfactory sense of the MT, it is possible that the Aramaic original read כִּרְעוּתֵיהּ 'according to his pleasure', which was corrupted into בארעתא = בָּאֲרָצֹות of the MT, which, if the suggestion offered is right, should be emended into כִּרְצֹנוֹ : cf. 8[4], 11[3,16,36]. Antiochus shall go where he pleases. This thought is in keeping with his imperious and overweening character. This suggestion has the merit of explaining the corrupt accentuation of רבות in the next verse.

Shall overflow, &c. Borrowed as in 11[10] from Isa. 8[8].

11[41]. *The glorious land.* See 11[16], 8[9] notes.

Tens of thousands. Here for רַבּוֹת = 'many' (lands) fem. we should obviously with De Wette, Bevan, Behrmann, Kamphausen, Prince, &c., read רִבּוֹת = 'tens of thousands'. Cf. 11[12], Neh. 7[71]. The feminine accentuation of רבות in the MT can be explained as due to the corrupt reading of בארצות in the preceding verse.

But these shall be delivered out of his hand [*Edom and Moab and the chief of the children of Ammon*]. As we have already pointed out, the designation of nations by their actual names, especially when the events occur near or in the time of the writer, is contrary to the usage of Apocalyptic. On this ground alone we excise the phrase 'Edom ... Ammon'. But independently of this fact, the history of the time is against its inclusion. For of these three peoples, two are specifically mentioned in 1 Macc. 5[1-8] as taking up arms against Judah in furtherance of the policy of Antiochus, i. e. the Edomites and the Ammonites.[1] As enemies of the Jews they are mentioned in Ps. 83[8-9 (7-8)] and in Judith 7[8,17,18], the latter and probably the former being composi-

---

[1] In 2 Macc. 4[26], 5[7] Jason the apostate high-priest twice found sanctuary with the Ammonites.

tions of the second cent. B.C. John Hyrcanus conquered the Edomites in 109 B.C. and compelled them to adopt Judaism.

Hence they cannot be regarded as other than confederates of Antiochus, and to speak of them as 'being delivered out of his hand' is absurd. Of the Moabites we have no mention. They were, however, hereditary foes of Israel,[1] and, though they had long disappeared from the stage of history, this is enough to explain their inclusion in an interpolated gloss.

But if we excise, as we must, the mention of these three nations from the text, how are we to explain the clause that precedes? They cannot naturally refer to the interpolated words that follow in the MT. Hence they are to be explained in reference to the words that precede. The writer *expected* Antiochus to make a third expedition. In the course of this expedition, whose ultimate goal was Egypt (11⁴²), Antiochus would overthrow tens of thousands of Judah. We have, therefore, to interpret this victory of Antiochus as a victory indeed, but not as a victory of annihilation. Cf. 11³⁴ where the same verb with the same nuance occurs. The clause 'but these shall be delivered out of his hand' is designed to teach the readers of the book that in some way the main body of the Jews should be delivered out of the hands of Antiochus. This is in keeping with the expectations of the writer. It would of course be possible to take אלה as an emendation of an original מאלה (= 'some of these') made after the incorporation of the false gloss above referred to.

[*The †chief†*], i. e. ראשית. If this is right, then it means the principal part of Ammon: cf. Amos 6¹; Jer. 49³⁵. But Buhl and Marti with the Pesh. emend ראשית into שְׁאֵרִית = 'the remnant of the children of Ammon'. This certainly improves the sense of the interpolation.

11⁴²⁻⁴³. Conquest of Egypt after the reduction of Palestine.

[1] The ancient Moabites had long disappeared, and their place been taken by Nabataean Arabs, to whom even Josephus gives this designation: *Ant.* i. 11. 5; cf. xiii. 13; xiv. 1. 4. It is significant that Moab is never once mentioned in 1 Macc. On the other hand, in Isa. 24-27 (assigned by many modern scholars to the 2nd cent, B.C.) Moab—only now a name with a religious significance—is mentioned in 25¹⁰, probably as typical of Israel's enemies. If the reference is not typical, and the present context is against its being so regarded, then the Nabataean Arabs may have early been regarded as identical with Moab as in Judith 7⁸ and Ps. 83⁷.

11⁴². *Stretch forth his hand:* i. e. to seize : cf. Esther 8⁷.

The land of the south. MT and versions have wrongly interpreted the original phrase into 'the land of Egypt': see note on 11⁸.

Shall not escape: i. e. לא תהיה לפליטה. The LXX—ἐν χώρᾳ Αἰγύπτου οὐκ ἔσται ἐν αὐτῇ διασωζόμενος—makes a far stronger statement : 'in the land of Egypt there shall not one escape'—thus reading בָּהּ פָּלִיט instead of לִפְלֵיטָה. The phrase תהיה · · · לפליטה is from Gen. 32⁹⁽⁸⁾.

11⁴³. *Precious things.* The word מכמנים is a ἅπ. λεγ., and is derived from the Aramaic כְּמַן.

The south. MT has wrongly as in preceding verse interpreted the original phrase into 'Egypt'; see note on 11⁸.

[*The Libyans and Ethiopians,* &c.] This is another interpolation like that in 11⁴¹. Since the Libyans and Ethiopians dwelt W. and S. of Egypt and are mentioned as following 'in his train' (lit. 'in his steps' במצעדיו = ברגליו, the classical phrase: cf. Exod. 11⁸; Judges 4¹⁰, 8⁵; 1 Kings 20¹⁰, &c : only here in this literal sense in the O.T. : figuratively in Ps. 37²³; Prov. 20²⁴), Egypt is represented as being beset on all sides. The Libyans and Ethiopians are mentioned in Nahum 3⁹ and Jer. 46⁹. The interpolator by such an addition seeks to intensify the contrast between Antiochus with his highest ambitions all but achieved and his sudden overthrow.

11⁴⁴. *Tidings out of the east.* As tidings (שְׁמוּעָה) drew away Sennacherib from Palestine (Isa. 37⁷; 2 Kings 19⁷), so tidings (שְׁמֻעוֹת) from the east and north shall cause Antiochus to retire in haste from Egypt.

To destroy and exterminate: i. e. להשמיד ולהחרים. The LXX has here ῥομφαίᾳ ἀφανίσαι καὶ ἀποκτεῖναι = בחרב להחרים ולהשמיד (or ולהמית). Cf. Deut. 7². בחרב is then a dittograph of החרים. The two verbs which occur in this order in 2 Chron. 20²³ would then mean 'to ban and to destroy'. But are not the Hebrew and the LXX here renderings of the Aramaic expression לְהַשְׁמָדָה וּלְהוֹבָדָה, which has already occurred in 7²⁶? If this is so, it is best to render as these 'to consume and to exterminate'. Th. τοῦ ἀφανίσαι (+ καὶ τοῦ ἀναθεματίσαι A Q) support this latter order as found in 7²⁶, where it renders τοῦ ἀφανίσαι καὶ τοῦ ἀπολέσαι. So also the Vulg. 'ut conterat et interficiat'.

11⁴⁵. *Shall plant:* i. e. יְטַּע, used only here in the O.T. in this

sense of pitching a tent, instead of יִפֶּה. Cf. Eccles. 12¹¹ for
a related use. Duhm, Cheyne, Marti, &c., take לְנֹטַע as corrupt
for לִנְטֹח where 'the spreading out of the heavens' is the idea,
not 'the planting' of them.

The tents of his palace : i. e. אָהֳלֵי אַפַּדְנוֹ. But the LXX, Th.,
Pesh., and Vulg. do not support this text. All four read אהלו =
'his tent'. Th., Aquila, and Vulg. regard אפדנו as a proper
name. Though this word passed into Aramaic from the Persian
and occurs frequently in Syriac, the Syriac translator could not
render it. The LXX reads τότε = Aramaic אדין. The word is
derived from Persian *apadâna* = 'treasury' or 'armoury', but
'palace' in Syriac. Text uncertain.

Between the seas and the glorious holy mountain. The 'seas'
here is a poetical plural (cf. Judges 5¹⁷; Deut. 33¹⁹) for the
Mediterranean Sea. The mountain is of course Mount Zion. The
text here implies that Antiochus died in Palestine between the
Mediterranean and Mount Zion, whereas he actually died at
Tabae in Persia in the winter of 165–164 B. C. It was a reasonable expectation on the part of the Jews that their greatest
persecutor should fall amid the scenes of his greatest crimes.
According to 8²⁵ he was to perish 'broken without hand'.
Moreover, the old eschatological expectations of the prophets
fixed on the neighbourhood of Jerusalem. This is emphasized
in Ezek. 38–39 according to which the nations that were hostile
to Israel were to fall on the mountains of Israel: cf. 38¹⁴⁻¹⁶,²¹,
39²,⁴; Joel 3²; Zech. 14² ˢqq·; 1 Enoch 90¹³⁻¹⁹. Even the
throne of judgement was to be set up 'in the pleasant land',
1 Enoch 90²⁰, and the wicked judged according to what was
written in the sealed books.

Yet he shall come to his end. Antiochus made a fresh attempt
to get hold of the treasures in the Elymaean temples. He tried
to break into a temple of Istar or Anaitis, but the people of the
place filled with religious frenzy succeeded in driving off his
forces. Soon afterwards he died at Tabae in Persia (Polyb.
xxxi. 11; 1 Macc. 6¹⁻⁴; 2 Macc. 9¹⁻²), as above mentioned.
See Bevan, *House of Seleucus*, ii. 160 seq.

INTRODUCTION TO CHAPTER XII.

The conventional division of this chapter from the preceding
one is based on a sound judgement. Both chapters constitute,

it is true, one vision, to which chapter 10 forms an introduction. But chapter 11 is wholly concerned with human history already past, 11$^{2-39}$, or on the eve of realization, 11$^{40-45}$, whereas chapter 12 passes from temporal to eternal things.

In this introduction I shall briefly draw attention to the methods pursued in order to recover the original Hebrew version and thereby in the main the Aramaic original. In the study of the text it has been found necessary to reject phrases and entire clauses as very early or late additions to the original text : and in the next place to emend by means of the versions— above all by means of the LXX—many corrupt passages in the text. There is a third point which is of no little interest to the student of religious development. In 12^2 owing to the mis-understanding of an Aramaic expression a new conception of the nature of the joys of the righteous and the sufferings of the wicked arose, helped no doubt by the occurrence of this expression (in part) already in Isa. 66^{24}.

I. *Interpolations.*

12^2. לחרפות is to be excised as an explanatory gloss on לדראון. The LXX actually incorporates three renderings of לדראון, one of which εἰς διασποράν is reasonably correct. The other two, εἰς ὀνειδισμόν and εἰς . . . αἰσχύνην, are further efforts of the translator to render in the margin this difficult phrase, both of which unhappily were incorporated subsequently in the text. Th. is here very unfortunate. He rejects the real rendering and adopts the two glosses into his text.

12^{10}. Excise יתלבנו as the gloss of an unintelligent scribe in 11^{35} and here. In both passages the LXX knows nothing of it.

12^{11,12}. When the original date fixed for the advent of the kingdom was not realized, either the original author—the style is quite his own, or a reviser in the year 165–164 b.c. in the second edition, added 12^{11,12} to correct the original prediction and adapt, if possible, its forecasts to actual events. Possibly 12^{11} was added in the second edition and 12^{12} in the third. If so, we have the remarkable fact that three editions of Daniel appeared in the vernacular, i. e. Aramaic in the course of slightly over three years.

12^{13}. Excise לקץ with LXX, Th., and context. See note *in loc.*

II. *Emendations* (a) *ancient and at the same time incorrect.*
     (b) *Emendations of the present corrupt MT under the guidance
     of the versions, mainly the LXX.*

(*a*) $12^{6,8}$. When $12^{11,12}$ were added in the second and third
editions, Jewish scholars after the Christian era (?) recognized
their incongruity with the statements in $12^{6,8}$, and so changed
ואמר (so LXX and Vulg.) in 12^6 into ויאמר—a change which
made the text questionable Hebrew, and אחוית (so LXX) in 12^8
into אחרית. A further result of this addition led to the attribu-
tion of an unparalleled meaning to עמד in 12^{13}, i.e. 'to rise in
the resurrection' = קום.

(*b*) 12^2. For אדמת עפר read with (LXX, Th.) Pesh. and
Vulg. עפר אדמה.

12^4. For the very corrupt text ותרבה הדעת ישטטו רבים read
under the guidance of the LXX עד ישטו (יסטו) הרבים ותרבה הרעה.
See notes *in loc.*

12^6. For ויאמר read with LXX, Vulg., and some manuscripts
of Th. וָאמר.

12^8. For אחרית with LXX read אחוית—another Aramaism like
דראין in 12^2. It is found in 5^{12}. See note *in loc.*

12^{10}. For יתבררו ויתלבנו ויצרפו read with LXX עד יצרפו ויתבררו.
Cf. 11^{35}, where again the LXX is right. Here Th. supports the
restoration of the עד. See note *in loc.*

III. *Aramaisms.*

12^2. דראון. See under *Interpolations* above and the note *in loc.*
12^8. אחוית אלה = אחוית אלין. Cf. 5^{12}.
12^{11}. מעת הוסר · · · ולתת. Here ל with inf. appears to be a
continuation of the preceding finite verb: cf. 2^{16}. But it could
be justified by Hebrew parallels. The Aramaic was possibly
מן־די אתעדי · · · , ולמנתן.

IV. *The Hebrew verb* עמד. This verb is a maid-of-all-work in
our author. In 12^1 it appears with על in a new construction =
'to protect', whereas in 8^{25}, 11^{14} the same phrase = 'to withstand'. In $8^{4,7}$, 11^{16} with לפני it bears the latter meaning, while
this same phrase in $1^{5,19}$ = 'to serve'. Again in 12^{13} owing to
the interpolation of $12^{11,12}$ it comes to mean unjustifiably 'to rise
from the dead'.

V. *A characteristic of Gehenna*—i.e. that the wicked should

suffer in the presence of the righteous arose from a false etymology of דראון. See note on 12².

VI. *Hebrew renderings of Aramaic phrases of our author.*

12⁷. חֵי עֹולָם = חַי עָלְמָא, 4³¹⁽³⁴⁾.

12⁷. עֶדָּן ועדנין ופלג עדן = מועד מועדים וחצי, 7²⁵.

VII. *Very late use (or misuse) of a Hebrew word.* יְאֹר which *in
all OT. writings before 200 B.C. is used only of the Nile*, is in
12⁵,⁶,⁷, 10⁴ used of the Euphrates. In Isa. 33²¹ (assigned to
163 B.C. by Duhm, Bickell, Marti; by other scholars to the
middle of the 4th cent. B.C.) it means 'watercourses'. In very
late Hebrew and late Aramaic it bears the same meaning.

12¹⁻³. These three verses form the close of the revelation of
the angel, and belong to what precedes. In fact 11⁴⁰⁻⁴⁵ and
12¹⁻³ form a unity, being a description of the last times of all,
i. e. the destruction of the great heathen power, 11⁴⁰⁻⁴⁵, followed
by tumults and troubles throughout the world, out of which,
however, the faithful shall be saved, 12¹. Then shall follow the
resurrection of the pre-eminently righteous Israelites as well as
of the apostates, and the age of everlasting blessedness on the
present earth, 12²⁻³.

12¹. *At that time*, i. e. the period of the overthrow of Antiochus.
Michael . . . the great prince. See 10¹³,²¹.

Shall . . . stand up : i. e. יעמד, which the LXX read as יעבר,
since it renders by παρελεύσεται: just as in 11¹ it read עמד as אמר
(i. e. εἶπεν).

Which standeth for the children of thy people, i. e. 'protects' :
cf. Esther 8¹¹, 9¹⁶. This phrase עמד על has exactly the opposite
meaning in 8²⁵, 11¹⁴, where it = 'to withstand', and is therefore
there used as the equivalent of עמד לנגד in 10¹³, or עמד לפני in 8⁴,⁷,
11¹⁶. For quite a different use of the last phrase see note on 1⁴.

A time of trouble such as never was, &c. This phrase constitutes a technical description of the last times : cf. Jer. 30⁷ 'Alas !
for that day is great, so that none is like it' : 1 Macc. 9²⁷ καὶ
ἐγένετο θλῖψις μεγάλη ἐν τῷ Ἰσραήλ, ἥτις οὐκ ἐγένετο ἀφ᾽ ἧς ἡμέρας οὐκ ὤφθη
προφήτης αὐτοῖς: Ass. Mos. 8¹, 'ira quae talis non fuit in illis';
Mark 13¹⁹: Matt. 24²¹: Rev. 16¹⁸ σεισμὸς ἐγένετο μέγας, οἷος οὐκ
ἐγένετο ἀφ᾽ οὗ ἄνθρωπος ἐγένετο ἐπὶ τῆς γῆς τηλικοῦτος σεισμὸς οὕτω μέγας.
It should be observed here that Rev. 16¹⁸ adheres more closely
to Th. than to the MT or LXX, as Th. reads θλῖψις, οἷα οὐ γέγονεν

Enoch is Pre-Maccabean

ἀφ' ἧς γεγένηται ἔθνος ἐν τῇ γῇ ἕως τοῦ καιροῦ ἐκείνου. So far as the
phrase in itself goes, it occurs in a non-technical sense in
Exod. 9^{18,24}. The phrase 'time of trouble' (עת צרה) has already
occurred in Jer. 30^{7}. It refers here of course to the gathering
of all the Gentile powers against Jerusalem.

Thy people : the true Israel.

Written in the book, i.e. of life. See note on 7^{10} : also my
notes on 1 Enoch 47^{3}. This book of life, which originally was
a register of the actual citizens of the theocratic community on
earth, has in the present passage become a register of the citizens
of the coming kingdom of God, whether living or departed.

12^{2}. In Pss. 49, 73 there are probably the first intimations of
the immortality of righteous souls. These psalms are the
utterances of mystics. It is probable also that in Ps. 17 we
have just such another utterance, while in 39 (i. e. omitting the
interpolated verses 39^{9(8),11—14(10—13)}), though the writer is convinced that every man is at his best estate altogether vanity,
yet there is the expression of an unconquerable hope in God:
'And now Lord what wait I for? My hope is unto thee' 39^{8(7)}.

These psalms were probably not written earlier than the
3rd cent. B. C. and possibly towards its close. They avoid all
definition of the nature of the life beyond. But the time came
when thought busied itself about the nature of the future life.

In 1 Enoch 22, which is pre-Maccabean in date, there is an
elaborate account of Sheol and its different divisions corresponding to the moral distinctions between the different classes
of men. From this Sheol only the pre-eminently good and bad
were to be raised, just as in our text, but the mediocre folk of
both classes were to remain for ever in Sheol. Thus in our
text and in 1 Enoch 22 there is taught a doctrine of the resurrection which in certain respects is morally conceived.

But this is a comparatively late form—that is logically—of
the original doctrine. In the O.T. the resurrection was derived
from a synthesis of the hopes of the righteous individual and
of the righteous nation. By the resurrection the righteous
individual was to be raised to a higher communion (*a*) with God
and (*b*) and to be restored to communion with the righteous community. Thus the communion of the righteous individual with
God was not temporally conditioned, because it was unbroken
by death. This is a truth too generally lost sight of—not only in

Judaism but also in Christianity, and particularly in the case of
our Lord. In His case there could be no breach wrought by
death in His full and perfect communion with the Father. But
to return to our immediate problem. Though the communion
of the righteous individual with God is not temporally conditioned, restoration to communion with the righteous community
is temporally conditioned as regards its external and complete
consummation, but not in its spiritual essence; for the spiritual
resurrection can be and is experienced in the present alike in
respect to God and man. Hence this life is for the faithful the
resurrection life, though but in its beginnings. This is the
teaching of the later Pauline Epistles, but as a fact of experience
it was true all along.

Thus in Judaism[1] the resurrection in its original form was
the prerogative of the righteous, as it is also in the N.T. save
in a few Judaistic passages.[2] The doctrine in its essential and
pure form—a resurrection of the righteous only—appears in the
comparatively late section in Isa. 26$^{1-19}$. But in our text, in
1 Enoch 22; Test. Benj. 10^8; 2 Macc.; 2 Bar.; 4 Ezra there are
declensions from the original conception. In these writers the
spiritual essence of the resurrection has been lost sight of, and
the resurrection—instead of being regarded as at once a Divine
gift and a personal achievement—came to be used as a sort of
vehicle for bringing certain classes of the righteous and of the
wicked before the Final Judgement, and, last stage of all, for
bringing all men before the Judgement Seat for the General
Resurrection. As generally conceived these latter developments are not Christian.

Many. Not all Israel but many in Israel. See preceding note.

Sleep in the dust: i.e. ישני עפר: cf. Isa. 26^{19} שכני עפר 'those
that dwell', &c.

That sleep in the dust of the earth. This rendering of the R.V.,
though it has the support of the LXX, Th., the Pesh., and Vulg.
is not a rendering of the MT, which reads ישני אדמת עפר =
'those who sleep in a land of dust'. Marti explains 'the dust'
as defining the term 'earth', i.e. earth which is dust (G.-K.,

[1] Cf. Pss. Sol. 3^{16}, 14^7, 15^{15}. There is no mention in these Pss. of the resurrection of the wicked: Sheol is their inheritance, 14^{5a,6}, 15^{11}, 16^2.
[2] See my *Eschatology*[2], pp. 397 seq., 407, 410 seq., 428-30, 444, 448-54:
Comm. on Revelation, I, p. cxvi: II, 194-198.

§ 128 *o*). Driver renders 'the dusty earth', which is simply impossible here, where abodes of the departed are spoken of. We must either, then, take עפר as a synonym for Sheol as in Job 7²¹, 17¹⁶, 20¹¹, 21¹⁶, and render 'in a land of dust'. The Babylonian Hades, which is the same as that of the ancient Hebrews, is described in the Descent of Ishtar, as 'the dark house . . . the house from which he who enters never emerges— where dust is their nourishment, clay their food'. For מִישֵׁנֵי the usual form would be מִישֵׁנֵי (Ges.-Kautzsch, § 102 *b*).

Otherwise we must for אדמת עפר read עפר האדמה. Cf. Gen. 13¹⁶; Exod. 8¹²,¹³, where we find עפר הארץ (=Aram. עפרא דארעא), which the LXX in the two latter passages renders τὸ χῶμα τῆς γῆς as Th. in the present passage. This is the better of the two methods of dealing with the text; for the LXX, Th., Pesh., and Vulg. presuppose this order. There is a difficulty in the text of the LXX but not in the order—ἐν τῷ πλάτει τῆς γῆς. Since πλάτος is a rendering of פתי in Dan. 3¹; Ezra 6³, the corruption may have arisen in the Aramaic original, i. e. בפתיא דאדמתא, where פתיא[1] may be corrupt for עפר. But the divergence is too great.

Shall awake: i. e. יקיצו. Used in Isa. 26¹⁹ in the same sense. In this verse of Isaiah three verbs are used of the resurrection: חיה, קום, הקיץ. Our author uses the third here (and owing to the interpolation of 12¹¹,¹² עמד becomes a synonym for קום in 12¹³).

Everlasting life. Here only in the O.T., but of frequent occurrence in Apocalyptic literature, in the Targums, the Talmuds, and other Jewish writings. It is found in 1 Enoch 15⁴,⁶, which is older than our author; Pss. Sol. 3¹⁶⁽¹²⁾.

Everlasting rejection: i. e. לדראון עולם. Here the MT retains לחרפות (לחרפה?: so LXX and Th. as Jahn recognizes) without a copula before לדראון, as also does the Vulg. 'ut videant semper'. לחרפה was originally a marginal gloss explaining לדראון, and was subsequently incorporated in the text. Here the MT and Vulg. preserve the first stage in this act of incorporation, before the copula was inserted. The LXX contains two renderings of לחרפה and one of לדראון. It reads οἱ δὲ εἰς ὀνειδισμόν, οἱ δὲ εἰς διασποράν καὶ αἰσχύνην αἰώνιον. Th. reproduces the renderings of the two glosses and omits the rendering of the original word of which they were glosses: οὗτοι εἰς ὀνειδισμὸν καὶ αἰσχύνην αἰώνιον.

---

[1] See *Aram. Pap.* (Cowley, 8⁴, 79²⁻⁴, 26¹⁸⁻²⁰).

The Pesh. with ܠܚܒܠ = 'in interitum' as its first phrase appears
to attest לדראון as that phrase, while it paraphrases the second
phrase as 'et opprobrium sociorum suorum aeternum'.

Rejecting, therefore, the explanatory gloss (or glosses) we
arrive at the original Hebrew version אלה לחיי עולם ואלה לדראון
עולם, the terse antithesis = 'some to everlasting life and some
to everlasting rejection'.

Much interest attaches to the Hebrew phrase דראון עולם, which
the LXX, when the glosses are rejected, rendered by εἰς διασποράν. Here it is manifest that the translator derived דראון
from the Aramaic דרי (the Syr ܕܪܐ) = διασπείρειν (= Hebr. זרה),
and the etymology may be right. At all events זרה is used of
the punishment of the wicked in Prov. 20²⁶, and of wickedness
20⁸, and of wicked nations Ezek. 29¹², 30²⁶. The word is
generally derived from דרא, of which the Arabic equivalent
root means 'to repel'. Thus it comes in any case to mean
'scattering', 'rejection'. This word occurs only once elsewhere
in the O.T., i.e. Isa. 66²⁴, where the LXX renders לדראון by
εἰς ὅρασιν, the Vulg. by 'ad satietatem visionis'. Since the Vulg.
renders the phrase לדראון עולם in our text by 'ut videant
semper', it clearly follows that the LXX and Vulg. translators
of this phrase in Isa. 66²⁴ and the Vulg. in Dan. 12² derived
דראון from the Hebrew ראה 'to see'. The Targum on Isa. 66²⁴ᵉ
takes the same view and paraphrases as follows: 'And the
wicked shall be judged in Gehenna until the righteous say over
them, We have seen enough' (מסת חזינא). The same interpretation of the Hebrew phrase appears several times in 1 Enoch
27³ 'In the last days there shall be unto them the spectacle of
righteous judgement in the presence of the righteous for ever':
48⁹ 'So shall they burn before the face of the holy': 62¹² 'They
shall be a spectacle for the righteous and for His elect'. From
the above facts we learn that for nearly 200 years B. C. Jewish
scholars derived this rare word in our text from ראה 'to see',
and from this mistaken etymology concluded that *Gehenna was
to be a place of punishment in the presence of the righteous.* Thus
the chief characteristic of this Jewish and subsequently Christian
conception was derived from a false etymology.

12³. This verse refers to the teachers and leaders of the
faithful. Amongst them would naturally be the martyrs and
confessors of Judaism, who with the teachers would be distin-

guished from the rest of the faithful Israelites. Cf. 1 Enoch 104²:
'Be hopeful; for aforetime ye were put to shame through ill
     and affliction;
But now ye shall shine as the lights of heaven:
Ye shall shine and shall be seen,
And the portals of heaven shall be opened to you.'
     Cf. also 4 Ezra 7⁹⁷,¹²⁵.
     They that be wise. Cf. 11³³,³⁵.
     Shall shine: i.e. יַזְהִירוּ. This verb is found nowhere else in
the O.T., though the noun זֹהַר = 'brightness' occurs once: i.e.
in Ezek. 8². The root has this meaning in some Aramaic
dialects and in Arabic.
     As the brightness of the firmament: i.e. כזהר הרקיע. But the
LXX has ὡς φωστῆρες τοῦ οὐρανοῦ = כמאורי השמים, 'as the lumi-
naries of heaven', i.e. the sun and moon. Does this imply
a different text or is it an interpretation of the above phrase in
the MT? This question is in part connected with the other
suggested in the first note on this verse. Are two classes of the
faithful referred to? or only the two forms in which their
loyalty to God displayed itself—in the faithfulness *alike by
precept and example* in the days of persecution? The things to
which the faithful are compared favour the former; for 'the
brightness of the firmament', i.e. the sun and moon, are clearly
distinguished in glory from the stars.
     It is hard indeed to divide them into two classes, and yet the
context on the whole favours such a division. 'The wise.' or
'the teachers' are of course faithful in their lives; but their
distinguishing characteristic is that they are the teachers of the
true faith. The rest who are likened to the stars have as their
distinguishing characteristic their loyalty to the God of Israel
even unto death. They too teach, but more by example than
precept. Indeed they may not be more than silent but faithful
disciples of the teachers.
     To return now to the text. The text of the LXX is at all
events a very old one, and not improbably a literal reproduction
of the Hebrew version. If so, then זהר הרקיע may have been
suggested by the verb יזהירו in the preceding clause and be due
to a reviser or the Massoretes. זֹהַר which literally means
'shining' is far from an apt expression in this context. In
Ezek. 8²—the only passage elsewhere in the O.T. where it

occurs—this meaning is quite apt. But this is not all. When the Aramaic equivalent of זהר occurs in the Mishnah of the Jer. Talmud, it is used only of the moon and not of the sun: see *NHWB*. i. 516.

They that turn many to righteousness : i. e. מַצְדִּיקֵי הָרַבִּים. It is noteworthy that the LXX has here οἱ κατισχύοντες τοὺς λόγους μου, which apparently goes back to (or דברי) מחזיקי בדברי = 'they who hold fast my words'. The text it presupposes should then be rendered (not 'they who strengthen my words' but 'they who hold fast my words'. The two classes referred to then would be : 'they who are wise', i. e. have a deep insight into matters like Daniel and are teachers like him : and they who hold fast such teaching at whatever cost.

Turn many to righteousness : i. e. not justify them technically but lead them to righteousness alike by precept and example as in Isa. 53[11]. The same idea is conveyed by the Aboth v. 26 (Taylor's ed.): 'Whosoever makes the many righteous (המזכה את הרבים), sin prevails not over him ; and whosoever makes the many to sin, they grant him not the faculty to repent'.

12[4]. *The angel's last commission to Daniel.*

Shut up the words and seal. The book was to be concealed and sealed. The words are repeated in 12[9]. With the former injunction cf. 8[26].

To the time of the end. The entire book, as it has already been said in 8[17,26], was written in the time of Antiochus' persecution. In that reign the seals were to be removed and the book understood : cf. Isa. 29[11,12,18,19]. Contrast Rev. 22[10], which is not a pseudepigraph, and was written at the time of the crises with which it deals.

†*Many shall run to and fro† :* i. e. יְשֹׁטְטוּ. The verb is admitted by many modern scholars to be an enigma or a corruption.[1] Two explanations are advanced. The first is that the words signify that many shall run to and fro in the book, i. e. shall diligently study it. But this verb could not be used of an earnest study of the book, but only of a superficial reading of it. Besides, how could it be studied, if it was sealed and

---

[1] In support of the MT Amos 8[12] 'Many shall run to and fro (ישוטטו) to seek the word of the Lord' is quoted. But the word in our text is used absolutely and metaphorically, and not so elsewhere in the O.T. Cf. Jer. 5[1] ; Zech. 4[10] ; 2 Chron. 16[9].

hidden? The second explanation is that many generations would be perplexed as to its meaning, and that only after many generations would its meaning leap to light. But neither explanation meets the difficulty that the book was not to be made known till the very crisis it dealt with had arrived. Nor does either agree with the universal and literal use of this verb elsewhere. Recently, Wright (*Daniel and his Prophecies*, p. 322) abandons the metaphorical use of this verb and suggests: 'Why should it not refer to the Jews . . . running to and fro through the world, and gradually increasing in learning the ways and works of God by their weary wanderings? By those wanderings they are even now being prepared more fully to learn the meaning of the visions which so deeply concern them.' But this suggestion also fails to explain how they are to learn the meaning of visions which are not to be disclosed till the hour of the actual events has struck.

Moreover there are still further difficulties. The LXX reads ἕως ἂν ἀπομανῶσιν οἱ πολλοί. The true explanation, if we can arrive at it, should account for the MT and the LXX. The LXX = עד יְשֹׁטוּ הרבים. Behrmann, following Schleusner, suggests that for ישטטו we should here read ישֹטו, and compares the LXX Ps. 40⁵ where μανίας ψευδεῖς is a rendering of שָׂטֵי כֹזב. This rendering may have been suggested to the translator by the Aramaic שְׁטָא, the participle of which שָׁטֵי is found frequently and means 'unreasonable', 'foolish'. Perhaps the confusion arose in the Aramaic original, which read (?) עד ישטון שׁגיאיא. Here ישטון stands for יסטון. If this were so, then the rendering should be 'till the many become apostates'—at all events in Targumic Hebrew. The nearest to יסטון in Hebrew would be ישוטו, which the LXX translator wrongly rendered by ἀπομαίνειν. The MT ישטטו could then have arisen from an accidental duplication of the ט in ישוטו.

Th. has διδαχθῶσιν, which is a corruption of διαχθῶσιν (as in Isa. 55¹²), a bad rendering of the MT. The Pesh. renders the MT metaphorically and the Vulg. literally by 'pertransibunt'. The one thing certain is that the text is uncertain.

†*And knowledge shall be increased*†, i. e. וְתִרְבֶּה הַדָּעַת. Here Bevan takes these words as corrupt. He thinks that the LXX καὶ πλησθῇ ἡ γῆ ἀδικίας supplies the solution, which (omitting ἡ γῆ) presupposes וְתִרְבֶּה הָרָעַת. This he renders 'and many shall be the calamities'. If the singular verb with a plural noun is

unsatisfactory, we can read ותרבינה הרעת. But Bevan adduces
similar constructions in Isa. 34[13]; Jer. 4[14], &c. In support of
this restoration he adduces 1 Macc. 1[9], which refers to the evils
wrought by the Seleucidae and Ptolemies on Palestine: καὶ
ἐπλήθυναν κακὰ ἐν τῇ γῇ = 'and they multiplied evils in the earth'.
This conjecture is regarded favourably by Driver, Wright, and
others. It is attractive, but these scholars have failed to recognize that in the LXX πίμπλημι is never a rendering of any mood
of רבה. πλησθῆναι means 'to be filled', whereas רבה = 'to be
multiplied'. Hence (1) πληθῇ may be a corruption of πληθύῃ
or of πληθυνθῇ as in Th. We should have מלא instead of רבה, if
the LXX were right: cf. Gen. 6[11] ותמלא הארץ חמס and the LXX
καὶ ἐπλήσθη ἡ γῆ ἀδικίας. Perhaps the LXX represents the original
text and the MT is only an editorial substitute.

Hence for 'and knowledge shall be increased' we might read
'and evils be increased' or 'and the earth be filled with iniquity'.
But here again the only certainty is the uncertainty of the text.

12[5-7]. Vision of the two angels, one of whom states the duration of the troubles just foretold.

12[5]. *Other two*, i. e. in addition to the glorious being who
appeared to Daniel in 10[5], clothed in linen, and who had
imparted to him the revelation in 10[11-14,19]-12[4].

The river: i. e. הַיְאֹר, an Egyptian loan-word, elsewhere in the
O.T. the regular name for the Nile. In Isa. 33[21] it is used,
however, of watercourses, and in Job 28[10] of mining shafts. But
where יְאֹר means 'a river' in the O.T., and especially where
this word is preceded by the article, it is used only to designate
the Nile. Hence its proper use was forgotten when Daniel
was written or translated from the Aramaic. In keeping with
this fact we note that in the Talmud and Rabbinic writings it
bears the general sense of river alike in Hebrew and Aramaic.
See Levy, *NHCW*. i. 213. In 10[4], where the same river is
referred to, the Hebrew designation is right, i. e. הנהר. In the
note on that passage we saw just grounds for identifying this
river with the Euphrates and not with the Tigris, as apparently
is done universally.

12[6]. *And ⌐I⌐ said to the man*. The speaker according to the
MT is one of the two angels mentioned in 12[5]. But not only is the
form of the Hebrew, which should have been ויאמר אחד מהם or
the like, against the above rendering, but from 12[8] it appears that

Daniel is no silent auditor as in 8[13 seqq]. but asks for an explanation of the angel's answer. The very form of the words 'And I heard but I understood not : then said I, O my lord, &c.', imply that Daniel has already spoken but wishes for more information. There is no nuance of remonstance in Daniel's words, even though they express deprecation of the angel's refusal. Thus both the form of the Hebrew and the context require not ויאמר but וָאֹמַר. Now the LXX εἶπα attests this reading : so also the Vulg. and the manuscripts A Q of Th. The passage in 8[13,14] is not a true parallel. If the dialogue between the two angels in that passage is correct in form, as we may reasonably suppose it is, Daniel does not intervene in any part of it. But he does certainly intervene in 12[8] here, and no doubt in 12[6] also.

The man clothed in linen. The same being who is described in 10[5,6].

The wonders : i. e. הפלאות the things prophesied in 11[31-36], 12[1]. The same word is used of the boastings of Antiochus in 8[24], 11[36].

12[7]. *He held up his right hand, &c.* The lifting up of the hand as an appeal to heaven in confirmation of an oath is mentioned in Gen. 14[22] ; Exod. 6[8] ; Deut. 32[40] ; and in Rev. 10[5], where the speaker is an angel as here. Here both hands are lifted up by the angel in confirmation of this solemn oath.

Him that liveth for ever : i. e. חי העולם. In 4[34] we have the Aramaic equivalent חי עלמא. The expression is a late one, but it is based on a 6th cent. B. C. one : Deut. 32[40] חַי אָנֹכִי לְעֹלָם.

For a time, times, and a half : i. e. מועד מועדים וחצי. Here again we have the Hebrew rendering of an Aramaic phrase of our author עדן ועדנין ופלג עדן in 7[25], where see note and on 8[14]. The three and a half years define the limit of the reign of the Antichrist.

†*And when they have made an end of breaking in pieces the power of the holy people, all these things shall be ended*†. We have here a fresh time determination, and it is entirely vague. It has no apparent connexion with the definite time determination just given by the angel, who has defined the period of evil as limited to three years and a half. But this is not all. The statement is not true in itself. The power of the holy people was not wholly broken in pieces, nor did our author ever expect that it would be. There is also a grammatical difficulty. Elsewhere

when כַּלּוֹת is followed by an inf. the inf. is preceded by לְ.
Furthermore, the fact that the Versions take different directions
shows that the Hebrew text is secondary. The LXX, as Bevan
recognized, shows the way to recover the original of the
Hebrew version. The LXX—ἡ συντέλεια χειρῶν †ἀφέσεως†[1] λαοῦ
ἁγίου καὶ συντελεσθήσεται πάντα ταῦτα—is so meaningless as regards
the first four words that Bevan reasonably regards them as
a literal rendering, and concludes accordingly that the translator
found יד נפץ and not נפץ יד. By reading וְכִכְלוֹת יַד נֹפֵץ עַם קֹדֶשׁ
under the guidance of the LXX he arrives at the following
clause: 'And when the power of the shatterer of the holy
people shall come to an end, all these things shall be ended'.
Antiochus is to be the last of the oppressors of Israel. The
preceding clause defines the temporal limits of the oppression:
this clause all but names the oppressor. Bevan thus recovers
the thought but not the form of the text. For this use of נפץ
he compares Judges 7[19]; Jer. 51[20]. For the כִּכְלוֹת יַד cf. Ps. 71[9]
ככלות כֹּחִי. For יד in the sense of power cf. Joshua 8[20]; Deut.
16[17]; 1 Chron. 18[3], &c. The above combination of the three
times and a half with the oppression of Antiochus has already
occurred in 7[25]—a fact which confirms Bevan's restoration of
the thought but not of the form [1] of the text.

12[8]. Daniel, as living at the time of Cyrus, is represented as
not understanding this time determination, and as therefore
seeking more explicit information. To the readers of the book
in the time of Antiochus the meaning of 12[7] (as it then stood)
was of course quite clear. This is the usual interpretation of
these words, but it must be confessed that it is not quite satisfactory that Daniel should (as in the MT) again ask 'What is
the end of these things?' when he has already been told it most
definitely. Thus, when in 12[6] he asked 'How long shall it be
to the end of the wonders?', and has in 12[7] been told their
actual duration and all but the actual name of the last oppressor
of the Jews, he cannot reasonably again ask 'What shall be the
end of these things?' (אחרית אלה MT and Th.). Driver seeks
to get over the difficulty by representing that, whereas קֵץ (12[6])

---

[1] For ἀφέσεως, which cannot be a rendering of נפץ, as Bevan assumes, is
apparently itself a corruption of ἀφα⟨νί⟩σεως, or even of ἀφανίζοντος. Hence read
נתץ and cf. Jer. 4[26] ἠφανίσθησαν (LXX) a rendering of נִתְּצוּ, or מַפֵּץ (= 'hammer'
or 'shatterer': cf. Jer. 51[20]) of which נַפֵּץ may be a corruption.

means the absolute end of a thing, אחרית means the closing or
latter part of it, and compares Job 8[7], 42[12]. But the opening
words of 12[8] prepare us for quite a different question. Daniel
says 'I heard but I did not understand'. He had heard perfectly what the angel had said, but failing to understand it, he
would naturally ask for an explanation of the angel's words.
On these grounds I cannot but regard the MT, which Th.
supports, as corrupt. The translators of the LXX, Pesh., and
Vulg. either found a different text or emended the existing one.
The Pesh. and Vulg. = מה אחרי אלה 'what will be after these
things?' This question, as it appears in Pesh. and Vulg.,
might apart from its context be reasonable enough. But it
is inexplicable alike from what precedes and what follows.
Daniel does not want to know *what follows the 3½ years of distress*
but to have further disclosures on this period, which he is
unable to understand. But the angel in 12[9] definitely refuses to
make them. Nor does the reading of the Pesh. and Vulg.
accord with what follows; for, if 12[11,12] were original, which
they are not, they would be no answer to the reading of the
Pesh. and Vulg. Hence we must fall back on the only remaining
authority, but happily it is the oldest and at the same time the
most satisfactory. The LXX reads τίς ἡ λύσις τοῦ λόγου τούτου;
Daniel in these words asks the angel to explain more clearly
the words he has just uttered. What then stands behind ἡ λύσις
τ. λόγου τούτου? Either (1) the loan-word (אלה) אחות = 'declaration
(i. e. an explanation) of these things'. אחוה is found in Job 13[17],
and is Aramaic both as respects its root and form (an Aram.
Aph'el Inf.). Or (2) there may have stood here the actual
Aramaic אֲחָוַת אלה, which we find in 5[12] of our text = אחות אחידין
'the solving of riddles'. Either word would serve as the original
of the LXX and account for the two divergent forms of the
text presupposed by the MT and Th. or the Pesh. and Vulg.
The Hebrew translator, being perfectly acquainted with the
meaning of this Aramaic word and knowing that the Aramaic
verb חוי (see Cowley, 30[16], 31[15], &c.), had been borrowed and
used in the Pss. and Job, allowed it to remain in his version.
How long it maintained its place we do not know. In the
2nd cent. A. D. at all events, if not earlier, two attempts were
made to transform this Aramaic word into a Hebrew one: one
survives in the MT and Th., and the other in the Pesh. and

Vulg., as we have seen above. Accordingly I have adopted the rendering of the LXX into my translation. אחרית אלה (or אחות) explains the corrupt MT אחרית אלה and the אחרי אלה which the Pesh. and Vulg. presuppose. λύσις bears in Classical Greek the meaning of 'interpretation': frequently in Aristotle: cf. also Orph. Arg. 37 σημείων . . . λύσεις.

12⁹. The angel refuses to give any explanation of his oracular disclosures as to the things belonging to the end. They are not for the prophet but for the readers of the distant future. The same view of prophecy is expressed in 1 Peter 1¹⁰⁻¹².

12¹⁰. This verse combines two statements already made. In 12⁴ the words of the book are to be shut up and sealed 'to the time of the end, till the many become apostates and the earth is filled with iniquity (so LXX): and in 11³⁵ 'some of them that be wise shall be wise so as to refine and make themselves pure to the time of the end' (on basis of LXX text restored).

Till many refine and make themselves pure: i. e. עד יצרפו ויתבררו, instead of the corrupt MT. See note on 11³⁵. Here as in 12⁴ we are to insert עד (LXX ἕως ἄν) at the beginning of the sentence under the guidance of the LXX. Even Th. appears originally to have had the same conjunction, seeing that it is not possible otherwise to explain the subjunctives ἐκλεγῶσιν καὶ ἐκλευκανθῶσιν κτλ. Q^mg inserts καὶ ἕως before ἐκλεγῶσιν, while Q^ℵ agrees with LXX in reading only two verbs.

The object of the final woes is twofold—to discipline the faithful so that they may come nearer their highest ideals, and to afford the wicked full opportunity to give full rein to their wickedness.

Here the Niph'al יצרפו is used reflexively just as the Hithp. which follows it. See Ges.-Kautzsch, § 51 c.

If we omit the 'till', then the sense of the text is changed, and the duty of deliberately choosing suffering and martyrdom is emphasized by our author with a view to the purification of character. But the oldest form of the text is decidedly against this thought.

None of the wicked shall understand, but they that be wise shall understand. The nemesis of wickedness is blindness and self-delusion: but the faithful shall grow in understanding.

Daniel, who in 12⁸ deplored his total lack of understanding, is here promised full understanding of the mysteries mentioned

by the angel in 12⁷. Since in 12² he has been given the promise
of everlasting life and here in 12¹⁰ a divine wisdom in all
things that concern the Kingdom, the book naturally comes to
a close here. The additions in 12¹¹⁻¹³, though called forth by
the emergencies of the time destroy the unity of the book, and
contain a misuse of a Hebrew verb or else represent the author
as forgetting his role as a writer of the sixth cent. B.C.

Here the Book ends, and ends not with the promise of future
blessedness to a solitary individual; for that had already been
declared to be the guerdon of all those who had been faithful at
a great cost (12²): but with the additional promise of spiritual
enlightenment to the divinely wise on the dark questions of
God's dealings with the faithful and with the world at large.
Even in 1¹⁷ the beginnings of wisdom were already given to the
faithful.

Two Early Additions—12¹¹ and 12¹², ¹³.

12¹¹,¹². Gunkel (*Schöpfung u. Chaos* 269) was the first to
suggest that 12¹¹,¹² were two successive glosses designed to
prolong the term of 1150 days predicted in 8¹⁴. This suggestion
is obviously right, and is accepted by most leading modern
scholars. In 12⁹ the angel definitely refused to give Daniel
any further information on the *meaning* of his disclosures (so
restored text). But the Massoretes or some earlier reviewer
introduced quite a different sense in 12⁸, and thereby represent
Daniel as again asking 'what shall be the end of these things'.
To this point we shall return later. In the meantime we find
in 12¹¹,¹² two new and different reckonings given by the angel—
reckonings, too, which are in direct conflict with the reckoning
of 1150 days already furnished in 8¹⁴. In 8¹⁴ 1150 days were
to elapse, from the doing away with the daily burnt offering,
till the cleansing of the sanctuary. These two reckonings start
from the same date, i. e. from the removal of the daily burnt
offering. Cf. 8¹⁴, 9²⁷, 11³¹. Both verses are without doubt to
be regarded as later additions, which were made successively
and possibly by the author himself with a view to bringing the
text into accord with history, by adjourning the date of the
fulfilment of the prophecy. As such, these additions, therefore,
must have originated about 165 B.C. Their style accords also
with that of our author. The period mentioned in 12¹¹, i. e.

1290 days, is easy to explain. It obviously defines the duration of the 3½ years. If in the 3½ years (= 42 months = 1260 days : cf. Rev. 11³, 12⁶) we insert an intercalary month, we have 43 months in the 3½ years, and if we take these months as consisting of 30 days each, we arrive at the number 1290. How the 1335 days is to be explained otherwise than on the ground of practical necessity, i. e. the fact that the prediction as to the 1290 days had not been fulfilled, I do not see. It amounts to 45 days or 1½ months more than the 1290 days.

To return now to the relations existing between 12⁸ and 12¹¹,¹²⁻¹³. We have seen in the note on 12⁸ that the reading of the Pesh. and Vulg., 'What shall be after these things?' is a late attempt to make something of a corrupt text, and likewise an attempt which is at variance with the context. In the same note also we saw that the reading of the MT and Th., 'What shall be the end of these things?' was not the question that Daniel would naturally put in accordance with the context, seeing that Daniel had already put this question in 12⁶, and in 12⁷ had received an answer, but in 12⁸ confessed that he *could not understand*. What Daniel wanted to know in 12⁸ was the meaning of the angel's disclosures in 12⁷. But owing to the additions made subsequently in 12¹¹,¹²⁻¹³ it was recognized later in the 2nd cent. A. D., or shortly before, that the text in 12⁶,⁸ needed to be adapted to the additions in 12¹¹,¹²⁻¹³. Hence the question in 12⁶ was transferred by the Massoretes—but not by the LXX nor the Vulg.—from Daniel to one of the angels mentioned ; and in 12⁸ the original question, 'What is the interpretation of these (difficulties) ?' was changed into 'What shall be the end of these things?' These two changes helped in some degree to account for the addition in 12¹¹,¹²⁻¹³.

FIRST ADDITION—BY THE AUTHOR (?)—12¹¹.

12¹¹. *From the time*, &c. : i. e. מֵעֵת הוּסַר, For the construction cf. Jer. 36² מִיּוֹם דִּבַּרְתִּי.

And a horror that appalleth set up : i. e. וְלָתֵת. Here ל with the infinitive appears as a continuation of the perfect הוּסַר in the preceding clause as in Aramaic מִן־דִּי אִתַּעֲדִּי · · · וּלְמִנְתַּן. Cf. 2¹⁶ for a like sequence of verbal forms but with a different nuance. On this sequence in Hebrew, see Driver, *Hebrew Tenses* § 206.

A horror that appalleth. Cf. 8¹³, 9²⁷, 11³¹.

12[12]. *Blessed is he that waiteth.* Cf. Pss. Sol. 18[7]. These
verses contain a further extension of the time limit, the first
extension having already been inserted in 12[11]. Thus 12[12]
belongs to the third edition of the Apocalypse.

The thousand three hundred and five and thirty days. This
term of 1335 days reappears in the *Ascension of Isaiah* 4[12],
from my Comm. on which I repeat the following note. In 4[12]
we read: 'He shall bear sway three years and seven months
and twenty-seven days.' 'Computed according to the Julian
reckoning this period amounts . . . to 1335 days, the actual
number found in Dan. 12[12] and adopted therefrom by our
writer. This period points back to the "time and times and
half a time" in Dan. 7[25], 12[7]; Rev. 12[14]; in other words, three
and a half years. The same period is otherwise described as
forty-two months in Rev. 11[2], 13[5], or as 1260 days in Rev. 11[3],
12[6], in which case the month was reckoned at 30 days, or as
1290 days in Dan. 12[11] and in the Διαθήκη 'Εζεκίου.

'The above three and a half years has a special significance in
apocalyptic literature as the period of the Antichrist, or the
period of the last and worst woes; cf. Rev. 13[5], 12[6,14], . . . This
apocalyptic period has affected . . . Luke 4[25] and James 5[17].
For though the famine in Elijah's time lasted, according to
1 Kings 18[1], three years, it is said in Luke 4[25]; James 5[17] to
have lasted three and a half years.'

12[13]. The book closes with words susceptible of two quite
different interpretations. That this verse is an interpolation
see Introd., § 14 k.

Go thou thy way. Here the MT adds לַקֵּץ 'to the end'. But
since both the LXX and Th. omit this phrase, and since it is
completely otiose, seeing that a few words later we have all
that it imports asserted in the fuller phrase לקץ הימים, I have
excised it from the text. Bevan takes it as synonymous with
this closing phrase. It is, therefore, tautologous. Robertson
Smith, according to Bevan, supposed 'that the first לקץ was
wrongly introduced by a scribe, whose eye, passing from the
preceding לך, caught the last letters of לגרלך in the second half
of the verse'.

Rest: i. e. in thy mind, not in the grave as in Isa. 57[2], or in
Sheol as in Job 3[17].

Both the LXX and Th. add here : ἔτι γάρ εἰσιν ἡμέραι καὶ ὧραι (Th. omits last two words) εἰς ἀναπλήρωσιν συντελείας. These may go back to the original. They imply that Daniel hopes to see and to share in the new kingdom of God on earth, and that in the flesh. Since the first edition of the book was written some time before the re-consecration of the Temple, such a statement as that in the LXX and Th. is perfectly justified. See note on 8[14].

Shalt stand : i. e. shalt live to see and share in the coming kingdom and inherit thy lot therein. עָמַד thus retains its normal meaning in Hebrew. But, when 12[11,12,13] was incorporated in the second and third editions by revisers in 165 B. C., and when the predictions they contained were not realized, then an *abnormal* and unjustifiable meaning, 'thou shalt arise', came of necessity to be attached to this verb. There is, so far as I can discover, no example of this meaning in Classical or late Hebrew : nor in Aramaic. Indeed it is not an Aramaic verb. Here the interpolator abandons the author's role as a writer in the sixth cent. B.C. and writes as a contemporary of the early Maccabees.

In thy lot : i. e. the Seer's lot in the kingdom whose advent was all but due. This was the original meaning of the words. Even St. Paul and the first generation of the Christian Church hoped to enter into life without passing through physical death.

But when the expectations of the Seer or his revisers were not fulfilled a secondary meaning came to be attached to this phrase—'thy lot'. After death he was to arise to share in the kingdom when it was established on the earth.

End of the days : i. e. קץ הימים, which is not synonymous with אחרית הימים in 10[14] or אחרית יומיא in 2[18], much less with עת קץ 'end of the days', which phrases have an eschatological reference to the advent of the kingdom. See note on 12[13] (Transl.).

TRANSLATION

SECTION I

i.e. Chapter I i-19, in the third year of Jehoiakim.

I. 1-2. Jehoiakim in the third year of his reign carried captive to Babylon and also other members of the seed royal and of the nobles. 3-4, 5ᵇ, 5ᵃ, 6-7. Nebuchadnezzar orders Ashpenaz to educate certain noble Jewish youths as pages for the king's service, whom Ashpenaz renamed. 8-17. Daniel and his companions out of loyalty to the Law refused the food assigned by the king, and on a diet of pulse and water proved their superiority physically, mentally, and spiritually to the other youths who accepted the royal regimen. 18-19. When brought before the king, he found none like them, and so they served as pages in the Court of the king.

I.   In the third year of the reign of Jehoiakim king of Judah came Nebuchadnezzar king of Babylon unto Jerusalem
2   and besieged it.   And the Lord gave Jehoiakim king of Judah into his hand.   And part of ⟨the seed royal and of the nobles and part of⟩[1] the vessels of the house of God he carried into the land of Shinar:[2] but the vessels he
3   brought into the treasure-house of his god.   And the king commanded †Ashpenaz† the master of his eunuchs, that he should bring in certain of the children of ⌐the
4   exiles of⌐[3] Israel both of the seed royal and of the nobles; youths in whom was no blemish, but well favoured and skilful in all kinds of wisdom, ⌐and literature⌐,[4] and cunning in knowledge, and understanding science, and such as had ability to stand in the king's palace; and that he should teach them the literature and the tongue of
5ᵇ the Chaldeans: *And that he should nourish them for

---

[1] Context requires the restoration of these words, lost through homoioteleuton.   See Comm. p. 7 sq.

[2] MT adds against Syrʰ and context ' to the house of his god '.

[3] Restored from Th (and LXX here corrupt).   See Comm. p. 12.

[4] Restored from LXX : cf. 1¹⁷.

three years, that at the end thereof they should stand
5ᵃ before the king.   And the king appointed for them a daily
portion of the king's meat, and of the wine which he drank.[1]
6 Now amongst these were, of the children of Judah, Daniel,
7 Hananiah, Mishael, and Azariah.   And the prince of the
eunuchs gave names unto them : unto Daniel (the name
of) Belteshazzar ; and to Hananiah (of) Shadrach ; and
to Mishael, (of) Meshach; and to Azariah, (of) Abed-nebo.[2]
8 But Daniel purposed in his heart that he would not defile
himself with the king's meat, nor with the wine which he
drank : therefore he requested the prince of the eunuchs
9 that he might not defile himself.   Now God made Daniel
to find favour and compassion in the sight of the prince
10 of the eunuchs.   And the prince of the eunuchs said unto
Daniel, I fear my lord the king, who hath appointed your
meat and your drink : lest he should see your faces worse-
liking than the youths that are of your own age and so ye
11 should make my head forfeit to the king.   Then said
Daniel to †the Melzar† ⌜the prince of the eunuchs who
had been appointed⌝ [3] over Daniel, Hananiah, Mishael,
12 and Azariah : Prove thy servants, I beseech thee, ten
days ; and let them give us pulse to eat, and water to
13 drink.   Then let our countenances be looked upon before
thee, and the countenances of the youths that eat of the
king's meat ; and as thou seest deal with thy servants.
14 So he hearkened unto them in this matter, and proved
15 them ten days.   And at the end of the ten days their
countenances appeared fairer, and they were fatter in
flesh, than all the youths which did eat of the king's meat.
16 So †the Melzar† kept taking away their meat, and the
17 wine that they should drink, and gave them pulse.   Now
as for these four youths, God gave them knowledge and
skill in all literature and wisdom : and Daniel had under-
18 standing in every kind of vision and dreams.   And at the
end of the days on which the king had commanded to
bring them in, the prince of the eunuchs brought them in

---

[1] With Marti I have transposed 5ᵇ before 5ᵃ. This change regularizes the
grammar and improves the sense.

[2] Text reads Abed-nego—an obvious corruption of Abed-nebo.

[3] So LXX. MT reads 'whom the prince of the eunuchs had appointed'.

19 before Nebuchadnezzar. And the king spake with them ;
and among them all was found none like Daniel, Hananiah,
Mishael, and Azariah : therefore stood they before the
king.[1]

SECTION II

i.e. Chapter II 1–49ᵃ, I 20–21, II 49ᵇ, in the second year
of Nebuchadnezzar.

II. 1-2. *Troubled by a dream Nebuchadnezzar summons his wise
men to make known to him his dream and its interpretation.*
*3–11. They reply that they are ready to interpret the dream, if
the king makes it known to them, but that they cannot meet both
demands. 12–16. Thereupon the king orders them to be slain,
but at the request of Daniel, who with his companions belonged to
the guild of the wise men, the decree is stayed and Daniel promises
to meet the demands of the king. 17–23. In answer to the prayers
of Daniel and his companions the secret is revealed to him and
thanksgivings are offered to God. 24–30. Daniel is brought at
his own request before the king and declares his readiness to make
known both the dream and its interpretation. 31–5. The dream.
36–45. Its interpretation. 46–7. Homage rendered by the
king to Daniel. 48–9ᵃ, I. 20–1, II. 49ᵇ. Daniel made chief
governor over all the wise men of Babylon. Since Daniel owed
so much to the intercessions of his three brethren, he requests the
king to reward them also. The king does so and, setting them
over the affairs of the province of Babylon, finds them ten times
wiser than all the other wise men of his realm. Daniel appointed
to be the chief governor next to the king.*

II.   And in the second year of the reign of Nebuchadnezzar,
        Nebuchadnezzar dreamed dreams : and his spirit was
2   troubled, and his sleep **brake from** [2] him. Then the king
        commanded to call the magicians, and the enchanters, and
        the sorcerers, and the Chaldeans for to tell the king his
        dreams. So they came in and stood before the king.

---

[1] I have restored 1²⁰⁻¹ to their original context after 2⁴⁹ᵃ. See Comm.
pp. 52–4.

[2] So with other scholars I have restored the text as in 6¹⁹ ⁽¹⁸⁾. Sym.
renders both passages alike. MT has ' was done for '—very questionable
Hebrew. See p. 26 sq.

3 And the king said unto them, I have dreamed a dream,
4 and my spirit is troubled to know the dream. Then spake
the Chaldeans to the king *and said*,[1] O king, live for ever :
tell thy servants the dream, and we will show the inter-
5 pretation. The king answered and said to the Chaldeans
the thing †is gone†[2] from me : if ye make not known unto
me the dream and the interpretation thereof, ye shall be
cut in pieces, and *your houses* be made a dunghill.[3]
6 But if ye declare the dream and the interpretation thereof,
ye shall receive of me gifts and rewards and great honour :
therefore declare me the dream and the interpretation
7 thereof. They answered the second time and said, Let
the king tell his servants the dream, and so will we show
8 the interpretation. The king answered and said I know
of a certainty that ye would gain time, because ye see the
9 word from me is sure : That if ye do not make known
unto me the dream, the judgement upon you is inevitable :
for lying and corrupt words ye have concerted to speak
before me, till the time be changed : therefore tell me the
dream, and so I shall know that ye can show me the
10 interpretation thereof. The Chaldeans answered before
the king and said, there is not a man upon the earth that
can show the king's matter : forasmuch as no king, be
he never so great and mighty, hath asked such a thing of
11 any magician, or enchanter, or Chaldean. And it is a
difficult thing that the king requireth, and there is none
other that can show it before the king, except the gods,
12 whose dwelling is not with flesh. For this cause the
king was angry and very furious, and issued a command-

[1] So Haupt, Kamphausen, Marti, &c., emend the corrupt MT text 'in
Aramaic'. See p. 28 sq.

[2] Better render 'the thing from me is sure', i. e. shall certainly be carried
out. See p. 30 sq.

[3] So MT, but the LXX 'your possessions be confiscated to the crown'.
Here the LXX is supported by the Vulg. See p. 31. The same rendering
is given in 3²⁹ i.e. ἡ οἰκία αὐτοῦ δημευθήσεται and in Ezra 6¹¹, both by the
LXX and Vulg., though in slightly different words, and again in 1 Esdras 6³¹
τὰ ὑπάρχοντα αὐτοῦ εἶναι βασιλικά. In 2⁵, 3²⁹ of our text Th. renders 'your
houses will be destroyed (διαρπαγήσονται)'. Jensen, K.B., vi. 363 suggests
that נוֹלִי (נוֹלִי) is a word from the Assyrian namâlu (nawâlu) 'ruin'. The
text is uncertain.

13 ment to destroy all the wise men of Babylon ; So the
decree went forth that the wise men should be slain ; and
⌐Daniel and his companions were sought to be slain¬[1]

14 Then Daniel returned answer with counsel and prudence
to Arioch the captain of the king's guard who had gone

15 forth to slay the wise men of Babylon. He answered
and said to Arioch the king's captain, Wherefore is the
decree from the king so severe ? Then Arioch made the

16 thing known unto Daniel. And Daniel went in and implored the king to give him time, and so he would make
it his task to show the king the interpretation.[2]

17 Then Daniel went to his house and made the thing known

18 to Hananiah, Mishael, and Azariah, his companions : and
*so they made it their task[3] to implore compassion from
the God of heaven concerning this secret; that Daniel
and his companions should not perish with the rest of

19 the wise men of Babylon. Then was the secret revealed
unto Daniel *in a vision on that self-same night.[4]   Then

---

[1] So LXX and Vulg. See p. 34. The MT has a conflation of constructions :
'sought Daniel and his companions to be slain '. Th. and Pesh. have the
active construction : ' sought Daniel and his companions to slay (them) '.

[2] In my note on this verse I have rendered this clause 'and (so) it would
be his task to show'. But the rendering above reproduces the peculiar
idiom ופשרא להחויא in the text with sufficient accuracy. The idiom
expresses intention ' and so he *would* show'. Here the ו = 'and so' as in
$2^{4, 9, 24, 49}$, 6^2. בעה is never followed by ל and the Inf. in Ezra or Daniel, but
by די. Cf. 2^{16}.

[3] In my note I have followed the MT and sought to make the best of
a very difficult construction, and to bring it into line with the same idiom in
2^{16}. But the idiom in 2^{16} follows after a request, whereas in 2^{18} it follows
after a simple statement of fact. Now our author uses ו to express an
intention : after a command in 2^{13}, 5^2, 6^3, or after a request 2^{49}, in which
case it can be rendered ' that ', but apparently *not after a mere statement of
fact*. The LXX reads καὶ παρήγγειλε ... ζητῆσαι i.e. למבעא ... ואמר
' and bade (them) ... implore'. In 3^4 where παραγγέλλω recurs in the LXX
it is a rendering of אמר. See Introd. § 20, t.

[4] So LXX ἐν ὁράματι ἐν αὐτῇ τῇ νυκτί = בחזוא בה ליליא. This is a
familiar idiom in our author. Observe also how forcible this text is. Daniel
and his companions receive an immediate answer to their prayer, whereas in
10^{13} owing to strife between the angelic patrons of the nations the vision is
delayed three weeks. We cannot conceive the translator recasting the text in
this fashion. In 7^2 there is a parallel expression בחזוא עם ליליא (MT, Vulg,
where the LXX and Pesh. have the ordinary expression ' in a vision of the
night'. Th. omits the phrase). But in 7^7 (LXX, Pesh., Vulg.: Th. omits), ^{18}
(LXX, Th., Vulg.: Pesh. omits) the ordinary expression ' in a vision of the

Daniel blessed the God of heaven. Daniel answered and said,

20   Blessed be the name of God
From everlasting to everlasting;
For wisdom and might are his:

21   And he changeth the seasons and the times:
He removeth kings and setteth up kings:
He giveth wisdom unto the wise,
And knowledge to them that know understanding.

22   He revealeth the deep and secret things:
He knoweth what is in darkness,
And the light dwelleth with him.

23   I thank and praise thee, O thou God of my fathers,
Who hast given me wisdom and insight[1]
And hast now made known unto me what we besought
of thee;
For thou hast made known unto us the king's matter.

24 Therefore Daniel went in unto Arioch, whom the king
had appointed to destroy the wise men of Babylon,[2] and
said thus unto him; Destroy not the wise men of Babylon:
bring me in before the king, and so I will show unto the
king the interpretation.

25 Then Arioch brought in Daniel before the king in haste,
and said thus unto him, I have found a man of the children
of the exiles of Judaea that will make known unto the

26 king the interpretation. The king answered and said to
Daniel, named Belteshazzar, Art thou able to make known
unto me the dream which I have seen, and the interpreta-

27 tion thereof? Daniel answered before the king and said,
The secret which the king hath demanded, it is not wise
men, enchanters, magicians, or determiners, that can show

28 (it) unto the king; but there is a God in heaven that

night' appears to be original. Our author thus appears to use two forms to
express this thought but never the third which the MT has in 7[7, 13] 'in the
night visions' (בחזוי ליליא). Moreover the context is against the plural.
7 contains but one vision, not a series of visions.

[1] So LXX φρόνησιν, as the context also requires. MT reads 'might'.
See note on p. 38.

[2] MT and Pesh. add 'he went' against LXX, Th., and Vulg.

revealeth secrets, and he hath made known unto the king
29 Nebuchadnezzar what shall be in the latter days. As for
thee, O king, Thy thoughts came ⟨into thy heart⟩[1] upon
thy bed, as to what should come to pass hereafter : and
he that revealeth secrets hath made known to thee what
30 shall come to pass. But as for me, this secret is not
revealed to me for any wisdom that I have more than any
living, but to the intent that the interpretation may be
made known to the king, and that thou mayest know the
28c the thoughts of thy heart. [Thy dream and the visions
of thy head upon thy bed, are these].[2]
31 Thou, O king, sawest, and behold a great image. This
image was great and its brightness was excellent : it stood
32 before thee ; and the aspect thereof was terrible. As for
this image, his head was of fine gold, his breast and his
33 arms of silver, his belly and his thighs of brass, his legs
34 of iron, his feet part of iron and part of clay. Thou
sawest till the stone was cut out ⌜from a mountain⌝[3]
without hands, which smote the image upon his feet
that were of iron and clay, and broke them in pieces.
35 Then was the *clay, the iron,[4] the brass, the silver and the
gold, broken in pieces together, and became like the chaff
of the summer threshing-floors ; and the wind carried them
away, that no place was found for them : and the stone
that smote the image became a great mountain, and filled
36 the whole earth. This is the dream ; and we will tell the
37 interpretation thereof before the king. Thou, O king,
art the king of kings, unto whom the God of heaven hath
given the kingdom, the power, and the strength, and the
38 glory ; and wheresoever the children of men dwell, the
beasts of the field and the fowls of the heaven hath he

[1] Restored. See note, p. 41 sq.

[2] I have restored this clause to its natural position if it belongs to the
original at all. It is omitted by the LXX. In any case it is wrongly read
at the close of 2^{28}. It is noteworthy that neither here nor in $4^{2\,(5),\,7\,(10)}$,
$7^{1,\,15}$ does the LXX contain the non-Semitic expression (see Comm., p. 42)
'visions of the head'. $4^{2\,b\,(5\,b),\,7\,(10)}$ occur in the large interpolation $4^{2\,b\,(5\,b)-7\,(10)}$.

[3] Restored with LXX, Th., Josephus, and 2^{45} where in the text definite
mention of 'the mountain' presupposes the prior occurrence of the indefinite
phrase 'a mountain'. So Justin, *Dial.* 70.

[4] So the order in Th., whereas MT, LXX, Vulg., read 'the iron, the
clay' wholly against the sense of the context. See 2^{45}.

given into thine hand, and hath made thee to rule over
39 them all: thou art the head of gold. And after thee shall
arise another kingdom inferior to thee; and another,
a third kingdom of brass, which shall bear rule over all
40 the earth. And the fourth kingdom shall be strong as
iron: forasmuch as iron breaketh in pieces and shattereth
all things [1] so shall it break in pieces and crush ⌜the whole
41 earth⌝.[2] And whereas thou sawest the feet and toes, part
of potter's clay, and part of iron, it shall be a divided
kingdom; but there shall be in it the strength of the iron,
forasmuch as thou sawest the iron mixed with miry clay.
42 And as the toes of the feet were part of iron, and part of
clay, so the kingdom shall be partly strong and partly
43 broken. And whereas thou sawest the iron mixed with
miry clay they shall mingle themselves with the seed of
men, but they shall not cleave one to another, even as
44 iron doth not mingle with clay. And in the days of those
kings shall the God of heaven set up a kingdom, which shall
never be destroyed, nor shall the sovereignty thereof be
left to another people; but it shall break in pieces and
consume all these kingdoms, and it shall stand for ever.
45 Forasmuch as thou sawest that a stone was cut out of the
mountain without hands, and that it broke in pieces the
clay, the iron, the brass, the silver, and the gold; a great
God hath made known to the king what shall come to
pass hereafter: and the dream is certain, and the inter-
46 pretation thereof sure. Then the king Nebuchadnezzar
fell upon his face, and worshipped Daniel, and commanded that they should offer an oblation and sweet
47 odours unto him. The king answered unto Daniel, and
said, Of a truth your God is [3]a God of gods[3] and a Lord of
kings, and a revealer of secrets, seeing that thou hast

---

[1] MT adds a dittograph on the preceding words: 'and as iron that
crusheth'. LXX defective and corrupt. See note on p. 47.

[2] On this phrase see note on p. 47 seq. Supplied from the LXX: cf. 7[23].
MT reads corruptly 'forasmuch as iron breaketh in pieces and shattereth all
things: and as iron that crusheth all these, shall it break in pieces and crush'.

[3] Not to be rendered 'the God of gods'. The emphatic forms are not
used. Daniel accommodates his words to the views of Nebuchadnezzar.
See note on 11[36] (Transl.) where the Hebrew repeats the same indefinite
phrase 'a God of gods'. In 2[45] we have the unemphatic phrase 'a great
God'—not 'the great God' as the R.V. renders.

48 been able to reveal this secret. Then the king made
Daniel great, and gave him many great gifts, and made
him to rule over the whole province of Babylon, and to
be chief governor over all the wise men of Babylon.
49ᵃ And Daniel requested the king to appoint[1] Shadrach,
Meshach, and Abed-nebo over the affairs of the province
I. 20 of Babylon. And in every matter of wisdom and understanding, concerning which the king inquired of them, he
found them ten times better than all the magicians and
21 enchanters that were in all his realm.[2] *And Daniel
II. 49ᵇ continued unto the first year of Cyrus the king.[3] But
Daniel was in the gate of the king.

SECTION III

i. e. Chapter III. 1-30, in the eighteenth year of Nebuchadnezzar.

III. 1-7. *In his eighteenth year Nebuchadnezzar dedicates a
golden image to do honour to his god and to celebrate his conquests from India to Ethiopia—including the conquest of Jerusalem in this year (see p. 56 seq.), and summons the rulers of
all the subject states to worship the image.* 8-12. *Shadrach,
Meshach, and Abed-nebo accused before the king of refusing to
render this worship.* 13-18. *Despite the king's threats they
maintain their loyalty to the God of Israel.* 19-27. *Therefore
they are cast into the burning fiery furnace, but are delivered
unharmed therefrom.* 28-30. *The king then recognizes them as
servants of the Most High God and issues a decree against any
nation that speaks against their God.*

III. 1 ⌜In the eighteenth year⌝[4] Nebuchadnezzar the king,
⌜when he had brought under his rule cities and provinces
and all that dwell upon the earth from India to Ethiopia⌝,[5]

---

[1] Literally 'requested the king and he appointed'. This Aramaic idiom
where the following coordinate clause expresses the fulfilment of the request
or command in the preceding clause recurs in 5²⁹, 6², ¹⁷, ²⁵. See notes on
2¹⁶, ¹⁸.

[2] On the necessity of transferring 1²⁰⁻²¹ to their original position here,
see p. 52 seq.

[3] This is probably a later addition.

[4] Restored to text in accordance with LXX and Th.

[5] Restored from LXX. These clauses supply the reason for the erection
of the great image by the king.

made an image of gold, whose height was threescore
cubits, and the breadth thereof six cubits : he set it up in
2 the plain of Dura, in the province of Babylon. Then
Nebuchadnezzar sent to gather together the satraps, the
deputies, and the governors, the judges, †the treasurers†,[1]
the counsellors, the sheriffs, and all the rulers of the
provinces, to come to the dedication of the image which
3 Nebuchadnezzar the king had set up.   Then the satraps,
the deputies, and the governors, the judges, †the trea-
surers†,[1] the counsellors, the sheriffs, and all the rulers
of the provinces were gathered together unto the dedication of the image that Nebuchadnezzar the king had set
4, 5 up. Then the herald cried aloud, To you it is commanded,
O peoples, nations, and languages, that at what time ye
hear the sound of the cornet, pipe, harp, sackbut, psaltery,
dulcimer, and all kinds of music, ye fall down and worship
the golden image that Nebuchadnezzar the king hath set
6 up : But whoso falleth not down and worshippeth shall
the same hour be cast into the midst of a burning fiery
furnace.
7 Therefore at that time, when all the peoples heard the
sound of the cornet, pipe, harp, sackbut, psaltery, and all
kinds of music, all the peoples, the nations, and the languages fell down and worshipped the golden image that
8 Nebuchadnezzar the king had set up.   Wherefore at that
time certain Chaldeans came near, and brought accusation
9 against the Jews.   They answered and said[2] : O king,
10 live for ever.   Thou, O king, hast made a decree that
every man that shall hear the sound of the cornet, pipe,
harp, sackbut, psaltery, and dulcimer and all kinds of
music, shall fall down and worship the golden image :
11 and whoso falleth not down and worshippeth shall be
12 cast into the midst of a burning fiery furnace.   There are
certain Jews whom thou hast appointed over the affairs
of the province of Babylon, Shadrach, Meshach, and

[1] Rejected by many scholars on various grounds. See p. 62.
[2] MT and all versions but the LXX (Th. is defective) add ' to Nebuchadnezzar the king', but the idiom of our author requires ' before ' and not ' to '
where a Divine or semi-divine being is addressed.   See p. 65 ; also
Introd., § 20. w.

Abed-nebo; these men, O king*, have not hearkened unto thy decree:[1] they serve not 'thy god',[2] nor worship the

13 golden image which thou hast set up. Then Nebuchadnezzar in his rage and fury commanded to bring Shadrach, Meshach, and Abed-nebo. Then these men were brought

14 before the king. Nebuchadnezzar answered and said unto them, Is it true,[3] O Shadrach, Meshach and Abed-nebo that ye serve not my god, nor worship the golden

15 image which I have set up? Now if ye be ready at what time ye hear the sound of the cornet, pipe, harp, sackbut, psaltery, and dulcimer, and all kinds of music to fall down and worship the image which I have made (well): but if ye worship not, ye shall be cast the same hour into the

---

[1] So with Th. (and also LXX and Vulg.) we should read לא שמעו מלכא לטעמך and not as the MT 'have not regarded thee'. See p. 66 sq.

[2] So *Qr.* לֵאלָהָךְ i.e. Bel. (*Kt.* לאלהיך): so also read in 3[18]. In 3[14] read לֵאלָהָי with Erfurt MS. (MT לֵאלָהָי): cf. 4[5] אֱלָהִי. Next in 4[5, 6, 15], 5[11] רוח אלהין קדישין = 'spirit of the holy gods'. Here Nebuchadnezzar speaks as an idolator. (Grotius, Driver, Behrmann, Marti, &c.). But Montgomery (p. 153), maintains that אלהין means 'god' and not 'gods', and quotes Sachau's edition of the *Aram. Pap.*, i.e. Aḥ. 126 (where the plural has a sing. verb). But Cowley always takes אלהן (whether in its absolute, construct, or emphatic forms) as a plural, and adopts Perles' suggestion that, in this solitary case out of twenty or more, אלהיא is a corruption of אלהא. Montgomery quotes the Phoenician inscription of Eshmunazar (fourth to third cent. B.C.) *CIS.* I. 3[9, 22] האלנם הקדשם, which (p. 227) he recognizes as polytheistic), yet he refers to Aḥ. 115 (Cowley) as supporting the sing. meaning of אלהן, and claims Lidzbarski, *Eph.* iii. 255 and Epstein as maintaining the same view, though he does not quote the Aramaic phrase. But Lidzbarski, Epstein, and Cowley agree in rendering this word as a plural: the first of the three translating רחים אלהן by 'götterliebend', Nöldeke, Epstein, and Cowley by 'beloved of (the) gods'. Similarly in 3[25] בר אלהין means 'son of the gods'. Montgomery finds that the plural *ilâni* 'gods' is used as a sing. in Akkadian, and tries to trace the like supposed use. But this fact still further strengthens the grounds for taking אלהן as a pl., seeing that in Aḥ., which was translated into Aramaic under Akkadian influences, the word is always, save in one corrupt passage, i.e. l. 115, treated as a pl. Bauer and Leander, *Gram. d. Biblisch. Aram.*, p. 305, writes : 'Hier bedeutet אלהן und אלהיא immer "(die) Götter", nur 6[17, 21] hat eine Lesart (unrichtig) אלהיך = "dein Gott"'. Ginsburg in both these passages reads the sing. form אלהך and אלהא.

[3] See note on p. 67, where Lidzbarski is quoted as showing that הַצְדָא ('true') is an Aramaic word and not of Persian origin.

midst of a burning fiery furnace; and what god is there
16 that can deliver you out of my hands? Shadrach,
Meshach, and Abed-nebo answered and said to [1]king
Nebuchadnezzar,[1] We have no need to answer thee in this
17 matter. ⌜For⌝[2] there is a God whom we serve who is able
18 to deliver us from the burning fiery furnace; and he will
deliver us out of thine hands, O king.[3] But if not, be it
known unto thee, O king, that we will not serve thy god,
nor worship the golden image which thou hast set up.
19 Then was Nebuchadnezzar filled with fury, and the form
of his visage was changed against Shadrach, Meshach,
and Abed-nebo: (wherefore) he spake and commanded
that they should heat the furnace seven times more than
20 it was wont to be heated. And he commanded certain
mighty men that were in his army to bind Shadrach,
Meshach, and Abed-nebo, (and)[4] to cast them into the
21 burning fiery furnace. Then these men were bound in
their mantles, their trousers, and their hats, and their
other garments, and were cast into the burning fiery
22 furnace. Therefore, because the king's commandment
was urgent and the furnace exceeding hot, the flame of
the fire slew those men that took up Shadrach, Meshach,
24 and Abed-nebo.[5] Then Nebuchadnezzar was alarmed,
and rose up in haste: he spake and said unto his counsellors, Did we not cast three men bound into the midst
25 of the fire? They answered and said †unto†[6] the king,
True, O king. He answered and said, Lo, I see four
men loose, walking in the midst of the fire, and they have
no hurt; and the aspect of the fourth is like a son of the

[1] I have followed the LXX, Th., and Vulg. in connecting the two words
'King Nebuchadnezzar'. The MT separates them 'to the king: O Nebuchadnezzar'.

[2] So LXX, Th., Pesh., Vulg. The MT reads corruptly 'if' and spoils
the force of the reply of the three Confessors. See p. 68 sqq.

[3] So LXX, Th., Pesh., Vulg. MT reads 'hand'.

[4] Restored on Marti's suggestion. See p. 71.

[5] The MT adds here against the LXX and the context 'And these three
men Shadrach, Meshach, and Abed-nebo, fell down bound into the midst of
the fiery furnace'. Seeing that they were 'hurled' into the furnace, it is
more than gratuitous to add that they 'fell down bound'. See p. 72 sqq.

[6] Here our author's usage requires 'before'. See Introd., § 20.

26 gods. Then Nebuchadnezzar came near to the mouth of the burning fiery furnace: he spake, and said, Shadrach, Meshach, and Abed-nebo, ye servants of the Most High God, come forth, and come hither. Then Shadrach, Meshach, and Abed-nebo came forth out of the midst of
27 the fire. And the satraps, the deputies, and the governors, and the king's counsellors, being gathered together, saw these men, that the fire had no power upon their bodies, nor was the hair of their head singed, neither were their mantles changed, nor had the smell of fire passed on
28 them. Nebuchadnezzar answered, and said, Blessed be the God of Shadrach, Meshach, and Abed-nebo, who hath sent his angel, and delivered his servants that trusted in him, and have changed the king's word, and have yielded their bodies ⌈to the fire⌉,[1] that they might not serve nor worship any other god except their own God.
29 Therefore, I make a decree that every people, nation, and language which shall speak anything amiss against the God of Shadrach, Meshach, and Abed-nebo, shall be cut in pieces, and their houses shall be made a dunghill: because there is no other god that is able to deliver after
30 this sort. Then the king caused Shadrach, Meshach, and Abed-nebo to prosper in the province of Babylon.

SECTION IV

i.e. Chapter IV and III. 31-3, in the eighteenth year of Nebuchadnezzar—the same year of his imperial conquests—the nemesis following quickly on the heels of his self-glorification.

IV. 1-2. *Nebuchadnezzar in the midst of his prosperity has a dream, which* 7ᵇ (10ᵇ)-15 (18) *he recounts and requests Daniel, the chief of his wise men to interpret.* 16 (19)-25 (28). *Daniel gives the interpretation.* 26 (29)-30 (33). *Its fulfilment within a year.* 31 (34)-34 (37). *The king's repentance and restoration.* [*Here the text has been so drastically revised that the recovery of its original form is impossible, though the substance may be accepted as trustworthy*]. III. 31-33 (MT=LXX iv. 34 c) *The king's Edict—closing the section as in* III. *and* VI.

[1] Restored from LXX and Th. Cf. 1 Cor. 13⁹.

IV. 1 (4) ⌜In the eighteenth year of his reign⌝[1] Nebuchadnezzar
     said : I Nebuchadnezzar was at rest in mine house, and
  2 (5) flourishing in my palace. I saw a dream which made me
     afraid ; and ⌜fear fell upon me.⌝[2]

7[b] (10[b]) Upon my bed I saw and behold a tree in the midst of
     the earth,
     [And the height thereof was great :][3]
  8 (11) And the tree grew and became strong,
     And the height thereof began to reach unto heaven
     And the sight thereof to the end of all the earth.
  9 (12) The leaves thereof were fair and the fruit thereof much
     [And in it was meat for all :][4]

[1] This note of time is preserved only by the LXX. It is in keeping with
our author's method throughout the book. See note on 3[1]: also Introd., § 4. *a–e.*

[2] Restored from LXX : IV. 2[b]–7[a] (5[b]–10[a]). *The MT and the Versions dependent on it make the following interpolation which is omitted by the LXX and
contains idioms at variance with our author's usage, to which attention is drawn
in the notes on pp. 79–82, 87–9. Observe the flagrant misuse of 'before' in
4[4] (7), 5 (8) ad fin. The interpolator or redactor has also thrown the text into confusion by abandoning the order of events observed in chapters 3 and 6, in both of
which the prescripts of the king are preceded by a large body of narrative. The
LXX which knows nothing of 4[2b–7 a] (5b–10 a) preserves the original order of the
text, according to which the king in his difficulty at once consulted Daniel, 4[15] (18),
and not first Daniel's subordinates and then Daniel. Again the LXX preserves
the narrative form and adds the imperial prescript at the end of the chapter as
in 3 and 6, whereas the MT attempts to cast the entire chapter into the form of
a prescript, but the redactor carelessly forgets in 4[16], 25–30 (19, 28 seqq.) to transform
the narrative form in the third person into that of the prescript form in the first.*
IV. 2[b]–7[a] (5[b]–10[a]). 2[b] (5[b]) And thoughts upon my bed and the visions of my
     head troubled me.
  3 (6) Therefore made I a decree to bring in all the wise men of Babylon
     before me, that they might make known unto me the interpretation of
  4 (7) the dream. Then came in the magicians, the enchanters, the Chaldeans,
     and the soothsayers : and I told the dream before them ; but they did
  5 (8) not make known unto me the interpretation thereof. But †at the last†
     Daniel came in before me, whose name was Belteshazzar, according to
     the name of my god, and in whom is the spirit of the holy gods : and I
  6 (9) told the dream before him : O Belteshazzar, master of the magicians,
     because I myself know that the spirit of the holy gods is in thee, and no
  7 (10) secret troubleth thee, ⌜hear⌝* the visions of my dream that I have seen,
     and tell the interpretation thereof. And the visions of my head.

[3] Bracketed as a dittograph of 8 (11) γ. A gloss from 4[18] (21).
[4] Bracketed as a dittograph of 9 (12) ε.

* Here with Th. I insert 'hear', i.e. ἄκουσον (= שְׁמַע). Even the interpolator of 4[3–7 a], 6–10 a) could not make the author represent the king as

> The beasts of the field were sheltering under it,
> And the fowls of the heaven dwelling in the branches
>   thereof,
> And all flesh was being fed of it.

10 (13) I saw* in the vision[1] of my head upon my bed and
behold a watcher, even a holy one, came down from
11 (14) heaven. He cried aloud and said thus,

> Hew down the tree and cut off his branches
> Shake off his leaves, and scatter his fruit :
> Let the beasts get away from under it,
> And the fowls from his branches.

12 (15) Nevertheless leave the stump of his roots in the earth,
> Even with a band of iron and brass, in the tender grass
>   of the field,
> And let it be wet with the dew of heaven,
> And let his portion be with the beasts in the grass of
>   the earth :

13 (16) Let his heart be changed from man's,
> And let a beast's heart be given unto him ;
> And let seven times pass over him.

14 (17) The sentence is by the decree of the watchers, and by
the word of the holy ones is the decision,[2] to the intent
that the living may know that the Most High ruleth in
the kingdom of men, and giveth it to whomsoever he will,
and setteth up over it the lowliest of men.

---

[1] So Th. LXX reads 'in my vision' (?) (ἐν τῷ ὕπνῳ μου) : MT, Pesh., and
Vulg. corruptly 'in the visions ("vision" Pesh. and Vulg.) of my head
upon my bed'—from the same hand as 4²ᵇ ⁽⁶ᵇ⁾ apparently. Perhaps the
LXX is simply an abbreviation of the text preserved by Th. Cf. LXX 7¹
for a like use of ὕπνος. See § 14. f.

[2] Montgomery (p. 237) appears to be right in assigning this meaning to
שאלתא. He compares שאילת דיניך in the Targ. of Jer. 12¹ where it
renders משפטים. Its parallel above פתגמא 'decree' supports this rendering.

requiring Belteshazzar to tell him the dream in 4⁷ ᵃ ⁽¹⁰ ᵃ⁾ seeing that the king
begins forthwith in the next clause, 4¹⁰ ᵇ, to recount his dream. See p. 89.

LXX (see MT in foot-note).

15 (18) I was greatly alarmed at these things and my sleep departed from my eyes. And I rose up early from my bed and called Daniel, the chief of the wise men and the master of the interpreters of dreams. And I told him the dream and he made known to me all its interpretation.[1]

16 (19) Then Daniel, whose name was Belteshazzar, was appalled for a while, and his thoughts alarmed him. The king answered and said, Belteshazzar, let not the dream or the interpretation alarm thee. Belteshazzar answered and said, My lord, the dream be to them that hate thee, and the interpretation to thine adversaries.

17 (20) The tree which thou sawest, which grew and became strong, whose height began to reach unto heaven, and the
18 (21) sight thereof to all the earth; whose leaves were fair and and the fruit thereof much, and in it was meat for all; under which the beasts of the field were dwelling and upon which the fowls of heaven were having their habita-
19 (22) tion: it is thou, O king, that art grown and become strong; for thy greatness is grown, and hath reached unto heaven,
20 (23) and thy dominion unto the end of the earth. And whereas the king saw a watcher, even an holy one, coming down from heaven, and saying, Hew down the tree, and destroy it; nevertheless leave the stump of the roots thereof in the earth, even with a band of iron and brass, in the tender grass of the field; and let it be wet with the dew of heaven, and let his portion be with the beasts of the field, till seven
21 (24) times pass over him; this is the interpretation, O king, it is the decree of the Most High, which is come upon my

---

[1] For 4[15 (18)] I have given a rendering of the LXX. The MT reads as follows: 'This dream I King Nebuchadnezzar have seen: and thou, O Belte-shazzar, declare the interpretation; forasmuch as all the wise men of my kingdom are not able to make known unto me the interpretation; but thou art able, for the spirit of the holy gods is in thee'.

On p. 93 I have shown that the MT here stands or falls with 4[2b–7 a (5b–10 a)]. It contains the form דנה חלמא 'this dream' a solecism in our author who elsewhere always places this pronoun after its noun (11 times). Further it contains another example of the late order 'King Nebuchadnezzar' instead of 'Nebuchadnezzar the King'. Here, however, it may be the Massoretes to whom this late order of the words is due, since the Pesh. and Vulg. support the older order

22 (25) lord the king: that thou shalt be driven from men, and thy dwelling shall be with the beasts of the field, and thou shalt be made to eat grass as oxen, and shalt be wet with the dew of heaven, and seven times shall pass over thee; until thou know that the Most High ruleth in the kingdom 23 (26) of men, and giveth it to whomsoever he will. And whereas commandment was given to leave the stump of the tree roots; thy kingdom shall be sure unto thee, after that 24 (27) thou shalt have known that the heavens do rule. Wherefore, O king, let my counsel be acceptable unto thee, and break off thy sins by righteousness, and thine iniquities by showing mercy to the poor ; if there may be a lengthen- 25 (28) ing of thy tranquillity. All this came upon Nebuchadnezzar 26 (29) the King.[1] At the end of twelve months he was walking 27 (30) on the roof of the royal palace of Babylon. The king answered, Is not this great Babylon, which I have built for a royal dwelling place, for the might of my power, and 28 (31) for the glory of my majesty? While the word was in the king's mouth, there fell a voice from heaven, To thee it is spoken, O Nebuchadnezzar the king: the kingdom is 29 (32) departed from thee. And thou shalt be driven from men, and thy dwelling shall be with the beasts of the field; thou shalt be made to eat grass as oxen, and seven times shall pass over thee ; until thou know that the Most High ruleth in the kingdom of men, and giveth it to whomsoever he will.

30 (33) The same hour was the thing fulfilled upon Nebuchadnezzar : and he was driven from men, and did eat grass as oxen, and his body was wet with the dew of heaven, till his hair was grown as eagles' feathers, and his nails as birds' claws.

---

[1] The A.V., R.V., and even the latest Commentary—that of Montgomery —misrepresent the MT, Th., Pesh., and Vulg. by transposing the words and rendering ' King Nebuchadnezzar '. This point is important since the latter order is late. The Aramaic of our author gives the late order once in three times, but there is no justification for wrongly exaggerating the lateness of the Aramaic. The offence is repeated in the A.V. and R.V. in 4[28].

MT

The MT IV. 31-4 (34-7) with the Versions in agreement with it can only be regarded as a redaction of the original. It reads as follows. The LXX varies greatly but observes the idioms of our author, whereas the MT does not always do so.

IV. 31 (34) And at the end of the days I Nebuchadnezzar lifted up mine eyes to heaven
And mine understanding returned to me,
And I blessed the Most High,
And praised and honoured him that liveth for ever.
For his dominion is an everlasting dominion,
And his kingdom from generation to generation.[1]

32 (35) And all the inhabitants of the earth are as persons of no account:
And he doeth according to his will in the army of heaven,
[And among the inhabitants of the earth][2]
And none can stay his hand,
Or say unto him[3] What doest thou?

33 (36) At the same time mine understanding returned unto me;
And for the glory of my kingdom my majesty and my splendour returned unto me,
And my counsellors and my lords sought unto me;
And I was established in my kingdom,
And excellent greatness was added unto me.

34 (37) Now I Nebuchadnezzar praise and extol and honour the King of heaven:[4]
For all his works are truth, and his ways judgement:
And those that walk in pride he is able to humiliate.

[1] If this couplet came from our author we should expect (though it has some support from 7[14], see below),
' And his kingdom is an everlasting kingdom
And his dominion from generation to generation ',
as it occurs in 3[33] MT, the genuineness of which is unquestioned. See p. 100 for a possible restoration of the text. In 7[14] however, we find:
' His dominion is an everlasting dominion which shall not pass away, and his kingdom that which shall not be destroyed.'
But see note on Transl. 7[14].

[2] An obvious dittograph and a weakening of the context. See line 1.

[3] Our author's usage here would require: 'say before him'.

[4] This title is not assigned to God by our author elsewhere. Is it also due to the redactor? Our author uses the phrases 'God of heaven', 2[18, 19, 44] or 'Most High' 4[21 (24)], 7[8], or 'God of gods' 2[47], or 'Lord of kings' 2[47], 'Lord of heaven' (5[23]), 'Most High God' 3[26], 5[18], &c.

LXX

There is nothing in the MT IV. 31-4 corresponding to the following clauses in the LXX. And yet all the clauses or expressions save two or three are those of our author. There is no misuse of his idioms such as we find in the MT IV. 31, 32. I have given Swete's numbering, but rearranged the order of the clauses. There is no hope of recovering the original form of IV. 31-4.

IV. 30[a] I Nebuchadnezzar, king of Babylon, was bound for seven years. They made me eat hay (χόρτον) as an ox,[1] and I eat of the grass of the earth.

    30[c] And my hair became as the †wings of an eagle, my nails as (the claws) of a lion.†[2] My flesh was changed and my heart (also).[3] I walked naked along with the beasts of the earth.[4]

    30[b] And after seven years I gave my soul unto prayer and I made supplication regarding my sins before [5] the Lord the God of heaven [6]—yea I prayed regarding mine iniquities[7] to the great God of gods.[8] And at the end of seven years [9] the time of my redemption came, and my sins and mine iniquities were paid in full before the God of heaven.[6]

    30[d] I saw a dream and thoughts took hold of me, and after an interval a deep sleep [10] seized me and a heavy slumber[11] fell upon me. And behold an angel called unto me from heaven [12] saying Nebuchadnezzar serve the holy God of heaven [6] and give glory to the Most High.[13] The

33 (36) sovereignty of thy nation is restored unto thee. At that time my kingdom was restored unto me and my glory given back unto me.

34 (37) To the Most High [14] I give thanks and praise.

    [1] Cf. 4[30 (33)].   [2] Cf. 4[30 (33)].

    [3] Cf. 4[13 (16)], 5[21].   [4] Cf. 4[13 (16)], 22 (25).

    [5] I. e. κατὰ πρόσωπον, i e. קְדָם. Contrast this correct idiom with the blunder in MT 4[32 (35)].

    [6] Cf. 2[18, 19, 37, 44].   [7] Cf. 4[24 (27)].

    [8] Cf. 2[47].   [9] Cf. 4[13 (16)], 23 (26).

    [10] Cf. 10[9].   [11] Cf. 10[9].   [12] Cf. 4[23 (26)].

    [13] Cf. 3[26], 4[17 (20), 24 (27)], &c.   [14] Cf. 4[33 (36)].

(Edict of Nebuchadnezzar´ the King.)

MT

III. 31 Nebuchadnezzar the King, unto all the peoples, nations, and languages that dwell in all the earth: 32 Peace be multiplied unto you. It hath seemed good before me to declare the signs and wonders that God the Most High hath wrought towards me.

33 How great are his signs! And how mighty are his wonders!

His kingdom is an everlasting kingdom,

And his dominion is from generation to generation.

LXX (third form of this Edict. See p. 103).

LXX IV. 34c, i.e. MT (III. 31) Nebuchadnezzar the King, unto all the nations and lands and all that dwell therein; (III. 32) Peace be multiplied alway. The deeds which the great God hath wrought towards me, it hath seemed good to me to declare unto you and to your wise men that he is God and that his wonders are great.

(III. 33) His kingdom is an everlasting kingdom, and his dominion is from generation to generation. And he sent letters concerning all that had befallen him to all the nations which were beneath his sovereignty.

SECTION V

i.e. Chapter V. 1–30, in the last year of Belshazzar.

V. 1–4. Belshazzar's feast, 5–7 a, ⌜7 b⌝, 8 a, 9, ⌜8 b⌝, 7 c; 8 c— handwriting on the wall : the king's alarm : wise men summoned but retire when they prove unable to interpret the writing : the king then offers extraordinary rewards : wise men return and again fail to interpret the writing. 10–16. The queen-mother summoned, by whose advice Daniel, as the chief of the wise men under Nebuchadnezzar, is brought before the king. 17–24. Daniel reproves the king for his pride, though he knew what had befallen Nebuchadnezzar for the same offence, and for his idolatry. 25–28. The writing and its interpretation. 29–30. Daniel rewarded and Belshazzar slain.

V.   Belshazzar the king made a great feast to a thousand of
2 his lords, and drank wine before the thousand. Belshazzar, whilst he tasted the wine, commanded to bring the golden

and silver vessels which Nebuchadnezzar his father had
taken out of the temple that was in Jerusalem ; that the
king and his lords and his wives and his concubines,
3 might drink therein. Then they brought the golden ⌐and
silver⌐[1] vessels that were taken out of the temple [2] of the
house [2] of God, which was at Jerusalem ; and the king
and his lords, and his wives and his concubines, drank in
4 them. They drank wine, and praised the gods of gold,
and of silver, of brass, of iron, of wood, and of stone.[3]
5 In the same hour came forth the fingers of a man's hand,
and wrote over against the candlestick upon the plaister
of the wall of the king's palace : and the king saw the
6 palm of the hand that wrote. Then the king's countenance
was changed and his thoughts alarmed him ; and the
joints of his knees were loosed, and his knees smote one
against another.

Restored Text of V. 7a–10a mainly on the basis of the LXX and Josephus.	MT dislocated, interpolated, and defective. V. 7a–10a.
7a The king cried aloud to bring in ⌐the magicians⌐,[4] the enchanters, the Chaldeans, and the soothsayers,[5] 7b ⌐that they should make known the interpretation of 8a the writing⌐.[6] Then came in all the king's wise men : but they could not read the writing, nor make known to the king the interpreta- 9 tion. Then was king Bel- shazzar greatly alarmed,	7a The king cried aloud to bring in the enchanters, the Chaldeans, and the soothsayers. The king an- swered and said to the wise men of Babylon : Whoso- ever shall read this writing, and show me the interpre- tation thereof, shall be clothed with purple, and have a chain of gold about his neck, and rule as one of three in the kingdom.

[1] Added in accordance with Th., Vulg., and context.

[2] The Pesh. and Vulg. omit, the last omitting 'of God' also.

[3] The LXX here adds and probably rightly : 'but the eternal God they praised not, in whose hand is their breath' or 'who has power over their breath'. See note *in loc.*

[4] Restored from the LXX.

[5] The MT adds 'And the king answered and said to the wise men of Babylon'. The LXX does not admit of this clause and Josephus omits it.

[6] Restored from the LXX and Josephus.

and his countenance was changed, and his lords were 8ᵇ confounded. ⌐Then the king made a decree, say- 7ᶜ ing⌐¹: Whosoever shall read this writing and declare to me the interpretation thereof, shall be clothed with purple, and have a chain of gold about his neck, and shall rule as ²one of three² in my kingdom. 7ᵈ ⌐And the magicians and enchanters and soothsayers came in, but none could read or make known the interpretation of the writ- 10ᵃ ing⌐.¹ ⌐Then the king called the queen⌐.³ (And) the queen⁴ came into the banquet house, and said, O

8 Then came in all the king's wise men: but they could not read the writing, nor make known to the king 9 the interpretation. Then was king Belshazzar greatly alarmed, and his countenance was changed, and his lords were confounded. 10 Then the queen by reason of the words of the king and his lords came into the banquet house.

king, live for ever; let not thy thoughts alarm thee, nor 11 let thy countenance be changed: there is a man in thy kingdom, ⌐whose name is Daniel⌐,⁵ ⌐one of the exiles of Judah⌐,⁶ in whom is the spirit of the holy gods; and in the days of thy father⁷ light and understanding and

---

¹ Restored from LXX and supported by Joseph. *Ant.* x. 11. 2.

² For a valuable note on the original expression 'one of three' see Montgomery, p. 256 seq. He writes: 'We are dealing here, then, with a customary official title, the numerical denotation of which has been lost. The Aramaic has preserved the two Akkadian case-forms of the noun *taltâ* and *taltî*, by true reminiscence, . . . תלתי is not emphatic but absolute; hence . . . we might translate "Thirdling". We have thus here a title which had lost its original significance, like " tetrarch "—in English.' If we accept this explanation ' it disposes with speculation as to the person of "the second" ruler'.

³ Restored from LXX τότε ὁ βασιλεὺς ἐκάλεσε τὴν βασίλισσαν.

⁴ MT adds 'by reason of the words of the king and his lords'. The queen could not enter the banquet-chamber unless invited by the king. See p. 127.

⁵ I have restored this clause on the evidence of the LXX and Josephus.

⁶ Restored on the evidence of the LXX and Josephus: cf. Th. 1³, 5¹³.

⁷ LXX adds 'the king'. Hence correct note on p. 130.

wisdom, like the wisdom of the gods, was found in him, and the king Nebuchadnezzar thy father, made him master of the magicians, enchanters, Chaldeans, and

12 soothsayers; forasmuch as an excellent spirit, and know-ledge and understanding, the *interpreting*[1] of dreams, and the *solving*[1] of riddles, and the loosing of spells were found in the same Daniel.[2] Now let Daniel be called, and he will show the interpretation.

13 Then was Daniel brought in before the king. The king spake and said unto Daniel, Art thou Daniel, which art of the exiles of Judah, whom the king my father brought

14 out of Judah? I have heard of thee that the spirit of the gods is in thee, and that light and understanding and

15 excellent wisdom is found in thee. And now the wise men, the enchanters, were brought before me to read this writing, and they made it their task to make known unto me the interpretation thereof: but they could not show the interpretation of the thing.

16 But I myself[3] have heard of thee, that thou canst give interpretations, and dissolve doubts: now if thou canst read the writing, and make known to me the interpretation thereof, thou shalt be clothed with purple, and have a chain of gold about thy neck, and shalt be as one of

17 three in the kingdom. Then Daniel answered and said before the king, Let thy gifts be to thyself, and give thy rewards to another; nevertheless I will read the writing unto the king, and make known unto him the interpretation.

18 As for thee, O king, the Most High God gave Nebu-

---

[1] On this emendation see note *in loc.*

[2] MT adds an incorrect gloss: 'Whom the king named Belteshazzar' against the LXX and Josephus.

[3] Since the text has here אנה שמעת I have taken the pronoun to be emphatic and not pleonastic. The pronoun is not inserted in 5[14], since the king speaks with little assurance, but, as he speaks with Daniel, he becomes assured, and so in 5[16] he says 'I myself, &c.' Cf. also 4[6 (9)], [27 (30)], where the same emphatic use of the pronoun occurs. This emphatic use of the pronoun with an inflected verb is found often in the *Aram. Pap.*—not only in the business documents when clear definition is indispensible; cf. Cowley 2[9, 11, 16], 5[3], &c., but even in Aḥ. 52, כען אנת לקבלוי אנה עבדת לך כן . . עבד לי 'Now do thou as I did to thee: do so to me'. Here the pronouns are certainly emphatic. But where the inflected verb is used (and not the participle) the pronoun is often omitted even in business documents.

chadnezzar thy father the kingdom, and greatness, and
19 glory, and majesty : and because of the greatness that he
gave him, all the peoples, nations, and languages trembled
and feared before him : whom he would he slew, and
whom he would he kept alive ; and whom he would he
raised up, and whom he would he put down.

20 But when his heart was lifted up, and his spirit was
hardened that he dealt proudly, he was deposed from his
21 kingly throne, and they took his glory from him : and he
was driven from the sons of men ; and his heart was
made like the beasts, and his dwelling was with the wild
asses ; he was fed with grass like oxen, and his body was
wet with the dew of heaven : until he knew that the
Most High God ruleth in the kingdom of men, and that
he setteth up over it whomsoever he will.

22 And thou his son, O Belshazzar, hast not humbled thine
23 heart, though thou knewest all this ; but hast lifted up
thyself against the Lord of heaven ; and they have
brought the vessels of his house before thee, and thou
and thy lords, thy wives and thy concubines, have drunk
wine in them ; and thou hast praised the gods of * gold
and silver,[1] of brass, iron, wood, and stone, which see′
not, nor hear, nor know : and the God in whose hand thy
breath is, and [2]whose are all thy ways, him thou hast
24 not glorified.[2]   Then was the palm of the hand sent from
25 before him, and this writing was inscribed.   And this is
the writing that was inscribed, MENE, TEKEL, PERES.[3]
26 This is the interpretation of the thing : MENE ; God
hath numbered thy kingdom and brought it to an end.
27 TEKEL ; thou art weighed in the balances and art found
28 wanting.   PERES ; thy kingdom is divided, and given
to the Medes and Persians.   Then Belshazzar [4] commanded them to clothe [4] Daniel with purple, and to put

---

[1] So Th. and Pesh. MT reads 'Silver and gold'. Cf. 5², where all the
authorities give the right order.

[2] So Th. (and LXX). MT reads 'whose are all thy ways, thou hast not
glorified'. See note *in loc.*

[3] So LXX, Th., Vulg., and Josephus. MT reads MENE, MENE, TEKEL,
UPHARSIN. See note *in loc.*

[4] Literally 'commanded and they clothed'. See note on 2⁴⁹. (Transl.)

a chain of gold about his neck, and make proclamation
concerning him that he should rule as one of three in the
30 kingdom. In that night Belshazzar the Chaldean king
was slain.

SECTION VI

i. e Chapter VI (V. 31–VI), in the first year of Darius.

VI. 1 (V. 31). *Darius receives the kingdom.* 2–4 (1–3). *Darius
resolves to set Daniel, who was already over all the satraps, over
the whole realm.* 5 (4)–10 (9). *The satraps therefore conspire and
approaching Darius prevail on him to issue a decree forbidding the
worship of any deity.* 11 (10)–18 (17). *Daniel, detected in the breach
of this decree, is accused by his enemies, who do not leave the
king's presence till at sunset the king yields, and Daniel is cast
into the den of lions.* 19 (18)–25 (24). *Daniel rescued therefrom,
and his enemies cast therein.* 26 (25)–28 (27). *Edict of Darius.*
29 (28). *Daniel at last set over the whole kingdom. Darius dies,
and Cyrus reigns in his stead.*

VI. 1 (V. 31) And Darius the Mede received the kingdom† being
2 (1) about threescore and two years old.[1] It pleased Darius†
and he set over the kingdom an hundred and twenty
3 (2) satraps, which should be throughout the whole kingdom ;
and over them three presidents, of whom Daniel was one ;
that these satraps might give account unto them, and that
4 (3) the king should have no damage. Then this Daniel was
distinguished above the presidents and satraps, because
an excellent spirit was in him, ⌐and he prospered in the
king's business which he carried out⌐;[2] and the king
5 (4) *thought to set him[3] over the whole realm. Then the

---

[1] Here the LXX reads πλήρης τῶν ἡμερῶν καὶ ἔνδοξος ἐν γήρει. That the
MT is here corrupt see p. 148 seq. The LXX is itself uncertain.

[2] Restored from the LXX. See p. 150.

[3] So MT, LXX, Pesh., and Vulg. Th. read 'set him' (κατέστησεν αὐτόν).
But MT, Pesh., and Vulg. combine two conflicting types of text, i. e. those
of the LXX and Th., which in themselves are consistent. But the LXX is
undoubtedly right. The king's intention to set Daniel over the kingdom
brought about the plot against Daniel. When the plot was defeated, the
king carried out his intention (LXX 6²⁹ (²⁸) καὶ Δανιὴλ κατεστάθη ἐπὶ τῆς
βασιλείας. Hence the MT is corrupt in 6²⁹ (²⁸). See p. 151 seq.

presidents and the satraps sought to find occasion against
Daniel as touching the kingdom : but they could find
none occasion nor fault; forasmuch as he was faithful.[1]

6 (5) Then said these men, We shall not find any occasion
against this Daniel, except we find it against him con-

7 (6) cerning the law of his God. Then these presidents and
and satraps ⌜drew near⌝[2] to the king and said thus

8 (7) ⌜before⌝[3] him, Darius, the king, live for ever. All the
presidents of the kingdom, the deputies, and the satraps,
the counsellors and the governors, have taken counsel
together that the king should establish a statute and
make a strong interdict, that whosoever shall ask a
petition of any god[4] for thirty days, save of thee, O king,

9 (8) he shall be cast into a den of lions. Now, O king, establish
the interdict, and sign the writing, that it be not changed,
according to the law of the Medes and Persians, which

10 (9) altereth not. Wherefore the king Darius signed the

11 (10) writing and the interdict. And when Daniel knew that
the writing was signed, he went into his house; now his
windows were open in his chamber towards Jerusalem ;
and he was wont to kneel upon his knees three times
a day, and he prayed and gave thanks before his God as

---

[1] MT, Pesh., and Vulg. add gloss ' neither was there any error or guilt found
in him ' against LXX and Th.

[2] So LXX, Th., and Pesh. Hence I suggest that קרבו originally stood
in the text. הרגשו (MT) has no support from any version or other authority
before the fourth century A.D. for the sense 'came tumultuously'. In
Aramaic two meanings are found (1) 'to be enraged or in tumult': (2) 'to
spy upon'. The former is the older : cf. Cowley, Aḥ. 29 : the latter is not
attested before the time of our author : cf. 6¹² (¹¹). The presence of הרגשו
in 6¹⁶ (¹⁵) is against the entire sense of the context. This Aramaic verb was
adopted by the Psalmist into Hebrew in Ps. 2¹ and nouns from the same
stem in 55¹⁵, 64³. Montgomery (p. 272 seq.) following in the wake of Briggs
discusses this word and concludes that it may be translated ' They acted in
concert '. But is there any foundation for this conjecture ? The old Aramaic
and the Arabic support the meaning usually assigned to this word in Ps. 2¹,
a meaning also which is upheld by the parallelism of the context. Neither
does 64³ (cf. 83³) afford it any countenance. 55¹⁵, it is true, is difficult, but
Duhm is probably right in regarding the MT as hopelessly corrupt.

[3] Here the LXX preserves the original text, where the MT and later
versions read ' unto him '. See my note on p. 154 seq. : Introd., § 20. w.

[4] MT adds ' or man ' against the LXX and Josephus and also against
common sense. See note in loc.

12 (11) he did aforetime. Then these men ¹ kept watch,¹ and found Daniel making petition and supplication before his God.

13 (12) Then they came near and spake before the king [concerning the inderdict of the king]² ; Hast thou not signed an interdict, that every man that shall make a petition unto any ³ god within thirty days, save unto thee, O king, shall be cast into the den of lions? The king answered and said, The thing is true, according to the law of the Medes and Persians which altereth not.

14 (13) Then answered they and said before the king: Daniel, which is one of the exiles of Judah ⁴ obeyeth not thy decree,⁴ nor the interdict that thou hast signed, but maketh his petition ⌜before his God⌝ ⁵ three times a day.

15 (14) Then the king when he heard these words was sore displeased, and set his heart on Daniel to deliver him :
and he laboured until the going down of the sun to
16 (15) rescue him. Then these men ⁶ said unto ⁷ the king, Know, O king, that it is a law of the Medes and Persians that no interdict nor statute which the king establisheth may
17 (16) be changed. Then the king commanded them to bring Daniel, and cast him into the den of lions. The king spake and said unto Daniel, Thy God whom thou servest
18 (17) continually, he will deliver thee. And a stone was brought and laid upon the mouth of the den ; and the king sealed

---

¹ See note on 6⁷ ⁽⁶⁾ for this meaning of הרגשׁו. It appears in modern times to be always wrongly rendered either as 'assembled together' or 'came tumultuously' in Daniel.

² This bracketed clause of the MT is not supported by LXX, Th. or the Pesh. : only by Vulg.

³ MT and Th. add 'or man'. See note on 6⁸⁽⁷⁾.

⁴ So Th., but LXX omits. MT, which is corrupt, reads 'regardeth not thee, O king'. See note on 3¹².

⁵ So LXX and Th. MT, Pesh., and Vulg. omit.

⁶ MT adds the impossible clause 'came tumultuously (or 'came in concert ') to the king'. It is omitted by Th. and what is more the LXX and Josephus (as well as Th.) *represent the satraps as present throughout the entire interview which lasted all the day*, 6¹²⁻¹⁶. Even in the MT 6¹⁵ ⁽¹⁴⁾, the words 'the king laboured till the going down of the sun' presuppose Daniel's adversaries as present all the day.

⁷ Daniel's enemies now become disrespectful to the king, since the king is convicted of seeking to break 'the law of the Medes and Persians which altereth not', and so they say 'unto' instead of 'before' as in 6¹³ ⁽¹²⁾, ¹⁴ ⁽¹³⁾.

it with his own signet, and with the signets of his lords ;
that nothing might be changed concerning Daniel.

19 (18) (a) Then the king went to his palace, (d) and his sleep
fled from him, (b) and he spent the night fasting : (c) neither
20 (19) were instruments of music brought before him.[1] Then
the king arose very early in the morning, and went in
haste unto the den of lions. And when he came near
unto the den to Daniel he cried with a lamentable voice :
the king spake and said to Daniel, O Daniel, servant of
the living God, is thy God, whom thou servest continually,
22 (21) able to deliver thee from the lions ?   Then spake Daniel
23 (22) unto the king, O king, live for ever.   My God hath sent
his angel, and hath shut the lions' mouths, that they have
not hurt me : forasmuch as before him innocency was
found in me ; and also before thee, O king, have I done
24 (23) no hurt.   Then was the king exceeding glad, and commanded that they should take Daniel up out of the den.
So Daniel was taken up out of the den, and no manner
of hurt was found upon him, because he had trusted in
25 (24) his God.   [2] And the king commanded, and those men
were brought which had accused Daniel, and were cast
into the den of lions, they and their wives and their
children [2] ; and the lions had the mastery of them, and
brake all their bones in pieces, or ever they came at the
bottom of the den.

26 (25) Then king Darius wrote unto all the peoples, nations,
and languages, that dwell in all the earth ; Peace be
27 (26) multiplied unto you.   I make a decree, that in all the

---

[1] By transposition of clause (d) immediately after clause (a) the text is
made intelligible.

[2] With the Vulg. (adducti sunt) for הַיְתִיו, I have read הֵתָיִו ‘ were brought ’
and for רְמֹו I have read with LXX, Th., Vulg., Josephus, רְמִיו ‘ were cast ’.
Thus אִנּוּן (= ‘ they ’), which only occurs elsewhere in the nominative, is
read as a nom. and not as an acc. as in the MT (= ‘ them ’).   See p. 161 sq.
The MT reads ‘ And the king commanded and they brought those men
which had accused Daniel, and into the den of lions they cast them, their
children and their wives ’.   In reading ‘ their wives and their children (so
LXX, Pesh., Vulg., Cyprian, Test. iii. 20) I have followed the usual O.T.
order.   The order in the MT and Th. ‘ their children and their wives ’ is
Greek rather than Jewish.   For the Semitic order ‘ wives and children ’ ;
see Cowley 30[15, 26], 31[14].

dominion of my kingdom men tremble and fear before
the God of Daniel :

For he is the living God and steadfast for ever,

And his kingdom one which shall not be destroyed,

And his dominion (one that shall be) for ever :

28 (27)   He delivereth and rescueth,

And he worketh signs and wonders

In heaven and in earth ;

(Even) he who hath delivered Daniel

From the power of the lions.

29   LXX

⌜So Daniel was set over the kingdom of Darius. King
Darius was gathered to his people and Cyrus the Persian
received his kingdom⌝.[1]

SECTIONS VII–X

The Visions of Daniel : i. e. Chapters VII–XII.

SECTION VII

i. e. Chapter VII, in the first year of Belshazzar.

VII. 1–8. *Daniel's vision of the four beasts, i. e. the four successive world powers.* 9–14. *Divine judgement on these powers.*
15–28. *The interpretation of the vision by an angel.*

VII. 1. In the first year of Belshazzar king of Babylon Daniel
saw a dream, [even visions of his head][2] upon his bed :
then he wrote the dream, even a complete account.[3]

---

[1] . So the LXX save that I have changed the order of the first two clauses.
The intention expressed in 6⁴⁽³⁾ is here carried out. In 6⁴ Th. represents
this intention as already carried out, and so omits 29ᵇ (28ᵇ) but the MT,
Pesh., and Vulg. represent a medley of the two types of text : see note on 6⁴⁽³⁾ :
also p. 151 seq.

Instead of the text in the LXX, which I have adopted, the MT, Pesh., and
Vulg. read : ' So this Daniel prospered in the reign of Darius and in the
reign of Cyrus the Persian.'

[2] Not in LXX. An interpolation. ' Visions of his head '—a non-Semitic
expression. See note on 2¹⁹, ²⁸ᶜ (Transl.): Comm. p. 42, *ad init.*

[3] MT adds ' he told ' against the LXX (and Th.).

2 I[1] saw in ⌈a vision of the night⌉,[2] and, behold, the four
3 winds of heaven *stirred up[3] the great sea.   And four
   great beasts came up from the sea, diverse one from
4 another.   The first was like a lion, and had eagle's
   wings : I beheld till the wings thereof were plucked, and
   it was lifted up from the earth, and made to stand upon
   two feet as a man, and a man's heart was given to it.
5 And behold another beast[4] like a bear, and it was raised
   up on one side, and three ribs were in its mouth between
6 its teeth : and it was said unto it, Arise, devour much
   flesh.   After this I beheld, and lo another ⌈beast⌉[5] like
   a leopard, which had upon the back of it four wings of
   a fowl ; the beast had also four heads ; and dominion was
7 given to it.   And after this I saw in ⌈a vision of the night⌉[6]
   and behold a fourth beast, dreadful and terrible and
   strong exceedingly ; and it had great iron teeth : it
   devoured and brake in pieces, and trod the residue with
   its feet : and it was diverse from all the beasts that were
8 before it ; and it had ten horns.   I was observing the
   horns and, behold, there came up among them another
   horn, a little one, before which three of the first horns
   were plucked up by the roots : and behold in this horn
   were eyes like the eyes of a man, and a mouth speaking
9 great things, ⌈and it made war with the saints⌉.[7]   I
   beheld till thrones were placed and ⟨one like unto⟩[8] an
   ancient of days did sit :

   His raiment was as snow, and the hair of his head was
      spotless as white[9] wool ;

---

[1] MT prefixes against LXX, Th., and Vulg., 'Daniel answered and said'.
[2] So [Th. ΓΑ], Pesh. Cf. 2[19] 'a vision of the night'. MT and Vulg. read
'my vision in the night'. LXX here only uses 'visions' in the plural in this
peculiar phrase. Καθ' ὕπνους νυκτός : always elsewhere it uses the sing. But
the LXX seems corrupt here as in 4[10].
[3] On this rendering see note on p.175. Otherwise render 'brake forth upon'.
[4] MT adds against LXX and Vulg. 'a second'.
[5] So LXX, Th., and Pesh. MT omits.
[6] So LXX, Pesh., Vulg. MT reads 'the night visions'. Th. om.
[7] Restored from LXX : Cf. parallel statements in 7[21,25].
[8] I have of necessity restored these words simply by reading עַתִּיק
instead of עַתִּיק. See note in loc. There has been a like loss of this letter
in 10[5]. Clem. Alex. Paed. ii. 10 preserves the original reading : ὡσεὶ παλαιὸς
ἡμερῶν : also the LXX in 7[13] ὡς παλαιὸς ἡμερῶν. But contrast 7[22].
[9] In the MT 'white' precedes 'as snow'. See note in loc.

His throne was fiery flames, the wheels thereof burning
fire.

10 A fiery stream flowed[1] from before him :
Thousand thousands ministered unto him,
Yea, ten thousand times ten thousand stood before him :
The judgement was set,
And the books were opened.

11 I beheld at that time because of the voice of the great
words which the horn spake,[2] till the beast was slain, and
its body destroyed, and it was given to be burned with
12 fire. And as for the rest of the beasts, their dominion
was taken away: yet, their lives were prolonged for a
season and a time.

13 I saw in ⌜a vision of the night⌝,[3]
And behold there came ⌜on⌝[4] the clouds of heaven one like
unto a son of man,
And he came even unto an ancient of days, and they[5]
brought him near before him.

14 And there was given him dominion, and glory and a
kingdom,
That all peoples, nations and languages should serve him :
[6]His dominion is an everlasting dominion which shall not
pass away.[6]
And his kingdom that which shall not be destroyed.

15 And my spirit was distressed ⌜therewith⌝[7] even the spirit
of me Daniel, and †the visions of my head† [8] troubled me.

---

[1] Only one verb appears in the LXX and Th.   The duplicate arose through
an explanatory gloss on a rare word.   See note *in loc.*

[2] MT adds 'I beheld' against LXX and Th.

[3] So LXX, Th., and Vulg. as in 2¹⁹, 7⁷.   MT 'the night visions'
Pesh. om.

[4] So LXX and Pesh.   MT, Th., and Vulg. read 'with'.   See note on p. 186.

[5] LXX, supported by pre-Theod., Tertullian, and Cyprian, reads, 'they
that stood before him'.

[6] Since T. Jos. xix 12 appears to quote this verse as follows : ἡ βασιλεία
αὐτοῦ ἔσται αἰώνιος ἥτις οὐ παρελεύσεται, is it possible that for 'dominion' in this
line we should read 'kingdom', and 'dominion' in the next line for 'kingdom'.
This would bring the phrasing into harmony with that on 3³³, 7²⁷ of our
text.   The contrast, however, in 7¹²,¹⁷ may have led our author to make
this change.   But in 7²⁷ the usual order is unquestionable.

[7] So LXX and Vulg.   MT reads 'in the midst of the (or its) sheath'.   See
note on p. 188 sq.

[8] Read 'my thoughts' οἱ διαλογισμοί μου with LXX.   'Vision of my head'
is non-Semitic.   See note on 2²⁸ ᶜ (Transl.).

16 I came near unto one of them that stood by and asked
   him the truth of all this. [1]And he told me,[1] and made me
17 know the interpretation of the things. These great beasts
   [which are four][2] are four kings which shall ⌜be destroyed
18 from⌝[3] off the earth. But the saints of the Most High
   shall receive the kingdom, and possess the kingdom[4] for
   ever and ever.

19 Then I desired to know the truth concerning the fourth
   beast, which was diverse from them all, exceeding terrible,
   whose teeth were of iron, and its nails of brass ; which
   devoured, brake in pieces and trod the residue with its
20 feet ; and concerning the ten horns that were on its head,
   and the other *horn* that came up, and before which three
   fell ; even concerning that horn that had eyes, and a
   mouth that spake great things, whose appearance was
21 more stout than its fellows. I beheld, and the same horn
   made war with the saints and prevailed against them ;
22 until the Ancient of Days came, and ⟨judgement was set
   and dominion⟩[5] was given to the saints of the Most High ;
   and the time came that the saints should take possession
23 of the kingdom. Thus he said,
   The fourth beast shall be a fourth kingdom upon earth,
   Which shall be diverse from all the kingdoms,
   And it shall devour the whole earth
   And shall thresh it and break it in pieces.

24   And as for the ten horns,
   Out of this kingdom shall ten kings arise :
   And another shall arise after them ;
   And shall be diverse from the former,
   And he shall put down three kings.

25 And he shall speak words against the Most High,
   And shall wear out the saints of the Most High :

---

[1] **LXX** reads ἀποκριθεὶς δὲ λέγει μοι i. e. וענה ואמר לי ' And he answered
and told me '.

[2] LXX omits.

[3] So LXX and without doubt correctly. MT reads ' arise out of '. Th. is
conflate. See note on p. 189 sq.

[4] MT Pesh. and Vulg. add ' for ever and ' against LXX and Th.

[5] Restored on Ewald's suggestion. Most scholars accept this restoration.

And it shall be his intention to change times and law;
And they[1] shall be given into his hand until time and
  times and half a time

26 But the judgement shall sit,
And his dominion shall be taken away,
So that it may be consumed and destroyed for ever.

27 And the kingdom and the dominion, and the greatness of
  the kingdoms under the whole heaven,
Shall be given to the people of the saints of the Most High :
Its kingdom is an everlasting kingdom,
And all dominions shall serve and obey it.

28 Here is the end of the matter. As for me Daniel, my
thoughts alarmed me much, and my countenance was
changed upon me : but I kept the matter in my heart.

SECTION VIII

i. e. Chapter VIII, the Vision of the Seer in the third year
of Belshazzar, in which he sees the victory of the
Greek over the Median and Persian empires, the
persecution of the Jews, and the suspension of the
Temple worship by Antiochus.

VIII. 1–8. *Vision of the ram and he-goat, i. e. Alexander.*
9–12. *'The little horn,' i.e. Antiochus IV.* 13–14. *Dialogue
between two angels overheard by the Seer who learns therefrom
that the time of this tyranny will last 1150 days.* 15–27. *Gabriel
appears to Daniel and interprets the vision.*

VIII. 1. In the third year of the reign of Belshazzar the king
  a vision appeared unto me, even unto me Daniel, after
2 that which appeared unto me aforetime. And I saw in
the vision ;[2] and I was in Shushan the palace,[3] which is
in the province of Elam ;[4] and I was by the ⌜water-gate⌝[5]

---

[1] i.e. the saints.

[2] MT adds against LXX, Th., Pesh., and Vulg. 'and it was so when
I saw'.

[3] Or 'fortress'.

[4] MT adds against LXX, Th. 'and I saw in the vision'.

[5] So LXX, Pesh., and Vulg. (אבול Aram.) here and in 8⁶. LXX and
Pesh. have same reading in 8³. MT in each case reads אובל ('river ').

3 of the Ulai. Then I lifted up mine eyes, and saw, and, behold, there stood before the ⌜water-gate⌝ a single ram which had two horns : and the two horns were high ; but one was higher than the other, and the higher came up

4 last. I saw the ram thrusting [2] westward, and northward, and southward ; [2] and no beasts could stand before him, neither was there any that could deliver out of his hand ; but he did according to his will, and magnified himself.

5 And I was observing, and behold, ⌜an he-goat⌝[3] came from the west over the face of the whole earth, and touched not the ground : and the goat had [4] †a notable† [4]

6 horn between his eyes. And he came to the ram that had the two horns, which I saw standing before the ⌜water-gate⌝,[1] and ran upon him in the fury of his power.

7 And I saw him come close to the ram, and he was moved with choler against him, and smote the ram, and brake his two horns ; and there was no power in the ram to stand before him : and he cast him down to the ground, and trod upon him : and there was none that could deliver

8 the ram out of his hand. And the he-goat magnified himself exceedingly : and when he was strong, the great horn was broken ; and there rose up ⌜*others*⌝[5] (even) four ⌜horns⌝[6] in its stead towards the four winds of heaven.

9 And out of one of them came forth [7] *another* horn, a *little* one,[7] which waxed exceeding great, towards the south,

---

[1] So LXX, Pesh., and Vulg. (אבול Aram.) here and in 8². LXX and Pesh. have same reading in 8³. MT in each case reads אובל (' river ').

[2] LXX reads : eastward and northward and westward and southward '.

[3] So LXX and Th. against MT which reads ' the he-goat '.

[4] So MT חָזוּת. Th. omits : LXX reads ἕν, i.e. אחת, i.e. κέρας ἕν. Hence render 'a horn '. Vulg. supports MT by its rendering *insigne*. But the description 'notable' lit. ' conspicuousness ' is not justified till the horn over-throws the ram, 'magnifies itself exceedingly ' and ' becomes strong' (8⁸). Thus it is rightly called גדלה ' great' in 8⁸,²¹.

[5] So LXX i.e. ἕτερα = אהרות. Th. and Vulg. om. MT חזות corrupt = 'four notable (horns) '. But is there any justification for calling Alexander's four successors 'notable'? Even Antiochus Epiphanes is at the outset called ' a little horn ' which afterwards ' waxed exceeding great ', 8⁹). The text is not to be translated ' four other horns ' but as above, the 'others' being in apposition. Otherwise we shall expect ארבע קרנות אחרות : cf. 12⁵ : Gen. 8¹⁰, ¹² : 41³,¹⁹.

[6] So LXX, Th., Vulg. MT omits.

[7] Emended by Bevan. See p. 203.

and towards the east, and towards the glorious land.
10 And it waxed great (even) to the host of heaven; and some
of the host, even of the stars, it cast down to the ground,
and trod upon them.

Emended Text of VIII. 11–12 (see pp. 204-9)	MT. VIII. 11, 12
11 Even unto the prince of the host it magnified itself, and by it the daily burnt offering was taken away, and the place cast down and the sanctuary laid desolate.	11 Yea, it magnified itself, (even) to the prince of the host; and it took away from him the daily burnt offering and the place of his sanctuary was cast down.
12 And the transgression was offered on ⟨the altar of⟩[1] the daily burnt offering; and truth cast down to the ground, and it did (its pleasure) and prospered.	12 †And the host was given over (to it) together with the daily burnt offering through transgression; and it cast truth to the ground† and it did (its pleasure) and prospered.
13 Then I heard a holy one speaking; and another holy one said unto that certain one which spake, How long shall be the vision while the daily burnt offering ⌜is taken away⌝[2] and the transgression that appalleth ⌜set up and the sanctuary laid waste to be trod-	
14 den under foot?⌝[3] And he said unto ⌜him⌝,[4] Unto two thousand and three hundred evenings and mornings; then shall the sanctuary be justified.	MT †to give both the sanctuary and the host to be trodden under foot†.

15 And it came to pass, when I, even I Daniel, had seen the
vision, that I sought to understand it; and, behold, there
16 stood before me as the appearance of a man.   And I

---

[1] Text appears to require this addition.   See p. 204 sqq.
[2] Restored by help of LXX and Th. (ἀρθεῖσα).
[3] Restored by help of LXX and Th.   See p. 210 sq.
[4] So LXX, Th., Pesh., and Vulg.   MT = ' to me '.

heard a man's voice between the (banks of) Ulai, which
called, and said, Gabriel, make this man to understand
17 the vision. So he came ⌜and stood⌝[1] near where I stood ;
and when he came, I was affrighted, and fell upon my
face : but he said unto me, Understand, O son of man ;
18 for the vision belongeth to the time of the end. Now as
he was speaking with me, I fell into a deep sleep with
my face to the ground : but he touched me and ⌜made me
19 to stand⌝[2] where I had stood. And he said, Behold,
I will make thee know what shall be in the latter time of
the indignation : for it belongeth to the appointed time
20 of the end. The ram which thou sawest that had the
two horns, they are the kings of Media and Persia.
21 And the he-goat[3] is the king of Greece : and the great
22 horn that is between his eyes is the first king. And as
for that which was broken, in the place whereof four
arose, four kingdoms shall arise out of his[4] nation, but not
23 with his power. And in the latter time of their kingdom,

	MT
when ⌜their transgressions are come to the full⌝[5] a king, insolent and skilled in double	when the transgressors are come to the full.
24 dealing shall stand up. And his power shall be mighty,[6] and he shall *devise* presumptuous things.[7]	
And shall prosper and do (his pleasure): and he shall destroy the mighty ones.	MT 24b–25a 'And he shall destroy the mighty ones and the holy people. And through his policy he shall cause craft to prosper in his hand.'
25 And [8] against the holy people shall his policy be directed, and he shall cause craft to prosper in his hand ;[8]	

[1] Restored with LXX, Th., and Vulg.
[2] LXX reads 'Waked me'. Perhaps we should read 'waked me and made me stand'. See p. 215.
[3] MT adds against LXX, Th., Pesh., and Vulg. 'the he-goat' הַשָּׂעִיר thus expressing the same idea in both Aramaic and Hebrew. See p. 216.
[4] LXX, Th., Vulg. ; but MT and Pesh. read 'the'.
[5] So LXX and Th. MT reads as in marg. See p. 217 sq.
[6] MT and LXX add 'but not by his own strength'. See p. 218.
[7] Emended. See p. 218. MT reads '†destroy† wonderfully'.
[8] Emended by Graetz, Bevan, &c. See p. 219 sq.

And he shall magnify himself in his heart, and in (their)
security shall he destroy many:

He shall also stand up against the prince of princes; but
he shall be broken without hands.

26 And the vision of the evenings and mornings which hath
been told is true:

And shut thou up the vision; for it belongeth to many
days (to come).

27 And I Daniel[1] was sick certain days; then I rose up and
did the king's business: and I was astonished at the vision,
but none understood it.

SECTION IX

i.e. Chapter IX, in the first year of Darius, being the
explanation of Jeremiah's prophecy of the seventy
years given by the Seer.

*IX. 1–2. Daniel reflects on Jeremiah's prediction and prays for
an interpretation. [4–20 an early interpolation which takes no
account of what precedes or follows, but contains a confession of
the sins of the nation, and prays for the restoration of Jerusalem.
20 serves to connect 4–19 with what follows.] 21–27. In answer
to Daniel's prayer Gabriel comes to him and explains the prediction
of the seventy weeks.*

IX. 1 In the first year of Darius the son of Ahasuerus, of the
seed of the Medes, who was made king over the realm of
2 the Chaldeans; in the first year of his reign I Daniel
understood by the books the number of the years, which,
according to the word of **God**[2] which came to Jeremiah
the prophet, were to be accomplished in the desolations
3 of Jerusalem, even seventy years. And I set my face
unto [the Lord] God,[3] to seek by prayer and supplications,
4 with fasting, and sackcloth, and ashes.   [And I prayed

---

[1] MT adds 'fainted and', which appears in the Hebrew to be a dittograph
of the word that follows. It is omitted in the LXX.

[2] Emended by help of LXX. MT reads 'Lord' (יהוה).

[3] The interpolator of the prayer 9[4-20] inserted 'the Lord' before 'God'.
אדני occurs frequently in the prayer, but not elsewhere in our author save
in 1[2].

unto the Lord my God, and made confession, and said,
O Lord, the great and dreadful God, which keepeth
covenant and mercy with them that love ⌜*thee*⌝[1] and keep
5 ⌜*thy*⌝[1] commandments; we have sinned and have dealt
perversely, and have done wickedly, and have rebelled,
and turned aside from thy precepts and from thy judgements : neither have we hearkened unto thy servants the
prophets, which spake in thy name to our kings, our
princes, and our fathers, and to all the people of the land.
7 O Lord, righteousness belongeth unto thee, but unto us
confusion of face, as it is this day; to the men of Judah,
and to the inhabitants of Jerusalem, and unto all Israel,
that are near, and that are far off, and in all the countries
whither thou hast driven them, because of their unfaithfulness wherein they have dealt unfaithfully against thee.
8 O Lord, to us belongeth confusion of face, to our kings,
to our princes, and to our fathers, because we have sinned
9 against thee. To the Lord our God belong compassions
and forgivenesses; for we have rebelled against him;
10 neither have we obeyed the voice of the Lord our God,
to walk in his laws, which he set before us by his servants
11 the prophets. Yea all Israel have transgressed thy law,
and have turned aside, so as not to obey thy voice:
therefore hath the curse been poured out upon us, and
the oath that is written in the law of Moses the servant
12 of God; for we have sinned against him. And he hath
confirmed his words, which he spake against us, and
against our judges that judged us, by bringing upon us
a great evil: for under the whole heaven hath not been
13 done as hath been done upon Jerusalem. As it is written
in the law of Moses all this evil is come upon us : yet we
have not entreated the favour of the Lord our God, that
we should turn from our iniquities, and have discernment
14 in thy truth. Therefore hath the Lord watched over the
evil and brought it upon us: for the Lord our God is
righteous in all his works which he doeth, and we have
15 not obeyed his voice. And now, O Lord our God, that
hast brought thy people forth out of the land of Egypt

---

[1] So LXX, Th., Vulg. MT reads 'him' and 'his' respectively.

with a mighty hand ⌐and a stretched out arm⌐,[1] and hast
gotten thee renown, as at this day ; we have sinned, [2] we
16 have done wickedly. O Lord according to all thy righteous
acts, let thine anger [2] and thy fury, I pray thee, be turned
away from thy city Jerusalem, thy holy mountain : because
for our sins, and for the iniquities of our fathers, Jerusalem
and thy people have become a reproach to all that are
17 round about us. Now therefore, O our God, hearken
unto the prayer of thy servant, and to his supplications,
and cause thy face to shine upon thy sanctuary that is
desolate, for †the Lord's sake†.[3] O *my God [4] incline thine
18 ear, and hear ; open thine eyes and behold our desolations,
and the city over which thy name has been called : for we
do not present our supplications before thee for our own
19 righteousness but for thy great compassions. O Lord,
hear ; O Lord, forgive ; O Lord, hearken and do ; defer
not for thine own sake, *O my God,[5] because thy name
hath been called over thy city and thy people.
20   And whiles I was speaking, and praying, and confessing
my ⌐sins⌐[6] and the ⌐sins⌐[6] of my people Israel, and presenting my supplication before the Lord my God for the
21 holy mountain of my God]   And whiles I was speaking
in prayer ⌐behold⌐,[7] the man Gabriel, whom I had seen
in the vision aforetime [8] when I was sore wearied,[8] touched
22 me about the time of the evening oblation. And he
instructed ⌐me⌐,[9] and talked with me, and said, O Daniel,
I am now come forth to make thee skilful of understanding.
23 At the beginning of thy supplications a word went forth,

[1] Preserved in LXX, which omits ' with a mighty hand '.

[2] Perhaps with several MSS. and the rendering in 1 Bar. ii 12 we should
translate ' We have done wickedly, O Lord, despite all thy righteous acts.
Let thine anger '.

[3] So MT. But read ' thy servants' sake, O Lord ' with the LXX. (So
Bevan suggests) : or ' thine own sake ' with Th., Vulg., and 1 Bar ii. 14.
See p. 233 seq.

[4] MT and Th. LXX reads Κύριε and 1 Bar. ii. 16.

[5] LXX reads δέσποτα.

[6] So LXX, Th., Pesh., Vulg. MT reads ' sin '.

[7] So LXX, Th., Vulg. MT omits.

[8] Such seems the best rendering of MT. (So Meinhold, Keil). Other
scholars refer the words to the angel and render ' being caused to fly swiftly '.
(Cf. LXX, Th., Vulg.), or ' being sore wearied '. See p. 235.

[9] Restored with Th. and Vulg.

and I am come to tell ⌈thee⌉;[1] for thou art ⌈a man⌉[2]
greatly beloved : therefore consider the word, and under-
24 stand the vision. Seventy weeks are decreed upon thy
people and upon thy holy city To complete the transgression, and to bring sins to the full, And to ⌈blot out⌉[3]
iniquity, and to bring in everlasting righteousness : To
seal up vision and prophet, and to anoint a most holy
25 place. Know therefore and discern that from the going
forth of the word ⌈to rebuild⌉[4] Jerusalem unto an anointed
one, a prince, shall be seven weeks : and threescore
and two weeks, it shall be rebuilt with square and moat.[5]
26ab ⌈And at the end of the times, even⌉[6] after the threescore
and two weeks, shall an anointed one be cut off and

26c †he shall have nothing† :[7] and | MT
the city and the sanctuary | 26c And the people of the
shall be destroyed,[8] ⌈together | prince that shall come
with⌉[9] a prince, and ⌈the end | shall destroy the city
shall come⌉[10] with a flood, and | and the sanctuary, and
even unto the end shall be | his end shall be
war ; — that which is deter- |

| MT

27a mined of desolations. And[11] a | 27a And he shall make a
stringent statute shall be issued | firm covenant with the
against the many[11] for one | many.

---

[1] Restored with two MSS., LXX, Th., Pesh., Vulg. MT omits.

[2] Restored with Th., Vulg., and Sym. Cf. 10¹¹,¹⁹.

[3] So LXX and Vulg. = למחות. MT reads לכפר (so Th., Aq.: Pesh.)
'treat as covered'. See p. 238 sq. The spurious work *De Pascha Compu-
tus* 13, attributed to Tertullian by its rendering, ut . . . deleantur . . . inju-
stitiae et expientur iniustitiae (= ולכפר . . למחות) attests the earlier
Hebrew phrase as well as the later that displaced it.

[4] So Pesh. and Vulg. Hence I emend להשיב to לשוב. MT is by some
scholars rendered 'to restore and build'. But MT gives no satisfactory
sense. See p. 242 sq.

[5] See p. 243 sq.

[6] So LXX and Pesh. MT reads, 'even in troublous times. And' :
see p. 244.

[7] See p. 247.

[8] So Bevan, Marti, and others, emending יַשְׁחִית into יְשָׁחֵת.

[9] So one MS. and five versions. See p. 247 sq.

[10] Emended by Von Gall and Marti on the basis of the LXX. See p. 248.

[11] On this restoration of the text see p. 249 sq.

27^b week : And so for the half of
the week the sacrifice and the
meat offering ⌐shall cease⌐ : [1]

27^c and ²*in its stead*² *shall be a*
horror that appalleth ; and that
until the annihilation that is
already determined shall be
poured out upon the desolator.

MT

27^c On the wing of horrors
shall be one that appalleth.

SECTION X

i. e. Chapters X–XII, constituting one vision accorded to
the Seer in the third year of Cyrus.

SECTION X^a

i. e. Chapters X–XI. 1.

X. 1–3. *In the third year of Cyrus the Seer prepares himself by*
prayer and fasting to receive a revelation on the future destinies
of Israel. 4–8. *An angel—not Gabriel—appears to the Seer,*
who forthwith falls into a deep sleep. 9–14. *Thereupon the angel*
touches the Seer and wakes him to full consciousness, and tells
him that owing to his prayer he has come to declare to him what
shall befall Israel in the latter days. 15–XI. 1. *But the vision*
makes the Seer dumb. Then the angel touches the Seers's lips
and removes his dumbness, and by touching him again enables
him to receive the revelation he is about to make to him.

X. 1 In the third year of Cyrus king of Persia a thing was
revealed unto Daniel, whose name was Belteshazzar ;
and the thing was true, and a hard service : and he understood the thing, and had understanding of the vision.
2 In those days I Daniel was mourning three whole weeks.
3 I ate no pleasant bread, neither came flesh nor wine into
my mouth, neither did I anoint myself at all, till three
4 whole weeks were fulfilled. And in the four and twentieth
day of the first month, I was by the side of the great
5 river,³ and I lifted up mine eyes, and looked, and behold

---

[1] So LXX, Th., and Vulg. MT reads ' he shall cause to cease '.

[2] So most scholars emend the MT which reads ' on the wing of '. See
p. 251.

[3] MT adds a wrong gloss ' which is Hiddekel '.

⟨one like unto⟩[1] a man clothed in linen, whose loins were
6 girded with [2]gold, yea with fine gold:[2] his body also was
like the beryl, and his face as the appearance of lightning,
and his eyes as torches of fire, and his arms and his feet
like the gleam of burnished brass, and the voice of his
7 words like the voice of a multitude. And I Daniel alone
saw the vision: for the men that were with me saw not
the vision; but a great quaking fell upon them, and they
8 fled to hide themselves. So I was left alone and saw
this great vision, and there was no strength left in me:
9 for my comeliness was turned into corruption,[3] Yet
I heard the voice of his words, and when I heard the
voice of his words I fell into a deep sleep *with my face
10 to the ground.[4] And behold   MT X. 10ᵇ
    a hand touched me, and   'set me tottering upon my
11 ⌜waked me⌝.[5] And he said   knees and upon the palms
unto me, O Daniel, thou man   of my hands.'
greatly beloved, understand the words that I speak unto
thee, and stand upright; for unto thee am I now sent:
and when he had spoken this word unto me I stood
12 trembling. Then he said unto me, Fear not, Daniel;
for from the first day that thou didst set thine heart to
understand, and to humble thyself before thy God, thy
words were heard: and I am come for thy words' sake.
13 But the prince of the kingdom of Persia withstood me
one and twenty days; but, lo, Michael, one of the chief
princes, came to help me: and *I left him*[6] there with ⌜the
14 prince of⌝[7] the kings of Persia. Now I am come to make

---

[1] I have here restored the כ before איש. Cf. 10¹⁶, ¹⁸, where it has been
preserved. See p. 256 sq.

[2] Behrmann (followed by Montg.) rightly emends MT אופז 'Uphaz'—
a *vox nulla*—into ופז: cf. Cant. 5¹¹ where with the LXX we should read
כתם ופז. Mention of gold from a definite country of this world is against
the character of Apocalyptic in such a context.

[3] The text adds here 'and I retained no strength'—a gloss drawn from
10¹⁶ which weakens what has been already said.

[4] So LXX and Pesh. MT reads 'on my face with my face to the ground'—
a conflate text.

[5] So LXX and Th. See p. 260 on the corrupt and conflate text of the MT,
and the translation given alongside above.

[6] With LXX and Th. and most scholars I have emended נותרתי into
הותרתיו. See note *in loc.*

[7] Restored with LXX and Th.

thee understand what shall befall thy people in the latter
15 days: for there is yet a vision for the days. And when
he had spoken unto me according to these words, I set
16 my face towards the ground, and was dumb. And behold
one like the similitude of the sons of men touched my
lips: then I opened my mouth and spake and said unto
him that stood before me, O my lord, by reason of the
vision my pangs have come upon me, and I retain no
17 strength. For how can the servant of this my lord talk
with this my lord? for as for me †straightway†[1] there
remained no strength in me, neither was there breath
18 left in me. Then there touched me again one like the
19 appearance of a man, and he strengthened me. And he
said, O man greatly beloved, fear not, peace be unto
thee, be strong, *and of a good courage.[2] And when he
spake unto me, I was strengthened, and said, let my lord
20a speak; for thou hast strengthened me. Then said he,
21a [3]Thou knowest wherefore I am come unto thee. And
now I will tell thee that which is inscribed in the writing
20b of truth. Howbeit[3] I am returning to fight with the
prince of Persia: and when I go forth, lo the prince of
21 b Greece shall come. And there is none that holdeth with
XI me against these, but Michael your prince. And as for
me in the first year of Darius the Mede, I stood up to
confirm and strengthen him.

SECTION X[b]

i. e. Chapters XI. 2–XII. 4.

XI. 2-4. *The Kings of Persia and the overthrow of the kingdom
of Persia by Alexander the Great; his empire divided on his
death into four kingdoms. 5-20. The Ptolemies and the Seleucidae before the time of Antiochus Epiphanes. Their conflicts for
the possession of Palestine. Utter defeat of Antiochus III the
Great by the Romans, and his death in 187 B.C. His successor
(187–175) dies through a conspiracy. 21-39. Rise of Antiochus
Epiphanes: his first Egyptian campaign (25-28)—the second*

---

[1] Pesh. and Vulg. om.

[2] So 6 MSS, LXX., Th., Pesh., Vulg. MT ' yea be strong '. See note
in loc.

[3] See p. 265 seq. for a recovery of the right order of the text.

*in 168 B.C. (29–39), and his attempts to pervert the Jews.
40–45. Transition from history to prophecy.*
XII. *1–3. The final woes and triumph of the righteous accompanied by the resurrection of the pre-eminently righteous and wicked. 4. The angel commands the Seer to seal and conceal the book.*

2 And now will I show thee the truth. Behold there shall stand up yet three kings of Persia; and the fourth shall be far richer than they all: and when he is waxed strong through his riches, he shall ⌜rouse himself against all the 3 kingdoms⌝[1] of Greece. And a mighty king shall stand up, and shall rule with great dominion, and do according to 4 a, b his will. And when he *is waxed strong,*[2] his kingdom shall be broken, and shall be divided towards the four 4 c winds of heaven: [3]but not to his posterity, for it shall be 4 e, f rooted up; and his kingdom shall be for the others 4 d besides these: but not according to his dominion where- 5 with he ruled.[3] And the king of the south shall be strong, ⌜but one of his princes shall be stronger than he⌝,[4] and 6 have dominion; and his dominion shall be a great dominion. And at the end of years they shall join themselves together; and the daughter of the king of the south shall come to the king of the north to make an agreement: but she shall not retain the strength of her arm, ⌜neither shall his seed stand⌝;[5] but she *shall be rooted up,*[6] and they that brought her, and *her son,*[7] and

---

[1] So Th. and practically LXX. MT reads '†stir up the realm'† or '†stir up all against the kingdom of Greece'†

[2] Emended with Graetz, Bevan, Driver, &c. MT reads 'shall stand up'. See note p. 275.

[3] Emended by transposition of clause (*d*) after (*f*) and of the *vav* from before לאחרים to the word that precedes it. MT reads 'but not to his posterity nor according to his dominion wherewith he ruled; for his kingdom shall be plucked up, even for others beside these'. See p. 276.

[4] So LXX, Th., Vulg., MT reads 'and one of his princes; and he shall be stronger'. See p. 277.

[5] So Th., Vulg., and Sym. MT reads 'neither shall he stand nor his arm'.

[6] So I emend the text with the help of the LXX. MT reads 'she shall be given'. See p. 279.

[7] So Von Gall, Marti, &c., emend the corrupt MT which reads 'he that begat her'. See p. 279.

7 he that obtained her in those times.　But out of a shoot
from her roots shall one stand up in his place, who shall
march against the army, and shall enter into the fortress
of the king of the north, and shall deal with them, and
8 shall prevail : and also their gods, with their molten
images, (and) with their goodly vessels of silver and of
gold, shall he carry captive into the **south** ;[1] and he shall
9 refrain some years from the king of the north.　And he
shall come into the realm of the king of the south, but
10 he shall return into his own land.　And his son shall
war, and shall assemble a multitude of great forces, and
[2] attack him,[2] and overwhelm, and pass beyond : and he
11 shall again carry the war even to his fortress.　And the
king of the south shall be moved with choler, and shall
go forth, and shall fight with this same king of the north :
and he shall raise a great multitude, but the multitude
12 shall be given into his hand.　And the multitude shall
be swept away, and his heart shall be uplifted : and he
shall cast down tens of thousands, but he shall not prevail.
13 And again the king of the north shall raise a multitude
greater than the former ; and he shall [3] attack him [3] at the
end [4] of years, with a great army and with great [5] substance.
14 And in those times there shall many stand up against the
king of the south : also the children of the violent among
thy people [6] shall lift themselves up to establish the
15 vision ; but they shall fall.　So the king of the north
shall come, and cast up earthworks, and take a well-
fenced city.

---

[1] MT interprets and so reads : ' Egypt '.

[2] So 13 MSS., Pesh. (and LXX), Cf. 11[13]. MT reads ' come on and on ' or
' come repeatedly '.

[3] So many MSS. and the LXX (though corrupt) εἰσελεύσεται [εἰς αυτὴν]
ἐπ' αὐτόν where the words in square brackets are a duplicate rendering.
Cf. 11[6,10]. MT reads ' come repeatedly '.

[4] MT adds ' of the times '.

[5] So LXX. MT reads ' much '. See note on 11[25] (Comm.).

[6] e. g. Tobiadae. Montgomery takes them to be a party of Zealots.

Restored Text	MT
15ᵈ⁻ᵉ And the forces of ⌜the king of⌝¹ the south shall² make a stand, even the *élite* of his troops, but the strength to withstand shall be lacking.	15ᵈ⁻ᵉ And the arms of the south shall not withstand, neither his chosen people, neither shall there be any strength to withstand.

16 And so he that cometh against him shall do according to his own will, and none shall stand before him : and he shall stand in the glorious land, and in his hand shall be

17 annihilation.   And he shall set his face to come with the strength of his whole kingdom, ⌜but shall instead make an agreement with him :⌝³ and he shall give him the daughter of women, to destroy it ;⁴ but it shall not

18 stand, neither shall it come to pass.   After this shall he turn his face to the isles, and shall take many :

Restored Text	MT
18ᶜ⁻ᵈ ⌜but a chief shall put an end to his contumely (even) **unto annihilation**: yea he shall requite him with his own contumely⌝.⁵	18ᶜ⁻ᵈ But a chief shall cause the reproach offered by him to cease : †yea moreover† he shall cause his reproach to turn upon him.

19 Then he shall turn his face toward the fortresses of his own land : but he shall stumble and fall, and shall not be

20 found.   Then shall stand up in his place one that shall cause an exactor to pass through with royal splendour : but within a few days he shall be destroyed, neither in

21 anger,⁶ nor in battle.   And in his place shall stand up a contemptible person, upon whom had not been bestowed the honour of the kingdom : but he shall come in time of

---

¹ So Th. (also LXX though corrupt).

² MT adds ' not ' against LXX and Th.

³ So LXX, Th., and Vulg.   MT reads corruptly ' and upright ones with him and he shall do '.   See p. 290.

⁴ ' Destroy it '.   See p. 290 seq.

⁵ So by means of the Versions I emend 18ᶜ,ᵈ.   For a discussion of this difficult passage see p. 292 seqq.   Bevan's emendation does not account for the MT nor for the Versions, nor yet does that of Marti.

⁶ Rather ' not in a fair face to face encounter '.   See p. 296 seq.

22 security, and shall obtain the kingdom by flatteries.[1]   And
  [2]armies shall be ***utterly*** swept away[2] from before him,
  and shall be broken ; yea also the prince of the covenant.
23 And from the time they shall
  make a league with him he shall
             Restored Text 23[b]–24[a]
             based on the LXX.
23[b] work deceitfully: for he shall
  take the field †and become
       'And he shall ⟨take the
       field⟩ with a small force
24 strong with a small people. In
       unexpectedly against a
  time of security he shall attack
       mighty force ⟨and⟩ lay
  even the fattest places of the
       waste a province.'
  province† ;[3] and he shall do
  that which his fathers have not done, nor his fathers'
  fathers ; he shall scatter among them prey, and spoil, and
  substance : yea, he shall devise his devices against the
25 strongholds, even for a time.   And he shall stir up his
  power and his courage against the king of the south with
  a great army ; and the king of the south shall war in
  battle with an exceeding great and mighty army : but he
  shall not stand, for they shall devise devices against him,
26 and ⌈his anxieties ***shall wear him out and*** shall work his
  ruin⌉,[4] and his army [5]***shall be swept away***[5] : and many
  shall fall down slain.
27 And as for both these kings, their hearts shall be to do
  mischief, and they shall speak lies at one table : but it
  shall not prosper ; for yet the end shall be at the time
28 appointed.   And he shall return into his land with great
  substance ; and his heart shall be against the holy
  covenant ; and he shall do ⟨his pleasure⟩ and return to his

---

[1] The MT word is here a corruption of the original and shorter form בחלקות.

[2] So Bevan by emending הַשֶּׁטֶף into הִשָּׁטֹף. MT reads 'with the arms of a flood shall they be swept away'. See p. 298.

[3] So MT. In the margin I have given a possible restoration of the text based on the LXX. This would probably mean that Antiochus with a small following of the people would reduce the entire people and lay Palestine waste. The reference to Palestine, if correctly interpreted, would be proleptic here. See p. 299 seq. Bevan transposes the *vav* in 24[a] and renders ' and by stealth he shall assail the mightiest men of (each) province' (comparing 8[25]). Text uncertain.

[4] So LXX and Th. MT corrupt: 'yea they that eat his meat shall work his ruin.' See p. 302 seqq.

[5] So Bevan, Driver, &c. point the text. MT reads 'shall overflow'.

29 own land. At the time appointed he shall return, and
come into the south; but it shall not be in the latter time
30 as it was in the former. For   MT
 ¹ *those who go forth from the*   Kittian ships.
 *west*¹ shall come against him; and he shall be cowed
 and shall return, and have indignation against the holy
 covenant, and shall do (his pleasure): and, he shall return
 and have regard unto them that forsake the holy covenant.
31 And armies sent by him shall make a stand, and they
 shall profane the sanctuary, even the fortress, and shall
 take away the daily burnt offering, and they shall set up
32 a horror that appalleth. And such as do wickedly against
 the covenant shall he pervert by flatteries: but the people
 that know their God shall be strong, and do (well).
33 And they that be wise among the people shall instruct the
 many: yet they shall fall by the sword and by flame, by
34 captivity and by spoil (many) days. Now when they shall
 be overthrown they shall be holpen with a little help: and
34ᵇ ² there shall join them many   MT
 ⌜in the city and many⌝ in ⌜their   34ᵇ 'Many shall join them-
35 *several homesteads*⌝.² And   selves to them with
35ᵇ some of them that be wise   flatteries.'
 ³ shall be wise so as *to refine*   MT
 and make themselves pure,³ to   35ᵇ shall fall, to refine
 the time of the end: because   amongst them and to
 it is yet for the time appointed.   purify [and to make
                                        them white.]
36 And the king shall do according to his will; and he shall
 exalt himself and magnify himself above every god, and
 shall speak marvellous things against ⁴a God of gods:⁴
 and he shall prosper till the indignation be accomplished:
37 for that which is determined shall be done. Neither
 shall he regard the gods of his fathers, nor the desire of

---

¹ See note on p. 305 for this emendation of the corrupt MT.

² See note p. 310 seq. for this emendation on the basis of the LXX.

³ See note on p. 311-12 for this emendation of the text on the basis of
the LXX. See 12¹⁰.

⁴ I.e. אַל אֵלִים. Contrast Deut. 10¹⁷, Ps. 136², where the article before
אֱלֹהִים gives the sense 'the God of gods', i.e. אֱלֹהֵי הָאֱלֹהִים. The Seer
is writing from the standpoint of Antiochus, just as in 2⁴⁷ (see note on
Transl.) he is writing from that of Nebuchadnezzar, and so describes the
God of Israel as a 'God of gods', i.e. אֱלָהּ אֱלָהִין. Cf. 2⁴⁵ also.

women, nor regard any god : for he shall magnify himself
38 above all. But instead thereof shall he honour the god
of fortresses : yea, a god whom his fathers knew not shall
he honour with gold, and silver, and with precious
stones and pleasant things.

MT

39 And he shall use for
the strongest fortresses[1] *the
people*[1] of a strange god ;
39 And he shall deal with the
strongest fortresses by the
help of a strange god ;

whomsoever he recognizes, he shall honour highly: and he
shall cause them to rule over the many, and shall divide the
40 land for a price. And at the time of the end shall the king
of the south make a thrust against him: and the king of the
north shall storm against him with chariots, and horse-
men, and with many ships ; and he shall enter into the
†countries†[2] and shall overwhelm and pass through.
41 And he shall come into the glorious land, and [3] *tens of
thousands*[3] shall be overthrown: yet these shall be
42 delivered out of his hand.[4] He shall stretch forth his
hand also upon the countries : and the land of the *south*[5]
43 shall not escape. And he shall have power over the
treasures of gold and silver, and over all the precious
things of the *south*.[6]
44 But tidings out of the east and out of the north shall
alarm him : and he shall go forth with great fury to
45 destroy and exterminate many. And he shall plant the
tents of his palace between the sea and the glorious holy
mountain ; yet he shall come to his end and none shall
help him.

[1] See p. 316 seq. for the above emendation.

[2] On a possible restoration of this unsatisfactory text see p. 319.

[3] So De Wette, Bevan, &c. emend the MT which reads 'many (lands)'.

[4] MT adds here against the universal usage of apocalyptic the names of
the contemporary and immediate enemies of the Jews, when they were
warring against Antiochus. The addition is : 'Edom and Moab and the
chief of the children of Ammon.' See pp. 319-20.

[5] MT interprets this word and reads 'Egypt', see p. 321 and note.

[6] MT and Versions add the gloss 'And the Libyans and the Ethiopians
shall be in his train', a gloss as unjustifiable in this literature as in that in
11[41]. Here also all the authorities have interpreted the word 'south' as
Egypt. See note on 11[8].

XII.　And at that time shall Michael stand up, the great
　　　prince which standeth for the children of thy people:
　　　and there shall be a time of trouble, such as never was
　　　since there was a nation even to that same time: and at
　　　that time thy people shall be delivered, every one that
　2　shall be found written in the book.　And many of them
　　　that sleep in the ¹ *dust of the earth* ¹ shall awake, some to
　3　everlasting life, and some to ² everlasting rejection.²　And
　　　they that be wise shall shine as the brightness of the
　　　firmament; and they that turn many to righteousness as
　4　the stars for ever and ever.　But thou, O Daniel, shut up
　　　the words and seal the book even unto the time of the
　　　end: †and many shall run to and fro and knowledge
　　　shall be increased†.³

SECTION Xᶜ

i.e. Chapter XII. 5–10.

*5–7. Vision of other two angels, one of whom states the duration
of the troubles just foretold.　8–9. The Seer declares his inability
to understand the things which he has just heard and asks for an
explanation of them.　But the angel refuses save in that he repeats
what has been already said in XI. 35, that the time of the end
would be a time of trial and probation.　[11–13. Two later and
successive additions designed to extend the period of 1150 days,
which were to elapse before the advent of the Kingdom on earth,
first to 1290 and then to 1335, in order to bring the prophecy
into accord with history.　13. Promise to the Seer that he will
live to see and inherit his lot in the coming Kingdom.*]

¹ So LXX, Th., Pesh., Vulg.　MT reads 'land of dust'.
² For the grounds for this text see note *in loc.*　The MT and the Versions
take different directions.　The difficulty arose from the word דראון.　MT =
'to shame (and) everlasting rejection'.　Here the first word was a marginal
interpretation of the second, which was incorporated into the text without
a copula.　The LXX gives three interpretations of this word, one of which
is right: Th. omits the right interpretation and reproduces the two wrong
interpretations.　See p. 328 seq.　T. Benj. 10⁸ supports in using this passage
the contrast of only the two opposites 'life' and 'rejection'.　See Introd.,
§ 14. *h.*　Comm., p. 323 *ad med.*: 328 sq.
³ So MT.　This thought seems wholly out of place.　If we follow the
LXX we obtain a text which is absolutely in keeping with the eschatological
thought of the time: 'till the many become apostates and the earth is filled
with iniquity.'　The darkest hour ushers in the dawn.　See p. 331 sqq.

5 Then I Daniel looked, and behold, there stood other two,
the one on the brink of the river on this side, and the
6 other on the brink of the river on that side. And *I said* [1]
to the man clothed in linen, which was above the waters
of the river, How long shall it be to the end of the
7 wonders? And I heard the man clothed in linen, which
was above the waters of the river, when he held up his
right hand and his left hand unto heaven, and sware by
him that liveth for ever that it shall be for a time, times,
and an half; [2] and when the power *of the shatterer* of the
holy people *shall come to an end* [2] all these things shall be
8 finished. And I heard, but I understood not : then said I,
O my lord, what is the *interpretation* [3] of these things?
9 And he said, Go thy way, Daniel : for the words are shut
10 up and sealed till the time of the end : [4] ⌐till⌐ many refine
and make themselves pure ; [4] And the wicked shall do
wickedly ; for none of the wicked shall understand : but
they that be wise shall understand.

Here the book ends, and ends—not with the promise of
future blessedness to a solitary individual ; for that had already
been declared to be the guerdon of all that had been faithful
at a great cost (12^2). The book closes with the further promise
of spiritual enlightenment to the divinely wise on the vexed and
dark questions of God's dealings with the faithful and the world
at large. It marks a great advance. As God is sole ruler of
the world, all history is one and all the kingdoms of the earth
subserve His will, and eternal life and divine wisdom are the
heritage of all that render Him pre-eminent service.

[1] So LXX—a reading required also by the context. MT = '(one) said '.
See p. 333 sq.

[2] Text as emended by Bevan on the basis of the LXX, which needs
however to be corrected otherwise than he assumes. MT = ' And when
they have made an end of breaking in pieces the power of the holy people '.
According to the emended text the duration of the oppression—$3\frac{1}{2}$ years—
and the oppressor are here mentioned together as in 7^{25}. See p. 334 sq.

[3] So LXX. MT = ' end '. See p. 335 sqq.

[4] So LXX. MT ' Many shall purify themselves [and make themselves
white] and be refined '. Here as in 11^{35} there is an interpolated clause in
the MT. But the order of the words here is likewise wrong. The ' smelting '
or ' refining ' should precede as in 11^{35} ' the purifying '. See p. 337. The
' till ' is preserved in the LXX and implied in Th.

(First Appendix XII. 11 added by the Author to bring his prediction into accordance with history by adjourning the date of its fulfilment.)

11 And from the time that the daily burnt-offering shall be taken away, and a horror that appalleth set up, there shall be a thousand two hundred and ninety days.

(Second Appendix XII. 12–13 made by a contemporary interpolator on the failure of the emended prediction in XII. 11.)

12 Blessed is he that waiteth, and cometh to the thousand three hundred and five and thirty days.

13 But go thou thy way[1] and take thy rest, for thou shalt stand in thy lot,[2] at the end of the days.

---

[1] MT adds against LXX and Th. 'to the end', i.e. till the end be.

[2] I.e. shalt live to inherit everlasting blessedness in the coming Kingdom on earth. Even S. Paul thought, according to his earlier Epistles, that he would live till the actual second Advent of Christ, and without passing through the gate of death become a citizen of the everlasting Kingdom of Christ. The words 'stand in thy lot' imply that the Seer will survive the coming of the Kingdom: not that he shall rise to share in it as it is universally taken. See p. 341. Here the interpolator has fallen from the role of one writing as it were from the 6th cent. B.C., and writes as a contemporary of the Maccabees and the real writer of the book. Hence the promise to the Seer that he will *survive* to inherit the Kingdom. עמד is not used of the resurrection from the dead. The interpolator should have used עת קץ 'time of the end' which in our author is always used eschatologically, as the following notes will show.

It is important for the student of Daniel to recognize these facts, as no lexicon or commentary has hitherto done so.

1°. 'End of the days' (קצת הימים, 1[18]: cf. 1[5, 15]: in Aramaic קצת יומיא 4[31 (34)]). This phrase is never used eschatologically in our author and never refers to the advent of the kingdom. But the interpolator did not recognize this fact and took this phrase to be synonymous with 'the time of the end', i.e. עת קץ. See 4° below. Our author always uses the phrase 'end of the days' to mark the close of some definite crisis in the lives of the personalities with whom he deals.

2°. 'End of years' (קץ שנים). This phrase has no eschatological meaning in our author but is used practically in the same sense as phrase 1°.

3°. 'The latter days' (אחרית יומיא 2[28]: אחרית הימים 10[14]). This phrase is used eschatologically in our author, as embracing the final period of history preceding the advent of the kingdom; also the emended text of 9[26 a] בקץ העתים: see p. 382 n. 6.

4°. 'Time of the end' (עת קץ). This phrase is always used eschatologically in our author and refers definitely to the advent of the kingdom: cf. 8[17], 11[35, 40], 12[4, 9]. This is the phrase the interpolator would have used, had he been familiar with our author's usage.

ADDENDA ET CORRIGENDA

The Prophets were not thinkers but mystics and forthtellers of the will of God, and dealt mainly with the present duties and destinies of man. The Apocalyptists were thinkers and *sought to explain all history as a unity*. The greatest of them, as our author, combined the teachings of Prophecy and Apocalyptic. So far as we know, he was the first to recognize this unity.

Owing to their lack of metaphysical gifts and their belief that the gifts of Prophecy had died out before the second century B.C., the educated Jews set no value on the lessons of Apocalyptic. The book of Daniel, written by the Great Unknown, was not recognized by the Massoretes as having a place among the lowliest of the prophets: even amongst the Hagiographa he was generally placed by them amongst the last three writers. In short the Massoretes were unable to appreciate Apocalyptic and were in fact ignorant of its gifts and character.

In profound contrast stands the judgement of the Early Christian Church. Not only did it admit this Great Unknown among the prophets, but dividing the prophets into two groups—the Four Major and the Twelve Minor—they actually included the Great Unknown in the first group. Who was answerable in the Christian Church for this? The Christian Church was right. Daniel is the only prophet who dealt with life both here and hereafter.

P. 283, l. 8 *for* $11^{8,29}$ *read* $11^{8,29,42,43}$.

P. 283, l. 18 *delete the article before* מצרים.

P. 287, l. 13 ab imo *for* עתים *read* העתים.

P. 311, l. 10 ab imo *for* אתם *read* אתם.

P. 311, l. 6 ab imo *for* ed. *read* rd.

P. 313, l. 13 ab imo *transpose* Sir. 37^7 *and* Dan. 11^{36e}.

P. 315, l. 19 *for* the *read* a.

P. 315, l. 21 *add*: see note on 11^{37} (Transl.).

P. 324, l. 4 ab imo *for* Again in 12¹³ owing to the interpolation of 12¹¹,¹² *read* In 12¹³ which is also as 12¹¹,¹² interpolated.

P. 328, l. 18 *for* עפר *read* עפרא.

P. 328, l. 22 *for* ' עמד becomes a synonym' *read* ' עמד wrongly becomes a synonym'.

P. 328, ll. 4, 8 ab imo *for* לחרפה *read* לחרפות.

P. 329, l. 10 *for* σποράν *read* σπορὰν αἰώνιον.

P. 341, l. 12 *for* in *read* after.

INDEX I

The black figures indicate page numbers.

---

* Although the words in brackets have been lost in the MT and Versions, they are preserved in Clem. Alex. *Paed.* ii. 10 ὡσεὶ παλαιὸς ἡμερῶν : also in LXX, Dan. 7^{13}. In any case they must be restored.

† The form אֲשְׁפְּנַז appears in an incantation text found in Nippur as Montg. in his *Aram. Incant. Texts* **145** shows.

* Cyrus King of Anshan became 'King of Persia' in the ninth year of his reign (See *Annalistic Tablet*, cxxii sq.). He and his successors were called 'Kings of Persia' only according to Hellenistic usage in order to distinguish them from the Greek dynasties that took their place.

* Contrast Deut. 10[17], Ps. 136[2] אלהי האלהים ' the God of gods'.

† The same phrase occurs in Cowley 30[2, 27-28], 32[3-5].

* Bauer-Leander is here wrong. 'King David' (המלך דוד) is early classical
Hebrew, but not classical Aram. In the later books of the O.T. the Hebrew
order is usually 'David the King' (ד" המלך).

† Observe that the translators of the Aramaic never interpret 'King of the
North ' as one of the Seleucids, though they interpret ' King of the South ' four
times as ' King of Egypt '.

‡ It would be wiser to read לא אשתמעו in both these passages instead of
לא שמעו which I have proposed in the sense of ' they have not obeyed '—which
the Versions require.

INDEX II

Some Aramaic and Hebrew words and phrases. The Hebrew appears to be from different translators of the Aramaic. Erroneous uses of both Aram. and Hebr. words due to the translators, Massoretic revisers as well as to the errors incidental to transmission. The brackets used have the same significance they have earlier in the book.

†אדמת־עפר† 392 n. 1

אדרגזר 61

אדר 44

†אובל† cviii, 199

†אופז† 258, 384 n. 2

אזדא 30, 346 n. 2

אחוית (אחידין) 130, 365.

אחרי 46

†אחרית† 335

אחשדרפניא 61

אחשורוש 224

אימתני 179

איתי c. Part—use in D 68 sqq.

אלהיא sing. (?) in Old Aram. 353 n. 2

אל אלים = 'a God of gods' 390 n. 4

אלה אלהין   ,,   ,,   350 n. 3, 390 n. 4

אלו 42

אלין 'these' peculiar to D: Introd., § 20. h, lxxxvii

אנבה 90

אנדע 32

אנון (Qr.) (Kt. אנין) only in nom. in D: Introd., § 20. h : 161 sq., 370 n. 2

אנשא (Kt. אנושא) 92

אנשים (Heb. due to error. Rd. אנשא) 93

אסר 155

אפדן 318, 322

אפים 296

אצל 201

ארגונא 125

ארו 42

אריותא 156

ארכבתה (but ברכוהי in 6^{11}) 119

ארכה 98

ארעא מך (contrast עלא מן 150) 46

אשמעה 209

אשף 27

אשר למה = lest (Aramaisms) 3, 20

אשתומם (Hebraism) 94

אתון 'furnace' 64

אתכרית 188

אתעקרו 179 sq.

באדין 34

בגו (Old Aram.) 189

בין[1] 224, 236, 255 al.

בינותי 224

בירה 198

---

[1] This verb is very variously used in our author by the translators. Thus in 8^{17}, 10^{12} (Hiph.) it means 'to understand'; in 8^5, 9^{23} (Hiph.) 'to give heed to'; in 1^{17} (Hiph.) ב 'to understand' but in 12^8 (Qal) 'to hear' but not 'to understand' c.; in 8^{27}, 9^{22} (abs.) 'to teach' (abs.). It has also other uses in the six Hebrew chapters.

חלקות 'flatteries' 308 sq.

+חלקלקות+ 11²¹, ³⁴, 297 sq.

איש חמודות 10¹¹, ¹⁹, 237

חרטמים 27

חרצא 118

(לא) חשיבין 100 sq.

טאב 161

טות 'fasting' 160

יְאֹר 12⁵, ⁶, ⁷ 'Nile' but in our author = 'Euphrates' 333

יבחלך (Jussive, Old Aram.: Introd. § 20. s), 4¹⁶ ⁽¹⁹⁾, 5¹⁰.

יבלא (Old Aram.) 'to wear out' 193

+ישטטו+ rd. ישטו Hebr. i.e. יסטו 332, 392 n. 3

יהוד 'Judaea' 39 sq.

יכל (= כהל) Use in D. differs from that in earlier Aramaic: Introd. § 20. y

+יכשלו+ rd. ישכילו 311

[ימחא] 101

ינתן 34

יעמדנא 217

+יעף+ 235

יצבא 192

+ישרים+ 11¹⁷ rd. מישרים as in 11⁶

ית 66

יִתֵּב 194

כ (with temporal meaning where Older Aram. has ל) 161

כדב (Old Aram.) 32

כהל Introd. § 20. y

כוין 156

כחדה 'together' 44

כל with suff. in Old Aram. but not in our Author: Introd. § 20. r

כלא = demonstrative pronoun 98

כל-קבל Introd. § 20. ff

כֵּלֵא 238

כנו 295

(כ)עתיק יומין 372 n. 8

[כפר] used by Massoretes to replace מחות as LXX and Vulg. prove, 238, 382 n. 3

כפיתו 71

כרסא 132

כשדים 13 sqq.

[כשים] 321

[כתים] 305 sq.

ל c. acc. very frequent in D., but not often earlier: Introd. § 20. x

ל c. Inf. = finite verb in D. 2¹⁶,¹⁸, 5¹⁵: Introd. § 20. t

[לבים] 321

+לדנא+ 188

(כ)לה חשיבין 100 sq.

להוא Jussive: see Introd. § 20. s

לחם 115

לחנתה 117

[ללבן] 313

+לצד+ (על rd. ?) 193

מאזניא 'balances' 137

מאניא 'vessels' 115

מגיחן 'stirred up' 175

מדע 13

מהימן 152

מהלכין 75

מזיה (c. suff.) cf. מֵאתֵא for מֵאתָא 62

מַחֵא 'kept alive' 132

[מחא 'strike'] 101 (cf. 2³⁴, ³⁵)

מישרים 'agreement' 278

מכמנים 321

מכשפים 27

(אשר ל)מלאות 225: Introd. § 20. t

---

[1] Not so in 9[15], which is a late, not an early interpretation as in 11[8,42,43].

†(צבא)(ו)† (rd. יצדא(?)) ¹ 204-9

צבו 159

†צוק† rd. קֵץ 244

צֶלֶם (an artificial form) 70

צפיר 200, 376 n. 3

קאמין (Kt.) 46

קְבֵל and compounds : Introd. § 20. ff

קדם ² (technical use in D.) 'before' divine or semidivine beings—hence it is interpolated in 3⁹, 4⁴⁽⁷⁾,⁵⁽⁸⁾,³²⁽³⁵⁾: Introd. § 20. w

קדישי עליונין 191

קטרין 118

קיתרס (Kt.) 63

קלל 258

קצין 292

קצת 10, 394 n. 2. 1°

קרנא 63

קרנים (dual) 199

קרציהון 65

רב טבחיא 34

רבית 96

(רִבְּוָן) 184

(רמיו) (MT רמו) 161, 370 n. 2

שבבא 63

†שְׁמַת† 159

שאלתא 93, 357 n. 2

שביבא 72

שגל 116 sq.

שוי 133

שיזב 68, 77

שלה (Kt. שלו Qr.) 77

שלוה 220

שלותך 98

שמיא 'heavens'—'God' (very late) 97

שמם 210, 251, 308

†שניהי† rd. שנין עלוהי 118 as in 5⁹

שנתה 161

שעתא 64

שרי 119

(אל) תהובד 2²⁴. Jussive. See Introd. § 20. s

תלתי 126

(ה)תמיד (עולת התמיד late for) 205, 307

תפתיא 62

תְּקֵל 133-7, 366 n. 3

תקפה 155

תקף 99

תִּרְאֶה 22

¹ See p. 377 n. 3 for text emended by help of Versions: p. 204 sqq.

² In 6⁷⁽⁶⁾, ¹⁴⁽¹³⁾ קדם to be restored on evidence of LXX. If a subject ignored 4¹⁶ or was disrespectful to the king, (contrast 6¹⁴⁽¹³⁾), he used ל and not קדם. after אמר. See 369 n. 7.